Springer Texts in Education

CW01084345

Springer Texts in Education delivers high-quality instructional content for graduates and advanced graduates in all areas of Education and Educational Research. The textbook series is comprised of self-contained books with a broad and comprehensive coverage that are suitable for class as well as for individual self-study. All texts are authored by established experts in their fields and offer a solid methodological background, accompanied by pedagogical materials to serve students such as practical examples, exercises, case studies etc. Textbooks published in the Springer Texts in Education series are addressed to graduate and advanced graduate students, but also to researchers as important resources for their education, knowledge and teaching. Please contact Natalie Rieborn at textbooks.education@springer.com or your regular editorial contact person for queries or to submit your book proposal.

More information about this series at https://link.springer.com/bookseries/13812

Hassan Mohebbi • Christine Coombe
Editors

Research Questions in Language Education and Applied Linguistics

A Reference Guide

 Springer

Editors
Hassan Mohebbi 🆔
European Knowledge
Development Institute
Ankara, Turkey

Christine Coombe 🆔
Higher Colleges of Technology (HCT)
Dubai Men's College
Dubai, United Arab Emirates

ISSN 2366-7672   ISSN 2366-7680   (electronic)
Springer Texts in Education
ISBN 978-3-030-79142-1   ISBN 978-3-030-79143-8   (eBook)
https://doi.org/10.1007/978-3-030-79143-8

© Springer Nature Switzerland AG 2021
This work is subject to copyright. All rights are reserved by the Publisher, whether the whole or part of the material is concerned, specifically the rights of translation, reprinting, reuse of illustrations, recitation, broadcasting, reproduction on microfilms or in any other physical way, and transmission or information storage and retrieval, electronic adaptation, computer software, or by similar or dissimilar methodology now known or hereafter developed.
The use of general descriptive names, registered names, trademarks, service marks, etc. in this publication does not imply, even in the absence of a specific statement, that such names are exempt from the relevant protective laws and regulations and therefore free for general use.
The publisher, the authors and the editors are safe to assume that the advice and information in this book are believed to be true and accurate at the date of publication. Neither the publisher nor the authors or the editors give a warranty, expressed or implied, with respect to the material contained herein or for any errors or omissions that may have been made. The publisher remains neutral with regard to jurisdictional claims in published maps and institutional affiliations.

This Springer imprint is published by the registered company Springer Nature Switzerland AG
The registered company address is: Gewerbestrasse 11, 6330 Cham, Switzerland

Much of the work on this volume has taken place during the global pandemic. We are grateful for the commitment that healthcare workers and educators have shown during this time and it is to them that this book is dedicated.

Contents

Part VI Technology and Technology-enhanced Instruction

Contributors

Rebekha Abbuhl Department of Linguistics, California State University Long Beach, Long Beach, CA, USA

Saleh Al-Busaidi Department of Curriculum and Instruction, Sultan Qaboos University, Muscat, Sultanate of Oman

Ali H. Al-Hoorie Jubail English Language and Preparatory Year Institute, Royal Commission for Jubail and Yanbu, Jubail Industrial City, Saudi Arabia

Jason Anderson Applied Linguistics, University of Warwick, Coventry, UK

Neil J. Anderson Department of English Language Teaching & Learning, Brigham Young University–Hawaii, Laie, HI, USA

Eileen N. Whelan Ariza Department of Teaching and Learning, College of Education, Florida Atlantic University, Boca Raton, FL, USA

Nikki Ashcraft Learning, Teaching & Curriculum-TESOL, University of Missouri, Columbia, MO, USA

Mahmood Reza Atai Department of Foreign Languages, Kharazmi University, Tehran, Iran

Dwight Atkinson University of Arizona, Tucson, AZ, USA

Esmat Babaii Department of Foreign Languages, Kharazmi University, Tehran, Iran

Gary Barkhuizen School of Cultures, Languages and Linguistics, University of Auckland, Auckland, New Zealand

Leslie Barratt Languages, Literatures, & Linguistics, Indiana State University, Terre Haute, IN, USA
Roi Et Rajabhat University, Roi Et, Thailand

Helen Basturkmen Applied Linguistics and Language Teaching, Faculty of Arts, University of Auckland, Auckland, New Zealand

Alessandro Benati CAES, Hong Kong University, Hong Kong, China

Phil Benson Multilingualism Research Centre, Macquarie University, Sydney, Australia

Tej K. Bhatia Department of Linguistics (LLL), Syracuse University, Syracuse, NY, USA

Maneka Deanna Brooks Department of Curriculum and Instruction, Texas State University, San Marcos, TX, USA

James Dean Brown Second Language Studies, University of Hawai'i at Mānoa, Honolulu, Hawai'i, USA

Tineke Brunfaut Department of Linguistics and English Language, Lancaster University, Lancaster, UK

Anne Burns School of Education, University of New South Wales, Sydney, Australia

Yuko Goto Butler Graduate School of Education, University of Pennsylvania, Philadelphia, PA, USA

Mónica S. Cárdenas-Claros Instituto de Literatura y Ciencias del Lenguaje, Pontificia Universidad Católica de Valparaíso, Viña del Mar, Chile

J. Elliott Casal Department of Applied Linguistics, The Pennsylvania State University, University Park, PA, USA
Department of Cognitive Science, Case Western Reserve University, Cleveland, OH, USA

Anna A. C.-S. Chang Department of Applied English, Hsing Wu University, New Taipei, Taiwan

Mahjabin Chowdhury Educational Psychology, Texas A&M University, College Station, TX, USA

Mary Ann Christison Department of Linguistics, University of Utah, Salt Lake City, UT, USA

Andrew D. Cohen Professor Emeritus, Program in Second Language Studies, College of Liberal Arts, University of Minnesota, Minneapolis, MN, USA

Christine Coombe Department of General Studies, Dubai Men's College, Higher Colleges of Technology, Dubai, United Arab Emirates

Elena Cotos English/Applied Linguistics and Technology, Iowa State University, Ames, IA, USA

Deborah Crusan Department of English Language and Literatures, Wright State University, Dayton, USA

Kata Csizér Department of English Applied Linguistics, School of English and American Studies, Eötvös University, Budapest, Hungary

Sara T. Cushing Department of Applied Linguistics & ESL, Georgia State University, Atlanta, GA, USA

Peter Davidson College of Humanities and Social Sciences, Zayed University, Dubai, UAE

Peter I. De Costa Department of Linguistics, Languages & Cultures and Department of Teacher Education, Michigan State University, East Lansing, MI, USA

Luciana C. de Oliveira School of Education, Virginia Commonwealth University, Richmond, VA, USA

C. J. Denman Office of Deputy Vice-Chancellor for Postgrasduate Studies and Research, Sultan Qaboos University, Muscat, Oman

Sandra C. Deshors Department of Linguistics, Languages, and Cultures, Michigan State University, East Lansing, MI, USA

David Deterding Universiti Brunei Darussalam, Gadong, Brunei

Slobodanka Dimova Centre for Internationalization and Parallel Language Use, University of Copenhagen, Copenhagen, Denmark

Krishna K. Dixit Centre for English Language Education (CELE), Dr. B. R. Ambedkar University, Delhi, India

Hilary Dumbrill Hamilton Lodge School & College for Deaf Learners, Brighton, UK

Martin East School of Cultures, Languages and Linguistics, Faculty of Arts, The University of Auckland, Auckland, New Zealand

Joy Egbert Department of Teaching and Learning, College of Education, Washington State University, Pullman, WA, USA

Rod Ellis School of Education, Curtin University, Perth, WA, Australia

Zohreh R. Eslami Teaching, Learning, and Culture, Texas A&M University, College Station, TX, USA
Department of Educational Psychology, Texas A&M University, College Station, TX, USA

Thomas S. C. Farrell Applied Linguistics, Brock University, St. Catharines, ON, Canada

Flora Debora Floris English Department, Petra Christian University, Surabaya, Indonesia

Lynne Flowerdew Department of Applied Linguistics and Communication, Birkbeck, University of London, London, UK

Eric Friginal Department of Applied Linguistics and ESL, Georgia State University, Atlanta, GA, USA

Glenn Fulcher School of Education, University of Leicester, Leicester, Leicestershire, UK

Nicola Galloway School of Education, University of Glasgow, Glasgow, UK
UCL Institute of Education, London, UK

María del Pilar García Mayo Departamento de Filología Inglesa, Universidad del País Vasco (UPV/EHU), Vitoria-Gasteiz, Spain

Kimberly L. Geeslin Department of Spanish & Portuguese, Indiana University, Bloomington, IN, USA

Zübeyde Sinem Genç Department of Foreign Language Education/English Language Teaching, Faculty of Education/Bursa Uludağ University, Bursa, Turkey

Zihan Geng Department of Teaching, Learning, and Culture, Texas A&M University, College Station, TX, USA

David Gerlach School of Humanities, Chair of TEFL, University of Wuppertal, Wuppertal, Germany

Marta Giralt School of Modern Languages & Applied Linguistics, University of Limerick, Limerick, Ireland

Aline Godfroid Second Language Studies and TESOL program, Department of Linguistics, Languages, and Cultures, Michigan State University, East Lansing, MI, USA

Greta Gorsuch Classical and Modern Languages and Literatures, Texas Tech University, Lubbock, TX, USA

Keith M. Graham Educational Psychology, Texas A&M University, College Station, TX, USA
College of Teacher Education, National Taiwan Normal University, Taipei, Taiwan

Kathleen Graves School of Education, University of Michigan, Ann Arbor, USA

Curtis Green-Eneix Department of Linguistics, Languages & Cultures, Michigan State University, East Lansing, MI, USA

Peter Yongqi Gu School of Linguistics & Applied Language Studies, Victoria University of Wellington, Wellington, New Zealand

Graham Hall English Language and Linguistics, Department of Humanities, Northumbria University, Newcastle upon Tyne, UK

Trude Heift Linguistics Department, Simon Fraser University, Burnaby, BC, Canada

Berna Hendriks Language and Communication/Centre for Language Studies, Radboud University, Nijmegen, The Netherlands

Alastair Henry Department of Social and Behavioural Studies, University West, Trollhättan, Sweden

Lana Hiasat Department of General Studies, Higher Colleges of Technology, Dubai, UAE

Nicky Hockly The Consultants-E, Swansea, United Kingdom

Barbara Hoekje Department of Communication, Drexel University, Philadelphia, PA, USA

Joanna Hoskin Language & Communication Science Division, City University of London, London, UK

Alex Housen Department of Linguistics & Literary Studies, Vrije Universiteit Brussel (VUB), Brussel, Brussels, Belgium

Li-Shih Huang Department of Linguistics, University of Victoria, Victoria, BC, Canada

Ken Hyland School of Education and Lifelong Learning, University of East Anglia, Norwich, UK
Jilin University, Changchun, China

Talia Isaacs UCL Institute of Education, University College London, London, UK

Yuseva Iswandari English Language Education, Sanata Dharma University, Yogyakarta, Indonesia

Noriko Iwashita School of Languages and Cultures, The University of Queensland, Brisbane, QLD, Australia

Mark A. James Department of English, Arizona State University, Tempe, AZ, USA

Mark D. Johnson Department of English, East Carolina University, Greenville, NC, USA

Johnathan Jones UCL Institute of Education, University College London, London, UK

Renee Jourdenais Graduate School of Translation, Interpretation, and Language Education, Middlebury Institute of International Studies at Monterey, Monterey, CA, USA

Carina Kaufmann Institute of English and American Studies, Goethe University Frankfurt, Frankfurt am Main/Hesse, Germany

Rubina Khan Department of English, University of Dhaka, Dhaka, Bangladesh

Mohadese Khosravi English Department, Kharazmi University, Tehran, Iran

Robert Kirkpatrick Gulf University for Science and Technology, Mubarak Al-Abdullah, Kuwait

Tamas Kiss Centre for English Language Studies, Sunway University, Subang Jaya, Malaysia

Friederike Klippel Department of English and American Studies, Ludwig-Maximilians-University, Munich, Germany

Ute Knoch Language Testing Research Centre, School of Languages and Linguistics, University of Melbourne, Parkville, VIC, Australia

Shaun Weihong Ko Department of Teaching, Learning, and Culture, Texas A&M University, College Station, TX, USA

James P. Lantolf Department of Applied Linguistics, The Pennsylvania State University, University Park, PA, USA
School of Foreign Studies, Xi'an JiaoTong University, Xi'an, China

Diane Larsen-Freeman Linguistics Department/School of Education, University of Michigan, Ann Arbor, Michigan, USA

Icy Lee Faculty of Education, The Chinese University of Hong Kong, Shatin, Hong Kong

Yuyun Lei East Asian Languages and Cultures, Wake Forest University, Winston-Salem, USA

Ronald P. Leow Department of Spanish & Portuguese, Georgetown University, Washington, DC, USA

Christine Lewis Universiti Brunei Darussalam, Gadong, Brunei

Shaofeng Li Florida State University, Tallahassee, USA

Yingying Liu Department of Applied Linguistics, The Pennsylvania State University, University Park, PA, USA

Wander Lowie Department of Applied Linguistics, University of Groningen, Groningen, The Netherlands

Xiaofei Lu Department of Applied Linguistics, The Pennsylvania State University, University Park, PA, USA

María José Luzón Department of English Studies, University of Zaragoza, Zaragoza, Spain

Elvenna Majuddin School of Linguistics and Applied Language Studies, Te Herenga Waka, Victoria University of Wellington, Wellington, New Zealand

Pauline Mak The Education University of Hong Kong, Hong Kong, China

Wolfgang Mann School of Education, University of Roehampton, London, UK

Juan de Dios Martínez Agudo Department of Didactics of Social Sciences, Languages and Literatures, Faculty of Education, University of Extremadura, Badajoz, Spain

Aya Matsuda Department of English, Arizona State University, Tempe, AZ, USA

Joshua Matthews School of Education, University of New England, Armidale, NSW, Australia

Lee McCallum Graduate School of Education, University of Exeter, Exeter, UK

Jim McKinley UCL Institute of Education, London, UK

Péter Medgyes Department of Language Pedagogy, Eötvös Loránd University, Budapest, Hungary

Sarah Mercer ELT Research and Methodology, University of Graz, Graz, Austria

James Milton Department of Applied Linguistics, Swansea University, Swansea, UK

Hassan Mohebbi European Knowledge Development Institute (EUROKD), Ankara, Turkey

Pat Moore Languages & Translation, Universidad Pablo de Olavide, Sevilla, Spain

Heiko Motschenbacher Departmnt of Language, Literature, Mathematics and Interpreting, Western Norway University of Applied Sciences, Bergen, Norway

Denise E. Murray Department of Linguistics, Macquarie University, Sydney, NSW, Australia
San José State University, San Jose, CA, USA

Liam Murray School of Modern Languages & Applied Linguistics, University of Limerick, Limerick, Ireland

Neil Murray Department of Applied Linguistics, University of Warwick, Coventry, UK

Akram Nayernia Faculty of Foreign Languages, Iran University of Science and Technology, Tehran, Iran

Raffaella Negretti Department of Communication and Learning in Science, Division for Language and Communication, Chalmers University of Technology, Gothenburg, Sweden

Jonathan Newton School of Linguistics and Applied Language Studies, Victoria University of Wellington, Wellington, New Zealand

Minh Thi Thuy Nguyen Department of English & Linguistics, University of Otago, Dunedin, New Zealand

Bonny Norton Language and Literacy Education, University of British Columbia, Vancouver, BC, Canada

M. Obaidul Hamid The University of Queensland, Brisbane, Australia

Rhonda Oliver School of Education, Curtin University, Perth, West Australia, Australia

Carmel O'Shannessy Australian National University, Canberra, Australia

Amol Padwad Centre for English Language Education (CELE), Dr. B. R. Ambedkar University, Delhi, India

Brian Paltridge English Department, City University of Hong Kong, Hong Kong, China
School of Education and Social Work, University of Sydney, Sydney, Australia

Spiros Papageorgiou Educational Testing Service, Princeton, NJ, USA

Hyunji (Hayley) Park Department of Linguistics, University of Illinois at Urbana-Champaign, Illinois, USA

Mirosław Pawlak Faculty of Pedagogy and Fine Arts, Adam Mickiewicz University, Kalisz, Poland
State University of Applied Sciences in Konin, Konin, Poland

Lia Plakans Department of Teaching and Learning, The University of Iowa, Iowa City, Iowa, USA

Luke Plonsky English Department, Northern Arizona University, Flagstaff, AZ, USA

Matthew E. Poehner Department of Curriculum and Instruction, The Pennsylvania State University, University Park, PA, USA

Phil Quirke Department of Education, Higher Colleges of Technology, Abu Dhabi, United Arab Emirates

Kashif Raza Werklund School of Education, University of Calgary, Calgary, Canada

John Read School of Cultures, Languages and Linguistics, University of Auckland, Auckland, New Zealand

Hayo Reinders Anaheim University, Anaheim, USA
School of Liberal Arts, King Mongkut's University of Technology Thonburi, Bangkok, Thailand

Willy A. Renandya English Language and Literature, National Institute of Education, Nanyang Technological University, Singapore, Singapore

A. Mehdi Riazi Department of Linguistics, Macquarie University, Sydney, Australia
College of Humanities and Social Sciences, Middlebury Institute of International Studies at Monterey, Monterey, CA, USA
College of Humanities and Social Sciences, Hamad Bin Khalifa University (HBKU), Doha, Qatar

Heath Rose Department of Education, The University of Oxford, Oxford, UK

Rachael Ruegg School of Linguistics and Applied Language Studies, Victoria University of Wellington, Wellington, New Zealand

Mavadat Saidi English Department, Shahid Rajaee Teacher Training University, Tehran, Iran

Masatoshi Sato Department of English, Universidad Andres Bello, Santiago, Chile

Ali Shehadeh Curriculum and Instruction, United Arab Emirates University, Al Ain, UAE

Jeff Siegel Linguistics, University of New England, Armidale, NSW, Australia

Anna Siyanova-Chanturia College of Foreign Languages, Ocean University of China, Qingdao, China
School of Linguistics and Applied Language Studies, Te Herenga Waka, Victoria University of Wellington, Wellington, New Zealand

Sophia Skoufaki Department of Language and Linguistics, University of Essex, Colchester, UK

Peter Smagorinsky Department of language and Literacy Education, The University of Georgia (emeritus), Athens, GA, USA

Richard Smith Department of Applied Linguistics, University of Warwick, Coventry, UK

Sharon L. Smith Department of Teaching and Learning, University of Miami, Coral Gables, FL, USA

Suhad Sonbul English Language Centre, Umm Al-Qura University, Makkah, Saudi Arabia

Jacqueline S. Stephen College of Professional Advancement, Mercer University Instructional Designer & Director of the Office of Distance Learning Assistant Professor, Mercer University, Atlanta, GA, USA
Department of Leadership Studies, Human Resources Administration and Development, Mercer University, Atlanta, GA, USA

Ekaterina Sudina English Department, Northern Arizona University, Flagstaff, AZ, USA

Pia Sundqvist Department of Teacher Education and School Research, University of Oslo, Oslo, Norway

Mona Syrbe College of Business, Rikkyo University, Tokyo, Japan

Etsuo Taguchi Department of Japanese, Daito Bunka University, Tokyo, Japan

Kyle Read Talbot ELT Research and Methodology, University of Graz, Graz, Austria

Elena Taylor Utah State University, Logan, UT, USA

Justin Taylor School of Foreign Languages, Bahçeşehir University, Istanbul, Turkey

Shelley K. Taylor Faculty of Education, The University of Western Ontario, London, ON, Canada

Brian Tomlinson University of Liverpool, Liverpool, Merseyside, UK
Anaheim University, Anaheim, CA, USA

Jonathan Trace Faculty of Environment and Information Studies, Keio University, Fujisawa, Kanagawa, Japan

Phuong Tran School of International Liberal Studies, Waseda University, Tokyo, Japan

Ruth Trinder Department of Foreign Language Business Communication, Vienna University of Economics and Business, Vienna, Austria

Salah Troudi Graduate School of Education, University of Exeter, Exeter, England

Ruanni Tupas Institute of Education, University College London, London, UK

Blake Turnbull Faculty of Global and Regional Studies, Doshisha University, Kyoto, Japan

Victoria Tuzlukova English for Humanities Department, Centre for Preparatory Studies, Sultan Qaboos University, Sultanate of Oman, Muscat, Oman

Hossein Vafadar School of Languages, Literacies and Translation, Universiti Sains Malaysia, Penang, Malaysia

Frank van Meurs Language and Communication/Centre for Language Studies, Radboud University, Nijmegen, The Netherlands

Marjolijn Verspoor Department of Applied Linguistics, University of Pannonia, Veszprem, Hungary

Paola Vettorel Department of Foreign Languages and Literatures, University of Verona, Verona, Italy

Britta Viebrock Institute of English and American Studies, Goethe University Frankfurt, Frankfurt am Main/Hesse, Germany

Julie Waddington Department of Subject-Specific Education, Faculty of Education & Psychology, University of Girona, Girona, Catalonia, Spain

Elvis Wagner Department of Teaching and Learning, Temple University, Philadelphia, PA, USA

Zhisheng (Edward) Wen School of Languages and Translation, Macao Polytechnic Institute, Macau SAR, China

Gillian Wigglesworth University of Melbourne, Melbourne, Australia

Mark Wyatt Department of English, Khalifa University, Abu Dhabi, United Arab Emirates

Daniel Xerri University of Malta, Centre for English Language Proficiency, Msida, Malta

Xun Yan Department of Linguistics, University of Illinois at Urbana-Champaign, Illinois, USA

Martha Young-Scholten School of English Literature, Language and Linguistics, Newcastle University, Newcastle upon Tyne, UK

Alla Zareva Department of English, Old Dominion University, Norfolk, VA, USA

Volume Introduction: Research Questions in Language Education and Applied Linguistics: Strategies for their Conceptualization and Development

Christine Coombe

In my own development as a teacher educator in general and as a teacher of research methods in particular, I am often called on to mentor students, both undergraduate and graduate, in choosing not only a research topic but also on the process of formulating research questions. In looking for relevant literature to help me in this mentoring process, I have more often than not come up short. In fact, White (2013) has described the neglect of research questions in both methods texts and the wider academic literature (p. 1) and goes on to point out that this lack is not specific to educational research but exists in the social sciences as well as the humanities.

1.1 Why the Need for This Book

This volume has three distinct purposes. The first purpose is to assist budding researchers in TESOL and Applied Linguistics to be better prepared to identify important research questions in a specific area within the field and provide a practical discussion on the identification and development of researchable problems. This process is considered "a cornerstone and precursor for a successful research effort" (Akhidime, 2017, p. 631).

The second purpose is to attempt to fill the gap in the literature on the importance of framing research questions. Indeed, given the central role that research questions play in the research process, it is surprising that they have received scant research attention. As noted by experts in the field (Andrews, 2003; White, 2009), relative to the vast literature on other elements of the research process, very little has been

C. Coombe (✉)
Department of General Studies, Dubai Men's College,
Higher Colleges of Technology, Dubai, United Arab Emirates
e-mail: ccoombe@hct.ac.ae

© Springer Nature Switzerland AG 2021
H. Mohebbi and C. Coombe (eds.), *Research Questions in Language Education and Applied Linguistics*, Springer Texts in Education,
https://doi.org/10.1007/978-3-030-79143-8_1

written on the subject of research questions. Many well-known and frequently used general texts on research methods either do not include the topic or devote only a few mere paragraphs to it (White, 2013, p. 3). This neglect is not limited to textbooks. The topic of research questions has attracted very little attention from academics as a subject of inquiry and/or discussion.

A third reason for this volume is for it to serve as a reference guide and stress reliever of sorts. Novice researchers sometimes go through bewilderment and frustration during this process as described by this first time thesis writer (Boraie & Gebril, 2015, p. 191).

> In my opinion, the most difficult thing when writing the research questions is choosing questions that have not been chosen by someone else in order to get useful results in the field of my study from which the reader could benefit from. Also, it is important to find the research gap first, then decide on my research questions, but the problem in my case for example, that it is the same gap in all researches that I have read, and they all end up their papers by writing that more research is needed to figure out this problem. So, how could I know that I have chosen the correct research questions that would really solve that issue? Another issue is the quality of the research questions, they should be clear to the reader, feasible and straight forward; the question should not carry more than one meaning. However, it seems challenging for me to decide whether they are supposed to be more general or narrowed down.

A closer look at this quotation shows the dilemmas that novice researchers usually face when developing their research questions. Therefore, another purpose of this book is to serve as a jumping off point for researchers and students of research to further delve into topics of interest to them by using these entries as a guide written by others who have researched these topics before them.

1.2   The Importance of Research Questions

According to Pole and Lampard (2002), curiosity is, or at least, should be the driving force behind the conduct of any research (as cited in White, 2013, p. 2). Research questions are an attempt to tame this curiosity by not asking questions haphazardly but rather in relation to what is already known about a topic of interest.

A key decision that a researcher should always make is whether a study is worth doing. The field of ELT and Applied Linguistics is vast with many potential questions that need to be asked and later researched. However, not all questions are good questions. Therefore, it is essential to know what good research questions are and what is involved in writing them.

In an editorial in the journal *Language Teaching Research*, Nassaji (2019, p. 283) shares his views on research questions. A good research question is not just any question we ask. Instead, it is a clear, specific, and goal-oriented query related to a problem that needs to be addressed (Nassaji, 2019, p. 283). Moreover, it is the soundness and appropriateness of the research question that determine the quality of the research.

Nassaji (2019) puts forward three essential characteristics of good research questions. First, an important characteristic of good research questions is that they are empirically testable. That is, they are stated in ways that can be observed and measured (p. 283). There are, however, instances where a research question may be testable but other reasons why it cannot be answered, including practical considerations and restrictions. Thus, a good research question is also one that is feasible given the time constraints, the resources and/or facilities required, and the skill set and expertise needed on the part of the researcher.

Another essential element of a good research question relates to the interest level of the topic under study. A good research question is also interesting, not only just to the researcher but also to others in the field and the wider academic community. This means that the researcher must know about and be aware of what is currently going on in the field and the direction in which the field is moving.

A third element as described by Nassaji (2019, p. 283) is that good questions are also theoretically, pedagogically, or empirically motivated and worthy of research. A research question is worthy of investigation if it in some way contributes to the research literature and adds to the current understanding of and knowledge base of the profession.

1.3 What is a Research Question?

In its most simplest form, a research question is meant to guide and center research. Developing a good research question is one of the first critical steps in the research process and it is essential to guide your research output whether it be a research paper, project, thesis or dissertation. It pinpoints exactly what you want to find out and gives your work a clear focus and purpose. Boraie and Gebril (2015, p. 190) liken research questions to a roadmap that shows you (the researcher) which path to follow to reach your destination and what resources you need to take with you. A road map can also help you plan for any expected challenges during the trip and hopefully make your journey easier by showing you the shortest way to reach your destination.

The essential elements of a research question differ depending on the scope and focus of the research. According to McCombes (2021, p. 1) all research questions should be:

- **Focused** on a single problem or issue
- **Researchable** using primary and/or secondary sources
- **Feasible** to answer within the timeframe and practical constraints
- **Specific** enough to answer thoroughly
- **Complex** enough to develop the answer over a space of time
- **Relevant** to your field of study or specialization and/or society more broadly.

Other criteria of good research questions mentioned in the literature are that a research question should be: (George Mason University Writing Center, 2018).

- **Clear** in that it provides enough specifics that one's audience can easily understand its purpose without needing additional explanation
- **Arguable** in that its potential answer is open to debate rather than accepted facts.

Patino and Ferreira (2016) developed a framework of six criteria of good research questions. The recommend that all research questions should meet certain criteria as summarized by the acronym 'FINGER' which stands for Feasible, Interesting, Novel, Good, Ethical and Relevant (Table 1.1).

Whereas the FINGER criteria outline the important aspects of the question in general, a useful format to use in the development of a specific research question is the PICO format (Farrugia et al., 2010, p. 279). This format recommends that the researcher consider the (P) population of interest, the (I) intervention being studied, the (C) comparison and the (O) outcome of interest. Often (T) timing is added to this framework. The PICOT approach helps researchers generate a question that aids in constructing the framework of the study (Table 1.2).

Table 1.1 FINGER criteria (Patino & Ferreira, 2016)

Feasible	This criterion relates to whether the researcher(s) have access to enough money, time, technical expertise and skills as well as research participants
Interesting	This criterion relates to whether the research findings will be of interest to the research community
Novel	This criterion relates to whether the research question will provide new findings and/or extend or refute previous findings
Good	This criterion asks the question: Will conducting the research prove beneficial to your career and fit into your career development plan?
Ethical	The research should be considered ethical by peers and the IRB and ensures that risk to participants is low or at an acceptable rate
Relevant	Results of the research should add to the knowledge base of the profession, improve scientific knowledge, inform policy and impact future research

Table 1.2 The PICOT framework (Farrugia et al., 2010, p. 279)

Population of interest	What population are you interested in studying?
Intervention used	What interventions are you using?
Comparison	What are you comparing the intervention to?
Outcome of interest	What do you intend to accomplish, improve or effect with your research?
Timing	What is the appropriate follow-up time to assess your outcome?

1.4 Writing Effective Research Questions

A poorly constructed research question may affect the choice of study design and potentially hamper the chance of determining anything of empirical significance, which can then have an impact on opportunities for publication and dissemination of research results. So, it is therefore important to review the process for formulating and developing good research questions.

The process of writing or developing a research question follows several steps (Brown & Coombe, 2015; McCombes, 2021):

- Choose a broad topic that is of interest to the researcher (and to the wider academic or professional community)
- Do some preliminary or background reading/research to find out about topical issues within your field of study and what other researchers before you have discovered about your topic
- Based on this background research narrow down your topic to a specific area that you want to focus on and in doing so consider your audience
- Identify a practical or theoretical research problem that you will try to answer
- Determine whether a problem/question should be researched by answering these questions:

  - Can you study the problem/question?

    Do you have access to the research site and/or participants?

    Do you have the time, resources and skills to carry out the research?
  - Should you study the problem/question?
    Does it advance knowledge?
    Does it contribute to the knowledge base of your field and to practice?
    Will your research fill a gap or void in the existing literature?

1.5 How This Book is Organized

In the early conceptualization of this book, co-editor Hassan Moehbbi and I, set forth what we consider to be a unique concept answering a need on both of our academic wish lists. Wouldn't it be great to have a book with short chapters written by experts in the field and up-and-coming scholars on their areas of expertise which included what they thought to be the most important areas of research and practice and included their personal recommendations on the most relevant sources of information and the most important research questions that needed to be answered in that field of study. With this in mind, we invited said widely-recognized scholars and up-and-coming academics to produce a short chapter with the following common sections. The first section asked authors to provide a brief, clear overview of the topic with any corresponding references. Section 1.2 asked authors to formulate 10 research questions that they felt needed answering or further study. The next section invited authors to provide a short five-entry annotated bibliography of selected sources that they felt would introduce those new to that field of study essential information about the topic. In essence, we invited authors to problematize areas of theory and practice, identify apparent gaps in the field that merited research and to do this in highly accessible language for our audience, namely teachers, graduate and undergraduate students and other students of research.

The results of this three-year project are 150+ chapters on diverse topics in the field of ELT and Applied Linguistics. The book was further sub-divided into 9 parts as follows:

Part 1: Teaching and teaching-related topics.
Part 2: Learning and learning-related topics.
Part 3: Assessment and assessment-related topics.
Part 4: Language skills and subskills.
Part 5: Teachers and teacher education.
Part 6: Technology and technology-enhanced instruction.
Part 7: Politics, policies and practices in language education.
Part 8: Research and research-related topics.
Part 9: Applied linguistics and second language acquisition.

The focus of Part 1 is on topics related to teaching in the language classroom. Part 1 is the biggest section of the book and features 33 entries on topics like blended learning, ESP and EAP, TEIL as well as inclusive language teaching and World Englishes among others. The focus switches over to learning and learning-related topics in Part 2. The 16 entries in this part center around issues like emergent bilingualism, learning beyond the classroom, learner and learning strategies and task engagement. Assessment and assessment-related topics are the focus of Part 3 with 27 entries. This part begins with a chapter on aligning language assessment to standards and frameworks and ends with entries on washback and writing assessment literacy. Part 4 features 11 entries on language skills and sub-skills. In addition to entries on reading, writing, listening and speaking, entries also feature topics like foreign accent, lexical inferencing and vocabulary development. Part 5 concentrates on topics of interest to teachers and teacher education. The 18 entries found in this part look at diverse topics such as emotionality, teacher motivation, teacher burnout, teacher identity, well-being, self-efficacy and teacher reflective practice. Technology and technology-enhanced instruction is the topic under study in Part 6 which features 11 entries. From online continuing professional development to game-based learning and digital literacies, this part includes a diverse range of topics for today's ELT professional and researcher. Part 7 includes 10 chapters on politics (i.e., textbook ideology and unequal Englishes), policies (i.e., English language education policies, policy enactment for leadership development), and practices (i.e., values in the language classroom and Englishization of higher education). The next part of the book (Part 8) centers around research and research-related topics with entries focusing on qualitative research methods, eye-tracking as a research tool and research paradigms in TESOL and language education. The last part of the volume focuses on 19 entries related to Applied Linguistics and Second Language Acquisition with chapters ranging from code-mixing and code-switching to multiple intelligences theory and plurilingualism.

As you browse the Table of Contents, you might see that some entries could fit under two (or more) of the above-mentioned parts. (i.e., Elvis Wagner's *Assessing Second Language Listening* which could be placed in either assessment or language skills and sub skills). This is a dilemma that we editors faced when putting together the book. As such in the second edit we asked entry authors to specify where they thought the best placement of their entry would be. In most instances, we were able to place entries as per the chapter authors' wishes. As far as the order of the chapters within each part is concerned, entries appear alphabetically based on the first letter of the first word of the entry title.

1.6 Closing Thoughts

Research ideas or questions can come from a variety of sources, including this volume which asked experts in the field as well as up-and-coming scholars to identify the most needed research questions in their academic specialty. Please note that these questions are not the only ones that can be asked, researched and subsequently answered; they represent just a sampling of the research questions out there. It is our hope that students of research will use the entries in this book as not only a springboard for research but also for discussion about the academic topics represented therein.

References

Akhidime, A. E. (2017). The importance and development of research problem: A didactic discussion. *International Journal of Economics, Commerce and Management, 8*, 631–640.

Andrews, R. (2003). *Research questions*. Continuum.

Boraie, D., & Gebril, A. (2015). Creating effective research questions. In J. D. Brown & C. Coombe (Eds.), *The cambridge guide to research in language teaching and learning* (pp. 190–197). Cambridge University Press.

Brown, J. D., & Coombe, C. (2015). *The cambridge guide to research in language teaching and learning*. Cambridge University Press.

Farrugia, P., Petrisor, B. A., Farrokhyar, F., & Bhandari, M. (2010). Research questions, hypotheses and objectives. *Canadian Journal of Surgery, 53*(4), 278–281.

McCombes, S. (2021). *Developing strong research questions*. May 14, 2021 at https://www.scribbr.com/research-process/research-questions/

Nassaji, H. (2019). Editorial: Good research questions. *Language Teaching Research, 23*, 283–286.

Patino, C. M., & Ferreira, J. C. (2016). Developing research questions that make a difference. *Jornal Brasileiro De Pneumologia, 42*(6), 403.

Pole, C. J., & Lampard, R. (2002). *Practical social investigation: Qualitative and quantitative methods in social research.* Prentice Hall.

The George Mason University Writing Center (2018). How to write a research question. May 14, 2021 at https://writingcenter.gmu.edu/guides/how-to-write-a-research-question

White, P. (2009). *Developing research questions: A guide for social scientists.* Palgrave.

White, P. (2013). Who's afraid of research questions? The neglect of research questions in the methods literature and a call for question-led methods teaching. *International Journal of Research & Method in Education*, 36(3), 213–227. https://doi.org/10.1080/1743727X.2013. 809413

Christine Coombe has a Ph.D from The Ohio State University. She is currently an Associate Professor of General Studies at Dubai Men's College. Christine is co-author or editor of numerous volumes on assessment including Assessment Practices (2003, TESOL Publications); A Practical Guide to Assessing English Language Learners (2007, University of Michigan Press); The Cambridge Guide to Second Language Assessment (2012, Cambridge University Press), and TESOL Encyclopedia of ELT (Vol. 8) (Wiley Blackwell, 2018). She has won many awards including: the 2002 Spaan Fellowship for Research in Second/Foreign Language Assessment; and the 2013 British Council's International Assessment Award. Her most recent honors were being named to TESOL's 50@50 and being the recipient of the 2018 James E Alatis Award which recognizes exemplary service to TESOL.

Part I
Teaching and Teaching-related Topics

Attending to Form in the Communicative Classroom

Martin East

How teachers should help students to develop their grammatical competence in communicatively-oriented classrooms is an issue of significant concern in English Language Teaching. So-called Communicative Language Teaching (CLT) is now widely established as the dominant model for language teaching and learning worldwide. CLT is built on extensive agreement that helping learners to develop their communicative or interactional competence is the primary goal (see, e.g., Hedge, 2000; Kramsch, 1986). Beyond that simple agreement, however, attention to grammar has stood out as an issue of contention (see, e.g., Mitchell et al., 2019). Debates reflect the perceived pedagogical effectiveness of a behaviourist top-down teacher-led position (the teacher as 'sage on the stage' who imparts grammatical knowledge to students from the front of the class) in contrast to a social constructivist learner-centred model (the teacher who, as 'guide on the side', encourages learners' self-discovery of the underlying grammatical rules).

Presentation-Practice-Production (PPP) exemplifies a traditional top-down approach to grammar within the CLT paradigm: the teacher first presents a grammatical rule to learners in an explicit front-of-class way. Learners then practise the rule using a range of targeted grammar exercises. Finally, learners may be asked to use the target rule in a communicative context, with communication focused on putting the rule into practice. Long (2000) described this teacher-led 'deductive' model as focus on forms (FonFs). FonFs arguably helps learners to develop their explicit grammatical knowledge. However, the production (communication) stage is frequently so restricted to practising the target forms that learners do not develop their ability to use language beyond limited confines (that is, the development of interactional competence is constrained).

M. East (✉)
School of Cultures, Languages and Linguistics, Faculty of Arts, The University of Auckland, Auckland, New Zealand
e-mail: m.east@auckland.ac.nz

© Springer Nature Switzerland AG 2021
H. Mohebbi and C. Coombe (eds.), *Research Questions in Language Education and Applied Linguistics*, Springer Texts in Education,
https://doi.org/10.1007/978-3-030-79143-8_2

Contrasting learner-centred and experiential approaches view language, in Brown's (2014) words, as "interactive communication among individuals," whereby the language classroom becomes "a locus of meaningful, authentic exchanges among users of language," and language learning becomes "the creation of meaning through interpersonal negotiation among learners" (p. 206). So-called task-based language teaching (TBLT) exemplifies these foci. However, TBLT itself has been subject to differences in application depending on stances taken to pedagogical effectiveness.

Strong TBLT, in which a pure focus on engaging in communicative tasks is seen as "the necessary and sufficient condition of successful second language acquisition" (Nunan, 2004, p. 21) might employ a largely focus on meaning or 'zero grammar'/non-interface approach whereby learners will work out the rules implicitly for themselves as they engage in language use. As an alternative, focus on form (FonF) is an 'inductive' approach whereby more explicit attention to grammar is contingent on learners first noticing patterns as they put language to use, built on the premise that "if the students can work out the rule for themselves, then they are more likely to remember it" (Ur, 2012, p. 81). Weak TBLT (or task-*supported* language teaching) extends the FonF approach to incorporate more traditional teacher-led exposition.

In summary, when it comes to the 'best' approaches to helping learners to acquire grammatical competence, the jury is still out. As Mitchell et al. (2019) put it, "[t]here can be no 'one best method' … which applies at all times and in all situations, with every type of learner" (p. 406).

The Research Questions

1. How can teachers improve their students' grammatical competence?
2. What beliefs do teachers hold about grammar teaching?
3. How do beliefs about grammar teaching influence teachers' pedagogical choices?
4. What are the comparative advantages of one approach to grammar over another?
5. What impact does direct instruction have on developing learners' grammatical competence?
6. What impact do focused or consciousness-raising tasks have on developing learners' grammatical competence?
7. How might explicit grammatical knowledge contribute to increased interactional competence?
8. Which approaches to grammar do learners favour, and why?
9. How do learner variables (age, proficiency, etc.) impact the stance taken by teachers to developing grammatical competence?
10. How can we effectively measure students' grammatical competence?

Suggested Resources

Spada, N., & Lightbown, P. (2008). Form-focused instruction: Isolated or integrated? *TESOL Quarterly, 42*(2), 181–207.

In this significant and informative article, Nina Spada and Patsy Lightbown begin from what they see as a foundational premise: that grammar teaching is important, and that there is growing agreement that form-focused instruction helps learners in communicative contexts to learn features of the target language that they might not acquire if they did not receive some level of instructional input. The article goes on to consider the role that instruction might play either in separate (i.e., isolated) activities or embedded within the context of communicative activities (i.e., integrated). The authors suggest that both kinds of instruction can be advantageous, depending on the grammatical feature at hand, and the characteristics of the learners and learning conditions. They argue furthermore that teachers and students see benefit in both instructional formats. The article provides a valuable rehearsal of the theory- and research-informed benefits of both approaches.

Larsen-Freeman, D. (2015). Research into practice: Grammar learning and teaching. *Language Teaching, 48*(2), 263–280.

This important article appears in *Language Teaching*'s 'Thinking Allowed' section which provides scope for suitably-qualified experts to consider different dimensions of a topic in which they have particular expertise. Here, Diane Larsen-Freeman reviews the second language acquisition and applied linguistics research literature on grammar learning and teaching. She considers areas where, with regard to practice, research has had little impact (the non-interface position) or modest impact (form-focused instruction), and where it could potentially have a larger impact (reconceiving grammar). Larsen-Freeman contends that, despite advances in research, grammar instruction remains largely traditional and teacher-led. Grammar teaching focuses on accuracy of form and rule learning, and mechanical exercises are perceived as the means to embed this rule learning. Larsen-Freeman suggests that one reason for this adherence to tradition is the gulf that exists between research and practice. As a consequence, researchers and teacher educators need to find ways of helping teachers to navigate the divide so that teachers can be encouraged to consider alternative approaches.

East, M. (2017). Research into practice: The task-based approach to instructed second language acquisition. *Language Teaching, 50*(3), 412–424.

This 'Thinking Allowed' piece discusses the phenomenon of task-based language teaching in instructed contexts. It builds on the argument that, despite considerable theoretical and empirical support, TBLT remains a contested endeavour. With regard to grammar in task-based classrooms, the article argues that the learner-centred inductive approach of focus on form, which relies on students' noticing of grammatical forms in the target language input, is under-developed in practice. Rather, a tendency persists to hold onto more traditional teacher-led approaches to grammar instruction. This tendency emerges among critiques of TBLT which suggest that, particularly in time-limited instructional contexts, TBLT's learner-centred and experiential approach does not provide an adequately structured environment that allows for sufficient exposure to frequent language, and processing and practising of grammatical concepts.

East, M. (2018). "If it is all about tasks, will they learn anything?" Teachers' perspectives on grammar instruction in the task-oriented classroom. In M.J. Ahmadian & M. P. García Mayo (Eds.). *Recent perspectives on task-based language learning and teaching* **(pp. 217–231). Berlin: De Gruyter Mouton.**

This book chapter directly addresses the issue of how grammatical accuracy might be attended to within a task-based language teaching approach to language pedagogy. Teachers' anxiety about a minimalist role for grammar instruction in the task-based classroom forms the backdrop of the chapter. It is argued that teachers often feel uncertain about the relationship between learner-centred tasks and explicit grammar explanation, particularly when TBLT is perceived as an experiential approach that eschews direct grammar instruction. The chapter proposes, however, that explicit teaching can be a viable component of task-oriented classrooms. The chapter reports on a study that investigated how practising school-based teachers facilitated form-focused instruction, illustrating teachers' attempts to draw on a 'directed noticing' approach. This approach clearly focused on the learners' ability to process language for themselves but was elicited in co-construction with the teacher.

East, M. (2018). Learning in the classroom. In A. Burns & J.C. Richards (Eds.). *The Cambridge guide to learning English as a second language* **(pp. 110–117). Cambridge, UK: Cambridge University Press.**

This book chapter builds on the contrasting theoretical perspectives that inform the development of grammatical competence as articulated by Long—focus on forms, focus on meaning, and focus on form. Situated within an interactionist perspective that encourages students to take part in authentic interaction with others, the chapter argues that language students require ample and adequate time to engage in communicative interaction in class. With this in mind, the chapter suggests a 'flipped classroom' model. In this model, form-focused instruction is constructed as something that could take place outside the classroom as a precursor to classroom work. Prior to class, students, scaffolded by appropriate support resources such as short instructional videos, work on the rules for themselves. The classroom then becomes primarily a place where the rules can be put into practice through a range of opportunities for communicative interaction among students.

References

Brown, H. D. (2014). *Principles of language learning and teaching* (6th ed.). Pearson.

Hedge, T. (2000). *Teaching and learning in the language classroom.* Oxford University Press.

Kramsch, C. (1986). From language proficiency to interactional competence. *The Modern Language Journal, 70*(4), 366–372.

Long, M. (2000). Focus on form in task-based language teaching. In R. D. Lambert, & E. Shohamy (Eds.), *Language policy and pedagogy: Essays in honor of A. Ronald Walton* (pp. 179–192). John Benjamins.

Mitchell, R., Myles, F., & Marsden, E. (2019). *Second language learning theories* (4th ed.). Routledge.

Nunan, D. (2004). *Task-based language teaching.* Cambridge University Press.

Ur, P. (2012). *A course in English language teaching.* Cambridge University Press.

Martin East is Professor of Language Education and current Head of the School of Cultures, Languages and Linguistics at the University of Auckland, New Zealand, where he primarily teaches courses in language teaching and learning. His research interests focus on two broad areas: innovative practices in language pedagogy and assessment, and the development of policies to support the teaching and learning of languages other than English in English-dominant contexts. His articles have appeared in a wide range of international journals, and he is the author of several books, including Task-Based Language Teaching from the Teachers' Perspective (2012), Assessing Foreign Language Students' Spoken Proficiency (2016) and Foundational Principles of Task-Based Language Teaching (2021). In 2017 Martin became President of the International Association for Task-Based Language Teaching.

Blended Learning

Lana Hiasat

The Blended learning approach is a shift from teachers using traditional face-to-face teaching strategies to creating productive and positive learning experiences in an online blended approach using educational technology tools. A general definition of blended learning is an instructional delivery mode that teachers combine both face-to-face instruction and online learning (Bonk & Graham, 2012). There are several models of blended learning that can occur at the following four levels: activity, course, department or program, and district or institutional levels. There is not a one best model of blended learning. The models of blended learning can be any of the following: rotation, flex, self-blend, or enriched virtual blend. There are many benefits as well as challenges in implementing the blended learning approach. Blended learning provides an increased community and collaboration, the possibility of an increased global connectedness, currency of course materials, and the freedom for students of learning anytime and anywhere (Bonk & Graham, 2012). Most recently from the academic year of 2019-2020 in the response to the COVID 19 pandemic, the blended learning approach became extremely important for all levels of educational institutions to continue offering a high level of education despite the lockdowns and other challenges of illnesses that happened to both faculty and students. Educators all around the world started swiftly studying and applying blended learning approaches and utilizing educational technology tools available to them.

Despite the many benefits of blended learning, there are several significant obstacles recorded in the literature to applying a blended learning curriculum as noted by several scholars (Lloyd et al., 2012; Murphy & Rodriguez-Manzanares, 2009; Wilson, 2004). The barriers of quality online resources and learning appear to be due to restrictions that are interpersonal, institutional, training and technology-related, and cost issues as Lloyd, Byrne, and McCoy (2012) have reported. Lack of

L. Hiasat (✉)
Department of General Studies, Higher Colleges of Technology, Dubai, UAE
e-mail: lhiasat@hct.ac.ae

© Springer Nature Switzerland AG 2021
H. Mohebbi and C. Coombe (eds.), *Research Questions in Language Education and Applied Linguistics*, Springer Texts in Education,
https://doi.org/10.1007/978-3-030-79143-8_3

updated technology, absence of required training, and low motivation were also some of the key barriers (Lloyd et al., 2012) mentioned. Motivational factors are also reported in the literature and they relate to both learners and the teachers' perspectives. Learner motivation in distance education courses is difficult because learners need to exercise a high level of independence (Murphy & Rodriguez-Manzanares, 2009). These mentioned barriers prior to the COVID 19 pandemic appeared the same especially notable barrier of quality online resources and student engagement online.

The quality and cost of distance education can be another set of barriers to online learning. Wilson (2004) has explained how educational leaders doubt that technology tools can replace the face-to-face classroom interactions that some claim are critical to education. Pogash (2012) found that the expensive reality of online education could create a barrier to online learning. For example, the large amounts of funding and technical support that the K12 California Virtual schools needed were evidence of the high cost of online learning (Pogash, 2012). Finally, online education is argued as not suitable for all learners because distance learning is a different approach from the traditional ways of studying (Milman, 2011). Therefore, it was believed that learners who were already low achievers would not succeed in the online environment (Milman, 2011).

Several researchers have suggested that there is a lack of a clearly defined road map on how to build online learning communities in general (for example, see Deng & Yuen, 2010; Liu et al., 2007). The lack of understanding of how blended learning approaches can reform schools and help them move away from the traditional view of teaching and learning is a concern that educational leaders can help address by further in-depth research. Such data driven research is needed to learn what works best in each context especially after the opportunity that the COVID 19 pandemic offered to create transformational changes in education.

The Research Questions

1. What are the contexts in which teachers create blended learning curricula?
2. How is the gamification of learning used in a blended learning environment?
3. What are the barriers that prevent language teachers from implementing a blended learning curriculum?
4. How is the blended learning approach used to create a smart learning environment?
5. What factors impact student satisfaction and dissatisfaction in blended learning courses?
6. How is virtual reality implemented in blended learning courses?
7. What are the cultural and contextual elements that impact the success of blended learning courses?

8. What are the characteristics of a successful teacher and learner in blended learning environments?
9. How do accreditation and benchmarking processes impact blended learning course design?
10. What are the educational policies that countries have implemented to reform schools when using blended learning curriculum?

Suggested Resources

Barber, W., Taylor, S., & Buchanan, S. (2014). Empowering knowledge-building pedagogy in online environments: Creating digital moments to transform practice. *Electronic Journal of e-Learning, 12*(2), 128–137. Retrieved from http://www.ejel.org/volume12/issue2/p128

Barber, Taylor, and Buchanan (2014) explored a specific teaching tool called digital moments to build online learning experiences in a constructivist approach. The emphasis in this study was on not only getting students to use technology as consumers but creators of new learning experiences. In their qualitative study, the authors were concerned with exploring how innovation, authentic, and risk-taking approaches could be applied in online communities. This study was based on a narrative design and story-telling approach to explore how learning happens in online communities. A four-phase project was planned to explore the effectiveness of the digital moments teaching strategy by first piloting this new teaching approach as phase one, then using the technology in an undergraduate course as phase two. In phase three the teaching strategy was used to examine using reflections and online interactions. In the final and fourth stage interviewing students on how the digital moments strategy affected their learning was conducted through interviews. Barber, Taylor, and Buchanan's study (2014) revealed the importance of building relationships in the online environment, encouraging risk taking, and establishing a human element in learning through empowerment, confidence, and dealing with the fear of technology use. This study placed a greater emphasis on establishing the human factor in online communities as an essential element. Such a conclusion was especially noticed in further studies when the transtion to fully online happened in many educational institutions. It can be also concluded from this study that technology tools are not the essential element in online communities but rather the relationship between teachers and students which is critical in improving student engagement.

Cuthbertson, W., & Falcone, A. (2014). Elevating engagement and community in online courses. *Journal of Library & Information Services in Distance Learning, 8*(3), 216–224. https://doi.org/10.1080/1533290X.2014.945839

Cuthbertson and Falcone (2014) discussed best practices for building online communities by focusing on motivational elements and what engages students. The authors stated that the level of community is correlated with the levels of engagement and student participation and discussed the following strategies that foster building online communities:

- Discussion forums: teachers should create spaces for students to share their experiences through discussion forums.
- Roles and responsibilities: teachers should assign individual students and groups roles and responsibilities within their discussion forums.
- Peer feedback: teachers should encourage students to offer peer feedback.
- Synchronous communication: in addition to asynchronous discussion, teachers should plan for live sessions to connect with their students in real time.
- Media rich environment: teachers should create assignments that utilize rich media that excite students to engage.

Cuthbertson and Falcone (2014) listed several applications for following the five strategies to engage students. This study emphasized how teachers engage learners and strategies that motivate them in building the online community.

Dlugash, M. (2014). Innovating schools. *Kennedy School Review, 14,* **75–79. Retrieved from** http://harvardkennedyschoolreview.com/innovating-schools/

Dlugash (2014) believes that education reform is an ongoing effort that is transformative and can indeed be transformed; however, the focus of reform may not be the right things. Policies to reform American education have been set as solutions for failing schools. Dlugash (2014) stated that polices to reform education did not focus on the organization and conceptualization of schools because the main reason behind failing schools in America is the defunct educational model as the author believes. The educational model is not meeting twenty-first century needs, and the core assumptions of schools need to change to become innovative and yet address the core standards of education. The author proposes new models of education based on innovation. The models are based on empowering students and their families, creating authentic assessments, promoting democratic values and a celebration of cultural heritages, empowering students through internships and community serving and serving students through individualized learning plans and assessments through a flexible model of online learning.

Hiasat, L. (2018). Blended and experiential learning for Emiratis in tertiary education. *Journal of Asia TEFL,* **15(3), 874–881.** https://doi.org/10.18823/asiatefl.2018.15.3.874

This article provides a summary of a qualitative case study of blended and experiential learning in tertiary education in one of the largest higher education institutions in the United Arab Emirates. Cultural complexities are addressed in this article when faculty implemented the blended learning approaches. The two major themes found in this case study were discussed as the following: culture in blended learning and technology based experiential learning. The list of findings included six important discoveries that the author listed. The recommendations provided can guide faculty, instructional designers, and educational leaders to implement blended learning in their institutions.

Hiasat, L., & Pollitt, A. (2019). Blended and experiential learning for Emiratis in tertiary education. *Journal of Asia TEFL, 15*(3), 874–881. https://doi.org/10. 4018/978-1-5225-6136-1

In this article, the authors describe the results of a case study that explored what elements created a smart learning environment. They specifically focused on what educators do to create such an environment. The article is focused around three main areas that are meant to prompt readers to evaluate their own learning environment. The first question is related to using appropriate technology, the second one is about applying suitable pedagogy, and the third relates to the context of teaching and learning. The authors presented a list of recommendations for learning resources, learning tools, learning communities, teaching communities, and learning and teaching methods. The authors' recommendations are in comparison to what common digital learning environments offer and suggestions on how to move towards a smart learning environment are also offered.

References

Bonk, C. J., & Graham, C. R. (2012). *The handbook of blended learning: Global perspectives, local designs*. John Wiley & Sons.

Deng, L., & Yuen, A. H. K. (2010). Exploring the role of academic blogs in a blended community: An integrative approach. *Research Practice Technology Enhanced Learning, 5*(2), 53–71. https://doi.org/10.1142/s1793206810000840

Liu, X., Magjuka, R. J., Bonk, C. J., & Lee, S. (2007). Does sense of community matter? An examination of participants' perceptions of building learning communities in online courses. *Quarterly Review of Distance Education, 8*(1), 9–24,87–88.

Lloyd, S., Byrne, M., & McCoy, T. (2012). Faculty-perceived barriers of online education. *MERLOT Journal of Online Learning and Teaching, 8*(1). Retrieved from: http://jolt.merlot.org/vol8no1/lloyd_0312.pdf

Milman, N. (2011). Is online learning for all learners? *Distance Learning, 8*(2). Retrieved from: http://www.infoagepub.com

Murphy, E., & Rodriguez-Manzanares, M. (2009). Teacher's perspectives on motivation in high school distance education. *International Journal of E-Learning and Distance, 23*(3), 1-4. Retrieved from: http://www.ijede.ca

Pogash, C. (2012). Online charters are expensive and problematic. *Opposing Viewpoints in Context*. Web. November 9, 2015. Retrieved from: http://assets.cengage.com

Wilson, D. (2004). The information revolution has not improved off-campus education. *The Information Revolution*. Retrieved from: https://www.homeworkmarket.com

Lana Hiasat is the Program Coordinator of the General Studies department at Dubai Men's College, UAE in addition to being English faculty. She has published in areas of emotional intelligence, smart learning, blended learning, educational leadership, intercultural intelligence, and online teaching and learning. She has co-chaired several international conferences including the latest one on happiness and wellbeing, TESOL Arabia, and the first general academic requirement (GARD) conference and is currently on the advisory board for TESOL Arabia in addition to chairing the research committee for her division on 16 campuses. Dr. Hiasat has been on the task force to write the national curriculum for the social sciences and moral education in the UAE in which role she has developed the curriculum for grades 10, 11, and 12 including assessments, teacher guides, and instructional audio and video recordings. She applied her research in emotional intelligence and training in future foresight to creating 21st century curriculum. Her research interests are in smart learning, blended learning, education 4.0, e-learning, educational leadership, and voluntary teaching and learning communities.

Content and Language Integrated Learning (CLIL)

4

Zohreh R. Eslami and Zihan Geng

Content and language integrated learning (CLIL) was proposed by the European Network of Administrators, Researchers and Practitioners (EUROCLIC) in the 1990s. CLIL refers to "any dual-focused educational context in which an additional language, thus not usually the first language of the learners involved, is used as a medium in the teaching and learning of non-language content" (Marsh, 2002, p. 15). Therefore, CLIL is an umbrella term for different teaching approaches, in which both a foreign language and the non-language subject are equally emphasized. CLIL is considered "the European label for bilingual education" (Muñoz, 2007, p. 28).

However, CLIL is far more than simply teaching a subject in a foreign language. In CLIL, the language serves both as a tool for learning and as a learning objective itself (Coyle, 2007). To realize the integration, language teachers and subject teachers need to work collaboratively to construct an appropriate curriculum and pedagogy based on the context (Coyle, 2006). The dual foci feature of CLIL leads to diverse models in practice. According to Grin (2005), there are 216 different CLIL programs in Europe depending on the age, language proficiency level, intensity of the program, and duration.

Coyle (1999) proposed the 4Cs pedagogical framework for CLIL— content, cognition, communication, and culture. The concept of content is not limited to the knowledge and skills teachers provide. It also entails the development of self-learning. Cognition is reflected in the thinking process of both subject and language acquisition. In other words, cognition is related to thinking, analyzing,

Z. R. Eslami (✉)
Department of Educational Psychology, Texas A&M University, College Station, TX, USA
e-mail: zeslami@tamu.edu

Z. Geng
Department of Teaching, Learning, and Culture, Texas A&M University, College Station, TX, USA
e-mail: gengzihan@tamu.edu

© Springer Nature Switzerland AG 2021
H. Mohebbi and C. Coombe (eds.), *Research Questions in Language Education and Applied Linguistics*, Springer Texts in Education,
https://doi.org/10.1007/978-3-030-79143-8_4

and constructing the new subject knowledge and language use. Successful communication should be fulfilled through meaningful content learning activities. In the meanwhile, the language should be accessible to learners to ensure effective communication. Finally, culture is embedded in content, cognition, and language. CLIL lesson plans should help raise students' intercultural awareness by introducing culturally relevant concepts and implementing multicultural tasks.

The dual emphases of CLIL require teachers to have both in-depth subject knowledge and sufficient linguistic competence (Marsh et al., 2010). Moreover, CLIL teachers should be able to provide comprehensible input and create a rich language learning environment. However, what challenges CLIL teachers most is to develop both language and content knowledge (Vázquez & Ellison, 2018). In other words, the goal of the delivery of the content should not just be comprehensibility of content but should also facilitate students' language development.

The Research Questions

1. How do CLIL teachers perceive their role in classroom teaching?
2. How do the language outcomes of CLIL students compare with non-CLIL students?
3. How do the content outcomes of CLIL students compare with students studying in their L1?
4. What are the main challenges CLIL teachers face and how can they be resolved?
5. How should students' language and content learning outcomes in CLIL be measured?
6. What teaching strategies help improve learning outcomes in CLIL programs?
7. What are effective practices for educating CLIL instructors?
8. How do different types of CLIL programs differ from each other? What variables contribute to the diversity of CLIL programs?
9. What are the attitudes toward CLIL of various stakeholders?
10. Whose culture should be included in the CLIL classroom? Local culture, target culture, or global culture? How does this affect the identities of CLIL instructors and students?

Suggested Resources

De Zarobe, Y. R. & Catalan, R. M. J. (Eds.) (2009). *Content and language integrated learning: evidence from research in Europe.* **Bristol: Multilingual Matters.**

The primary purpose of this volume is to provide an overview of CLIL programs in Europe. It first discusses the conceptual framework of CLIL models along with the potential issues. Then it provides empirical CLIL research in the European context. The theoretical framework section contains three chapters: the development of CLIL programs in Spain, the features of successful CLIL programs in different countries, and the importance of involving all CLIL stakeholders. The second part of this volume, which is composed of nine chapters, offers a wide range of empirical CLIL studies. The research areas include: pronunciation, vocabulary, morphological knowledge, lexical choice and production, syntactic knowledge, the role of first language (L1), communicative competence, and spoken and written language production. The studies addressed in these chapters show how foreign language could be acquired efficiently in CLIL classroom contexts.

Dalton-Puffer, C. (2007). *Discourse in content and language integrated learning (CLIL) classrooms.* **Amsterdam, the Netherlands: John Benjamins.**

This volume is based on data from CLIL studies in Austria. The chapters in this volume provide investigations of the discourse, that is, the language use and communication in CLIL classrooms. This book provides an in-depth analysis of the kind of communicative abilities exemplified in CLIL classrooms. It examines teacher and student talk at the secondary school level from different discourse-analytic perspectives, taking into consideration the interpersonal pragmatics of classroom discourse. The analysis reveals how CLIL classroom interaction is tightly shaped by its institutional context, which in turn effects the different ways students experience, use and develop the target language. The research presented in this book submits that CLIL programs require more explicit language learning goals in order to fully achieve their potential for promoting the learners' appropriation of a foreign language as a medium of learning.

The extensive data and citation record used in this book offers valuable reference material for comparison purposes and for locating resources. Dalton-Puffer's volume can be considered a key contribution to understanding CLIL classrooms.

Dalton-Puffer, C., Nikula, T., & Smit, U. (Eds.). (2010). *Language use and language learning in CLIL classrooms.* **Amsterdam, the Netherlands John Benjamins.**

This edited volume explores the fast spreading practice in mainstream education to teach content subjects through a foreign language. The introductory and concluding chapters provide a comprehensive synthesis of current CLIL research as well as critically discussing the unresolved issues relating to both theoretical concerns and research practice. Current empirical research in CLIL is presented by the different individual contributions from a range of European contexts. The book includes three different parts. Part one includes two chapters and focuses on the theoretical issues related to CLIL. Part two and three include chapters related to CLIL at the secondary and the tertiary levels. The chapters have different foci ranging from theoretical to empirical, from learning outcomes to classroom talk, investigating both the written and spoken mode across secondary and tertiary educational contexts. This volume is a valuable resource not only for researchers and teachers but also for policy makers as it represents the multifaceted state of affairs of CLIL in diverse educational contexts. The editors provide a well synthesized reflective and significant prospective view by summarizing the findings of the field and outlining contentious issues in CLIL.

Ball, P., Kelly, K., & Clegg, J. (2015). *Putting CLIL into practice*. **Oxford: Oxford University Press.**

This volume offers a new methodological framework for the CLIL classroom, focusing on how to monitor input and support output. It contains a wide range of new ideas and numerous criteria, guidelines, and sample materials. The chapters provide real-life examples and practical guidelines to help CLIL teachers to successfully use CLIL in their own contexts. The authors offer different types of assessment and diverse courses of action based on the possible scenarios we can find in real institutions and educational systems.

The book clearly offers a classroom-based vision of CLIL through a reader-friendly narrative. The volume provides support for both novice and expert CLIL teachers and discusses criteria required to ensure the success of CLIL classrooms. Each chapter ends with a useful summary and recommendations for further reading in addition to a glossary.

In sum, this volume is a highly relevant and useful read as it offers a vast range of ideas, activities and checklists on all aspects of CLIL that reflect the authors' concern with conceptual foundations as well as their experience as CLIL consultants and language-teaching experts. The book is an important contribution to the development of teaching methodology in CLIL and will promote awareness and understanding related to effective pedagogy in CLIL contexts around the globe.

Graham, K. M., Choi, Y., Davoodi, A., Razmeh, S. & Dixon, L. Q. (2018). Language and Content Outcomes of CLILand EMI: A Systematic Review. *LACLIL, 11*(1), 19–37.

Graham et al. (2018) use a systematic literature review approach to examine current literature on the effect of CLIL (Content Based Instruction/CBI in their terminology) on language and content outcomes. Twenty-five articles were used in this review. The review revealed mixed findings for both language and content outcomes. As the researchers indicate, based on the reviewed studies, CLIL either exceeds non-CLIL courses or there is no significant difference. The researchers submit that due to a large number of methodological flaws found in the literature the results should be interpreted cautiously.

Furthermore, as authors state literature from CLIL classrooms in Spain is well represented in their review, while other countries remain understudied and thus this review synthesis may not reflect the realities of CLIL in other contexts. In order to add clarity and validity about the effect of CLIL on student outcomes, the authors suggest for future research on CLIL outcomes to extend the studies to other countries and also consider the methodological flaws identified in the reviewed studies. Furthermore, other varieties of CLIL, such as English Medium Instruction (EMI), deserve more attention.

References

Coyle, D. (1999). Theory and planning for effective classrooms: Supporting students in content and language integrated learning contexts. In J. Masih (Ed.), *Learning through a foreign language* (pp. 46–62). CILT.

Coyle, D. (2006). Developing CLIL: Towards a theory of practice. In *Monograph 6* (pp. 5–29). APAC.

Coyle, D. (2007). Content and language integrated learning: Towards a connected research agenda for CLIL pedagogies. *International Journal of Bilingual Education and Bilingualism, 10*(5), 543–562.

Grin, F. (2005, March). *Added value of CLIL.* Paper presented at the Changing European Classroom—The Potential of Plurilingual Education conference, Luxembourg.

Marsh, D., Mehisto, P., Wolff, D., & Frigols-Martin, M. (2010). *European framework for CLIL teacher education: A framework for the professional development of CLIL teachers.* European Centre for Modern Languages, Council of Europe.

Marsh, D. (2002) *CLIL/EMILE: The European dimension: Actions, trends and foresight potential.* European Commission.

Muñoz, C. (2007). CLIL: Some thoughts on its psycholinguistic principles. *Revista Española De Lingüística Aplicada, 1*(1), 17–26.

Vázquez, V. P., & Ellison, M. (2018). Examining teacher roles and competences in content and language integrated learning (CLIL). *Linguarum Arena: Revista De Estudosem Didática De Línguas Da Universidade Do Porto, 4,* 65–78.

Zohreh R. Eslami is a Professor at the Department of Teaching, Learning, and Culture at Texas A&M University in College Station and currently serves as the Liberal Arts Program Chair at Texas A&M University at Qatar. Her research has examined intercultural and cross-cultural communication, English as an International language, sociocultural perspectives of teaching, acquisition of, and English-medium instruction. Her publications include over one hundred journal papers, book chapters and conference proceedings.

Zihan Geng is a Ph.D. candidate at the Department of Teaching, Learning, and Culture at Texas A&M University in College Station. She currently works as a graduate research assistant at the Center for Research & Development in Dual Language & Literacy Acquisition at Texas A&M University. Zihan has more than three years' teaching experience in China and in the U.S. Her research interests include English as a second/foreign language, second language acquisition, task-based language teaching (TBLT), content and language integrated learning (CLIL), and professional development for teachers. She has presented research in different conferences related to second language acquisition such as the Second Language Research Forum (SLRF).

Content-Based Language Teaching

5

Zübeyde Sinem Genç

Content-based language teaching (CBLT), also known as content-based instruction (CBI), or content and language integrated learning (CLIL), first appeared in the field of language teaching in the mid-1980s deriving its origins from immersion education and the language-across-the-curriculum movement. In the late 1980s, it was viewed as an approach to teaching a second/foreign language by pioneers such as Benesch (1988), Brinton et al. (1989), Cantoni-Harvey (1987), Crandall (1987) and Short, Crandall and Christian (1989). CBLT can be briefly defined as the integration of language teaching with content instruction, where language teaching is organized 'around meaningful content or subject matter, rather than the more traditional focus on grammar or skills or more recently, on tasks'. (Crandall, 2012: 149).

CBLT has taken a prominent place among the approaches to teaching a foreign language in the twenty-first century with the support of the theories and empirical findings on second language acquisition and cognitive psychology. In this respect, CBLT offers language learners the necessary conditions and opportunities to be exposed to comprehensible input in meaningful contexts, and to interact in the target language through negotiating on meaning, leading to the production of comprehensible output. Further support for CBLT has been provided by the sociocultural approaches to learning a second language. The Zone of Proximal Development as proposed by Vygotsky (1978) finds a working and sound place in CBLT where learners can work with teachers and more capable peers to handle increasingly complex texts and tasks when engaged in group work (Lantolf & Appel, 1994). CBLT has been in use more than ever in the US as reflected in English Language Proficiency Standards released by TESOL in 2006, and in European countries usually referred to as content and language integrated learning (CLIL). The reasons for its popularity lie in the strong theoretical underpinnings explained above, and the benefits CBLT offers to teachers and students in various

Z. S. Genç (✉)
Department of Foreign Language Education/English Language Teaching, Faculty of Education/Bursa Uludağ University, Bursa, Turkey

© Springer Nature Switzerland AG 2021
H. Mohebbi and C. Coombe (eds.), *Research Questions in Language Education and Applied Linguistics*, Springer Texts in Education, https://doi.org/10.1007/978-3-030-79143-8_5

contexts. Language learning becomes more meaningful and motivating because language is contextualized within the topics/subject matters students want and need to learn more about. Furthermore, as Crandall (2012) states, "it offers a natural context for developing learning strategies and academic skills. Through the use of relevant and motivating content, learners can be provided with opportunities to develop note-taking, paraphrasing, summarizing, predicting, and confirming/disconfirming skills" (p: 153). The techniques used in content-based language classrooms include information management, modifying input, using contextual clues, checking for understanding, vocabulary instruction, schema-building activities, learner grouping strategies, hands-on activities, critical thinking, language- and discourse-rich activities, and text-analysis and construction.

Depending on the purpose, needs and teaching context, models of CBLT range from more content-driven to more language-driven (Met, 1999). Commonly used varieties are known as total immersion, partial immersion, sheltered instruction observation protocol (SIOP), adjunct model, theme-based model and language classes with frequent use of content for language practice (Snow, 2014).

However, CBLT has its own challenges and problems. One major challenge is to justify its validity as a way to teach a foreign language for learners and other stakeholders who are not familiar with the principles of CBLT, as they may feel that they waste their time and do not really focus on learning the language. For those who wish to implement CBLT, it is quite a challenge to determine how much content learning and how much language instruction would take place in the program. Related to this challenge, it is very crucial to organize a working collaboration, and distribution of roles and responsibilities between content instructors and language teachers. Another difficulty commonly faced is to find appropriate materials and authentic texts for learners with different goals, needs and proficiency levels, especially for lower levels. As Snow (2014) noted that "getting teachers to design lessons that truly integrate language and content in the manner proposed by current research has proven to be a difficult proposition" (p. 446), professional development of both language teachers and content instructors is yet another great challenge.

The Research Questions

1. What professional and situational variables guide the process of determining the roles and responsibilities of language and content teachers?
2. What are the perceptions of language and content teachers on the obstacles in the implementation of CBLT in various teaching contexts? What possible solutions can be offered?
3. What are the needs of pre-service and in-service teachers in terms of professional development to better prepare for CBLT?
4. How can we identify and develop appropriate and engaging content and materials for learners at lower proficiency levels?

5. What types of language tasks and innovative teaching strategies will make the content/subject matter more comprehensible?
6. What instructional conditions will create better learning opportunities for students within CBLT framework?
7. How should teachers design assessment procedures to assess the foreign language and targeted content?
8. How can we improve CBLT programs through integrating more recent technology into the teaching and assessment procedures?
9. What kinds of content-related and language-related pre-, while- and post-reading tasks are appropriate for better outcomes in learners' performance in the target language?
10. How does classroom interaction in a content-based lesson contribute to learners' language development and better content comprehension?

Suggested Resources

Escobar Urmeneta, C. (2019). An introduction to content and language integrated learning (CLIL) for teachers and teacher educators. *CLIL Journal of Innovation and Research in Plurilingual and Pluricultural Education,* **2(1), 7–19.** https://doi.org/10.5565/rev/clil.21

The paper presents a comprehensive overview of the Content and Language Integrated Learning (CLIL) taking all stakeholders into consideration. Providing a rationale for implementation, it contextualizes CLIL within the European Union policy and identifies common features found in CLIL programs around Europe. The paper also describes key characteristics of CLIL classroom interaction. The author warns teachers and teacher educators of certain practices commonly observed in CLIL settings which may undermine its effectiveness, and points to the importance of the standards in CLIL teacher education.

Lightbown, P. M. (2014). *Focus on content-based language teaching.* **Oxford, UK: Oxford University Press.**

The book presents a strong connection between theory and practice, pointing to the prominent research findings and evidence-based instructional practices in content-based language teaching. Activities encouraging comparison and reflection, and the extracts from real classrooms guide teachers to make the connection between research on content-based language teaching and their own teaching contexts, which actually help them overcome the challenges of teaching a foreign language alongside another subject.

Lin, A. M. Y. (2016). *Language across the curriculum & CLIL in English as an additional language (EAL) contexts: Theory and practice.* **Singapore: Springer**.

The book is a recent contribution to the field of content-based language learning with its comprehensive account of how language across curriculum and CLIL can be implemented, by systematically reviewing theories and literature regarding the issue, especially in EAL contexts. The strength of the book lies in its concrete and practical examples that teachers and educators can refer to in their attempts to incorporate CLIL in language classes. The book also explicitly addresses the challenges and needs experienced by teachers while providing practical and working suggestions to overcome them.

Thompson, G. & McKinley, J. (2018). Integration of content and language learning. In J. I. Liontas, M. Delli Carpini & S. Abrar-ul-Hassan (Eds.). *TESOL encyclopedia of English language teaching.* **Hoboken, NJ: Wiley**.

This section, which has taken place within the huge comprehensive resource "TESOL Encyclopedia of English Language Teaching", introduces the major approaches to content-based language learning. Among the approaches introduced are bilingual education, immersion, content-based instruction (CBI), content-based language teaching (CBLT), content and language integrated learning (CLIL), and English medium instruction (EMI). It is a valuable addition to the literature as it distinguishes the differences between these approaches and clarifies the confusion created by multiple use of the terms in CLIL. The authors also raise a number of questions about the implications of EIL for content-integrated approaches.

Valcke, J. & Wilkinson, R. (Eds.) (2017). Integrating *content and language in higher education: Perspectives on professional practice.* **Frankfurt: Peter Lang**.

The book includes a collection of papers reporting on how Higher education institutions have coped with the shift to English-medium instruction. The papers focus on critical issues in English-medium instruction at tertiary level and the impact of this change on professional development for university teachers, curriculum and course developers, language experts, as well as quality assurance. The topics covered in the book include teacher perceptions of teaching CLIL courses, teachers' beliefs on the roles of languages and learning in CLIL, the challenges and benefits of collaboration between content and language specialists, and perspectives on professional practice in the integration of content and language in higher education, which all make the book a good source for those interested in integrating CLIL in higher education.

References

Benesch, S. (Ed.). (1988). *Ending remediation: Linking ESL and content in higher education.* TESOL.

Brinton, D., Snow, M. A., & Wesche, M. (1989). *Content-based second language instruction.* Heinle & Heinle.

Cantoni-Harvey, G. (1987). *Content-area language instruction: Approaches and strategies.* Addison-Wesley.

Crandall, J. A. (Ed.). (1987). *ESL through content-area instruction.* Prentice Hall Regents.

Crandall, J. A. (2012). Content-based instruction and content and language integrated learning. In A. Burns & J. C. Richards (Eds.), *The Cambridge guide to pedagogy and practice in second language teaching* (pp. 149–160). Cambridge University Press.

Lantolf, J. P., & Appel, G. (Eds.). (1994). *Vygotskian approaches to second language research.* Ablex.

Met, M. (1999). Content-based instruction: Defining terms, making decisions. *NFLC Reports.* The National Foreign Language Center.

Short, D., Crandall, J. A., & Christian, D. (1989). *How to integrate language and content instruction: A training manual.* Washington, DC: Center for Applied Linguistics. (ERIC Document Reproduction Service No. ED 305824)

Snow, M. A. (2014). Content-based and immersion models of second/foreign language teaching. In M. Celce-Murcia, D. M. Brinton, & M. A. Snow (Eds.), *Teaching English as a Second or foreign language* (pp. 438–454). National Geographic Learning.

Vygotsky, L. S. (1978). *Mind in society: The development of higher psychological processes.* Harvard University Press.

Zübeyde Sinem Genç is Professor at the ELT Department, Faculty of Education, Bursa Uludag University (BUU), Turkey. She received her Ph.D. from Indiana University of Pennsylvania, USA, specializing in TESOL and SLA. She also taught undergraduate and graduate courses in USA. She designed the intensive English curriculum for the School of Foreign Languages at BUU. She has articles in national and international journals such as Teacher Development (British Education indexed), Asian EFL Journal, English Language Teaching (Canada), and Education and Science (SSCI). She is the author of book chapters in various books published by Cambridge University Press, John Benjamins, Peter Lang, Wiley, and TESOL. She is the editor of the book titled Updating Perspectives on English Language Teaching and Teacher Education, published by Peter Lang.

Creativity and Language Teaching

Tamas Kiss

Creativity is becoming increasingly popular in applied linguistics research as testified by recently published books (e.g. Jones, 2016; Jones & Richards, 2016; Maley & Kiss, 2018) on the topic which is understandable, since 21st c. frameworks of education put creativity in the focus of attention. Work in this area dips into a wider pool of knowledge, based on the conceptual and empirical work of linguists, psychologists, and educational theorists, e.g. Rhodes (1961), Csikszentmihalyi (1990), Amabile (1996), and Johnson (2010)—just to name a few, without any attempt to be exhaustive.

In applied linguistics, creativity studies have mainly focused on the 'linguistics', rather than on the 'applied' (Maley & Kiss, 2018). Looking at how linguistic creativity is manifested in everyday language use (e.g. Carter, 2004; Cook, 2000) we find that "[l]inguistic creativity is not simply a property of exceptional people but an exceptional property of all people" (Carter, 2004, p. 13). This suggests that a major part of language teaching could focus on encouraging and developing creativity, rather than on the memorization of formulaic language patterns. Although such linguistic building blocks are important, (after all, creativity needs technical expertise), classroom teaching should move beyond this to encourage creativity if learners are to enjoy language use like they enjoy other forms of creative acts, such as music, film or dance.

When it comes to language teaching, creativity research can be categorised into Rhodes' (1961) four Ps model: Person, Process, Product, and Press. Person creativity focuses on either the language teacher or the language learner as a creative individual. Researchers investigate whether creative potential has an impact on teaching, materials design, language proficiency, or the acquisition of certain language skills. When Process creativity is examined, most scholars are interested in the activities that shape creative thinking and performance. These studies look at

T. Kiss (✉)
Centre for English Language Studies, Sunway University, Subang Jaya, Malaysia
e-mail: tamask@sunway.edu.my

© Springer Nature Switzerland AG 2021
H. Mohebbi and C. Coombe (eds.), *Research Questions in Language Education and Applied Linguistics*, Springer Texts in Education,
https://doi.org/10.1007/978-3-030-79143-8_6

creative writing, the use of literature and technology in language teaching. Interestingly, there is not much research interest in the outcomes of creative processes, i.e. in students' or teachers' creative Products. Finally, Press creativity examines contextual factors that impede or facilitate language teachers to be creative or to promote creativity in their classrooms. Studies on teacher cognition can also be listed here as what teachers think, know, or believe will shape the learning environments they create (Maley & Kiss, 2018).

Interestingly, although we know a lot about creativity, we know very little. This paradox firstly stems from the fact that research findings are often contradictory and this prevents the development of sound theories on language learning and creativity. For example, Ottó (1998) investigated the relationship of Hungarian EFL learners' creativity and their language proficiency, measured by the use of a modified version of the Torrance Test for Creative Thinking, and the learners' grades in English. He found a significant correlation between the two. In contrast, Albert's (2006) study, which aimed to establish if there was a connection between creativity and Hungarian learners' language proficiency and aptitude using similar methodology, did not support that claim. Her conclusion was that creativity doesn't have an impact on student performance and aptitude.

Secondly, research into creativity and language learning/teaching is fragmented, at best inconclusive (Maley & Kiss, 2018). There is little evidence that scholars build on previous work to develop and test ideas in a systematic manner; needless to say, this suggests that there is a lot to do in this area.

The Research Questions

1. *Individual versus collective creativity:* Are language learners more creative when they work individually or when they collaborate with others? Is there a difference in their creative language output?
2. *Complex dynamic systems and creativity:* How does creative thought self-organize and emerge in L2 learners' cognitive processes?
3. *Critical pedagogy:* To what extent does critical pedagogy contribute to language learners' ability to generate, evaluate, expand, and elaborate on ideas in creative writing activities?
4. *Curriculum and syllabus:* How can creativity develop in the L2 classroom and yet align with the goals of a standardized, exam-oriented curriculum?
5. *Language testing and creativity:* To what extent do standardized language tests measure and reward, if at all, creative language use?
6. *Learners' perception of creativity:* Do students see the need to be linguistically creative?
7. *Creativity and language teacher education:* How do L2 teacher education programmes prepare teacher learners to be creative classroom practitioners?

8. *Praise, reward, evaluation and feedback:* What impact does corrective feedback have on L2 learners' creative language use?
9. *Culture and creativity:* How does membership in different cultural groups affect L2 learners' creative writing? Is there a difference between the creative products of Oriental and Western L2 learners?
10. *Competition versus collaboration:* What difference, if any, can be observed in L2 learners' creative language use in competitive and collaborative classrooms?

Suggested Resources

Maley, A. & Kiss, T. (2018). *Creativity and and English language teaching: From inspiration to implementation*. Basingstoke: Palgrave Macmillan.

One of the latest book-length publications on creativity and language teaching offers a very comprehensive review of the development of concepts and ideas, integrating theory, practice, and research. The book starts with outlining general creativity theories from a variety of fields before focusing on the role of creativity in education. Then, it narrows down the focus to applied linguistics and discusses how creativity is cultivated in the language classroom and how creative ideas have contributed to ELT in terms of new language teaching methodologies and directions for research. The book also offers practical ideas and principles for creative materials design and teaching, suggestions on how one can become a creative teacher—and creative person. Finally, a comprehensive review of research on creativity in English language teaching is provided, pinpointing areas where further study would be necessary.

Carter, R. (2004). *Language and creativity: The art of common talk*. London: Routledge.

In this excellent book the author sets out to explain and prove that linguistic creativity can be observed everywhere, claiming that "ordinary language, in so far as it exists, is the exception rather than the rule" (p. 81). Using the CANCODE corpus extensively, he draws on clines between such polar 'opposites' as literary versus 'ordinary language', written versus spoken discourse, formal versus informal language use. He argues that there are many forms of creative language in everyday use, including repetition, alliteration and assonance, rhythm and rhyme, word play, humour, etc. He also claims that creative language use is more often found in social and informal contexts than in settings which have higher demand for following generic conventions. This work is very useful for anyone who wishes to understand the creativity of spoken discourse.

Cook, G. (2000). *Language play, language learning.* **Oxford: Oxford University Press**.

The interconnected nature of 'play' and creativity is the focus of Cook's work. The author is serious about playfulness; he argues that language play is not confined to children, but it is present in a large part of adult language use. One of the areas he looks at is repetition as it creates internal rhythm and structure. He mentions the sometimes weird and strange, even nonsensical nature of nursery rhymes, folk stories, and other chants, pointing out the very strong rhythmical power in these language samples. Although they do not conform to conventional meaning, he argues, rhythm is the sense they make. Another interesting area of Cook's book is the focus on the duality of play: competitive and collaborative. This is an area which definitely needs more study in applied linguistics and L2 classrooms.

Jones, R. H. & Richards, J. (Eds.) (2016). *Creativity in language teaching: Perspectives from research and practice.* **Abingdon, VA: Routledge**.

This edited volume contains papers which investigate creativity from several aspects. It starts with chapters that discuss the issue from a theoretical perspective, and then moves on to discuss creativity in the language classroom and curricular designs. Mention must be made to Kathleen Graves' paper which discusses five dimensions of the curricular conceptual space and argues that small, loosely structured contexts are more supportive of creative projects. This idea is also presented in Susan Ollerhead and Anne Burns' chapter, who propose that "teachers may need to act as resisters or subversers of […] prescribed conditions" (p. 227). An interesting feature of the book is that each chapter contains a 'questions for discussion' section which encourages the reader(s) to engage with the text at a deeper level. Finally, there are some suggestions for further research at the end of the chapters.

Jones, R. H. (Ed.) (2016). *Routledge handbook of language and creativity.* **London: Routledge**.

This up-to-date and scholarly collection of essays on creativity is a valuable resource especially for those who are interested in the interlink of language and creativity, rather than how creativity is present in language classrooms. The majority of the papers, i.e. 26 chapters, are organised in three main parts: (1) Dimensions of language and creativity, (2) Literary creativity, and (3) Multimodal and multimedia creativity. Part 3 is especially interesting as it portrays new literary practices by looking at how creativity is enacted in multimodal texts and in computer-mediated communication. Yet, for those interested in the 'applied' part of applied linguistics, the volume offers little. Part 4 focuses on creativity in language teaching and learning (5 chapters only), containing such gems as Tan Bee Tin's paper who argues that "language learning tasks should be set up to instigate a creative desire in language learners" (p. 433).

References

Albert, Á. (2006). Learner creativity as a potentially important individual variable: Examining the relationships between learner creativity, language aptitude and level of proficiency. In M. Nikolov & J. Horváth (Eds.), *UPRT 2006: Empirical studies in English applied linguistics* (pp. 77–98). Pécs: Lingua Franca Csoport.

Amabile, T. M. (1996). *Creativity in context*. Westview Press.

Carter, R. (2004). *Language and creativity: The art of common talk*. Routledge.

Cook, G. (2000). *Language play, language learning*. Oxford University Press.

Csikszentmihalyi, M. (1990). *Flow: The psychology of optimal experience*. Harper Row.

Johnson, S. (2010). *Where good ideas come from*. Allen Lane/Penguin.

Jones, R. H. (Ed.). (2016). *Routledge handbook of language and creativity*. Routledge.

Jones, R. H., & Richards, J. (Eds.). (2016). *Creativity in language teaching: Perspecitves from research and practice*. Routledge.

Maley, A., & Kiss, T. (2018). *Creativity and English language teaching: From inspiration to implementation*. Palgrave Macmillan.

Ottó, I. (1998). The relationship between individual differences in learner creativity and language learning success. *TESOL Quarterly, 32*(4), 763–773.

Rhodes, M. (1961). An analysis of creativity. *Phi Beta Kappa, 42*(7), 305–310.

Tamas Kiss is an Associate Professor at the Centre for English Language Studies, Sunway University, Malaysia. He has been involved with language teacher education programmes in Europe, the Middle East, South Asia, Latin America and South East Asia, working with language teachers in more than 20 countries. His main research interests include language pedagogy, language teacher education, creativity, intercultural communication, the link between complex dynamic systems and education, and the role of culture in language teaching materials. He recently published a co-authored book with Alan Maley (2018) *Creativity and English Language Teaching: From inspiration to implementation*.

Discourse Analysis

7

Brian Paltridge

Discourse analysis is interested, among other things, in the organizational structures of texts. One way in which this might be examined is through identifying the *schematic structures* of texts; that is, the discourse structure of texts such as arguments, reports, descriptions, and explanations which come together in the writing of larger texts such as in academic essays or assignments. Another way of looking at discourse structures might be through an analysis of the stages, or *moves,* of a text in terms of their communicative function within the text (Swales, 1990). This area of research is referred to as *genre analysis* (Tardy, 2019).

Conversation analysis is an approach to the analysis of spoken discourse that looks at the way in which people manage their everyday conversational interactions. It examines how spoken discourse is organized and develops as speakers carry out these interactions. Conversation analysis has examined aspects of spoken discourse such as sequences of related utterances (adjacency pairs), preferences for particular combinations of utterances (preference organization), turn taking, feedback, repair, conversational openings and closings, discourse markers, and response tokens. Conversation analysis works with recordings of spoken data and carries out careful and fine-grained analyses of the data (see Wong & Waring, 2010; Waring, 2018).

Multimodal discourse analysis considers how texts draw on modes of communication such as pictures, film, video images and sound in combination with words to make meaning. It has examined print genres as well as genres such as web pages, films, and television programs. It considers how multimodal texts are designed and how the colour, focus and positioning of multimodal elements contribute to the making of meaning in texts (Bezemer & Jewitt, 2018).

B. Paltridge (✉)
English Department, City University of Hong Kong, Hong Kong, China
e-mail: brian.paltridge@sydney.edu.au

School of Education and Social Work, University of Sydney, Sydney, Australia

© Springer Nature Switzerland AG 2021
H. Mohebbi and C. Coombe (eds.), *Research Questions in Language Education and Applied Linguistics*, Springer Texts in Education,
https://doi.org/10.1007/978-3-030-79143-8_7

Critical discourse analysis explores connections between the use of language and the social and political contexts in which it occurs. It explores issues such as gender, ethnicity, cultural difference, ideology and identity and how these are both constructed and reflected in texts. A critical analysis may include a detailed textual analysis and move from there to an explanation and interpretation of the analysis. It might proceed from there to deconstruct and challenge the text/s being examined. This may include tracing underlying ideologies from the linguistic features of a text, unpacking particular biases and ideological presuppositions underlying the text, and relating the text to other texts and to people's experiences and beliefs.

Discourse analysts has also examined the notion of *identity,* mostly taking a post-structural perspective, seeing identity as something that is both socially constructed and in constant process. One way in which this might be examined is through the ways in which people, through the language choices that they make, *index* a particular identity (see Strauss & Feiz, 2014). A further way in which identity has been explored is through the use of *narrative analysis* (see Barkhuizen, 2013); that is, the collection of stories in the form of journals, letters, autobiographies, memoirs, interviews and orally told stories that enable us to gain insights into the identities that people display through their use of discourse.

The Research Questions

1. Choose examples of a written genre you would use in your classroom and analyse the discourse structures of the texts. How could you use your analysis in your teaching?
2. Choose a spoken text you would use in your classroom and analyse it from the point of view of conversation analysis. How could you use your analysis in your teaching?
3. Look at a textbook that is commonly used in language teaching classrooms. What genres are focused on in the textbook and how do these relate to the target students' learning needs?
4. Look at a textbook that is commonly used in language teaching classrooms. What identities are portrayed in the textbook and how are they constructed through the use of language?
5. Choose a text which contains images or other multimodal elements. Analyse the text from a multimodal perspective. How could you use this analysis in the classroom?
6. Choose a text you would use in your classroom and analyse it from a critical perspective. How could you use this analysis in your classroom?
7. Choose a spoken and written text on the same topic. What are some of the differences in the use of discourse between the two texts and how could you use this kind of analysis in the classroom?
8. Ask students to keep a diary focusing on their use of language in the classroom. How does their use of language index their identity as a learner?

9. Keep a diary focusing on your use of language in the classroom. How does your use of language index your identity as a teacher?
10. Find an example of discourse analysis in published research and consider how you could draw on this analysis in the classroom.

Suggested Resources

Flowerdew, J. (2013). *Discourse in English language education.* **London: Routledge**

Discourse in English Language Education discusses major concepts and questions in discourse studies and their applications to language education. Topics covered include systemic functional linguistics, genre, register, speech acts, politeness, conversation analysis, critical discourse analysis and corpus linguistics. Texts that are analysed include casual conversation, newspapers, fiction, radio programs, classroom interactions, blogs and real-life learner texts. There are discussion questions at the end of each chapter which are designed to encourage reflection and engagement with the topics covered in the book.

Gee, J. & Handford, M. (Eds.), (2011). *The Routledge handbook to discourse analysis.* **London: Routledge**

This handbook contains chapters on a wide range of areas including conversation analysis, genre analysis, corpus-based studies, multimodal discourse analysis and critical discourse analysis. Educational and institutional applications of discourse analysis are discussed as well as topics such as identity, power, ethnicity, intercultural communication, cognition and discourse. The chapters are written by contributors from around the world, each a leading researcher in their respective field.

Hyland, K., Paltridge, B. & Wong, L. L. C. (Eds.), (2021). *The Bloomsbury handbook of discourse analysis* **(2nd ed.). London: Bloomsbury**.

This set of specially commissioned chapters discusses a range of approaches and issues in researching discourse. Assumptions underlying methods and approaches are discussed as are research techniques and instruments appropriate to the goal and method of the research. The second part of the book provides an overview of key areas of discourse studies such as genre analysis, conversation analysis, narrative analysis, multimodal analysis and critical discourse analysis. In each chapter the authors include a sample study which illustrates the points they are making and identify resources for further reading on the particular approach or issue under discussion.

Jaworski, A. & Coupland, N. (Eds.), (2014). *The discourse reader* **(3rd ed.). London: Routledge**.

The Discourse Reader covers the foundations of modern discourse analysis and represents major methods and traditions. Seminal pieces of work are republished in the book as well as new readings by Jan Blommaert, Norman Fairclough, James

Paul Gee, Barbara Johnstone, Ron Scollon and Don Zimmerman, among others. In the introduction to their book, Jaworski and Coupland provide definitions of the term 'discourse' and discuss traditions in the analysis of discourse. Strengths and limitations of discourse studies are also discussed.

Paltridge, B. (2021). *Discourse analysis* **(3rd ed.). London: Bloomsbury**.

In a series of eleven chapters this book examines different approaches to discourse, looking at discourse and society, discourse and pragmatics, discourse and genre, discourse and conversation, discourse grammar, corpus-based approaches to discourse, multimodal discourse analysis, discourse and digital media, and critical discourse analysis. The final chapter presents a practical approach to doing discourse analysis. The book includes chapter summaries which outline the key areas that have been covered. Technical terms are explained in each chapter and examples are drawn from films, television, newspapers, the classroom and everyday life. Each chapter ends with tasks, suggestions for student projects, and recommendations for further reading.

References

Barkhuizen, G. (Ed.) (2013). *Narrative research in applied linguistics*. Cambridge University Press.

Bezemer, J., & Jewitt, C. (2018). Multimodality: A guide for linguists. In L. Litosseliti (Ed.), *Research methods in linguistics* (2nd ed., pp. 281–304). Bloomsbury.

Strauss, S., & Feiz, P. (2014). *Discourse analysis: Putting our worlds into words*. Routledge.

Swales, J. M. (1990). *Genre analysis: English in academic and research settings*. Cambridge University Press.

Tardy, C. M. (2019). *Genre-based writing: What every ESL teacher needs to know*. University of Michigan Press.

Wong, J., & Waring, H. Z. (2010). *Conversation analysis and second language pedagogy*. Routledge.

Waring, H. Z. (2018). *Discourse analysis. The questions discourse analysts ask and how they answer them*. Routledge.

Brian Paltridge is Professor of TESOL at the University of Sydney and visiting professor in the English Department at City University of Hong Kong. His publications include *Ethnographic Perspectives on Academic Writing* (with Sue Starfield and Christine Tardy, Oxford University Press, 2016), *Getting Published in Academic Journals* (with Sue Starfield, University of Michigan Press, 2016), *The Discourse of Peer Review* (Palgrave Macmillan, 2017), and *Writing for Research Purposes* (Shanghai Foreign Language Education Press, 2018). He has recently published a second edition of *Thesis and Dissertation Writing in a Second Language* (Routledge, 2020), and a third edition of his book *Discourse Analysis* (Bloomsbury, 2021).

English Academic Vocabulary Teaching and Learning

Sophia Skoufaki

Academic vocabulary is defined as the vocabulary used in academic writing and speech across scientific disciplines but opinions vary on which words these are exactly. The Academic Word List (AWL) (Coxhead, 2000) embodies the traditional conceptualization of academic vocabulary in that it distinguishes English academic vocabulary from English frequent vocabulary. It includes words which do not appear in the General Service List (GSL) (West, 1953), a list of the most common 2000 English word families. However, research comparing the AWL and wordlists containing frequent words other than the GSL indicates a large overlap between the AWL and frequent words (e.g., Masrai & Milton, 2018). The Academic Vocabulary List (AVL) (Gardner & Davies, 2014) exemplifies this recent understanding that academic words span all frequency bands; it consists of words from all frequency bands of the Corpus of Contemporary American English. Since many English academic words are high-frequency, students across levels of education (primary, secondary, higher) do not only need to recognize but also use appropriately many academic words in their speech and writing. Therefore, this recent reconceptualization of English academic vocabulary calls for research in English academic vocabulary teaching and learning, especially since English is dominant in academia worldwide (Melitz, 2018) and academic vocabulary knowledge can predict academic achievement (e.g., Schuth et al., 2017).

Research examining students' academic vocabulary knowledge and use would have pedagogical implications about which, if any, academic words need to be taught. For example, a reasonable suggestion is that the most frequent academic words would need to be prioritized for teaching, as the more frequent a word is, the more useful it is. Research on students' knowledge of academic vocabulary (e.g., Skoufaki et al., 2017) would indicate which aspects of frequent academic vocabulary require teaching. Research on the relevant effect of lexical characteristics

S. Skoufaki (✉)
Department of Language and Linguistics, University of Essex, Colchester, UK
e-mail: sskouf@essex.ac.uk

© Springer Nature Switzerland AG 2021
H. Mohebbi and C. Coombe (eds.), *Research Questions in Language Education and Applied Linguistics*, Springer Texts in Education,
https://doi.org/10.1007/978-3-030-79143-8_8

(such as word length or whether a second-language word has a first-language cognate or not) on academic word learning (e.g., Perez Urdaniz & Skoufaki, 2019) may also indicate what makes some academic words harder to learn than others and, consequently, what kinds of academic words should be taught.

Research on which, if any, aspects of vocabulary knowledge should be focused on during this teaching is also necessary due to challenges specific to academic word learning. For example, the more frequent an academic word is, the more likely it is to be polysemous and, if it is polysemous, the more meaning senses it is likely to have (Skoufaki & Petrić, 2019). Research aiming to identify the meaning sense (s) of frequent academic words which tend to be shared across disciplines would help teachers to choose the meaning senses which are the most worthwhile to teach in primary and secondary school and in English for General Academic Purposes (EGAP) courses.

Other avenues for future research are the examination of language teaching materials, language course curricula or classroom activities in terms of how well (a) they cater for students receptive and productive academic-vocabulary needs and (b) they agree with recommendations on academic vocabulary instruction stemming from research projects suggested above.

The Research Questions

1. Which kinds of English academic vocabulary knowledge (in terms of the receptive-productive continuum and more specifically, e.g., in terms of syntactic properties, meaning senses, collocations) are particularly challenging for primary-/secondary-school/university students?
2. Which kinds of English academic vocabulary knowledge (e.g., meaning-form link, collocations) are focused on in primary/secondary schools or in university presessional/insessional courses?
3. To what extent do the kinds of English academic vocabulary knowledge focused on in educational settings map onto the ones that are particularly challenging for native/non-native primary-/secondary-school/university students?

Research questions inspired by Skoufaki and Petrić (2019)

4. Which English polysemous academic words have meanings which are shared across scientific disciplines and, therefore, lend themselves to English for General Academic Purposes (EGAP) instruction?
5. For which English polysemous academic words are some meaning senses known to university students thanks to their General English knowledge?

Research questions inspired by Perez Urdaniz and Skoufaki (2019)

6. What is the relevant effect of lexical characteristics (e.g., English word frequency, cognateness) on AVL-word receptive/productive knowledge of EFL learners who are native speakers of a language rich in English cognates (e.g., Spanish, Japanese)?
7. Do lexical-characteristic effects on AVL-word receptive/productive knowledge vary depending on the learners' proficiency level?
8. What is the effect of English word frequency vis a vis first-language (L1) loanword frequency on AVL-word receptive/productive knowledge of EFL learners with L1s rich in English cognates?

Research questions inspired by Coxhead, Dang and Mukai (2017)

9. Which is the academic-word/formulaic expression overlap between EAP presessional/insessional teaching materials and university lectures/tutorials/lab sessions?
10. Which is the academic-word/formulaic expression overlap between EAP presessional/insessional teaching materials and students' assignments?

Suggested Resources

Coxhead, A., Dang, T. N. Y. & Mukai, S. (2017). Single and multi-word unit vocabulary in university tutorials and laboratories: Evidence from corpora and textbooks. *Journal of English for Academic Purposes, 30, 66–78.*

This study exemplifies research which compares academic vocabulary used by experts and taught in textbooks to make recommendations on the academic vocabulary that needs to be included in English for academic purposes textbooks. A corpus was created from laboratory communication, another from tutorials and a final one from three EAP textbooks. The overlap between the lexical items that the textbook analysis indicated as potentially useful to university students and the lexical items which were actually used in the laboratory and tutorials corpora was not complete; the textbook corpus included lexical items which did not occur in the one or the other communication corpus. The researchers discuss the pedagogical implications of the study for textbook creators and academics. They also call for similar studies with larger corpora that offer better balance across academic subdisciplines.

Csomay, E. & Prades, A. (2018). Academic vocabulary in ESL student papers: A corpus-based study. *Journal of English for Academic Purposes*, *33*, 100–118.

This study exemplifies research that examines academic vocabulary use by second language learners. It examines which academic vocabulary is used in second language learners' writing produced in the context of a composition course taken by international students at a university in the USA. The effect of three factors (namely, text type, proficiency level and whether a piece of writing was in its first or second draft) on the number of academic words in students' writing was examined. The relationship between the amount of academic vocabulary used and the holistic ratings given to these pieces of writing was also examined.

Paquot, M. (2010). *Academic vocabulary in learner writing. From extraction to analysis.* **London: Continuum.**

This book can be used as an introduction to research on academic vocabulary for linguists and language teachers because it strikes a good balance between theoretical and pedagogical considerations in relation to academic vocabulary use and instruction. It reports on a comparative study of English academic vocabulary use in expert and undergraduate English as a Foreign Language student writing conducted with the aim to identify aspects of vocabulary use that could benefit from EAP teaching. The thorough literature review on academic vocabulary research and the detailed and accessible summary of the procedures followed to extract and analyse academic vocabulary in the two corpora will be helpful to students who are starting to research academic vocabulary use through corpus linguistics methods.

Perez Urdaniz, R. & Skoufaki, S. (2019). Spanish L1 EFL learners' recognition knowledge of English academic vocabulary: The role of cognateness, word frequency and length. *Applied Linguistics Review*. **Advance online publication.** https://doi.org/10.1515/applirev-2018-0109

This study exemplifies research on the relative effect of lexical characteristics on academic word knowledge. It examines the extent to which cognateness, word frequency and length predict the ability of L1-Spanish EFL learners to recognise written English academic words. Findings suggest that word frequency was the most important predictor, followed by cognateness and finally a frequency by cognateness interaction whereby word frequency is more predictive of IF for non-cognates than cognates. Various suggestions for partial replications of this study are mentioned in the final section of this article.

Spencer, S., Clegg, J., Lowe, H. & Stackhouse, J. (2017). Increasing adolescents' depth of understanding of cross-curriculum words: an intervention study. *International Journal of Language and Communication Disorders*, *52*, 652–668.

This article reports on an intervention study. It illustrates the challenges that polysemous academic words can pose to teachers and learners. Participants were 35 adolescents at risk of educational underachievement at a British secondary state school. Participants received a ten-week instruction of 10 academic words. This instruction was administered in the Spring term to one participant subgroup and in the Summer term to another.

After the intervention, one of the tests administered to them asked them to define each word. Despite the focus of the programme on only 10 words, the comparison of the pre- and the post-intervention test results indicates that the Spring-term intervention led to an average increase of only one meaning definition, which was not a statistically significant gain. The Summer-term intervention led to a significant increase in the results of the word-definition test, but still the average number of meanings known increased only by 2.69.

References

Coxhead, A. (2000). A new academic word list. *TESOL Quarterly, 34*, 213–238.

Gardner, D., & Davies, M. (2014). A new academic vocabulary list. *Applied Linguistics, 35*, 305–327.

Masrai, A., & Milton, J. (2018). Measuring the contribution of academic and general vocabulary knowledge to learners' academic achievement. *Journal of English for Academic Purposes, 31*, 44–57.

Melitz, J. (2018). English as a lingua franca: Facts, benefits and costs. *The World Economy, 41*, 1750–1774.

Schuth, E., Köhne, J., & Weinert, S. (2017). The influence of academic vocabulary knowledge on school performance. *Learning and Instruction, 49*, 157–165.

Skoufaki, S., Petrić, B., & Demetriou, L. (2019). *Delineating polysemy in English academic vocabulary: A lexicographic and corpus analysis.* Third international Conference on Corpus Analysis in Academic Discourse (CAAD'19). Castelló de la Plana, 14–15 November, 2019.

Skoufaki, S., Petrić, B., & Chatsiou, K. (2017). *British students' knowledge of polysemous academic English vocabulary.* BAAL Vocabulary Studies Special Interest Group conference. Reading, 3–4 July, 2017.

Perez Urdaniz, R., & Skoufaki, S. (2019). Spanish L1 EFL learners' recognition knowledge of English academic vocabulary: The role of cognateness, word frequency and length. *Applied Linguistics Review*. Advance online publication. https://doi.org/10.1515/applirev-2018-0109

West, M. (1953). *A general service list of English words.* Longman, Green & Co.

Sophia Skoufaki is an Associate Supervisor in Applied Linguistics at the University of Essex. She has a Ph.D. in Applied Linguistics from the University of Cambridge. Her current research is on (a) English academic vocabulary learning and use by university students in the UK and (b) polysemy in English academic vocabulary. Her other research interests are figurative language processing and coherence in written discourse. Her research has appeared in journals such as *Applied Linguistics Review, English for Specific Purposes, Metaphor and Symbol and Text & Talk.*

English for Academic Purposes

Helen Basturkmen

English for academic purposes is the branch of English for Specific Purposes that is concerned with teaching and research to meet the language needs of those in study and research settings. There are two main areas of EAP. The first area is English for study purposes. This area aims to help students acquire the English they need to successfully participate in academic events, such as lectures and seminars, and complete student written genres, such as essays and laboratory reports. Most English for study purposes enquiry to date has concerned the needs of students in tertiary level education, although it is recognized that learning English for study purposes starts in school settings. The second area is English for professional academic purposes. This area concerns the needs and interests of professional academics in events and genres of key relevance to their work, such as grant proposals, research articles and academic presentations.

In English for study purposes, a dichotomy is made between English for General Academic Purposes, or EGAP, and English for Specific Academic Purposes, or ESAP. In the former, research and instruction focuses on pedagogic genres that are considered common across disciplines, such as essays, lectures, and seminars and on linguistic features common across academic texts, such as complex nouns or academic vocabulary. Research and instruction also focus on language skills, including listening to lectures, academic reading and writing. EGAP instruction is often provided to students at the onset of university study when students' disciplines may still be unclear. It is expected that the common genres or the features of the general academic register focused on in instruction will be transferred to writing or speaking in the students' disciplines at a later time. ESAP instruction is for students from a particular discipline or disciplinary area and it focuses on disciplinary uses of language and the specific genres or variants of common genres, such

H. Basturkmen (✉)
Applied Linguistics and Language Teaching, Faculty of Arts, University of Auckland, Auckland, New Zealand
e-mail: h.basturkmen@auckland.ac.nz

© Springer Nature Switzerland AG 2021
H. Mohebbi and C. Coombe (eds.), *Research Questions in Language Education and Applied Linguistics*, Springer Texts in Education,
https://doi.org/10.1007/978-3-030-79143-8_9

as essays, that students in the discipline require. Instruction often includes a focus on the disciplinary expectations for writing as well as the linguistic features of disciplinary written discourse. Although students may have encountered these expectations and features during disciplinary study, their knowledge of them may be largely tacit. Writing instruction may thus aim to help learners become more aware of language and communication in their discipline.

A great deal of inquiry in the area of English for professional academic purposes has concerned research publication. For example, there have been many genre analytic studies of research articles. These studies often aim to describe typical rhetorical patterns and linguistic features in particular sections of the research article, such as, the literature review or discussion.

The Research Questions

1. What genres do students need for successful participation in any one discipline?
2. To what extent do academic language needs vary across disciplines?
3. How do learners acquire disciplinary vocabulary?
4. How do learners acquire academic genres?
5. To what extent do learners transfer content from EGAP type writing courses to writing in their disciplines?
6. What is the rhetorical structure of a particular academic genre? (Select a genre about which limited information is currently available).
7. How do EAP teachers develop their understanding of the features of academic English?
8. How do ESAP teachers overcome gaps in their knowledge of disciplinary language use and genres?
9. What are the expectations and values for research article writing in any one discipline?
10. What kinds of information about research genres do novice academic staff find useful?

Suggested Resources

De Chazal, E. (2014). *English for academic purposes.* **Oxford: Oxford University Press.**

English for academic purposes provides a comprehensive overview of research and practice in EAP. Chapter One traces the emergence of EAP, introduces EAP's key features, explains how EAP differs from general English language teaching and identifies key theoretical influences. Chapter Two focuses on teaching and learning. It examines arguments for an EGAP approach, compares EGAP and ESAP approaches and discusses the topic of EAP teacher competencies. The remainder of the work includes chapters on academic texts, academic language, critical thinking, reading, writing, speaking, listening, materials development, assessment and technologies. The chapters highlight key research and present both typical and best practice. This work offers a good starting point for researchers wishing to understand the range of topics that can be explored in EAP.

Nesi, H. & Gardner, S. (2012). *Genres across disciplines: student writing in higher education.* **Cambridge: Cambridge University Press.**

This book provides descriptions of language and organization in the kinds of assessed writing required of students in university settings. The work is based on findings from a large-scale, corpus-based, research project conducted in the UK. The study investigated genres of student writing at four different levels (year one, year two, year three and taught postgraduate) across over 30 disciplines. The work presents a classification and description of 13 genre families and highlights disciplinary variation in genre writing. For example, the work describes disciplinary variants of the explanation genre family, a genre that functions to enable students to develop coherent and detailed knowledge of an aspect of their field. This is a very valuable resource for researchers in the area of student academic writing.

Flowerdew, J. & Costley, T. (Eds.) (2017). *Discipline-specific writing: Theory into practice.* **Abingdon: Oxon: Routledge.**

This work brings together chapters by researchers from a range of higher education contexts with chapter topics chosen to reflect various stages that would be involved in the preparation and delivery of discipline-specific writing courses. These stages, include for example, a chapter on investigation of the local and socio-cultural context for a disciplinary course, design options in course development and specific writing language assessment. A number of chapters focus on particular content areas, such as the role of grammar in the discipline-specific writing curriculum or perspectives on teaching vocabulary in discipline-specific academic writing. Some chapters focus on approaches, such as using genre analysis to teach writing in the disciplines and critical literacy approaches. The work includes chapters about research and practice in a particular disciplinary area, such as teaching writing for science and technology and using annotated bibliographies to develop student writing in social sciences.

Hyland, K. & Shaw, P. (2016). *The Routledge handbook of English for academic purposes.* **Abingdon, Oxon: Routledge.**

This handbook provides over 40 chapters by experts in the field of EAP. Each author explains their specialist subject through a synthesis of literature and with reference to concepts, theories, issues and practices. Part One *Conceptions of EAP* includes for example a chapter on general and specific EAP, Part Two *Contexts for EAP* a chapter on EAP in Latin America, Part Three *EAP and language skills* a chapter on listening to lectures, Part IV *Research perspectives* a chapter on genre analysis, Part V *Pedagogic genres* a chapter on seminars, Part VI *Research genres* a chapter on research blogs and Part VII *Pedagogic contexts* a chapter on EAP for postgraduate students. Part VIII *Managing learning* includes for example chapters on EAP teacher development and needs analysis for curriculum design.

Basturkmen, H. (Ed.) (2015). *English for academic purposes: Critical concepts in linguistics***. Abingdon, Oxon, UK: Routledge**.

This work brings together key research studies, concepts and issues that have characterised the field of EAP. It provides a selection of previously published articles and chapters to help the reader understand how contemporary perspectives and research interests have emerged. The selection includes discussions of theory, debates as well as reports of empirical studies. Volumes One and Two focus on descriptions of academic English. Volume Three focuses on EAP teaching and Volume Four on EAP learning. Each volume begins with an introduction by the editor to explain why publications have been included, to introduce key concepts and provide background information on the topic.

Helen Basturkmen teaches on the MTESOL program at the University of Auckland, where she convenes courses on ESP and Discourse Analysis. Her research describes language use in specific settings and draws on discourse analytic approaches. She also conducts research into the design features of ESP/EAP instruction. Her articles regularly appear in international journals, including *System, Language Teaching, The Modern Language Journal, Applied Linguistics, English for Specific Purposes Journal, Journal of English for Academic Purposes, Language Awareness, Language Learning* and *TESOL Quarterly*. She has written two books on ESP (Routledge, 2006; Palgrave Macmillan, 2010) and edited the four-volume work *English for Academic Purposes* in the *Critical Concepts in Linguistics Series* (Routledge, 2015).

English for Specific Purposes

10

Helen Basturkmen

English for specific purposes (ESP) refers to the field of language teaching that aims to support learners with the linguistic needs of their study or work area, and research into language use in work or study areas. ESP instruction does not aim to develop a general linguistic competence but rather to develop the particular set of linguistic competencies that will enable learners to enter or make progress in their chosen field of study, such as economics, profession, such as accounting, or occupation, such as tour guiding. For example, instruction in English for Accounting might include a focus on the technical vocabulary and written genres used in the profession, such as financial reports. ESP instruction often groups learners in relation to their roles in target settings. For example, in teaching an English for the Heath Care sector program, learners might be divided into their specialisms, with one group receiving instruction in English for nursing and another group receiving instruction in English for pharmacists.

Needs analysis is a key course design process in ESP. Needs analysis is both a pre-course design procedure as well as a procedure used in course refinement to ensure the continuing relevance of instructional content. Analysis is typically made of communication in the target situations that learners face or will face in their study or work domain (target situation analysis, TSA) and the learners' current level of linguistic competencies in relation to the level needed for successful participation in the target situation (present situation analysis, PSA). In addition, analysis may be made of learner subjective needs and the teaching situation. The latter may include analysis of the teachers' knowledge of ESP, for example. Questionnaire and interviews are typical data collection techniques, but often these are supplemented with other techniques. For example, job shadowing might be used in a TSA in order to gain an understanding of the types of communicative events and demands related

H. Basturkmen (✉)
Applied Linguistics and Language Teaching, Faculty of Arts, University of Auckland, Auckland, New Zealand
e-mail: h.basturkmen@auckland.ac.nz

© Springer Nature Switzerland AG 2021
H. Mohebbi and C. Coombe (eds.), *Research Questions in Language Education and Applied Linguistics*, Springer Texts in Education,
https://doi.org/10.1007/978-3-030-79143-8_10

to a specific role in an institution, and performance tests might be used in PSA to gauge how much learners already know and can do in relation to a particular key task in the target situation.

Although it is possible to teach ESP to learners with beginners' levels of English proficiency, most ESP courses are for learners with intermediate or advanced levels of English proficiency. Learners are most often adults or young adults. A fundamental assumption is that learners will find ESP instruction motivating because it integrates language teaching with contexts, texts and activities from their work or study area of interest. ESP courses can be devised for pre-experienced learners, that is, learners with little or no experience of the target setting, during-experience learners, who are taking the ESP course at the same time they are working or studying in a specific field and post-experience learners, who have experience of working or studying in a field but are no longer doing so.

The Research Questions

1. How do the language learning needs of pre-experience and during- or post-experience ESP learners compare in any given setting?
2. How motivating do learners find ESP courses?
3. How do learners perceive their own language learning needs for any given target setting?
4. What are the relative values of different needs analysis techniques?
5. What is the technical vocabulary of any given workplace?
6. What kinds of knowledge and teacher education do ESP teachers require?
7. How do ESP teachers collaborate with subject specialists?
8. To what extent does ESP teaching draw on learning activities and tasks from target study and work areas?
9. In what ways can ESP instruction support learners in exploring their own needs and language use in target settings?
10. How do teachers draw on findings from needs analysis in ESP curriculum development?

Suggested Resources

Gollin-Kies, S. Hall, D.R. & Moore, S.H. (2015). *Language for specific purposes*. Basingstoke: Palgrave Macmillan.

Language for Specific Purposes is an up-to-date, general introduction to ESP. It traces the history of ESP and describes current trends in teaching and research. The book has four main parts. Part One provides an overview of key concepts and issues in the field and identifies a number of trends that impact on the development of

ESP. Part Two concerns ESP teaching. Part Three concerns ESP research and it provides information about research as well as summaries of studies on particular topics, such as, case studies in needs analysis. Chapter 12 suggests a range of research projects that readers might wish to pursue and for each project outlines a research question, problem and research procedure. Part Four lists key literature, online sites and associations relevant to the interests of ESP researchers and practitioners.

Basturkmen, H. (2010). *Developing Courses in English for Specific Purposes.* **Basingstoke, UK: Palgrave Macmillan.**

This book examines how teachers devise ESP courses. The first part of the work examines three topics in course design, analyzing needs, investigating specialist discourse and developing a curriculum, with reference to the ESP literature. The second part reports four cases studies that were based on interviews with course developers. In the interviews, the course developers, who were highly experienced ESP teachers, were asked about the processes and procedures they had used in developing a particular ESP course. Two of the cases are work-related (an English for medical doctors' course and an English for new police recruits course) and two of the cases are study-related (an academic literacies course in Visual Communication and an English for thesis writers course). The case studies bring to light the steps the teachers had taken to develop their courses as well as the rationale behind their decision-making.

Brown, J. D. (2016). *Needs analysis and English for specific purposes.* **London: Routledge.**

This work provides a guide to the theory and practice of needs analysis in ESP. It provides practical tools and a stage-by-stage process that teachers can use. Part One, Getting ready to do an ESP needs analysis, provides definitions, introduces the various type of analysis that can be conducted and discusses how to select and sequence data collection procedures. Part Two, Doing the ESP needs analysis, focuses on strategies for collecting data and ways of analyzing and interpreting data. Part Three, Using the needs analysis results, discusses how results can be used in curriculum design and provides guidance on how to report a needs analysis project.

Serafini, E.J., Lake, J.B. & Long, M.H. (2015). Needs analysis for specialised learner populations: Essential methodological improvements. *English for Specific Purposes, 40,* **11–26.**

This first part of the article critically examines research methodologies and the development of research design in needs analysis in ESP by means of an analysis of reported needs analysis studies in two periods of time, 1984–1999 and 2000–2014. For each period, the authors identify positive trends or improvements and less positive trends in the design and reporting of needs analyses. This provides a close analysis of developments and highlights limitations in methodologies. The second part of the article reports a needs analysis study conducted by the writers to investigate the English language needs of non-native English speakers working in a national research institution in the US. The study illustrates methodological rigor in ESP needs analysis research design and reporting.

Kirkgöz, Y. & Dikilitaş, K. (Eds.) (2018). *Key issues in English for specific purposes in higher education.* **Switzerland: Springer.**

This volume provides a set of research–based studies on ESP in higher education settings in a diverse set of contexts. It aims to shed light on the range of ESP-related practices and issues at this point in time. In the opening chapter, the editors provide background information about the current situation. They describe how ESP has become a fast track area of growth due in large part to the increasing prevalence of English-Medium Instruction (EMI) globally and they distinguish key terms, such as Content and Language Integrated Learning (CLIL) and EMI. The first main part of the book includes studies related to ESP materials development, the second part studies concerning ESP teacher development and the third part studies concerning curricular issues. The final part of the work focuses on perspectives of ESP, CLIL or EMI in different countries.

Helen Basturkmen teaches on the MTESOL program at the University of Auckland, where she convenes courses on ESP and Discourse Analysis. Her research describes language use in specific settings and draws on discourse analytic approaches. She also conducts research into the design features of ESP/EAP instruction. Her articles regularly appear in international journals, including *System, Language Teaching, The Modern Language Journal, Applied Linguistics, English for Specific Purposes Journal, Journal of English for Academic Purposes, Language Awareness, Language Learning and TESOL Quarterly.* She has written two books on ESP (Routledge, 2006; Palgrave Macmillan, 2010) and edited the four-volume work English for Academic Purposes in the Critical Concepts in Linguistics Series (Routledge, 2015).

English-Medium Instruction

11

Keith M. Graham and Zohreh R. Eslami

English-Medium Instruction (EMI) is defined by Macaro et al. (2017) as "the use of the English language to teach academic subjects in countries or jurisdictions where the first language of the majority of the population is not English" (Macaro et al., 2017, p. 37). EMI is distinguished from other content-based approaches, such as content and language integrated learning (CLIL), for having "no explicit English language-related learning outcomes" (Airey, 2016, p. 73).

Very little is known about the effectiveness of EMI, neither for language nor content outcomes. Studies that have compared EMI students to non-EMI students have either found only higher receptive skills (Yang, 2015) or no difference (Lei & Hu, 2014). Investigations of EMI content outcomes have been equally mixed, finding either L1 instruction to be superior (Li, 2017) or no difference (Dafouz et al., 2014; Joe & Lee, 2013).

While the empirical evidence of EMI effectiveness is limited, there is a growing literature on instructor and student attitudes toward EMI. Attitudes of instructors are generally positive toward EMI (Macaro et al., 2017). However, student attitudes are more diverse based on a variety of variables (Graham & Eslami, 2019).

EMI is a phenomenon that has spread around the world (Dearden, 2015). Although research on EMI has been increasing in recent years (Macaro et al., 2017), it has not kept pace with EMI's rapid growth. EMI is multi-dimensional with many dimensions remaining left unexplored, therefore, providing rich opportunities for researchers.

K. M. Graham · Z. R. Eslami (✉)
Educational Psychology, Texas A&M University, College Station, TX, USA
e-mail: zeslami@tamu.edu

K. M. Graham
College of Teacher Education, National Taiwan Normal University, Taipei, Taiwan

© Springer Nature Switzerland AG 2021
H. Mohebbi and C. Coombe (eds.), *Research Questions in Language Education and Applied Linguistics*, Springer Texts in Education,
https://doi.org/10.1007/978-3-030-79143-8_11

The Research Questions

1. How do the language outcomes of EMI students compare with non-EMI students?
2. How do the content outcomes of EMI students compare with students studying in their L1?
3. What prerequisite language ability is ideal for EMI instructors and students?
4. What teaching strategies help improve learning outcomes in EMI courses?
5. What are effective practices for training EMI instructors?
6. How does EMI differ between the various academic disciplines?
7. What are the attitudes toward EMI of various stakeholders?
8. What is the effect of EMI on local contexts?
9. How does EMI affect the identities of EMI instructors and students?
10. What role do other languages play (e.g., translanguaging) in EMI classrooms?

Suggested Resources

Macaro, E. (2018). *English Medium Instruction.* **Oxford, U.K.: Oxford University Press**.

Macaro provides the most comprehensive overview of research on EMI to date. EMI has been used along with other acronyms to describe teaching content through English. The first chapter of this volume addresses this lack of consensus in terminology. The second chapter reviews language policies guiding EMI in Europe, Asia, the Middle East, and Africa. Chapters three and four look in-depth at instructors' and students' perceptions and beliefs about EMI. Chapter five asks two important questions regarding the rapid spread of EMI: (1) Which English should be taught? and (2) Who should teach in English? Chapter six examines the pros and cons of EMI implementation, connecting to existing research studies. The next three chapters take a narrower look into EMI classrooms, discussing classroom interactions, teacher roles, and learner strategies. The book concludes with a revisit to the drivers and cost-benefits of EMI as well as future directions.

Doiz, A., Lasagabaster, D., & Sierra, J. M. (2013). *English-medium instruction at universities: Global challenges.* **Buffalo: Multilingual Matters**.

This volume by Doiz, Lasagabaster, and Sierra critically examines EMI from a variety of perspectives in Europe, Asia, Africa, and North America. Parts one and two examine the expansion of EMI and the demands it places on stakeholders. Van der Walt and Kidd suggest biliteracy practices as one means of lowering the demand. Part three offers an examination of the threat of EMI in multilingual areas of Hong Kong and Spain. Of particular concern is how English seems to be crowding out local mother tongues. Part four extends the conversation about bilingualism/multilingualism in EMI with a chapter examining international and immigrant students in the U.S. and detrimental monolingual policies. The section concludes with a chapter by Shohamy who outlines three issues with EMI: (1) difficulty learning content through a foreign language, (2) the disadvantage of minority students for whom English is a third language, and (3) assessment validity.

Fenton-Smith, B., Humphreys, P., & Walkinshaw, I. (2017). *English medium instruction in higher education in Asia-Pacific: From policy to pedagogy.* Cham, Switzerland: Springer.

Fenton-Smith, Humphreys, and Walkinshaw focuses exclusively on EMI in the Asia-Pacific, offering case studies from a variety of countries. Part one focuses on policy and implementation. A theme that emerges is a top-down policy implementation, which often lacks the appropriate planning. The section also showcases countries with longer histories of EMI such as Pakistan and Singapore whose implementations are connected more with politics and colonialization rather than internationalization. The second section transitions to an examination of EMI stakeholders, mainly instructors and students. The first few chapters of this section examine instructor training and attitudes toward EMI and the second half transitions to examining the multilingual practices within EMI. For those who take a broader view of EMI as inclusive of international student instruction in Anglophone countries such as Australia, this volume uniquely provides both justification for such definitions as well as research in this area.

Zhao, J., & Dixon, L. Q. (2017). *English-medium Instruction in Chinese universities: Perspectives, discourse and evaluation.* New York: Routledge.

Whereas the preceding books on this reading list have looked at EMI in multiple countries, Zhao and Dixon take an in-depth look at EMI in one country—China. The book is comprised of nine studies conducted in EMI institutions around China. The studies fall into three categories. The first section, "Perspectives", offers three studies addressing the varied attitudes toward EMI in China. "Discourse" takes the reader into EMI classrooms and offers analysis on the discourse of instructors and course materials. The final section, "Evaluation," evaluates EMI in terms of content outcomes, implementation aligned with policy, and instructor questioning practices. This book acts as a great model for any researchers who would like to develop a varied research agenda studying EMI in a single country.

Dafouz, E., & Smit, U. (2016). Towards a dynamic conceptual framework for English-medium education in multilingual university settings. *Applied Linguistics*, 37(3), 397–415.

Our final recommendation for reading is an article rather than a book. We feel this article is a must-read for anyone doing research on EMI as Dafouz and Smit set out a framework for understanding the multidimensional nature of EMI. The ROADMAPPING framework lays out six dimensions of EMI: Roles of English, Academic Disciplines, Language Management, Agents, Practices and Processes, and Internationalization/Glocalization. This conceptual framework acted as a guide for us as we developed our research questions for this chapter as well as our own research, and we believe it can be a valuable asset for anyone creating an EMI research agenda.

References

Airey, J. (2016). EAP, EMI, or CLIL. In K. Hyland & P. Shaw (Eds.), *The Routledge Handbook of English for Academic Purposes*. Routledge.

Dafouz, E., Camacho, M., & Urquia, E. (2014). Surely they can't do as well': A comparison of business students' academic performance in English-medium and Spanish-as-first-language-medium programmes. *Language and Education, 18*(3), 223–236.

Dearden, J. (2015). *English as a medium of instruction—A growing global phenomenon*. British Council: https://ora.ox.ac.uk/objects/uuid:4f72cdf8-b2eb-4d41-a785-4a283bf6caaa

Graham, K. M., & Eslami, Z. R. (2019). Attitudes toward EMI in East Asia and the Gulf: A systematic review. *Language Problems and Language Planning, 43*(1), 8–31.

Joe, Y., & Lee, H. (2013). Does English-medium instruction benefit students in EFL contexts? A case study of medical students in Korea. *Asia-Pacific Education Researcher* (Springer Science & Business Media B.V.), *22*(2), 201–207.

Lei, J., & Hu, G. (2014). Is English-medium instruction effective in improving Chinese undergraduate students' English competence? *International Review of Applied Linguistics in Language Teaching, 52*(2), 99–126.

Li, M. (2017). Evaluation of learning outcomes in an education course: Does it work? In J. Zhao & L. Q. Dixon (Eds.), *English-medium Instruction in Chinese universities: Perspectives, discourse and evaluation* (pp. 147–164). Routledge.

Macaro, E., Curle, S., Pun, J., An, J., & Dearden, J. (2017). A systematic review of English medium instruction in higher education. *Language Teaching, 51*(1), 36–76.

Yang, W. (2015). Content and Language Integrated Learning next in Asia: Evidence of learners' achievement in CLIL education from a Taiwan tertiary degree programme. *International Journal of Bilingual Education and Bilingualism, 18*(4), 361–382.

Keith M. Graham is currently working at National Taiwan Normal University. He received his PhD from Texas A&M University in 2020. His research focuses on using qualitative and quantitative methodologies for exploring teaching English as an international language, particularly English medium instruction and content and language integrated teaching.

Zohreh R. Eslami is a Professor in the Educational Psychology Department at Texas A&M University. Her research has examined intercultural communication, English as an International language, sociocultural perspectives of teaching, acquisition of, and English-medium instructions. Her publications include over one hundred and fifty journal papers and book chapters.

Focus on Form in Second Language Instruction

12

Alessandro Benati

Language is not something to be learned the way a person learns anything else (e.g., play tennis, drive a car, playing chess, etc.). Language is a complex, abstract, and implicit system. It is complex because it means acquiring a number of elements (lexicon, phonology, morphology, syntax, etc.). It is abstract as language representation bears no resemblance to rules found in language textbooks. Much of the grammatical information is stored in lexical entries with embedded features. There are also many aspects of language that are universal and governed by abstract principles.

This complex and abstract system is also implicit as we know we have language in our heads, but we don't really know what the contents are. This implicit system is a vast network of forms and lexical items in our mind/brain. A network is a map of grammatical and lexical items linked to each other through connections demonstrating semantic (relation based on meaning such as between *boring* and *interesting*), lexical (root word relationship such as *interest* and *interesting*) and formal relationship (a relationship between on grammatical form that does not change the meaning of the root but when added produces a new word such as *boring* and *bored*). The network grows in our head as we process more language and make the right connections.

Considering the main characteristics of this complex, abstract and implicit system, we can draw the following implications for language instruction:

- Language is too abstract and complex to be taught and learned explicitly. Language cannot be equated to the rules and paradigms that appear in textbooks;
- Explicit rules and paradigm lists can't become the abstract and complex language system because the two things are completely different.

A. Benati (✉)
CAES, Hong Kong University, Hong Kong, China
e-mail: abenati@hku.hk

© Springer Nature Switzerland AG 2021
H. Mohebbi and C. Coombe (eds.), *Research Questions in Language Education and Applied Linguistics*, Springer Texts in Education,
https://doi.org/10.1007/978-3-030-79143-8_12

Instruction is often characterized by paradigmatic explanations of specific linguistic forms or structures. This paradigmatic explanation is followed by pattern practice and substitution drills. However, research investigating the role of instruction in second language acquisition has provided the following main findings:

- Instruction does not affect the stage-like or the ordered nature of acquisition. For example, the way that L2 learners can string together elements to produce a sentence is constrained by internal processing procedures which follows a predictable order (e.g. we have access to the use of single words before more complex syntactic structures to string elements of the language together in a sentence. L2 learners acquire different morphological features in a fixed and predicted order over time);
- Internal mechanisms inside the learner's mind/brain process and organize language in ways that can't be manipulated by outside forces such as instruction and practice;
- Input provides the essential data for acquisition. Language that learners hear and see in communicative contexts forms the data on which the internal mechanisms operate. L2 learners must be exposed to input and that input must be comprehensible and meaning bearing in order to facilitate acquisition. However, input might not be sufficient in second language acquisition as L2 learners often miss some formal features in the input that are crucial to build their language system. Therefore, a *focus on form* element might be required.
- Instruction has a limited and constraint role. It does not alter the route but it might facilitate the rate of acquisition if L2 learners are exposed to language input where simultaneous attention is brought to both meaning and how that meaning is encoded.

Considering the limited role for instruction, the nature of language and the role of input in second language acquisition, we should consider a type of *focus on form* that, on one hand, enhances the grammatical features in the input, and on the other hand, provides L2 learners with opportunities to focus on meaning to make language connections. The question is to determine what type of *focus on form* is more successful in terms of helping learners internalize the grammatical features of a target language.

The term *focus on form* is characterized by any pedagogical interventions which provide a focus on meaning and a focus on form. Learners' attention is being focused on specific linguistic properties in the course of a communicative task. A series of pedagogical interventions to instruction under the umbrella of *focus on form* are available.

Structured input aims at helping L2 learners to correctly process a form and to make appropriate form-meaning connections. During, structured input practice, the input is manipulated in particular ways to make L2 learners become dependent on form to get meaning.

Input enhancement aims at helping L2 learners to notice a form in the input. Various ways of enhancing the input have been proposed which differ in terms of explicitness and elaboration. In order to help L2 learners notice a particular form, instructors could provide L2 learners with typographical cues such as bolding and italics to draw their attention to grammatical forms in the text (textual enhancement). A different pedagogical intervention would be to modify a text so that a particular target item would appear over and over again so that the text will contain many more exemplars of the same feature (input flood).

Consciousness raising aims at helping L2 learners to pay attention to grammatical forms in the input while at the same time provides the necessary input learners need to acquire a second language.

Recast aims at helping learners resolve a breakdown in communication and at the same time focus on form. This is the case when L2 learners produce something non-native-like during a conversation, and the interlocutor responds by recasting what the learner says in a native-like way (reproducing the form in a correct way). Thus, the main focus is on meaning with only a brief sidestep to formal features of language as the conversation continues.

Dictogloss aims at helping L2 learners to use their grammar resources to reconstruct a text and become aware of a particular form.

Structured output aims at helping L2 learners to exchange previously unknown information and it requires them to access a particular form in order to process meaning.

These types of *focus on form* approaches can in certain cases and conditions enhance and speed up the way languages are learned and are an effective way to incorporate a *focus on form* (while keeping meaning in focus) in second language instruction. Traditional instruction is not an appropriate way to provide *focus on form*. Paradigmatic explanation about rules followed by drill practice is not an effective way to provide a focus on form in the language classroom. *Focus on form* should ensure that L2 learners first process input correctly and efficiently. It should help L2 learners notice and process forms in the input and eventually make correct form-meaning connections.

The Research Questions

1. Is a *focus on form* component beneficial no matter the target form?
2. Is a *focus on form* component in second language instruction beneficial no matter what type of pedagogical interventions is used?
3. Are the effects of *focus on form* durative?
4. Would different types of *focus on form* be equally effective as a pedagogical intervention for improving learner's performance (e.g. making form-meaning connections, accuracy in interpreting language input)?

5. What are the characteristics of the learner (individual differences) who benefits most from *focus on form* type of instruction? For the ones who benefit the least, would more practice (top-up *focus on form*) help them to improve more?
6. How effective is *focus on form* on discourse-level interpretation and production tasks?
7. How effective is *focus on form* when measured through online tests (e.g. self-paced reading, eye-tracking, ERPs)?
8. Can learners transfer/apply the positive effects of *focus on form* they received on a particular feature to other features of the target language?
9. Would *focus on form* be more beneficial if provided in addition to explicit information?
10. How would a type of *focus on form* such as structured input affect learner's mental representation (internal system) in a way that other types of focus on form pedagogical intervention do not and cannot?

Suggested Resources

Benati, A. (2020). *Key questions in language teaching*. Cambridge: Cambridge University Press.

This book provides readers with an introduction to the main concepts and issues in language teaching such as the role and nature of language, communication and *focus on form*. Grounded in research, theory and empirical evidence, the book provides, practitioners with effective options for providing a *focus on form* component in language instruction. The author suggests that instructors should move from input to output when it comes to focus on form (e.g. structured input follow by structured output practice).

Benati, A., Laval, C., & Arche, M. (2014). *Advances in instructed second language acquisition research*. London: Bloomsbury.

This collection of chapters offers a number of perspectives on the form that instruction might take to optimize the development of mental representation. The book is divided into two parts. In the first section, VanPatten and Rothman suggest that the notion of 'rule' does not take into consideration the nature of mental grammars. In the second section, the results of four empirical studies investigating the effects of different types of *focus on form* are presented. The volume is very useful in providing additional evidence about the relationship between the type of input L2 learners are exposed to in the classroom and the grammatical knowledge they develop.

Nassaji, H., & Fotos, S. (2011). *Teaching grammar in second language classrooms.* **New York: Routledge.**

This book, designed specifically for language teachers, presents and examines the various options for effectively and efficiently incorporating a *focus on form* component in second language instruction. In each chapter, a clear and easy description of each option is provided along with its theoretical and empirical background. Guidelines for developing and implementing each option are fully listed and described.

VanPatten, B., Smith, M., & Benati, A. (2019). *Key questions in second language acquisition.* **Cambridge: Cambridge University Press.**

This introductory book carefully explores the main issues that have driven the field of second language acquisition research. It explains important linguistic concepts, and how and why they are relevant to second language acquisition. Topics such as the role of instruction and *focus on form* are presented via a 'key questions' structure that enables the reader to understand how these questions have motivated research in the field, and the problems to which researchers are seeking solutions.

Wong, W., Simard, D. (2016). *Focusing on form in language instruction.* **New York: Routledge.**

This Routledge E-module is written in a concise and clear way to introduce the readers to key concepts such as the nature of language, the importance of language input in building learners' language system, and the role of *focus on form*. The module also presents in details the characteristics of pedagogical interventions such as structured input, textual enhancement and dictogloss text reconstruction.

Alessandro Benati is Director of CAES at the University of Hong Kong. He has previously worked at the University of Greenwich, London, Middlesex, Portsmouth and the University of Sharjah. He is honorary visiting professor at the University of York SJ. Alessandro is internationally known for his research in second language acquisition and language teaching. He has published ground-breaking research with James Lee on the pedagogical framework called processing instruction. He is author and co-author of books and articles in international high-ranked journals, editor of the journal *ISLA* and the CUP Elements Series in SLA. He has coordinated international high-impact research projects and he is a member of the AHRC Peer Review College and the REF Panel 2021.

A Genre-Based Approach to Writing Instruction in the Content Areas

13

Luciana C. de Oliveira and Sharon L. Smith

The ability to write in different contexts and for diverse purposes is fundamental to students' success across content areas. However, literacy instruction within disciplines often proves challenging to teachers, as knowledge is communicated in distinct ways (Schall-Leckrone, 2017). With the goal of "mak[ing] the distribution of knowledge in schools more equitable" (Rose & Martin, 2012, p. 6), a group of educational linguists and researchers, often referred to as the Sydney School, put forth a genre pedagogy based on systemic-functional linguistics. *Genre* refers to the way language is used as a meaning-making resource to accomplish a social purpose (Hyland, 2007). This genre-based approach to writing instruction focuses on how language can be used to build content-specific knowledge, highlighting the relationship between texts and their contexts (Gebhard & Harman, 2011).

Building on this work, scholars have identified genres used in common disciplinary areas (e.g., Derewianka & Jones, 2016) and examined how knowledge of them can be facilitated. In English language arts, genre pedagogy has been used to move students from narrative to expository to arguments (Rose & Martin, 2012). In social studies, educators have examined how a genre-based approach to writing provides a way for students to examine and to interpret events, to tell powerful stories, and to establish positions (e.g., Coffin, 2006; Schall-Leckrone, 2017). Other researchers have looked at the language of science and how genre pedagogy can facilitate students' learning of both science content and how to write in science, especially scientific reports and explanations (e.g., Acurso et al., 2016). The area where there has been the least amount of research is mathematics, with work done on the genre of word problems (de Oliveira et al., 2018).

L. C. de Oliveira (✉)
School of Education, Virginia Commonwealth University, Richmond, VA, USA
e-mail: deoliveiral@vcu.edu

S. L. Smith
Department of Teaching and Learning, University of Miami, Coral Gables, FL, USA
e-mail: sls334@miami.edu

© Springer Nature Switzerland AG 2021
H. Mohebbi and C. Coombe (eds.), *Research Questions in Language Education and Applied Linguistics*, Springer Texts in Education,
https://doi.org/10.1007/978-3-030-79143-8_13

Most of the existing work has been isolated to very specific contexts and grades, leaving large gaps across genres, content areas, and academic levels. As current research positions genre pedagogy as a promising approach to writing instruction, there is much work that needs to be done in this area, both vis-a-vis studies that examine each genre in every content area at every grade level and those that address questions that cut across disciplines and contexts and provide a continuum of understanding.

The Research Questions

1. How can genre be taught in different writing contexts and with different students (e.g. elementary, secondary, higher education and L1 and L2 learners)?
2. How can differentiation be utilized when teaching genre to students at varying academic levels?
3. How does teachers' knowledge of genre impact student's academic achievement across content areas?
4. What specific knowledge about genre do content-area teachers need to have?
5. What is the optimal instructional sequence for teaching writing using a genre-based approach?
6. How can a genre-based approach to writing promote equity among marginalized and minoritized groups of learners?
7. How do genres differ across content areas (English language arts, mathematics, science, and social studies)?
8. What knowledge about language do teachers need in order to address genre in the classroom?
9. What preparation do pre-service teachers and in-service teachers need in order to address genre in different content areas?
10. What preparation do elementary and secondary teachers need in order to address genre in the classroom? Is this kind of preparation different for each group of teachers?

Suggested Resources

Brisk, M. E. (2015). *Engaging students in academic literacies: Genre-based pedagogy for K-5 classrooms.* **New York: Routledge.**

This book is a resource with specific information on how to plan and implement genre-based writing instruction for elementary students across the disciplines. It draws on systemic functional linguistics, a theory of language that examines how language is used as a social, meaning-making resource across contexts. *Engaging Students in Academic Literacies* leads educators in fostering students' writing by focusing on the structures and features across genres. Brisk discusses how genre pedagogy, with its focus on academic language, is especially effective with English language learners. This text provides concrete ways, strategies, and examples to help teachers design, implement, and reflect upon genre theory in the classroom.

Derewianka, B., & Jones, P. (2016). *Teaching language in context* **(2nd ed.). South Melbourne, Australia: Oxford University Press**.

Teaching Language in Context is centered around language, how it enables learning, and how teachers' understanding of language fosters students as they read and write across genres. This text introduces educators to the language that teachers and students encounter across disciplinary areas in elementary and secondary schooling. It provides practical strategies related to the language demands that students encounter, the planning, creating, and evaluating of language-focused activities, the analysis of texts and materials, and the scaffolding of students as they work with various genres. This second edition of *Teaching Language in Context* takes a multimodal approach to examining texts and the relationship between images and texts.

Gebhard, M. (2019). *Teaching and researching ELLs' disciplinary literacies: Systemic functional linguistics in action in the context of U.S. school reform.* **New York: Routledge**.

This book provides a comprehensive structure for teaching and learning multilingual learners in content area classes from a systemic-functional linguistic perspective. The book highlights supports for multilingual learners' development of disciplinary literacies, based on work in K-12 classrooms.

Humphrey, S. (2017). *Academic literacies in the middle years: A framework for enhancing teacher knowledge and student achievement.* **New York: Routledge**.

This text presents a framework for professional learning that was designed to foster educators' understandings of language and how it creates meaning across content areas. The framework is grounded in systemic functional linguistic theory and is composed of a metalinguistic toolkit. The book teaches how to design literacy interventions, specifically looking at exploring narratives, writing responses and factorial explanations, and persuading audiences. Throughout the text, examples of how teachers have applied specific metalinguistic toolkits with students in diverse disciplinary classrooms. *Academic Literacies in the Middle Years* aims to provide teachers with the knowledge about language necessary to provide their students with the academic language and literacy skills needed to succeed in school.

de Oliveira, L. C., & Iddings, J. (2014). (Eds). *Genre pedagogy across the curriculum: Theory and application in U.S. classrooms and contexts.* **London: Equinox Publishing**.

This volume provides the most recent scholarship using a theory of genre emerging from Systemic Functional Linguistics (SFL). It describes both theoretical and practical applications of a language-based curriculum from elementary through to university level within a U.S. context. While there are other genre-based pedagogies in the United States, SFL-based genre pedagogies illuminate the importance of language and linguistic choice within the curriculum, aiming to make these choices explicitly understood by scholars, teachers and students. Each chapter shows how this pedagogy can be adapted and used across many different disciplines and student age groups.

Martin, J. R., Maton, K., & Doran, Y. J. (Eds.) (2019). *Accessing academic discourse: Systemic functional linguistics and legitimation code theory.* **New York: Routledge**.

This volume brings together the longstanding theory of systemic functional linguistics with new developments in the sociological legitimation code theory. Authors present chapters that advance the inter-disciplinary connections between these two theories. Chapters present key ideas and new conceptual advancements, studies, and guidelines for developing curriculum and pedagogy to support access to academic discourse in classrooms.

References

Acurso, K., Gebhard, M., & Selden, C. (2016). Supporting L2 elementary science writing with SFL in an age of school reform. In L. C. de Oliveira & T. Silva (Eds.), *Second language writing in elementary classrooms* (pp. 126–150). Palgrave Macmillan.

Coffin, C. (2006). *Historical discourse: The language of time, cause, and evaluation.* Continuum.

de Oliveira, L. C., Sembiante, S., & Ramirez, J. A. (2018). Bilingual academic language development in mathematics for emergent to advanced bilingual students. In S. Crespo, & S. Celedón-Pattichis, & M. Civil (Eds.), *Access and equity: Promoting high quality mathematics in grades 3–5* (pp. 81–98). National Council of Teachers of Mathematics.

Derewianka, B., & Jones, P. (2016). *Teaching language in context* (2nd ed.). Oxford University Press.

Gebhard, M., & Harman, R. (2011). Reconsidering genre theory in K-12 schools: A response to school reforms in the United States. *Journal of Second Language Writing, 20*, 45–55. https://doi.org/10.1016/j.jslw.2010.12.007

Hyland, K. (2007). Genre pedagogy: Language, literacy and L2 writing instruction. *Journal of Second Language Writing, 16*, 148–164. https://doi.org/10.1016/j.jslw.2007.07.005

Rose, D., & Martin, J. R. (2012). *Learning to write/reading to learn: Genre, knowledge and pedagogy in the Sydney school.* Equinox.

Schall-Leckrone, L. (2017). Genre pedagogy: A framework to prepare history teachers to teach language. *TESOL Quarterly, 51*(2), 358–382. https://doi.org/10.1002/tesq.322

Luciana C. de Oliveira, is Associate Dean for Academic Affairs and Graduate Studies in the School of Education and a Professor in the Department of Teaching and Learning at Virginia Commonwealth University, Richmond, VA, USA. Her research focuses on issues related to teaching multilingual learners at the elementary and secondary levels. She served in the presidential line of TESOL International Association (2017–2020) and was a member of the Board of Directors (2013–2016). She was the first Latina to ever serve as President (2018–2019) of TESOL.

Sharon L. Smith Ph.D. is currently working as an elementary teacher in Miami-Dade County Public Schools. She holds Bachelor's degrees in Elementary Education and Spanish from Purdue University and a Ph.D. in Teaching and Learning from the University of Miami. Her research currently focuses on action research and the application of critical, humanizing literacies in the elementary school context with a specific focus on honoring and sustaining the stories of diverse children.

Global Englishes and Teaching English as an International Language

14

Heath Rose and Mona Syrbe

The related fields of Global Englishes and English as an International Language examine the growth of English as the world's foremost global lingua franca (see Galloway & Rose, 2015; Rose & Galloway, 2019). There is currently tremendous scope to explore the implications of the spread of English as a global language on English language teaching practices. While theoretical arguments have been made for curricular change, there is a dearth of research that explores classroom-level implementation of such innovation.

First, there is a need for classroom-based research into approaches and materials to effectively bring Global Englishes into the classroom. Syrbe (2018) notes that while Global Englishes approaches tie in well with progressive components of global curricula, many elements of teaching English will need to be reconsidered. Action research is required to examine different approaches, resources, as well as student and teacher perceptions toward teaching English as an international language. A central question here surrounds material use and selection. It is paramount to carry out more research evaluating existing materials in terms of their incorporation and representation of English as a global language. Research could follow the foundations provided by Syrbe and Rose (2018) and Rose and Galloway (2019). The key task for future research will be to develop a framework delineating constructs of Global Englishes, based on which qualitative and quantitative text and content analyses can be carried out. Beyond that, there is a lack of research into real world materials and resources used to expose learners to Global Englishes.

Second, the changed use of English entails a changed understanding of what it means to be proficient in this global language. Global speakers use English with a variety of interlocutors from diverse backgrounds and have been observed to make

H. Rose (✉)
Department of Education, The University of Oxford, Oxford, UK
e-mail: heath.rose@education.ox.ac.uk

M. Syrbe
College of Business, Rikkyo University, Tokyo, Japan

© Springer Nature Switzerland AG 2021
H. Mohebbi and C. Coombe (eds.), *Research Questions in Language Education and Applied Linguistics*, Springer Texts in Education,
https://doi.org/10.1007/978-3-030-79143-8_14

extensive use of communication and pragmatic strategies. In this sense, Global Englishes communication focuses on content and effectiveness rather than standard English norms. This naturally has implications for testing and assessment practices and requires us to re-consider test design on all levels, including test constructs and test content. Research is needed to address the question of how to include the use of non-native speakers and speakers of different varieties of English into tests, and how to measure communicative effectiveness and the use of communication strategies rather than norm-benchmarked accuracy (Hall, 2014).

Third, attitudes are of interest to researchers as they influence the way we use English and react to diverse speakers of the language. So far, research has explored teacher and learner attitudes associated with different English varieties. However, current methods rely on static varieties, which are inapt for measuring the complexity of Global Englishes. There is further scope for research to explore how Global Englishes education can positively influence attitudes. Beyond the ELT classroom, this also extends to teacher education. Despite the positive effects of greater exposure to Global Englishes, research has found deeply ingrained standard language ideologies in teachers (Suzuki, 2011), highlighting the necessity to investigate ways to change such beliefs.

The Research Questions

1. What are students' linguistic and communicative needs in terms of using English as an international language?
2. How globally-oriented are English language teaching materials and textbooks?
3. What are student/teacher attitudes toward the use of materials that contain Global Englishes content?
4. What are the psychological, linguistic and/or sociolinguistic effects of teaching English as an international language for learners?
5. What barriers are associated with teaching English as an international language in various contexts, and how can teachers overcome these?
6. What underpins learner attitudes towards Global Englishes, and how can attitudes be changed?
7. How can teacher education best prepare teachers to teach Global Englishes?
8. What is the role of standardized testing in a global English-using community?
9. In what ways can assessment practices be changed to incorporate Global Englishes?
10. How does the teaching of Global Englishes affect specific learning outcomes such as comprehensibility of accents?

Suggested Resources

Rose, H. & Galloway, N. (2019). *Global Englishes for Language Teaching.* **Cambridge: Cambridge University Press**.

This book outlines a number of concrete proposals for innovation in English language teaching praxis, under the umbrella term of Global Englishes Language Teaching. Within this framework, the authors offer a detailed examination of how a Global Englishes perspective permeates into the fields of TESOL and second language acquisition. The book is divided into two parts, the first on theory and the second on research, and unites discussions on the pedagogical implications of the global spread of English. While the book is intended for a researcher audience, practitioners will find many of the ideas in the book illuminating, especially if teaching in global contexts.

Rose, H., Syrbe, M., Montakantiwong, A., & Funada, N. (2020). *Global TESOL for the 21st Century: Teaching English in a Changing World.* **Bristol: Multilingual Matters**.

This multi-authored volume explores a variety of teaching-related questions, divided into four sections. The first section examines theoretical foundations by looking at key concepts and frameworks, providing a useful resource for methodology. The second part addresses classrooms and curricula, specifically materials, norms, and testing and thus offers a good basis for a variety of teaching and testing related research projects. The third section focuses on teachers and learners of English, providing insight for research into attitudes and teacher education. The fourth section outlines ideas for researching curriculum change.

McKay, S. L. & Brown, J. D. (2016). *Teaching and Assessing EIL in local contexts around the world.* **New York: Routledge**.

The first three chapters of this book cover themes related to EIL such as contexts of EIL classrooms, EIL teachers, learners, and classroom interactions, as well as EIL student needs. The remaining chapters address individual language skills such as grammar, oracy and literacy. These are especially useful for ELT teachers as they provide practical guides on how to approach these skills from an EIL perspective. One key assumption of the book is that "all teaching and assessing of English must be based on locally defined goals and standards" (McKay & Brown, 2016, p. xiii). This concept feeds into many of the research questions we outline above that are related to needs, practices, materials and assessment. This book provides a great source of information from which to build pedagogically-grounded research projects.

Matsuda, A. (2012) (Ed.). *Principles and Practices of Teaching English as an International Language.* **Bristol: Multilingual Matters.**

This edited collection provides a comprehensive overview of some of the main topics related to teaching EIL. This book is organised into two sections: the first focuses on key principles of EIL, and the second showcases EIL programs, courses and pedagogical ideas. The second part offers useful information on already implemented EIL-informed teaching and teacher education, and thus relates to our research questions connected to teacher education and classroom implementation. Some of the chapters touch on developing and testing communication strategies (e.g. chapters five and six) and could provide a basis for research into testing.

Galloway, N. & Rose, H. (2015). *Introducing Global Englishes.* **Abingdon, UK: Routledge.**

This book provides a comprehensive overview and analysis of the field of Global Englishes from the history of the language to implications for the ELT classroom. In its first two chapters this book looks at history and change of English, analyzing diversity within the language and its current role. This role is critically discussed in chapter 3, while chapters 4 and 5 focus on describing and understanding new varieties of English, both of which are interesting to establish teaching and testing content. The following chapters (6 and 7) examine how English is used as a lingua franca in contact situations and are useful for research into establishing students' needs for using English globally. From an educational perspective, chapters 8 and 9 are highly relevant as they address attitudes and ELT implications, both of which are key issues in research.

References

Galloway, N., & Rose, H. (2015). *Introducing global Englishes.* Routledge.

Hall, C. J. (2014). Moving beyond accuracy: From tests of English to tests of "Englishing." *ELT Journal, 68*(4), 376–385.

Rose, H., & Galloway, N. (2019). *Global Englishes language teaching.* Cambridge University Press.

Suzuki, A. (2011). Introducing diversity of English into ELT: Student teachers' responses. *ELT Journal, 65*(2), 145–153.

Syrbe, M. (2018). Evaluating the suitability of teaching EIL for the German classroom. *International Journal of Applied Linguistics.* https://doi.org/10.1111/ijal.12214

Syrbe, M., & Rose, H. (2018). An evaluation of the global orientation of English textbooks in Germany. *Innovation in Language Learning and Teaching, 12*(2), 152–163.

Heath Rose is an Associate Professor of Applied Linguistics at the University of Oxford's Department of Education, where he is course director for the MSc in Applied Linguistics for Language Teaching. He has edited and authored numerous books including *Global Englishes for Language Teaching* (2019), *Doing Research in Applied Linguistics* (2017), and *Introducing Global Englishes* (2015). He has published on topics related to language education in such journals as *Applied Linguistics, The Modern Language Journal, TESOL Quarterly, ELT Journal and Higher Education*.

Mona Syrbe is an Assistant Professor at Rikkyo University in Tokyo, where she teaches Academic English. Her research has centered on the implications of Global Englishes on materials and high-stakes tests. She has published articles concerning teaching EIL in the *International Journal of Applied Linguistics* and *Innovation in Language Learning and Teaching*. She has co-authored a chapter on assessing EIL for the *TESOL Encyclopedia of English Language Teaching* (2018) and co-authored a textbook titled *Global TESOL for the 21st Century* (2020).

Identity in Language Learning and Teaching

15

Bonny Norton

Identity in language education and applied linguistics is best understood with reference to changing conceptions of the individual, language, and learning. These changes, in turn, are associated with broader trends in the social sciences, and represent a shift from a predominantly psycholinguistic approach to language education to include a greater focus on sociological and cultural dimensions of language learning (Douglas Fir Group, 2016). From the mid-1990s, when Norton challenged essentialist views of the language learner, developed her theory of investment, and highlighted issues of power in language learning (Norton, 2013; Norton Peirce, 1995), there has been a vibrant and expanding body of research on identity in language education and applied linguistics (Preece, 2016). Drawing on poststructuralist theory (Weedon, 1997), much of this research takes the position that identity is multiple, changing, and a site of struggle, and the extent to which a learner speaks, reads, or writes, is associated with the learner's perceived value in a given institution or community (Bourdieu, 1991). In this regard, social processes marked by inequities of gender, race, class, ethnicity, and sexual orientation may serve to position learners in ways that silence and exclude. As Norton argues, such learners, who may be highly motivated, may not be *invested* in the language practices of their classrooms or communities, and thus paradoxically positioned as "poor" or unmotivated language learners. At the same time, these learners, through the exercise of human agency, may resist marginalization through both covert and overt acts of resistance. What is of central interest is that the very articulation of power, identity, and resistance is expressed in and through language.

While these ideas about language and identity have already proved highly generative, they are also responding to a new social order, characterized by technological innovation, mobility, and unpredictability (Blommaert, 2013). There is increasing interest in the way advances in technology are impacting language

B. Norton (✉)
Language and Literacy Education, University of British Columbia, Vancouver, BC, Canada
e-mail: bonny.norton@ubc.ca

© Springer Nature Switzerland AG 2021
H. Mohebbi and C. Coombe (eds.), *Research Questions in Language Education and Applied Linguistics*, Springer Texts in Education,
https://doi.org/10.1007/978-3-030-79143-8_15

learning and teaching, and the ways in which the forces of globalization are implicated in identity construction. To investigate language learning in the digital era, in which learners navigate relationships both online and offline, Darvin and Norton (2015) have developed an expanded model of investment, which occurs at the intersection of identity, capital, and ideology. Through this critical lens, researchers are examining more systematically how microstructures of power in communicative events are indexical of larger ideological structures. By providing a multi-layered and multidirectional approach, the model demonstrates how power circulates in society and constructs modes of inclusion and exclusion through and beyond language. The interaction of language learners with material objects, for example, can enable language learners to reframe their relationships with others to claim more powerful identities from which to speak (Toohey, 2018). Further, issues of identity are seen to be relevant not only to language learners, but also to language teachers, teacher educators, and researchers (Barkhuizen, 2017). The research questions that accompany this summary are an extension of this expanding body of research, as addressed by Norton and Costa (2018).

The Research Questions

1. In two families with contrasting socioeconomic histories, how is social class implicated in the digital literacy practices of each family?
2. How do the linguistic practices and identities of language learners in diaspora sites change over time?
3. In the context of a transnational study with youth, to what extent do digital innovations build transnational identities across different language learner communities?
4. How does educational policy impact teacher practices and teacher identity in a given community?
5. With reference to a designated group of diverse language learners or teachers, to what extent is Darvin & Norton's, (2015) model of investment useful as a tool for the analysis of intersectionality?
6. How are the identities of lingua franca speakers negotiated in an online chat room or other social media sites?
7. How does a heritage language course impact the identities of college students in a given community?
8. To what extent do the identities of language learners in study abroad programs change over time and space?
9. In what ways does the practice of translation impact the translator's identity and investments in a given text?
10. With reference to a multiracial group of non-native teachers of English, to what extent is race implicated in teacher experiences of legitimacy as English language teachers?

Suggested Resources

Barkhuizen, G. (Ed.) (2017). *Reflections on language teacher identity research.* **New York: Routledge**.

This is a highly readable collection of reflections on language teacher identity research. Barkhuizen has invited leading researchers to draw on their own experiences as teachers and researchers to explore the many dimensions of language teacher identity. The editor's introduction helps readers navigate the many contributions, and the authors address their respective areas of expertise from both theoretical and methodological perspectives. Key ideas, theories, and research about language teacher identity are presented in a succinct and engaging style.

Darvin, R. & Norton, B. (2015). Identity and a model of investment in applied linguistics. *Annual Review of Applied Linguistics,* **35, 36–56**.

This article locates Norton's early work on identity and investment within the social turn of applied linguistics, and then presents an expanded model of investment, occurring at the intersection of identity, ideology, and capital. The authors argue that the changing social world, characterized by new technologies and changing patterns of mobility, calls for new questions, analyses, and theories of identity. The model addresses the needs of learners who navigate their way through online and offline contexts and perform identities that have become more fluid and complex. The model thus depicts the increasingly complex relationship between identity, investment, and language learning. The article was awarded the 2016 TESOL Distinguished Research Award.

De Costa, P & Norton, B. (Guest Eds, 2017). Transdisciplinarity and language teacher identity [Special Issue]. *The Modern Language Journal, 101 (S1)*.

This special issue draws on the exciting work of the Douglas Fir Group (DFG, 2016) to engage the following two broad questions: (a) In what ways is language teaching "identity work"? and (b) To what extent does a transdisciplinary approach to language learning and teaching offer insight into language teacher identity? Beginning with an introductory article by the co-editors on the "good language teacher", the special issue considers how the transdisciplinary framework of the DFG might contribute to our understanding of language teacher identity. The DFG focus on macro, meso, and micro dimensions of language learning at the ideological, institutional, and classroom levels, respectively, proved useful to the diverse contributors. A central finding from the special issue is the need to recognize the rich linguistic and personal histories that language teachers bring into the classroom in order to promote effective language learning.

Norton, B. (2013). *Identity and language learning: Extending the conversation* **(2nd Edition). Bristol, UK: Multilingual Matters.**

In this highly-cited second edition, Norton defines identity as "how a person understands his or her relationship to the world, how that relationship is structured across time and space, and how the person understands possibilities for the future." Drawing on a longitudinal case study of immigrant women in Canada, Norton draws on this construct of identity to explain the language learning experiences of the participants. Her construct of investment, conceptualized as a sociological complement to the psychological construct of motivation, is also integral to the analysis. The book concludes with a compelling Afterword by Claire Kramsch, which addresses Norton's impact on the field with respect to the three influential concepts of identity, investment, and imagined communities.

Preece, S. (Ed.). (2016). *The Routledge handbook of language and identity.* **Oxon: Routledge.**

This 37-chapter volume provides a comprehensive and highly readable overview of research on language and identity in the field of language education and applied linguistics. Contributors are leading researchers from diverse regions of the world, and Preece has organized the contributions into five sections, which include theoretical perspectives, categories of identity, key issues for researchers, case studies, and future directions. The sheer scope and scale of the research on language and identity is striking, and the future of language and identity research in the digital age is particularly exciting.

References

Barkhuizen, G. (Ed.). (2017). *Reflections on language teacher identity research.* Routledge.

Blommaert, J. (2013). *Ethnography, superdiversity and linguistic landscapes: Chronicles of complexity* (Vol. 18). Multilingual Matters.

Bourdieu, P. (1991). *Language and symbolic power* (J. B. Thompson, Ed.; G. Raymond & M. Adamson, Trans.). Polity.

Darvin, R., & Norton, B. (2015). Identity and a model of investment in applied linguistics. *Annual Review of Applied Linguistics, 35,* 35–56.

Douglas Fir Group. (2016). A transdisciplinary framework for SLA in a multilingual world. *The Modern Language Journal, 100*(S1), 19–47.

Norton, B. (2013). *Identity and language learning: Extending the conversation.* Multilingual Matters.

Norton, B., & De Costa, P. I. (2018). Research tasks on identity in language learning and teaching. *Language Teaching, 51*(1), 90–112.

Norton Peirce, B. (1995). Social identity, investment, and language learning. *TESOL Quarterly, 29*(1), 9–31.

Preece, S. (Ed.). (2016). *Routledge handbook of language and identity.* Routledge.

Toohey, K. (2018). *Learning English at school: Identity, sociomaterial relations and classroom practices* (2nd, Revised edition). Multilingual Matters.

Weedon, C. (1997). *Feminist practice and poststructuralist theory* (2nd ed.). Blackwell.

Bonny Norton, FRSC, is a University Killam Professor and Distinguished University Scholar in the Department of Language and Literacy Education, University of British Columbia, Canada. Her research interests are identity and language learning, digital literacy, and international development. She is committed to open technology in language education, and is playing a leading role in the development of the Global Storybooks initiative (https://globalstorybooks.net/). A Fellow of the Royal Society of Canada and the American Educational Research Association, her work has been translated into Chinese, Japanese, Korean, Portuguese, German, and French. Her website is: http://www.educ.ubc.ca/faculty/norton/.

Inclusive Language Teaching

16

David Gerlach

Catering to students with different abilities and special educational needs has become an important paradigm in many educational systems around the world. The UN Convention on the Rights of Persons with Disabilities, ratified by most UN members, has contributed a lot to the efforts of including learners with disabilities in regular schools and classrooms. Inclusive education is considered an overall developmental process that stretches beyond particular social systems, communities, or state borders (Booth & Ainscow, 2011). Yet, in many places, inclusive practices and mainstreaming have led to categorisation and stigmatisation of learners who are put into certain categories of special educational needs (SEN) such as language impairments, social-emotional difficulties, or neurodevelopmental disorders (e.g. autism spectrum disorder). Although these diagnoses might help special education teachers and therapists to create support strategies for these learners, they are not helpful for regular school teachers in their everyday approaches to language teaching. The idea behind inclusive teaching is to create a learning environment that would enable learners with a large number of different abilities to gain access to (in this case) a foreign language. The 'foreignness' of the language itself, the change of perspective, and the tenets of inter- and transcultural learning allow for a genuine interaction with the topics and aspects of language learning. If teaching and learning is concentrated around a common topic with scaffolded activities and tasks, differentiation and individualised language learning can take place in a motivating way. Task-Based Language Teaching (TBLT; see the chapter in this book) offers means of differentiation and language scaffolding that allows for different products being the result of lesson plans created and assessed at different levels of learner competence.

As far as assessment and the evaluation of learners' progress is concerned, different regulations in different educational systems allow for disability compen-

D. Gerlach (✉)
School of Humanities, Chair of TEFL, University of Wuppertal, Wuppertal, Germany
e-mail: gerlach@uni-wuppertal.de

© Springer Nature Switzerland AG 2021
H. Mohebbi and C. Coombe (eds.), *Research Questions in Language Education and Applied Linguistics*, Springer Texts in Education,
https://doi.org/10.1007/978-3-030-79143-8_16

sations for students with certain difficulties, and even gifted students who need special assistance (Gerlach, 2017).

Although a lot of research on inclusive education from the perspective of general (school) education or special education appears in relevant publications, the research on learning foreign languages in inclusive classrooms is still rather limited. Of late, the main perspectives have dealt with important issues of policy development, legislation, and exemption from language classes (e.g. Wight, 2015), and specific learning difficulties in the context of foreign language learning (Sparks, 2016). Wight (2015) also sums up the importance of foreign language learning for students to become literate adults despite their learning difficulties. Yet, research on the aforementioned methodological approaches towards inclusive language teaching (and if they really work), as well as what teachers and learners need in those language learning environments, still remains widely unexplored. E.g. we do not know much about effective means of differentiation in inclusive settings or if different SEN require certain (or different) approaches when fostering certain language skills. In addition to that, the role of additional teachers, e.g. SEN teachers, who can support the language teacher during his/her lessons, still remains under-researched and also begs the question of how good the additional teacher needs to be, in the language taught in that classroom, to make inclusive language teaching fruitful for the learners in need.

The Research Questions

1. What is 'inclusive language teaching'?
2. What means of differentiation might be employed given certain (specific) learning difficulties and special educational needs (SEN)?
3. What means of assessment is most effective for certain (specific) learning difficulties and SEN?
4. What methods, techniques, and approaches can be applied effectively in heterogeneous groups of learners?
5. How far can certain language skills and competences be fostered for both learners with special educational needs and those without?
6. How far can the teaching of literature or culture attribute to inclusive language teaching?
7. How can assistive technologies effectively help learners with difficulties or SEN in learning a foreign language?
8. What disability compensations exist in different educational systems for learners with SEN and how are they put into practice by teachers/schools/institutions?
9. What beliefs do teachers have of effective inclusive language teaching and how do these beliefs show in their everyday practice?
10. What teacher knowledge is necessary to create inclusive language learning environments?

Suggested Resources

Kormos, J., & Smith, A. M. (2012). *Teaching Languages to Learners with Specific Learning Differences.* **Bristol: Multilingual Matters.**

The book introduces its readers to the social construct of "disability" and its implications for education and teaching before it deals with specific learning differences, especially dyslexia and associated learning differences. The authors' approach is therefore inclusive in the sense that it immediately seeks solutions to— or at least ways of dealing with—different learning difficulties without focusing on pathological or disability constructions. In addition to dyslexia and difficulties such as Specific Language Impairment, Dyspraxia, ADHD and Asperger's Syndrome, the authors focus on the cognitive and emotional dimensions of language learning, how difficulties can be identified in language teaching as well as means of accommodating these learning differences.

Kormos, J., & Kontra, E. H. (2008). *Language Learners with Special Needs: An International Perspective.* **Bristol: Multilingual Matters.**

This edited volume presents research on different learning difficulties and challenges from different countries around the world, among which are Canada, Hungary, Norway, Poland, the United States, and the United Kingdom. Although dyslexia is, again, a strong focus due to its immediate influence on language learning, the authors also present research on language aptitude, language anxiety, learners with ADHD, and deaf EFL learners. Apart from raising more research questions, the papers give insights into addressing learning difficulties in inclusive classroom settings. Interestingly, the final chapters deal with teachers' perceptions of dyslexic language learners as well as their views on inclusive education within a TEFL landscape.

Oxford Position Paper: Inclusive Practices in English Language Teaching.

Based on the works and expertise of a panel of experts from schools, universities, curriculum developers and policymakers, this comprehensive position paper presents both an overview of the most common difficulties and challenges found in inclusive language learning settings (with a focus on English language teaching). These challenges (e.g. dyslexia, autism, ADHD, social, emotional and behavioral difficulties, different mother tongues due to refugee history of students) are seen as causes of difficulties in language learning and discussed within a frame of both professional development opportunities for language teachers, as well as guidelines for inclusive teaching, testing, and assessment. In addition to that, the authors stress the importance of cooperation and collaboration between the different stakeholders to provide fruitful learning environments for all language learners.

Although this position paper deals with many issues in a summarised, very practice-oriented form and addresses primarily teachers and policymakers, many open questions remain that could be dealt with in research (seminars) and in strong cooperation with language teachers who struggle with learning differences of their students.

References

Booth, T., & Ainscow, M. (2011). *Index for inclusion. Developing learning and participation in schools.* Centre for Studies on Inclusive Education.

Gerlach, D. (2017). Reading and spelling difficulties in the ELT classroom. *ELT Journal, 71*(3), 295–304.

Sparks, R. L. (2016). Myths about foreign language learning and learning disabilities. *Foreign Language Annals, 49*, 252–270.

Wight, M. C. S. (2015). Students with learning disabilities in the foreign language learning environment and the practice of exemption. *Foreign Language Annals, 48*, 39–55.

David Gerlach is a full professor of Teaching English as a Foreign Language (TEFL) at the University of Wuppertal, Germany. He has earned a PhD in school pedagogy with a special focus on the teaching and learning of foreign languages from the University of Marburg. David's research focuses on inclusive language teaching with a special focus on developmental dyslexia and reading and spelling difficulties in the context of English language classrooms. In addition to that, he is interested in professional development of teachers in institutionalised contexts and reflective practice. He has authored and co-authored several publications on inclusive TEFL, dyslexia and foreign language teaching/learning, and teacher professionalisation and development.

Increasing Reading Fluency

Neil J. Anderson

The most important issue that should be addressed by researchers engaged in the examination of reading fluency is the definition of reading fluency. The definition must be clear and measureable.

Zadeh et al. (2012) emphasize in their work that for both first and second language reading there is not an agreed upon definition of reading fluency. That can be troublesome for researchers. However, it is clear when examining definitions of reading fluency that researchers define it simply as the number of words read per minute either silently or orally (Carver, 2000; Dubin & Bycina, 1991; Grabe & Stoller, 2011; Jensen, 1986; Nuttall, 2007; Taguchi et al., 2006, 2012).

Grabe (2009) defines reading fluency as "the ability to read rapidly with ease and accuracy, and to read with appropriate expression and phrasing" (p. 291). Note that this definition highlights three elements of fluency. First, the idea of reading with ease, points out the importance of automaticity. Second, accuracy assumes that we recognize the words when we see them. Third, oral reading is key to this definition of fluency. Notice what is lacking in this definition of reading fluency; there is no explicit inclusion of comprehension while reading.

Anderson (2018) defines reading fluency as "reading at an appropriate rate with adequate comprehension" (p. 2213). This definition is unique among definitions of reading fluency for several reasons. First, it combines both reading rate and reading comprehension in the definition. Anderson explains that various conditions determine appropriate rate and adequate comprehension. Variables such as whether the subject is reading orally or silently must be considered. Also, the grade or age level of the reader will also determine appropriate rate. Younger readers read slower than

N. J. Anderson (✉)
Department of English Language Teaching & Learning, Brigham Young University–Hawaii, Laie, HI, USA
e-mail: neil.anderson@byuh.edu

© Springer Nature Switzerland AG 2021
H. Mohebbi and C. Coombe (eds.), *Research Questions in Language Education and Applied Linguistics*, Springer Texts in Education,
https://doi.org/10.1007/978-3-030-79143-8_17

older readers, both silently and orally. Adequate comprehension will be determined by the reading purpose. Far too many readers assume they need to have 100% comprehension of what they have read. That percentage of comprehension is rarely needed for most reading tasks.

It is important to consider why the development of reading rate should be considered in isolation of reading comprehension. Is there a scenario in the real world of reading when we would give preference to reading rate with no expectation of comprehension? The reverse question is also relevant. Is there a scenario in the real world of reading when we desire 100% comprehension and at the same time we do not care how long it takes an individual to reach that level of comprehension? Refer to Anderson (2018) for additional explanations of appropriate rate and adequate comprehension.

Zadeh et al. (2012) give support to Anderson's (2018) definition when they point out that the frameworks that predict successful reading suggest "that it may be of theoretical value to consider an expanded [simple view of reading] framework, in which reading fluency (rate) and reading comprehension are treated as distinct, yet related, parallel outcome behaviors" (p. 167). Because reading rate and reading fluency are "distinct, yet related" (p. 167) behaviors, both could be combined into a single definition of reading fluency.

The Research Questions

1. Based on a careful review of publications, what is the strongest definition of reading fluency?
2. Should reading rate be separated from reading comprehension in order to better understand the relationships between the two critical components of reading?
3. Using Anderson's (2018) four quadrants of reading fluency, what are typical movement patterns through the quadrants?
4. What is the minimal reading fluency that a second language learner of English should have to successfully navigate through college/university reading assignments?
5. How does silent reading fluency differ from oral reading fluency for the same individuals?
6. Does reading fluency vary by language proficiency level?
7. How does reading fluency vary across learners when reading online versus reading hard copy?
8. How long does it take to break the cycle of word-by-word reading to fluent reading?
9. How does reading fluency correlate with course grades for students at different levels of academic achievement?
10. What classroom pedagogical activities could teachers draw upon to facilitate the development of reading fluency?

Suggested Resources

Anderson, N. J. (2018). (Ed.). *The TESOL Encyclopedia of English Language Teaching,* **Volume IV, Teaching Reading, 1ˢᵗ Edition. Edited by John I. Liontas (Project Editor: Margo DelliCarpini) Hoboken, NJ: John Wiley & Sons, Inc.**

This resource is key to success in both L2 reading research and classroom pedagogical practices. As noted earlier, various factors ultimately influence the development of reading fluency (as defined by Anderson). This volume of the TESOL Encyclopedia includes 39 entries on a variety of second language reading topics central to research and pedagogical instruction. Researchers may want to review each entry to determine the impact each has on the development of reading fluency. Each entry follows a consistent format: framing the issue, making the case, pedagogical implications, references, and suggested readings. The entries could play a key role in using appropriate classroom activities to then research the impact on reading fluency.

Evans, N., Anderson, N. J., & Eggington, W. (Eds.) (2015). *ESL readers and writers in higher education: Understanding challenges, providing support.* **New York, NY: Routledge.**

This resource is valuable for researchers focusing on university learners of English as a second/foreign language. The 15 chapters focus on challenges that readers (and writers) face in university contexts and what support can be provided by institutions to address the challenges. This resource is valuable for researchers because of the contextual variables that influence the development of reading in adult learners. The support provided within university contexts could be a factor that ultimately influences reading fluency.

Anderson provides a key chapter in this volume that focuses on the academic reading expectations and challenges of university readers. Data gathered from 114 university departments across five majors resulted in the identification of 12 overall reading expectations that faculty have of readers and 15 challenges that faculty view in their learners.

Grabe, W. & Stoller, F. L. (2011). *Teaching and researching reading* **(2nd ed.). Harlow, UK: Pearson.**

Grabe and Stoller provide an extremely valuable resource on both aspects of teaching and researching reading. It is important for both of these areas to be combined. Research should inform effective classroom practices and the realities of classroom practices should inform research. This resource allows us to keep both perspectives in mind.

The book is divided into five sections: understanding L2 reading, exploring research in reading, teaching reading using evidence-based practices, investigating reading through action research, and resources. The area of reading fluency is addressed within the section on action research. Key questions related to word recognition, oral reading and classroom practices are addressed in the chapter on reading fluency that can help inform any research project examining the questions raised in this entry.

Newton, J. M., Ferris, D. R., Goh, C. C. M., Grabe, W., Stoller, F. L., & Vandergrift, L. (2018). *Teaching English to second language learners in academic contexts.* **New York, NY: Routledge**.

Developing reading fluency while engaged in academic reading is extremely challenging, thus the need for examining this language skill and the need for additional research on this topic. One short section addresses the question of how fluent should L2 readers become. The authors suggest that reading at 200 words-per-minute is an appropriate goal to work towards, but they also recognize that when reading difficult texts, as in academic contexts, L2 readers will read slower just as L1 readers read more slowly when reading difficult texts.

In terms of building an effective reading curriculum, the authors suggest one (of 12) key principles that should be considered: Reading fluency—at word and passage levels—is essential for efficient reading comprehension abilities. One essential element addressed in this principle is that readers will vary their reading rate depending of the reading purpose. That is an important element to keep in mind when engaging in research on reading fluency.

Zadeh, Z. Y, Farnia, F., & Geva, E. (2012). Toward modeling reading comprehension and reading fluency in English language learners. *Reading & Writing,* **25, 163–187**.https://doi.org/10.1007/s11145-010-9252-0

This research article is valuable because of its focus on the simple view of reading (SVR) and the initial development of reading fluency and reading comprehension in young second language learners. The study follows 179 language learners from first grade through third grade (n = 308 in first grade, but due to attrition data was available from only 179 participants in year three). This article emphasizes the central role of phonological awareness, naming speed, and oral language in the long-term development of reading fluency and reading comprehension. Perhaps one of the most important outcomes of this research is the importance of early identification of foundational components of reading success even before reading problems emerge in second language readers.

References

Anderson, N. J. (2018). Silent reading fluency. In J. I. Liontas (Ed.), *The TESOL Encyclopedia of English Language Teaching* (1st ed., pp. 2212–2221) (Project Editor: Margo DelliCarpini; Volume Editor Neil J Anderson), John Wiley & Sons, Inc.

Carver, R. P. (2000). *The causes of high and low reading achievement.* Lawrence Erlbaum Associates.

Dubin F., & Bycina, D. (1991). Academic reading and the L2/EFL teacher. In M. Celce-Murcia (Ed.), *Teaching English as a second or foreign language* (2nd ed., pp. 195–215). Newbury House.

Grabe, W. (2009). *Reading in a second language: Moving from theory to practice*. Cambridge University Press.

Grabe, W., & Stoller, F. (2011). *Teaching and researching reading* (2nd ed.). Longman.

Jensen, L. (1986). Advanced reading skills in a comprehension course. In F. Dubin, D. E. Eskey, & W. Grabe (Eds.), *Teaching second language reading for academic purposes* (pp. 103–124). Additions-Wesley Publishing.

Nuttall, C. (2007). *Teaching reading skills in a foreign* language (3rd ed.). Heinemann.

Taguchi, E., Gorsuch, G., & Sasamoto, E. (2006). Developing second and foreign language reading fluency and its effect on comprehension: A missing link. *The Reading Matrix, 6*, 1–18.

Taguchi, E., Gorsuch, G., Takayasu-Maass, M., & Snipp, K. (2012). Assisted repeated reading with an advanced-level Japanese EFL reader: A longitudinal diary study. *Reading in a Foreign Language, 24*, 30–55. http://nflrc.hawaii.edu/rfl/April2012/

Zadeh, Z. Y., Farnia, F., & Geva, E. (2012). Toward modeling reading comprehension and reading fluency in English language learners. *Reading & Writing, 25*, 163–187. https://doi.org/10.1007/s11145-010-9252-0

Neil J Anderson is a Professor of English Language Teaching and Learning at Brigham Young University–Hawaii. Professor Anderson is the author/co-editor of over 50 books, book chapters, and journal articles. His interests include second language reading, language learner strategies, learner self-assessment, motivation in language teaching and learning, and ELT leadership development. Professor Anderson served as President of TESOL International Association from 2001–2002. He was a Fulbright Teaching and Research Scholar in Costa Rica (2002–2003) and in Guatemala (2009–2010). Professor Anderson was the 2014 recipient of the TESOL International Association James E. Alatis Service Award. In 2016, Professor Anderson was recognized as one of the 50 individuals who has made a significant contribution to the profession of teaching English to speakers of other languages.

Instructional Pragmatics

18

Zohreh R. Eslami and Shaun Weihong Ko

There are various definitions of pragmatics in the literature emphasizing different dimensions of this construct. One of the most encompassing definitions is provided by LoCastro (2003). She defines pragmatics broadly as: "the study of speaker and hearer meaning created in their joint actions that include both linguistic and non-linguistic signals in the context of socioculturally organized activities" (p. 15). As shown in her definition of pragmatics, LoCastro addresses the interactional and dynamic nature of pragmatics explicitly and gives due credit to the speaker–hearer interaction, and the co-constructed meaning in interactional discourse in a socio-culturally relevant context.

Due to the complexity of pragmatics and the need for multiple mapping of form, meaning, function, and context, second language (L2) learners experience great difficulty in learning pragmatics (Taguchi, 2015). In addition, norms and conventions for linguistic and non-linguistic means to perform social functions, are often culture specific as defined by specific cultural and social norms.

Instructional pragmatics aims to foster L2 learners' comprehension and production of socially appropriate language (Bardovi-Harlig, 2013). Instructional pragmatic studies have expanded rapidly during the last two decades as pragmatic competence is shown to be amenable to instruction as viewed within the common SLA frameworks of attention and noticing, explicit/implicit instruction, inductive/deductive approach, input processing, skill acquisition and practice, collaborative dialogues, and sociocultural theory (Taguchi, 2015).

The findings of two meta-analysis studies (Jeon & Kaya, 2006; Plonsky & Zhuang, 2019) and one systematic literature review (Taguchi, 2015) on pragmatic

Z. R. Eslami (✉)
Department of Educational Psychology, Texas A&M University, College Station, TX, USA
e-mail: zeslami@tamu.edu

S. W. Ko
Department of Teaching, Learning, and Culture, Texas A&M University, College Station, TX, USA

© Springer Nature Switzerland AG 2021
H. Mohebbi and C. Coombe (eds.), *Research Questions in Language Education and Applied Linguistics*, Springer Texts in Education,
https://doi.org/10.1007/978-3-030-79143-8_18

instruction have indicated that explicit instruction (i.e., with provision of metapragmatic information) tends to be more effective than implicit instruction which provides mere exposure to contextualized pragmatic input. Furthermore, the effects of different teaching approaches (e.g., deductive vs. inductive teaching, input processing, skill acquisition and practice) have been empirically investigated. The findings of these studies are inconclusive at this point due to the complex role of different factors (e.g., learners' proficiency, learning styles, motivation and attitudes, the extent of exposure to the target language and culture, and other individual differences such as age, gender, agency, and personality; the frequency, salience, and level of complexity of the target structure and the intensity and duration of instruction) that influence the effectiveness of the instructional intervention, as well as differential effects of the assessment measures used in previous studies.

Researchers and educators in instructional pragmatics continue to explore creative ways to include pragmatics in a classroom as seen in several recent resource books, teachers' guides, and websites (e.g., Bardovi-Harlig & Mahan-Taylor, 2003; Ishihara & Cohen, 2010; Houck & Tatsuki, 2011; Martınez-Flor & Uso-Juan, 2006; Sykes & Cohen, 2006). These resources in pragmatics teaching demonstrate how we can incorporate key elements of pragmatics into classroom activities and tasks. Future research needs to consider diverse theoretical approaches for instruction and examine the opportunities for the transfer of training to real world interaction and use of online language (Taguchi, 2015).

The Research Questions

1. What does it mean to be competent in pragmatics and what elements are involved in the construct of pragmatic competence?
2. How do learners' characteristics and contextual variables shape pragmatic development trajectories?
3. What is the role of instruction for development of pragmatic competence?
4. Which instructional methods are more effective in developing learners' pragmatic competence?
5. Which pragmatic targets are more amenable to instruction?
6. What is the role of English as a Lingua Franca (ELF) in connection to pragmatic norms, discourse patterns and learners' agency?
7. Is there an interaction between effects of instruction and characteristics of assessment tasks? Explain through examples.
8. To what extent do different language learning environments (i.e., ESL and EFL) mediate pragmatic learning in regards to speech act production and comprehension?
9. How can we empirically assess the effectiveness of corpus-based materials on L2 pragmatic instruction?
10. What are empirically validated frameworks that guide the development of physical and digital materials that utilize corpus methodologies and data?

Suggested Resources

Culpepper, J., Mackey, A., & Taguchi, N. (2018). Second language pragmatics: From theory to Research. New York, NY: Routledge.

This book reconceptualizes L2 pragmatics and explore new theoretical frameworks and methodological techniques from the general field of pragmatics, with the intention to benefit all types of pragmatics in L2 context. The book has 8 chapters which are organized into three parts, namely: language production, language comprehension and awareness and interactional competence. Part 1 provides a general accounts of the constructs of productive ability in pragmatics (i.e., pragmalinguistics and sociopragmatics) and provides methods for data collection. Part 2 delves into pragmatic comprehension and then discusses measures for collecting meta-pragmatic awareness. Part 3 integrates pragmatic production and comprehension by discussing the concept of interaction competence and methods for collecting the dynamic development of co-construction of action. This is an important textbook that puts forward innovative methodologies along with their appropriate data collection methods for comprehension, production and interactional ability.

Ishihara, N., & Cohen, A.D. (2010). *Teaching and learning pragmatics: Where language and culture meet.* **London, UK: Longman-Pearson.**

This book illustrates how pragmatics research findings can be applied to instruction. The book has 15 chapters which are organized into three parts, followed by extensive pedagogical resources and extensive references. The first part introduces key terms and constructs in pragmatics and provides readers with data collection methods and online databases for research and instruction. Part two provides theoretical foundations for pragmatics instruction and offers guidelines for textbook analysis and classroom observation. Finally, the authors discuss issues regarding teaching, learning and assessing L2 pragmatics in part three. This book is an indispensable resource for teachers and teacher educators.

Taguchi, N., & Kim, Y. (2018). *Task-based approaches to teaching and assessing pragmatics.* **Amsterdam, The Netherlands: John Benjamins.**

This volume is the first book-length treatment of the area of task-based language teaching (TBLT) and L2 pragmatics by exploring how instruction and assessment of pragmatics can be integrated into TBLT. The 12 chapters were written by internationally renowned scholars and addressed a variety of constructs (e.g., speech acts, interactional features, genres and honorifics), data collection methods (e.g., quasi-experimental and qualitative) and topics (e.g., instructed SLA, technology- enhanced teaching, task complexity and discursive pragmatics). Collectively, chapters in this volume illustrate how the two fields can together advance the current practice of language teaching for socially-situated and real-world communication.

Eslami, Z. R., Mirzaei, A., & Dini, S. (2015). The role of asynchronous computer mediated communication in the instruction and development of EFL learners' pragmatic competence. *System, 48,* **99–111.** https://doi.org/10.1016/j.system.2014.09.008

Situated within the explicit/implicit instructional paradigm, Eslami and her colleagues (2015) examined different forms of digital tools (i.e., email, oral and written chats) in promoting L2 pragmatic development of Iranian users of English. Iranian university students received random assignment into either an explicit or an implicit instruction group and received pragmatic instruction on request giving provided by 18 native English speaking (NES) and highly proficient nonnative English speaking (NNES) students at a U.S. university. Results indicated online pragmatic tutoring, coupled with corrective feedback in L2 pragmatics were effective for developing learners' pragmatic competence.

Bardovi-Harlig, K., Mossman, S., & Su, Y. (2017). The effect of corpus-based instruction on pragmatic routines. *Language Learning & Technology, 21,* **76–103.**

Bardovi-Harlig et al. (2017) investigated the relative effectiveness of teacher-developed corpus-based materials (CM group) and teacher-guided corpus search (CS group) on learning English conventional expressions. The CM group received corpus materials with underlined conventional expressions and guided practice for noticing the conventional expressions whereas the CS group performed guided corpus searches. Oral discourse completion task was used to assess the treatment outcomes. The results revealed statistically significant interactions between pretest scores and treatment types on scores of speech act and conventional expressions. Moreover, post-hoc analysis detected differences between the speech act scores of the CM and control group, an indication that corpus-based materials are effective in raising learners' pragmatic competence.

References

Bardovi-Harlig, K. (2013). Developing L2 pragmatics. *Language Learning, 63,* 68–86.
Bardovi-Harlig, K., & Mahan-Taylor, R. (2003). *Teaching pragmatics.* Office of English Programs, U.S. Department of State.
Houck, N., & Tatsuki, D. (2011). *Pragmatics from research to practice: New directions.* TESOL.
Jeon, E. H., & Kaya, T. (2006). Effects of L2 instruction on interlanguage pragmatic development. In N. John, & L. Ortega (Eds.), *Synthesizing research on language learning and teaching* (pp. 165–211). John Benjamins.
LoCastro, V. (2003). *An introduction to pragmatics: Social action for language teachers.* The University of Michigan Press.
Martinez-Flor, A., & E. Uso-Juan (2006). A comprehensive pedagogical framework to develop pragmatics in the foreign language classroom: The 6Rs approach. *Applied Language Learning, 16,* 39–64.

Plonsky, L., & Zhuang, J. (2019). A meta-analysis of second language pragmatics instruction. In N. Taguchi (Ed.), *Routledge handbook of SLA and pragmatics* (pp. 287–307). Routledge.

Sykes, J., & Cohen, A. D. (2006). Dancing with words: Strategies for learning pragmatics in Spanish. Retrieved 14 January, 2019, from Regents of the University of Minnesota: www. carla.umn.edu/speechacts/sp-pragmatics/home.html

Taguchi, N. (2015). Instructed pragmatics at a glance: Where instructional studies were, are, and should be going. *Language Teaching, 48*, 1–50.

Zohreh R. Eslami is a Professor at the Department of Teaching, Learning, and Culture at Texas A&M University in College Station and currently serves as the Liberal Arts Program Chair at Texas A&M University at Qatar. Her research has examined intercultural and cross-cultural communication, English as an International language, sociocultural perspectives of teaching, acquisition of, and English-medium instruction. Her publications include over one hundred journal papers, book chapters and conference proceedings.

Shaun Weihong Ko is a Ph.D. Candidate in the Department of Teaching, Learning and Culture at Texas A&M University. His primary research interests are L2 pragmatics, task-based language teaching and digital game-mediated communication.

Interactionist Approach to Corrective Feedback

19

Rebekha Abbuhl

Corrective feedback (CF) is a common technique for helping learners recognize errors in their second language (L2) production. It has also been the subject of much research over the past 30 years and has been approached from a wide variety of theoretical angles. One of these is the Interactionist approach, which posits that CF has the potential to draw learners' attention to problems in their L2 production, provide opportunities for modified output (i.e., to self-correct), and to hear models of targetlike input (Gass, 2003; Long, 1996).

More specifically, interactionist researchers believe that when learners receive CF during meaningful, communicative tasks or conversations, their attention can be brought to 'mismatches' between their own forms and the targetlike forms. This in turn may facilitate form-meaning mappings to a greater degree than if the CF was provided during a decontextualized grammar drill. The CF can be provided by the teacher or a peer and can take many forms, including recasts (reformulating a learner utterance in a more targetlike manner), prompts (discourse moves that encourage learners to self-correct), and metalinguistic explanations (detailed information on the nature of the learner error), among others. These discourse moves can provide negative evidence, or information about what is not possible in the target language. This is believed to be useful if not necessary for the development of fluency and accuracy in the L2.

Interactionist researchers have sought to identify an optimal type of CF given a set of learner characteristics (e.g., aptitude, working memory capacity, anxiety levels), contextual variables (e.g., the pedagogic orientation of the classroom), and linguistic target features (and in particular, the difficulty of the target) (Ellis &

R. Abbuhl (✉)
Department of Linguistics, California State University Long Beach, Long Beach, CA, USA
e-mail: Rebekha.abbuhl@csulb.edu; rabbuhl@csulb.edu

© Springer Nature Switzerland AG 2021
H. Mohebbi and C. Coombe (eds.), *Research Questions in Language Education and Applied Linguistics*, Springer Texts in Education,
https://doi.org/10.1007/978-3-030-79143-8_19

Shintani, 2013). Highlighting the interpersonal nature of CF, interactionist researchers have also investigated the characteristics of the interlocutors involved, including age (see Oliver & Azkarai, 2017 for a review), the relative proficiency of the interlocutors (e.g., native speaker, foreign language learner, heritage language learner; e.g., Mackey et al., 2003), and interpersonal dynamics (such as the learner's perceived competence of the interlocutor and the degree of cooperation between the two (Sato & Ballinger, 2016).

A number of avenues for future research have been identified in the literature. These include more research on linguistic targets beyond morphosyntax; investigating a wider variety of L2 learners, including less literate learners and those in non-instructional contexts (Tarone, 2010); examining the amount of CF that needs to be provided to best facilitate acquisition (Li, 2018); investigating the long-term effect of CF; and researching the extent to which interpersonal dynamics intersect with cognitive factors and feedback characteristics.

The Research Questions

1. What can teachers do to promote learner noticing and retention of CF?
2. What factors need to be considered in deciding what CF to use with a particular group of learners?
3. How much CF needs to be given to facilitate acquisition of a particular linguistic target?
4. How do different types of CF impact the development of various phonological targets?
5. How do different types of CF impact the development of various pragmatic targets?
6. How do different types of CF impact the development of L2 vocabulary?
7. To what extent do interpersonal dynamics between learners and their interlocutors influence the effect of CF on various L2 targets?
8. To what extent do characteristics of the learners' interlocutors (e.g., age, proficiency level) impact the efficacy of CF?
9. To what extent do learners' levels of motivation affect their attention to and retention of CF?
10. How do considerations of learner identity (e.g., class, political inequality) mediate the effects of various forms of CF?

Suggested Resources

Long, M. (1996). The role of the linguistic environment in second language acquisition. In W. Ritchie & T. Bhatia (Eds.), *Handbook of second language acquisition* **(pp. 413–468). New York: Academic Press**.

Considered one of the foundational articles for the interactionist approach to second language acquisition, Long (1996) provides a detailed overview of the role of input (positive and negative evidence), output, and attention in L2 development. The role of corrective feedback in both first and second language acquisition is discussed.

Mackey, A. (2007). *Conversational interaction in second language acquisition.* **Oxford: Oxford University Press**.

This edited collection of empirical studies showcases research conducted in the area of interaction-driven L2 learning, including CF. The chapters on CF address perceptions of interactional feedback, the role of literacy in the processing of oral CF, individual difference factors in the processing of recasts, recasts in computer-mediated communication, and recasts in communicative EFL classes. Chapters on the effect of interactional feedback on linguistic development are also included, as is a meta-analysis on interaction research in SLA.

Mackey, A. (2012). *Input, interaction, and corrective feedback in L2 learning.* **Oxford: Oxford University Press**.

This book covers the theoretical and historical foundations of the Interactionist approach, providing detailed information on the key components involved: input, interaction, output, attention, and corrective feedback. The author also provides an overview of the methodologies used for studying interaction-based L2 learning and discusses the role of context and individual differences. Chapter 7 focuses on feedback, providing a detailed discussion of different types of feedback with examples drawn from the literature. Directions for future research, such as a greater focus on interpersonal and social factors, are also included.

Nassaji, H. (2015). *The interactional feedback dimension in instructed second language learning.* **London: Bloomsbury**.

This monograph focuses on CF from an interactionist perspective. In the first section, the author discusses multiple perspectives on CF before discussing the interactionist approach in particular. The second section overviews both descriptive and experimental research on CF, while the third focuses on the various factors that may influence the effectiveness of CF, including learners' perceptions and views. The fourth section highlights classroom practice. Each chapter ends with questions for discussion.

Nassaji, H., & Kartchava, E. (2017). *Corrective feedback in second language teaching and learning: Research, theory, applications, implications.* **New York: Routledge.**

This edited collection is divided into four parts: oral corrective feedback, computer-mediated feedback, written feedback, and student and teacher issues in feedback. Individual chapters synthesize existing research to discuss theoretical perspectives on oral feedback, factors influencing the effectiveness of peer feedback, the timing of feedback, feedback delivered in computer-mediated contexts, feedback on writing, teachers' and learners' beliefs on corrective feedback, and non-verbal feedback. Future directions and pedagogical implications are also provided.

References

Ellis, R., & Shintani, N. (2013). *Exploring language pedagogy through second language acquisition research.* Routledge.

Gass, S. (2003). Input and interaction. In C. Doughty & M. Long (Eds.), *The handbook of second language acquisition* (pp. 224–255). Blackwell.

Li, S. (2018). Data collection in the research on the effectiveness of corrective feedback: A synthetic and critical review. In A. Gudmestad & A. Edmonds (Eds.), *Critical reflections on data in second language acquisition* (pp. 33–61). John Benjamins.

Long, M. (1996). The role of the linguistic environment in second language acquisition. In W. Ritchie & T. Bhatia (Eds.), *Handbook of second language acquisition* (pp. 413–468). Academic Press.

Mackey, A., Oliver, R., & Leeman, J. (2003). Interactional input and the incorporation of feedback: An exploration of NS–NNS and NNS–NNS adult and child dyads. *Language Learning, 53*, 35–66.

Oliver, R., & Azkarai, A. (2017). Review of child second language acquisition (SLA): Examining theories and research. *Annual Review of Applied Linguistics, 37*, 62–76.

Sato, M., & Ballinger, S. (2016). *Peer interaction and second language learning: Pedagogical potential and research agenda.* John Benjamins.

Tarone, E. (2010). Second language acquisition by low-literate learners: An under-studied population. *Language Teaching, 43*, 75–83.

Rebekha Abbuhl has a Ph.D. in Applied Linguistics from Georgetown University. She is currently an Associate Professor of Linguistics at California State University Long Beach, where she teaches courses in language acquisition, research methods, and pedagogy. She has taught English as a foreign language and worked as a teacher trainer in Hungary, Japan, Ukraine, and Vietnam.

Issues in Teaching and Assessing Language as Communication

20

Barbara Hoekje

Teaching language as communication has been the dominant paradigm in English language teaching since *communicative competence* (Hymes, 1974) and its pedagogical applications (Canale & Swain, 1980; Widdowson, 1978) provided a framework for language teaching, learning, and assessment. Modern languages also adopted functionally oriented curriculum and assessment frameworks; e.g., American Council on the Teaching of Foreign Languages (ACFTL) in the United States and the Common European Framework of Reference (CEFR) in the European Union. Communicative language ability (Bachman, 1990) became the key measure of language ability given worldwide flows of students and workers; high stakes standardized language exams such as TOEFL and IELTS were also revised to reflect a communicative approach. Despite its widespread adoption, however, contradictions arising from the communicative language teaching model are still unresolved, including the following:

(1) The role of content and meaning. Teaching language as communication requires something to be communicated—namely, content. Yet current models of communicative competence do not have a systematic way to account for content or meaning. See Widdowson (2001) in Suggested Resources.
(2) The role of the interlocutor. In current models, communication is understood as a joint interactional achievement between speaker and interlocutor, raising issues for curriculum, task design and assessment. Hoekje (2016) (Suggested Resources) describes issues of variability in a performance test for international doctors resulting from interlocutor factors.
(3) The role of gesture. Communication is a multi-modal activity, relying on gesture, gaze, and surrounding visual and auditory context to make meaning. Gesture and gaze have traditionally been excluded from the linguistic analysis

B. Hoekje (✉)
Department of Communication, Drexel University, Philadelphia, PA 19104, USA
e-mail: hoekje@drexel.edu

© Springer Nature Switzerland AG 2021
H. Mohebbi and C. Coombe (eds.), *Research Questions in Language Education and Applied Linguistics*, Springer Texts in Education,
https://doi.org/10.1007/978-3-030-79143-8_20

of meaning. Peng, Zhang, and Chen (2017; Suggested Resources) discuss an alternate approach that integrates diverse semiotic resources.

(4) The status of the communicatively competent speaker. Models of language use based on the notion of "communication" must theorize competence outside of an increasingly untenable "native/nonnative" distinction (Davies, 2008; Suggested Resources).

(5) The nature of the target language use context. Communicative competence locates the speaker in a speech community with stable, learnable norms. Yet language use in the twenty-first century occurs with multilingual speakers in often transitory settings, across cultural divides of history, experience, and imagination. Kramsch (2006, Suggested Resources) describes the need for a different kind of communicative competence, a symbolic competence.

Developments in the twenty-first century will bring these issues more prominently into view, due to advances in communication technology, continued globalization, and increased reliance on high stakes assessment. As new tools facilitate the analysis of the multimodal nature of communication, models of language and communication that allow for the integration of these multiple semiotic resources will come more prominently into use in language teaching and assessment.

The Research Questions

1. What is the relationship of language to other modalities such as gesture, eye contact and context in communication?
2. How do multimodal resources affect communicative language ability, for example, on a speaker's "willingness to communicate" outside of the second language classroom?
3. How can "topic" as a form of meaning be accounted for in communicative language teaching?
4. What models exist for the collaboration of language experts with content experts in language for specific purposes (LSP) assessment and instruction?
5. What models exist to account for the impact of the interlocutor on speaker comprehensibility?
6. How do factors related to listener background affect interlocutor (or other audience) judgments of speaker comprehensibility and accuracy?
7. How can studying successful communicators of all backgrounds help change the focus of the field from communicative problems to communicative successes in second language studies?
8. How can the nature of speaker competence in communication be modelled without reference to the notion of "native speaker" norms?
9. How do multilingual speakers in online settings negotiate new norms of language use?
10. How does "symbolic competence" relate to other forms of intercultural communicative competence?

Suggested Resources

Davies, A. (2008). The native speaker in applied linguistics. In A. Davies & C. Elder (Eds.), *The handbook of applied linguistics*, 431–450. Malden, MA: Blackwell.

Davies provides a trenchant analysis of the "native speaker" concept in relation to psycholinguistic capabilities (e.g., intuitions on grammaticality) and sociolinguistic issues of use, in particular the notion of norms in various contexts of World Englishes and dialectal varieties, and the identity of the speaker in relation to these norms. Davies concludes that the status of "native speaker" both as myth and reality in applied linguistics relates to the "langue/parole" (language vs. speech) dichotomy first identified by Saussure and taken up in modern linguistics in the "competence" vs. "performance" distinction identified by Noam Chomsky. For Chomsky, issues of language use ("performance") had no theoretical interest compared to a native speaker's intuition ("competence"); Hymes' response identifying the components of a "communicative competence" which would take into account a speaker's knowledge of the "possible, the feasible, the appropriate, and the done" set into motion the "communicative turn" in language teaching.

Hoekje, B. (2016). "Language," "communication," and the longing for the authentic in LSP testing. *Language Testing 33*(2), 289–299. https://doi.org/10. 1177/0265532215607921.

This article was written as commentary to a special issue of *Language Testing* devoted to performance testing in healthcare, the revision of the Occupational English Test (OET). The revision involved the collaboration of applied linguists with domain experts in medicine, nursing, and physiotherapy. Because the OET was designed as a "weak" performance test to assess "only language," the question of what could be assessed within a communicative model of language was central. This article argues that the full power of the communicative competence model was incompletely realized in the face of a sociohistorical conception of language in English language teaching which relied on a native speaker/non native speaker dichotomy and was inadequate to address the role of content and meaning in task completion, provide descriptively adequate accounts of context, or account for the variation introduced by the interlocutor, among other issues.

Kramsch, C. (2006). From communicative competence to symbolic competence. *The Modern Language Journal 90*(2), 249–252.

Kramsch argues that Hymes'original notion of communicative competence was reduced in foreign language education to notions of functional efficiency and informational transfer. Yet today what is needed to communicate with others goes beyond the informational—what is needed is a deep understanding of our own and others' histories, memories, and imaginings. In a complex world, students need a more *symbolic competence* fed by literature at all levels of the language curriculum.

Peng, J.-E., Zhang, L., & Chen, Y. (2017). The mediation of multimodal affordances on willingness to communicate in the English as a foreign language classroom. *TESOL Quarterly 51*, 2, 302–331.

This article acknowledges the multimodal nature of communication as an activity involving diverse semiotic resources, among them gesture and gaze in addition to language. The researchers investigated students' "willingness to communicate" (WTC) in an EFL classroom in relation to the teacher's gaze and gesture using a Halliday systemic functional framework of multimodal discourse analysis (SF MDA). By directly acknowledging the multimodal nature of communication, and with new analytical tools designed for video, the connection between language and other semiotic resources such as gesture and gaze can be investigated.

Widdowson, H. (2001). Communicative language testing: the art of the possible," in C. Elder et al., (Eds.), *Experimenting with uncertainty: Essays in honour of Alan Davies*, **pp. 12–21. New York and Cambridge: Cambridge University Press.**

One of the earliest advocates for communicative approach in language teaching, Widdowson (1978) also foresaw how treating language as "communication" would involve issues—such as the role of meaning—that were incompletely specified in Hymes' model. In this article, written more than two decades later, Widdowson critiques the subsequent, pedagogical adaptations of the model with discourse and strategic components and the move within assessment toward communication "authenticity" as inadequate to address the central problem of meaning. He proposes instead Halliday's social semiotic model of language where meaning potential is explicitly addressed and where the communicative potential of "language" can be taught and assessed.

References

Bachman, L. (1990). *Fundamental considerations in language teaching*. Oxford University Press.
Canale, M., & Swain, M. (1980). Theoretical bases of communicative approaches to second language teaching and testing. *Applied Linguistics, 1*(1), 1–47.
Hymes, D. (1974). *Foundations in sociolinguistics*. University of Pennsylvania Press.
Widdowson, H. (1978). *Teaching language as communication*. Oxford University Press.

Barbara Hoekje is associate professor of communication in the Department of Communication at Drexel University where she teaches courses on language, sociolinguistics, intercultural communication, and discourse analysis. Her work has focused on issues of spoken language assessment and use in US higher education; language program administration; medical discourse, and international students in US higher education. Recent work has focused on immigrant families and school communication within a social justice framework of school leadership.

Language Teaching in Difficult Circumstances

Jason Anderson, Amol Padwad, and Richard Smith

"Teaching in difficult circumstances" (TiDC) refers to teaching in contexts where a number of challenging factors are present (cf. West, 1960). These may include:

1. Large classes, typically over 40 learners;
2. A lack of basic resources, including textbooks, furniture, stationery, electricity, and even suitable classrooms;
3. Low school readiness of learners;
4. Inadequate pre-service and in-service training and support for teachers;
5. Excessive workload for teachers and other staff.

Because any of these factors can influence classroom practices independently of the others, several have their own bodies of literature, especially "teaching in large classes", but also "teaching in low-resource contexts" and "teaching in low-income/developing countries". TiDC can be seen as a superordinate label for all these, but also a referent to contexts where two or more regularly co-exist. Difficult circumstances are often contrasted with "privileged contexts" in the TiDC literature (e.g., Kuchah, 2018). While difficult circumstances may exist at any level of economic development, they are more likely, and often are relatively extreme, in sub-Saharan Africa and the Indian subcontinent. They can be further exacerbated by political crises and natural disasters (cf. Phyak's "super difficult circumstances", 2015).

Given the large numbers of teachers working in developing countries worldwide, difficult circumstances are the norm for many language teachers. However, they

J. Anderson (✉) · R. Smith
Applied Linguistics, University of Warwick, Coventry, UK
e-mail: R.C.Smith@warwick.ac.uk

A. Padwad
Centre for English Language Education (CELE), Dr. B. R. Ambedkar University Delhi, Delhi, India

© Springer Nature Switzerland AG 2021
H. Mohebbi and C. Coombe (eds.), *Research Questions in Language Education and Applied Linguistics*, Springer Texts in Education,
https://doi.org/10.1007/978-3-030-79143-8_21

have tended to be "dysfunctionally" ignored in mainstream language teaching research and discourse (Smith, 2011). With the exception of the Lancaster-Leeds project led by Dick Allwright and Hywel Coleman in the late 1980s (e.g., Coleman, 1989), there seemed to be little interest in researching TiDC until 2008, when the Teaching English in Large Classes research and development network was founded by Fauzia Shamim and Richard Smith. There are now a number of publications and resources on the TELCnet website (bit.ly/telcnet-home) although there are still many needs for further research.

Research to date has involved investigating challenges (e.g., Kuchah & Shamim, 2018), learner needs or expectations (e.g., Khati, 2010) and context-appropriate (e.g., Kuchah, 2013) or methodologically-specific (e.g., Panhwar, 2016) initiatives. Emphasis has been placed on the particular value of engaging learner and teacher autonomy (Amritavalli, 2007; Smith et al., 2018), while a focus on multilingual practices has also become prominent (see Coleman, 2017). Recent teacher development initiatives range from grass-roots practical guides for teachers (e.g., Anderson, 2015; Shamim et al., 2010) to participatory approaches involving exploratory action research (Smith & Rebolledo, 2018), researching with children (Pinter et al., 2016), small and larger communities of practice (Padwad & Dixit, 2014; Smith & Kuchah, 2016), as well as usage of mobile phone technology for large-scale interventions (Solly & Woodward, 2018).

Desiderata include: a more robust and critical conceptualization of 'difficult circumstances'; further documentation of effective teaching practices in difficult circumstances (Westbrook et al., 2013); further development of bottom-up proposals for appropriate TiDC methodology (Smith, 2011; Smith et al., 2017); critical discussion of fundamental issues of agency, ethics and politics (including language policy: Mohanty, 2010); elicitation of more first-person narratives and, fundamentally, underpinning all of this, more involvement of learners and teachers themselves in the research and development process (cf. Smith et al., 2018).

The Research Questions

1. What challenges/issues/concerns are specifically related to difficult circumstances, and how are they being addressed in different contexts?
2. What are the opinions, beliefs and insights of students learning languages in difficult circumstances, and how can these usefully inform teaching practices?
3. What are the opinions, beliefs and insights of teachers teaching languages in difficult circumstances, and how do these impact their teaching practices?
4. What are the teaching practices of effective language teachers working in difficult circumstances, and to what extent do these differ both from those of less effective teachers and those of teachers working in more privileged contexts?

5. How can models, ideas and resources for good practice in difficult circumstances be disseminated effectively via pre-service and in-service teacher education?
6. What roles can professional development communities play in the lives and development of teachers working in difficult circumstances?
7. What are the roles of learner and teacher autonomy in meeting the challenges of difficult circumstances?
8. How can the existing languaging (L1, L2, translingual) resources of learners studying in difficult circumstances be engaged in the learning of new languages and the development of their multilingual competence?
9. How can teachers be encouraged to research their own practice and contribute to the development of appropriate methodologies?
10. In light of research, how can 'difficult circumstances' be better conceptualized, and how can they be improved?

Suggested Resources

Kuchah, K., & Shamim, F. (2018). *International perspectives on teaching English in difficult circumstances.* **London: Palgrave Macmillan.**

A thirteen-chapter edited volume of perspectives on teaching English in difficult circumstances from around the world, in four sections: 1. Policy decisions and the creation of difficult circumstances; 2. Developing contextually responsive pedagogy and materials for teaching English in difficult circumstances; 3. Difficult circumstances in non-mainstream ELT: Contexts of confinement, conflict and special needs; and 4. Approaches to teacher development in difficult circumstances. Kuchah's comprehensive introduction provides an authoritative overview of the history of research in the area of TiDC, as well as analyses from relevant current perspectives within English language teaching, while Shamim's conclusion considers potential future directions for the field. The range of authors and perspectives covering contexts as diverse as prison education and refugee camps is a reflection of the true diversity of difficult circumstances worldwide.

Ojha, L. P. (2015). *Teaching English in difficult circumstances.* **Special issue of** *NELTA ELT Forum.* **Online:** https://neltaeltforum.wordpress.com/2015/07/

This special issue of the online *ELT Forum* journal of NELTA is dedicated to the theme of teaching English in difficult circumstances and contains articles by practising teachers on how they have tried to deal with various practical challenges in their teaching contexts. These include teaching large classes, coping with a lack of resources, developing learner autonomy, improving strategies for reading lessons and a personal teacher's perspective on developing her own language proficiency for English language teaching. The issue also contains an interview with Richard

Smith in which he discusses common concerns associated with difficult circumstances and suggests some ways of addressing them.

Shamim, F., Negash, N., Chuku, C., & Demewoz, N. (2010). *Maximizing learning in large classes: Issues and options.* **London: British Council. Online:** https://www.teachingenglish.org.uk/sites/teacheng/files/ELT-16-screen.pdf

This accessible, practical resource was developed by teachers and teacher educators at a Hornby regional school in Ethiopia. It includes a six-chapter introduction to large class contexts, challenges and potential solutions that draws extensively on the expertise of African and Asian teacher educators, including foci on increasing student involvement, managing large classes, assessment and feedback in large classes and maximizing use of resources. This is followed by 27 useful activities submitted by local teachers but potentially of use to language teachers around the world working in difficult circumstances, requiring few, if any resources. The book is written in non-academic English, making it accessible for all.

Smith, R., Kuchah, K., & Lamb, M. (2018). Learner autonomy in developing countries. In A. Chik, N. Aoki, & Smith, R. (Eds.), *Autonomy in language learning and teaching: New research agendas* **London: Palgrave Pivot. Online:** https://link.springer.com/content/pdf/10.1057%2F978-1-137-52998-5_2.pdf

This chapter provides a rationale for encouraging learner autonomy in language learning in difficult circumstances, summarizing findings from historical and exploratory research in a range of low-income contexts around the world (e.g., Bangladesh, Cameroon, India and Indonesia). It discusses the nature of out of class learning, exploring the emerging role that ICT, especially through mobile phone use and participation in online social networks, is playing in facilitating autonomous learning. It also looks at participatory approaches to research in learner autonomy conducted both with and by teachers and learners. The chapter calls for more research, firstly into IT-mediated autonomous learning outside the classroom, secondly into grass roots projects developing learner autonomy, and thirdly for research both with and by teachers and learners themselves.

Smith, R., Padwad, A. & Bullock, D. (2017). *Teaching in low-resource classrooms: Voices of experience.* **London: British Council. Online:** https://www.teachingenglish.org.uk/sites/teacheng/files/pub_30325_bc_teach_in_low_resource_report_a4_v4_online.pdf

A free resource that gives voice to 34 teachers of English working in difficult circumstances in Bangladesh, India, Nepal and Pakistan, who share their perspectives, challenges and solutions directly in this edited volume. It reports findings of an "enhancement approach", building on positive stories of success which document practical strategies and ideas that other teachers may benefit from. The book also includes stories of teacher inquiry, including both practical research questions and potential solutions regarding issues such as managing group work in large classes, correcting large quantities of written work, and teaching learners from diverse backgrounds in the same class. In line with the overall bottom-up approach of the TELC network, the editors promote the idea that "there is particular value in teachers in difficult circumstances collaboratively sharing examples of successful teaching as a starting point for their own further development" (p. 3). Associated website and video resources are freely available online: http://www. teachingenglish.org.uk/low-resource-classrooms.

References

Amritavalli, R. (2007). *English in deprived circumstances: Maximising learner autonomy.* Foundation.

Anderson, J. (2015). *Teaching English in Africa: A guide to the practice of English language teaching for teachers and trainees.* East African Educational Publishers.

Coleman, H. (1989). *The study of large classes: Report no. 2.* Lancaster-Leeds Project, Lancaster, UK.

Coleman, H. (Ed.). (2017). *Multilingualism and development: Selected proceedings of the 11th language & development conference, New Delhi, India 2015.* British Council.

Khati, A. R. (2010). Exploring common expectations from students in large multilevel secondary level English classes. *Journal of NELTA, 15,* 98–105.

Kuchah, K. (2013). *Context-appropriate ELT pedagogy: An investigation in Cameroonian primary schools (Unpublished doctoral dissertation).* University of Warwick.

Kuchah, K. (2018). Teaching English in difficult circumstances: Setting the scene. In K. Kuchah & F. Shamim (Eds.), *International perspectives on teaching English in difficult circumstances* (pp. 1–25). Palgrave Macmillan.

Kuchah, K., & Shamim, F. (Eds.). (2018). *International perspectives on teaching English in difficult circumstances.* Palgrave Macmillan.

Mohanty, A. K. (2010). Languages, inequality and marginalization: Implications of the double divide in Indian multilingualism. *International Journal of the Sociology of Language, 205,* 131–154.

Padwad, A., & Dixit, K. (2014). Exploring continuing professional development: English teachers clubs in central India. In M. Beaumont & T. Wright (Eds.), *Experiences of second language teacher education* (pp. 153–174). Palgrave Macmillan.

Panhwar, A. H. (2016). *Using cooperative learning to enhance student engagement with language support classes in Pakistani higher education (Unpublished doctoral dissertation).* Anglia Ruskin University.

Phyak, P. (2015). Editorial (July 2015 Issue): *EFL teachers in 'super-difficult circumstances'.* Retrieved from http://eltchoutari.com/2015/07/editorial-efl-teachers-in-the-super-difficult-circumstance 2/

Pinter, A., Mathew, R., & Smith, R. (2016). *Children and teachers as co-researchers in Indian primary English classrooms.* British Council.

Shamim, F., Negash, N., Chuku, C., & Demewoz, N. (2010). *Maximising learning in large classes: Issues and options.* British Council. http://www.teachingenglish.org.uk/sites/teacheng/files/ELT-16-screen.pdf

Smith, R. (2011). Teaching English in difficult circumstances: A new research agenda. In T. Pattison (Ed.), *IATEFL 2010 Harrogate conference selections.* IATEFL.

Smith, R., & Kuchah, K. (2016). Researching teacher associations. *ELT Journal, 70*(2), 212–221.

Smith, R., & Rebolledo, P. (2018). *A handbook for exploratory action research.* British Council.

Smith, R., Padwad, A., & Bullock, D. (2017). *Teaching in low-resource classrooms: Voices of experience.* British Council.

Smith, R., Kuchah, K., & Lamb, M. (2018). Learner autonomy in developing countries. In A. Chik, N. Aoki, & R. Smith (Eds.), *Autonomy in language learning and teaching: New research agendas.* Palgrave Pivot. https://link.springer.com/content/pdf/10.1057%2F978-1-137-52998-5_2.pdf

Solly, M., & Woodward, C. (2018). Using mediated authentic video as a potential innovative solution for training at scale: A view from Bangladesh. In K. Kuchah, & F. Shamim (Eds.), *International perspectives on teaching English in difficult circumstances.* Palgrave Macmillan.

West, M. (1960). *Teaching English in difficult circumstances.* Longmans, Green.

Westbrook, J., Durrani, N., Brown, R., Orr, D., Pryor, J., Boddy, J., & Salvi, F. (2013). *Pedagogy, curriculum, teaching practices and teacher education in developing countries.* EPPI-Centre, University of London.

Jason Anderson is an award-winning author, teacher educator, consultant and researcher in both language teaching and mainstream education. He has worked in over twenty countries worldwide, including longitudinal grass roots support of teachers working in difficult circumstances in both Africa and Asia. He has also worked on top-down teacher development initiatives, both pre-service and in-service, for organizations including UNICEF, British Council and national ministries of education. As well as his interest in teaching in difficult circumstances, he has conducted research on translingual practices, initial certification courses, teacher reflection, lesson planning and aspects of language teaching history. He is currently the series editor for Delta Publishing's Ideas in Action series.

Amol Padwad is Professor and Director, Centre for English Language Education, Ambedkar University Delhi. He is also the Secretary of Ainet Association of English Teachers (AINET-India). He has been actively engaged in promoting teacher development, teacher networking and associations and teacher research, and has carried out studies in these areas. He pioneered the English Teachers' Clubs—self-help teacher development groups—in rural towns of central India, some of which have been running for over fifteen years. His recent publications include *Continuing professional development* (with Rod Bolitho) and *Teaching in low-resource classrooms: Voices of experience* (with Richard Smith and Deborah Bullock).

Richard Smith is a Professor in ELT and Applied Linguistics at the University of Warwick, UK. Founder of the Warwick ELT Archive (www.warwick.ac.uk/elt_archive) and the AILA Research Network on History of Language Learning and Teaching (http://hollt.net), he has been active in the fields of historical research, learner autonomy, teaching in difficult circumstances, and teacher-research in language education. In 2008, he co-founded TELCnet (the Teaching English in Large Classes research and development network: http://bit.ly/telcnet-home). In recent years, he has been involved in projects with teachers from Chile, India, Peru and Nepal and has produced open access books for teachers in difficult circumstances including *A handbook for exploratory action research* (with Paula Rebolledo) and *Teaching in low-resource classrooms: Voices of experience* (with Amol Padwad and Deborah Bullock).

Materials in the Language Classroom

Kathleen Graves

Materials are a pervasive, taken-for-granted aspect of language instruction and thus difficult to define in theoretically useful ways. According to Tomlinson (2012, p.143) they *are* "anything that can be used to facilitate the learning of a language, including coursebooks, videos, graded readers, flash cards, games, websites and mobile phone interactions…" Mishan and Timmis (2015) define them more economically as digital or physical artifacts with a pedagogic purpose. Materials are thus broadly understood as any resource that is used by teachers and learners to promote language learning. Materials may be specifically designed for language learning (a graded reader, flash cards, a coursebook) and may be produced by individual teachers or groups of teachers, institutions and publishing companies. Materials may also be 'purposed' for language learning (a website, a white board, an advertisement, a video game).

The most ubiquitous type of material is the textbook, which is the primary teaching resource used by language teachers around the world (Richards, 2014). Textbooks are produced locally, regionally or globally. Scholarship on textbooks has mainly focused on their content, on how to evaluate their appropriateness for a given context, and on how teachers adhere to, adapt or resist them. In terms of their content, all materials, including textbooks, represent views of language and how language is learned, e.g., as grammar rules or as interaction. Textbooks also represent a hidden curriculum: who is represented (e.g. gender, country of origin) and how (e.g. types of occupations, activities, aspirations), the topics and tasks that are included (e.g. shopping, celebrities) or excluded (e.g. religion, politics) and whose voices are heard (varieties of English).

K. Graves (✉)
School of Education, University of Michigan, Ann Arbor, USA
e-mail: gravesk@umich.edu

© Springer Nature Switzerland AG 2021
H. Mohebbi and C. Coombe (eds.), *Research Questions in Language Education and Applied Linguistics*, Springer Texts in Education,
https://doi.org/10.1007/978-3-030-79143-8_22

Research on teachers' use of textbooks shows that they adapt or resist textbooks for a variety of reasons based on contextual factors and on their own beliefs and experience. Adaptations and resistance may occur when they are unfamiliar with a topic or deem it inappropriate for their learners, when the methodology is at odds with their beliefs about how languages are learned, when the content does not contribute to exam-preparedness, when they need to control the class, and when they do not have time.

Despite the fact that all teachers use materials to teach, materials have been neglected in teacher education. Particularly in pre-service education, teachers are rarely asked to evaluate or adapt published materials or to develop their own materials according to the principles and theories they are taught in their methodology courses, linguistics courses, language acquisition courses, or language assessment courses.

Technology has expanded what materials offer both in the range of content and the affordances for language use and interaction. Mobile and digital technology enable learners to direct their own learning (e.g. via apps on mobile phones), to communicate with others (e.g. via videoconferencing platforms), and to create their own content (e.g. using interactive whiteboards).

There is very little empirical research about how materials are actually used by learners in the classroom. Research on materials use is needed to help us understand the kinds of language, interaction and meaning-making that different types of materials might evoke or constrain. Focusing on materials use would also help us better understand the contingent, emergent and generative nature of materials.

The Research Questions

1. How do we determine that something is 'a material'?
2. What are usable ways to categorize materials theoretically and practically?
3. How do teachers and learners use the same materials differently?
4. How are materials other than textbooks used by teachers in classrooms?
5. How do learners use different kinds of materials?
6. How are classroom interactions shaped by materials?
7. What agency do learners have around materials?
8. How do the materials students use shape the language they use?
9. How do digital technologies and devices contribute to language learning?
10. How does the hidden curriculum of materials influence teachers and learners?

Suggested Resources

Garton, S. & Graves, K. (Eds.) (2014). *International perspectives on materials in ELT*. **Basingstoke, UK: Palgrave Macmillan.**

This book brings together the perspectives of researcher-practitioners from 14 different countries. Part 1 examines global and local materials: their differences (Argentina), adapting global textbooks for a specific context (Bahrain), and how culture is represented in them (Algeria). Part 2 looks at how materials are used in language classrooms, largely from the perspective of teachers: their attitudes towards adaptation (Ghana) and toward educational reform (Albania), how to draw on their students cultural and linguistic backgrounds (US), and how to adapt materials for multi-level classes (Thailand). Part 3 looks at how different forms of technology are used as a means for language learning: mobile phones (Bangladesh), computer writing programs (Portugal), students teaching each other using interactive whiteboards (Italy.) The final section looks at teacher education, or lack thereof: learning how to develop literacy activities (US/Korea), learning how to evaluate and adapt textbooks (Brazil), and teachers' lack of preparation for new textbooks (Japan.)

Harwood, N. (Ed.) (2014). *English language teaching textbooks: Content, consumption, production.* **Basingstoke, UK: Palgrave Macmillan**.

This edited volume takes a critical look at global English course books on three levels: their content, how they are used and how they are produced. The chapters are based on robust, well-supported research. The section on textbook content includes chapters on the ideology of textbooks in the era of neo-liberalism and an analysis of the types of reading comprehension questions found in textbooks, finding an emphasis on lower order thinking skills. The chapters on textbook use are noteworthy in their focus on how teachers actually use textbooks in their classrooms in a variety of contexts. Similarly, the chapters on textbook production provide an insider's perspective on what it is like to actually write textbook materials for global consumption.

McGrath, I. (2013). *Teaching materials and the roles of EFL/ESL teachers.* **London: Bloomsbury**.

In this book, McGrath seeks to bridge gaps between producers and choosers of materials on the one hand, and users of materials on the other, and between theories of how materials should be written and used, and how they are actually used in practice. He uses his considerable expertise in the area of materials development to first examine the 'theory' side of materials, from the perspective of publishers, coursebook writers, teacher educators and policy-makers. He then explores the 'practice' side of materials, from the perspectives of teachers, how they evaluate and adapt their materials and the role that learners and context play in these decisions. This is followed by a lucid discussion of the implications of these apparent divides for different stakeholders: teachers, managers, materials writers, ministries and publishers. He concludes the book with a proposal to bridge the gap with a practice-based approach to teacher education.

Mishan, F. & Timmis, I. (2015). *Materials development for TESOL.* **Edinburgh: Edinburgh University Press.**

This book was written to be used as a core text for courses in materials development. It starts with an exploration of what materials are and what they are for. The authors then propose a 'principled' approach to materials development based on principles of SLA such as the need for affective and cognitive challenge as well as input and output. Subsequent chapters examine the relationship between materials and context, as well as how materials can be evaluated and adapted. A chapter is devoted to the ways technology has changed the materials landscape. Three chapters focus on developing materials for the four skills, vocabulary, and grammar, using the principles described earlier. The concluding chapter describes the materials design journey from conceptualization to realization. A notable feature of the book are the two further readings in each chapter that serve as a complement or counterpoint to the ideas of the two authors.

Tomlinson, B., & Masuhara, H. (2018). *The complete guide to the theory and practice of materials development for language learning.* **London: Wiley Blackwell.**

Tomlinson and Masuhara have been hugely influential in the field of materials research through their publications and projects, and as founders of MATSDA (The Materials Development Association) in 1993. In this book they bring together everything they have learned in the last decades. Half of the chapters are devoted to documenting and reflecting on how the field has developed and include chapters on materials evaluation, development, adaptation, publication and research. The other half focus on specific aspects of materials development such as teaching the four skills, materials for different age groups, developing digital materials, as well as the nitty gritty of visuals, layout and design and writing instructions for activities. Each chapter reviews research related to the chapter focus, how the focus has been informed by practice, and how research-derived principles can inform practice. The book is a useful reference manual for materials developers, publishers, teachers, teacher educators and applied linguists.

References

Mishan, F., & Timmis, I. (2015). *Materials development for TESOL.* Edinburgh University Press.
Richards, J. (2014). The ELT textbook. In S. Garton & K. Graves (Eds.), *International perspectives on materials in ELT* (pp. 19–36). Palgrave Macmillan.
Tomlinson, B. (2012). Materials development for language learning and teaching. *Language Teaching, 45*(2), 143–179.

Kathleen Graves is Clinical Professor Emerita of Education at the University of Michigan. Her research focuses on how a language curriculum is designed and enacted and the role of teachers in curriculum renewal. She is the co-author of two global coursebook series, *East West (OUP)* and *Icon (McGraw-Hill)*. She is the editor/author of *Teachers as course developers* (CUP) and *Designing language courses: A guide for teachers (Heinle)* and series editor of TESOL's Language Curriculum Development series for which she co-edited *Developing a new curriculum for school-age learners*. She is co-editor of *International perspectives on materials in ELT (Palgrave)* and co-author of *Teacher Development Over Time (Routledge)*.

Motivation in Practice

Julie Waddington

Considerable advances have been made in the field of motivational research over recent decades. Despite this, questions have been raised about the extent to which the research has been transferred, or not, into practice. At the beginning of the twenty-first century, work by some specialists explicitly aims to address this question. It is in this spirit that one of the most prominent figures in the field presents a practical approach for teachers, aiming to make complex theories more accessible and to provide a stepwise model encouraging teachers to gradually introduce different motivational strategies into their practice (Dörnyei, 2001). Nevertheless, and as suggested in the revised version of Dörnyei's *Teaching and researching motivation*, co-authored by Ema Ushioda (2011), a decade later the field still tends to be dominated by positivist-quantitative approaches focusing on aspects of the construct itself rather than on the pedagogical implications of such theories.

Developments since then have continued to stress the need to bridge the gap between research and theory, aiming to present the latter in more accessible ways on the one hand, and to link theories with specific strategies that can be implemented by teachers on the other. In this regard, different authors have contributed innovative ideas to help transfer theory into practice, while others have worked to shift the balance away from positivist-quantitative approaches to qualitative methods that resonate more with teachers and whose findings may have a more direct practical application (Lasagabaster et al., 2016).

While general consensus exists on the importance of transferring theory into practice, some authors have also highlighted the need to resist universalising tendencies implying that one motivational model may fit all. In this vein, and after presenting a clear and accessible account of key motivation theories, Lamb (2016)

J. Waddington (✉)
Department of Subject-Specific Education, Faculty of Education & Psychology,
University of Girona, Girona, Catalonia, Spain
e-mail: julie.waddington@udg.edu

© Springer Nature Switzerland AG 2021
H. Mohebbi and C. Coombe (eds.), *Research Questions in Language Education and Applied Linguistics*, Springer Texts in Education,
https://doi.org/10.1007/978-3-030-79143-8_23

insists on the need to take the learning context fully into account when considering learning-related and teaching-related motivational issues and to adopt different research strategies depending on the context. Following such an approach, Waddington (2017) presents a study which strategically uses one particular model (Dörnyei's process-oriented model, 2001) in order to explore teacher understandings of motivation and to identify how they (primary teachers) implement motivational strategies in their practice. The findings support the claim advanced by previous authors that theory has not transferred into practice and that much work needs to be done to develop understandings of motivation. At the same time, the study also shows the high predisposition shown by teachers and the benefits of providing focused training to develop understandings. The benefits of focused training, and the positive pedagogical implications of it, are also reported by Ellis and Read (2015) in a longitudinal study evaluating their own primary teacher training course carried out annually over a period of 20 years.

Finally, in addition to practical, teacher-training based approaches aimed at transferring theory into practice, recent proposals suggest that teachers and learners could work together to research motivation, focusing on issues of interest to them and adopting small-scale qualitative approaches which may generate interesting and relevant results, while simultaneously boosting their own motivation levels (Ushioda, as cited in Lamb, 2016).

The Research Questions

1. How has motivation been conceived in research on foreign language teaching?
2. How do language teachers understand motivation?
3. How do language learners understand motivation?
4. To what extent have motivation theories influenced language teaching practice?
5. Are some approaches to motivation more present in the classroom than others? Which ones and why?
6. Are some approaches to motivation neglected in the classroom? Which ones and why?
7. What are the barriers to maintaining motivation in language teaching?
8. How do teachers assess the extent to which their practice is motivational?
9. What research instruments are available to measure motivation in practice?
10. To what extent is motivation covered within teacher training programs?

Suggested Resources

Lamb, M. (2016). Motivation. In G. Hall (Ed.). *The Routledge Handbook of English Language Teaching* **(pp. 324–338). Oxon, UK: Routledge.**

The chapter starts by addressing the first research question proposed in Sect. 2, by discussing what the term motivation actually refers to. The chapter then goes on to present some of the different perspectives and psychological approaches drawn on in motivational theories. After considering the construct from a learning point of view, the second part of the chapter focuses more on the effects of teaching and its motivational dimension, taking in possible demotivating effects as well as specific strategies aimed at boosting learner motivation. The author stresses the partiality of the research results obtained up to now and the need to consider each different learning context, avoiding the imposition of one single motivational model as universally applicable. The chapter ends by setting out future pathways for ELT motivation theory and research, and also highlights the importance of teacher motivation in an increasingly demanding and complex profession.

Lasagabaster, D., Doiz, A., & Sierra, J. M. (Eds.) (2016). *Motivation and Foreign Language Learning: From Theory to Practice.* **Amsterdam: John Benjamins Publishing.**

The editors of this book claim that motivational research has been predominantly driven by quantitative approaches focusing more on the general construct than on practical paths that teachers might follow. Arguing that this does not help bridge the gap between research and practice, they present a collection of chapters from well-known authors that aim to present motivational theories and models in an accessible way, while also linking them to practical strategies. Considering the teachers, the learners and the learning context, the book analyses how these three different dimensions interact with motivation. The collection is divided into two sections; with the first presenting some innovative ideas regarding language learning motivation, and the second focusing on different approaches to foreign language learning and motivation. The emphasis throughout is on the pedagogical implications of motivational research and its application.

Waddington, J. (2017). Teacher understanding and implementation of motivational strategies in ELT. *ELT Journal, 72*(2), 162–174.

This article addresses the second research question proposed in Sect. 2, by exploring how teachers understand and implement motivational strategies in an ELT context. It also contributes towards bridging the gap between research and practice by presenting a qualitative approach which can be replicated in other contexts. The study identifies initial understandings of the concept of motivation and specific ways in which teachers aim to implement motivational strategies in their classrooms. On the one hand, the findings indicate that teachers' understandings of motivation are limited and do not reflect the theoretical advances made over recent decades in ELT-related motivational research. On the other hand, results suggest that changes in understanding can be achieved through focused training activities, in a way which can help shift the emphasis from current teacher-centered approaches to more learner-sensitive environments.

Dörnyei, Z. & Ushioda, E. (2011). *Teaching and researching motivation.* **Harlow: Pearson Education.**

In this substantially revised edition of Dörnyei's, 2001 book, co-author Ema Ushioda provides a valuable contribution which critiques the predominant positivist approach to motivation studies and presents a case for more qualitative research in this field. The book is divided into four sections, with two to four chapters per section. Section one concentrates on defining the construct and presenting different theoretical approaches, before advocating a dynamic systems approach and proposing the use of qualitative, exploratory and longitudinal research approaches. Section two outlines different motivational strategies for teachers and considers the important link between teacher beliefs and learner motivation. Section three and four will be of particular interest to researchers; with section three describing the differences between quantitative and qualitative research and discussing the strengths and weaknesses of mixed methods research, and section four providing useful links and resources to carry out further motivational research, including questionnaires used in previous studies.

Dörnyei, Z. (2001). *Motivational Strategies in the Language Classroom.* **Cambridge, UK: Cambridge University Press.**

This book takes a practical approach to teaching motivational strategies in the language classroom, starting with some thought-provoking questions on motivation itself, before going on to provide some background knowledge, introducing key theorists and approaches. The author then presents an instructional model, intended to help teachers identify the different aspects involved in motivating learners. Referred to as the process-oriented model, this helps organize the different stages of motivational teaching practice as follows: Creating the basic motivational conditions; Generating initial motivation; Maintaining and protecting motivation; Encouraging positive retrospective self-evaluation. Having split the teaching/ learning process into these different component parts, the author then dedicates a chapter to each and provides useful strategies to address each part. The stepwise approach presented encourages teachers to incorporate new ideas into their practice in a manageable and realistic way and provides teacher trainers with a useful tool to organize training sessions on motivation.

References

Dörnyei, Z. (2001). *Motivational strategies in the language classroom.* Cambridge University Press.
Dörnyei, Z., & Ushioda, E. (2011). *Teaching and researching motivation.* Routledge.

Ellis, G., & Read, C. (2015). Course design and evaluation in primary teacher education. In C. N. Giannikas, L. McLaughlin, G. Fanning, & N. D. Muller (Eds.), *Children Learning English: From research to practice* (pp. 115–131). Garnet Education.

Lamb, M. (2016). Motivation. In G. Hall (Ed.), *The Routledge handbook of English language teaching* (pp. 324–338). Routledge.

Lasagabaster, D., Doiz, A., & Sierra, J. M. (Eds.). (2016). *Motivation and foreign language learning: From theory to practice*. John Benjamins Publishing.

Waddington, J. (2017). Teacher understanding and implementation of motivational strategies in ELT. *ELT Journal, 72*(2), 162–174.

Julie Waddington teaches on the degree programmes in Early Childhood Education and Primary School Education at the University of Girona, Catalonia. She also enjoys working with in-service teachers in action research projects and as a trainer for the Catalan Ministry of Education. With a Ph.D. in Literature and Critical Theory, she enjoys applying critical theory to language education and has published and presented widely on different topics, including motivation, foreign languages in the early years, storytelling methodologies and identity-related issues. As a member of the Culture & Education research group (University of Girona), she has also developed and published work on Funds of Knowledge approaches to promote more interest-based and inclusive learning environments.

Second Language Writing Instruction

24

Ken Hyland

Writing is one of the most important skills that second language students need to develop, and the ability to teach it is central to the expertise of a good language teacher. Writing in English has established itself as a key metric in the life chances of millions of people: a measure of educational success, academic competence, professional advancement and institutional recognition. As a result, research on the topic has grown massively, extending beyond conventional academic, school and workplace texts into the features of new electronic genres such as blogs, webpages and wikis. But Second language writing is not just finished texts and research also explores how writers create texts, how these processes and texts are different from those in a first language, and what texts and writing mean to writers, all this as well as seeking to gain greater understanding of writing is taught, analyzed and learnt.

One important variable of the teaching context is whether students are learning to express themselves in writing (learning-to-write) or to develop some area other than writing itself (writing-to-learn). Most research in L2 writing refers to Learning-to-Write contexts, how we can understand and teach writing as an additional language. In contrast, Writing -to-Learn Language refers to writing as a tool for language acquisition and Writing-to-Learn Content aims at enhancing student learning about content subjects, prompting learning and critical thinking.

Various theories supporting teachers' efforts to understand L2 writing and learning have developed since the subject emerged as a distinctive area of scholarship in the 1970s. Structural, functional, content, expressive, process and genre views can be seen as complementary and overlapping perspectives, representing potentially compatible means of understanding the complex reality of writing and how it might best be taught. But these theories are not open curriculum options as

K. Hyland (✉)
School of Education and Lifelong Learning, University of East Anglia, Norwich, UK
e-mail: k.hyland@uea.ac.uk; K.Hyland@uea.ac.uk

Jilin University, Changchun, China

© Springer Nature Switzerland AG 2021
H. Mohebbi and C. Coombe (eds.), *Research Questions in Language Education and Applied Linguistics*, Springer Texts in Education,
https://doi.org/10.1007/978-3-030-79143-8_24

instruction is often constrained by local teaching contexts and always informed by teachers own views of what writing is and how it should be taught.

So, although the "pure" application of a particular theory may be quite rare, it is usual for one to predominate. Most common are varieties of process models, which privilege the writer as an independent producer of texts and recognize that writing depends on basic cognitive processes. Teachers are encouraged to develop these by helping students to plan a text, define a rhetorical problem, propose solutions and evaluate outcomes through a process of brainstorming, redrafting and responding to feedback. The second main approach looks beyond composing processes to see writing as attempts to communicate with readers. Genre is an approach concerned with helping learners create coherent, purposeful texts that will be seen as effective by readers, following certain rhetorical conventions for organizing messages to help readers to recognize a social purpose, such as telling a story, crafting a business email, describing a technical process or whatever. In general, the value of scaffolding students writing development through an explicit awareness of language, a knowledge of target texts, and opportunities to redraft and receive feedback, are now key tenets of much writing instruction. Teachers have also embraced new practices to teach writing, turning to electronic, online and social media resources, being more sensitive to students' writing goals and target contexts, as well as making greater use of corpora, automated feedback and what the web has to offer. *Language* teachers are quickly becoming *writing* teachers.

The Research Questions

1. How do students best learn to write?
2. How should teachers intervene in students' writing and at what stage?
3. What are the main similarities and differences between writing in an L1 and an L2?
4. What information about the students and the context is most useful to have in preparing a writing course for L2 students?
5. To what extent does culture or first language influence writing in a second language?
6. What are the main features of key instructional and target genres and how can teachers best make these salient to learners?
7. What factors influence plagiarism/textual borrowing and how should this be treated by teachers?
8. What kinds of feedback (teacher, peer, automated, oral) are most effective in encouraging student engagement and promoting writing improvement?
9. What affordances and drawbacks do the internet and social media present for L2 writing instruction?
10. How are different kinds of writing most fairly and effectively assessed?

Suggested Resources

Casanave, C. (2017). *Controversies in second language writing 2nd ed.* **Ann Arbor, MI: University of Michigan Press.**
Christine Pearson Casanave's book is an excellent resource for teachers, scholars, and administrators who find themselves grappling with various key concerns in the field. She focuses on five broad issues: contrastive rhetoric, "paths to improvement" (fluency and accuracy, process and product, and error correction), assessment, "interaction" (issues related to audience and plagiarism), and politics and ideology. Rather than simply relate the various views available on these topics, however, she encourages readers to think about their own assumptions and teaching contexts. In other words, she prompts teachers to become self-reflective by examining their own writing experiences, their preferred teaching and learning styles, and the pedagogical theories that have influenced them. She advises teachers to develop a "coherent and internally consistent belief system" for teaching writing that will evolve throughout their teaching careers.

Crusan, D. (2010). *Assessment in the second language writing classroom.* **Ann Arbor, MI: University of Michigan Press.**
This book is strongly recommended for teachers looking for an intelligent, informative and authoritative book on L2 writing assessment uncomplicated by statistics. The book is for teachers working in a range of different contexts including mixed population classes. There are a number of learned books which cover the theoretical aspects of writing assessment, but none focus as heavily on practical classroom aspects of writing assessment. Topics include key issues such as validity, reliability, fairness, biases, washback and developing rubrics and prompts. The book also covers Large-scale and classroom tests, the influence of technology, internet plagiarism, the politics of assessment and the machine scoring of writing and its effects on second language writers. This is an accessible, thought-provoking presentation of the conceptual and practical dimensions of writing assessment, both for the classroom and on a larger scale.

Hyland, K. (2019). *Second language writing 2nd ed.* **Cambridge: Cambridge University Press.**
Hyland introduces the theory and practice of teaching writing to second language learners. Written for pre-service teachers and those new to teaching writing, it sets out the key issues of needs analysis, course design, lesson planning, creating texts, tasks and materials, giving feedback and assessing L2 writing. Importantly, it shows how current research can inform classroom practice and includes a chapter on how teachers and teacher-trainees can conduct research of their own. The book includes recent work on automated feedback, plagiarism, social media, Virtual Learning Environments and teacher workload issues. It takes the stance that student writers not only need realistic strategies for drafting and revising, but also a clear understanding of genre to structure their writing experiences according to the

expectations of particular communities of readers and the constraints of particular contexts. There are review exercises, reflection questions, examples and a glossary to help new teachers.

Hyland, K. & Hyland, F. (Eds.) (2019). *Feedback in second language writing: Contexts and issues* **2nd ed. Cambridge: Cambridge University Press.**
This edited volume provides an up to date overview of current insights and understandings on feedback on second language writing. Chapters written by experts in various areas of feedback emphasize the potential that feedback has for helping to create a supportive teaching environment, for conveying and modelling ideas about good writing, for developing the ways students talk about writing, and for mediating the relationship between students' wider cultural and social worlds and their growing familiarity with new literacy practices. The book includes updated chapters from the first edition on culture, appropriation, interaction, peer feedback and a state-of-play chapter on the impact of error correction on writing. It also adds new chapters on developing areas such as student engagement and participation with feedback, the links between SLA and feedback research, automated computer feedback and the use by students of internet resources and social media as feedback resources.

Manchon, R. & Matsuda, P. (eds.). (2016). *Handbook of Second and Foreign Language Writing.* **Berlin: Mouton.**
This edited collection provides an up-to-date view of theory and research in the field by internationally recognised authors. It offers a fairly comprehensive overview of developments and future directions in L2 writing in six parts: "Mapping the terrain," "Population and contexts," "Learning writing," "Teaching and assessing writing," "Researching writing" and "Interdisciplinary relations." In the introduction, Rosa Manchón argues that L2 writing research is an evolving, interdisciplinary field of inquiry and the chapters which follow demonstrate this through critical interpretations of research in a wide range of areas. In addition to showing how the field evolved, the volume provides state-of-the-art surveys of basic and applied research, overviews of research methods in L2 writing research, critical reflections on future developments, and explorations of existing and emerging interactions with other fields of inquiry.

Ken Hyland is Professor of Applied Linguistics in education at the University of East Anglia. He was previously a professor at UCL/IOE and the University of Hong Kong and has taught in Africa, Asia and Europe. He is best known for his research into writing and academic discourse, having published 240+ articles and 30 books on these topics with over 65,000 citations on Google Scholar. A collection of his work was published as *The Essential Hyland* (Bloomsbury, 2018). He is the Editor of the *Bloomsbury Discourse Series* and Routledge *Innovations and Challenges in Applied Linguistics*, was founding co-editor of the *Journal of English for Academic Purposes* and was co-editor of *Applied Linguistics*.

Task-Based Language Teaching

25

Rod Ellis

Task-based language teaching is an approach that aims to facilitate the acquisition of a second or foreign language (L2) by engaging learners in the performance of tasks. A task is an instructional activity that requires a primary focus on meaning, some kind of gap that is filled by completing the task, the free use of the students' own linguistic resources, and a communicative outcome. An example is the Heart Transplant Task where students are given information about four people in need of a heart transplant, told that only one heart is available, and asked to decide which of the four people should be given the new heart. Such tasks cater to incidental learning by providing learners with L2 input, drawing attention to linguistic form, and offering opportunities for using the L2 communicatively.

Task-based language teaching draws on second language acquisition research and aims to take account of what this research has shown. Learners acquire an L2 naturally and gradually through trying to use the language. They do not acquire the L2 in a linear fashion but rather organically, working on different aspects of the language at the same time. Task-based teaching aims to foster natural language acquisition by helping learners to perform tasks. It contrasts, therefore with mainstream approaches to language teaching, which seek to present and practise discrete bits of language one at a time.

A task-based lesson can consist of three phases—a pre-task phase, a main task phase and a post-task phase—although not all lessons need to include all three phases. In the pre-task phase, students perform activities designed to prepare them to do the task. For example, they may be given the task materials and asked to plan what they want to say before they start performing or they might be asked to listen to a model performance of the task before performing the task themselves. In the main task phase students perform the task either with the teacher, in small groups or individually. A key feature of the main task phase is focus-on-form; that is,

R. Ellis (✉)
School of Education, Curtin University, Perth, WA, Australia
e-mail: rod.ellis@curtin.edu.au; r.ellis@auckland.ac.nz

© Springer Nature Switzerland AG 2021
H. Mohebbi and C. Coombe (eds.), *Research Questions in Language Education and Applied Linguistics*, Springer Texts in Education,
https://doi.org/10.1007/978-3-030-79143-8_25

attention is drawn to the correct use of the language that the students are attempting to use. This can be done in a variety of ways—for example, through corrective feedback or by stopping the task and providing a brief explicit description of a key grammatical feature. Teachers will also need to make a note of the linguistic problems that students experienced so they can address these in the post-task stage of the lesson.

There are many problematic issues in task-based teaching that need to be addressed. One concerns the selection and sequencing of tasks in a task-based course. Should tasks be based on the target-tasks that learners have to perform in real life (e.g. making a hotel booking) or should they address topics that are of general interest to students (e.g. deciding which restaurant to take a friend to?) The answer may depend on the particular students. How can tasks be sequenced so that they increase in difficulty? Currently, there is no clear answer to this question but current research is investigating what makes tasks more or less difficult. Another problem concerns the implementation of task-based teaching. Many teachers in state schools are used to the more traditional, linear teaching of a language and consequently resist adopting an approach where there is no pre-determined language to teach in each lesson. The solution to this problem requires well-designed teacher education courses to prepare teachers for task-based teaching but these are often not available.

The Research Questions

1. What is task-based language teaching?
2. What factors need to be taken into account in deciding what tasks to use with a particular group of learners?
3. What principles inform the sequencing of tasks in a task-based syllabus?
4. What kinds of pre-task teaching activities are compatible with a task-based approach?
5. How can teachers ensure that students pay attention to form while they are performing a task?
6. What kinds of post-task activities can a teacher make use of?
7. How can tasks be used to assess learners' progress?
8. How can a teacher tell whether a task has 'worked'?
9. What problems do teachers face in task-based language teaching?
10. How can a balance between task-based and more traditional language teaching be achieved?

Suggested Resources

Skehan, P. (1998). *A cognitive approach to language learning.* **Oxford: Oxford University Press.**

In this book Peter Skehan lays out the cognitive theory of language learning that informs his own view of TBLT. He proposes that people possess a dual-system of language—an exemplar-based system that they draw on in everyday, fluent speech and a rule-based system that they draw on when they need to express more complex ideas. He also suggests that, L2 learners' working memory is limited in capacity with the result that they experience difficulty in attending to complexity, accuracy and fluency concurrently, leading to trade-offs (e.g. they may prioritize fluency over complexity and accuracy or accuracy over complexity). The relevance of this to TBLT is that different tasks will predispose L2 learners to draw on their exemplar-based or rule-based systems and to prioritize one aspect of production over the others. It follows that in order to ensure balanced L2 development learners need to experience a variety of tasks and task conditions.

Willis, J, & Willis, D (200). *Doing task-based teaching.* **Oxford: Oxford University Press.**

This book is strongly recommended for readers who want a more practical account of TBLT. Both authors have been involved in workshops for teachers and their book set out to address the kinds of questions that teachers often asked them—for example, what exactly is a task? Can you use TBLT with beginners? What about the grammar? How can I use the tasks I find in my textbook? The practical nature of the book is also reflected by the inclusion of examples of TBLT provided by teachers in the field. The book provides a clear explanation of the principles that inform TBLT, sample materials and lesson plans, and guidance on how to adapt existing course materials to include a task-based element. However, readers should approach the book critically as it presents a particular version of TBLT and there are other versions!

Long, M. (2015). *Second language acquisition and task-based language teaching.* **Malden, MA: Blackwell-Wiley.**

Long's book is arguably the most comprehensive account of theory and research related to TBLT. A notable strength of the book is that Long frames TBLT as not just based on theories of second language acquisition but also on general principles of education. There are chapters devoted to both. Long adopts the view that the tasks in a task-based course should be based on the target tasks that learners need to perform in real life and argues that identifying these requires a needs analysis. He discusses issues of critical importance in TBLT such as the selection and grading of tasks, the methodological principles and procedures involved in implementation, and task-based assessment. He also reports on studies that have evaluated the effectiveness of TBLT. Long offers a particular view of TBLT—one that not all proponents of TBLT agree with—and the book needs to be read with this in mind.

Annual Review of Applied Linguistics (2016), 36, 5–33.

The topic of this volume of ARAL is task-based teaching. It includes a key article by Michael Long addressing what he sees as the issues and non-issues in task-based language teaching and an article by Peter Skehan in which he examines research that has investigated task design and the implementation conditions. There is also an interesting article by Philp and Duchesne that approaches tasks from the perspective of 'engagement' and suggests various indicators of students' level of involvement in a task. Other articles address the aspects of task-based production that researchers have investigated (Plonsky & Kim), how best to measure accuracy in task-based production (Foster and Wigglesworth), oral versus written tasks (Gilabert, Manchón & Vasylets) University of Murcia, technology mediated TBLT (Ziegler), the role of the teacher in TBLT (Van den Branden), teachers' perspectives on task difficulty (Révész) and the role that explicit instruction plays in the pre-task stage of a lesson (Li, Ellis & Zhu).

Ellis, R. (2018). *Reflections on task-based language teaching.* **Bristol, UK: Multilingual Matters.**

Ellis has put together a collection of some of his previously published papers on TBLT along with some new chapters. The book starts with a brief history of TBLT and a chapter that outlines two different perspectives on TBLT—what he calls the psycholinguistic and sociocultural perspectives. He argues that both approaches should inform TBLT. The bulk of the book consists of chapters on researching TBLT and on task-based pedagogy. Ellis addresses a number of important issues such as the role of input-based tasks and the place of explicit instruction in TBLT. He also points out that there have been a number of misconceptions about TBLT and addresses these. He takes the stance that TBLT is not monolithic but an 'approach' that can be realized in different ways depending on the particular instructional context. He presents the case for a modular syllabus that incorporates both a task-based and a structural component. In the final chapter in the book he attempts to answer some of the questions about TBLT that teachers often ask.

Rod Ellis is currently a Research Professor in the School of Education, Curtin University (Perth, Australia). He is also a professor at Anaheim University, a visiting professor at Shanghai International Studies University as part of China's Chang Jiang Scholars Program, and an Emeritus Professor of the University of Auckland. His published work includes articles and books on SLA, language teaching and teacher education. His latest book (co-authored) is *Task-based Language Teaching: Theory and Practice* published by Cambridge University Press in 2020. Other recent publications include *Understanding Second Language Acquisition* (2015, Oxford University Press) and *Reflections on Task-based Language Teaching* (Multilingual Matters, 2018). He has held university positions in six different countries and has also conducted numerous consultancies and seminars throughout the world. He was appointed a Fellow of the Royal Society of New Zealand (2014).

Teacher and Learner Perspectives on Vocabulary Learning and Teaching (VLT)

Jonathan Newton

Teachers bring to the classroom a variety of beliefs, attitudes, identity construc-tions, perceptual frames and knowledge about second language vocabulary learning and teaching (VLT) all of which shape their decision-making and classroom practice. Given the importance of teachers, and the large body of research on language teacher cognition (Borg, 2006; Darvin & Norton, 2015), it is surprising that so little research on either teacher cognition or vocabulary teaching has addressed the relationship between teacher cognition and VLT. By way of example, in a recent and expansive handbook of vocabulary studies (Webb, 2019) that includes contributions from many leading scholars in the field, only two chapters address the topic of the current article (Gu, 2019; Newton, 2019) and then only briefly. That said, the limited amount of published research on this topic has revealed some promising emerging themes as discussed below, and these offer rich potential for more research.

In a small but rather elegant study which deserves to be replicated in other contexts, Folse (2010) observed one week (25 h) of classes in an intensive English program at a North American university. He found a low occurrence of episodes with an explicit vocabulary focus. By contrast, Xie (2013) found quite the opposite in her study into the vocabulary teaching practices of four university EFL teachers in two Chinese universities. Here, the teachers overwhelming chose a heavily transmission-oriented stance which involved presenting lexical information in English first and then in Chinese, mostly in the form of explicit definitions of words without examples. They also deliberately and explicitly taught every word they thought to be difficult. In other words there appeared to be no awareness of the value of using word frequency information to determine whether it was worth spending time on a new word (Nation, 2013). This final point is echoed in a study

J. Newton (✉)
School of Linguistics and Applied Language Studies, Victoria University of Wellington,
Wellington, New Zealand
e-mail: jonathan.newton@vuw.ac.nz

© Springer Nature Switzerland AG 2021
H. Mohebbi and C. Coombe (eds.), *Research Questions in Language
Education and Applied Linguistics*, Springer Texts in Education,
https://doi.org/10.1007/978-3-030-79143-8_26

by McCrostie (2007) which found that a group of 21 native speaker English teachers were no better at judging the frequency of low and high frequency words than a comparison group of native speaker first year university graduates, and neither group was successful in judging the frequency of words in the middle frequency range.

The role of learner cognition in VLT is also under-researched (cf., for example, Chou, 2018; Simon & Taverniers, 2011), despite the fact that learners typically view learning vocabulary as a major hurdle (Meara, 1980). There is however a long tradition of research in the related areas of learner beliefs (e.g., Ellis, 2008; Gu, 2010; Horwitz, 1999) and vocabulary learning strategies (e.g., Gu, 2019; Segler et al., 2002). A range of learner factors are likely to impact on VLT, including what learners believe about the value of vocabulary, what they know about the lexicon and about VLT, their educational background and previous L2 learning experiences, their willingness and capacity to engage with VL, the nature of their first language and its proximity to the language they are learning, and their experience of learning other languages.

There is, therefore, scope for more research on the relationship between teacher and learner factors and VLT. Such research is needed if we are to bridge the divide between the well-established body of existing theoretically-oriented research on VLT and the practical concerns of teachers and learners.

The Research Questions

1. How familiar are teachers with (findings from) second language vocabulary research and how do they view its relevance to their teaching practice?
2. What knowledge do teachers have of the structure and nature of the lexicon and how do they put this knowledge to use in teaching vocabulary and guiding learning?
3. What beliefs do teachers hold concerning effective vocabulary teaching and learning and how are these beliefs reflected in their pedagogic decision-making and classroom practice?
4. What use do teachers and learners make of technology for vocabulary learning and with what perceived or measurable value?
5. With respect to RQs 1–4, how do contextual factors (e.g. class size, educational sector, curriculum) and teacher demographic factors (e.g. years of service, level of educational achievement, language learning experience) affect VLT?
6. What VLT content is present in pre-service language teacher education programmes and in in-service Teacher Professional Development and Learning (TPDL), what is the uptake of this content by teachers, and what is its impact on vocabulary learning attainments?
7. How is VLT represented in commercially available textbooks for language learners and to what extent does VLT in textbooks align with teachers' VLT preferences and with theoretically and empirically motivated VLT principles?

8. What is the vocabulary profile of commercially available textbooks for language learners (i.e. distribution of vocabulary across frequency bands) and to what extent does this align with known information about the expected vocabulary size of learners who use the textbooks?

9. What effect does classroom instruction focused on awareness raising concerning VLT and/or the nature and structure of the lexicon (especially with regards frequency bands) have on how learners learn vocabulary, how motivated they are to learn, and vocabulary learning attainment?

10. What factors (learner and/or contextual factors) predict effective and sustained independent vocabulary learning by learners, and, conversely, predict ineffective and discontinued independent vocabulary learning?

Suggested Resources

Burns, A., Freeman, D., & Edwards, E. (2015). Theorizing and studying the language-teaching mind: Mapping research on language teacher cognition. *The Modern Language Journal, 99*(3), 585–601. https://doi.org/10.1111/modl.12245

This article is the final piece in a special issue of MLJ on language teacher cognition. Here, the authors seek to conceptualize 'ontologically and methodologically past and current trajectories in language teacher cognition research and synthesizing various themes that arise across this body of work' (p. 585). As such, this is an important 'state of the art' account of teacher cognition research and provides a valuable overview of the field as well as useful summaries of preceding articles in this special issue. To quote the authors' concluding statement, research on teacher cognition has moved the research community in the direction of the lived complexity of the work of language teaching, how that work is learned, and how it is carried out. The present challenge is how to think beyond our current empirical structures and categories to capture this mental work. To paraphrase Yeats's observation, we may no longer be able to separate the dancer from the dance (pp. 507–508).

Webb, S. (Ed.). (2019). *The Routledge handbook of vocabulary studies*. Milton: Routledge.

The past decade has seen a remarkable resurgence of research on VLT and nowhere is this better reflected than in Webb's handbook of vocabulary studies. In this book, major scholars in the field bring their expertise to bear on key issues in teaching, researching and measuring vocabulary. While, as I note above, teacher cognition is not strongly represented in the book, the currency and breadth of the research presented here makes it a key resource for researchers interested in VLT.

Gao, X., & Ma, Q. (2011). Vocabulary learning and teaching beliefs of pre-service and in-service teachers in Hong Kong and mainland China. *Language Awareness, 20*(4), 327–342. https://doi.org/10.1080/09658416.2011.579977

Gao and Ma (2011) undertook a larger scale study of beliefs concerning vocabulary instruction involving pre- and in-service teachers in Hong Kong and Mainland China. Using a questionnaire (Likert-scale and open-ended questions) and follow-up interviews, the research found general agreement among the four groups on the efficacy of learning through memorization and the value of contextual use. Responses to the open-ended questions also revealed general agreement on the need to explicitly teach lexical knowledge. However, the groups differed on questions of strategy use and how much emphasis should be placed on putting words to use as part of the learning process. Perhaps the most interesting finding from the study concerns the effect of the teachers' own language learning experiences on their beliefs. Teachers who as learners had experienced an excess of copying and dictation as a primary form of vocabulary learning showed a stronger preference for alternatives such as directly teaching word meaning. While there are aspects of survey design in the study that perhaps deserved more attention, the findings from the study highlight some valuable themes and trends which deserve further research.

Darvin, R., & Norton, B. (2015). Identity and a model of investment in applied linguistics. *Annual Review of Applied Linguistics, 35*, 36–56.

Davin and Norton's (2015) model of identity and investment provides a potentially valuable tool for understanding motivations and disincentives for second language vocabulary learning. The model brings together analyses of capital, identity and ideology. To explain *capital,* they employ Bourdieu's concept of social, cultural and economic capital to argue that, regardless of motivational dispositions, language learners need an expectation of return to invest in language learning. Davin and Norton further argue for the crucial role of *identity* in the process of language learning, which involves joining a community of practice of target language speakers. If students do not value that community or they perceive classroom teaching as inappropriate, they will resist learning the language. Norton (2013, p. 4) defines identity as "the way a person understands his or her relationship to the world, how that relationship is structured across time and space, and how the person understands possibilities for the future". *Ideology* enables the multi-layered complexity of social influences to be considered in relation to learners and their willingness to invest in learning. The intersections between capital, identity and ideology reveal sites of synergy and contestation which, in their interplay, shape the degree to which a student is willing, able, and resourced to engage in language learning, including vocabulary learning. Specifically, these intersections bring *affordances* for language learning, expose systematic *patterns of control,* and *position* the language learner. Given the considerable amount of independent effort required to build a substantial second language lexicon, a model of investment provides a useful theoretical starting point for understanding learner agency in vocabulary learning.

References

Borg, S. (2006). *Teacher cognition and language education: Research and practice.* Continuum.

Chou, I. (2018). Exploring Taiwanese students' perceptions of active explicit vocabulary instruction: A case study in an English medium course. *International Journal of Education & Literacy Studies, 6*(1), 17.

Darvin, R., & Norton, B. (2015). Identity and a model of investment in applied linguistics. *Annual Review of Applied Linguistics, 35*, 36–56.

Ellis, R. (2008). Learner beliefs and language learning. *Asian EFL Journal, 10*(4), 7–25.

Folse, K. S. (2010). Is explicit vocabulary focus the reading teacher's job? *Reading in a Foreign Language, 22*(1), 139.

Gu, Y. (2010). Learning strategies for vocabulary development. *Reflections on English Language Teaching, 9*(2), 105–118.

Gu, P. Y. (2019). Strategies for learning vocabulary. In S. Webb (Ed.), *The Routledge handbook of vocabulary studies* (pp. 271–287). Routledge.

Horwitz, E. K. (1999). Cultural and situational influences on foreign language learners' beliefs about language learning: A review of BALLI studies. *System, 27*(4), 557–576. https://doi.org/10.1016/S0346-251X(99)00050-0

McCrostie, J. (2007). Investigating the accuracy of teachers' word frequency intuitions. *RELC Journal, 38*(1), 53–66. https://doi.org/10.1177/0033688206076158

Meara, P. (1980). Vocabulary acquisition: A neglected aspect of language learning. *Language Teaching, 13*(3–4), 221–246.

Nation, I. S. P. (2013). *Learning vocabulary in another language.* Cambridge University Press.

Newton, J. (2019). Approaches to learning vocabulary inside the classroom. In S. Webb (Ed.), *The Routledge handbook of vocabulary studies* (pp. 255–270). Routledge.

Segler, T. M., Pain, H., & Sorace, A. (2002). Second language vocabulary acquisition and learning strategies in ICALL environments. *Computer Assisted Language Learning, 15*(4), 409–422. https://doi.org/10.1076/call.15.4.409.8272

Simon, E., & Taverniers, M. (2011). Advanced EFL learners' beliefs about language learning and teaching: A comparison between grammar, pronunciation, and vocabulary. *English Studies, 92*(8), 896–922. https://doi.org/10.1080/0013838X.2011.604578

Webb, S. (Ed.). (2019). *The Routledge handbook of vocabulary studies.* Routledge.

Xie, X. (2013). Vocabulary explanation in English-major university classrooms in China. *ELT Journal, 67*(4), 435–445. https://doi.org/10.1093/elt/cct031

Jonathan Newton is an Associate Professor at Victoria University of Wellington, New Zealand. He has worked as a language teacher and teacher educator for more than 30 years, with wide experience of engaging with teachers from across Asia. He has published more than 60 book chapters and articles in leading applied linguistics journals on topics focused on classroom language teaching. He has co-authored three books, one with Paul Nation, *Teaching ESL/EFL Listening and Speaking* (2009, Routledge), a second with Nicky Riddiford, *Workplace Talk in Action: An ESOL Resource* (2010, VUW Press), and a third with four co-authors, *Teaching English to Second Language Learners in Academic Contexts: Reading, Writing, Listening, and Speaking* (2018, Routledge).

Teachers' Relational Practices and Students' Motivation

27

Alastair Henry

Language learning is a social practice. At a minimum level, it involves interaction with others. As applied linguistics shifts into a social era, psychological constructs such as motivation and willingness to communicate are being reframed as relational phenomena. Research is beginning to investigate the influences that relationships in language classrooms have on students' learning behaviors.

In educational psychology the positive impact that meaningful relationships with teachers and peers have on motivation, engagement and achievement is well-established. As Martin and Dowson (2009) make clear, positive relations with important others provide the "cornerstones of young people's capacity to function effectively in social, affective, and academic domains" (p. 351). From a synthesis of over 800 meta-analyses, positive teacher–student relationships have been identified as central to students' engagement in learning, and their academic attainment (Hattie & Yates, 2013).

Because positive relationships with teachers have important influences on student's *emotional responses* to learning, the teacher–student relationship is of particular importance in language classrooms (Henry & Thorsen, 2018). In a state-of-the-art review of the motivational dimension of language teaching, Lamb (2017) identifies the teacher–student relationship as of paramount importance for motivation and engagement. As he explains, the aspects of teacher behavior with the greatest impact on students' motivation are those that involve interpersonal qualities, and which "relate to the human side of teaching" (p. 330). Research by Noels and colleagues (Noels et al., 1999) shows that teacher support of students' autonomy plays a central role in shaping motivation, while Joe et al. (2017) highlight important correlations between the classroom social climate, and the satisfaction of the basic psychological needs of autonomy and relatedness.

A. Henry (✉)

Department of Social and Behavioural Studies, University West, Trollhättan, Sweden

e-mail: alastair.henry@hv.se; al.henry@hv.se

© Springer Nature Switzerland AG 2021

H. Mohebbi and C. Coombe (eds.), *Research Questions in Language Education and Applied Linguistics*, Springer Texts in Education,
https://doi.org/10.1007/978-3-030-79143-8_27

The teacher's empathic capacity, and ability to create connections with students is foundational in the development of the types of learner-centered, facilitative classroom environments in which successful language learning can take place (Mercer, 2016). In line with the recognition that motivation in L2 classrooms is best understood as a *relational phenomenon* that is shaped by teachers' empathy and responsiveness, research is now focusing on teachers' social and emotional intelligence, and their capacity to develop empathic relationships (Gkonou & Mercer, 2018). As Henry and Thorsen (2019) have demonstrated, in attuning to students' interests, concerns, experiences and emotions, teachers' empathic capacity can be manifested both in the design of learning activities, and in 'in-the-moment' interactions. Because it is at the "very localised level of students' learning experience that the real potential for engaging (or disengaging) their motivation may lie" (Ushioda, 2013, p. 236), there is a need for research that focuses on how connections are created in interpersonal interactions and activity designs, and how teachers' perspective taking practices shape students' engagement (Henry, 2021).

The Research Questions

1. What is characteristic of language teachers' social intelligence (SI) and emotional intelligence (EI) in particular contexts of learning?
2. What are the relationships between language teacher's beliefs about effective teaching, and particular aspects of SI and EI?
3. What relationships exist between particular types of teacher relational practice, and students' motivation, engagement and achievement?
4. How do language teacher relational practices differ in relation to factors such as the target language, class size, and relational maturity?
5. How is language teacher empathy manifested in interactions with students, and what influences do these interactions have on engagement?
6. How does a teacher's knowledge of his/her students as unique individuals influence instructional design, feedback and support, and classroom interactions?
7. How do teachers orient to students' cultural frames of reference? What are the characteristics of self-expression and identity work in language classrooms?
8. How do teachers create spaces for students' agency, and how does scope for agency affect engagement?
9. How do teachers make themselves present to students in interpersonal interactions, and what impact do in-the-moment connections have on motivated behavior?
10. What are the characteristics of an effective relational practice, and in what ways do teachers' relational profiles differ?

Suggested Resources

Stevick, E. (1980). *Teaching Languages: A Way and Ways.* **Rowley, MA: Newbury House**.

This is a classic book by one of the pioneers of language teaching. As relevant today as when it was published, it has had a profound influence on many of the leading voices in language education. With a point of departure in the recognition that "the language classroom can be a place of alienation for student and teacher alike", Stevick brings the humanist philosophy of Ernest Becker (1924–1974) and Martin Buber (1878–1965) to the "narrow back yard of the language teacher" (p. 22). Arguing that what is really important in the language classroom is what goes on *inside* and *between* the people in it, Stevick introduces a number of central concepts focusing on the relationality of learning and teaching. Among these are 'counseling learning', 'reflective listening' and 'community learning'. For Stevick, the power of the teacher is subordinate to the teacher's responsibility for ensuring that the resources of *all* of the members of the classroom community are utilized in a task at hand. The role of the teacher is thus to 'understand' and to 'know' the students, and to 'direct' their learning. To avoid practice pitfalls that can lead to alienation, Stevick maps out a humanistic approach that is summarized in seven steps (and seven hazards inherent in such a way of teaching). Stevick's philosophy and approach are succinctly set out in the following paragraph, which captures the essence of an effective relational practice:

> If we, in our zeal to be "humanistic," become too "learner-centered" with regard to "control," we undermine the learner's most basic need: which is for security. We may find that we have imposed our own half-baked anarchy on the class. Absence of structure, or of focus on the teacher, may well be all right in certain kinds of psychological training, but not in our classrooms. In a task-oriented group like a language class, the student's place is at the center of a space which the teacher has structured, with room for him to grow into. In this kind of relationship, there are two essentials for the teacher: faith that the student will in fact grow into that space and understanding of where the student is in that space at any given moment. When both these ingredients are present, there is the possibility of true 'humanism' in teaching. (p. 33).

Arnold, J. & Murphey, T. (2013). *Meaningful Action: Earl Stevick's Influence on Language Teaching.* **Cambridge: Cambridge University Press**.

This book, carefully put together by Arnold and Murphey, and which pays tribute to the career of Earl Stevick, focuses on the notion of 'meaningful action'. As the editors explain, taking meaningful action involves the agency of the teacher and the student, and encompasses self-determination, autonomy, motivation, self confidence and self-esteem, risk-taking, socialization and belonging. In language learning that is meaningful, there is a *harmony* both within the learner and in the productive relationships between the people in the classroom. There is also a *depth* of purpose, where participants in language learning experience a sense of connection and belonging.

With a list of contributors that reads like a 'Who's Who' of contemporary language education—Heidi Byrnes, Zoltán Dörnyei, Diane Larsen-Freeman, David Nunan, Rebecca Oxford and Scott Thornbury, among many others—the book is divided into three parts: "Meaning-making inside and between the people in the classroom", "Meaningful classroom activity", and "Frameworks for meaningful language learning". It is in Part A where the relational aspects of instructed language learning, and the connections between teachers and students are most in focus. Topics central in the essays in this section include, for example, agency and interpersonal validation (Kristjánsson), meaningful self-esteem and teacher confirmation (Arnold), the co-creation of experience (Puchta), trust (Candlin & Crichton), learner-centeredness (Nunan), and the embodiment and embeddedness of 'meaningful action' in social contexts (Thornbury). In Part B, although the focus is on meaningful activity in the language classroom, Arnold and Murphey make clear that experiences that enhance the student's sense of agency and connect to their lives outside the classroom provide the conditions for investment in learning. They argue that teachers can increase the meaningfulness of learning "through their interactions and relationships with learners" (p. 127). In this section, essays focus on the development of community in the language classroom (Maley), and how meaningfulness emerges through the skill of the teacher in creating a positive social atmosphere (Underhill).

Dörnyei, Z. (2001). *Motivational Strategies in the Language Classroom.* **Cambridge: Cambridge University Press**.

Aimed at practitioners and providing a practical approach to working with strategies designed to generate and maintain motivation in classrooms, this book provides important insights into language teachers' relational practices, and the influences they can have on engagement and motivation. Drawing on work conducted with Kata Csizér on the motivational techniques used by Hungarian teachers of English (Dörnyei & Csizér, 1998), Dörnyei describes how this research revealed the teacher's own way of being and behaving to be the single most important way of developing and enhancing students' motivation.

While nearly all of the 35 macro-strategies described in the book have an interpersonal dimension, 4 strategies directly involve elements of a motivation-enhancing relational practice:

- Teachers should demonstrate and talk about their own enthusiasm for the course content and materials and show students how it affects them personally. Teachers should demonstrate how the L2 interests them, is enjoyable, and enriches their life.
- Teachers should show concern for their students' learning, show their capacity for care, and demonstrate their mental and physical availability.
- Teachers should develop personal relationships with students and demonstrate a capacity for acceptance. They should show students that they care about them and pay attention to them.

- Teachers need to create a pleasant and supportive atmosphere in the classroom that establishes norms of tolerance, encourages risk-taking, and enables accommodations to be made to students' personal choices.

Dörnyei, Z., & Csizér, K. (1998). Ten commandments for motivating language learners: Results of an empirical study. *Language Teaching Research*, *2*(3), 203–229.

Mercer, S. & Kostoulas, A. (2018). *Language Teacher Psychology***. Bristol: Multilingual Matters**.

While there is an extensive body of research into the psychology of language *learning*, work on the psychology of language *teaching* is only beginning to take place. In this edited volume, Sarah Mercer and Achilleas Kostoulas collect together seventeen specially written contributions on various aspects of language teacher psychology. In the book's introduction, the editors provide a reasoned justification for the need for research into language teacher psychology and map out its terrain. Major topic areas in this emerging landscape include teacher cognitions, teacher identities and teacher motivation. Within this research area, a range of constructs are to be found. These include teacher resilience, teacher immunity, teacher well-being and teachers' social and emotional intelligence, all of which are in focus in various chapters of the book.

Among the contributions, several focus on relational practices. In their chapter on language teacher motivation, Hiver, Kim and Kim consider teacher motivation in the classroom context, and how this links to classroom dynamics and development within the teaching profession. In another chapter where relational practices are in focus, Dewaele and Mercer investigate the ways in which aspects of teacher psychology influence teacher–student relationships. Among a number of interesting results, they report that teachers' language proficiency and linguistic self-efficacy are related to more positive attitudes to students, and to increased enjoyment when interacting with lively students. In another chapter with a focus on the interpersonal dimensions of teacher/learner psychologies, Saleem describes how the emotions and cognitions of teachers and students can be understood as interacting with one another, and how teachers can both inspire learners and be inspired by them. The anthology ends with the editors' encouragement of future research into all aspects of language teacher psychology, and their underscoring of the importance of research agendas that can support the development of effective language teaching.

Gkonou, C. & Mercer, S. (2016). *Understanding emotional and social intelligence among English language teachers***. London: British Council**.

In this book, Gkonou and Mercer report on an extensive mixed-methods study of language teachers' emotional intelligence (EI) and social intelligence (SI) carried out in Austria and the United Kingdom. The book is invaluable for researchers interested in understanding L2 motivation as a relational phenomenon. This is not only because of the array of findings about the characteristics of language teachers' emotional and social competencies, but also because the authors map out the concept space of these important constructs, and explain how teacher beliefs, behaviors and social orientations influence the fostering of positive interpersonal relationships. Importantly, the study shows how a teacher's relational skills constitute a necessary foundation for successful language teaching. As Gkonou and Mercer explain, while teaching can be based on the most inspiring and innovative materials and resources, in the absence of appropriate interpersonal dynamics, such affordances are unlikely to achieve their full potential. The study points to the importance of EI and SI for the *sustainability* of effective language learning and teaching, Gkonou and Mercer's findings showing how these capacities are beneficial not only for the classroom relational climate, but also for teacher wellbeing and resilience.

References

Gkonou, C., & Mercer, S. (2018). The relational beliefs and practices of highly socio-emotionally competent language teachers. In S. Mercer & A. Kostoulas (Eds.), *Language teacher psychology* (pp. 158–177). Multilingual Matters.

Hattie, J., & Yates, G. (2013). *Visible learning and the science of how we learn.* Routledge.

Henry, A. (2021). Motivational connections in language classrooms: A research agenda. *Language Teaching, 54*(2), 221–235.

Henry, A., & Thorsen, C. (2018). Teacher-student relationships and L2 motivation. *The Modern Language Journal, 102*, 218–241.

Henry, A., & Thorsen, C. (2019). Weaving webs of connection: Empathy, perspective taking, and students' motivation. *Studies in Second Language Learning and Teaching, 9*, 31–53.

Joe, H.-K., Hiver, P., & Al-Hoorie, A. H. (2017). Classroom social climate, self-determined motivation, willingness to communicate, and achievement: A study of structural relationships in instructed second language settings. *Learning and Individual Differences, 53*, 133–144.

Lamb, M. (2017). The motivational dimension of language teaching. *Language Teaching, 50*, 301–346.

Martin, A. J., & Dowson, M. (2009). Interpersonal relationships, motivation, engagement, and achievement: Yields for theory, current issues, and educational practice. *Review of Educational Research, 79*, 327–365.

Mercer, S. (2016). Seeing the world through your eyes: Empathy in language learning and teaching. In P. D. MacIntyre, T. Gregersen, & S. Mercer (Eds.), *Positive psychology in SLA* (pp. 91–111). Multilingual Matters.

Noels, K. A., Clément, R., & Pelletier, L. G. (1999). Perceptions of teachers' communicative style and students' intrinsic and extrinsic motivation. *The Modern Language Journal, 83*, 23–34.

Ushioda, E. (2013). Motivation and ELT: Looking ahead to the future. In E. Ushioda (Ed.), *International perspectives on motivation: Language learning and professional challenges* (pp. 233–239). Palgrave Macmillan.

Alastair Henry is Professor of Language Education at University West, Sweden. He is a co-editor of *The Palgrave Handbook of Motivation for Language Learning*, and his work has been published in journals such as *Applied Linguistics, Language Learning The Modern Language JournalLanguage Teaching Research* and *Journal of Teacher Education*. He was PI for the large-scale ethnographic project, 'Motivational Teaching in Swedish Secondary English' (MoTiSSE), which investigated the relational practices of teachers who were successful in motivating their students. This project generated numerous research papers, including an article on teacher–student relationships in The *Modern Language Journal*, and a 'Research Agenda' article in *Language Teaching*. A book for practitioners has also been published *Motivational Practice: Insights from the Classroom* (2019, Studentlitteratur).

Teaching English as an International Language

28

Aya Matsuda

Teaching English as an International Language (TEIL) is an emerging paradigm in ELT that acknowledges the linguistic, functional, and cultural diversity associated with the English language today (Matsuda & Matsuda, 2018). It does not assume or promote the idea that there is one variety of English that should be used for international communication. EIL, rather, refers to the function that English performs as a lingua franca for people from various linguistic and cultural backgrounds, both L1 and other users of English.

Although the TEIL paradigm is still evolving, its vision and practices are gaining traction. In 2008, TESOL International Association passed a position statement on English as a Global Language, which "encourages the recognition and appreciation of all varieties of English" (Teachers of English to Speakers of Other languages, 2008). In 2014, *TESOL Journal* published a special issue on "Critical Perspectives on World Englishes," which suggests that world Englishes and their implications for ELT are considered essential information for ELT professionals.

The paradigm may be called differently, reflecting different intellectual traditions —e.g. *English as a Lingua Franca* (ELF)-*aware Pedagogy* (e.g., Bayyurt & Sifakis, 2015), *Global Englishes Language Teaching* (GELT) (e.g., Galloway & Rose, 2015), *WE-informed ELT* (Matsuda, 2020)—but they are "united in the desire to move away from teaching for native-speaker competence" (Alsagoff, 2012, p. 116) and commonly include the following components (see also Alsagoff et al., 2012; Marlina & Giri, 2014; Matsuda, 2012; McKay, 2002; Selvi & Yazan, 2013):

- **Exposure to different varieties of English** so that learners develop awareness of the pluralistic nature of English used in the world today and are less likely to be startled, surprised, confused, overwhelmed or feel underprepared when they encounter varieties of English different from the one they are learning.

A. Matsuda (✉)
Department of English, Arizona State University, Tempe, AZ, USA
e-mail: aya.matsuda@asu.edu

© Springer Nature Switzerland AG 2021
H. Mohebbi and C. Coombe (eds.), *Research Questions in Language Education and Applied Linguistics*, Springer Texts in Education,
https://doi.org/10.1007/978-3-030-79143-8_28

- **Exposure to different types of English users**, including so-called NNESs, which helps learners gain a clearer vision of how they will be using English and with whom, picture themselves as a legitimate user of the language, and set realistic goals regarding how proficient they can be.
- **Cultural content from diverse contexts** to reflect the definition of "English-speaking cultures" that has broadened because of the global spread of English. Although it is impossible to know all cultural assumptions that future interlocutors may have, knowing that it goes beyond the mainstream US/UK culture is critical for the successful use of EIL.
- **Critical perspectives on EIL** as well as sensitivity and a sense of responsibility as an EIL user, which would allow learners to use English effectively to meet their own needs while resisting any oppression from the dominance of English and respecting the needs of others.

The Research Questions

1. What are students', teachers', and teacher educator's beliefs and attitudes toward different varieties of English?
2. Do students, teachers, and teacher educators perceive so-called nonnative English speakers as legitimate users of EIL? Why/why not? What can be done to empower students to see themselves as a legitimate user of English?
3. How do teaching materials (e.g., textbooks) capture the diversity in English forms, users, and uses today? How can gaps in the (re)presentation be compensated?
4. Which assessment tools are effective in assessing the proficiency in EIL, which is naturally linguistically diverse?
5. Does the exposure to different varieties alone increase the awareness and lead to positive attitudes, or is additional scaffolding necessary?
6. Does the exposure to different cultures alone increase the awareness and lead to positive attitudes, or is additional scaffolding necessary?
7. What are common communication strategies used in EIL communication? How can they be introduced in EIL classrooms?
8. What kind of challenges do teachers face when they attempt to practice TEIL? How do they overcome those challenges?
9. How is the notion of TEIL introduced in teacher education programs across the world? What do teachers learn and what do they apply in their actual teaching?
10. What skills, knowledge, and experience do teachers need in order to successfully practice TEIL in their classroom?

Suggested Resources

Alsagoff, L., McKay, S. L., Hu, G., & Renandya, W. A. (Eds.). (2012). *Principles and practices for teaching English as an International Language.* **New York/London: Routledge**.

This edited volume explores the pedagogical implications of the global spread of English and its role as an international language, highlighting particularly the importance of socially sensitive pedagogy. It starts with a set of theoretical chapters that call for changes, which apply to multiple areas and overall assumptions about ELT, and then moves to a set of more practical chapters that address specific topics that are typically included in teacher education courses (e.g., curricular development, teaching materials, teaching various skills, grammar, literature). Each chapter includes activities called "Exploring the Ideas" and "Applying the Ideas" to help teachers implement new ideas and reflect on them.

Galloway, N., & Rose, H. (2015). *Introducing global Englishes.* **Arbingdon, UK: Routledge**.

This book is not specifically about TEIL, except the one chapter that is devoted the topic, but it is one of the most comprehensive and balanced presentations of the linguistic, cultural, and functional diversity and heterogeneity of English today that TEIL embraces. It covers such topics as the history of English, language changes and variation, language attitudes, and forms and uses of English in different parts of the world today, drawing from the work of WE, ELF and EIL scholars. The presentation is accessible but also thoughtful and nuanced, making it a great resource for teachers who are interested in learning the complexity of the English-speaking world that they are preparing their students for.

Marlina, R. (Eds.) (2018). Special Issue: Teaching English as an international language (TEIL): Realistic or idealistic? *RELC Journal, 49*(1).

This special issue is only 6 years newer than Alsagoff et al. (2012) and Matsuda (2012), but clearly shows that the TEIL paradigm has matured and evolved during that time. Scholars of TEIL and other relevant fields engage in the critical examination of the current status of TEIL and respond to common and prevalent questions among language practitioners, emerged from the increased awareness and interests in the concept. One of such questions is whether "teaching EIL is simply an ideological fantasy"—authors, focusing on different aspects of TEIL, demonstrate that TEIL is neither utopian or idealistic but real and realistic. In addition, the chapters in this volume collectively show the current state and future direction of not only TEIL practices but also TEIL scholarship/research, bringing pedagogy and research closer.

Matsuda, A. (Ed.). (2012). *Principles and practices of teaching English as an International Language*. **Bristol, UK: Multilingual Matters**.

This edited volume lays out the principles of TEIL by critically examining the traditional practices in ELT in light of the current use of EIL and suggest changes in assumptions and practices that are needed in order to prepare competent users of EIL. Part I explores how the linguistic, cultural and functional variety of English today complicates the ELT practices, focusing on different aspects of teaching including the selection of instructional variety, teaching materials, and assessment. Part II is a showcase of EIL-based programs, courses, and activities from different geographical and institutional contexts, which collectively show how ideas presented in Part I are practiced in real contexts.

Matsuda, A. (Ed.) (2017). *Preparing teachers to teach English as an international language*. **Bristol, UK: Multilingual Matters**.

Building on Matsuda (2012), this edited volume explores ways to prepare teachers to teach English as an international language. It attempts to present theoretically-grounded models for EIL-informed teacher education by creating a space for the exploration of EIL teacher education that cuts across English as a Lingua Franca, World Englishes, and other relevant scholarly communities. The volume begins with two chapters that present the principles of EIL-informed teacher education, followed by the descriptions of existing teacher education programs, courses, units in a course, and stand-alone activities. These pedagogical ideas were created and situated in their particular geographical and institutional contexts, but the detailed description allows readers to adopt and adapt those ideas for their own contexts.

References

Alsagoff, L. (2012). Identity and the EIL learner. In L. Alsagoff, S. L. McKay, G. Hu, & W. A. Renandya (Eds.), *Principles and practices for teaching English as an International Language* (pp. 104–122). Routledge.

Alsagoff, L., McKay, S. L., Hu, G., & Renandya, W. A. (Eds.). (2012). *Principles and practices for teaching English as an international language*. Routledge.

Bayyurt, Y., & Sifakis, N. C. (2015). Developing an ELF-aware pedagogy: Insights from a self-education programme. In P. Vettorel (Ed.), *New frontiers in teaching and learning English* (pp. 55–76). Cambridge Scholars Publishing.

Galloway, N., & Rose, H. (2015). *Introducing global Englishes*. Routledge.

Marlina, R., & Giri, R. A. (Eds.). (2014). *The pedagogy of English as an international language: Perspectives from scholars, teachers, and students*. Springer.

Matsuda, A. (2020). World Englishes and English language teaching. In C. Nelson, Z. Proshina, & D. R. Davis (Eds.), *The handbook of World Englishes* (2nd ed.) (pp. 686–702). Wiley-Blackwell.

Matsuda, A. (Ed.). (2012). *Principles and practices of teaching English as an international language*. Multilingual Matters.

Matsuda, A., & Matsuda, P. K. (2018). Teaching English as an international language: A WE-informed paradigm for English language teaching. In E. L. Low & A. Pakir (Eds.), *World Englishes: Re-thinking paradigms* (pp. 64–77). Routledge.

McKay, S. L. (2002). *Teaching English as an international language: Rethinking goals and approaches*. Oxford University Press.

Selvi, A. F., & Yazan, B. (2013). *Teaching English as an international language*. TESOL.

Teachers of English to Speakers of Other Languages. (2008). *Position statement on English as a global language*. Retrieved from www.tesol.org/s_tesol/bin.asp?CID=32&DID= 10884&DOC=FILE.PDF

Aya Matsuda is Associate Professor of Applied Linguistics at Arizona State University, where she currently directs programs in linguistics, applied linguistics, and TESOL. Her research interests include the use of English as an international language and the pedagogical implications of the global spread of English. Her work focusing on these issues has appeared in various books and journals including *JALT Journal, RELC Journal, TESOL Quarterly*, and *World Englishes*. Her edited volumes, *Preparing teachers to teach English as an international language* (2017) and *Principles and practices of teaching English as an international language* (2012), were published by Multilingual Matters. Matsuda has served on the Board of Directors for TESOL International Association (2015–2018) and as the secretary-treasurer of the International Association for World Englishes (2015–2019).

Teaching for Transfer of Second Language Learning

Mark A. James

A fundamental goal of second language (L2) education is to promote learning that students will apply in new situations. For example, in an English-as-a-second-language course for engineering students at a Canadian university, a goal might be to help students learn to write lab reports so this learning can be applied in other courses with labs. This goal involves *learning transfer*, which occurs "when learning in one context or with one set of materials impacts on performance in another context or with another set of materials" (Perkins & Salomon, 1994, p. 6452). If L2 education does not promote learning transfer, the value of that education is questionable.

Fortunately, there are steps educators can take to try to promote transfer of L2 learning. Research that has investigated transfer of various types of L2 learning (e.g., grammar, pronunciation, vocabulary) across a range of contexts (e.g., new activities, new topics) points to the potential benefit of general teaching techniques such as providing students with learning activities that are similar to activities in target contexts, having students learn general principles, and having students do large amounts of practice that varies (e.g., listening to different speakers) (James, 2018). Since these techniques have been linked to students' transfer of L2 learning, they are worth considering in further efforts to teach for such transfer.

However, such efforts do not guarantee that students' L2 learning will transfer. Outside L2 education, there are numerous examples of failed attempts to promote transfer (Detterman, 1993), and there is evidence that transfer is influenced not only by teaching methodology but also by factors over which teachers have less control, such as students' motivation to transfer learning and students' perceptions of support for transfer in target contexts (Haskell, 2001). Furthermore, within L2 education, research has shown that transfer of L2 learning is not inevitable, even when opportunities for transfer are immediate (James, 2009). With this in mind, it is

M. A. James (✉)
Department of English, Arizona State University, Tempe, AZ, USA
e-mail: Mark.A.James@asu.edu

© Springer Nature Switzerland AG 2021
H. Mohebbi and C. Coombe (eds.), *Research Questions in Language Education and Applied Linguistics*, Springer Texts in Education,
https://doi.org/10.1007/978-3-030-79143-8_29

no surprise that transfer of L2 learning has been highlighted as a key concern (Larsen-Freeman, 2013) and a priority for research (Long, 2015; Swales, 1990).

The Research Questions

1. What teaching techniques are most effective for promoting transfer of L2 learning?
2. Are teaching-for-transfer techniques more effective with some kinds of L2 learning than others (e.g., grammar vs. vocabulary; skills vs. strategies)?
3. How do students judge a L2 learning activity and an activity in a target context as similar or different?
4. Is there a relationship between students' motivation to transfer L2 learning and students' transfer of L2 learning?
5. What goals do students have for transferring L2 learning?
6. What do students believe causes their successful or unsuccessful transfer of L2 learning?
7. What phases are there in students' motivation to transfer L2 learning? (For example, what leads a student to attempt L2 learning transfer in the first place? How does a student sustain an attempt at L2 learning transfer? How does a student evaluate an attempt at L2 learning transfer?)
8. How can L2 teaching increase students' motivation to transfer L2 learning?
9. Is there a relationship between support for transfer in target contexts and students' transfer of L2 learning?
10. How can L2 teaching prepare students for target contexts where there will be no support for transfer?

Suggested Resources

Perkins, D.N., & Salomon, G. (1988). Teaching for transfer. *Educational Leadership, 46*, 22–32.

This article focuses on learning transfer from a teaching perspective, presenting a practical framework that can be used as a basis for teaching for transfer. The article points out that transfer can occur in two ways: *low-road transfer*, which is automatic and is triggered by similarities between learning activities and activities in target contexts, and *high-road transfer*, which is deliberate and therefore is less reliant on similarities between activities. The article also recommends two general techniques for teaching for transfer: *hugging* involves providing students with a learning context that resembles target contexts, and this can promote low-road transfer; *bridging* involves encouraging students to think abstractly about what they are learning (e.g., to identify general principles), and this can promote high-road transfer.

Haskell, R.E. (2001). *Transfer of learning: Cognition, instruction, and reasoning.* **San Diego, CA: Academic Press Inc.**

This book provides a broad review of transfer research across the main areas in which this research has been conducted (e.g., psychology, education, human resources development). The book also presents a relatively comprehensive theory of how to teach for transfer. This theory includes principles that reflect a variety of general teaching techniques, such as providing students with learning activities that are similar to activities in target contexts and helping students to develop an abstract understanding of what they are learning. Besides teaching techniques, this theory also includes principles that reflect characteristics of students (e.g., students' motivation to transfer learning), and features of target contexts (e.g., students' perceptions of support for transfer in those contexts).

Larsen-Freeman, D. (2013). Transfer of learning transformed. *Language Learning, 63* **(supplement 1), 107–129.**

Emphasizing the importance of transfer of L2 learning as an issue in the language sciences, this article examines the history of research on transfer of learning in general and of L2 learning more specifically. The article's main argument is that transfer should be viewed not as the export or re-use of intact L2 knowledge, but instead as the transformation of what has been learned. The article also recommends general techniques for teaching for transfer of L2 learning, including providing students with classroom activities that are similar to activities beyond the classroom, providing students with hints or reminders to transfer what they learn, having students work with multiple iterations of ideas and activities, and helping students to learn the process of adaptation (e.g., by providing them with feedback as they try).

James, M.A. (2014). Learning transfer in English-for-academic-purposes contexts: A systematic review of research. *Journal of English for Academic Purposes, 14,* **1–13.**

This article describes a systematic review of research in L2 education contexts from a teaching-for-transfer perspective. This review involved application of the transfer taxonomy (Barnett & Ceci, 2002), an analytic tool that focuses on key details in research findings, for example what kind of learning transferred and where and when this transfer occurred. This was the first application of the transfer taxonomy specifically to research on L2 teaching, and it involved using the taxonomy to analyze 41 studies of teaching in English-for-academic-purposes contexts. Results of this analysis showed that transfer in these contexts involved various kinds of learning (e.g., grammar, pronunciation, vocabulary) and occurred across varying "distances" (e.g., between situations that were very similar, and between situations that differed in important ways).

James, M.A. (2018). Teaching for transfer of L2 learning. *Language Teaching,* *51*, 330–348.

This article describes a historical timeline of scholarly work related to teaching for transfer of L2 learning. The timeline covers a period of over 100 years, beginning with the earliest published experimental research on learning transfer. The timeline includes descriptions of 51 sources, most of which are specific to L2 education but some of which are more general and provide broader context. The article also describes three major themes in the timeline: (a) transfer of L2 learning has continued to be seen as important to L2 teaching; (b) conceptualization of transfer of L2 learning has evolved; (c) understanding of teaching for transfer of L2 learning has expanded and become increasingly detailed.

References

Barnett, S. M., & Ceci, S. J. (2002). When and where do we apply what we learn?: A taxonomy for far transfer. *Psychological Bulletin, 128*, 612–637.

Detterman, D. K. (1993). The case for the prosecution: Transfer as an epiphenomenon. In D. K. Detterman & R. J. Sternberg (Eds.), *Transfer on trial: Intelligence, cognition, and instruction* (pp. 1–24). Ablex.

Haskell, R. E. (2001). *Transfer of learning: Cognition, instruction, and reasoning.* Academic Press.

James, M. A. (2009). "Far" transfer of learning outcomes from an ESL writing course: Can the gap be bridged? *Journal of Second Language Writing, 18*, 69–84.

James, M. A. (2018). Teaching for transfer of L2 learning. *Language Teaching, 51*, 330–348.

Larsen-Freeman, D. (2013). Transfer of learning transformed. *Language Learning, 63*(supplement 1), 107–129.

Long, M. (2015). *Second language acquisition and task-based language teaching.* Wiley-Blackwell.

Perkins, D. N., & Salomon, G. (1994). Transfer of learning. In T. Husen & T. N. Postlethwaite (Eds.), *The international encyclopedia of education* (2nd ed., Vol. 11, pp. 6452–6457). Pergamon.

Swales, J. M. (1990). *Genre analysis: English in academic and research settings.* Cambridge University Press.

Mark A. James is an associate professor of applied linguistics in the English department at Arizona State University. He has taught English-as-a-foreign/second-language and applied linguistics courses in a variety of contexts in Canada, Japan, Puerto Rico, and the USA. He is interested in curriculum, teaching, and learning issues in second language education in general, and his current research focuses on theoretical and practical aspects of learning transfer. His work in this area has been published in a variety of professional journals (e.g., *Journal of English for Academic Purposes, Language Teaching*), encyclopedias (e.g., *TESOL encyclopedia of English language teaching* (2017, Wiley)), and edited books (e.g., *Effective second language writing* (2010, TESOL)).

Jeff Siegel

Marginalized varieties are vernacular forms of language that are often considered to be "broken" or incorrect versions of the recognized standard language to which they are related. They include ethnic dialects (such as African American English), regional dialects (such as Liverpool English) and many creole languages (such as Hawai 'i Creole). Although marginalized varieties are as systematic and rule-governed as the standard, they are frequently dismissed as lazy or careless speech. Teaching speakers of these varieties in the formal education system presents many challenges.

In general, students who speak a marginalized variety are expected to acquire the standard school language, but without any specific instruction. The students' vernacular home language is ignored in the classroom and not used as a bridge to learning the standard. One rationale is that any reference to the students' existing linguistic knowledge would lead to linguistic interference (or "negative transfer"). Another is that it would waste valuable time that could be devoted solely to the standard. These views and other unfounded arguments against using marginalized varieties in the classroom have been frequently rebutted (e.g. Siegel, 2006). Nevertheless, when bridging programs are actually introduced, they are often met with ill-informed (and sometimes racist) resistance, for example with the Ebonics debate in the 1990s (Rickford, 2002).

The result is that students who come to school speaking a marginalized variety are truly disadvantaged in many ways. First, they have to learn how to read and write in the standard—a variety of language that differs significantly from their home language and learn content in subjects such as mathematics in this variety as well. Second, as they are often unaware of the subtler linguistic differences between their home language and the standard, they may become frustrated by constant correction and not being allowed to express themselves in the variety they feel

J. Siegel (✉)
Linguistics, University of New England, Armidale, NSW, Australia
e-mail: jsiegel@une.edu.au

© Springer Nature Switzerland AG 2021
H. Mohebbi and C. Coombe (eds.), *Research Questions in Language
Education and Applied Linguistics*, Springer Texts in Education,
https://doi.org/10.1007/978-3-030-79143-8_30

comfortable with. In many contexts they have to compete with classmates who speak varieties closer to the standard. Other disadvantages can arise from negative attitudes of teachers, who often know very little about their students' home language. For example, teachers may assume that students' errors are a result of carelessness or lack of intelligence rather than systematic differences between their home variety and the standard. There are also issues of social identity, as students may be averse to learning and using the standard because it is seen as closely associated with a different social group (see, for example, Fordham, 1999).

Various pedagogical approaches have been tried to alleviate some of these disadvantages. The **instrumental approach** uses the students' home variety as a medium of instruction to teach initial literacy and in some cases content subjects such as mathematics, science, and health. This approach has been implemented in creole-speaking contexts where all the students in the classroom are speakers of the same home variety, which is clearly distinguished from the standard. In the **accommodation approach**, marginalized varieties are accepted in the classroom to a limited extent. Students are given opportunities to speak or write in their home language, or their own interactional patterns and stories are utilized for teaching the standard. In the **awareness approach**, the students' home varieties are used as a resource for learning the standard and for education in general. Teaching programs using this approach have at least two of three components: accommodation, sociolinguistic and contrastive. The accommodation component includes the students' home language in the classroom in various ways, as in the approach of the same name. The sociolinguistic component introduces students to variation in language, the many different kinds of varieties that exist (such as types of dialects and creoles), and the history of their own way of speaking. The contrastive component involves students discovering the rule-governed nature and linguistic characteristics of their own varieties and how they differ from those of other students and from the standard. An advantage of the awareness approach is that it can be used in classrooms where students have a variety of linguistic backgrounds.

References to descriptions of, and research on, these various types of approaches can be found in works listed in the suggested resources.

The Research Questions

General questions. These questions focus on a teaching and learning context where students speak a particular marginalized variety at home. (Answering these questions will require some linguistic analysis, observation, and interviews with teachers and students.)

1. What are some of the linguistic and pragmatic differences between the marginalized variety and the standard variety to which it is related?
2. What are the attitudes of teachers to the marginalized variety and the students who speak it?

3. How familiar are teachers with the linguistic and pragmatic differences between the marginalized variety spoken by their students and the standard language?
4. What are the attitudes of speakers of the marginalized variety towards their own home language?
5. What are the attitudes of speakers of marginalized varieties towards the standard variety and its speakers?
7. Devise an experimental study similar to that of Fogel & Ehri (2000). How effective in learning the standard is contrasting its features with those of a marginalized variety?

Evaluations of approaches. These questions focus on the effectiveness of particular educational approaches for teaching students who speak a marginalized variety. (Answering these questions will require access to an existing program using one of the approaches or instituting a pilot program that does so. Again, observation and interviews will be necessary.)

8. How does the use of a particular approach (instrumental, accommodation, or awareness) affect the attitudes of teachers towards the marginalized variety and its speakers?
9. How does use of a particular approach (instrumental, accommodation, or awareness) affect the attitudes of students with regard to their own variety and the standard?
10. Is there any evidence that the use a of particular approach improves the educational experience and academic performance of speakers of a marginalized variety? (An example of evidence would be a comparison of students' results before and after the adoption of the approach.)

Reference

Fogel, H. & Linnea C. E. (2000). Teaching elementary students who speak Black Englih Vernacular to write in Standard English: Effects of dialect transformation practice. *Contemporary Educational Psychology* 25(2): 212–235.

Suggested Resources

Hart Blundon, P. (2016). Nonstandard Dialect and Educational Achievement: Potential Implications for First Nations Students. *Canadian Journal of Speech-Language Pcathology & Audiology, 40*(3). 218–231.

Focusing on the language of First Nations students in Canada, this article provides an excellent overview of the differences between a standard language or dialect and a marginalized variety (here referred to as a "nonstandard language variety/dialect"). It goes on to describe the issues relating to the educational achievement of students who speak nonstandard dialects.

Migge, B., Léglise, I. & Bartens, A. (2010). *Creoles in Education: An Appraisal of Current Programs and Projects*. **Amsterdam/Philadelphia: John Benjamins**.

Several chapters in this book describe instrumental programs using creoles to some extent as the medium of instruction and vehicle for learning initial literacy. Pilot or preliminary programs have been implemented in Jamaica, the Caribbean coast of Nicaragua and the islands of San Andres, Providence and Santa Catalina, which are part of Colombia. Evaluations of these programs all show that using the creole as the initial educational language has several benefits, including easier and quicker acquisition of literacy, more positive attitudes toward the creole among students and teachers, and, unexpectedly for many educators, better performance in the main language of education (English or Spanish). Other chapters describe established programs in the ABC Islands (Aruba, Bonaire and Curaçao) and northeastern Brazil where the creole is used as the medium of instruction. Projects in Hawai'i and French Guiana aim to raise awareness among educators and society in general about creoles and linguistic diversity.

Nero, S. J. (2006). *Dialects, Englishes, Creoles, and Education*. **Mahwah, NJ: Erlbaum**.

This edited volume contains chapters on teaching speakers of English-based creoles (Hawai'i, Jamaican), expanded pidgins (West African), African American English, World Englishes (Indian, Philippine, West African) and Hispanized English. The focus of several of the contributions is on teaching speakers of these varieties who have migrated to North America from other regions (the Caribbean, West Africa, India and the Philippines). Other contributions consider wider issues such as the reconceptualization of the field of English Language Teaching in general, the standard language ideology, power dynamics in the classroom, and the placement of students in appropriate language-teaching programs.

Yiakoumeti, A. (2012). *Harnessing Linguistic Variation to Improve Education (Rethinking Education, vol. 5)* **Bern: Peter Lang**.

This volume advocates the use of indigenous languages. minority languages, nonstandard varieties (regional, ethnic and social), and contact languages (pidgins and creoles) in formal education. Five of the chapters are specifically relevant to the issues and methodologies involved in teaching speakers of marginalized varieties. One is concerned with the teaching of World Englishes and advocates a language awareness approach. Two chapters deal with educational programs for speakers of indigenous ethnic dialects in Canada and Australia. Another chapter focuses on the benefits of bringing expanded pidgins and creoles into the classroom. The final chapter discusses uninformed popular views (or myths) about unstandardized dialects and their use in the education system.

Rickford, J. R., Sweetland, J., Rickford, A. & Grano. T. (2013). *African American, Creole, and Other Vernacular Englishes in Education: A Bibliographic Resource.* **New York: Routledge, and Urbana, IL: National Council of Teachers of English.**

This book is the ultimate bibliographic resource for anyone interested in research on educational issues concerning speakers of English-related marginalized varieties. It includes over 1600 references, each coded for a particular category of language variety: (1) African American English, (2) anglophone pidgins and creoles, (3) Asian and Asian American English, (4) Latino/a Englishes, (5) Native American English, and (6) other vernacular Englishes. Each entry is also coded for the specific topics it covers, including assessment and achievement; bidialectalism and contrastive analysis; culture and curriculum; [linguistic] features; ideology, attitudes and/or identity; controversies about vernacular Englishes in schools; language or dialect awareness approach; materials for instruction; reading; vernacular literacy or dialect readers; writing; strategies for instruction; and language transfer or interference. Coding is given for particular types of references, such as edited volumes, overviews, reviews or other bibliographies and video resources.

Siegel, J. (2010). *Second Dialect Acquisition.* **Cambridge: Cambridge University Press.**

This is the only book completely on the topic of acquiring an additional dialect, including the acquisition of standard dialects by speakers of creoles and unstandardized dialects. The first part of the book covers second dialect acquisition in naturalistic contexts. It discusses previous research in the area and some methodological issues. It also summarizes the individual and linguistic factors affecting acquisition, and the special difficulties that often make second dialect acquisition more difficult than second language acquisition. The remaining part of the book turns to classroom contexts. It discusses the obstacles faced by speakers of marginalized varieties in the formal education system and the arguments that have been made against special teaching programs for these speakers. The book goes on to describe various modern educational approaches that are being used to help students acquire the standard, and the results of evaluative research. The final chapter provides explanations for the research results and suggests a more critical approach.

References

Fordham, S. (1999). Dissin "the standard": Ebonics as guerrilla warfare at Capital High. *Anthropology & Education Quarterly, 30*(3), 272–293.

Rickford, J. R. (2002). Linguistics, education, and the Ebonics firestorm. In J. E. Alatis, H. E. Hamilton, & A.-H. Tan (Eds.), *Linguistics, language and the professions (Georgetown University round table on languages and linguistics, 2000)* (pp. 25–45). Georgetown University Press.

Siegel, J. (2006). Keeping creoles and dialects out of the classroom: Is it justified? In S. J. Nero (Ed.), *Dialects, Englishes, creoles, and education* (pp. 39–67). Erlbaum.

Jeff Siegel is Emeritus Professor in Linguistics at the University of New England in Australia, and a Fellow of the Australian Academy of Humanities. He is a member of the editorial boards of *Language in Society*, the *Journal of Pidgin and Creole Languages* and the *Journal of Portuguese and Spanish-lexified Creoles*. Jeff's main area of research has been on language contact, concentrating on the origins of pidgins, creoles and new dialects, and on the use of these varieties in formal education. Recently, he has changed his focus to language documentation, working on Nama, a Papuan language of southern New Guinea. He is author of *The Emergence of Pidgin and Creole Languages* (OUP, 2008) and *Second Dialect Acquisition* (CUP, 2010).

Teaching Suprasegmentals in English as a Lingua Franca Contexts

Christine Lewis and David Deterding

Nowadays, English is spoken more widely as a Lingua Franca around the world, between people who do not share a first language, than as a first language in places such as the UK and the USA; and the key concern of people involved in English as a Lingua Franca (ELF) communication is whether or not they are understood, so there is often little desire to adhere to native-speaker patterns of speech that do not have much impact on intelligibility.

Clearly, some features of pronunciation contribute to enhancing intelligibility more than others, but which features are important and which are not so crucial remains contentious. This particularly affects suprasegmental features, those aspects of pronunciation that extend beyond individual consonants and vowels. For example, it is uncertain how important the following features of speech are in achieving a high level of intelligibility in ELF contexts: standard patterns of word stress; stress-based rhythm; fluent linking of words; native-speaker intonational tones; and the placement of the intonational nucleus to signal key information. Research needs to be conducted on each of these features to determine how important it is for successful communication, so that guidance can be given to teachers in the ELF-based classroom about what they should focus on and what might be left for individual variation.

Particularly contentious is the role of word stress. While many teachers believe that word stress represents the fundamental framework on which the pronunciation of a word is built, others suggest that word stress is not important in ELF contexts, particularly with varieties of English in which there is little vowel reduction, so that the contrast between stressed and unstressed syllables may not be very salient. This needs to be investigated in a wide range of ELF contexts, and it seems likely that word stress will be found to be far more important in some contexts than in others.

One other area that needs substantial research is the teachability of various suprasegmental features. For example, it has been suggested that the rules for

C. Lewis (✉) · D. Deterding
Universiti Brunei Darussalam, Gadong, Brunei

© Springer Nature Switzerland AG 2021
H. Mohebbi and C. Coombe (eds.), *Research Questions in Language Education and Applied Linguistics*, Springer Texts in Education,
https://doi.org/10.1007/978-3-030-79143-8_31

lexical stress assignment are too complicated to be easily taught, yet at the same time, others suggest that the basic contrast between stressed and unstressed syllables can easily be learned. This needs further investigation. A related and vital question is how suprasegmental features of speech can best be taught.

As ELF-based teaching becomes increasingly accepted to ensure that learners of English can function successfully in the modern globalized world, such research questions take on fundamental importance. Currently, there is a paucity of advice based on solid research into suprasegmentals in ELF contexts, so it is hard to provide suitable support for innovative teachers who want to adopt ELF-based teaching. It is hoped that this gap in the research can soon be addressed.

The Research Questions

1. Which suprasegmental features are most important for the intelligibility of English and should take priority in the English as a Lingua Franca (ELF) classroom?
2. Which suprasegmental features are teachable in ELF settings?
3. To what extent do variations in word stress result in misunderstandings in ELF settings?
4. How can word stress patterns of English be taught in L1 cultures that have fixed-syllable word stress?
5. How do learners from a variety of L1 backgrounds hear prominence?
6. Which patterns of intonation are most important for ELF?
7. How essential is stress-timed rhythm for intelligibility in international contexts?
8. To what extent does vowel reduction contribute to the intelligibility of English? Should it be taught in the ELF classroom?
9. Which native-speaker fast-speech processes interfere with intelligibility and should possibly be only taught as receptive skills?
10. How does speech rate affect intelligibility in English in international settings? Should we teach our students to speak rapidly?

Suggested Resources

Jenkins, J. (2000). *The phonology of English as an international language.* **Oxford: Oxford University Press**.

This book is seminal in establishing priorities in ELF-based teaching, proposing a Lingua Franca Core of those features of pronunciation that are essential for international intelligibility while arguing that other features of English pronunciation do not need to be taught. The book suggests that word stress, intonational tunes, and stress-based rhythm are not essential for achieving a high level of intelligibility.

Cruttenden, A. (2014). *Gimson's pronunciation of English* **(8th ed.). London: Taylor and Francis.**

This classic volume, now in its 8th edition, continues to provide essential information about how English is actually pronounced. While it focuses on native-speaker accents, particularly those of the UK, it also offers advice to learners of English and concurs that not all features of native-speaker pronunciation need to be imitated, especially fast speech linking patterns that may result in the omission of consonants.

Celce-Murcia, M., Brinton, D. M., & Goodwin, J. M. (2010). *Teaching pronunciation: A course book and reference guide* **(2nd ed.). Cambridge, England: Cambridge University Press.**

This reference work combines the theoretical and practical aspects of teaching the pronunciation of North American English, including the instruction of suprasegmentals. Though focused on the North American context, the pedagogical suggestions and activities found in this guide can be explored and investigated in ELF contexts in future research.

Levis, J. M. (2018). *Intelligibility, oral communication, and teaching pronunciation.* **Cambridge, England: Cambridge University Press.**

This book evaluates intelligibility in pronunciation teaching and oral communication. It investigates the concept of intelligibility as well as research on the impact on intelligibility of various features of speech including word stress, rhythm and intonation, and it provides a substantial discussion research in classroom contexts.

Walker, R. (2010). *Teaching the pronunciation of English as a Lingua Franca.* **Oxford: Oxford University Press.**

There is a shortage of materials for teachers who want to pursue innovative ELF-based teaching, but this book provides an invaluable first step, offering practical advice for teachers, and, for example, emphasizing the importance of students accommodating to the needs of their listeners rather than attempting to adhere to irrelevant native-speaker norms of pronunciation.

Christine Lewis has an MA TESOL from San Francisco State University, and she is pursuing her PhD in Applied Linguistics at Universiti Brunei Darussalam. Her thesis focuses on the effects of innovative word stress on intelligibility in English as a Lingua Franca (ELF). This work has developed from her 15 years of experience teaching English pronunciation both in the U.S. and in ELF settings. She has published on pronunciation in ELF, World Englishes and globalisation, and also the pragmatics of ELF communication.

David Deterding is a visiting professor at Universiti Brunei Darussalam. His research focuses on the pronunciation of English in Southeast Asia, particularly Brunei, Singapore, Hong Kong and China, the intelligibility of English in international settings, and the pronunciation of indigenous Brunei languages. His most recent books have been on Brunei English (published by Springer) and misunderstandings in ELF (published by De Gruyter).

Translanguaging in Teaching/Learning Languages

32

Leslie Barratt

A major issue in language teaching is which languages are used in class. While early language teaching involved translating from the students' language to the target language (TL), later methods used only the TL. More recently, the pendulum has shifted back to permitting the student's language, usually the official language of instruction, but nowadays also home and local languages (Cummins, 2007; Mahboob & Lin, 2016). In this shift, translanguaging pedagogy has emerged as a promising approach for language teaching, particularly for teaching in multilingual contexts because it builds on a common practice of multilingual communities known as translanguaging.

Put simply, translanguaging can be described as people's multicompetence in all of their linguistic tools in their communication. As Canagarajah (2011:1) stated, "For multilinguals, languages are part of their repertoire that is accessed for their communicative purposes." Accordingly, a multilingual speaker might use only the single language common to all while interacting in monolingual contexts, but that same speaker could employ a much greater range of their linguistic repertoire in contexts where the interlocutors also speak the other languages. Further, individuals do not translanguage in a vacuum but translanguage in concert with other people who are also translanguaging to negotiate meaning. (Canagarajah, 2011). Hence, translanguaging is a social phenomenon as well as an individual one.

The strategic use of translanguaging in teaching, or translanguaging pedagogy, is promising in a constructivist framework for two reasons. First, constructivism involves starting where the learners are, i.e. with what they know and with their experiences. Teachers activate students' prior knowledge to teach new knowledge and skills. Whether learners are monolingual or multilingual, they already know and use at least one language. For the goal of adding an additional language,

L. Barratt (✉)
Languages, Literatures, & Linguistics, Indiana State University, Terre Haute, IN, USA
e-mail: Leslie.Barratt@indstate.edu

Roi Et Rajabhat University, Roi Et, Thailand

© Springer Nature Switzerland AG 2021   171
H. Mohebbi and C. Coombe (eds.), *Research Questions in Language Education and Applied Linguistics*, Springer Texts in Education,
https://doi.org/10.1007/978-3-030-79143-8_32

translanguaging pedagogy should be ideal since it scaffolds learners as they develop their linguistic repertoire for their own purposes. Translanguaging pedagogy also fits well with a second aspect of constructivism, that learning is a social activity because learners must test the knowledge they have constructed themselves with other people's knowledge, and this examination occurs through social interaction. Hence, the social nature of translanguaging leads educators naturally to consider translanguaging pedagogy.

Despite these reasons, translanguaging pedagogy is not common globally, nor is it taught in many teacher preparation programs, adopted by many educational systems, nor been examined extensively across varied contexts. Research is needed on how speakers negotiate the process of translanguaging, which translanguaging teaching and learning strategies are effective, and what attitudes stakeholders have toward translanguaging and translanguaged communication in order to ascertain how it can and should be employed in education.

The Research Questions

1. What translanguaging teaching techniques are effective for helping students enhance language skills, vocabulary, and/or grammar?
2. What translanguaging strategies do learners make use of? Which of these are effective?
3. Can translanguaging strategies be developed (i.e. taught and/or learned)?
4. How different is student achievement in the TL between using the home language, the language of instruction, all languages, and the TL only? (This could be a replication of Khanyakham, P. (2018). The Effect of Translanguaging Pedagogy for Vocabulary Learning. M. A. Thesis, Roi Et Rajabhat University. Paper in Proceedings of 2nd National and International Research Conference 2018: 2nd NIRC 2018, February, 2018, Buriram Rajabhat University).
5. To what extent will previously known languages (home, local, official, etc.) be strengthened when used as bridges to learn a TL?
6. How does translanguaging pedagogy affect learners' attitudes toward their ownership of the languages they use?
7. Does translanguaging pedagogy facilitate confidence, engagement, or WTC?
8. Does translanguaging pedagogy have an effect on metalinguistic awareness?
9. Does translanguaging pedagogy help literacy skills if the learners' languages have similar or different orthographic systems?
10. What kinds of assessment are useful in a translanguaging pedagogy model?

Suggested Resources

Canagarajah, S. (2011). Translanguaging in the Classroom: Emerging Issues for Research and Pedagogy. *Applied Linguistics Review* **2, 1–28**.

Much of Canagarajah's work is relevant to researchers of translanguaging. However, this article can serve as an overall introduction to translanguaging and to the research that has been conducted and could be conducted on the subject. Canagarajah presents a broad view of the translanguaging from various disciplines and introduces the alternative terminology used in those fields as well. His critical analysis of previous scholarship will benefit those who research this topic. Also, extremely useful is his discussion of the areas that have lacked scholarship and need to be studied, such as the process of translanguaging (rather than the product), the strategies and possible stages in the process, how translanguaging operates in non-face-to-face genres, such as in writing and in social media, and people's attitudes toward translanguaging. Finally, Canagarajah provides a case study that examined how one writer navigated the process of translanguaging.

Creese & Blackledge (2010). Translanguaging in the Bilingual Classroom: A Pedagogy for Learning and Teaching? *The Modern Language Journal* **94, 103–115**.

In this article the authors describe four "interlocking case studies" that examined multilingual schools, the complementary or community language schools, across various cities in the UK. The research investigated how bilingualism operated in these schools and, in particular how translanguaging was enacted as a bilingual pedagogy. The extracts and analyses afterwards clearly demonstrate how speakers use their full linguistic repertoire to create an inclusive social situation as well as to convey meaning to their audience. Examples also illustrate how teachers and students negotiate language use and identities in a language lesson. In addition to the research findings, this article is also valuable for its brief discussion of various bilingual approaches that preceded translanguaging pedagogy as well as its summary of insights and skills developed in a translanguaging classroom.

Garcia, L. Ibarra Johnson, S. & K. Seltzer. (2017). *The Translanguaging Classroom: Leveraging Student Bilingualism for Learning.* **Philadelphia: Caslon Publishing**.

Many works by Ofelia Garcia will be useful to researchers of translanguaging. Although this book was written as a guide for teachers or pre-service teachers in how to develop their translanguaging pedagogy practice, it also would be useful to the researcher. Anyone who wants to understand how theories of language acquisition support translanguaging pedagogy will benefit from reading the first two chapters, and those who plan to conduct classroom research will find the entire work an invaluable resource for the study because of its clear explication of the authors' instructional design cycle, the lesson plans, the dynamic assessment process, the teacher stance, and the teaching strategies. In addition, the supplemental materials and activities at the end of each chapter encourage reflection and may thus assist those who are trying to narrow their research questions.

MacSwan, J. (2017). A Multilingual Perspective on Translanguaging. *American Educational Research Journal 54*(1), 167–201. https://doi.org/10.3012/0002831216683935.

This article provides a critical examination of the literature on the nature of translanguaging and counters the prevailing viewpoint that multilinguals have a unitary system in their mental model rather than separate grammars for each named language. MacSwan uses examples from scholarship on code-switching, bilingualism, and neurolinguistics to argue that the research in these latter fields points to differentiation of languages even among young bilinguals. In this article, MacSwan proposes an alternative mental model, a "multilingual perspective on translanguaging." He suggests further that codeswitching is an instance of translanguaging and concludes with various benefits of translanguaging pedagogy. In addition to providing an alternative view of translanguaging theory, this article also includes many sources in the text and reference list.

2016 Special issue of Journal of Language, Identity & Education (**Volume 16 Number 4**).

This special issue contains six articles on translanguaging pedagogy. First, Cenoz provides an overview of trends in translanguaging theory and translanguaging pedagogy. She also proposes a difference between pedagogical translanguaging and spontaneous translanguaging. The next two articles both report on using translanguaging to promote bilingualism and to protect minority languages: Jones studied protecting Welsh from English while Leonet, Cenoz, and Gorter studied protecting Basque from Spanish and English. Next, Lin and He examined the natural translanguaging that occurs in a content and language integrated learning (CLIL) classroom in Hong Kong with minority students and discuss the implications for CLIL. Garcia-Mateus and Palmer also consider minority language students, but their research concerns identity. Their results indicate that translanguaging helped develop bilingual identities as well as metalinguistic awareness. Finally, Garcia discusses the theoretical basis for translanguaging pedagogy and argues that language policies must be flexible to promote multilingualism.

References

Canagarajah, S. (2011). Translanguaging in the classroom: Emerging issues for research and pedagogy. *Applied Linguistics Review, 2,* 1–28.

Cummins, J. (2007). Rethinking monolingual instructional strategies in multilingual classrooms. *Canadian Journal of Applied Linguistics, 10,* 221–240.

Mahboob, A., & Lin, A. (2016). Using local languages in English language classrooms. In W. H. Renandya & H. P. Widodo (Eds.), *English language teaching today: Building a closer link between theory and practice.* Springer.

Leslie Barratt is Professor Emerita of Linguistics at Indiana State University. Professor Barratt taught at Indiana State University (1980–2015), first in the English Department and then in the Department of Languages, Literatures, and Linguistics, which she chaired. With graduate degrees in linguistics and education, she has taught in various contexts, including K-12, intensive ESL, undergraduate and graduate linguistics, ESL/EFL, and TESL. She taught as a Fulbright Senior Lecturer in Hungary (1987–88) and China (1995–96) and as Professor at Roi-Et Rajabhat University (2015–18). Her research spans World Englishes, language acquisition and loss, language teaching, linguistic universals, on-going changes in English, and linguistic differences. As a lifelong language learner, Dr. Barratt is particularly interested in any aspect of language change or variation that causes difficulty for learners.

Translanguaging with SLIFE Students for More Inclusive Teaching

33

Eileen N. Whelan Ariza

Consciously or unconsciously, multilinguals use their entire linguistic repertoire while communicating. This phenomenon is "translanguaging," a "theoretical lens that offers a different view of bilingualism and multilingualism" (Vogel & García, 2017, p.1). Bilinguals use languages separately and switch from one language to another during discourse when "codeswitching." Translanguaging encourages multilinguals to use all language skills to communicate in academic or linguistic activities. (Garcia & Wei, 2014). By separating two specific cognitive tasks, students can focus on one cognitive process at a time (Ariza, 2018) and then determine which language will be used to express those thoughts.

Worldwide, students migrate due to poverty, war, disasters or gender discrimination (females prohibited from attending school). Students escape from great challenges, seeking life in more stable countries, and may not receive adequate education (e.g. secondary education). Students with limited or interrupted formal education (SLIFE) have nonexistent, limited or interrupted formal education (DeCapua, 2016). Students lack basic literacy in home languages, presenting serious problems in the new classroom with foreign vocabulary and English script. Basic academic skills and instruction are needed for accelerated learning. Although lacking traditional academic preparation, students have life skills that include intensive decision-making from exposure to global issues. Mainstream teachers can incorporate inclusive teaching strategies that provide differentiated instruction for diverse learners. (Mastropieri & Scruggs, 2010). Teachers should provide accommodation strategies and scaffolding techniques to connect learning for all students with different languages and varying levels of academic proficiency.

E. N. W. Ariza (✉)
Department of Teaching and Learning, College of Education, Florida Atlantic University, Boca Raton, FL, USA
e-mail: EARIZA@fau.edu; eariza@fau.edu

© Springer Nature Switzerland AG 2021
H. Mohebbi and C. Coombe (eds.), *Research Questions in Language Education and Applied Linguistics*, Springer Texts in Education,
https://doi.org/10.1007/978-3-030-79143-8_33

Translanguaging builds background knowledge, deepens understanding, critical thinking, and uses the home language to bridge learning the target language. (Garcia & Wei, 2014). Strategies include using native languages in collaborative grouping, multilingual texts, stories, word walls with multiple languages, cognates, native language brainstorming, and other tactics promoting crosslinguistic transfer and conversation. Visuals and graphic organizers promote decoding skills. Scaffolding techniques help differentiate and accommodate a variety of diverse learners and include sentence starters, story maps, word webs, KWL charts, templates and organization graphics. By using pedagogical devices, teachers help clarify academic expectations that provide inclusive educational practices for learners of all levels of language and academic proficiencies.

The Research Questions

1. Based on the standard definition of translanguaging, describe the literacy practices that you have implemented with the emerging bilingual or multilinguals to ensure meaningful instruction in your learning environment. What are your findings?
2. SLIFE students need to be served linguistically and academically, and are central members of your classroom. What are at least three recognized characteristics of this population of learners, and describe how you will implement at least three strategies to advance their language skills, using their current linguistic knowledge and abilities. Keep a record of your techniques, strategies, and results. As a result of your findings, what will you change or implement?
3. Classroom teachers need to know about the processes of translanguaging and what students can do to best learn, using the knowledges they already possess. Upon watching an assigned video of a bilingual teacher in the emerging bilingual classroom:

   a. Describe how you would integrate translanguaging into the Morning Message
   b. Describe how you would engage the emerging bilingual/multilingual in your reading groups.
   c. Describe how you would engage the emerging bilingual/multilingual student in project-based learning activities.
   d. Describe how you would use the student's first language to help interpret meaning for the additional language/s?
   e. Chart your strategies and graph your findings.

4. Scenario: You and your colleagues are attending a school-wide meeting where your building administrator has informed you that 10 SLIFE students will be enrolled in your school next year. Many of the teachers feel unprepared to meet the needs of these students. One of your assigned "service" responsibilities has been to work with these students. How will you assist your peer teachers to address the needs of these new students? What will you teach the teachers about how they can use translanguaging to take advantage of their students' previous language knowledge? How will you be able to evaluate the progress that students will make?

5. In the schools where you serve, what do you theorize will be the most effective translanguaging strategies you could implement? Describe the implementation used in your content/subject area, and share the findings.

6. There are many barriers to teaching SLIFE students. Translanguaging offers support for students because students already possess multiple repertoires of language knowledge that they can use to make sense of literacy in the home and the target language. Describe how your professional development and tacit knowledge of translanguaging have prepared you to succeed in teaching learners in your own classroom, or a class that you are observing. Share your findings.

7. What specific knowledge, skills, and competencies do teachers need to possess to use translanguaging in their instruction, and describe why you believe they are necessary for effective instruction for emerging bilingual learners? Based on your knowledge of skills, competencies, and best practices to assist SLIFE students, describe that steps that are needed to create a learning environment which will best serve these students. Show evidence.

8. What is inclusive teaching and what issues will inclusive teaching address within a translanguaging environment? Observe a classroom of English learners where students receive inclusive remedies. What practices are included in the daily classroom, and what appear to be the most successful strategies for inclusive teaching? Describe what you are seeing or doing, for what reasons, and provide a summary of successes or failures.

9. Classrooms where students are from different countries and possess different literacy and academic levels in the home languages present unique learning problems. How can you determine the knowledge students come with when they arrive at your classroom? What strategies could you implement to support L1 (the home language) that will interface with the target language?

10. Based on your knowledge of skills, competencies, and best practices to assist students who do not know the language/s of instruction, or academic content in either the home language or the target language, how will you create a learning environment which will best serve these students? How can you best assess learning gains? Describe your findings.

Suggested Resources

Allard, E. C. (2017). Re-examining teacher translanguaging: An ecological perspective. *Bilingual Research Journal*, *40*(2), 116–130. https://doi.org/10.1080/15235882.2017.1306597.

Translanguaging is a practice that multilingual people use when they utilize their entire linguistic repertoire to make sense out of the target language. Research shows that these practices can offer pedagogical assistance resulting in successful classroom instruction. This paper reports on an ethnographic study carried out by two teachers in a suburban ESOL program. Results showed that the participation and academic performance of ELs improved due to this infusion of translanguaging strategies but contradictions appeared in the interpersonal arena. The author suggests that the most successful way to exploit the benefits of translanguaging are when they are connected to practices that support multilingualism inside and outside the classroom.

Cenoz, J. (2017). Translanguaging in school contexts: International perspectives. *Journal of Language, Identity & Education*, *16*(4), 193–198. https://doi.org/10.1080/15348458.2017.1327816.

This special issue examines the development of translanguaging and the differences between .translanguaging and codeswitching within the study of bilingualism and multilingualism. Different contexts determine how bilingual and multilingual education occur. Pedagogical translanguaging and spontaneous translanguaging are discussed and the differences are explained as specific teaching strategies in the classroom versus discursive practices that bilingual and multilingual speakers employ during conversation. The studies described in this issue highlight instructional differences students have and discuss the need for differentiated instruction to reach the individual multilingual and bilingual learner in international perspectives.

DeCapua, A. (2016). Reaching students with limited or interrupted formal education through culturally responsive teaching. *Language and Linguistics Compass*, *10*(5), 225–237.

This article addressed the beliefs, values, norms, and ways of thinking concerning students with limited or interrupted formal education (SLIFE) with the aim of teaching in a culturally responsive manner. SLIFE students come from countries where the education in the home language might have been incomplete due to war, strife, unrest, or inability to attend school. They arrive in the new country lacking adequate academic preparation in their own languages and are expected to learn in the target language. The author suggests that knowing the cultural backgrounds of the students can inform curriculum and pedagogical practices that will best serve the needs of SLIFE students, who differ greatly from the typical English learner.

Garcia, O & Kleyn, T. (Ed.). (2016). *Translanguaging with multilingual students: Learning from classroom moments.* **New York, NY: Routledge.**

This book looks at the kind of linguistic behaviors taking place in classrooms today. Six empirical ethnographies are presented in this book, using a Transformative Action Research design. They show how translanguaging techniques are used in lesson planning to determine how, when, and why translanguaging is used, or not used, in the American classroom context. The studies are based on schools in New York, but the authors try to link the findings and theories to a more global perspective so that teachers worldwide can use these types of pedagogical techniques for emerging bilinguals and multilinguals.

Santamaria, L. J. (2009). Culturally responsive differentiated instruction: Narrowing gaps between best pedagogical practices benefiting all learners. *Teachers College Record, 111***(1), 214–247.**

This publication reports findings on a 5-year qualitative study of data derived from observations, teacher conversations, administrators, students, and parents in two elementary schools in San Diego County, California, to determine how to create differentiated instructions for culturally and linguistically diverse (CLD) learners. The schools are high achieving, academically sound, and were chosen specifically to dispel myths about high levels of poverty and low English proficient students leading to lower student achievement. Findings show that best teaching practices consider all learners in a classroom setting and considerations must be made for differences inherent to academic, cultural, linguistic, and socioeconomic diversity.

References

Ariza, E. N. W. (2018). *Not for ESOL teachers: What every classroom teacher needs to know about the linguistically, culturally, and ethnically diverse student* (3rd ed.). Kendall/Hunt Publishing.

DeCapua, A. (2016). Reaching students with limited or interrupted formal education through culturally responsive teaching. *Language and Linguistics Compass, 10*(5), 225–237.

García, O., & Wei, L. (2014). *Translanguaging: Language, bilingualism and education.* Palgrave Macmillan.

Mastropieri, M. A., & Scruggs, T. E. (2010). *The inclusive classroom: Strategies for effective differentiated instruction.* Merrill.

Vogel, S., & García, O. (2017). Translanguaging. In G. Noblit (Ed.), *Oxford research encyclopedia of education* (pp. 1–21). Oxford University Press.

Eileen   N.   Whelan   Ariza   Ed.D., Multilingual/Multicultural Education, UMass, Amherst; MATESOL, Spanish, Bilingual/Multicultural Ed, School of International Training, Brattleboro, Vermont. Teaching Fellow, Harvard University; Professor, Florida Atlantic University. Fulbright Scholar, Mexico, Costa Rica, and Malta, also Fulbright Alumni Ambassador. Researches ESOL, USA and overseas, cross-cultural communication, and preparation of mainstream teachers teaching English learners. Ariza has won multiple teaching awards, authored/co-authored several popular textbooks (*Not for ESOL teachers: What every classroom teacher needs to know about the linguistically, culturally, and ethnically diverse student.* [3nd Ed]; *Why TESOL? Theories and issues in teaching English as a second language for K-12 teachers* (5th Ed.), and *Fundamentals of teaching English to speakers of other languages in K-12 mainstream classrooms*, (4th Ed), Dubuque, IA: Kendall/Hunt, and over 85 peer reviewed publications.

World Englishes, English as a Lingua Franca and ELT

34

Paola Vettorel

Research into Global Englishes, comprising World Englishes (WE) and English as a Lingua Franca (ELF), has amply shown how complex the plurality of English has become today. As to WE, on the one hand we have native (ENL) varieties that have developed out of the first diaspora and are part of Kachru's Inner Circle. On the other hand, we have Outer Circle varieties, that are linked to colonization processes and to the second diaspora; here English constitutes a second language (ESL) and coexists with the local ones; these varieties are thus characterised by nativisation processes operating territorially.

Nowadays migration fluxes, technological developments, the media and digital communication entail that contact with different English*es* takes place alongside its extended use as a lingua franca of communication, beyond and across traditional speech community boundaries.

English as a Lingua Franca (ELF) refers to the use of English as a contact language among speakers belonging to different linguacultures and speaking different mother tongues (Seidlhofer, 2011). Research into ELF has thrived over the last decades, with three main phases of development: in the 1990s the main aim was to identify the linguistic elements characterizing ELF as a potential variety; in the 2000s the focus shifted onto the pragmatic factors that lead to effective communication in complex, hybrid and fluid ELF settings. More recently, ELF is seen as part of multilingual and translanguaging frameworks (e.g. Jenkins, 2015).

The pedagogical implications of WE and ELF have been a widely investigated area, with a growing body of literature from several contexts (e.g. Bowles & Cogo, 2015; Sifakis & Tsantila, 2019). Research has focused above all on teacher education, materials evaluation and classroom practices. Teacher education has been identified as a fundamental step to foster awareness of the current sociocultural diversity of use, users and contexts for World Englishes and ELF, essential to

P. Vettorel (✉)
Department of Foreign Languages and Literatures, University of Verona, Verona, Italy
e-mail: paola.vettorel@univr.it

© Springer Nature Switzerland AG 2021
H. Mohebbi and C. Coombe (eds.), *Research Questions in Language Education and Applied Linguistics*, Springer Texts in Education,
https://doi.org/10.1007/978-3-030-79143-8_34

promote critical reflection upon current ENL-based pedagogical models. Developing such critical awareness would foster the inclusion of a WE- and ELF-aware perspective both in ELT materials and in devising WE/ELF-aware activities (e.g. Sifakis et al., 2018). In course-book evaluation, criteria would focus on: awareness-raising and WE and ELF-related activities (characters/settings, sociolinguistic variation, plurilingual speakers/repertoires); promotion of the use of English in outside-school environments; communication and intercultural strategies; different perspectives on culture(s), including the learners' one(s). Classroom practices should include 'authentic' WE and ELF materials, such as audio and video resources available on the web and promote opportunities for communication with peers in international settings, for example through telecollaboration.

The Research Questions

1. How have World Englishes and English as a Lingua Franca contributed to problematizing 'traditional' SLA assumptions (e.g. the native speaker model)?
2. In what ways, and in which contexts, can English as a 'multilingua franca' be observed?
3. In what ways, and to what aims, is creativity in language use exploited in WE and in ELF?
4. Are examples, and experiences, of WE and ELF present in your teaching/learning context?
5. What are the implications of WE and ELF for teacher education?
6. What are the implications of WE and ELF for classroom practices?
7. What are the implications of WE and ELF for ELT materials?
8. In what ways can WE and ELF be integrated into ELT classroom practices?
9. What pedagogical implications do WE and ELF have for communicative competence?
10. What implications do WE and ELF have for intercultural communicative competence?

Suggested Resources

Bayyurt, Y., and Akcan S. (eds). (2015). *Current perspectives on pedagogy for English as a Lingua Franca.* **Berlin: Mouton de Gruyter**.

This collection of essays covers major areas in the implications of ELF for ELT, from 'teaching and learning' to teacher education, assessment and materials. Data and case studies in different contexts—from primary to tertiary education in Europe and elsewhere—provide evidence for the importance of taking ELF research findings into account in pedagogic practices. The studies also show how

ELF-informed teacher education plays a fundamental and pivotal role in familiar-izing pre- and in-service teachers with the complex reality of ELF, and thus in encouraging them to develop critical innovative ELF-aware pedagogic practices. Alternative, ELF-aware ways to carry out language assessment are also discussed, based on functional competence in authentic ELF contexts, rather than on formal ENL accuracy. The importance of developing critical reflection on ELT materials with teachers is also set forward, one that takes account of intercultural ELF communication.

Matsuda, A. (ed). (2017). *Preparing teachers to teach English as an interna-tional language.* **Bristol: Multilingual Matters.**

The contributions in this volume deal with a range of possibilities and ideas to incorporate EIL-informed practices in teacher education and TESOL programmes, providing several pedagogic ideas from research in the areas of World Englishes, Global Englishes and English as a Lingua Franca. After a section on theoretical frameworks, the book presents descriptions of teacher preparation programmes and courses that are wholly or partly based on an EIL-informed perspective. The experiences are set in different geographical and educational contexts, thus pro-viding a varied range of proposals to draw upon for other settings, too. The last section consists of fifteen lessons and activities related to teacher education for both L1 and L2 users, that can equally be integrated into, or adapted for, other contexts, either as awareness-raising moments or as integral parts of a course.

Seildhofer, B. (2011). *Understanding English as a Lingua Franca.* **Oxford: Oxford University Press.**

Seidlhofer's book examines the global development of English as a Lingua Franca in its complexity. ELF is conceptualized as 'any use of English among speakers of different first languages for whom English is the communicative medium of choice' (p. 7), including native and non-native speakers communicating in intercultural contexts. Given its widespread lingua franca role, the need for a reconceptualization of English is called for throughout the chapters, discussing issues like 'assumptions and presumptions' about English, standard language ideologies and 'real' English, ownership in relation to (non)nativeness and variation. Form and function and how the 'virtual language' is creatively exploited in ELF are then discussed and illus-trated with examples of ELF usage from the VOICE corpus. After looking into ELF misconceptions, the pedagogical implications of ELF are discussed, with a call for the need to rethink native-like competence, processes and aims in teaching and learning 'English', starting from teacher education.

Sifakis, N.C., and Tsantila, N. (eds). (2019). *English as a Lingua Franca for EFL contexts.* **Bristol: Multilingual Matters.**

This edited volume presents a comprehensive view on pedagogical perspectives on ELF, with contributions from outstanding scholars in the field. After a 'Founda-tions' section setting the theoretical framework, ELF in ELT pedagogy, materials, teacher education and assessment are examined, taking a variety of contexts into account. The essays included in the different sections present innovative perspectives on different, important aspects in the pedagogy of ELF. A particularly interesting element is the way in which the chapters are structured, from the initial expected outcomes to the research questions guiding the reader into active reflection on the issues that are set forward; the research questions in particular can constitute an effective means to support reflection and contextualization in the readers' own educational settings. The volume thus represents a welcome addition to the implementation of ELF pedagogy.

References

Bowles, H., & Cogo, A. (Eds.). (2015). *International perspectives on English as a lingua franca. Pedagogical insights*. Palgrave Macmillan.

Jenkins, J. (2015). Repositioning English and multilingualism in English as a lingua franca. *Englishes in Practice, 2*(3), 49–85.

Seidlhofer, B. (2011). *Understanding English as a lingua franca*. Oxford University Press.

Sifakis, N. C., & Tsantila, N. (Eds.). (2019). *English as a lingua franca for EFL contexts*. Multilingual Matters.

Sifakis, N. C., Lopriore, L., Dewey, M., Bayyurt, Y., Vettorel, P., Cavalheiro, L., Siqueira, S. P., & Kordia, S. (2018). ELF-awareness in ELT: Bringing together theory and practice. *Journal of English as a Lingua Franca, 7*(1), 179–184.

Paola Vettorel is assistant professor in the Department of Foreign Languages and Literatures—University of Verona. Her main research interests include ELF and its implications in ELT. Among her publications: (2014) *English as a Lingua Franca in wider networking. Blogging Practices*. Berlin: De Gruyter Mouton; (2015) (ed.) *New frontiers in teaching and learning English*. Newcastle-upon-Tyne: Cambridge Scholars; (2016) WE- and ELF-informed classroom practices: proposals from a pre-service teacher education programme in Italy. *Journal of English as a Lingua Franca* 5/1; (2018) ELF and Communication Strategies: Are they taken into account in ELT materials? *RELC Journal* 49/1; (2019) Communication strategies and co-construction of meaning in ELF: Drawing on "Multilingual Resource Pools", *Journal of English as a Lingua Franca* 8(2).

Part II
Learners and Learning-related Topics

María del Pilar García Mayo

Shehadeh (2018: viii) has recently mentioned that Task-based language teaching (TBLT) research (Ellis et al., 2020) has expanded in scope to new boundaries, one of which being TBLT in foreign language contexts. A foreign language (FL) context is one where the teaching of the language other than the learner's native language takes place in the learner's own country, mostly as a school subject. So far, numerous studies have been carried out within a TBLT framework with adults in second language (L2) and FL contexts (Long, 2015) and with children in English as a Second Language (ESL) contexts (Oliver, 2008) but only recently has research being devoted to children in FL contexts (García Mayo, 2018; Shehadeh, 2018).

The early learning of English as a FL in school settings has grown tremendously in the past twenty years (Enever, 2018; Pinter, 2011), with estimated figures of half a billion primary-aged children around the world, as reported by Ellis and Knagg (2013). One of the reasons put forward by governments is that their citizens should have a good command of the FL in order to compete in a globalized world. They have extrapolated the successful findings in immersion settings (Lyster, 2007), where the earlier is usually the better, to FL contexts where conditions are clearly different regarding the number of pupils per classroom, exposure to appropriate input and curriculum time available (Huang, 2016).

There is a real need to chart the territory, to study what actually happens in real classroom contexts in order to advance the agenda on child FL learning, which, together with child second language (L2) learning, should be studied in its own right (Oliver & Azkarai, 2017). Findings from this population will help to make decisions about appropriate educational provision, to inform policy makers and to maximize children's learning opportunities. As Johnstone (2009:38) put it "Simply

M. d. P. García Mayo (✉)
Departamento de Filología Inglesa, Universidad del País Vasco (UPV/EHU),
Vitoria-Gasteiz, Spain
e-mail: mariapilar.garciamayo@ehu.eus

© Springer Nature Switzerland AG 2021
H. Mohebbi and C. Coombe (eds.), *Research Questions in Language
Education and Applied Linguistics*, Springer Texts in Education,
https://doi.org/10.1007/978-3-030-79143-8_35

to assume that all will be well just because the starting age has been lowered is a recipe for confusion."

A task is an instructional activity that requires a primary focus on meaning (Ellis, 2018), which makes it a particularly interesting pedagogical tool for children because there are certain capacities that they bring to the language classroom such as the ability to grasp meaning by drawing on paralinguistic features (intonation, gesture and facial expressions), their willingness to focus on communication rather than accuracy and their instinct for play and fun and for interaction and talk (Halliwell, 1992; Philp et al., 2008). Recent research with English as a foreign language (EFL) children has been carried out mainly from cognitive and socio-cultural perspectives and has shown that young learners (i) negotiate for meaning with age- and proficiency-matched peers, (ii) focus on formal aspects of the FL without the teacher's intervention; (ii) rely on their L1 to a lesser extent the younger they are, and (iv) display more collaborative patterns when they repeat the same type of task (García Mayo, 2018).

More research is clearly needed, and is being carried out, on child task-based language learning but we should be aware of the challenges ahead such as the difficulty of accessing schools and ethical issues (informed consent) related to doing research with this young population (García Mayo, 2021), and the importance of teacher training in task-based language lessons, among others.

The Research Questions

1. Does learning setting play a role in the FL context? Specifically, are there any differences between the oral and written production of children enrolled in mainstream FL programs (3–4 h of weekly exposure to the foreign language) and those in Content and Language Integrated (CLIL) programs (with many more hours of weekly exposure)?
2. What are the main conversational adjustments that children use when completing communicative tasks?
3. What role does task repetition play? Does it foster attention to formal aspects of the language by children? Is there any difference between same-task and procedural task repetition?
4. Does pre-task planning have any impact on children's attention to formal aspects of the language?
5. What role do individual differences (engagement, motivation, working memory) play in child task-based interaction?
6. What is the oral-written connection in child task-based interaction? That is, does child oral interaction in collaborative tasks play a role when the children have to produce written output? In other words, is there any transfer of knowledge from language-related episodes correctly resolved in oral interaction to the children's written production?

7. Does corrective feedback in the form of models and/or reformulations benefit children's oral and written output?
8. What types of dyadic patterns are established by children in task-based interaction? Are they influenced by pair-formation methods (proficiency-paired vs. self-selected)?
9. How can teachers best be trained to use tasks with young children in FL contexts?
10. How can we improve teacher-researcher collaboration?

Suggested Resources

Pinter, A. (2011). *Children Learning Second Languages.* **New York: Palgrave McMillan**.

In this book Annamaria Pinter provides a rationale for the focus on children's second language (L2) learning and shows similarities and differences compared to the L2 process by adult language learners. The main aim of the volume is " […] to illustrate a variety of contexts where languages are learnt in childhood, to discuss links between existing research on child second language learning and classroom practice, and to enable practitioners to carry out their locally based research" (p. 1). The book consists of four sections. In the first one Pinter provides a background to child L2 acquisition and pedagogy (theories of child development, first and second language learning processes and contexts for language acquisition in childhood). The second section presents an overview of findings from research studies and the third advances issues in future research and practice. Finally, section four features numerous resources in child second language acquisition and pedagogy. The book is a very good introduction to this field of study and highlights interesting research lines and pedagogical applications.

Murphy, V.A. (2014). *Second Language Learning in the Early School Years: Trends and Contexts*. **Oxford: Oxford University Press**.

This volume has a twofold purpose. On the one hand, Victoria Murphy reviews the major issues that emerge from research investigating the development of L2 learning in childhood across a range of contexts. Thus, each chapter of the book focuses on one of those contexts, namely: bilingual development in young children, heritage language learners, minority language learners, majority language learners (immersion education) and, finally, instructed foreign language learning in primary school. A second aim is to consider the notion that 'younger is better' for L2 learning in each of those contexts. Chapter 6, focusing on foreign language learning in primary school, considers policy issues in different countries that have lowered the age at which foreign language instruction is introduced (Japan, Turkey, France, Vietnam and China, among others), how these decisions have been implemented and a range of different types of FL outcomes ("competence in and progression of the FL, motivation and attitudes toward the FL, effect of the FL on aspects of the L1, individual or learner characteristics which influence FL learner, and how FL instruction impacts on the teacher.") (p. 142).

García Mayo, M.P. (ed.) (2017). *Learning Foreign Languages in Primary School. Research Insights*. **Bristol: Multilingual Matters.**

The main aim of the volume is to advance the research agenda on child foreign language learning in order to contribute to studies on child L2 acquisition theory building, improve methodologies for this population (ages 6–12) and inform stakeholders. The twelve chapters in this volume report on research conducted in primary schools with 11 of the 12 papers focused on learners of English as a foreign language, thus reflecting the global trend for early introduction of English in school settings. All the contributions contain data gathered from primary school children while performing different tasks, answering questionnaires or providing feedback on diagnostic tests. The first languages of the children are Chinese, English, Hungarian, Persian and Spanish and, except for the data reported in one of the chapters where the children were exposed to Esperanto, French, German and Italian, the L2 learned as a foreign language was always English. The following topics are dealt with in the volume: the influence of learner characteristics on word retrieval, explicit L2 learning and language awareness, meaning construction, narrative oral development, conversational interaction, L1 use, feedback on written production, intercultural awareness raising and feedback on diagnostic assessment.

Enever, J. & Lindgren, E. (eds.) (2017). *Early Language Learning. Complexity and Mixed Methods*. **Bristol: Multilingual Matters.**

This volume comprises fifteen chapters with data from children in different instructional contexts such as English as an additional language (EAL), English as a second or foreign language (L2/FL), French as a modern foreign language (MFL) and content and language integrated learning (CLIL) classrooms in fourteen different countries. Among the issues considered in the contributions are individual differences (age, motivation, working memory capacity), conversational adjustments, language development and assessment of children's output. The editors write the introduction and the conclusions and reflect on the potential contribution of mixed-methods research for the field of early language learning. Considering the dynamic nature of the learning process, they also emphasize the need to charter young learners' progress longitudinally and to analyze data from a multidisciplinary perspective.

Enever, J. (2018*). Policy and Politics in Global Primary English*. **Oxford: Oxford University Press.**

Anyone interested in the complexities of policy making in the introduction of English as a foreign language at both pre-primary and primary levels worldwide should read this book. Organized in two parts, the first part explores the rapid growth of English as the language of choice in foreign language pre-primary and primary school contexts and focuses on the global forces that shape this tendency.

The second part addresses broad social issues that can be identified as influencing the growth of English in the pre-primary and primary years (regional policies, global forces in assessment, accountability and transparency). The book displays very informative figures of the thirteen countries to which the different schools examined belong: Chile, China (Shanghai), Colombia, Germany, India, Italy, Poland, Portugal, Slovenia, Spain, Sweden, Uruguay and Vietnam. It also examines numerous issues such as the importance of good quality exposure to the foreign language, teacher training, commitment and support from schools and governmental bodies, development of age-appropriate classroom materials, avoidance of high-stakes assessment, development of positive attitudes and motivation, and integration of other languages in multilingual environments.

References

Ellis, R. (2018). *Reflections on task-based language teaching*. Multilingual Matters.

Ellis, G., & Knagg, J. (2013). British council signature event: Global issues in primary ELT. In T. Pattison (Ed.), *IATEFL, 2012 Glasgow conference selections* (pp. 20–21). IATEFL Publications.

Ellis, R., Skehan, P., Li, S., Shintani, N., & Lambert, C. (2020). *Task-based language teaching. Theory and practice*. Cambridge University Press.

Enever, J. (2018). *Policy and politics in global primary English*. Oxford University Press.

Halliwell, S. (1992). *Teaching English in the primary classroom*. Longman.

Huang, B. H. (2016). A synthesis of empirical research on the linguistic outcomes of early foreign language instruction. *International Journal of Multilingualism, 13*(3), 257–273.

Johnstone, R. (2009). An early start: What are the key conditions for generalized success? In J. Enever, J. Moon, & U. Raman (Eds.), *Young learner English language policy and implementation. International perspectives* (pp. 31–42). IATEFL young Learner Special Interest Group.

Long, M. H. (2015). *Second language acquisition and task-based language teaching*. Wiley-Blackwell.

Lyster, R. (2007). *Learning and teaching languages through content*. John Benjamins.

García Mayo, M. P. (Ed.). (2017). *Learning foreign languages in primary school. Research insights*. Multilingual Matters.

García Mayo, M. P. (2018). Child task-based interaction in EFL settings: Research and challenges. *International Journal of English Studies, 18*(2), 119–143.

García Mayo, M. P. (2021). Are you coming back? It was fun' Turning ethical and methodological challenges into opportunities in task-based research with children. In A. Pinter, & K. Kuchah (Eds.), *Ethical and methodological issues in researching young learners in school contexts* (pp. 68–83). Multilingual Matters.

Oliver, R. (2008). "How young is too young?: Investigating negotiation of meaning and feedback in children aged five to seven years." In A. Mackey, & C. Polio (Eds.) *Multiple perspectives on interaction: Second language research in honor of Susan M. Gass* (pp. 135–156). Routledge.

Oliver, R., & Azkarai, A. (2017). Review of child second language acquisition (SLA): Examining theories and research. *Annual Review of Applied Linguistics, 37*, 62–76.

Philp, J., Oliver, R., & Mackey, A. (Eds.). (2008). *Second language acquisition and the younger learner. Child's play?* John Benjamins.

Pinter, A. (2011). *Children learning second languages*. Palgrave McMillan.

Shehadeh, A. (2018). New frontiers in task-based language teaching research. In M. A. Ahmadian, & M. P. García Mayo (Eds.), *Recent perspectives on task-based language learning and teaching* (pp. vii–xxi). De Gruyter.

María del Pilar García Mayo is Professor of English Language and Linguistics at the University of the Basque Country (Spain). She investigates the L2/L3 acquisition of English morphosyntax (generative perspective) and conversational interaction by EFL adults and children. Her published work includes numerous articles and book chapters in top journals and edited collections with Cambridge University Press, De Gruyter, John Benjamins, Multilingual Matters and Springer. She has authored one book and edited seven volumes and five special issues (*Bilingualism: Language and Cognition, International Journal of Applied Linguistics, International Journal of Educational Research Language Teaching for Young Learners and System*). She coordinates the *Language and Speech* research group and is the editor of *Language Teaching Research.*
(http://www.laslab.org/pilar).

Emergent Bilingualism in Foreign Language Education

Pat Moore and Blake Turnbull

For some time now, foreign language education (FLE) has been grappling with the dogma of what Howatt (1984) referred to as the 'monolingual principle': monolingual ideologies of language separation—dual monolingualism—in the classroom, coupled with (mythicized) monolingual native speakerdom personifying the goal of target language competence. Aside from the biological impossibility of producing native speakers, this mindset sidesteps several key questions crucial to FL contexts not least the naturally occurring, indeed unavoidable, interaction between students' languages and the cognitive and communicative consequences of this contact. New trends towards the development of FL learners' complete linguistic systems ties in with what Cook (1992) has termed 'multicompetence,; highlighting the logical goal of FLE: the development of bilingualism in some form.

Named languages—arguably socio-political constructions of the nation state (Makoni & Pennycook, 2007)—are sets of linguistic features, styles, and resources that speakers draw upon to communicate. They may manifest externally as linguistic systems adhering to determined 'grammars' (e.g., English, Japanese, Spanish, etc.); however, internally, they comprise a speaker's holistic linguistic repertoire. To illustrate: The Common European Framework of Reference for Languages states that multicompetence is "not seen as the superposition or juxtaposition of distinct competences, but rather as the existence of a complex or even composite competence on which the user may draw" (Council of Europe, 2001, p.168).

P. Moore (✉)
Languages & Translation, Universidad Pablo de Olavide, Sevilla, Spain
e-mail: pfmoox@upo.es

B. Turnbull
Faculty of Global and Regional Studies, Doshisha University, Kyoto, Japan
e-mail: bturnbul@mail.doshisha.ac.jp

© Springer Nature Switzerland AG 2021
H. Mohebbi and C. Coombe (eds.), *Research Questions in Language Education and Applied Linguistics*, Springer Texts in Education,
https://doi.org/10.1007/978-3-030-79143-8_36

The re-conceptualization of FL learners as possessing multicompetence, aligned to the 'multilingual turn' in language education (May, 2013), challenges traditional understandings of bilingualism and redefines those who fall within the spectrum. The term 'emergent bilingualism' has gained traction in recent years in reference to those "in the beginning stages of moving along a bilingual continuum" (García, 2009, p. 397). It is vital that FLE education moves to recognize the multicompetence of emergent bilinguals and go beyond 'allowing' the L1 for scaffolding to actively encouraging students to engage in translanguaging, that is, "the deployment of a speaker's full linguistic repertoire without regard to watchful adherence to the socially and politically defined boundaries of named languages" (Otheguy et al., 2015, p. 281). In doing so, FLE could, and arguably should, come to incorporate bilingual approaches, techniques and strategies that develop and evaluate students' holistic repertoires to better prepare students for life beyond the classroom.

The Research Questions

1. What is emergent bilingualism?
2. How does bilingualism emerge in FL contexts?
3. What beliefs[1] do stakeholders express regarding (emergent) bilingualism in diverse FL contexts?
4. Do beliefs towards language use in content-based approaches like CLIL and CBI, where subject teachers are tasked with contributing to FL development, differ from typical FL contexts?
5. What does educational policy, as expressed for example through official curricula, say about language use and emergent bilingualism in FL contexts?
6. How are beliefs relating to emergent bilingualism manifested in FL classroom practice?
7. What happens when FL educators go 'beyond' the use of the L1 for scaffolding learning?
8. What affordances (if any) for emergent bilingualism are to be found in published (print/on-line) FLE materials?
9. The recently revised *Common European Framework of Reference for Languages*[2] includes a new set of descriptors devised to describe plurilingual competence. How useful are they in practice?
10. If the goal is bilingualism, assessment proscribing L1/other language use becomes illogical. So, how should emergent bilinguals be assessed?

---

[1]In the literature we might find 'beliefs', 'attitudes', 'opinions', 'reactions', etc.

[2]See https://rm.coe.int/cefr-companion-volume-with-new-descriptors-2018/1680787989.

Suggested Resources

Cook, V., & Li, W. (Eds). (2016). *The Cambridge handbook of linguistic multi-competence*. **Cambridge, UK: Cambridge University Press**.

Drawing on the psycholinguistic, sociolinguistic, and SLA-based research of 29 globally distributed scholars, this edited volume presents an exploration of multi-competence and the mental systems of bi-/multilingual individuals and communities. Evidence is presented against the monolingual perspective (a commonly perpetuated principle in foreign language education) in favor of a bilingual perspective from multiple positions in language education and bi-/multilingualism research. The relevance of this to emergent bilingualism in foreign language education is that it supports new perspectives on the complex minds of speakers of two or more languages. It works to develop the idea that FL users are a unique set of emergent bilinguals with cognitive functions unrelated to the monolingual native speaker. A 15-page bibliography of multi-competence and related topics is provided at the end of the volume for further reading. This is an essential reference in the reframing of foreign language education as a bilingual event.

Cenoz, J. & Gorter. D. (Eds.) (2011). Special Issue: Toward a Multilingual Approach in the Study of Multilingualism in School Contexts. *The Modern Language Journal*, **95(3)**.

This special issue of the MLJ is devoted to the question of multilingual approaches and multilingualism in educational contexts. The contributors, Applied Linguists who are also multilingual, address the question from a variety of stances—both conceptual and empirical, and in a variety of contexts—encompassing foreign, second, regional and heritage languages in bi-, tri- and multilingual scenarios. The special issue focuses on multilingual practices and the ways which multilinguals creatively and fluidly meld and merge the languages, codes and dialects in their repertoires both in learning and in communication, and the corollaries of such behavior. It includes contextualized discussion of both practice and policy. In the concluding section, Cenoz and Gorter outline directions for future research.

Moore, P. (2018). Becoming Bilingual in the EFL Classroom. *ELT Journal*, **72(2), 131–140**.

In this article, Moore presents and discusses classroom-based research conducted with advanced (C1+) EFL students in a university context. Bemused by their reluctance to consider themselves bilingual, she decided to adopt a declaredly pro-bilingual stance in her teaching. She devised a set of translanguaging activities which involved students using an expanded repertoire in the classroom and she took advantage of an interactive writing task to gather data relating to their reactions to the praxis. This article groups their comments into three strands: reactions to the ideas in theory, reactions to in-class practice, and reflections upon outside class behavior. It was interesting how many of the students commented on significant differences between in-class and *hors* class behavior. Analysis of the texts further revealed what Moore terms 'bilingual interaction': writers displaying a cognizance of their reader's linguistic profile while composing their texts.

Turnbull, B. (2020). Towards new standards in foreign language assessment: Learning from bilingual education. *International Journal of Bilingual Education and Bilingualism*, *23(4)*, **488–498**. https://doi.org/10.1080/13670050.2017. 1375891.

Turnbull attempts to disrupt the construct of foreign language learners as double monolinguals by examining the way in which bi- and translingual strategies can be incorporated into the foreign language classroom for testing and assessment purposes from structural-, task-, and knowledge-based perspectives. He begins with an overarching examination of the historic trends in both foreign language and bilingual education assessment, before analyzing new standards of holistic language assessment laid out by bilingual education scholars and the way in which these could be implemented in the foreign language classroom. Turnbull dismisses the summative monolingual-based forms of assessment that have reigned prevalent in traditional foreign language education, suggesting instead that bilingual-based evaluative models must be employed to holistically assess foreign language learners' complete linguistic repertoires as the emergent bilinguals that they are.

Moate, J. & Ruohotie-Lyhty, M. (2020). The emotional journey of being and becoming bilingual. *International Journal of Bilingual Education and Bilingualism*, *23(2)*, **213–226**. https://doi.org/10.1080/13670050.2017.1348464.

In a longitudinal study, premised on the importance of identity and emotion in FL contexts, Moate and Ruohotie-Lyhty gathered personal narratives from a group of Finnish pre-service English teachers reflecting on their 'relationship' with English. Applying dialogical and narrative approaches, the researchers identify two recurrent themes: Bilingualism as striving and Bilingualism as a gift, correlating with the notions of becoming and being bilingual. Both storylines shared common themes: relating to belonging, to confidence and to going beyond but they were conceptualized differently. For example, strivers were more likely to measure themselves against native-speaker norms (a community towards which they might aspire but could never belong) and this resulted in a lack of confidence, whereas those who saw bilingualism as a gift were generally more confident. They already felt part of a community (of English users), indeed for them English was often a tool for achieving other goals rather than an end in itself.

References

Cook, V. (1992). Evidence for multicompetence. *Language Learning, 42*(4), 557–591.
Council of Europe. (2001). *Common European framework of reference for languages: Learning, teaching, assessment.* Cambridge University Press.
García, O. (2009). *Bilingual education in the 21st century: A global perspective.* Blackwell.
Howatt, A. (1984). *A history of English language teaching.* Oxford University Press.

Makoni, S., & Pennycook, A. (2007). *Disinventing and reconstituting languages.* Multilingual Matters.

May, S. (Ed.). (2013). *The multilingual turn: Implications for SLA, TESOL and bilingual education.* New York, NY: Routledge.

Otheguy, R., García, O., & Reid, W. (2015). Clarifying translanguaging and deconstructing named languages: A perspective from linguistics. *Applied Linguistics Review, 6*(3), 281–307.

Pat Moore has been in ELT since the mid-eighties. She has worked in the private and public sectors at all levels and with all ages in Brazil, China, France, Greece, Portugal, Spain and the UK. She has been at the Universidad Pablo de Olavide in Seville since 2004. Nowadays most of her teaching revolves around teacher development, both with pre-service (EFL) teachers and in-service content teachers who want to move into bilingual (CLIL) education. Her research interests are centered on questions pertaining to (foreign) language education and bilinguality, particularly with regards to classroom praxis, assessment and stakeholder perspectives.

Blake Turnbull is an assistant professor at Doshisha University, Japan. He completed his Ph.D. in foreign language acquisition and education at Kyoto University, Japan, and has an MA degree in ESL applied linguistics from the University of Otago, New Zealand. His main research interests center on EFL education, bilingualism, and translanguaging. He has published papers and given presentations on topics including those approaching foreign language education from a bilingual perspective, various stances on language learner and teacher beliefs, and new advances in English education in a Japanese EFL context.

Extramural English in Language Education

Pia Sundqvist

The term *extramural English* (*EE*) was coined in 2009 (Sundqvist, 2009). It comes from Latin and the prefix, *extra*, means 'outside' and the stem, *mural*, means 'wall.' In the field of language teaching and learning, EE refers to 'English outside the walls of the classroom', which was the phenomenon Sundqvist investigated in her study. More specifically, the question was whether adolescent foreign/second language (L2) learners in Sweden who, on their own initiative, engaged informally with English outside of school appeared to learn something from doing so. It turned out that they did. The participants in the study took part in many English-mediated activities, such as watching television or films, watching music videos, reading blogs, and playing video games. Based on EE data collected with the help of survey instruments and language data collected with speaking tests and vocabulary tests, Sundqvist (2009) ran statistical tests and could conclude that there was a statistically significant positive correlation between learners' total time spent on EE and oral proficiency on the one hand, and vocabulary on the other. She also found that some EE activities (reading, playing video games, and using the Internet) were more important for oral proficiency and vocabulary than other examined activities (watching tv, watching films, and listening to music).

In the decade that has followed since this first study, EE has become an established term in the field and the phenomenon of informal learning of English outside of school has become a concern for English language education. Ushioda (2013, p. 233) talks about "motivational dissonances between students' in-class and out-of-class contexts" and emphasizes that in settings where English is an important medium of youth culture, that is, in countries where children and adolescents are heavily engaged in EE, teaching English in the classroom has become a great

P. Sundqvist (✉)
Department of Teacher Education and School Research, University of Oslo, Oslo, Norway
e-mail: pia.sundqvist@ils.uio.no

© Springer Nature Switzerland AG 2021
H. Mohebbi and C. Coombe (eds.), *Research Questions in Language Education and Applied Linguistics*, Springer Texts in Education,
https://doi.org/10.1007/978-3-030-79143-8_37

challenge. This is the case in the Nordic countries and many other European countries as well as in Asia, so it is a global trend linked to the status of English in the world.

Without a doubt, findings from EE studies have implications for language education. There is a gap between learning English formally and informally that needs to be bridged. While the English teacher used to be the most important source of English and sometimes the only English role model for learners, that is simply not the case any longer. As a consequence, L2 English teachers are facing increasing challenges as students' motivation for learning English cannot be taken for granted anymore.

To make amends, researchers have suggestions for how teachers may draw on their students' EE experiences in teaching. Thorne and Reinhardt (2008) propose 'Bridging Activities', where students are encouraged to bring texts they find relevant to the classroom, and teachers help raise language awareness by working linguistically with these texts. Sundqvist and Sylvén (2016) offer summaries of EE research and theory, as well as pedagogical guidance. Finally, there is a lot to learn from in-service teachers who succeed in teaching English in contexts where EE plays a significant role in young people's lives, as shown and theoretically explained in a volume by Henry et al. (2019).

The Research Questions

1. How do students experience learning from EE activities as compared with learning from English classroom tasks?
2. How and to what extent does learners' involvement in EE vary over time?
3. What differences in EE habits can be found in relation to various background variables, such as first language (L1) and socio-economic status?
4. What connections, if any, are there between EE and individual differences, for example, aptitude, working memory, and personality traits?
5. What is most important for different aspects of L2 English proficiency (vocabulary, writing proficiency, oral proficiency, listening comprehension, reading comprehension etc.), the total time learners spend on EE, or the types of EE activities learners engage in?
6. What tasks can teachers use to draw more on EE in their teaching?
7. Research has shown gender-related differences when it comes to young people's EE habits; what influence may gender-related differences have on teaching English?
8. Why do some EE activities, such as pleasure reading and playing digital games, seem to be particularly influential for L2 English proficiency?
9. What problems may teachers face if they do not acknowledge students' involvement in EE activities?

10. What teaching strategies may be suitable in an L2 English classroom when the class consists of students with varying degrees of involvement in EE (from very low to very high)?

Suggested Resources

Sundqvist, P., & Sylvén, L. K. (2016). *Extramural English in Teaching and Learning: From Theory and Research to Practice.* **London: Palgrave Macmillan.**

In this book, Pia Sundqvist and Liss Kerstin Sylvén give a thorough account of extramural English theory and research and they also discuss pedagogical implications of EE. In the first part of the book, central findings from empirical studies are discussed in relation to theory. The key term itself is elaborated upon and a theoretical framework for how EE may be understood is proposed. Important topics are addressed, such as the role of age in language learning and in relation to EE, as well as the role of motivation. Chapter five is a research overview of EE, which shows the importance for professionals working in language education to consider the topic of EE seriously. The second part of the book is more hands on and it is especially relevant to teachers and student teachers. Altogether, this volume addresses how teachers may deal with current challenges in the English classroom.

Benson, P., & Reinders, H. (Eds.). (2011). *Beyond the Language Classroom.* **Basingstoke: Palgrave Macmillan.**

This volume centers on language learning beyond the classroom and includes a collection of data-based case studies from around the globe as well as advice on how teaching materials can be created for the purpose of learning languages independently in out-of-school settings. The editors, Phil Benson and Hayo Reinders, stress the need for research in such settings, not least due to the rapid growth of technology that competes with language learning in the classroom. In contrast to what has often been the case in L2 research—that is, a focus on adult university students—in this volume, there are also contributions that target school-age learners.

Sylvén, L. K., & Sundqvist, P. (Eds.). (2017). Special issue. Computer-Assisted Language Learning (CALL) in Extracurricular/Extramural Contexts, *CALICO Journal, 34*(1). https://doi.org/10.1558/cj.31822.

This special issue of the *CALICO Journal* is most likely the first with an explicit focus on extramural language studies. More precisely, the issue contains contributions that can be characterized as computer-assisted language learning (CALL) studies, in extracurricular as well as extramural contexts. Whereas extracurricular L2 studies are connected to an educational context in the pursuit of learning a target language, such as in evening schools and language clubs, extramural L2 studies do not have such a connection. In total, there are six studies from around the globe focusing on different target languages. The studies include participants from primary school to university level and CALL is examined from a range of perspectives. Three of the studies cover the role of gaming in L2 learning, the fourth has a focus on captions when watching TV, the fifth a focus on so-called eTandem, and the sixth treats EE in general.

Reinders, H. (Ed.). (2012). *Digital Games in Language Learning and Teaching*. Basingstoke: Palgrave Macmillan.

This book is important work that focuses on a specific EE activity, namely digital gameplay. Whereas playing games has been a popular free time interest for a long time, it took some time before language researchers took a serious interest in the topic. Over the last two decades or so, the pedagogical benefits of playing games have steadily caught the attention of L2 researchers, as gaming encourages interaction (both in writing and orally) and the use of English. That is, it is not uncommon that gamers interact in English regardless of their native language, as English is the default language in many online games (Waters, 2007). With this volume, the potential of digital game play is examined from both an L2 and a teaching perspective. Chapter topics include, for example, interaction in massively multiplayer online role-playing games, learner autonomy, and willingness to communicate.

Henry, A., Sundqvist, P., & Thorsen, C. (2019). *Motivational Practice: Insights from the Classroom*. Lund: Studentlitteratur.

This volume provides a rich account of how L2 English teachers in Sweden, who are successful in motivating their students, create engaging learning opportunities through various classroom tasks and projects as well as through their own way of being. It is clear that the teachers who are described in the book manage to negotiate classroom relationships very well. Further, the book illustrates how motivation may emerge thanks to sound teacher-student relationships and the type of classroom activities the teachers plan for and carry out. The authors draw on research conducted in a project called MoTiSSE (Motivational Teaching in Swedish Secondary English). The purpose of the book is to help in-service and preservice teachers of English to develop abilities that will enable them to develop lessons that students find relevant, engaging, and meaningful.

References

Henry, A., Sundqvist, P., & Thorsen, C. (2019). *Motivational practice: Insights from the classroom*. Studentlitteratur.

Sundqvist, P. (2009). *Extramural English matters: Out-of-school English and its impact on Swedish ninth graders' oral proficiency and vocabulary* (Dissertation). Karlstad University, Karlstad. https://www.diva-portal.org/smash/get/diva2:275141/FULLTEXT03.pdf

Sundqvist, P., & Sylvén, L. K. (2016). *Extramural English in teaching and learning: From theory and research to practice*. Palgrave Macmillan.

Thorne, S. L., & Reinhardt, J. (2008). "Bridging activities", new media literacies, and advanced foreign language proficiency. *CALICO Journal, 25*(3), 558–572.

Ushioda, E. (2013). Motivation and ELT: Looking ahead to the future. In E. Ushioda (Ed.), *International perspectives on motivation: Language learning and professional challenges* (pp. 233–239). Palgrave Macmillan.

Pia Sundqvist is Associate Professor of English Language Education at the University of Oslo, Norway. Her main research interest is informal language learning, especially extramural English and the relation between digital gameplay and aspects of L2 English proficiency. Other research areas include the assessment of L2 oral proficiency and English language teaching. She is the author of *Extramural English in Teaching and Learning* (with Liss Kerstin Sylvén, Palgrave Macmillan, 2016) and of *Motivational Practice* (with Alastair Henry and Cecilia Thorsen, Studentlitteratur 2019). Sundqvist has contributed with articles in journals such as *Language Learning & Technology, ReCALL, System, TESOL Quarterly,* and *Journal of Pragmatics.*

Language Learning Strategies

38

Mirosław Pawlak

Language learning strategies (LLS), or "actions chosen by learners for the purpose of language learning" (Griffiths, 2018, p. 19) have been the object of empirical inquiry for over four decades since specialists identified their adept use as one of the characteristics of good language learners (e.g., Rubin, 1975). Since then major advances have been made, which have involved the identification of different types of LLS, examination of factors mediating the use of strategic devices (e.g. age, gender, learning style, personality), investigation of their link with attainment, and appraisal of the contribution of strategies-based instruction. In addition, major classifications of LLS have been proposed, also with respect to specific target language domains (e.g., vocabulary, listening, reading, grammar), and a number of data collection instruments have been designed to tap into strategic learning (cf. Cohen, 2011; Cohen & Griffiths, 2015; Grenfell & Macaro, 2007; Griffiths, 2018; Griffiths & Oxford, 2014; Oxford, 2011, 2017; Pawlak, 2011, 2021; Pawlak & Oxford, 2018).

With time, it became obvious that the sheer quantity of LLS use does not automatically translate into greater effectiveness of language learning and that it is necessary to look at the application of strategic devices in context. In particular, the strategies employed need to be matched to the task in hand, the individual profile of the learner, and they need to be adeptly combined into clusters or chains (Ehrman et al., 2003; McDonough, 1999). Another problem is that correlational studies cannot tell the whole story about the value of LLS, because it is not clear whether it is frequent strategy use that contributes to proficiency or, rather, achievement is responsible for greater reliance on strategies. The evidence concerning the contribution of instructing students in the use of LLS is also tenuous,

M. Pawlak (✉)
Faculty of Pedagogy and Fine Arts, Adam Mickiewicz University, Kalisz, Poland
e-mail: pawlakmi@amu.edu.pl

M. Pawlak
State University of Applied Sciences in Konin, Konin, Poland

© Springer Nature Switzerland AG 2021
H. Mohebbi and C. Coombe (eds.), *Research Questions in Language Education and Applied Linguistics*, Springer Texts in Education,
https://doi.org/10.1007/978-3-030-79143-8_38

greater strategy use is not always shown to be accompanied by greater attainment, and there are factors that mediate the efficacy of such pedagogic intervention (cf. Plonsky, 2011).

It is these and other problems that have triggered considerable criticisms against the strategy concept that have culminated in proposals that specialists should focus on how learners go about self-regulating their learning rather than how they employ LLS (Dörnyei, 2005). However, the field has been able to withstand such appeals and, even as its critics admit, "the question of learning strategies is an area that continues to demand our attention and compels us to offer a considered re-examination" (Dörnyei & Ryan, 2015, p. 141). LLS research has also managed to reinvent itself by laying more emphasis on situated use of strategies and trying to align itself with new theoretical stances, such as complex dynamic systems theories (Larsen-Freeman & Cameron, 2008). This said, it would be premature to abandon what has been achieved so far and reject research tools that have been used in previous empirical investigations, in particular questionnaires employed to assess LLS use, such as the *Strategy Inventory for Language Learning* (SILL) (Oxford, 1990). Rather, as with other strands of research on individual differences, it makes more sense to combine the old and the new by integrating the macro-perspective relaying on data obtained from large numbers of participants, and the micro-perspective, which explores the use of LLS in a situated manner.

The Research Questions

1. What are patterns of LLS use in less studied domains (e.g., grammar, pro-nunciation, culture)?
2. How do learners use LLS in technology-enhanced environments?
3. How do learners use LLS in content-based language instruction (e.g. study abroad)?
4. How do senior learners employ LLS when learning different skills and subsystems?
5. How is the use of LLS for learning skills and subsystems mediated by other variables and clusters of such variables (e.g., beliefs, boredom, willingness to communicate)?
6. How do learners use LLS in different kinds of learning tasks (e.g., meaning and form-oriented)?
7. How does LLS use change over time (e.g., over a longer period, in a given lesson)?
8. How is the use of LLS related to attainment in terms of explicit and implicit knowledge?
9. What are the best ways to teach LLS in different contexts?
10. What are the best tools to tap into LLS use, both in general and in specific tasks?

Suggested Resources

Cohen, A. D. (2014). *Strategies in learning and using a second language*. London and New York: Routledge.

The book is a substantially revised version of a previous publication. It comprises eight chapters in which the author attempts to disentangle the definitional and terminological confusion which surrounds the concept of strategies for learning and using a second language, and overviews methods used in LLS research, issues involved in strategies-based instruction as well as the empirical evidence for such pedagogic intervention. Importantly, Andrew Cohen also considers the use of strategies for choosing the language of thought and for dealing with assessment. The volume is invaluable reading not only for researchers and teacher educators, but also for teachers who are interested in fostering strategic learning, and undergraduate and graduate students working on their theses.

Cohen, A. D., & Macaro, E. (Eds.). (2007). *Language learner strategies: Thirty years of research and practice*. Oxford: Oxford University Press.

This edited collection constitutes an early attempt to confront theoretical issues in the study of LLS and to synthesize existing empirical evidence based on thirty years of research. It brings together 12 chapters by leading scholars in the field which are divided into two parts. Part One, *Issues, theories, and frameworks*, addresses claims and critiques aimed at LLS, surveys opinions of experts in this domain, and zooms in on such issues as the psychological and sociolinguistic perspectives on LLS, factors influencing strategy use, the research methods that can be applied in the study of strategies, grammar as a neglected facet of LLS research, and the question of strategies-based instruction. Part Two, *Reviewing thirty years of empirical LLS research*, summarizes the main results of studies that have focused on strategies related to listening, reading, vocabulary, writing and communication. The book closes with a chapter by the editors who consider key issues in light of the book contents and provide a research agenda for the field.

Griffiths, C. (2018). *The strategy factor in successful language learning: The tornado effect*. Bristol: Multilingual Matters.

This is a revised and expanded version of the book published in 2013. Carol Griffiths offers a comprehensive, state-of-the-art overview of the field, approaching many key themes from a new perspective. In the first part, she touches on a number of conceptual issues, such as the definition, characteristics, classification, theoretical bases, and effectiveness of strategies but particularly valuable are her ruminations on the research methods that can be used in strategy research. The following two parts offer insights into how LLS can be explored from a quantitative and qualitative perspective as well as pointing to areas in need of empirical investigation in both cases. The final part zooms in on critical issues related to how strategies can be of relevance to classroom pedagogy, focusing in particular on teachability of LLS, relevant training programs, the findings of previous research, the main principles of successful SBI, and the myriad of variables that can affect its effectiveness. The book is full of useful information and fresh ideas and it is a must-read for anyone interested in the field, whether they are researchers, teacher trainers or practitioners.

Oxford, R. L. (2017). Teaching and researching language learning strategies. Self-regulation in context. New York and London: Routledge.

The volume is a substantial expansion on an earlier book published in 2011. Rebecca Oxford undertakes the ambitious task of confronting many of the existing controversies regarding LLS and makes a successful attempt to portray strategies as complex dynamic systems that need to be investigated in context. In the ten chapters the book is comprised of, the author offers a content-based definition of strategies, links their use to agency, autonomy, self-regulation, motivation and emotions, underscores the need to investigate them in context, shows how her view of LLS can be applied to specific skills and subsystems, and illustrates some vital innovations related to how LLS can be taught, assessed and investigated. This landmark volume is a true treasure for anyone interested in language learning strategies. It represents a major step forward in the field and it is bound to shape research in the years to come.

Oxford, R. L., & Pawlak, M. (2018). *Language learning strategies: Linking with the past, shaping the future.* **Special issue of** *Studies in Second Language Learning and Teaching, 8(2).*

Just like Cohen and Macaro (2007), this special issue of *Studies in Second Language Learning and Teaching* offers a state-of-the-art overview of the field, but ten years later. The 14 papers by scholars from all over the world address different domains of LLS research, including those that have so far received little attention, such as strategies employed for learning and using grammar, pronunciation and pragmatics or culture. Importantly, the papers go beyond what is currently known and seek to expand the field by showing, for example, how speaking strategies can be approached more broadly than communication strategies, investigating the application of LLS in L2 and L3, tying strategy use to self-direction, self-regulation and autonomy, as well as demonstrating the importance of strategic learning in technology-enhanced situations. The final paper by Mirosław Pawlak and Rebecca Oxford considers the future of the field with respect to research foci, methodological issues and the connection between empirical investigations and classroom practice.

Oxford, R. L., & Amerstorfer, C. M. (Eds). (2018). *Language Learning Strategies: Situating strategy use in diverse contexts.* **London: Bloomsbury.**

This edited collection comprises 12 papers which illustrate the importance of individual as well as contextual characteristics in shaping the use of LLS. Part One, titled *Theoretical foundations of individuals' situated, self-regulated language learning strategies in authentic contexts*, focuses on the application of complex dynamic systems theories, the link between theoretical issues and classroom practice, and the extent to which successful strategy use is moderated by individual differences. Part Two, *Research methodologies for exploring learning strategies and individual differences*, stresses the contribution of innovative techniques in strategy research (i.e., narratives, decision tree models) and the need for a mixed-methods approach. Part Three, *Studies of learning strategies emphasizing diverse contexts and individual difference factors*, focuses on LLS use in different national contexts (i.e., China and Greece) and with respect to less studied domains (i.e., pronunciation). Part Four, *Preparing teachers for presenting strategy instruction to learners*, considers key issues in strategy-based instruction but also reports results of studies focusing on affective strategies and the development of assessment tools for assessing LLS use among young learners. The volume closes with a summary chapter by the editors in which they summarize the lessons from investigating LLS in a situated manner and consider the future directions of this line of inquiry.

References

Cohen, A. D. (2011). *Strategies in learning and using a second language.* Routledge.

Cohen, A. D., & Griffiths, C. (2015). Revisiting LLS research 40 years later. *TESOL Quarterly, 53*, 414–429.

Dörnyei, Z. (2005). *The psychology of the language learner: Individual factors in second language acquisition.* Lawrence Erlbaum.

Dörnyei, Z., & Ryan, S. (2015). *The psychology of the language learner revisited.* Routledge.

Ehrman, M., Leaver, B., & Oxford, R. L. (2003). A brief overview of individual differences in second language learning. *System, 31*, 313–330.

Grenfell, M., & Macaro, E. (2007). Claims and critiques. In A. D. Cohen & E. Macaro (Eds.), *Language learner strategies: Thirty years of research and practice* (pp. 9–28). Oxford University Press.

Griffiths, C. (2018). *The strategy factor in successful language learning: The tornado effect.* Multilingual Matters.

Griffiths, C., & Oxford, R. L. (2014). The twenty-first century landscape of language learning strategies: Introduction to this special issue. *System, 43*, 1–10.

Larsen-Freeman, D., & Cameron, L. (2008). *Complex dynamic systems and applied linguistics.* Oxford University Press.

McDonough, S. (1999). Learner strategies. *Language Teaching, 32*, 1–18.

Oxford, R. L. (1990). *Language learning strategies: What every teacher should know.* Heinle & Heinle.

Oxford, R. L. (2011). *Teaching and researching language learning strategies.* Pearson Education.

Oxford, R. L. (2017). *Teaching and researching language learning strategies. Self-regulation in context.* Routledge.

Pawlak, M. (2011). Research into language learning strategies: Taking stock and looking ahead'. In J. Arabski & A. Wojtaszek (Eds.), *Individual differences in SLA* (pp. 17–37). Multilingual Matters.

Pawlak, M. (2021). Investigating language learning strategies: Prospects pitfalls and challenges. *Language Teaching Research 25*(5), 817–835.

Pawlak, M., & Oxford, R. L. (2018). Conclusion: The future of research into language learning strategies. *Studies in Second Language Learning and Teaching, 8*, 523–532.

Plonsky, L. (2011). Systematic review article: The effectiveness of second language strategy instruction: A meta-analysis. *Language Learning, 61*, 993–1038.

Rubin, J. (1975). What the "good language learner" can teach us. *TESOL Quarterly, 9*, 41–51.

Mirosław Pawlak is Professor of English in the Department of English Studies, Faculty of Pedagogy and Fine Arts of Adam Mickiewicz University, Kalisz, Poland, and Department of Language and Communication, Faculty of Humanities and Social Sciences, State University of Applied Sciences, Konin, Poland. His main areas of interest are SLA theory and research, form-focused instruction, corrective feedback, pronunciation teaching, classroom discourse, learner autonomy, communication and learning strategies, grammar learning strategies, motivation, willingness to communicate, boredom, and study abroad. He is editor of the journals *Studies in Second language Learning and Teaching* and *Konin Language Studies*, as well as the book series *Second Language Learning and Teaching*, published by Springer.

Language Proficiency and Academic Performance

39

Saleh Al-Busaidi

The debate about the role of language proficiency in academic achievement is a perennial one. There have been many attempts to understand this relationship. Cummins (1980, 1984, 1992) was one of the first scholars to offer a conceptual framework of language proficiency. He divides language proficiency into two levels, a surface and deep level. The surface level, known as Basic Interpersonal Communicative Skills (BICS), depicts the visible quantifiable formal aspects of language such as grammar, vocabulary and pronunciation. This type of language is used in everyday communication such as knowledge, basic understanding, and application in concrete situations. The second level is the Cognitive Academic Language Proficiency (CALP) level, which deals with the less visible features through the "the manipulation of language in de-contextualized academic situations" and includes such skills as analysis, synthesis, and evaluation (Cummins, 1984, p. 137). For Cummins, CALP is more essential to academic achievement than BICS.

A similar perspective into what constitutes language proficiency was offered by Spolsky (1989) through what he called 'the preference model of language proficiency'. Spolsky claims that proficiency can take different levels and that language users possess varying degrees of proficiency and skills. The preference model suggests that students normally learn the second/foreign language for specific purposes and that a student who possesses general language knowledge may not be able to function well in academic situations that require an academic variety of the language. Spolsky recognizes the complexity of language learning and calls upon language education to be more precise and realistic in its goals and outcomes of learning. This is particularly important when academic competence is the target. Saville-Troike (1984) believes that academic competence consists of at least three

S. Al-Busaidi (✉)
Department of Curriculum and Instruction, Sultan Qaboos University, Muscat, Sultanate of Oman
e-mail: asad@squ.edu.om

© Springer Nature Switzerland AG 2021
H. Mohebbi and C. Coombe (eds.), *Research Questions in Language Education and Applied Linguistics*, Springer Texts in Education,
https://doi.org/10.1007/978-3-030-79143-8_39

main components: language proficiency, subject-area knowledge, and study/academic skills. She thinks that learners need to be given sufficient training in each of these areas to be able to cope with the rigorous demands of academia.

English language proficiency has increasingly become an important entry criterion in English-medium higher education institutions around the globe. Language preparation programs vary quite tremendously in their focus. Some take a narrow view to language education and focus primarily on teaching the linguistic aspects of the language, while others may broaden their scope to include study and academic skills, content-area vocabulary and knowledge. Yet other programs have gone for the integrated language-content design where language is taught through specific content (Brinton et al., 1989).

Many studies have investigated the interplay between language proficiency and achievement, and the impact such intensive language study has on learners' academic achievement. However, there have not been any conclusive findings about the degree of influence language proficiency has on achievement. While some studies reported a positive relationship between the two (e.g. Al-Busaidi, 2017; Fakeye, 2014; Leki & Carson, 1994; Maleki & Zangani, 2007; Racca & Lasaten, 2016; Stoffelsma & Spooren, 2019), others did not find a clear-cut positive relationship (e.g. Dev & Qiqieh, 2016; Light & Teh-Yuan, 1991; Light et al., 1987). Yet, other studies found the predictive power of language proficiency not to have a lasting effect (e.g. (Farley et al., 2019). The discrepancy in findings is due to several plausible reasons such as the ambiguity surrounding the key concepts such as language proficiency and academic achievement (Graham, 1987), variations in research design and data collection techniques, and the nature of the language program (Flowerdew & Miller, 1997) or other factors related to the discipline (Racca & Lasaten, 2016), teaching methods, assessments, and gender (Al-Busaidi, 2017). Hence, further research is needed to better define the key concepts and look more deeply into the socio-educational factors that can affect this relationship. Such research can potentially benefit program planners and curriculum designers in developing more focused and effective programs.

The Research Questions

1. How does language proficiency affect academic success?
2. What alternative language curriculum designs increase the impact of language proficiency on academic performance?
3. How does language proficiency affect academic achievement in different disciplines?
4. Which of the four language skills is/are the most influential in determining academic achievement?
5. What assessment techniques could best predict learners' future academic performance?

6. What is the relationship between the duration of language instruction and academic achievement?
7. What factors (learner factors, teacher factors, program factors) best explain the relationship between language proficiency and academic achievement?
8. What role does learners' motivation play in the relationship between language proficiency and academic success?
9. How do students' different language proficiency levels impact their academic achievement?
10. What is the relationship between entry-level language requirements and academic achievement?

Suggested Resources

Al-Busaidi, S. (2017). Predicting academic achievement. *The Asian EFL Journal,* **101(5), 4–29.**

This study investigated the extent to which English language proficiency could predict academic achievement at a university setting. It also explored the relationship between gender and college and academic success. The data was drawn from the English language placement test scores and grade point averages of 857 undergraduate students from three cohorts, 2010, 2011 and 2012 at Sultan Qaboos University (SQU) in the Sultanate of Oman. The results showed a strong relationship between English language proficiency and academic success. Language proficiency accounted for 13.5% of academic performance. Gender and college were also found to affect achievement. The findings showed that the three factors, language proficiency, college, and gender could predict 24% of students' success. However, gender was found to have the strongest predictive effect among the three factors. The findings of this study imply that there are many other factors that come into play.

This study has particular relevance to the Arabian Gulf region where the proficiency level of school leavers is deemed inadequate for academic study and therefore students undergo intensive preparatory instruction for one or two years before they are allowed to start their academic studies.

Ozowuba, G. U. (2018). Relationship between English proficiency and academic achievement of Nigerian secondary school students (Unpublished doctoral dissertation). Walden University, United States of America.

This quantitative correlational study investigated the relationship between English proficiency and academic achievement among secondary school students in Nigeria, where English enjoys the official language status. The results revealed a strong positive relationship between English proficiency and four subjects (English, biology, government, and mathematics). This study could be of interest to researchers from contexts where English is spoken as a second language.

Adamson, H. D. (1992). *Academic Competence: Theory and Classroom Practice: Preparing ESL Students for Content Courses*. **New York: Longman**.

This book discusses the concept of academic competence. It provides a theoretical rationale for the teaching of language through content, citing practical examples of programs and classroom activities that language teachers can use to prepare their students for content-area courses. The author draws connections between these classroom practices and second language acquisition theories. There is also an account of ESL students' experiences in content-area courses about their insights. The book combines theory with practice and can be a very useful resource for understanding the relationship between language and content learning while at the same time learning about some practical ideas for teaching language through content.

Oliver, R., Vanderford, & Grote, E. (2012). Evidence of English language proficiency and academic achievement of non-English-speaking background students. *Higher Education Research & Development*, *31*(4), 541–555.

This is a large-scale research study involving 5675 international undergraduate and postgraduate students studying in Australia. The study aimed at establishing the extent to which students' language proficiency upon entry, as determined by standardized English tests or completion of English instruction, was sufficient in ensuring their academic success. The study used data over a period of three years. The researchers concluded that standardized tests were a better predictor of students' potential academic achievement compared to other forms of evidence of English proficiency. Such large-scale research has implications for other contexts with similar student demographics.

Rivera, C. (1984). Language Proficiency and Academic Achievement. *Multilingual Matters 10*. **Available from:** https://www.researchgate.net/publication/309679144_Language_Proficiency_and_Academic_Achievement_Multilingual_Matters_10 **[Accessed on November 02, 2018].**

This volume contains seven papers selected from the Language Proficiency Assessment Symposium in Warrenton, VA, March 14–18, 1981. The symposium was part of the National Institute of Education's Assessment of Language Proficiency of Bilingual Persons Project. The Assessment of the Language Proficiency of Bilingual Persons (ALPBP) project aimed at improving teachers' understanding of the constructs of language proficiency and the different and more practical and constructive ways to assess language proficiency for better-informed decisions about student entry and exit. The papers in this volume address language proficiency from sociolinguistic and ethnographic perspectives for the purpose of offering a working definition of communicative language proficiency. The emphasis is on language use.

The authors also discuss the relationship between a learner's first and second language development on the one hand and his/her performance in school on the other. Jim Cummins, for example, argues that the confusion about language proficiency is due to the lack of an adequate theoretical framework for relating language proficiency to academic achievement. He offered a theoretical framework that attempted to explain the nature of this relationship. The validity of the framework is debated in this volume. Although the research in these papers was conducted in a bilingual context, many of its implications are applicable to EFL contexts.

Ulibarri, D. M., Spencer, M. L., & Rivas, G. A. (1981). Language proficiency and academic achievement: a study of language proficiency tests and their relationship to school ratings as predictors of academic achievement. *NABE Journal*, **5(3), 47–80**.

This is an empirical research study that tested the comparability of three language assessment instruments (Language Assessment Scale (LAS), Bilingual Syntax Measure (BSM), and the Basic Inventory of Natural Languages (BINL)) and their relationship to achievement tests of over 1100 school students in the USA. Data from students' academic achievement test scores, and school ratings of students' language and achievement status were also collected and used in the analysis. One main distinctive feature of this study is the use of multiple assessment tools that could potentially help make more accurate claims about the relationship between language proficiency and academic success.

References

Al-Busaidi, S. (2017). Predicting academic achievement. *The Asian EFL Journal, 101*(5), 4–29.

Brinton, D. M., Snow, M. A., & Wesche, M. B. (1989). *Content-based second language instruction*. Newbury House.

Cummins, J. (1984). *Bilingual and special education: Issues in assessment and pedagogy*. Multilingual Matters Ltd.

Cummins, J. (1992). Language proficiency, bilingualism, and academic achievement. In P. Richard-Amato & M. Snow (Eds.), *The multicultural classroom: Readings for content-area teachers*. Longman.

Cummins, J. (1980). The entry and exit fallacy in bilingual education. *NABE Journal, 4*, 25–60.

Dev, S., & Qiqieh, S. (2016). The relationship between English language proficiency, academic achievement and self-esteem of non-native-English-speaking students. *International Education Studies, 9*(5), 147–155.

Fakeye, D. (2014). English language proficiency as a predictor of academic achievement among EFL students in Nigeria. *Journal of Education and Practice, 5*(9), 38–41.

Farley, A., Yang, H. H., Min, L., & Ma, S. (2019). Comparison of Chinese and western English language proficiency measures in transnational business degrees. *Language, Culture and Curriculum, 32*(3), 1–16. https://doi.org/10.1080/07908318.2019.1630423

Flowerdew, J., & Miller, L. (1997). The teaching of academic listening comprehension and the question of authenticity. *English for Specific Purposes, 16*(1), 27–46.

Graham, J. (1987). English language proficiency and the prediction of academic success. *TESOL Quarterly, 21*(3), 505–521.

Leki, I., & Carson, J. (1994). Students' perceptions of EAP writing instruction and writing needs across the disciplines. *TESOL Quarterly, 28*(1), 81–101.

Light, R., & Teh-Yuan, W. (1991). Soviet students at US. Colleges: Social perspectives, language proficiency, and academic success. *TESOL Quarterly, 25*(1), 179–185.

Light, R., Xu, M., & Mossop, J. (1987). English proficiency and academic performance of international students. *TESOL Quarterly, 21*(2), 251–260.

Maleki, A., & Zangani, E. (2007). A survey on the relationship between English language proficiency and the academic achievement of Iranian EFL students. *The Asian EFL Journal Quarterly, 9*(1), 86–96.

Racca, R., & Lasaten, R. (2016). English language proficiency and academic performance of Philippine science high school students. *International Journal of Languages, Literature and Linguistics, 2*(2), 44–49.

Saville-Troike, M. (1984). What really matters in second language academic achievement? *TESOL Quarterly, 18*(2), 199–219.

Spolsky, B. (1989). *Conditions for second language learning.* Oxford University Press.

Stoffelsma, L., & Spooren, W. (2019). The relationship between English reading proficiency and academic achievement of first-year science and mathematics students in a multilingual context. *International Journal of Science and Mathematics Education, 17*(5), 905–922. https://doi.org/10.1007/s10763-018-9905-z

Saleh Al-Busaidi is an associate professor of English as a foreign language at the College of Education, Sultan Qaboos University (SQU), Sultanate of Oman. He received his BA in TEFL at SQU in 1995, his M.A. in TEFL at the University of Exeter, United Kingdom in 1997, and his PhD in curriculum studies at the University of Illinois at Urbana-Champaign, USA in 2003. He served as the Director of the Language Centre at SQU (2010 – 2016). He has also chaired and taken part in many committees and project teams in and outside SQU. Dr. Al-Busaidi has also served on several audit and accreditation review panels. Dr. Al-Busaidi has participated in many national and international conferences and symposia. He has published many journal articles and book chapters on a range of topics. His main research interests are: learner autonomy, material development, study/academic skills, academic readiness and language acquisition.

Learner Strategies

40

Li-Shih Huang

After Rubin (1975) first defined strategies used by "good language learners," early research attempted to identify learner strategies as researchers asked, what do "good language learners" do? Especially important in this era was the pioneering work of Naiman et al. (1978). The past four decades have witnessed renewed interest in this area, new existential debates, and a resurgence of research, which has evolved to focus extensively on general strategy use in second language learning vis-à-vis other individual learner variables (e.g., cultural/linguistic background, aptitude, personality type, gender, motivation, and willingness to communicate; Ehrman & Oxford, 1989; Oxford & Nyikos, 1989). It has further dealt with (a) the role of learner strategies in more successful language learning in key language skill domains and subdomains (e.g., speaking, reading, writing, listening, vocabulary, pronunciation, and grammar; see Huang, 2012; Vandergrift & Goh, 2012; Zhou & Huang, 2018); (b) strategies in specific contexts or subcontexts (e.g., Chen et al., 2013; Oxford & Amerstorfer, 2018; Oxford & Ehrman, 1995); (c) attention in task-specific strategies (e.g., Huang, 2013); and (d) use of different methodologies (e.g., strategy inventories, diaries, verbal stimulated recalls, key-stroke logging, and eye-tracking; Bax, 2013; Donato & McCormick, 1994; Guo & Huang, 2020; Wengelin et al., 2009).

Over the years, defining, operationalizing, and categorizing strategies, their theoretical frameworks, and methods to elicit strategic behaviours have been extensively discussed and analyzed (e.g., Cohen & Macaro, 2007; Thomas & Rose, 2018). The existential debate peaked with Dörnyei's (1995) proposal (see also Tseng et al., 2006) to replace strategies with self-regulated capacity and Gao's (2007) subsequent article titled "Has Language Learning Strategy Research Come to an End?" More recently, however, Dörnyei and Ryan (2015) have acknowledged the interdependent nature of strategies and self-regulation and stated that "neither

L.-S. Huang (✉)
Department of Linguistics, University of Victoria, Victoria, BC, Canada
e-mail: lshuang@uvic.ca

© Springer Nature Switzerland AG 2021
H. Mohebbi and C. Coombe (eds.), *Research Questions in Language Education and Applied Linguistics*, Springer Texts in Education,
https://doi.org/10.1007/978-3-030-79143-8_40

self-regulation, nor learning strategy has to become a casualty of the controversy, caught in the cross-fire of the various arguments" (p. 169). Meanwhile, the decades of findings have been undeniably supported by the relevance of the strategic component within the various language ability models or constructs of communicative competence put forward during the past few decades (Swain et al., 2009). Notably, the field has wrestled with recent efforts to merge learner strategies with related concepts such as self-regulation, agency, and autonomy (Oxford, 2011). Most recently, Thomas and Rose's (2018) conceptual article has persuasively postulated the need to "disentangle the concept of self-directed learning from definitions of learner strategies" (p. 248) and introduced their "regulated language learning strategies continuum," where self-regulation can be conceptually separate from learner strategies.

Overall, the focus of research has been mainly on strategy instruction, with limited attention to the inductive, awareness-raising approach to developing learners' strategic competence (e.g., Feyton et al., 1999; Huang, 2010, 2012). With the findings from Plonsky's (2011) meta-analysis of 61 primary studies focused on strategy instruction, which found a small-to-medium overall effect on L2 learning performance from this approach, disagreement about the teachability as well as feasibility of strategy instruction appears to have lessened. But as Plonsky (2011) pointed out, wide-ranging variations can be found across studies; further, "there is also an advantage for longer interventions as well as those that focus on only a few strategies" (p. 1010). Because the effectiveness of strategy instruction hinges on its length, whether the time devoted to it justifies the gains remains a central concern for instructors with limited instructional time (Rees-Miller, 1993). For language-teaching professionals, research has not yet addressed lingering questions such as: What is the optimal length of instruction, factoring in the cost–benefit ratio? Which strategies should be selected for instruction, given the wide range identified in the literature?

The current state of knowledge points to strategic behaviours as being dependent on learner, task, and context. The search for ways to help learners improve performance remains one of the lasting quests of teachers, learners, and researchers alike. Ultimately, the key to moving the field forward lies in addressing the challenges pertaining to definitions and categorizations, underlying theory, and methodological issues, and examining complex relationships among key variables by testing mediation and moderation effects with significant implications for the validity of strategic competence (e.g., Huang, 2013; Plonsky, 2011).

The Research Questions

1. *Instructional approach*: What are the prolonged effects of direct, explicit strategy instruction and an indirect, implicit strategy awareness approach to strategy development on learners' task performance in speaking, listening, reading, and/or writing?

2. *Strategy use and performance features*: What are the effects of direct, explicit strategy instruction or an indirect strategy awareness approach to strategy development on learners' performance as measured by different linguistic features (e.g., fluency, lexical diversity and complexity, syntactic complexity, and grammatical accuracy)?

3. *Transferability of strategies*: Are learner strategies transferable across different task types or contexts by learners at different proficiency levels?

4. *Interface of skill domains*: How does learners' strategy use differ in performing various types of integrated (i.e., tasks involving multiple skills, such as reading-to-write or listening-to-speak) versus non-integrated tasks?

5. *Mediational methods*: Do the methods used to develop learners' awareness of strategy use and to elicit data related to learners' strategy use play a role in identifying learners' strategic behaviours? What is the relationship between methods used and learning outcomes, as measured by language and strategic development?

6. *Learner variables*: What role do learners' demographic factors play in their reported and/or observed strategic behaviours?

7. *Strategic development across proficiency levels*: What strategic behaviours do learners at different proficiency levels (e.g., beginner, intermediate, and advanced) use in performing specific task types? How do their strategic behaviours change over time as they progress through or across proficiency levels?

8. *L1 literacy and L2 strategy use*: What are the effects of L1 literacy on young or adult learners in relation to learners' strategy use in L2/FL speaking, listening, reading, writing, and/or vocabulary learning?

9. *Mediation and moderation*: What potential mediational variables or intervening processes explain the association between variables (e.g., proficiency and strategic behaviours)? What are the potential moderating effects of certain individual or a bundle of individual or task variables on the relationship between strategy use and language performance?

10. How do language-learning experiences shape monolingual, bilingual, and multi-/plurilingual speakers' strategy use in performing identical tasks?

Suggested Resources

Cohen, A. D. (2011). Strategies in learning and using a second language (2nd ed.). Routledge.

In this updated, lengthened version of one of the seminal works in this area, originally published more than a decade ago, Cohen follows a similar approach in providing coverage designed to appeal to researchers, teacher trainers, language teachers, and program administrators. This volume revisits and updates the central issues concerning language learning and language use strategies, focusing mainly on adult learners. It also deals with several key issues important either to researchers seeking a general overview or to restoration of interest after the recent existential debate by one of the field's leading thinkers. For example, the volume pays attention to (a) the clarification, differentiation, and interpretation of key terms; (b) wide-ranging research methods for assessing L2 learner strategies in order to ensure rigour, with detailed treatment of the verbal report method; (c) frameworks for implementing strategy instruction; (d) a review of strategy instruction research regarding its rationale and effects; (e) the differential use of strategies by bi- or multilinguals; and; (f) strategic behaviours in language assessment. Researchers interested in test-taking strategies will find the chapter on this topic and the relevant research beneficial.

Griffiths, C. (Ed.) (2008). *Lessons from the good language learners*. **Cambridge University Press**.

This 23-chapter volume on the topic of good language learners, divided into two sections ("learner variables" and "learning variables"), addresses what makes a good language learner, why some learners are more successful than others, and how learners' characteristics relate to their strategy use. The first section covers the key grounds of learner variables (e.g., age, personality, gender, motivation, metacognition, autonomy, beliefs, culture, and aptitude) and the way they relate to strategy use. The second features various learning variables, including vocabulary, grammar, functional competence, pronunciation, the four skill domains (listening, speaking, reading, and writing), teaching and learning methods, strategy instruction and error corrections, and task types. The final chapter thoughtfully attempts to thread together all themes in the preceding chapters under four headings ("learner identity," "learner self-regulation," "the learning situation," and "the learning destination") and to explore the implications for teaching. This accessible edited collection of a variety of small-scale studies with their own "questions for further research" sections provides readers contemplating research in this area a cornucopia of insights and ideas to consider for further work.

Huang, L. S. (2013). Cognitive processes involved in performing the IELTS speaking test: Respondents' strategic behaviours in simulated testing and non-testing contexts. *IELTS Research Reports Online Series, 1*, **51**.

For researchers interested in learner strategies in the testing context, an area less discussed in the literature, this report provides a unique look at 40 intermediate and advanced learners' strategic behaviours in performing the three tasks in the IELTS Speaking Test in both simulated testing and non-testing situations using video-stimulated recall. The results suggested there were statistically significant differences in the identified strategic behaviours between the two contexts, with a moderate effect size; behaviors also varied across tasks, with a large effect size. The results also pointed to a significant interaction between a task and its context, with a moderate effect size, but no statistically significant differences for learners at the two proficiency levels. Critical points to highlight are the task and context variables.

Further, for readers interested in pursuing research in test-takers' and learners' cognitive processes and strategic behaviours, there are issues pertaining to methodological implications and to specific directions for future research. Such research should involve an adequate sample size based on power analysis, as well as an inter-disciplinary approach that involves examining mediating variables in order to move the field forward.

Oxford, R. L. (2011). Teaching and researching language learning strategies. Pearson Education Ltd.

This is the volume that launched the Strategic Self-Regulation Model (S^2R) informed by self-regulation theory, which shifted the focus of language-learning strategies and modified the strategic categories used extensively in the literature. Among the model's changes is the use of meta-strategies for each strategy category, including meta-cognitive, meta-sociocultural-interactive, and meta-affective. After presenting the S^2R model, the volume examines authentic uses of strategy assessment by reviewing data collection methods and quality issues, followed by different teaching approaches and factors to consider. It then looks at learner strategies, including both a guide to conducting research on S^2R and a synthesis of studies focused on various skill domains, and finally considers numerous resources, including those for researchers. Those interested in this research area may find useful chapters related to issues considered in the first section, the overview of research studies using different methodologies, and research gaps to consider in designing studies. Readers may also wish to refer to the second edition published in 2017, in which the first section proposes an integrated definition of language learning strategies through critically examining existing definitions.

Thomas, N., & Rose, H. (2018). Do language learning strategies need to be self-directed? Disentangling strategies from self-regulated learning. *TESOL Quarterly*, *53*(1), 248–257. https://doi.org/10.1002/tesq.473.

This conceptual article, which tracks the development of language learning strategy definitions, argues that the movements to link learner strategies with other related concepts such as self-regulation, self-regulated learning, agency, and autonomy have not clarified definitional criticisms. Drawing on the "self-determination continuum," the authors put forward their own *Regulated Language Learning Strategies Continuum* to advance the argument that although those concepts can be related to language learning strategies, they do not have to be interdependent with them or integrated into their definitions. Their conceptualization of language learning strategies has, moreover, pedagogical implications for devising ways to help learners move along the continuum in order to regulate themselves in deploying strategic behaviours.

References

Bax, S. (2013). The cognitive processing of candidates during reading tests: Evidence from eye-tracking. *Language Testing, 30*(4), 441–465. https://doi.org/10.1177/0265532212473244

Chen, L., Zhang, R., & Liu, C. (2013). Listening strategy use and influential factors in web-based computer assisted language learning. *Journal of Computer Assisted Learning, 30*(3), 207–219. https://doi.org/10.1111/jcal.12041

Cohen, A. D., & Macaro, E. (Eds.). (2007). *Language learner strategies: Thirty years of research and practice*. Oxford University Press.

Donato, R., & McCormick, D. (1994). A sociocultural perspective on language learning strategies: The role of mediation. *The Modern Language Journal, 78*(4), 453–464. https://doi.org/10.2307/328584

Dörnyei, Z. (1995). On the teachability of communication strategies. *TESOL Quarterly, 29*, 55–85. https://doi.org/10.2307/3587805

Dörnyei, Z., & Ryan, S. (2015). *The psychology of the language learner revisited*. Routledge.

Ehrman, M., & Oxford, R. (1989). Effects of sex differences, career choice, and psychological type on adults' language learning strategies. *The Modern Language Journal, 73*(1), 1–13. https://doi.org/10.2307/327261

Feyton, C. M., Flaiyz, J., & LaRocca, M. (1999). Consciousness raising and strategy use. *Applied Language Learning, 10*(1–2), 15–38.

Gao, X. (2007). Has language learning strategy research come to an end? A response to Tseng et al. *Applied Linguistics, 28*, 615–620. https://doi.org/10.1093/applin/amm034

Guo, X., & Huang, L-S. (2018). Are L1 and L2 strategies transferable: an exploration of the L1 and L2 writing strategies of Chinese graduate students. *The Language Learning Journal*. https://doi.org/10.1080/09571736.2018.1435710.

Huang, L.-S. (2010). Do different modalities of reflection matter? An exploration of adult second-language learners' reported strategy use and oral language production. *System, 38*(2), 245–261. https://doi.org/10.20429/ijsotl.2012.060227

Huang, L. S. (2013). Cognitive processes involved in performing the IELTS speaking test: Respondents' strategic behaviours in simulated testing and non-testing contexts. *IELTS Research Reports Online Series, 1*, 51.

Huang, L.-S. (2013). Cognitive processes involved in performing the IELTS speaking test: Respondents' strategic behaviours in simulated testing and non-testing contexts. *IELTS Research Report Series*, No. 1. IELTS Australia.

Naiman, N., Fröhlich, M., Stern, H., & Todesco, A. (1978). *The good language learner*. The Ontario Institute for Studies in Education.

Oxford, R. L. (2011). *Teaching and researching language learning strategies*. Pearson Education.

Oxford, R. L., & Amerstorfer, C. M. (2018). *Individual learner characteristics: Situating strategy use in diverse contexts*. Bloomsbury.

Oxford, R. L., & Ehrman, M. E. (1995). Adults' language learning strategies in an intensive foreign language program in the United States. *System, 23*(3), 359–386. https://doi.org/10.1016/0346-251X(95)00023-D

Oxford, R. L., & Nyikos, M. (1989). Variables affecting choice of language learning strategies by university students. *The Modern Language Journal, 73*(3), 291–300. https://doi.org/10.1111/j.1540-4781.1989.tb06367.x

Plonsky, L. (2011). The effectiveness of second language strategy instruction: A meta-analysis. *Language Learning, 61*(4), 993–1038. https://doi.org/10.1111/j.1467-9922.2011.00663.x

Rees-Miller, J. (1993). A critical appraisal of learner training: Theoretical bases and teaching implications. *TESOL Quarterly, 27*(4), 679–689. https://doi.org/10.2307/3587401

Rubin, J. (1975). What the good language learner can teach us. *TESOL Quarterly, 9*, 41–51.

Swain, M., Huang, L.-S., Barkaoui, K., Brooks, L., & Lapkin, S. (2009). The speaking section of the TOEFL iBT™ (SSTiBT): Test-takers' reported strategic behaviors, *TOEFL iBT™ Research Series No.* TOEFLiBT-10. *Educational Testing Service.* https://doi.org/10.1002/j.2333-8504.2009.tb02187.x

Thomas, N., & Rose, H. (2018). Do language learning strategies need to be self-directed? Disentangling strategies from self-regulated learning. *TESOL Quarterly, 53*(1), 248–257. https://doi.org/10.1002/tesq.473

Tseng, W. T., Dörnyei, Z., & Schmitt, N. (2006). A new approach to assessing strategic learning: The case of self-regulation in vocabulary acquisition. *Applied Linguistics, 27,* 78–102. https://doi.org/10.1093/applin/ami046

Vandergrift, L., & Goh, C. C. M. (2012). *Teaching and learning second language listening: Metacognition in action.* Routledge.

Wengelin, Å., Torrance, M., Holmqvist, K., Simpson, S., Galbraith, D., Johansson, V., & Johansson, R. (2009). Combined eye-tracking and keystroke-logging methods for studying cognitive processes in text production. *Behavior Research Methods, 41*(2), 337–351. https://doi.org/10.3758/BRM.41.2.337

Zhou, C., & Huang, L-S. (2018). An exploration of strategies used by Chinese graduate students in electrical engineering and education: Integrating questionnaire, task performance, and post-task recall data. *Asian-Pacific Journal of Second and Foreign Language Education, 3*(15),1–22. https://doi.org/10.1186/s40862-018-0054-2

Li-Shih Huang completed her Ph.D. at the Ontario Institute for Studies in Education of the University of Toronto. Currently, she is an Associate Professor of Applied Linguistics at the University of Victoria (UVic). Li-Shih has been the recipient of the UVic's Humanities Teaching Excellence Award, TESOL's Mary Finocchiaro Award for Excellence in Pedagogical Materials Development, and the Award for an Outstanding Paper on NNEST Issues. Li-Shih's scholarly interests include areas such as needs and outcomes assessment, strategic behaviours in language learning and language testing, and reflective learning. She has received numerous research grants from the Social Sciences and Humanities Research Council of Canada (SSHRC), the Educational Testing Service (ETS®), and the International English Language Testing System (IELTS™) for her work in those areas.

Learning Beyond the Classroom

Hayo Reinders and Phil Benson

The field referred to as 'learning beyond the classroom' (LBC) (also known as 'learning in the wild') comprises a wide range of research agendas in areas as diverse as informal and non-formal learning, community-based learning, self-access learning, language advising, naturalistic learning, study abroad, lifelong learning, lifewide learning and many others. What all of these areas have in common is that they operate on a number of continua that make them distinct from formal/traditional educational environments. The first of these is 'location', which refers to the physical or virtual space in which learning takes place. From learning in fixed, physical spaces, to learning in the home, at work or in the community, location is often considered a defining characteristic of learning beyond the classroom. However, it is only one element – formality is an equally important aspect and refers to the extent to which learning is linked to educational qualifications or structured by educational institutions. Clearly this is not a black-and-white proposition. Highly structured and regulated university degrees, certificates of attendance at community courses, and entirely naturalistic learning are only some of the points on a continuum of options. A third dimension of learning beyond the classroom is pedagogy, or the degree to which teaching is involved. Formal, curricular classroom teaching represents one end of the continuum and self-instruction another. Yet, learners regularly combine two or more types of learning with different degrees of formality. And even learning that on the surface may appear not to involve teaching may in fact be more like a formal instructional endeavour than it

H. Reinders (✉)
Anaheim University, Anaheim, USA
e-mail: info@innovationinteaching.org

School of Liberal Arts, King Mongkut's University of Technology Thonburi, Bangkok, Thailand

P. Benson
Multilingualism Research Centre, Macquarie University, Sydney, Australia
e-mail: philip.benson@mq.edu.au

© Springer Nature Switzerland AG 2021
H. Mohebbi and C. Coombe (eds.), *Research Questions in Language Education and Applied Linguistics*, Springer Texts in Education,
https://doi.org/10.1007/978-3-030-79143-8_41

seems at first glance. For example, a learner who slavishly and uncritically follows the highly structured, carefully sequenced and rigidly controlled structure of a self-study resource, may have simply had the teacher's voice transferred from the classroom to the book. The final dimension is 'control', which refers to the way decisions are distributed between the learner and others. In traditional, transmissive environments, all decisions are made by the 'sage on the stage'. In completely autonomous forms of learning, all decisions rest with the learner. Again, however, many hybrid options are possible; learners may consciously and purposively decide on some occasions to follow the teacher, if they have considered the options and decided it is the most suitable for their purpose at a given moment in time.

Clearly, for research in this area to be productive, it is firstly important that all of these elements are acknowledged and carefully identified and described in any study, so that meaningful comparisons between research findings can be made. Secondly, it is important that the interaction between the four dimensions are considered; rather than a static view of a learner in one context, it is vital that a more dynamic and holistic approach is taken that recognises the learner and his or her activities as part of a wider ecology of learning, some elements of which are likely to be more structured and formal and others less so.

This calls for new research questions and new ways of investigating them. Learning beyond the classroom is a fascinating and highly complex area of study as well as one in which a lot of terrain remains to be explored. The research questions below were adapted from Reinders and Benson (2017) and represent a starting point for some of the most urgent areas of investigation to be carried out.

The Research Questions

1. Document the settings and resources for LBC that are available to a group of learners with which you work. How do they make use of these settings and resources and how do they connect them with classroom learning?
2. Many new online and offline settings for LBC have emerged in recent years. Using an in-depth study, answer the question: How is one emerging setting used for LBC by an individual or small number of language learners?
3. What configuration of LBC settings is available in a particular study abroad programme and what uses do students make of them?
4. Using Critical Incident Analysis, what key experiences exist in LBC and what is their potential to inhibit or facilitate the language learning process?
5. What information can a case study of a learner's efforts to learn a language beyond the classroom give us, in particular, focusing on the strategies used to identify, take advantage of, and/or create opportunities to learn and use the language? What are the factors that affect the learner's success in these efforts?
6. Using Social Network Analysis, in what ways do learners use technology for LBC in one particular setting (e.g. in an online community, or in an online role-playing game) to identify how learners create opportunities for language learning within them?

7. What differences can be revealed on survey results of teachers' beliefs about LBC with observations of classroom practices relating to LBC, using mixed-method research study?
8. What are the outcomes of an action research project in which you design and evaluate an out-of-class learning project for a group of learners that you teach?
9. What are the outcomes of an action research project in which you design and evaluate an initiative or programme to help students make better use of the resources for LBC in their local environments?
10. How effective is teachers' advice to students on improving their LBC?

Suggested Resources

Reinders, H. (2020). A framework for learning beyond the classroom. In: Raya, M. & Vieira, F. (Eds.), *Autonomy in language education: Theory, research, and practice* (pp. 63–73). Routledge.
This chapter presents a framework of pedagogical practices for enhancing learning beyond the classroom. It distinguishes between the locations where learning beyond the classroom takes place, its degree of formality, the type of pedagogy and the locus of control and places these in a broader ecology of learning that combines learning in class with learning beyond it. It presents a pedagogical sequence of instructions based on encouraging, preparing, supporting and involving learners in/for language learning beyond the classroom.

Benson, P. & Reinders, H. (eds.) (2011). *Beyond the language classroom.* Basingstoke: Palgrave Macmillan.

One of the first volumes to appear on the topic of learning beyond the classroom, this edited book brings together perspectives from around the world on the theory and practice of many forms of non-traditional learning and teaching, including home tutoring, learning in social networks, learning by older learners, tandem learning in virtual spaces and learning in the family.

Nunan, D. & Richards, J. (eds.) (2015). *Language learning beyond the classroom.* New York: Routledge.

Covering examples of learning beyond the classroom involving extensive reading, listening, vocabulary learning, pronunciation and other language skills, the 28 chapters in this book cover a wide range of contexts, including study abroad, cultural encounters, the use of television and songs, language exchange, dialogue journals, the use of projects and many others. The chapters consider both the linguistic as well as the cultural, social and affective aspects of learning beyond the classroom. The chapters cover initiatives originating in the classroom and extending outwards, as well as types of learning that are located entirely outside of formal education.

Lai, C. (2017). *Autonomous language learning with technology beyond the* *classroom.* **London: Bloomsbury**.

Focusing on the uses of technology for autonomous language learning beyond the classroom, this book covers key concepts and theoretical frameworks, and the roles of learners, teachers, and resource and environment design. The book concludes by identifying key areas and methods for future research in the field.

Sockett, G. (2014). *The online informal learning of English.* **Basingstoke: Palgrave Macmillan**.

This book focuses on informal, self-directed English language learning by students who use online media for leisure and entertainment for social communication. It examines the extent of this phenomenon among European students, effects on language acquisition and implications for the teaching of English in the twenty-first century. The book concludes with a discussion of research methodologies for studying online informal language learning.

Cole, J., & Vanderplank, R. (2016). Comparing autonomous and class-based learners in Brazil: Evidence for the present-day advantages of informal out-of-class learning. *System*, **61, 31–42**.

A data-based study comparing the language proficiency of Brazilian adults who have learned English to advanced levels with and without classroom instruction. The study shows that it is possible to reach high levels of proficiency without classroom instruction and provides evidence that LBC may be more effective in some respects than classroom learning.

Hayo Reinders (www.innovationinteaching.org) is TESOL Professor and Director of Research at Anaheim University, USA, and Professor of Applied Linguistics at KMUTT in Thailand. He is founder of the globalInstitute for Teacher Leadership and editor of Innovation in Language Learning & Teaching. His interests are in out-of-class learning, technology and language teacher leadership.

Phil Benson is Professor of Applied Linguistics at Macquarie University, Sydney, Australia, where he teaches a Master's degree course on Language Learning beyond the Classroom. He has taught English as a foreign language and Applied Linguistics in North Africa, the Middle East, Malaysia, Japan and Hong Kong. He has published extensively on autonomy and informal language learning, study abroad, and narrative approaches to language learning research.

Long-Term English Learners

Maneka Deanna Brooks and Peter Smagorinsky

This entry focuses on a population of students who have come to be called long-term English learners (LTELs). LTEL is a term that appeared in the early 2000s (e.g., Freeman et al., 2002), although similar terms have been used by practitioners and researchers. This population of students, who are considered to be learning English as a second language, has been referred to variably in the research literature as long-term limited English proficient students (Olsen & Jaramillo, 1999), long term English learners (Olsen, 2010), and long-term English language learners (Menken et al., 2012). Other terms for this population that have been used among practitioners include ESL lifers (Valdés, 2001) and low-literacy students (Ruiz-de-Velasco et al., 2000).

There is not a single set of criteria that researchers or policymakers have used to identify a student as an LTEL. The most frequently used criterion is the number of years a student has been identified as a student who is learning English within the school system. However, there is even variation in the minimum number of years a student must remain classified as "learning English" to be considered a LTEL. For example, the minimum number of years can range between five and seven (Menken et al., 2012; U.S. Department of Education, 2016). Despite differences in identification criteria, LTELs are commonly described as academically struggling students who are orally bilingual for social purposes; yet, they have limited academic language and literacy abilities (e.g., Olsen, 2010). However, extant research demonstrates that these dominant narratives are overly homogenous and erase students' linguistic, literate, and academic abilities (e.g., Brooks, 2016; Thompson, 2015).

M. D. Brooks (✉)
Department of Curriculum and Instruction, Texas State University, San Marcos, TX, USA
e-mail: maneka@txstate.edu

P. Smagorinsky
Department of language and Literacy Education, The University of Georgia (emeritus),
Athens, GA, USA

© Springer Nature Switzerland AG 2021
H. Mohebbi and C. Coombe (eds.), *Research Questions in Language Education and Applied Linguistics*, Springer Texts in Education,
https://doi.org/10.1007/978-3-030-79143-8_42

The origin of the LTEL label in the U.S. educational system does not limit its use to national boundaries. Cushing-Leubner and King (2015) note that it is also used in Canada and Australia. In contexts where the official label does not exist, the beliefs about bilingual students that accompany the LTEL label may still be present. For example, Flores (2017) and Rosa (2016) note that the predominant narrative that describes LTELs as bilinguals with less than "full" proficiency in two languages reflects the discredited concept of Scandinavian origin: semilingualism. Notably, similar conceptions about bilingual young people are encompassed in the Flemish term zerolingual (Jaspers, 2011). Ideas about bilinguals who seemingly speak a language, but lack linguistic proficiency, are international.

Given the predominance of deficit perspectives about this population, research must continue to interrogate the LTEL label and accompanying ideologies (Brooks, 2017). Specifically, scholars should attend to the role of raciolinguistic ideologies (Flores & Rosa, 2015) and multilingual perspectives on language teaching, learning, and assessment (García & Wei, 2014; Gorter & Cenoz, 2017; Kibler & Valdés, 2016; Makalela, 2016). Moreover, the field must not overlook the consequences of extended classification as "learning English" for students' academic trajectories (e.g., Umansky, 2016). Finally, there is a need to develop instructional approaches that center equity and build upon the linguistic, literate, and academic strengths of this student population (e.g., Ascenzi-Moreno et al., 2013).

The Research Questions

1. How do educators, counselors, and school leaders conceptualize the linguistic and academic abilities of students who are considered to be long-term English learners (LTELs)?
2. How has the institutionalization of the LTEL label impacted course placement practices in K-12 settings?
3. What are the educational histories of students who have been identified as learning English for more than five years?
4. How can English language assessments be designed to recognize the skilled use of minoritized Englishes as proficient uses of language?
5. How do teachers who identify as monolingual and bi/multilingual articulate the perceived potentials and limitations of multilingual group-work?
6. What aspects of the reclassification process serve as roadblocks to students being identified as proficient in English?
7. How do language teacher educators engage in pedagogy that legitimizes dynamic linguistic practices of language-minoritized students and raise awareness about language and power? (Flores & Rosa, 2015)
8. What are the educational experiences of students who are dually-identified as LTELs and in need of special education services?

9. What does LTELs language use in "non-academic" contexts reveal about their linguistic abilities?
10. How can researchers and practitioners collaborate to integrate new understandings of multilingualism into instruction for students considered to be long-term English learners? (Kibler & Valdés, 2016)?

Suggested Resources

Brooks, M. D. (2015). "It's like a script": Long-term English learners' experiences with and ideas about academic reading. *Research in the Teaching of English*, *49*(4), 383–406.

In this year-long multiple case study of five adolescent long-term English learners (LTELs), Brooks examines participants' classroom reading experiences and individual ideas about reading. This focus on reading as it is instantiated in their day-to-day lives is a move away from the predominant perspective in research that had focused primarily on standardized test scores. The findings illustrate how students' day-to-day experiences with reading and their understanding of what counts as successful reading is distinct from the reading assessed as English proficiency. Reading on assessments is silent and individual, whereas their classroom experience emphasized oral language, teacher interpretation of meaning, and group reading of texts. As a result, Brooks points out that low standardized test scores cannot be solely attributed to English proficiency. Students must be treated holistically to understand that performances may be a reflection of history of experiences with instruction and thus warrant a different approach to education.

Estrada, P., & Wang, H. (2018). Making English learner reclassification to fluent English proficient attainable or elusive: When meeting criteria is and is not enough. *American Educational Research Journal*, *55*(2), 207–242.

An essential factor in the educational history of LTELs is that they have not been reclassified as proficient in English for multiple years. In this article, Estrada and Wang draw on quantitative and qualitative data from two districts over the course of multiple years to examine patterns in reclassification. They call attention to the phenomenon of students who meet the criteria of English proficiency without being reclassified as proficient in English. Specifically, their findings document how reclassification criteria and policies can facilitate or impede ELs' exiting the LTEL classification. In addition, the authors identify the role of the school staff in hindering the reclassification of students who meet eligibility criteria. Families and students were frequently absent from these decision-making processes. Together, this research underscores the fact that immediately assuming that a student's on-going classification as an EL is solely related to their "limited English proficiency" ignores the bureaucratic processes involved.

Flores, N., Kleyn, T., & Menken, K. (2015). Looking holistically in a climate of partiality: Identities of students labeled long-term English language learners. *Journal of Language, Identity & Education*, *14*(2), 113–132.

Flores and colleagues' study calls attention to the role of *epistemic racism* in the lives of students who are considered to be LTELs. This epistemic racism positions an idealized monolingualism that is situated in White supremacy as "the unmarked societal norm" (p. 118). The authors argue that epistemic racism's integration into the foundation of social institutions, like schools, results in the erasure of the linguistic abilities of students of color. The authors' analysis of interviews of 28 LTEL high school students, classroom observations, and written classroom artifacts provides concrete examples as to how this phenomenon occurs. Furthermore, Flores and colleagues use of student interviews provide a forum for adolescents to talk about their own experiences and self-understandings. This focus on LTELs' discussions of their own identities was absent from previously published literature. Together, these contributions provide a necessary framework for research and practice that resists deficit perspectives about this population.

Kibler, A.K., Karam, F.J., Futch Ehrlich, V.A., Bergey, R., Wang, C., & Elreda, L.M. (2018). Who are 'Long-term English learners'? Using classroom interactions to deconstruct a manufactured learner label. *Applied Linguistics*, *39*(5), 741–765.

Kibler and colleagues' multiple case study of six students in sixth-grade examines US-educated adolescents classified as EL's peer-to-peer and teacher-student oral interactions. The focal students, who had varied histories of academic success, had been educated in the same district since kindergarten. Rather than relying on static characterizations of students linguistic and academic abilities, this study situates students' oral language use within their classroom-based opportunities for interaction. The six participants demonstrated diverse ways of interacting. Among other factors, the authors found that the focal students' interaction with peers and teachers reflected their individual identities, various interpersonal dynamics, and the way in which teachers' structured opportunities for communication. Specifically, the findings noted limited opportunities for "substantive dialogic academic discourse" (p. 21). This research challenges simplistic notions about students who are considered to be LTELs. Moreover, it emphasizes the consequence of how educators construct opportunities for oral interaction through assignments and interpersonal engagement.

Kibler, A. K., & Valdés, G. (2016). Conceptualizing language learners: Socioinstitutional mechanisms and their consequences. *The Modern Language Journal*, *100*(S1), 96–116.

Kibler and Valdés illustrate that language learner categories are a by-product of transforming language, a system of communication, into an academic subject. This process is what Valdés terms in her earlier work 'curricularization.' The authors analyze these categories to demonstrate how they are embedded with, among other beliefs, particular understandings about language, language learning, language teaching. Through highlighting the lack of neutrality of language learner labels, they underscore their significance for how teaching and learning occurs. Within this broader examination of language learner categories, the authors analyze the LTEL label. Kibler and Valdés highlight the way in which embedded conceptualizations of language and language learning within popular and scholarly understandings of this category can limit LTEL students' educational opportunities and minimizes their existing abilities. Recognizing the significance of labels, the authors call for research-practice collaborations that are situated in multilingual perspectives that challenge deficit characterizations of these student populations.

References

Ascenzi-Moreno, L., Kleyn, T., & Menken, K. (2013). *A CUNY-NYSIEB framework for the education of 'long-term English learners': 6–12 grades.* New York: CUNY-NYSIEB. Retrieved from www.nysieb.ws.gc.cuny.edu/files/2013/06/cuny-nysiebframework-for-ltels-Spring-2013-final.pdf

Brooks, M. D. (2016). "Tell me what you are thinking": An investigation of five Latina LTELs constructing meaning with academic texts. *Linguistics and Education, 35,* 1–14.

Brooks, M. D. (2017). "She doesn't have the basic understanding of a language": Using spelling research to challenge deficit conceptualizations of adolescent bilinguals. *Journal of Literacy Research, 49*(3), 342–370.

Cushing-Leubner, J. & King, K. A. (2015). Long-term English learners, and language education policy. In A. Yiakoumetti (Ed.) *Multilingualism and language in education: Current sociolinguistic and pedagogical perspectives from Commonwealth countries* (pp. 199–220). Cambridge University Press.

Flores, N. (2017). The specter of semilingualism in the bilingualism of Latino students. *Texas Education Review, 5*(1), 76–80. Retrieved from http://txedrev.org/

Freeman, Y. S., Freeman, D. E., & Mercuri, S. (2002). *Closing the achievement gap: How to reach limited-formal-schooling and long-term English learners.* Heinemann.

García, O., & Wei, L. (2014). *Translanguaging: Language, bilingualism and education.* Palgrave MacMillan.

Gorter, D., & Cenoz, J. (2017). Language education policy and multilingual assessment. *Language and Education, 31*(3), 231–248.

Jaspers, J. (2011). Talking like a "zerolingual". Ambiguous linguistic caricatures at an urban secondary school. *Journal of Pragmatics, 43,* 1264–1278.

Kibler, A. K., & Valdés, G. (2016). Conceptualizing language learners: Socioinstitutional mechanisms and their consequences. *The Modern Language Journal, 100*(S1), 96–116.

Makalela, L. (2016). Ubuntu translanguaging: An alternative framework for complex multilingual encounters. *Southern African Linguistics and Applied Language Studies, 34*(3), 187–196.

Menken, K., Kleyn, T., & Chae, N. (2012). Spotlight on "long-term English language learners": Characteristics and prior schooling experiences of an invisible population. *International Multilingual Research Journal, 6,* 121–142.

Olsen, L., & Jaramillo, A. (1999). *Turning the tides of exclusion: A guide for educators and advocates for immigrant students.* California Tomorrow.

Olsen, L. (2010). *Reparable harm: Fulfilling the unkept promise of educational opportunity for California's long term English learners.* Californians Together.

Rosa, J. D. (2016). Standardization, racialization, languagelessness: Raciolinguistic ideologies across communicative contexts. *Journal of Linguistic Anthropology, 26*(2), 162–183.

Ruiz-de-Velasco, J., Fix, M., & Chu Clewell, B. (2000). *Overlooked & underserved: Immigrant students in U.S. secondary schools.* The Urban Institute.

Thompson, K. D. (2015). Questioning the long-term English learner label: How categorization can blind us to students' abilities. *Teachers College Record, 117*(12), 1–50.

U.S. Department of Education. (2016). *Non-regulatory guidance: English learners and Title III of the elementary and secondary education act (ESEA), as amended by the every student succeeds act (ESSA).* Retrieved from https://www2.ed.gov/policy/elsec/leg/essa/essatitleiiiguidenglish learners92016.pdf

Umansky, I. M. (2016). Leveled and exclusionary tracking: English learners' access to academic content in middle school. *American Educational Research Journal, 53*(6), 1792–1833.

Valdés, G. (2001). *Learning and not learning English: Latino students in American schools.* Teachers College Press.

Maneka Deanna Brooks is an assistant professor of reading education at Texas State University. Dr. Brooks' research agenda centers on everyday educational practices that impact the educational trajectories of bilingual adolescents. Her publications span the topics of bilingualism, adolescent literacy instruction, language proficiency and assessment, course placement, and teacher education. Dr. Brooks' work has been published in the *Journal of Literacy Research, Research in the Teaching of English, Language and Education*, and other venues.

Peter Smagorinsky is Distinguished Research Professor in the College of Education at The University of Georgia and Distinguished Visiting Scholar at the Universidad de Guadalajara, Mexico. His work takes a sociocultural perspective on literacy teaching and learning, teacher education, the teaching of the school discipline of English/Language Arts, neurodiversity, and related phenomena. He is the faculty advisor to the *Journal of Language and Literacy Education*, an open-access, refereed journal published by graduate students in his department.

Materials Development for Language Learning

43

Brian Tomlinson

Materials development is a relatively new academic field and until the nineteen nineties it was considered by most academics to be a practical pursuit to be discussed as an adjunct to language teaching methodology. However, towards the beginning of this century publications began to appear which discussed the theoretical principles as well as the procedures of materials development (e.g. Tomlinson, 1998). These publications tended to focus on such topics as materials evaluation, materials adaptation and materials writing and there were few reports of research studies on materials development. However, very quickly materials development became academically respectable and more and more post-graduate students and university researchers began to research aspects of materials development. Many of these studies have since been reported in Folio (the journal of MATSDA, the Materials Development Association—www.matsda.org) in academic journals and in such books as Tomlinson and Masuhara (2010), Tomlinson (2013, 2016), McGrath (2013), Harwood (2010, 2014), Garton and Graves (2014) and Mishan and Timmis (2015). For a review of the rapid progress of materials development from a practical pursuit to a principled academic discipline informed and driven by research see Tomlinson (2012) and Tomlinson and Masuhara (2018).

So far materials development research has mainly concerned itself with issues related to authenticity of texts and tasks, to the imposition of ideologies, to censorship, to materials evaluation, to materials adaptation and to the comparative effects of different pedagogical approaches. The measurement has been mainly of effects on learner impressions and attitudes but there is a welcome move towards more empirical research and to the measurement of the effects of materials on actual learner performance (see Tomlinson and Masuhara (2018). Obviously, the effects of materials on performance can never be entirely isolated from the effects of other variables such as teacher/learner rapport, teacher supplementation, learner moti-

B. Tomlinson (✉)
University of Liverpool, Liverpool, Merseyside, UK

Anaheim University, Anaheim, CA, USA

© Springer Nature Switzerland AG 2021
H. Mohebbi and C. Coombe (eds.), *Research Questions in Language Education and Applied Linguistics*, Springer Texts in Education,
https://doi.org/10.1007/978-3-030-79143-8_43

vation, learner out of class experience and time available for learning. However, indications of the likely effects of types of materials will be very welcome.

The Research Questions

1. Do delayed post-treatment tests of communicative effectiveness indicate a greater increase in communicative competence for B1/2 level learners who have followed a text-driven approach (TDA) than those who have followed a presentation, practice, production (PPP) approach?
2. Do delayed post-treatment tests of communicative effectiveness indicate a greater increase in communicative competence for B1/2 level learners who have followed a text-driven approach (TDA) than those who have followed a task-based approach (TBLT) which is not driven by texts?
3. Can affective engagement be demonstrated to be a more powerful determiner of text accessibility than text complexity?
4. Does evidence from questionnaires, interviews and actual projects indicate that students are less resistant to innovation in materials development than teachers are?
5. Do students who are asked to read the same text a number of times at spaced intervals acquire more language from the text than students who are asked to return to the text a number of times at spaced intervals for different purposes?
6. Can it be demonstrated that materials which follow a language awareness approach in which learners make discoveries about the use of grammar for themselves are more likely to help learners develop grammatical competence than materials which teach grammar through a presentation, practice, production (PPP) approach?
7. Do teachers who use a set of materials as a resource to exploit help their learners to achieve greater communicative competence than teachers of equivalent learners who use the same set of materials as a script to follow?
8. Can it be demonstrated that materials developed by a large team of varying experience and talents are more likely to be effective in helping learners to develop communicative competence than those developed by a single author?
9. Can it be demonstrated that a textbook with accompanying digital resources is more likely to be effective in facilitating the development of communicative competence than a stand alone textbook?
10. Do materials featuring texts focusing on controversial topics achieve more affective and cognitive engagement than those featuring texts focusing on uncontroversial topics?

Suggested Resources

Garton, S. & Graves, K. (Eds.). (2014). *International perspectives on materials in ELT*. **Basingstoke: Palgrave Macmillan**.

This collection of chapters from practitioner researchers around the world is driven by a conviction that there has been insufficient published research on the development of language learning materials and especially on the use of materials by teachers and by learners in the classroom. The book therefore tries to close this gap in the literature by including chapters which report empirical research and a number of chapters which investigate how materials are actually used in the classroom. These chapters report, for example, on how materials are actually used in classrooms in Algeria, Bahrain, Eastern Europe and Ghana. The book is also distinctive in providing research reports on the effectiveness of such digital materials as mobile phones, digital games and Web 2.0 tools.

Harwood, N. (Ed.). (2014). *English language teaching textbooks: content, consumption, production*. **Basingstoke: Palgrave Macmillan**.

Like Garton and Graves (2014) this is a collection of chapters from around the world reporting on principled research of aspects of materials development. It focuses on the "content" of textbooks (including the linguistic, topic and ideological content), the "consumption" of textbooks (i.e. how they are actually used) and the "production" of coursebooks (i.e. how textbook writers develop their materials). Some of the chapters focus on the content and the effects of global coursebooks, some on the classroom use of EAP and ESP textbooks and some on how authors have actually gone about designing, writing and delivering their textbooks.

Tomlinson, B. (2012). Materials development. *Language Teaching* **45 (2), 143–179**.

This state-of-the-art article reports the origins and development of the field of materials development for language learning and reviews the literature on the evaluation, adaptation, production and exploitation of language learning materials. It also reviews and comments on the literature on the many controversial issues in the field, on the electronic delivery of materials and on research in materials development. The section on research draws attention to the need for more empirical research on materials development and refers to a number of recent PhD studies which have conducted empirical research on, for example, the effects of comprehension-based materials for beginners of Bahasa Indonesia, materials designed to remedy reticence in Vietnam and the comparative effects of input-based and production-based vocabulary materials. The section on controversial issues reports debates and discussions on issues but is able to report very little research as of yet. This is a rich area for researchers with opportunities for pioneering research on the value of, for example, global textbooks, authentic texts and authentic tasks, the value of controversial topics, the effects of humanizing materials and the role played by ideology in materials.

Tomlinson, B. & Masuhara, H. (Eds.). (2010). *Research for materials development in language learning: Evidence for best practice.* **London: Continuum**.

This is probably the first book to devote itself to reporting research studies conducted on the effects of different types of language learning materials and of different approaches to the design and delivery of language learning materials. Altogether there are reports of twenty-seven research studies from fourteen countries spread around the world on such topics as extensive reading, authenticity, process drama, text-driven approaches, form-focused approaches and materials evaluation. The book also provides in Chap. 1 (pp. 1–20) a review of the published research to date on language learning materials and in Chaps. 25 and 26 (pp. 399–424) suggestions for applications of the results reported in the studies to second language acquisition theory and research and to the development of materials for language learning.

Tomlinson, B. & Masuhara, H. (2018). *The complete guide to the theory and practice of materials development for language learning.* **Hoboken, NJ: Wiley**.

This is a book which provides a critical review of the recent world literature on all aspects of the theory and practice of materials development for language learning. In addition, the authors draw on their extensive experience of teaching, teacher training, materials development and research to suggest and illustrate approaches to materials evaluation and adaptation and to the development of materials for different ages, levels and purposes. Of particular interest to researchers should be Chap. 2 on Issues in Materials Development (pp. 25–51) and Chap. 15 on Materials Development Research (pp. 355–388), a chapter in which the authors report the rapidly increasing attention being given to the study of the effects of different pedagogical approaches in the design, writing and use of language learning materials. In this chapter also the authors propose areas of research which they think "would be very informative and which could stimulate improvements in materials development leading to more durable and effective acquisition of language and more successful development of communication skills." (p. 366).

References

Garton, S., & Graves, K. (Eds.). (2014). *International perspectives on materials in ELT*. Palgrave Macmillan.

Harwood, N. (Ed.). (2010). *Materials in ELT: Theory and practice*. Cambridge University Press.

Harwood, N. (Ed.). (2014). *English language teaching textbooks: Content, consumption, production*. Palgrave Macmillan.

McGrath, I. (2013). *Teaching materials and the roles of EFL/ESL teachers*. Bloomsbury.

Mishan, F., & Timmis, I. (2015). *Materials development for TESOL*. Edinburgh University Press.

Tomlinson, B. (Ed.). (1998). *Materials development in language teaching*. Cambridge University Press.

Tomlinson, B. (2012). Materials development. *Language Teaching, 45*(2), 143–179.

Tomlinson, B. (Ed.). (2013). *Applied linguistics and materials development*. Bloomsbury.

Tomlinson, B. (Ed.). (2016). *SLA and materials development*. Routledge.

Tomlinson, B., & Masuhara, H. (Eds.). (2010). *Research for materials development in language learning: Evidence for best practice*. Continuum.

Tomlinson, B., & Masuhara, H. (2018). *The complete guide to the theory and practice of materials development for language learning*. Wiley.

Brian Tomlinson has worked as a teacher, teacher trainer, curriculum developer, film extra, football coach and university academic in Indonesia, Italy, Japan, Malaysia, Nigeria, Oman, Singapore, UK, Vanuatu and Zambia, as well as giving presentations in over seventy countries. He is Founder and President of MATSDA (the international Materials Development Association), an Honorary Visiting Professor at the University of Liverpool and a TESOL Professor at Anaheim University. He has over one hundred publications on materials development, language through literature, the teaching of reading, language awareness and teacher development and has recently co-authored with Hitomi Masuhara *The Complete Guide to the Theory and Practice of Materials Development for Language Learning* (published by Wiley in 2018) and *SLA Applied: Connecting Theory to Practice* (published by Cambridge University Press in 2021).

Metacognition in Academic Writing: Learning Dimensions

44

Raffaella Negretti

Metacognition refers to the unique human ability to reflect on one's own knowledge and thinking. This ability is crucial for learning and agency: metacognition allows us to assess what we know and do not know (including relevant previous experiences), set realistic goals, plan, monitor, and evaluate our performance. Theories of metacognition agree on two components. Metacognitive knowledge (or awareness), comprises knowledge of the person, the task, and strategies. Metacognitive regulation (or control) includes metacognitive skills such as planning, monitoring, control and evaluation (Winne & Azevedo, 2014). Inaccurate metacognition hampers our potential for learning, individual development, and academic achievement (Dunlosky & Thiede, 2013; Dunning et al., 2003).

As with any other area of learning, the development of academic writing expertise requires metacognition (Hacker et al., 2009, 2018). However, the communicative nature of academic writing poses some interesting challenges to the study of metacognition. Academic writing is contextual and situated, with a variety of purposes, genres and readers. This requires students to develop metacognition of how to meet the rhetorical expectations of academic writing tasks in different situations. Second, academic writing itself encompasses a variety of facets: rhetorical, processual, formal, and subject-specific (Tardy, 2009). Thus, learning to write for academic purposes requires the development of metacognition of strategies to address and integrate these complex facets in writing.

Research on metacognition in academic writing has focused on the connection between different metacognitive processes and writing quality and/or regulation (e.g. Escorcia et al., 2017; Hawthorne et al., 2017; Negretti, 2012; Qin & Zhang, 2019). However, when considering the social and communicative nature of academic writing and the intersection with applied linguistics and genre theory, many

R. Negretti (✉)
Department of Communication and Learning in Science, Division for Language and Communication, Chalmers University of Technology, Gothenburg, Sweden
e-mail: negretti@chalmers.se

© Springer Nature Switzerland AG 2021
H. Mohebbi and C. Coombe (eds.), *Research Questions in Language Education and Applied Linguistics*, Springer Texts in Education,
https://doi.org/10.1007/978-3-030-79143-8_44

questions are still open. For example, we still do not know enough about how students metacognitively engage with academic writing genres across contexts (see Driscoll et al., 2020), how metacognitive knowledge develops and impacts academic writing regulation and/or the accuracy of students' metacognitive judgments over time, and importantly how metacognition can support L2 writing pedagogy (see Lee & Mak, 2018) and subject-specific writing in higher education (see McGrath et al., 2019).

The Research Questions

1. What dimensions of metacognition promote effective self-regulation of academic writing, in students with different backgrounds, levels, and across contexts?
2. Assuming that academic writing expertise is multifaceted (cf. genre expertise, Tardy, 2009), how can we foster students' metacognitive awareness of the various facets of genre knowledge, and their eventual integration?
3. How can metacognitive knowledge of strategies for academic writing be fostered, and what are the effects on writing quality/performance?
4. What individual factors and/or contextual elements affect metacognitive accuracy in students' evaluation of their own academic writing?
5. In relation to calibration (accuracy of metacognitive judgments), what kind of metacognitive scaffolds—rubrics, concept maps, reflections etc.—facilitate students' accurate assessment of their academic writing?
6. What type of metacognitive training may promote transfer of writing across contexts?
7. How can metacognitive training be implemented in subject-specific courses that require students to produce academic texts?
8. What is the effect of different types of metacognitive scaffolds for the promotion of genre awareness and/or genre knowledge in the academic writing classroom?
9. How can metacognition about academic writing practices and pedagogy be promoted in teachers' professional development? (both academic writing and content teachers).
10. How can specific educational situations, such as collaborative writing or digital learning, promote metacognition in academic writing?

Suggested Resources

Clark, I. (2016). Genre, Identity, and the Brain: Insights from Neuropsychology. *The Journal of General Education, 65*(1), 1–19.

A pioneering scholar in her work on academic writing, in this paper Prof. Irene Clark explores the connection between learning to write, the development of genre knowledge, identity, and neuroplasticity. She discusses the changes in the brain that occur as we learn, and especially how the development of knowledge about academic genres—and our performance of these genres—influences our identity. After a review of research on neuroplasticity, the article addresses the implications of this research for academic writing, with a focus on genre and identity, and proposed pedagogical approaches to foster awareness and agency, touching upon the role of metacognition. A recommended, thought-provoking read for any researcher and teacher of academic writing.

Driscoll, D.L.; Paszek, J., Gorzelsky, G., Hayes, C.L., & Jones, E. (2020). Genre knowledge and writing development: Results from the writing transfer project. *Written Communication, 37*(1), 69–103..

The study reported is an example of how genre theory and metacognition theory can come together to inform research on academic writing in HE, with a focus on transfer. The study explores the development of genre knowledge and genre awareness in first-year, first-language (L1) students taking general writing courses, across four different institutions, and its long-term impact on student's wring performance. The study corroborates Tardy's (2009) theoretical model of genre knowledge development and shows that development of *nuanced* genre knowledge, beyond formal conventions, correlates with writing performance. Based on their findings, the authors make recommendations for pedagogy, and specifically the importance of promoting metacognitive strategies that raise students' awareness of their own strategies for completing a writing task, as well as their proficiency in regard to particular types of written genres.

Yeh, H. C. (2015). Facilitating metacognitive processes of academic genre-based writing using an online writing system. *Computer Assisted Language Learning, 28*(6), 479–498.

The paper by Yeh reports on an educational intervention aimed at promoting metacognition in academic writing with L2 students. The study also combines metacognition and genre pedagogy, illustrating an intervention that scaffolds the development of metacognitive strategies to address relevant aspects of genre: the communicative, rhetorical, textual, and social dimensions of writing. The study also explores how online digital environments can support metacognitive training in academic writing. Yeh shows that students made greater improvements in academic writing performance after experiencing metacognitive processes, and that collaborative efforts in metacognition supported students' development of metacognitive awareness about the academic genre and its demands, as well as their ability to monitor problems and apply their genre knowledge to their writing.

Negretti, R. (2017). Calibrating genre: Metacognitive judgments and rhetorical effectiveness in academic writing by L2 graduate students. *Applied Linguistics, 38*(4), 512–539.

This paper takes up the question of metacognitive accuracy (calibration) in academic writing, in this case with graduate (M.A. and Ph.D.) students. Adopting a qualitative approach, it aims to investigate why students make more or less accurate judgments about the rhetorical effectiveness of their texts, when compared with the expectations of academic writing teachers. Considering the situated and idiosyncratic nature of academic writing practices, the issue of calibration is worth further consideration, especially since it is often the least proficient students who make the most inaccurate judgments about their performance. Based on Hacker et al. (2009), this paper suggests that calibration of writing includes both aspects of depth of monitoring and alignment of criteria. It also proposes a rubric for the assessment of rhetorical effectiveness of research genres, based on Swales' work in English for Specific Purposes, which could be adopted for self-assessment and as a pedagogical tool for academic writing.

Negretti, R., & McGrath, L. (2018). Scaffolding genre knowledge and metacognition: insights from an L2 doctoral research writing course. *Journal of Second Language Writing, 40*, 12–31.

This study addresses the issue of how to implement metacognition in academic writing pedagogy. It reports on the development of metacognitive scaffolds in a writing-for-research course with doctoral students in the sciences, combining metacognition theory and genre pedagogy. It also explores the question of what stands the test of time in terms of writing pedagogy, by examining how the participants reported using genre knowledge metacognitively a few months after taking the course in academic writing. As such, the study provides inspiration and a concrete starting point for further pedagogical intervention studies that aim to incorporate metacognitive training in academic writing, and raises relevant points for the study of the relationship between metacognitive knowledge and writing transfer.

References

Driscoll, D. L., Paszek, J., Gorzelsky, G., Hayes, C. L., & Jones, E. (2020). Genre knowledge and writing development: Results from the writing transfer project. *Written Communication, 37*(1), 69–103.

Dunlosky, J., & Thiede, K. (2013). Four cornerstones of calibration research: Why understanding students' judgments can improve their achievement. *Learning and Instruction, 24*, 58–61.

Dunning, D., Johnson, K., Ehrlinger, J., & Kruger, J. (2003). Why people fail to recognize their own incompetence. *Current Directions in Psychological Science, 12*(3), 83–87.

Escorcia, D., Passerault, J. M., Ros, C., & Pylouster, J. (2017). Profiling writers: Analysis of writing dynamics among college students. *Metacognition and Learning, 12*(2), 233–273.

Hacker, D. J. (2018). A Metacognitive model of writing: An update from a developmental perspective. *Educational Psychologist, 53*(4), 220–237.

Hacker, D. J., Keener, M. C., & Kircher, J. C. (2009). Writing is applied metacognition. *Handbook of metacognition in education* (pp. 154–172). Routledge.

Hawthorne, K. A., Bol, L., & Pribesh, S. (2017). Can providing rubrics for writing tasks improve developing writers' calibration accuracy? *The Journal of Experimental Education, 85*(4), 689–708.

Lee, I., & Mak, P. (2018). Metacognition and metacognitive instruction in second language writing classrooms. *TESOL Quarterly, 52*(1).

McGrath, L., Negretti, R., & Nicholls, K. (2019). Hidden expectations: Scaffolding subject specialists' genre knowledge of the assignments they set. *Higher Education, 78*(5), 835–853. https://doi.org/10.1007/s10734-019-00373-9

Negretti, R. (2012). Metacognition in student academic writing: A longitudinal study of metacognitive awareness and its relation to task perception and evaluation of performance. *Written Communication, 29*(2), 142–179.

Qin, L. T., & Zhang, L. J. (2019). English as a foreign language writers' metacognitive strategy knowledge of writing and their writing performance in multimedia environments. *Journal of Writing Research, 12*(2), 394–413.

Tardy, C. M. (2009). *Building genre knowledge.* Parlor Press.

Winne, P., & Azevedo, R. (2014). Metacognition. In R. Sawyer (Ed.), *The cambridge handbook of the learning sciences* (pp. 63–87). Cambridge University Press.

Raffaella Negretti is associate professor of academic and scientific writing at Chalmers University of Technology, Department of Communication and Learning in Science, Division for Language and Communication. Her research addresses the topics of academic writing, genre pedagogy, and self-regulation/metacognition. Her work has been published in *Written Communication, Journal of Second Language Writing, English for Specific Purposes Journal, Applied Linguistics, and Higher Education*. She received a PhD in Educational Psychology and a M.A. in ESL at the University of Hawaii at Mano'a, USA, and an undergraduate degree in Foreign Languages and Literatures from Verona University (Laurea cum laude).

Second-Language Strategy Instruction

45

Luke Plonsky and Ekaterina Sudina

The basic premise underlying second-language (L2) strategy instruction (SI) is quite straightforward: Researchers or teachers instruct learners on strategies to help them become more effective and efficient learners and users of the target language. SI also draws support from theory as it is argued to promote learner autonomy/self-regulation (Rose et al., 2018) as well as strategic competence (Bachman & Palmer, 1996). Dozens of studies have sought to test these ideas. One group receives a treatment wherein they are taught one or more strategies. Their performance on a posttest is then compared to a control group that does not receive SI.

Results in this body of research are often encouraging but can vary substantially. In order to consolidate findings in this domain, the body of empirical work on SI has been synthesized on a number of occasions. Building on an earlier study, Plonsky (2019), meta-analyzed the effects of SI both overall and across different learner contexts, treatments, and outcomes. Looking across the entire sample of 77 studies and 112 unique experimental groups, Plonsky found an overall effect of SI of $d = 0.69$ [95% CIs: 0.53, 0.86]. This result indicates that, on average, experimental group participants outperform control or comparison group participants by approximately two-thirds of a standard deviation. Such a difference can be interpreted as a moderate effect in the context of L2 research, comparable to meta-analytic effects of instruction on L2 vocabulary or pronunciation. More practically speaking, such a benefit should also assuage concerns expressed by some regarding the place of SI in the L2 classroom (e.g., whether SI is worthy of valuable class time). The study also found that the effects of SI vary across different contexts, treatments, and outcomes. Larger effects were observed, for example, (a) among intermediate and advanced learners ($d = 0.74$ versus 0.39 for beginners), (b) when fewer strategies are taught ($d = 0.86$ versus 0.58 for larger numbers of

L. Plonsky (✉) · E. Sudina
English Department, Northern Arizona University, Flagstaff, AZ, USA
e-mail: ekaterina.sudina@nau.edu

© Springer Nature Switzerland AG 2021
H. Mohebbi and C. Coombe (eds.), *Research Questions in Language Education and Applied Linguistics*, Springer Texts in Education,
https://doi.org/10.1007/978-3-030-79143-8_45

strategies, (c) when interventions are sustained over longer periods of time (e.-g., > 2 weeks $d = 0.65$ vs. 0.49 when < 2 weeks) and (d) for certain skills (e.g., speaking [$d = 1$] and reading [$d = 0.82$]; see also Taylor et al., 2006) than for other skills such as listening ($d = 0.06$).

Despite the availability of robust synthetic findings, there is no shortage of un- and under-addressed questions that remain in the realm of L2 SI, several of which we propose below. There are also a number of valid concerns regarding the transparency of empirical efforts in this area that merit attention in future studies.

The Research Questions

1. What kinds of interactions might exist between the effectiveness of strategy instruction and learners' individual differences such as motivation, aptitude, working memory, and so forth?
2. Which strategies and techniques for teaching strategies are most effective for different proficiency levels, ages, and L1-L2 combinations?
3. To what extent do L3 learners transfer their L2 strategies? Can learners be taught to do so?
4. What types of strategies can most effectively be taught to heritage language learners?
5. What are the relative effects of SI that is integrated into other class activities vs. taught as an isolated course component?
6. Which strategies are most effective for each target skill (reading, writing, listening, speaking, pronunciation, grammar, pragmatics)?
7. To what extent does instruction on test taking strategies improve test performance?
8. Which strategies are most effective for distance or hybrid learners and how can SI be most effectively taught to such students?
9. When and how can SI be most effectively delivered to study abroad learners?
10. Which measures are most appropriate for estimating the effects of strategy instruction on different L2 skill areas?

Suggested Resources

Chamot, A.U. (2005). Language learning strategy instruction: Current issues and research. *Annual Review of Applied Linguistics, 25,* **112–130.**

The aim of the article is to synthesize key findings of noteworthy and representative language learning strategy intervention studies. The author discusses the methods employed by second language research to determine the strategies that learners use and proceeds to identify the characteristics of a "good language learner," emphasizing the role of comparative studies of language learning strategies—chosen by more and less successful learners—in teaching those strategies. A significant part of the article is devoted to an overview of classroom-based research on explicit strategy instruction including the following: (1) listening comprehension, (2) oral communication, (3) reading comprehension, (4) vocabulary, and (5) writing strategies studies. The author then addresses specific issues related to learning strategy instruction, reviews four metacognitive models, and indicates their applicability to teaching strategies in the language classroom. The article concludes with Chamot's suggestions for future research.

Grenfell, M. J., & Harris, V. (2017). *Language learner strategies: Contexts, issues and applications in second language learning and teaching.* **London: Bloomsbury.**

The purpose of this book is to present a comprehensive overview of language learner strategy (LLS) research in relation to teaching and learning as well as delve into the concept of strategy-based instruction (SBI). The volume is divided into three parts: (1) basics: principles and practice, (2) strategies in practice: from theory to research, and (3) applications. The authors strive to bridge the gap between theory and practice by highlighting and addressing burning issues in research on LLS such as the scarcity of information on research design which limits both study interpretability and the possibility of subsequent replications, and the lack of research on the learning strategies of bilinguals mastering a third language as opposed to a plethora of studies of monolingual learners' strategy use. Specialists with prior knowledge of the topic would find this volume particularly valuable and insightful.

Griffiths, C. (2018). *The strategy factor in successful language learning: The Tornado Effect (2nd ed.).* **Bristol: Multilingual Matters.**

This book aims to address the strategy construct from four different perspectives: conceptual, quantitative, qualitative, and pedagogical. The author introduces and analyses the key concept of the 'Tornado Effect' which refers to the spiral rather than linear relationship of strategy use to effective language learning and use. A powerful, enticing introduction immediately captures the attention of the intended audiences—teachers, students, and researchers—by illustrating through personal narratives the importance of strategy use in successful language development. Rich in similes and metaphors (hardly the most salient features of academic prose), this volume discusses how learner, contextual, and target (or goal-specific) variables relate to the learner's choice of strategy and identifies potentially underexplored areas that require further examination.

Oxford, R. L. (2011). *Teaching and researching language learning strategies.* **Harlow: Pearson Longman.**

Written in an open, clear style, in this volume, Oxford provides the reader with an in-depth overview of language learning strategies, with particular focus on the Strategic Self-Regulation (S^2R) Model of Language Learning and its practical applications. The book consists of 9 chapters organized into 4 sections: the strategic self-regulation (S^2R) model of language learning; authentic uses of strategy assessment and strategy assistance; researching learning strategies; and resources. Each chapter begins with a quotation from a famous author followed by a list of preview questions and an overview of the chapter and ends with a brief annotated bibliography of recommended further readings. Of particular relevance to the present discussion, Chap. 6 discusses pedagogical implications of direct versus separate strategy instruction as well as strategy instruction in distance learning, whereas Chap. 7 aims to help the reader design, conduct, and evaluate various learning strategy studies. Exploring the basic concepts first, the book is readily accessible even to novice researchers and educators without special background knowledge.

Plonsky, L. (2011). The effectiveness of second language strategy instruction: A meta-analysis. *Language Learning, 61*, **993–1038**.

Recognizing the vast body of empirical work on L2 strategy instruction, this study brings together findings in this area via meta-analysis. More specifically, effect sizes from 61 primary studies comprised of 95 unique samples were aggregated (averaged) to determine the overall effect of strategy instruction. The summary effect of $d = 0.49$, though somewhat smaller than other areas of instructed SLA (see Plonsky, 2017), indicates that learners receiving SI generally score approximately one-half of a standard deviation above control or comparison groups that do not receive any such treatment. Although these overall effects are useful and can help settle debates concerning whether SI should have a place in the L2 classroom, a secondary set of analyses (i.e., moderator analyses) examining variability in the effects of SI are perhaps of greater theoretical and practical interest. The study also provides concrete recommendations for improving and expanding future efforts in this domain.

References

Bachman, L. F., & Palmer, A. S. (1996). *Language testing in practice.* Oxford University Press.

Plonsky, L. (2017). Quantitative research methods in instructed SLA. In S. Loewen & M. Sato (Eds.), *The Routledge handbook of instructed second language acquisition* (pp. 505–521). Routledge.

Plonsky, L. (2019). Recent research on language learning strategy instruction. In A. U. Chamot & V. Harris (Eds.), *Learning strategy instruction in the language classroom: Issues and implementation* (pp. 3–21). Multilingual Matters.

Rose, H., Briggs, J. G., Boggs, J. A., Sergio, L., & Ivanova-Slavianskaia, N. (2018). A systematic review of language learner strategy research in the face of self-regulation. *System, 72,* 151–163.

Taylor, A., Stevens, J. R., & Asher, J. W. (2006). The effects of explicit reading strategy training on L2 reading comprehension. In J. Norris & L. Ortega (Eds.), *Synthesizing research on language learning and teaching* (pp. 213–244). John Benjamins.

Luke Plonsky is Associate Professor of Applied Linguistics at Northern Arizona University, where he teaches courses in SLA and research methods. Recent and forthcoming publications in these and other areas can be found in *Applied Linguistics Language Learning,* and *The Modern Language Journal,* among other journals and volumes. He has also written and edited several books. Luke is Senior Associate Editor of *Studies in Second Language Acquisition,* Managing Editor of *Foreign Language Annals,* Co-Editor of the de Gruyter Mouton Series on Language Acquisition, and Co-Director of the IRIS (iris-database.org). Luke held previous faculty appointments at Georgetown University and University College London. He has also taught in China, Japan, The Netherlands, Poland, Puerto Rico, and Spain. Luke received his Ph.D. in Second Language Studies from Michigan State University.

Ekaterina Sudina is a doctoral student in the Applied Linguistics program at Northern Arizona University. Ekaterina's research interests include individual differences in second language acquisition (SLA), quantitative research methods (scale development and validation in particular), and L2 reading and writing. Her professional experience includes teaching English, Russian, and French in the United States and Russia. Ekaterina is also a Fulbright alumna who earned a master's degree in TESOL from Southern Illinois University Carbondale.

Second Language Linguistic Competence and Literacy of Adult Migrants with Little or No Home Language Literacy

46

Martha Young-Scholten

Worldwide there are 773 million adults, two-thirds of them women, without basic home language print literacy due to poor access to formal education (UNESCO, 2019). Lack of access to education accompanies political unrest, and adult refugees from countries with low literacy rates such as Afghanistan, Iraq or South Sudan who resettle in post-industrialized countries will be expected to integrate into society and acquire the language and learn to read and write in it. Parental illiteracy is connected to social exclusion, poor health, young parenthood, children's poor school performance, increased likelihood of bearing learning-disabled children, and criminality (Bynner, 2001; Dalglish, 1982).

These adult migrants share inexperience with formal schooling and of confronting the challenge of learning to read for the first time ever in a new language. As a population, they are far more varied than foreign language learners. Learners in a single classroom might come from a score of countries and their ages typically range from 17 to 70. Research reveals that the majority of those with little or no formal schooling fail to gain sufficient oral language and literacy skills in the L2 and remain on the margins of society.

Resettlement of such adult migrants is not new; for example, the USA welcomed pre-literate Hmong refugees in the 1970s. Yet in research terms, these adults have also remained at the margins. This is unexpected because when, for example, formal-linguistics-based SLA began to emerge as a field of inquiry in its own right, adult migrants were the focus of major studies from the 1970s to early 1990s in Europe whose focus was on working class adults, including migrant workers. These studies led to hypotheses which shaped generative-linguistics-based SLA research for at least a decade (e.g. Clahsen & Muysken, 1986; DuPlessis et al., 1987; Schwartz & Eubank, 1996; Vainikka & Young-Scholten, 1994).

M. Young-Scholten (✉)
School of English Literature, Language and Linguistics, Newcastle University,
Newcastle upon Tyne NE1 7RU, UK
e-mail: martha.young-scholten@newcastle.ac.uk

© Springer Nature Switzerland AG 2021
H. Mohebbi and C. Coombe (eds.), *Research Questions in Language Education and Applied Linguistics*, Springer Texts in Education,
https://doi.org/10.1007/978-3-030-79143-8_46

This body of research led Hawkins in his 2001 book to conclude that L2 learners follow a predictable route of morphosyntactic development largely independent of age at initial exposure, native language, type of exposure or educational background. But educational background remains underexplored, with many more adult migrants now who fit the profile of those studied in the 1970s and 1980s. Formal and applied linguistics SLA has moved on without addressing all the issues relevant to this population of second language learners. Lack of an adequate research base on this population is connected to worldwide continued insufficiency of educational support for these learners combined with inadequate specialist training and continued professional development for those who teach them.

The Research Questions

1. What effect does lack of literacy have on the acquisition of morphosyntax and phonology?
2. What differences do we see across languages in non-literate migrants' acquisition of syntax, phonology, the lexicon and reading?
3. What developmental route do such learners follow in their emergent literacy?
4. How is linguistic competence (morphosyntax, phonology, the lexicon) connected to development of reading comprehension?
5. How do such learners co-construct knowledge within a Vygotskyan framework?
6. What roles are played by psychological factors such as motivation and identity?
7. Do those who are multilingual at the start differ from those who are monolingual?
8. What pedagogical approach, method, technique and materials work best?
9. How should the home language be approached by teachers working with these learners?
10. How do teacher knowledge and skills affect learner success?

Suggested Resources

Condelli, L., Spruck Wrigley, H., Yoo, K., Sebring, M. and Cronen, S. (2003). *What Works for Adult ESL Literacy Students.* **Volume II. Final Report. Washington, DC: American Institutes for Research and Aguirre International.**

This was a study of 495 adult literacy students who spoke 30 different native languages attending 38 ESOL classes in 13 schools and seven states in the U.S.A. 33.1% had no formal education/home language literacy. Students were assessed at intake, three months and nine months later on literacy and speaking tests, asked about literacy practices and classroom practice observed. Reading skill growth correlated with regular attendance; explanations in learners' home, weekly instructional hour and use of real world materials/connection to outside classroom. Oral skill growth correlated with regular attendance; explanations in learners' home languages; length of classes; focus on oral language with varied practice and interaction.

Kurvers, J. (2015). Emerging literacy in adult second-language learners: A synthesis of research findings in the Netherlands. *Writing Systems Research* **7(58–78).**

This article summarizes Kurvers and colleagues' research on the development of literacy by adult migrants in the Netherlands with little or no formal schooling. One study compared the conceptions of spoken and written language of adults with some and without any formal schooling to children who had not yet learned to read and found that the metalinguistic skills of the adults without school differed more from those with some school and less from the pre-reading children. The second looked at early reading development by adults with no home language literacy and found that their development follows stage models proposed for children. In the third study the literacy skills of about 300 adult low- and non-literate learners were assessed to see how their success was connected to external factors. Results showed considerable variation in relation to age, education, attendance, contact with Dutch speakers, time spent on small-group or individual work, use of multimedia, portfolio assessment and use of home language in the classroom.

Tarone, E., Bigelow, M. and Hansen, K. (2009). *Literacy and Second Language Oracy.* **Oxford: Oxford University Press.**

This seminal book begins with an overview of research on the relationship of phonological awareness to the development of Roman alphabet literacy and the small body of work on migrant adults. It includes the results of a study which aimed to examine the role conscious processing plays in the acquisition of morphosyntax under the Noticing Hypothesis, using the stages of question formation proposed by Pienemann and Johnston (1987). Studied were eight Somalis between 15 and 27 with three to seven years' US residence and 'low' or 'moderate' English literacy. One had had seven years' schooling prior to immigration. An oral testing instrument included spot-the-difference story completion, story recall, elicited imitation and repetition of the researchers' recasted questions. Recast results showed that those with moderate literacy were significantly better at recalling and accurately repeating them. The story retelling data showed more frequent use of verbs erroneously lacking inflection by the low literates.

Haznedar, B., J. K. Peyton & M. Young-Scholten. (2018). Teaching adult migrant. *Critical Multilingualism Studies* **6(1), 155–183.**

Adult migrants are under pressure to linguistically integrate as quickly as possible and this means focusing entirely on their learning of the majority language and supporting their children in mastering it. This contribution aims to raise awareness among the language practitioners who work with low-/non-literate migrants of the individual and social benefits bilingualism and the downside of shifting away from an exclusive focus on the majority language at the expense of the home language. Discussion goes beyond use of the home language in the classroom to the positive effect of gaining enough literacy in the home language as a foundation for literacy in the majority language and to maintenance of the home language in the community through support of children's bilingualism and biliteracy. Migrants with little formal schooling lack the social capital to organize the sort of bilingual programs common among the middle-class and describes a new international initiative to form a hub of links to resources in learners' heritage languages.

Literacy Education and Second Language Learning by Adults http://www.leslla.org, https://drive.google.com/drive/folders/1vblFpCOMMncLHExEo3Z_IJLU5zgZTJpA, https://drive.google.com/drive/folders/1kJtA47vjoRP3KJD5IhNbbNtVh7ZxgSyJ.

LESLLA was established in 2005 to recognize the need for unity among those who work with this learner population. This multi-disciplinary forum for researchers, practitioners and policy makers holds an annual symposium, alternating between English-speaking and non-English-speaking countries and publishes proceedings. At their symposia since 2005, there have been around 450 plenaries, panels, papers, posters, workshops, and demonstrations, a proportion of which are published in proceedings. Presentation topics include: agency/autonomy/empowerment/identity; acquisition of morphosyntax, phonology, vocabulary; attendance; decoding; digital skills; comprehension; health literacy; heritage languages; interaction with children's schools; numeracy; oral skills; pragmatics; practitioner awareness, knowledge and skills; trauma; visual skills; workplace; writing. Most of the presentations are descriptions or overviews of practice, of programmes, of testing/assessment and of training and continued professional development. Far fewer report on studies of the acquisition of morphosyntax, phonology, vocabulary or reading from a psycholinguistic perspective. Making up the remainder are systematic studies with multiple variables; action research; ethnographic research and policy (Peyton and Young-Scholten 2020).

References

Bynner, J. (2001). *Outline of the research, exploratory analysis and summary of the main results.* Institute of Education, Centre for Longitudinal Studies.

Clahsen, H., & Muysken, P. (1986). The availability of Universal Grammar to adult and child learners—A study of the acquisition of German word order. *Second Language Research, 2,* 93–119.

Dalglish, C. (1982). *Illiteracy and the offender.* Huntington Publishers.

DuPlessis, J., Solin, D., Travis, L., & White, L. (1987). UG or not UG, that is the question: A reply to Clahsen and Muysken. *Second Language Research, 3,* 56–75.

Hawkins, R. (2001). *Second language syntax. A generative introduction.* Blackwell.

Peyton, J. K., & Young-Scholten, M. (eds.) (2020). Teaching adult immigrants with limited formal education: Theory, researchand practice. Bristol: Multilingual Matters.

Schwartz, B. D., & Eubank, L. (1996). Introduction: What is the 'L2 initial state'? *Second Language Research, 12*, 1–5.

UNESCO Institute for Statistics. (2017). Fact sheet no. 45. September.

Vainikka, A., & Young-Scholten, M. (1994). Direct access to X'-theory: Evidence from Korean and Turkish adults learning German. In T. Hoekstra & B. D. Schwartz (Eds.), *Language acquisition studies in generative Grammar* (pp. 265–316). Benjamins.

Martha Young-Scholten (Ph.D., University of Washington, Seattle) is professor of SLA at Newcastle University, UK and is *Second Language Research* and *Linguistic Approaches to Bilingualism* editorial board member and de Gruyter Mouton and Narr/Francke/Attempo Verlag series co-editor. Since the 1980s she has conducted generative-linguistics-based research on the acquisition of German and English morphosyntax and phonology by adults without formal instruction in the language. In co-founding of leslla.org in 2005, she narrowed her focus to the acquisition of linguistic competence and development of reading by adult migrants without home language literacy. She was a partner in the 2013–2015 EU-funded DigLin project and led the three-phase EU-funded project EU-Speak in 2010–2018 which culminated in on-line professional development modules in English, Finnish, German, Italian, Spanish and Turkish.

Task Engagement in Language Learning

Joy Egbert

The term "task" in general can be understood to mean an activity that has clear goals and a specific beginning and end; for language tasks, the definition includes that language use is necessary. Task "engagement" is commonly recognized as a learner's involvement during a task. Task engagement is important because it can mediate factors external to the classroom, and the more deeply learners are involved in a task, the better their performance on that task (Christenson et al., 2012; Dörnyei & Ushioda, 2011).

Recently there has been increased interest in task engagement in the literature, and there is growing agreement on the specific elements of task engagement. Currently the most salient features of an engaging task are that it:

- Is authentic to learners. This means that learners consider the task to contain knowledge, processes, and/or products that have value to them outside of the classroom.
- Is deeply interesting. Authenticity may support interest for some learners, while some may be interested in topics, processes, or tools that are new to them or that address their hobbies, academic goals, or leisure activities.
- Provides opportunities for social interaction. Social interaction is that which involves interlocutors who can supply feedback, negotiate meaning, collaborate, and even empathize.
- Supports a challenge/skills balance. Csikszentmihályi (1990) and others posit that tasks should aim for a balance where the task challenge is just above learners' current skill levels in order to avoid boredom, anxiety, or apathy.
- Supports an autonomy/task structure balance. Linked to challenge and skills, different students will require different amounts of task structure. Some will be

J. Egbert (✉)
Department of Teaching and Learning, College of Education, Washington State University, Pullman, WA, USA
e-mail: jegbert@wsu.edu

© Springer Nature Switzerland AG 2021
H. Mohebbi and C. Coombe (eds.), *Research Questions in Language Education and Applied Linguistics*, Springer Texts in Education,
https://doi.org/10.1007/978-3-030-79143-8_47

able to work more independently, and others will need specific instructions and a clear idea of the organization of the task. There is a certain balance that will help engage each learner.

- Includes effective scaffolding. Scaffolding includes just-in-time feedback, resources that are available as needed, sufficient time, and other supports that facilitate learners' task processes.

These concepts have been supported by recent studies (e.g., Gao et al., 2017), but much about task engagement is still unknown. Research has not produced a strong model of task engagement, and the strength of each element that leads to deep engagement for language learners is not yet clear. Questions about the impacts of culture on task engagement, the roles of technology in supporting task engagement, and aspects of tasks (e.g., content, assessment, objectives, group structure) that interact with the engagement elements are under investigation.

The Research Questions

1. What does it mean to be engaged in a language task?
2. What are the concepts that make up task engagement?
3. How are the concepts related to each other?
4. What level of each concept is necessary for language learners to be engaged?
5. Does culture play a role in task engagement? If so, how?
6. How can task engagement mediate factors external to the class?
7. How can teachers know when a student is engaged?
8. How should the concepts that comprise task engagement be measured?
9. How is task engagement related to task outcomes in content and language?
10. What roles can technology use play in engaging English language learners?
11. What are the connections between language learning and task engagement principles?

Suggested Resources

Almetev, Y. (2018). Theory of Flow: Implications for foreign language education. *European Proceedings of Social and Behavioral Sciences.* https://doi.org/10.15405/epsbs.2018.04.02.41.

This proceedings article explores flow as optimal for student learning and leading to higher willingness to communicate (WTC). It provides a description of the components of flow that also contribute to a broader definition of task engagement. Almetev explains that engagement is important to explore because: (1) it is something that teachers can affect, and; (2) a focus on engagement helps young learners to see how fun learning can be.

Christenson, S. L., Reschly, A. L., & Wylie, C. (Eds.). (2012). *Handbook of research on student engagement.* **New York, NY: Springer.**

This edited book provides an extensive overview of the concept of engagement. Starting with the history of the term and its many definitions, it then offers sections on links between engagement and motivation, contextual influences on engagement, engagement and student outcomes, and measures of engagement. The book addresses school, classroom, and task engagement and discusses models, methods, and the future of engagement research. This is a must-read for engagement researchers.

Csikszentmihályi, M. (2014). *Flow and the foundations of positive psychology: The collected works of Mihaly Csikszentmihalyi.* **New York, NY: Springer.**

This book lays out the foundations of Flow Theory and presents many studies by Csikszentmihályi and his colleagues that are based on its assumptions. It presents the author's personal experiences, historical accounts of theory development and changing definitions of human experience, realizations about information processing and attention, discussions of methodology, and a focus on diverse samples that provide readers with a thorough understanding of the study of optimal experience. The Experience Sampling Method (ESM), a way of measuring flow and optimal experience, is comprehensively presented and ESM forms are included. Limitations of flow research are also discussed. Overall, this text provides both fundamental information and sample studies that any researcher working in the area of engagement should become familiar with.

Dörnyei, Z., Henry, A., & Muir, C. (2016). *Motivational currents in language learning: Frameworks for focused interventions.* **New York: Routledge.**

Dörnyei and his colleagues have been investigating motivation in language learning contexts for years, and their books are worth reading for researchers and teachers interested in motivation and/or engagement. In this text, the authors describe "directed motivational currents" (DMCs), which integrate aspects of Flow Theory (Csikszentmihályi, 1990), various motivation theories, and elements of task engagement. They explain how the construct of DMCs is positioned differently from these grounding concepts; the authors define it as the presence of sustained engagement over the life of a project, which might include a number of tasks. This book lays out the foundation for DMCs and provides clear examples and pedagogical suggestions. A number of studies based on DMCs have recently been published, and these too are worth reading. Also look for Mercer and Dörnyei's *Engaging students in contemporary classrooms* forthcoming from Cambridge University Press. More information can be found at https://www.zoltandornyei.co.uk/.

Egbert, J. (2003). A study of flow theory in the foreign language classroom. *The Modern Language Journal, 87*(4), 419–518.

This is one of the first studies exploring the concept of Flow (Csikszentmihályi, 1990), or optimal engagement, in language learning tasks. It provides a theoretical framework that links language learning and task engagement, and it presents a model of the proposed relationships. The multi-method study, which examined seven tasks completed by secondary school Spanish language students, employed both numeric and descriptive data. The role of technology use in flow was also explored. Recommendations for future research are included; many of them remain unexamined. This study can provide researchers with both theoretical and methodological frameworks for future study.

Meltzer, J., & Hamann, E. (2004). Meeting the literacy development needs of adolescent English language learners through content area learning—Part one: Focus on motivation and engagement. *Faculty Publications: Department of Teaching, Learning and Teacher Education, 51*. Education Alliance at Brown University. Access from http://digitalcommons.unl.edu/teachlearnfacpub/51.

Even though it was published over a decade ago, this paper can be considered seminal in the area of engagement and English language learners (ELLs). Focusing on secondary ELLs and literacy practices, it presents a thorough review of the literature and explains the development of the first author's "Adolescent Literacy Support Framework" that focuses on motivation and engagement. The paper provides a thorough investigation of motivation and engagement, looking at a variety of models and literatures. This paper provides a standard for in-depth literature review and is an exemplar of how to synthesize the literature in ways that move the field forward.

References

Christenson, S. L., Reschly, A. L., & Wylie, C. (Eds.). (2012). *Handbook of research on student engagement*. Springer.
Csikszentmihályi, M. (1990). *Flow: The psychology of optimal experience*. Harper Perennial.
Dörnyei, Z., & Ushioda, E. (2011). *Teaching and researching motivation* (2nd ed). Pearson Education Limited.
Gao, L., Bai, X., & Park, A. (2017). Understanding sustained participation in virtual travel communities from the perspectives of IS success model and flow theory. *Journal of Hospitality and Tourism Research, 41*(4), 475–509. https://doi.org/10.1177/1096348014563397

Joy Egbert is Professor of English Language Learners and Education Technology at Washington State University (WSU) in Pullman. Her publications include over a dozen books and many articles on computer-assisted language learning, teacher education, and ESL methods. Her most recent book, edited with Gisela Ernst-Slavit, is *Views from Inside: Languages, Cultures, and Schooling for K-12 Educators* (2018, IAP). She is the immediate past Editor of *TESOL Journal* and a leader of WSU's Teaching Academy. She has travelled and presented workshops around the world and is interested in understanding language learners' task engagement.

Vocabulary Knowledge and Educational Attainment

James Milton

The vocabulary knowledge of very young children learning their first language is considered crucial in influencing their subsequent educational attainment. Children whose upbringing results in a large vocabulary will tend to be educationally successful. Children with small vocabularies are not.

The premise behind the proposed study is described in the *Oxford Language Report, why closing the word gap matters*. They call it the Word Gap (report available at oxford.ly/wordgap). It is also called the *Matthew Effect*. The argument is,

- That language input varies from child to child and the scale of this input conditions language uptake.
- Language uptake will also vary and, crucially, vocabulary knowledge will vary among children of the same cohort in school and this conditions educational success.
- Children with big vocabularies will handle school and its various tasks, and will do better, than those who come to school with smaller vocabularies.

Hart and Risley's work (e.g. 1995) is a particularly widely cited expression of this idea. And there is an abundance of work on the learning of vocabulary that appears to support individual parts of this thesis. The link between variation in vocabulary knowledge and educational success is widely accepted. Variation in vocabulary is thought to become measurable very early in the learning process, as early as one year of age, and studies also show that vocabulary size and successful academic outcomes correlate However, it is less easy to show that these relationships are causal and studies which attempt to test this idea have drawn negative results. Hart and Risely's work in particular has been challenged on the basis of its

J. Milton (✉)
Department of Applied Linguistics, Swansea University, Swansea, UK
e-mail: j.l.milton@swansea.ac.uk

© Springer Nature Switzerland AG 2021
H. Mohebbi and C. Coombe (eds.), *Research Questions in Language Education and Applied Linguistics*, Springer Texts in Education,
https://doi.org/10.1007/978-3-030-79143-8_48

methodology and both the scale of language input available to children is questioned, as are Hart and Risely's calculations of vocabulary size.

Part of the Word Gap problem is thought to be that among young children language input is diminishing and that vocabulary knowledge of some learners at least is also falling with consequent damage to subsequent educational progress and achievement. But at the same time, you get the political and educational establishment maintaining equally firmly that things are actually getting better. Nick Gibb, the schools minister, is the latest to propound that literacy standards are rising (https://www.telegraph.co.uk/education/2017/12/04/phonics-revolution-reading-standards-england-best-generation/)—Something that cannot happen if vocabulary levels fall.

This kind of disagreement, and an absence of studies to seriously address these issues, stem from the absence of good, reliable and objective measures which can define whether there is a problem and if so how big it is and will probably also define how the problem might be addressed.

The Research Questions

1. Can good testing methodologies be created to measure vocabulary knowledge equivalently in non-literate pre-school NS English speakers, and literate 18-year-olds?
2. How many words do 'normal' speakers of English acquire each year through childhood?
3. Which words do they acquire?
4. Are there frequency and other effects present in the learning that takes place?
5. How much variation is there among these learners?
6. Is the variation qualitative or quantitative?
7. Are the volumes of knowledge sufficiently small, in low-performing speakers, to compromise comprehension and communication?
8. Can the differences in language input noted by Hart and Risely, and linked to socio-economic status, be replicated?
9. Can any variation in input be linked causally to vocabulary uptake?
10. Can variation in vocabulary size be linked causally to educational performance among NS with well-developed lexicons?

Suggested Resources

Stanovich, K. E. (1986). Matthew effects in reading: Some consequences of individual differences in the acquisition of literacy. *Reading Research Quarterly, 22,* **360–407.**

Stanovich explains how Matthew effects might work in relation to reading, vocabulary and educational attainment. These Matthew effects could be seen where slow-starters with small vocabularies would read less, grow smaller vocabularies, and fair less well in educational attainment than fast-starters with larger vocabularies. A feature of an educational system would be an ever widening gap between the knowledge of the slow-starters and the fast-starters.

Hart, B. & Risley, T. (1995). *Meaningful differences in the everyday experience of young American children.* **Baltimore: Paul H. Brookes Publishing.**

Hart and Risely's work is particularly influential in articulating the causal relationship between language input, vocabulary learning and educational attainment, and in investigating it empirically. Their studies suggest that there is huge variation in the language experience of very young children associated with socio-economic status (SES). They suggest a 30-million-word difference between the language experience of high SES children and low SES children, and explain the difference in measurable vocabulary knowledge which they observe between these groups to the difference in input.

Oxford University Press (2018). *Why Closing the Word Gap Matters: Oxford Language Report.* **retrieved from [oxford.ly/wordgap].**

This study repeats Hart and Risely's premise, called a Word Gap rather than a Matthew effect, and conducts a study of teachers to find support for it. Their results are said to suggest that teachers think that about a half of all primary age learners are hindered in their work and progress by having small vocabularies. Teachers believe the issue of inadequate lexical knowledge in school children is getting worse and this is affecting educational performance. A word gap is thought to affect the ability to work independently, to follow what is going on in class, and the ability to perform well in milestone exams such as GCSE. The solution, the teachers believe is much wider and more extensive reading.

Nation P. (2018). A brief critique of Hart, B. & Risley, T. (1995). Retrieved from [https://www.victoria.ac.nz/lals/about/staff/publications/paul-nation/Hart_and_Risley_critique.pdf].

Nation does not question the premise and the conclusions contained in Hart and Risely's study, but he does criticise their method, which challenges the conclusions they draw. He suggests experimental effect may have conditioned the results they get for language input. And he points out that the measure for vocabulary size they use is really a measure of vocabulary output and is sensitive to size as a consequence. It calls into question their assertion that the high SES group really knows more words, just that they speak more.

Shaywitz, B. A., Holford, T. R., Holahan, J. M., Fletcher, J. M., Stuebing, K. K., Francis, D. J. &. Shaywitz S. A. (1995). A Matthew effect for IQ but not for reading: Results from a longitudinal study. *Reading Research Quarterly,* **30, 894–906.**

This is a serious attempt to investigate whether the Matthew effects, or Word Gap effects, can be observed in relation to reading, vocabulary and educational attainment. The kinds of effects Stanovich describes, a widening gap in educational performance between groups with different vocabularies for example, are not visible in their data.

Biemiller, A. & Slonim, N. (2001). Estimating root word vocabulary growth in normative and advantaged populations: Evidence for a common sequence of vocabulary acquisition. *Journal of Educational Psychology,* **93, 498–520.**

This is an attempt to use an appropriately constructed vocabulary size test to assess both the vocabulary knowledge of grade school learners in North America, and whether differences exist between advantaged and disadvantaged children. Their results suggest learners learn 600–700 base words per year. There are differences between their two learner groups and the advantaged groups have on average a 40% larger vocabulary than their disadvantaged counterparts on entry to grade school by age 6. By the age of 11 however, this difference has almost entirely disappeared although it is not clear whether this is a result of ceiling effect or the leveling effect of the educational system.

Wilson, S., Thorne, A., Stephens, M., Ryan, J., Moore, S., Milton, J. & Brayley, G. (2016). English Vocabulary Size in Adults and the Link with Educational Attainment. *Language in Focus: International Journal of Studies in Applied Linguistics and ELT,* **2(2), 44–69.**

This is principally a study of the way vocabulary size grows with age in adults. But it does draw attention to one very important observation of the relationship between vocabulary size and educational performance. They point out that the vocabulary size of both educationally successful and unsuccessful participants is large enough for both to achieve close to complete coverage. Consequently, both should have the words at least for full comprehension and communicability. This challenges the idea that differences in vocabulary size actually determine educational success; they may correlate but something else must be affecting both.

Reference

Hart, B., & Risley, T. (1995). *Meaningful differences in the everyday experience of young American children*. Paul H. Brookes Publishing.

James Milton is Professor of Applied Linguistics at Swansea University, UK. After working in Nigeria and Libya he moved to Swansea in 1985 and set up the Centre for Applied Language Studies and the Department of Applied Linguistics and established with Paul Meara the Vocabulary Assessment Research Group. This group has been very prolific and has produced a wide variety of assessment measures for the understanding of vocabulary knowledge. This long-term interest in measuring lexical breadth and establishing normative data for learning and progress has led to many publications including *Modelling and Assessing Vocabulary Knowledge* (CUP 2007 with Michael Daller and Jeanine Treffers-Daller), *Measuring Second Language Vocabulary Acquisition* (Multilingual Matters 2009) and *Dimensions of Vocabulary Knowledge* (2014 with Tess Fitzpatrick).

Vocabulary Learning Strategies

49

Peter Yongqi Gu

Vocabulary learning is arguably one of the most salient, important, difficult and long-lasting tasks in language learning. Deliberate efforts in learning vocabulary strategically may make the learning process more efficient, effective, and even more pleasant.

Vocabulary learning strategies (VLS) are learners' conscious efforts in managing their own learning of vocabulary in order to make it more effective and more efficient, in increasing their vocabulary size and depth, and in being able to use the vocabulary learned automatically and appropriately. Strategic vocabulary learning is an intentional, dynamic and iterative process. It is normally triggered by a difficult or novel vocabulary learning task. We start by noticing a vocabulary item or chunk and then focus our attention on it. Next, we quickly analyse the learning task, ourselves as learners and the learning environment before we form an attack plan. The plan is then executed, and we monitor its effectiveness along the way and evaluate its degree of success in achieving the learning goal. Often this evaluation will necessitate a re-analysis of the task and redeployment of strategies, making strategic vocabulary learning a spiraling and complex problem-solving process.

Whenever a new, important or difficult task is identified, strategic learners go through the choice, use, and evaluation of strategic learning cycles. This means that the nature of the learning task is important in determining what strategies are the most appropriate and most effective. At the same time, who the learner is and what strategy repertoire is available determine what strategies are triggered. Whether a strategy is needed and how effective it is are influenced by contextual affordances and constraints as well.

Research on vocabulary learning strategies in second language acquisition started in the late 1980s. Three decades of research on vocabulary learning

P. Y. Gu (✉)
School of Linguistics & Applied Language Studies, Victoria University of Wellington, Wellington, New Zealand
e-mail: peter.gu@vuw.ac.nz

© Springer Nature Switzerland AG 2021   273
H. Mohebbi and C. Coombe (eds.), *Research Questions in Language Education and Applied Linguistics*, Springer Texts in Education,
https://doi.org/10.1007/978-3-030-79143-8_49

strategies have produced very fruitful findings that are now guiding the practices inside the language classroom. Many exploratory studies have resulted in the discovery of naturally occurring strategies second language learners normally use for learning vocabulary. These have resulted in the compilation of a number of strategy indices. Questionnaire studies making use of these indices have been able to establish how vocabulary learning strategies are related to vocabulary size and general language proficiency. It has also been found that the choice, use, and effectiveness of VLS are mediated by task, learner, and contextual factors, and that the configurations of factors and relationships are complex, dynamic, and situated.

The following list of ten research questions help to strengthen existing research findings and shift our efforts from surface-level explorations to more in-depth examinations and explanations. The last research question also highlights the need for the application of our research findings.

The Research Questions

1. What naturally occurring strategies can be found in the learning of vocabulary at various levels of proficiency in different learning contexts?
2. How are learners' choice and use of vocabulary learning strategies related to the learning of single words and multiword units?
3. To what extent can strategy instruction enhance the learning of vocabulary in short-, medium- and long-terms?
4. To what extent do individual differences such as motivation, personality, and learning styles influence the choice and use of vocabulary learning strategies?
5. To what extent does task knowledge (what vocabulary learning involves, e.g., receptive vs. productive; breadth, depth, automaticity, and appropriateness) influence the choice and use of vocabulary learning strategies?
6. What contextual affordances and constraints influence the choice, use, and effectiveness of vocabulary learning strategies?
7. How is the complex, dynamic and situated nature of strategy choice, execution, and growth related to the outcomes of vocabulary learning?
8. How is the simultaneous use of strategy clusters or strings in sync related to the outcomes of vocabulary learning?
9. To what extent do vocabulary learning strategies differ in their usefulness among ESL/EFL learners, English Language Learners, in CLIL or English as a medium of instruction programmes, or in children's learning of their first language?
10. To what extent can research findings on vocabulary learning strategies make a difference to learning and teaching in the language classroom?

Suggested Resources

Gu, Y. (2003). Vocabulary learning in a second language: Person, task, context and strategies. *TESL-EJ, 7*(2), 1–25.

This is a comprehensive review of research on vocabulary learning strategies. The review is based on a tetrahedral model of language learning strategies that sees vocabulary learning strategies being influenced by learners, tasks and learning contexts. Instead of searching for the best strategies that produce the best results, the author argued that the choice, use, and effectiveness of vocabulary learning strategies depend on the task, the learner, and the learning context. At the end of the review, a list of ten summary points and future research directions are presented. Looking back at the last decade and more since the publication of this article, the overwhelming majority of the research directions listed have barely been touched upon.

Gu, Y. (2020). Strategies for learning vocabulary. In S. Webb (Ed.), The Routledge handbook of vocabulary studies (pp. 271–287). London: Routledge.

This is a latest review of research on vocabulary learning strategies. If the focus of the 2003 review was placed on charting the domain and outlining overall directions, this review zoomed in onto a number of specific areas where empirical research is urgently needed. For example, an analysis of the task of vocabulary learning revealed the apparent lack of research on strategies for the learning of productive vocabulary, of the depth, automaticity and appropriateness of vocabulary, and the learning of multiword units. Seeing vocabulary as contextualised and dynamic competence that is situated in authentic language use also requires strategic learning that demands new research perspectives and methodologies. In addition, a learner perspective would entail research efforts that fully appreciate the skill, will, and co-construction of strategies and self- and co-regulation of vocabulary learning. Finally, it was argued that contextually responsive and practically useful research on vocabulary learning strategies should include studies such as L1 acquisition, ELL achievement, CLIL, and study abroad contexts.

Mizumoto, A., & Takeuchi, O. (2009). Examining the effectiveness of explicit instruction of vocabulary learning strategies with Japanese EFL university students. *Language Teaching Research, 13*(4), 425–449.

This is an empirical study examining of effects of a 10-week strategy instruction programme over a four-month period among a group of 204 EFL learners. Metacognitive and cognitive strategies for vocabulary learning were introduced to the experimental group on a weekly basis using the first 30 min of a 90-min class. A questionnaire on vocabulary learning strategies and a questionnaire on motivation were administered before and after the experiment. The results indicated in general the usefulness in strategy instruction on both vocabulary learning and on increased strategy use, especially among learners who used strategies at a low or moderate level at the beginning of the study.

Ranalli, J. (2013). Online strategy instruction for integrating dictionary skills and language awareness. *Language Learning & Technology, 17*(2), 75–99. http://dx.doi.org/10125/44325.

Technology-assisted vocabulary learning is a rapidly developing line of practice that deserves more research attention. This article presents an attempt to teach dictionary skills in a five-week, online strategy instruction course designed to teach web-based dictionary use. Sixty-four learners in a university ESL composition course at Iowa State University participated in the study. Eleven tutorials on vocabulary depth of knowledge, dictionaries, and pattern grammar were presented to the strategy instruction group (N = 32) in an automated, online course that lasted five weeks. The dictionary practice (control) group (N = 32) then swapped roles with the strategy instruction group and received the same online training within the following five weeks. Results showed that the strategy instruction group significantly outperformed the dictionary practice group in selecting the correct dictionary for the vocabulary task, and in exploiting the chosen dictionary in both identifying and correcting errors involving lexical patterns. The study shows promise for the integration of technology in developing learners' expertise in using vocabulary learning strategies.

Cohen, A. D., & Wang, I. K. H. (2018). Fluctuation in the functions of language learner strategies. *System, 74*, 169–182. https://doi.org/10.1016/j.system.2018.03.011.

This is a unique study that focused on explicating the micro functions of strategy use in the completion of a vocabulary fine-tuning task by six Chinese learners of English. It has long been thought that strategies serve different purposes and that learners normally employ clusters, pairs and sequences of strategies to tackle a given task. This study, however, demonstrated that even a single strategy served multiple micro functions and that these micro functions fluctuated on a moment-to-moment basis. The authors were able to identify six patterns of strategy functions: (1) a one-way linear progression from one function to the next, (2) simultaneous occurrence of two or more functions, (3) a linear progression plus simultaneous occurrence, (4) bi-directional fluctuation, (5) bi-directional fluctuation plus simultaneous occurrence of functions, and (6) Simultaneous occurrence of functions plus micro-fluctuation of functions. The methodological innovation employed in this study showcases one way in which the complex, dynamic and situated nature of vocabulary learning strategies can be studied.

Peter Yongqi Gu is an Associate Professor at the School of Linguistics and Applied Language Studies at Victoria University of Wellington, New Zealand. Dr. Gu's main academic interests include learner autonomy and learning strategies, vocabulary acquisition, and language testing and assessment. Dr. Gu has three decades of experience teaching English and training ESL teachers in mainland China, Hong Kong SAR (China), Singapore, and New Zealand.

Working Memory

50

Zhisheng (Edward) Wen

The term working memory (WM) generally refers to our cognitive ability to simultaneously maintain and process a small amount of information in our head temporarily so as to complete some mental tasks (Baddeley, 2003). Interpreted in this way, WM encompasses two key functions, namely, storage and processing, which are presumably essential for multiple facets of cognitive activities such as arithmetic calculation, logical reasoning, planning, and language comprehension etc. Indeed, since the inception of the classic model of WM proposed by Baddeley and Hitch (1974), the relationship between WM and language has been a central topic of interest for both developmental and cognitive psychologists alike (Gathercole & Baddeley, 1993). With the advent of a multitude of WM models (Miyake & Shah, 1999), research probing into the WM-language connection subsequently diverged into two major paradigms, namely, the British and North American traditions, with well-defined research agendas and distinctive research methodologies (Wen, 2012).

To begin with the British camps, most explorations investigating the WM-language nexus are based on Baddeley's (2003, 2015) classic tri-partite modality-based model of WM that conceives, (a) the phonological loop that stores and processes sound-based information from the input; (b) the visuo-spatial sketchpad that handles visual and spatial information; and (c) the central executive that allocates cognitive resources between the two storage buffers. Among these putative WM components, the phonological component (i.e., phonological WM) has received the most attention by Baddeley and colleagues and its instrumental roles in language acquisition are most researched and best understood (Gathercole & Baddeley, 1993). It is becoming increasingly clear that phonological WM (consisting of a phonological short-term store and an articulatory rehearsal mechanism) both facilitates and empowers the storage, chunking, consolidation, and

Z. (Edward) Wen (✉)
School of Languages and Translation, Macao Polytechnic Institute, Macau SAR, China
e-mail: edwardwen@ipm.edu.mo

© Springer Nature Switzerland AG 2021
H. Mohebbi and C. Coombe (eds.), *Research Questions in Language Education and Applied Linguistics*, Springer Texts in Education,
https://doi.org/10.1007/978-3-030-79143-8_50

retrieval processes of newly acquired phonological forms, thus rendering it a *'language learning device'* (Baddeley et al., 1998). Expanding on this assumption, it can be further hypothesized that phonological WM (as indexed by such storage-based memory recall procedures as the nonword repetition span task) underpins the acquisition of sound-based and serial-order-based linguistic sequences or chunks in language, thus subserving such domains as lexis or vocabulary, phrases or formulas, and grammatical structures or constructions in L1 and L2. (Wen, 2016).

On the other hand, WM-language explorations conducted by most cognitive psychologists based in North America have generally been subscribed to the attention- and executive-oriented views of WM as proposed by Cowan (1999) and Engle (2002). In line with these conceptual WM models, cognitive psychologists are more interested in exploring the modulating effects of executive aspects of WM such as information updating, task-switching, inhibitory control as they are related to sentence processing and reading comprehension etc. (Cowan, 2011). In terms of assessment procedures, they have discarded the storage-only WM measures adopted by their British counterparts, and instead opted to implement more complex WM span tasks such as the reading span task (Daneman & Carpenter, 1980) or its domain-general variant of the operation span task (Engle, 2002) that are purported to tap into the dual functions of storage and processing. Empirical evidence accumulated from this body of research converges on the positive role executive WM is impacting on selective language processes during listening, speaking, reading, writing in L1 and L2, as well as interpreting performance between the two. (Wen et al., 2015).

Overall results from recent research syntheses and meta-analytic studies of WM and second language (e.g., Grundy & Timmer, 2017; Linck et al., 2014) have largely lent support to the WM-language nexus postulated by cognitive psychologists, though finer-grained details regarding its multiple facets remain to be seen. Looking to the future then, given the fact that bilinguals or multilinguals are likely to outnumber monolinguals, the time has now become ripe to further explore how these emerging consensus benchmarks of WM theories and models gleaned from current cognitive science and neuroscience (Oberauer et al., 2018) can be seamlessly integrated to inform theories of SLA and vice versa (Wen, 2016). The ultimate goal then may lie in pinpointing to what extent WM may serve as a central language aptitude in constraining and shaping human language design, acquisition, processing, and long-term development (Wen, 2019).

The Research Questions

1. Given the many theoretical models of working memory in cognitive sciences, how can the construct be best conceptualized and measured in language research?

2. How does working memory shape language design and structure from a cross-linguistic perspective?
3. How does working memory impact on native language acquisition vs. L2 acquisition?
4. Should we use the same assessment procedures from current practice in cognitive psychology to measure working memory in L2 research?
5. Does working memory play a bigger role in L1 as opposed to L2 learning, or vice versa?
6. How does working memory impact on the acquisition of L1 vs. L2 vocabulary?
7. How does working memory impact on the acquisition and processing of L1 vs. L2 formulas or collocations?
8. How does working memory influence L1 vs. L2 sentence processing?
9. How does working memory modulate L2 task-based speech planning and performance in terms of complexity, accuracy, fluency and lexis?
10. How can working memory be improved or trained to facilitate first and second language learning?

Suggested Resources

Linck, J., Osthus, P., Koeth, J. T., & Bunting, M. (2014). Working memory and second language comprehension and production: A meta-analysis. *Psychonomic Bulletin & Review, 21, 861–83.*

In this highly cited review article in current working memory and second language studies, the authors report results of a meta-analysis of primary data (with 748 effect sizes) from 79 sample empirical studies involving 3707 participants. The results of the meta-analysis point to an overall estimated population effect size (ρ) of 0.255, confirming a positive association between working memory and relevant L2 processing and proficiency outcomes. In addition, the authors also found larger effect sizes for the executive control aspects of WM as opposed to the storage component, and larger effect sizes for verbal measures (such as the reading span task) as opposed to nonverbal measures (such as the operation span task). Overall, this large-scale meta-analysis provides compelling evidence for the asserted role between WM (as measured by established memory span tasks in cognitive psychology) and L2 learning and processing.

Wen, Z., M. Mota & McNeill, M. (2015). *Working memory in second language acquisition and processing.* **Bristol, UK: Multilingual Matters.**

This edited volume features chapters by scholars in both cognitive psychology and applied linguistics that discuss essential theoretical and methodological issues concerning the pivotal roles of WM in specific domains of second language acquisition and processing. Its foreword and introductory theoretical chapters are written by leading WM theorists in cognitive psychology. The subsequent sections contain empirical chapters providing original data and innovative insights into more specific relationships concerning WM and second language (sentence) processing, L2 instruction, L2 performance and development etc. Each section concludes with a commentary chapter written by a noted SLA researcher who not only reflects upon their unique perspectives on WM and SLA, but also offers suggestions for future research. Overall, the volume is a compendium of comprehensive and innovative insights into the intricate relationship between WM and second language learning and processing.

Wen, Z. (2016). *Working memory and second language learning: Towards an integrated approach.* **Bristol: Multilingual Matters.**

This research monograph is a first attempt to integrate emerging WM theories in cognitive psychology with current SLA theories. It is divided into three parts, with the first two parts reviewing the extensive literature of both WM research in cognitive science (concerning theories, models, and measurement issues) and applied linguistics research (synthesizing research studies exploring WM effects). Building on these reviews, the third part proposes an integrated perspective on theorizing and measuring WM in SLA, which culminates in the formulation of the overarching Phonological/Executive (P/E) model. Specifically, it is postulated that phonological WM mainly underpins those chunking-based *acquisitional* and *developmental* aspects of SLA domains (such as vocabulary/lexis, formulaic sequences and morpho-syntactic constructions/grammatical structure); while executive WM is posited to modulate selective online and offline processes in L2 sub-skills learning and processing, as well as some *real-time* performance dimensions during L2 comprehension, production and interaction processes. The book also discusses the implications of the integrative perspectives on L2 task-based performance and language aptitude research in SLA.

Grundy, J. G. & Timmer K. (2017). Bilingualism and working memory capacity: A comprehensive meta-analysis. *Second Language Research, 33*(3), **325–340.**

In this comprehensive meta-analysis, the authors investigated the effects of bilingualism on WM capacity. 27 empirical studies were analyzed, involving 88 effect sizes and 2901 participants. The overall results revealed a significant small to medium population effect size of 0.20, indicating a greater WM capacity for bilinguals as opposed to monolinguals. Moderator analyses also revealed the largest effects in children as opposed to other age groups. Furthermore, it was also found that whether the task was performed in bilinguals' L1 or L2 modulated the effect size of the bilingual advantage, pointing to the importance of defining language variables that influence critical cognitive outcomes.

Oberauer, K., et al. (2018). Benchmarks for models of working memory. *Psychological Bulletin, 144*(9)**, 885–958.**

An authoritative position paper written by currently active WM research camps and theorists in a recent issue of *Psychological Bulletin* (2018) that aims to develop consensus benchmarks for constructing WM models in cognitive psychology and neuroscience based on agreed-upon criteria. Based on these consensus benchmarks, future research in language learning and bilingualism can have a solid ground for proposing novel, empirical and testable hypotheses regarding the WM-language nexus.

Wen, Z., & S. Li. (2019). Working memory in L2 learning and processing. In Schwieter, J. W., & Benati, A. (Eds.). *The Cambridge handbook of language learning* **(pp. 365–389).** **Cambridge: Cambridge University Press.**

Building on empirical studies and meta-analytical studies, the current chapter aims to characterize WM by teasing out consensus, controversies and debates over its nature and structure. Then results and findings of empirical studies looking into the distinctive effects of phonological WM and executive WM as they relate to L2 domains such as vocabulary and grammar and the processing of L2 skills are reviewed and synthesized, portraying a comprehensive picture depicting the WM-SLA association.

References

Baddeley, A. D. (2003). Working memory and language: An overview. *Journal of Communication Disorders, 36*(3), 189–208.

Baddeley, A. D. (2015). Working memory in second language learning. In Z. Wen, M. Mota, & A. McNeill (Eds.), *Working memory in second language acquisition and processing* (pp. 17–28). Multilingual Matters.

Baddeley, A. D., Gathercole, S. E., & Papagno, C. (1998). The phonological loop as a language learning device. *Psychological Review, 105*, 158–173.

Baddeley, A. D., & Hitch, G. (1974). Working memory. In G.A. Bower (Ed.), *The psychology of learning and motivation (*Vol. 8). Academic Press.

Cowan, N. (1999). An embedded-processes model of working memory. In A. Miyake & P. Shah (Eds.), *Models of working memory: Mechanisms of active maintenance and executive control* (pp. 62–101). Cambridge University Press.

Cowan, N. (2011). Working memory and attention in language use. In J. Guandouzi, F. Loncke, & M. J. Williams (Eds.), *The handbook of psycholinguistics and cognitive processes* (pp. 75–98). Psychology Press.

Daneman, M., & Carpenter, P. A. (1980). Individual differences in working memory and reading. *Journal of Verbal Learning and Verbal Behaviour, 19*, 450–466.

Engle, R. W. (2002). Working memory capacity as executive attention. *Current Directions in Psychological Science, 11*, 19–23.

Gathercole, S., & Baddeley, A. (1993). *Working memory and language*. Lawrence Erlbaum Associates.

Grundy, J. G., & Timmer K. (2017). Bilingualism and working memory capacity: A comprehensive meta-analysis. *Second Language Research, 33*(3), 325–340. 0267658316678286.

Linck, J. A., Osthus, P., Koeth, J. T., & Bunting, M. F. (2014). Working memory and second language comprehension and production: A meta-analysis. *Psychonomic Bulletin and Review, 21*(4), 861–883. https://doi.org/10.3758/s13423-013-0565-2

Miyake, A. & Shah, P. (1999). Models of working memory: Mechanisms of active maintenance and executivecontrol. New York: Cambridge University Press.

Oberauer, K., et al. (2018). Benchmarks for models of working memory. *Psychological Bulletin, 144*(9), 885–958.

Wen, Z. (2012). Working memory and second language learning. *International Journal of Applied Linguistics, 22*, 1–22. https://doi.org/10.1111/j.1473-4192.2011.00290.x

Wen, Z. (2016). *Working memory and second language learning: Towards an integrated approach*. Multilingual Matters.

Wen, Z. (2019). Working memory as language aptitude: The Phonological/Executive Model. In Z. Wen, P. Skehan, A. Biedron, S. Li, & R. Sparks (Eds.), *Language aptitude: Advancing theory, testing, research, and practice*. Routledge.

Wen, Z., Mota, M., & McNeill, M. (2015). *Working memory in second language acquisition and processing*. Multilingual Matters.

Zhisheng (Edward) Wen Ph.D., is an Associate Professor at Macao Polytechnic Institute, having taught at universities for 20 years. Dr. Wen has research interests in second language acquisition, cognitive sciences and translation studies, particularly the roles of working memory and language aptitude. He has published extensively in international and local journals. His monograph *Working memory and second language learning* was published by Multilingual Matters in 2016. He is leading editor of *Working memory in second language acquisition and processing* (Multilingual Matters, 2015), *Language aptitude: Advancing theory, testing, research and practice* (Routledge, 2019), and *Researching L2 task performance and pedagogy in honour of Peter Skehan* (John Benjamins, 2019). Forthcoming books include *"Cognitive individual differences in second language acquisition"* and *"Cambridge handbook of working memory and language"*.

Part III

Assessment and Assessment-related Topics

Approaches in Aligning Language Assessments to Standards and Frameworks

Spiros Papageorgiou

The terms *frameworks* and *standards* are sometimes used interchangeably in the language testing literature. They might refer to a set of guidelines on which tests are constructed or the learning outcomes used to assess and report learner progress and achievement (see discussion of these terms in Papageorgiou, 2016). In recent years, educational reforms around the world have resulted in increased interest in aligning language assessments to proficiency frameworks and standards, such as the Common European Framework of Reference (CEFR; Council of Europe, 2001) or the *ACTFL Proficiency Guidelines* (American Council on the Teaching of Foreign Languages, 2012). One of the reasons for this trend is the desire of educators and policy-makers to define language proficiency in a way that is useful, understandable and easy to communicate (Figueras, 2012). For example, when the CEFR was published in 2001, it aimed, among other things, to facilitate how stakeholders could communicate expected outcomes of their language programs and curricula or levels of learner progress. The alignment of language tests to the proficiency levels of the CEFR has dominated relevant research for nearly two decades and has been advocated as a way to facilitate score interpretations across different educational contexts (Council of Europe, 2009). However, researchers have noted issues with the use of the CEFR for designing test specifications, setting minimum score requirements for its levels, and comparing scores across tests designed for different purposes (see Papageorgiou & Tannenbaum, 2016).

A common approach to aligning tests to the levels of the CEFR, and consequently to other standards, is the one recommended in the *Manual* published by the Council of Europe (2009). The approach consists of two main stages: content alignment (Specification stage) and setting of cut scores (Standardization stage). For content alignment, the *Manual* provides forms to be completed for each language skill (Council of Europe, 2009, pp. 25–34). The forms require the developer of an

S. Papageorgiou (✉)
Educational Testing Service, Princeton, NJ, USA
e-mail: spapageorgiou@ets.org

© Springer Nature Switzerland AG 2021
H. Mohebbi and C. Coombe (eds.), *Research Questions in Language Education and Applied Linguistics*, Springer Texts in Education,
https://doi.org/10.1007/978-3-030-79143-8_51

exam to describe various aspects of the test content for each language skill in relation to the CEFR, for example communicative language activities, tasks, communication themes and text types. The intended CEFR level for each language skill should also be specified. The completed forms constitute a claim of how test content covers aspects of language ability described in the CEFR.

The second stage involves establishing one or more minimum scores (cut scores) on the test. The cut scores are used to classify test takers' demonstrated performance according to CEFR levels. Cut scores are established following a well-researched process in the educational measurement literature called "standard setting" (Cizek & Bunch, 2007). During standard setting, a panel of experts is required, under the guidance of one or more meeting facilitators, to make judgments about the difficulty of test questions (items or tasks), which results in cut score recommendations to the examination provider. Statistical information about the test (e.g., item difficulty estimates and distribution of test scores) is also used to help panelists with their judgment task. A fairly common practice in standard setting meetings is to conduct more than one round of judgments. Between rounds, the panel discusses individual judgments, receives statistical information about items and scores, and repeats the judgments. Even though the panel will offer a recommended cut score, the decision whether to accept or adjust (lower or raise) this score rests with the examination provider. Procedures for validating the recommended cut scores are also presented in the *Manual* (Council of Europe, 2009, pp. 89–118).

The Research Questions

1. What are the factors affecting panelists' decision making during standard setting?
2. How do panelist characteristics relate to decisions panelists make during standard setting?
3. What types of information provided by standard setting facilitators seem to improve the accuracy and consistency of the panelists' cut score judgments?
4. What types of activities can improve the panelists' understanding of the standards on which cut scores are set?
5. What types of data can be used to validate the cut score recommendation made by a panel?
6. How can information from other sources of data be consolidated with a panel's recommendation, so that cut scores are useful to teachers and students?
7. How can technology be used to facilitate the implementation of standard setting procedures?
8. How can the association between levels of different language standards or frameworks be explored?

9. In what ways does standard setting support the argument for the use of a language assessment and its scores?
10. What evidence should be collected to demonstrate the positive consequences of a selected cut score on teachers, students and other stakeholders?

Suggested Resources

Cizek, G. J., & Bunch, M. (2007). *Standard setting: A guide to establishing and evaluating performance standards on tests*. **London: Sage Publications**.

This book is written with a focus on the practicalities and "how-to" of standard setting, as the authors point out in the preface. The first part of the book contains an overview of fundamental topics on standard setting. The second part focuses on the procedures for implementing some of the most popular standard setting methods. The third part describes some of the challenges and future directions in the practice of standard setting. This is a highly recommended book for those who need to be involved in standard setting activities.

Cizek, G. J. (Ed.) (2012). *Setting performance standards: Concepts, methods, and innovations* **(2nd ed.). New York, NY: Routledge**.

This second edition of the volume is the perhaps the most comprehensive publication on the topic of standard setting, with chapters by several well-known authors in the field. The book contains 27 chapters in four sections that offer a detailed treatment of foundational concepts, applications of several standard setting methods, and address important issues for researchers and practitioners to consider. The volume is highly recommended for readers who want to solidify their understanding of standard setting procedures.

Figueras, N., & Noijons, J. (Eds.). (2009). *Linking to the CEFR levels: Research perspectives*. **Arnhem: CITO. Retrieved from** http://www.ealta.eu.org/documents/resources/Research_Colloquium_report.pdf

This freely available edited volume includes papers from a research colloquium in which professionals from the field of language testing exchanged views and discussed their work on aligning language assessments to the CEFR levels. The papers reflect the structure of the colloquium. In the first part expert discussants present their views on critical issues related to the process of aligning assessment to the CEFR levels. In the second part, practitioners offer reports of their alignment projects. The unique combination of theoretical and applied papers is a strong feature of this volume.

Papageorgiou, S., Wu, S., Hsieh, C.-N., Tannenbaum, R. J., & Cheng, M. M. (2019). *Mapping the TOEFL iBT® test scores to China's Standards of English Language Ability: Implications for score interpretation and use* **(Research Report No. TOEFL-RR-89). Princeton, NJ: Educational Testing Service. Retrieved from** https://doi.org/10.1002/ets2.12281

This publication reports on the research collaboration between Educational Testing Service (ETS) in the United States and the National Educational Examination Authority (NEEA) in China. The research project aimed to build an argument for aligning the scores of the TOEFL iBT test to the levels of China's Standards of English Language Ability (CSE), a localized framework for English as a foreign language. This technical report demonstrates the different steps in building a robust alignment claim, including: establishing construct congruence between the test and the CSE; establishing recommended minimum test scores (cut scores), set by local experts, to classify language learners into the CSE proficiency levels; collection of scores by test takers and evaluations of the test takers' proficiency levels by their teachers, based on the CSE; consideration of the results of other alignment studies in the local context. Because of the detailed description of the above steps, this report will be of interest to those engaging in similar alignment projects.

Tschirner, E. (Ed.) (2012). *Aligning Frameworks of Reference in Language Testing: The ACTFL Proficiency Guidelines and the Common European Framework of Reference for Languages.* **Tübingen, Germany: Stauffenburg Verlag.**

This is a unique edited volume in that it explores the relationship between the levels of two language standards, the CEFR and the ACTFL Proficiency Guidelines. Both language standards have been particularly influential in different geographical areas and share the common element of describing language proficiency through multi-level language proficiency scales. This common element raises the question of how the CEFR and ACTFL levels relate to each other. The book chapters are based on papers presented in two conferences on the relationship between the CEFR and the ACTFL levels held in 2010 and 2011. The book is organized in three parts, ranging from theoretical issues to empirical studies trying to establish a link between the CEFR and the ACTFL levels through tests linked to these levels. This volume makes an important contribution to the relevant literature in that it demonstrates that correspondence between the levels of the two standards is not as straightforward as it might seem.

References

American Council on the Teaching of Foreign Languages. (2012). *ACTFL proficiency guidelines*. Retrieved from http://www.actfl.org/sites/default/files/pdfs/public/ACTFLProficiencyGuidelines 2012_FINAL.pdf

Cizek, G. J., & Bunch, M. (2007). *Standard setting: A guide to establishing and evaluating performance standards on tests*. Sage.

Council of Europe. (2009). *Relating language examinations to the common European framework of reference for languages: Learning, teaching, assessment*. A Manual. Retrieved from https://www.coe.int/en/web/common-european-framework-reference-languages/

Council of Europe. (2001). *Common European framework of reference for languages: Learning, teaching, assessment*. Cambridge University Press.

Figueras, N. (2012). The impact of the CEFR. *ELT Journal, 66*(4), 477–485.

Papageorgiou, S. (2016). Aligning language assessments to standards and frameworks. In D. Tsagari & J. Banerjee (Eds.), *Handbook of second language assessment* (pp. 327–340). De Gruyter Mouton.

Papageorgiou, S., & Tannenbaum, R. J. (2016). Situating standard setting within argument-based validity. *Language Assessment Quarterly, 13*(2), 109–123.

Spiros Papageorgiou is a Managing Senior Research Scientist at Educational Testing Service (ETS) in Princeton, New Jersey, United States. Spiros received his doctoral degree specializing in language testing from Lancaster University, UK. In his current position at ETS Spiros conducts research on language assessment, and his interests include standard setting, score reporting and interpretation, and listening assessment. He has published widely on these topics and recently co-edited (with Professor Kathleen M. Bailey) the volume *Global perspectives on language assessment: Research, theory, and practice*. He has served as a member-at-large of the Executive Boards of the International Language Testing Association (ILTA) and the Midwest Association of Language Testers (MwALT).

Assessing L2 Signed Language Ability in Deaf Children of Hearing Parents

Wolfgang Mann, Joanna Hoskin, and Hilary Dumbrill

There are 34 million children worldwide who have a disabling hearing loss of more than than 30 dB in the better hearing ear (World Health Organisation, 2018). Within this population many children with a hearing loss greater than 90 dB grow up bilingual, learning a signed language such as American Sign Language (ASL), British Sign Language (BSL) as well as the spoken and/or written form of the language of the hearing linguistic majority in which they live. Those with a deaf parent may be exposed to signed language as L1 from birth. However, as most deaf babies are born to hearing parents (Mitchell & Karchmer, 2004), signed language is generally not used in the home unless parents are motivated to learn it. Acquiring a new language as L2 in a different modality can be very complex for both deaf children and their parents (Humphries et al., 2012) if there are no role models available, for instance deaf native signers.

The lack of a language that is easily accessible from birth, the shortage of signed language assessments, and limited spoken language tests that are suitable for use with deaf children, pose a considerable challenge for practitioners and researchers (Herman, 2015; Herman & Morgan, 2011). Additional complications may arise in the form of conflicted information and recommendations that parents receive from professionals following the diagnosis of the hearing loss (Humphries et al., 2012). While the risk of delayed language exposure has been reduced in many Western countries through the introduction of newborn hearing screening programs and

W. Mann (✉)
School of Education, University of Roehampton, London, UK
e-mail: Wolfgang.Mann@roehampton.ac.uk

J. Hoskin
Language & Communication Science Division, City University of London, London, UK
e-mail: Joanna.Hoskin@city.ac.uk

H. Dumbrill
Hamilton Lodge School & College for Deaf Learners, Brighton, UK
e-mail: Hilary.Dumbrill@hamiltonlsc.co.uk

© Springer Nature Switzerland AG 2021
H. Mohebbi and C. Coombe (eds.), *Research Questions in Language Education and Applied Linguistics*, Springer Texts in Education,
https://doi.org/10.1007/978-3-030-79143-8_52

early access to cochlear implantation (Knoors & Marschark, 2012), this does not guarantee that each implanted child will be successful in acquiring spoken language.

Additionally, most of the currently available research tends to be based on very small samples or case studies.

Despite the undisputed advances in technology and their potential benefits for a deaf child, many children enter school with considerable language issues, or no language at all. Aside from language these children also lack the skills needed to benefit from classroom learning, e.g., memory, focus, theory of mind, etc. This can lead to difficulties with learning, developing relationships and a child's self-identity. Those assessments and interventions available may indicate needs that cannot be met within local provision, but attendance at specialist provision, if far from home, may introduce a number of other issues, including cost, travel, and separation from family and local communities.

Another layer of difficulty comes with the increasing number of deaf children who present with additional needs, such as Attention Deficit Hyperactivity Disorder (ADHD) or Autism Spectrum Disorder (ASD) (Marshall & Morgan, 2015). These children may perform poorly even if instruments are used that have been specifically developed for signed language. One reason could be that despite the growing number of assessments being developed for signed languages in different countries, including the UK, USA, and Germany, there is still an overall lack of breadth of assessments measuring different aspects of signed language: vocabulary, morpho-syntax, narrative skills, etc. Without the proper assessment batteries, which exist for many spoken languages, the information provided by a single signed language test is rather limited, even more so because these tests tend to focus on outcome rather than learning. Consequently, children who perform poorly may give the impression that they lack the knowledge or skills required to successfully complete a task even though the true reason for their poor performance may be different, for instance unfamiliarity with testing. Recent research which has used a more dynamic assessment approach to explore the child's response to different types of mediated learning shows promising results (Hoskin, 2017; Mann et al., 2014, 2015).

The Research Questions

1. How can we improve hearing professionals' (clinicians, educators, practitioners) working knowledge of the typical development of signed language in deaf children?
2. How do professionals working with deaf children perceive the role of a sign therapist?

3. What information is needed by professionals working with deaf children to determine interventions for signed language—universal, targeted or specialist and what role does dynamic assessment play?
4. What are the key training needs of hearing and deaf professionals in delivering language interventions to deaf children?—How can these be met?
5. How can we improve our understanding of systemic interventions in cases of language deprivation (the child, the family, the school, the community, society)?
6. How do parents of deaf children perceive the information they are given and the access to support available?
7. What barriers stop professionals working with deaf children from using signed language assessments (more consistently)?
8. How can teachers (be motivated to) get more involved in the development of signed language assessments?
9. How confident do professionals feel to recommend signed language to the parent/carer of a young hearing impaired/deaf child?
10. What knowledge and values lead professionals working with deaf children to recommend signed language for a particular deaf child?

Suggested Resources

Glickman, N. & Hall, W. (Eds.). (2019). *Language Deprivation and Deaf Mental Health*. **New York: Routledge**.

This book provides background and context for current signed language discussions from a USA perspective. It highlights the implications of not ensuring deaf children have good opportunities to learn an accessible language in their early years.

Humphries, T., Kushalnagar, P., Mathur, G., Napoli, D. J., Padden, C., Rathmann, C., & Smith, S. R. (2012). Language acquisition for deaf children: Reducing the harms of zero tolerance to the use of alternative approaches. *Harm Reduction Journal*, *9*(1), 16.

This paper explores the issue of whether deaf children should be supported to learn a signed language whatever their audiological and listening management. It takes a standpoint that early learning of language is critical for children's development and highlights the risks involved with late language development.

Knoors, H., & Marschark, M. (2012). Language planning for the twenty-first century: Revisiting bilingual language policy for deaf children. *The Journal of Deaf Studies and Deaf Education*, *17*(3), 291–305.

This paper offers an interesting and thought-provoking discussion of the role of signed language and bilingual education for deaf children in the twenty-first century. These children have better chances than ever to access spoken language due to growing universal newborn hearing screening services and considerable techno-logical advances specifically in the form of cochlear implants. The authors raise the point that to successfully address these changes, while also acknowledging the diverse makeup of the deaf population, a carefully implemented, differentiated language policy is needed.

Mann, W. (2018). Measuring deaf learners' language progress in school. In H. Knoors & M. Marschark (Eds.). *Evidence-Based Practices in Deaf Education* **(pp. 171–188). Oxford: Oxford University Press.**

This chapter provides some background on language assessment of deaf popula-tions and introduces the concept of dynamic assessment, an interactive approach which embeds intervention within the assessment procedure. Following a brief overview of the available research the chapter offers suggestions for practitioners on how to use dynamic assessment in the classroom.

Marschark, M. (2018). *Raising and educating a deaf child: A comprehensive guide to the choices, controversies, and decisions faced by parents and educators (3rd edition).* **Oxford: Oxford University Press.**

This book provides an overview of some of the questions asked by parents when they discover their child is deaf. It provides an evidence base from which parents can begin to make informed decisions about language and education that will work for their family and situation. It is also helpful for practitioners and educators new to working with deaf children.

References

Herman, R. (2015). Language assessment of deaf learners. In H. E. T. Knoors & M. Marschark (Eds.), *Educating Deaf Learners: Creating a Global Evidence Base* (pp.197–212). Oxford University Press. https://doi.org/10.1093/acprof:oso/9780190215194.003.0009

Herman, R., & Morgan, G. (2011). Deafness, language and communication. In K. Hilari & N. Botting (Eds.), *The Impact of Communication Disability Across the Lifespan* (pp. 101–121). J&R Press Ltd.

Hoskin, J. H. (2017). *Language Therapy in British Sign Language: A study exploring the use of therapeutic strategies and resources by Deaf adults working with young people who have language learning difficulties in British Sign Language (BSL)* Doctoral dissertation, UCL (University College London). https://discovery.ucl.ac.uk/id/eprint/10022827/

Humphries, T., Kushalnagar, P., Mathur, G., Napoli, D. J., Padden, C., Rathmann, C., & Smith, S. R. (2012). Language acquisition for deaf children: Reducing the harms of zero tolerance to the use of alternative approaches. *Harm Reduction Journal, 9*(1), 16.

Knoors, H., & Marschark, M. (2012). Language planning for the 21st century: Revisiting bilingual language policy for deaf children. *The Journal of Deaf Studies and Deaf Education, 17*(3), 291–305.

Mann, W., Peña, E. D., & Morgan, G. (2014). Exploring the use of dynamic language assessment with deaf children, who use American Sign Language: Two case studies. *Journal of Communication Disorders, 52*, 16–30.

Mann, W., Peña, E. D., & Morgan, G. (2015). Child modifiability as a predictor of language abilities in deaf children who use American Sign Language. *American Journal of Speech-Language Pathology, 24*(3), 374–385.

Marshall, C., & Morgan, G. (2015). Investigating Sign Language Development, Delay, and Disorder in Deaf Children. In M. Marschark & P. E. Spencer (Eds.), *The Oxford Handbook of Deaf Studies in Language* (pp. 1–27). Oxford University Press. https://doi.org/10.1093/oxfordhb/9780190241414.013.21

Mitchell, R. E., & Karchmer, M. (2004). Chasing the mythical ten percent: Parental hearing status of deaf and hard of hearing students in the United States. *Sign Language Studies, 4*(2), 138–163.

World Health Organisation (2018, November 12). *Deafness and hearing loss.* Retrieved from http://www.who.int/news-room/fact-sheets/detail/deafness-and-hearing-loss

Wolfgang Mann is a Reader in the School of Education at University of Roehampton (London, UK). His published work includes articles, chapters and books on signed language acquisition, -assessment and -teaching, dynamic assessment, vocabulary development, and online reading. He is currently co-editing a book on issues related to signed and spoken language assessment to be published by Oxford University Press in 2020. Other recent publications include *Measuring deaf learners' language progress in school* in 2018 (*OUP*) and *Lexical-semantic organisation in American Sign Language and English in 2016 (Language Learning)*. Wolfgang is a co-developer of the guidelines for signed language test development, evaluation and use (https://www.hfh.ch/fileadmin/files/documents/Dokumente_FE/E.16_Haug_2016_guidelines_sign_language_tests.pdf). He is a research associate at the Deafness Cognition and Language Research Centre (DCAL) at University College London (UCL).

Joanna Hoskin is a Specialist Speech & Language Therapist who has worked with with d/Deaf children and adults in education, mental health and residential settings, including at national tertiary settings. She has researched and published on intervention strategies for d/Deaf children who had language, emotional or self-regulation issues. For her Ph.D. she explored how Deaf practitioners work with children who have language-learning difficulties in BSL. This led to the development of a short course run at City, University of London to support co-working with Deaf practitioners and SLTs. Joanna is keen to support the translation of research findings into practical tools that are accessible to people working with deaf children and young people.

Hilary Dumbrill is a Specialist Speech and Language Therapist who has worked in all areas of special educational need and currently works in a non-maintained special school for d/Deaf children in the UK. She is also a trained Play Therapist registered with the British Association of Play Therapists. Hilary feels strongly that attachment, relationships, language and communication are crucial to the development of memory, learning, social skills and the maintenance of mental health. Everyone needs an accessible language, a means of communication and conversation partners.

Assessing Second Language Listening

53

Elvis Wagner

Because the ability to understand spoken language is such an important aspect of second language (L2) proficiency, the assessment of L2 listening is a vital component of any test or assessment that purports to be assessing a learner's communicative competence. Assessing L2 listening ability generally involves presenting spoken input to test-takers, and then test-takers have to respond in some way (e.g., answer comprehension questions, provide a spoken response, complete a task, etc.). But because listening (like reading) is an internal process, assessing listening ability presents unique challenges to test developers; indeed, Buck (2001) argues that listening is the most difficult of the four skills to assess, and thus test developers should focus on those aspects of language that are unique to listening when creating assessment tasks.

When testing L2 listening, test developers have to find or create the spoken input that will be provided for the test-takers, and selecting the most appropriate input presents a number of choices for the test developers. First, test developers need to decide if appropriate spoken texts should be found from existing texts, or whether they should create spoken texts specifically for their particular test. It seems that most test developers choose to create their own spoken texts, as doing so makes it easier to address the test specifications (Wagner, 2014). But creating a spoken text also presents issues (e.g., the need for recording devices, the speakers to speak the texts, editing expertise, etc.), and these texts often result in spoken language that is quite different from real-world spoken language, which presents real validity concerns (Wagner, 2014). Another decision for listening test developers is which variety of the target language to present to test-takers. For example, in most high-stakes L2 English assessments, standard American or standard British is often used, at the expense of local and regional varieties of English, and rarely is L2-accented English used, even though these varieties are often part of the construct

E. Wagner (✉)
Department of Teaching and Learning, Temple University, Philadelphia, PA, USA
e-mail: elviswag@temple.edu

© Springer Nature Switzerland AG 2021
H. Mohebbi and C. Coombe (eds.), *Research Questions in Language Education and Applied Linguistics*, Springer Texts in Education,
https://doi.org/10.1007/978-3-030-79143-8_53

of interest (Wagner, 2016). Another decision is whether the spoken text should be presented to test-takers audio-only, or audio-visually (Wagner, 2010). Finally, listening is, by its very nature, fundamentally intertwined with speaking, and thus test developers who are interested in assessing test-takers' communicative competence have to decide whether to assess listening and speaking separately, or interactively (Ockey, 2014).

How test developers decide to address these issues in their assessments can have a real impact on the validity of that particular test, and these decisions also need to be addressed when making an argument supporting the validity of that test for a particular purpose. In addition, these decisions can also impact how test-takers (and teachers, and curriculum and materials designers) prepare for the test. That is, the choices test developers make can have a real washback effect on learning systems, and it is important that test developers consider the potential washback effect and try to make that washback effect as positive as possible.

The Research Questions

1. How does the use of spoken texts that include the characteristics of real-world spoken language affect L2 listening test-taker performance?
2. How does the use of audio-visual texts affect L2 listening test-taker performance?
3. How does the assessment of test-takers' ability to understand academic spoken language differ from the assessment of the ability to understand conversational spoken language?
4. In an interactive listening/speaking test task, to what extent does listening ability affect test-taker performance?
5. To what extent should listening and speaking be assessed together (interactively), and to what extent should they be assessed separately?
6. How does the accent of the speaker affect L2 listening test-taker performance?
7. To what extent should different varieties and accents (including non-standard varieties, local varieties, and L2-accented speech) be used as spoken input on L2 listening tests?
8. How can technology best be used to assess L2 listening ability?
9. How does test anxiety affect L2 listening test-taker performance; to what extent is L2 listening anxiety part of the construct of L2 listening ability?
10. How can L2 listening tests provide a positive washback effect on the teaching of L2 listening?

Suggested Resources

Buck, G. (2001). *Assessing Listening*. **Cambridge: Cambridge University Press.**

This book is the first resource for language testing researchers interested in the assessment of L2 listening. In fact, this book is relevant not only for those interested in listening assessment, but researchers and instructors interested in the teaching and learning of L2 listening ability as well. Buck provides a useful and thorough overview of L2 listening comprehension, and then focuses on what is unique to listening (as opposed to speaking, reading, and writing). He reviews a number of influential L2 listening taxonomies, and also presents a useful "default" definition of L2 listening ability. The book is full of useful examples of creating tasks and providing suitable texts for L2 listening instruction and assessment.

Geranpayeh, A., & Taylor, L. (Eds.) (2013). *Examining listening: Research and practice in assessing second language listening*. **Cambridge: Cambridge University Press**.

This volume broadly examines how second language listening proficiency can and should be assessed. The editors present a test validation framework based on a socio-cognitive perspective that has six components: Test taker characteristics; cognitive validity; context validity; scoring validity; consequential validity; and criterion-related validity. The listening tasks from the suite of Cambridge ESOL tests are analyzed in relation to these six components of the framework. The editors argue that it is vital that test developers provide a clear and full definition and explanation of the constructs that underlie their tests. Of particular interest is the chapter "Cognitive Validity" by John Field.

Gilmore, A. (2007). Authentic materials and authenticity in foreign language learning. *Language Teaching, 40,* **97–118**.

In this "state-of-the-art" article, Gilmore reviews the idea of authenticity in relation to foreign language learning, especially focusing on materials used in the teaching (and testing) of L2 listening. He starts with a discussion of how "authenticity" has been defined and operationalized in the literature, and the debate about what it means in relation to L2 teaching and learning. He then focuses on four areas related to authenticity: the difference between authentic spoken language and textbook discourse; the debate around English as a world language; how the ideas of motivation and authenticity intersect; and how the characteristics of spoken texts and task design affect listening performance and language acquisition. Gilmore also provides a number of reasons why materials and test developers might be reluctant to utilize authentic materials and tasks for L2 listening.

Ockey, G., & Wagner, E. (2018). *Assessing L2 listening: Moving towards authenticity*. **Amsterdam: John Benjamins**.

In this book, Ockey and Wagner identify four themes that are prominent in the current research focused on L2 listening assessment: the use of authentic, real-world spoken texts; the use of different accents and speech varieties as spoken input; the use of audio-visual texts; and assessing listening as part of an interactive speaking/listening construct. The authors provide an overview of the literature for each of the four themes, and then two or three empirical studies related to each of the themes is presented. Ockey and Wagner argue that what underlies each of these themes is the notion of authenticity, and that by utilizing authentic tasks and texts that have more of the characteristics of real world language tasks, test developers can better and more effectively assess test takers' communicative competence and can also provide a positive washback effect on educational systems.

Vandergrift, L., & Goh, C. (2012). *Teaching and learning second language listening: Metacognition in action*. **New York, NY: Routledge**.

Vandergrift and Goh's book provides a comprehensive overview of theoretical models of L2 listening comprehension, and then provides a detailed pedagogical model for L2 listening instruction. Their pedagogical model focuses on the idea of metacognition, which they define as "the ability of learners to control their thoughts and to regulate their own learning" (p. 5), which is vital in developing L2 listening ability. While the book does not focus on L2 listening assessment, it provides a plethora of examples of theoretically, methodologically, and pedagogically sound L2 listening tasks, and these tasks can be applied to listening tests and assessments as well. In addition, throughout the book Vandergrift and Goh provide an insightful review and critique of L2 listening research.

References

Buck, G. (2001). *Assessing Listening*. Cambridge University Press.

Ockey, G. J. (2014). The potential of the L2 group oral to elicit discourse with a mutual contingency pattern and afford equal speaking rights in an ESP context. *English for Specific Purposes, 35*, 17–29.

Wagner, E. (2010). The effect of the use of video texts on ESL listening test-taker performance. *Language Testing, 27*, 493–510.

Wagner, E. (2014). Assessing listening. In A. Kunnan (Ed.), *Companion to language assessment* (Vol. 1, pp. 47–63). Wiley-Blackwell.

Wagner, E. (2016). Authentic texts in the assessment of L2 listening ability. In J. V. Banerjee & D. Tsagari (Eds.), *Contemporary second language assessment* (pp. 103–123). Bloomsbury Academic.

Elvis Wagner is currently an Associate Professor in the College of Education at Temple University (Philadelphia, USA), where he is the coordinator of the TESOL and World Languages Education programs. He received his Ed.D. in Applied Linguistics/Second Language Assessment from Teachers College, Columbia University. His research focuses on the teaching and testing of second language oral communicative competence, on how L2 listeners process and comprehend unscripted, spontaneous spoken language, and how this type of language differs from the scripted spoken texts learners often encounter in the L2 classroom. He is currently an Associate Editor of *Language Assessment Quarterly*. He won the ILTA "Best Article in Language Testing" award for his (2008) article "Video Listening Tests: What Are They Measuring" published in *Language Assessment Quarterly*.

Assessing Second Language Pronunciation

54

Johnathan Jones and Talia Isaacs

Pronunciation assessment (PA) is a resurgent subfield within applied linguistics that traverses the domains of psycholinguistics, second language acquisition (SLA), speech sciences, sociolinguistics, and more recently, computational linguistics. Though the terms 'pronunciation' and 'assessment' are sometimes defined in different ways by different authors, here we regard pronunciation as the vocal articulation of consonants and vowels (segmentals) combined with aspects of oral speech that extend beyond individual sounds, including stress, rhythm and intonation (suprasegmentals). Assessment is used here in a broad sense to refer to any means of systematically harvesting information about a second language (L2) learner to describe or make a decision about his/her pronunciation ability. PA may stand alone, such as part of a needs analysis to determine whether a learner is able to accurately perceive and/or produce particular pronunciation features in his/her L2. Alternatively, PA may be incorporated into larger assessments of language proficiency, such as a scoring criterion in L2 oral production scales as part of the speaking component of proficiency testing.

As outlined in Isaacs and Harding (2017), pronunciation research and practice is couched in (and before) the earliest traces of applied linguistics. However, a predilection toward a native speaker ideal, combined with mechanical drills to achieve that ideal, pushed pronunciation—and PA with it—to the fringes of applied linguistics research and practice in the late twentieth century; it was viewed as incompatible with communicative language teaching (Levis & Sonsaat, 2017). After decades of relative desertion, PA is emerging as a locus of research and is establishing new footing within the language assessment community.

J. Jones (✉) · T. Isaacs
UCL Institute of Education, University College London, London, UK
e-mail: johnathan.jones.17@ucl.ac.uk

T. Isaacs
e-mail: talia.isaacs@ucl.ac.uk

© Springer Nature Switzerland AG 2021

H. Mohebbi and C. Coombe (eds.), *Research Questions in Language Education and Applied Linguistics*, Springer Texts in Education,
https://doi.org/10.1007/978-3-030-79143-8_54

Technological and philosophical demands have helped fuel PA's renaissance. Fully automated L2 speaking tests, for instance, draw heavily on pronunciation features that are readily machine detectable. While machine scoring of speech garnered rigorous debate when it was first introduced in large-scale L2 proficiency testing in the first decade of the twenty-first century, it is now tacitly accepted as here to stay, and consequently, so too is PA. From the perspective of trends within applied linguistics and L2 teaching more generally, PA's revival corresponds with a shift from a "native like" standard to a model driven by intelligibility—the extent to which a speaker's utterance may be understood by the interlocutor (Munro & Derwing, 2019). Within this revised scope, PA is arguably better equipped to address the increasing use of English as a lingua franca on the global stage and to provide learners with more realistic L2 learning and assessment goals.

A preeminent focus of PA research is, therefore, better understanding of what constitutes intelligibility, and, specifically which linguistic aspects, speaker characteristics, listener/interlocutor/rater variables, and environmental factors contribute most to successfully perceiving and producing L2 speech.

PA is primed for growth over the coming years, with research emphasis likely to be placed on refining our understanding of intelligibility, identifying factors which influence human judgments of pronunciation, optimizing technology-mediated PA, and moving beyond the overriding focus of most of the existing research on English to examine other world languages.

The Research Questions

1. What is the role of pronunciation in the construct of L2 speaking? In theoretical models of communicative competence/communicative language ability? And how does it relate to other language components?
2. How can the features that are most important for L2 intelligibility and comprehensibility best be targeted in pronunciation assessment, including in classrooms where L2 learners are from mixed first language (L1) backgrounds?
3. How can pronunciation assessment (PA) best be addressed in teacher training to promote both familiarity with key concepts in L2 pronunciation, and assessment literacy?
4. How is pronunciation most effectively integrated with other language skills, such as grammar and vocabulary when providing feedback for formative assessment purposes?
5. How can PA be used to help improve workplace safety/communications in language for specific purposes environments (e.g., ensuring adequate L2 speaking and listening ability for professionals in aviation, medical, and higher education sectors)?
6. What is an appropriate standard for assessing L2 pronunciation in settings where the target language is the majority language of the society? And in

settings where there is no established L1 norm and interlocutors' L2 is used as the shared medium of communication?

7. After conducting a needs analysis for an L2 learner in terms of perceiving and/or producing key pronunciation features, which linguistic factors are most appropriate for helping determine whether remediation is needed?

8. How can we optimize the listening prompts that we use to make them more authentic representations of the language that learners are likely to encounter outside of instructed contexts (e.g., language varieties represented)?

9. How can sources of variance that may bias listeners' judgments of L2 pronunciation be minimized to promote fairer assessments (e.g., listener familiarity with L1- accented speech)? How can this best be implemented in both research contexts and operational assessments?

10. How can technological innovations such as automatic speech recognition, automated scoring, and dialogue systems be harnessed to target L2 pronunciation features that are important for aural/oral communication, including testing learners' abilities and providing them with meaningful feedback?

Suggested Resources

Celce-Murcia, M., Brinton, D., & Goodwin, J., with Griner, B. (2010). *Teaching pronunciation: A course book and reference guide* (2nd ed.). Cambridge, UK: Cambridge University Press.

There is, as yet, no book dedicated to the topic of guiding teachers on how to assess L2 pronunciation, including designing, administering, and scoring pronunciation tests and feedback provision for formative assessment purposes. Celce-Murcia et al.'s (2010) influential volume, now in its second edition, constitutes a wide-ranging pronunciation reference for L2 English teachers. In contrast to other pronunciation books for teachers, which either explicitly avoid covering assessment or have scant coverage of the topic, this book includes a 'Testing and Evaluation' chapter. It provides examples of sample items that could be used for diagnostic assessment; overviews formal language tests; discusses formative assessment, including feedback (self, peer, and teacher); and introduces testing pronunciation in the classroom. However, the chapter is largely descriptive, with little citation of relevant research, and focuses primarily on age-old practices, such as discrete-point items prototyped in the early 1960s. Beyond a few paragraphs on eliciting extemporaneous speech samples as part of needs analyses, the chapter bypasses coverage of integrated assessment, an indicator of modern assessment practices. Therefore, while serving as a helpful general resource for teachers, particularly given the dearth of practical resources, the book remains a glaring reminder of the gap between PA research and practice.

Isaacs, T. (2018). Shifting sands in second language pronunciation teaching and assessment research and practice. *Language Assessment Quarterly, 15,* **273–293.**

This state-of-the-art article provides a comprehensive sampling of topics under the PA umbrella as part of a special issue on the L2 speaking construct, with the inclusion of an article on PA attesting to its presumed importance in assessing speaking. The article uncovers trends—historical and recent—in pronunciation research, teaching, and assessment to orient PA within the broader context of L2 speaking assessments. It concludes by arguing for the importance of interdisciplinary research in this area and setting out directions for an ambitious research agenda for the future. Content coverage, reflected in an extensive reference list, includes discussions of accent discrimination and scapegoating, pronunciation teaching and assessment goals and targets, major global constructs, models from speech sciences research with potential applications for applied PA, the role of pronunciation in L2 speaking scales, rater effects, PA in interactional exchanges and lingua franca communication, automated assessment, and the potential for human and machine integrated scoring. The article is densely written and it would be worthwhile to unpack it in a larger work or series of works.

Isaacs, T., & Harding, L. (2017). Pronunciation assessment. *Language Teaching, 50,* **347–366.**

This research timeline delineates evolutions in PA and includes an annotated bibliography of seminal works, including research articles, curricular materials, and language tests. The article motivates the topic with a general introduction before presenting a tabular summary of key developments or milestones in the field, which are placed in chronological order and are tagged with at least one of six themes. The themes depict a PA meronomy consisting of operational assessments and scoring systems, practitioner-oriented guides, theoretical frameworks, and empirical studies. The article is an accessible reference for language practitioners and researchers, highlighting key themes and their interrelationships by tracing the historical developments through the discussion of the featured work.

Isaacs, T., & Trofimovich, P. (Eds.). (2017). *Second language pronunciation assessment: Interdisciplinary perspectives.* **Bristol, UK: Multilingual Matters.**

This open access volume is the first edited collection dedicated to the topic of PA. The book features chapters on key issues, including rating scale validation, revisiting the role of the native speaker and standard language, pronunciation and lingua franca communication, researching factors that impact intelligibility and comprehensibility, and investigating factors that may compromise the validity of formal and informal judgments of pronunciation (e.g., topic familiarity, listener attitudes). A novel contribution of this volume is its inclusion of chapters on how examining other language skills, including assessing fluency and assessing writing, can inform the topic of pronunciation assessment. Readers will benefit from the cogent exposition of current trends and future directions, though given the book's overall progressive approach, it would have benefited from a greater focus on automated pronunciation assessment and potential interchange with mobile- or web-based applications.

Kang, O., & Ginther, A. (Eds.). (2018). *Assessment in second language pronunciation*. **Abingdon, UK: Routledge**.

In this edited collection, leading researchers share foundational concepts in PA and explore the intersection between PA and technology. Readers will find numerous merits to this volume, including an updated exposition of accent, intelligibility, and comprehensibility; theoretical justifications for PA; the development of PAs in the context of World Englishes; and factors which affect rating and scoring. Those seeking information on recent technological advancements in PA and the role of pronunciation in automated scoring will benefit from three chapters devoted to technology and PA. One shortcoming, however, is that the book largely neglects perception as it pertains to PA, focusing almost exclusively on oral production. Given that L2 teachers are part of the book's target audience, it would have been auspicious to include at least one chapter on perception in PA. Overall, however, the book represents one of two edited works featuring PA and remains an essential collation of theory and practice.

References

Isaacs, T. & Harding, L. (2017). Research timeline: Pronunciation assessment. *Language Teaching, 50*, 347–366.

Levis, J., & Sonsaat, S. (2017). Pronunciation in the CLT era. In O. Kang, R. I. Thomson, & J. S. Murphy (Eds.), *The Routledge handbook of English pronunciation* (pp. 267–283). Routledge.

Munro, M. J., & Derwing, T. M. (2019). Phonetics and second language teaching research. In W. F. Katz & P. F. Assmann (Eds.), *The Routledge handbook of phonetics* (pp. 473–495). Routledge.

Johnathan Jones is a Ph.D. candidate researching the efficacy of traditional assessment methods in L2 speech perception testing at the UCL Centre for Applied Linguistics, UCL Institute of Education, University College London. Holding a Master of Applied Linguistics with a specialization in Language Testing (University of Melbourne), and credentials in Linguistics and Psychology (University of British Columbia), his work in pronunciation assessment merges the domains of language testing, applied linguistics, and speech perception. Though his academic work examines theoretical and methodological gaps in research and assessment, his interests are practical, refining assessments to better reflect language learners' present abilities.

Talia Isaacs is an Associate Professor of Applied Linguistics and TESOL at the UCL Centre for Applied Linguistics, UCL Institute of Education, University College London. She has disseminated extensively on L2 pronunciation assessment, including empirical studies, state-of-the-art articles, workshops, presentations/symposia, media pieces, radio interviews, blogs, a research timeline, and videos/podcasts. She is co-editor of *Assessing second language pronunciation: Interdisciplinary perspectives* (2017, Multilingual Matters), co-created the *L2*

English comprehensibility global and analytic scales (2018), both of which are open access, and has led numerous research projects and consultancies on analyzing and scoring L2 speech. Her research activities in applied linguistics are wide ranging, and she has designed courses in the areas of language testing, second language acquisition, L2 pedagogy and curriculum, oral communication, and research methodology.

The Assessment of Target-Language Pragmatics

Andrew D. Cohen

In assessing pragmatics during the late 1970s and into the 1980s, it was considered special to isolate and describe, say, apology behavior in a native language (L1) and in a target language (TL), rather than to focus on the discourse context within which that specific speech act or any other was ensconced. Nor was there concern for either multiple speech acts nor for the reality of having the speech acts as a part of a larger discourse. By the early 1990s, the focus was now on clusters of speech acts, like greetings, apologies, and requests, all performed within the same speech event (Hudson et al., 1992, 1995). Likewise, in the late 1990s into the early 2000s, Kasper (2004) started emphasizing the importance of viewing pragmatic behavior within the framework of conversational analysis. Shortly thereafter, Félix-Brasdefer (2006) wrote a paper detailing how teachers could teach speech act performance embedded within a discourse context, using a refusal to an invitation as the speech act area in focus. And so, the approach of focusing on isolated pragmatic features without concern for the larger context—where researchers were engaged in assessing what amounted to a reduced picture—was replaced by a more inclusive, discursive approach.

Interactional competence has now clearly emerged as a major variable in determining the nature of the pragmatic assessment to be undertaken. Experts would admonish us from simply paying lip service to the notion that pragmatic ability involves knowledge of a form-function-context relationship in assessment (Taguchi, 2018). Interactional competence adds another layer to the definition of pragmatic ability: the ability to adapt to the changing course of interaction and to achieve a communicative goal in collaboration with interlocutors. The argument is made that the analysis of conversational structure, such as turn-taking, adjacency pairs, pre- and post-sequences, and preference organizations, can reveal how par-

A. D. Cohen (✉)
Professor Emeritus, Program in Second Language Studies, College of Liberal Arts, University of Minnesota, Minneapolis, MN, USA
e-mail: adcohen@umn.edu

© Springer Nature Switzerland AG 2021
H. Mohebbi and C. Coombe (eds.), *Research Questions in Language Education and Applied Linguistics*, Springer Texts in Education,
https://doi.org/10.1007/978-3-030-79143-8_55

ticipants monitor the changing course of a conversation and adapt to the change by designing their contributions in a sequentially appropriate manner.

Currently, there is also a pullback from speech acts because they only represent one aspect of pragmatics. Nonetheless, they represent an area that is crucial for learners, has high face validity, and is fun for learners to engage in. Despite the plethora of studies conducted on L1 and TL requesting behavior, as well as a fair number on apologizing, complaining, complimenting, thanking, and greeting, there is still much of speech act performance that is not being adequately assessed. Item construction is problematic in trying to create deviant items with regard to a norm (Ellis & Roever, 2021), and it is easier to create items which fail pragmalinguistically as opposed to sociopragmatically. Sociopragmatics often involves a fine line as to what is or is not acceptable in a given TL community, especially given the variation L1 and speakers in that community—such as asking someone what their monthly salary is, the cost of their new home or new car, or whether they are engaged in trying to have a baby using in vitro fertilization.

Finally, the assessment of pragmatics needs to add an important distinction between construct-relevant and construct-irrelevant test-taking strategies. While the former can be inferred to be referred to as test-management strategies, the latter are being referred to as "test-deviousness strategies" in that their true purpose may be to assist respondents in avoiding having to access their language knowledge or lack thereof (see Cohen. 2021).

The Research Questions

1. To what extent can a bottom-up, micro-generic approach to analyzing a naturally-recorded interaction as it unfolds turn-by-turn inform the assessment of TL pragmatics?
2. What features contribute to the assessment of sociopragmatic ability in a student respondent? What types of items and tasks effectively distinguish high performers from low performers in terms of their TL sociopragmatic ability?
3. How can we assess the pragmatic effect of prosodic elements used in interaction to express tentativeness, politeness, or degrees of directness or indirectness, such as through pitch direction, pitch range, pauses, loudness, tempo, and voice quality?
4. To what extent should test-wiseness strategies—such as purposely ignoring elements in the prompt for role-play—be penalized in pragmatics assessment?
5. How does the language in naturally-occurring TL speech acts compare with that collected in oral response items and tasks for assessment purposes?
6. What does assessing L2 speakers in real-life situations in which there are genuine affective, relational, and material consequences to how they interact with others add to an understanding of learners' pragmatic ability?
7. In what ways can and should nonverbal behavior be included in pragmatics assessment—such as facial expressions and gestures?

8. To what extent can teachers be impartial, objective gatherers of pragmatics data on their own students for high-stakes assessment?

9. How does the teacher go about determining the norms to use in assessment? To what extent should they reflect the local variety or varieties of spoken language?

10. If there are two or more raters of TL pragmatic performance, what means can be used to ensure against numerous threats to rater reliability?

Suggested Resources

Bardovi-Harlig, K. & Shin, S-Y. (2014). Expanding traditional testing measures with tasks from L2 pragmatics research. *Iranian Journal of Language Testing, 4*(1), 26–49.

This article discusses the principles of language assessment as applied to tests of pragmatics. It reports on current interest in pragmatics testing in language programs through informal interviews conducted with researcher-teachers on current practices in pragmatics testing. Tasks used in pragmatic research that are considered innovative in the context of assessment, are presented, and then the authors discuss the potential of each task to enhance task authenticity, its practicality for testing, and its potential for broadening the construct representation. They include oral production (oral for oral), written production (written for written), and audio and/or audio-visual conversational excerpts with written/read interpretations. The tasks cover conventional expressions, pragmatic routines, conversational implicature, pragmaticality judgments, sociopragmatic judgments, interaction of grammar and pragmatics, and speech act identification tasks. The production tasks simulate turn taking by providing unanticipated turns through computer generation or audio presentation, requiring responses from the test takers.

Eslami, Z. & Mirzaei, A. (2014). Speech act data collection in a non-Western context: Oral and written DCTs in the Persian language. *Iranian Journal of Language Testing, 4*(1), 137–154.

The study compared two measures used frequently to assess pragmatic competence: written discourse completion tasks (WDCT) and oral discourse completion tasks (ODCT), exploring the validity of using these two forms of DCTs in non-Western contexts. Twenty-Four Iranian university students responded to both measures eliciting requests. The response length, range and content of the expressions, formality level, and spoken vs. written language forms were analyzed. The findings showed that the two measures elicited different production samples from the students. ODCTs elicited longer, more elaborate responses, and more linguistic forms representing the spoken variety of the language than did the WDCTs. In WDCTs students mixed different styles (spoken and written) and used both formal and informal linguistic devices in one situation. Their findings indicate that WDCTs may be inappropriate for collecting data in Persian language, which has marked differences between spoken and written varieties and highly complicated stylistic variations. Studies like this underscore the fact that more work is needed to both extend the range and scope of speech act studies to non-Western languages and refine the methodologies used to measure pragmatic competence.

Félix-Brasdefer, J. C. (2018). Role plays. In C. R. Hoffmann & W. Bublitz (Eds.), *Pragmatics of social media* (pp. 303–329). Berlin/Boston: De Gruyter Mouton.

This chapter offers a comprehensive account of the role-play method commonly used in cross-cultural and interlanguage pragmatics. Role plays have been used to investigate different aspects of the learners' pragmatic competence (e.g. pragmalinguistic and sociopragmatic knowledge). This chapter focuses on the conceptualization of the role-play method for research and assessment purposes, looks at the structure of the role-play task and instructions of the task for the role-play taker and role-play conductor, reviews existing varieties of role plays, and explains procedures for the coding and analysis of role-play data. The distinction between closed and open role play is explained, as well as the relevance of the role-enactment approach. This chapter ends with an overview of key issues of validity and reliability, and methodological and ethical issues for researchers using the role-play method.

Ishihara, N. (2009). Teacher-based assessment for foreign language pragmatics. *TESOL Quarterly, 43*(3), 445–470.

Ishihara contends that despite the growing interest in teaching L2 pragmatics, the issue of assessment of learners' pragmatic skills, particularly in the context of the classroom, seems to be less prominently discussed, even though the assessment is an integral part of the instruction. This qualitative case study aims to demonstrate an operationalization of a principle of pragmatics within the classroom context and demonstrate the effectiveness of teacher-based assessment of pragmatic competence grounded in Vygotsky's sociocultural theory. In freshman English courses at a Japanese university, the teacher researcher implemented pragmatics-focused instruction for 58 EFL students throughout a semester based on empirically established information on speech acts in English. The instructor used collaboratively developed authentic assessment tools, such as reflective writing, rubrics, role-plays, and self/peer-assessment, and facilitated interaction and assessment in the learning process. These assessments were designed (a) to elicit learners' pragmalinguistic competence to use community norms, (b) to elicit their sociopragmatic awareness of the consequences of their own pragmatic language choice, and (c) to evaluate the extent of the match between learners' intention (*illocution*) and interlocutors' interpretation (*perlocution*).

Roever, C., & Ikeda N. (October, 2020). Testing L2 pragmatic competence. In G. Schneider and E. Ifantidou (eds.), *Handbook of developmental and clinical pragmatics***. Berlin: Mouton de Gruyter.**

The chapter traces the evolution of L2 pragmatics assessment, which has been characterized by the attempt to provide adequate coverage of a broad construct such as L2 pragmatics. This has led to several paradigm shifts, with early tests focusing on clearly-defined speech acts, followed by instruments incorporating other aspects of pragmatics (such as implicature, style level, routine formulae), and with recent tests taking a much more holistic approach and assessing the ability to engage in extended interactions. At the same time, the need for establishing contexts of interaction has led pragmatics tests to struggle with practicality, which might account for their rare use in real-world settings. The authors contend that the ideal scenario would be the testing of interaction with an avatar and an automated speech recognition engine. They cite research by Ikeda (2017) demonstrating the value of collecting monologic data from respondents in that such data require fewer resources, but on the other hand they do not get at interactional competence. This chapter returns time and again to the point that pragmatics needs to assess discourse competency, while also stressing that the speech acts are just one part of pragmatic ability.

References

Cohen, A. D. (2021). Test-taking strategies and task design. In G. Fulcher & L. Harding (Eds.) *Routledge handbook of language testing* (2d. ed.). Abingdon, UK: Routledge.

Ellis, R., & Roever, C. (2021). The measurement of implicit and explicit knowledge. *The Language Learning Journal. 49*(2), 160–175.

Félix-Brasdefer, C. (2006). Teaching the negotiation of multi-turn speech acts: Using conversation-analytic tools to teach pragmatics in the FL classroom. In K. Bardovi-Harlig, C. Félix-Brasdefer, & A. S. Omar (Eds.), *Pragmatics and Language Learning* (pp. 167–197). National Foreign Language Resource Center, University of Hawai'i.

Hudson, T., Detmer, E. & Brown, J. D. (1992). *A framework for testing cross-cultural pragmatics* (Technical Report #2). Second Language Teaching and Curriculum Center, University of Hawaii at Manoa.

Hudson, T., Detmer, E., & Brown, J. D. (1995). *Developing prototypic measures of cross-cultural pragmatics (Technical Report #7)*. Second Language Teaching and Curriculum Center, University of Hawai'i at Manoa.

Kasper, G. (2004). Speech acts in (inter)action: Repeated questions. *Intercultural Pragmatics, 1* (1), 125–133.

Taguchi, N. (2018). Data collection and analysis in developmental L2 pragmatics research: Discourse completion test, role play, and naturalistic recording. In A. Gudmestad & A. Edmonds (Eds.), *Critical reflections on data in second language acquisition* (pp. 7–32). Amsterdam: John Benjamins.

Andrew D. Cohen Professor Emeritus, University of Minnesota, lives in Oakland, CA. He authored *Assessing language ability in the classroom* (Heinle & Heinle/Cengage Learning, 2nd ed., 1994), co-edited *Language learning strategies* with Ernesto Macaro (Oxford University Press, 2007), co-authored *Teaching and learning pragmatics* with Noriko Ishihara (Routledge, 2014, with translations into Japanese, Korean, and Arabic), authored the second edition of *Strategies in learning and using a second language* (Routledge, 2011), and most recently authored *The learning of pragmatics from native and nonnative language teachers* (Multilingual Matters, 2018). His article "Considerations in assessing pragmatic appropriateness in spoken language" (*Language Teaching*, 2019, https://doi.org/10.1017/S0261444819000156) deals with the topic of his entry in this volume. Copies of most of his papers are available for download on his website: https://z.umn.edu/adcohen.

Classroom Assessment & Assessment as Learning

56

Jonathan Trace

Second language classroom assessment sits at a challenging crossroads for both researchers and teachers. As an essential component of the curriculum, assessment in the classroom is not merely a measure of performance and achievement towards learning outcomes, but it should also promote and facilitate the learning process. Expanding beyond the standard definition of classroom tests as summative measures of achievement and diagnostic alone, tests have more recently been utilized for both formative purposes as well as a way to create learning-oriented opportunities (LOIs; Carless et al., 2006). Inherent in such an expanded definition is the realization that LOIs can, should, and do take on many possible forms, varying along multiple dimensions, including how they are planned, reported, interpreted, and connected to learning processes. This affordance for variation, however, still needs to be reconciled with the core principles of assessment, such as reliability, standards, consequences, and validity, as LOIs remain linked to the use and interpretation of performances (Stoynoff, 2012).

Hill and McNamara (2011) define classroom assessment as the way in which teachers view student performance to influence, "teaching, learning (feedback), reporting, management or socialization purposes" (p. 396). While this definition is helpful in understanding the broader purposes of classroom assessment, it leaves blank a description of what it can and does look like, as well as the particular commonalities that can be drawn across its uses in classrooms. Broadly speaking, LOIs can take the form of traditional measures like multiple-choice tests or performance assessments, though classrooms also provide opportunities for (a) longitudinal and personalized assessments, such as portfolios or project-based assessments (e.g., Cresswell, 2000), (b) alternative and democratic forms of assessment (Shohamy, 2001) in the form of rubrics that are co-developed with learners and self- and peer-assessment (e.g., Goto Butler & Lee, 2010), and

J. Trace (✉)
Faculty of Environment and Information Studies, Keio University, Fujisawa, Kanagawa, Japan
e-mail: tracej@sfc.keio.ac.jp

© Springer Nature Switzerland AG 2021
H. Mohebbi and C. Coombe (eds.), *Research Questions in Language Education and Applied Linguistics*, Springer Texts in Education,
https://doi.org/10.1007/978-3-030-79143-8_56

317

(c) individualized and process-based approaches to assessment including formative and dynamic assessment (e.g., Poehner, 2007; Popham, 2008). What appears to be common amongst these approaches is that they provide teachers and learners with learning-rich opportunities to not only measure what they have acquired, but also the processes involved through the use of feedback.

Research on classroom-based assessment has therefore taken on many different forms over the years, from comparisons to large-scale assessments, to descriptions of its use (Rea-Dickins, 2001), to theoretical frameworks (Turner & Purpura, 2016). The search for common ground from which to make generalizable or, at the very least, applicable claims about standards, uses, and interpretations of these LOIs remains an ongoing one, however. There is still much to be explored about how to make assessment in the classroom not only effective for learning purposes, but also accessible for teachers. In addition to the reality that many teachers are not experts in assessment research, the stigma of assessments as necessary, cumbersome, and an imposition rather than an asset remains. Steps to raise the awareness of how teachers can beneficially incorporate assessment into the things they already do within their classrooms is necessary, as it further assists both teachers and learners in using assessment as a learning tool in the classroom.

The Research Questions

1. What are identifiable and common features of second language classroom assessment across learning contexts?
2. What are the standards for validity and reliability in classroom-based assessment?
3. What do classroom teachers perceive and experience as the main challenges that they face in designing and using assessments?
4. To what degree are learners aware of the uses of classroom assessment (for learning)?
5. What is the role of validity and reliability in self- and peer-assessment in the classroom?
6. What are the implications of learning-oriented assessment for second language curriculum design (i.e., needs, objectives, materials)?
7. How can classroom-based assessment practices be linked to research in second language acquisition?
8. How can individualized assessments (i.e., continuous or dynamic assessment) be implemented effectively into language classrooms?
9. To what degree can assessment in the classroom address social and interactive components of language learning?
10. What are the qualities of effective feedback for learning-oriented assessment purposes?

Suggested Resources

Brown, J. D., (Ed.) (2013). *New ways of classroom assessment.* Alexandria, VA: TESOL International Association.

A volume aimed more at teachers than researchers, *New ways in classroom assessment* is collection of in-practice teacher descriptions of assessment activities designed for use in the language classroom. While the purpose is to generate ideas for classroom assessment, it also provides an excellent look at the many forms that assessment can take across a number of different language contexts. Assessment types are broken down into sections for alternative assessments, alternative feedback types, assessments for group and pairwork, ways to incorporate assessment into the daily curriculum, and oral and written assessments.

As the editor notes, the activities within highlight the strong connection between assessment, teaching, and learning, and it is partially because of this that the contents are referred to as *activities* rather than tests. Each contribution is described in terms of the processes involved, the potential context(s) it can be used within, and ways of providing feedback, advice and modifications, while also including suggested readings, appendices, and sample materials.

Brown, J. D., & Hudson, T. (2002). *Criterion-referenced language testing.* Cambridge: Cambridge University Press. https://doi.org/10.1017/CBO9781139524803

This seminal work in language assessment literature is recommended as a resource for those interested in understanding classroom assessment in relation and in contrast to traditional, large-scale language testing paradigms. It bridges theoretical concepts of language assessment, such as validity and reliability, and connects them to the practical considerations of using assessment in the classroom.

It begins with a discussion of how classroom assessment differs from large-scale, norm-referenced testing, then follows up by linking their use to program, classroom, and learning-specific needs and uses. Furthermore, it provides details through a multitude of examples about strategies for designing and writing items and activities. Given the authors' quantitative backgrounds, it also covers ways to analyze test and item function, score reliability and dependability, and validity via a number of both simple and advanced statistical methods. Though challenging on the surface, the authors provide examples and use beginner-friendly terminology and descriptions to make these approaches accessible to even neophyte researchers. The volume concludes with a practical discussion of interpreting and providing feedback to learners and other stakeholders involved.

Brown, J. D., & Trace, J. (2017). Fifteen ways to improve classroom assessment. In: E. Hinkel (Ed.), *Handbook of research in second language teaching and learning* (3rd ed.) (pp. 490–505). New York: Routledge. https://doi.org/10.4324/9781315716893-35

This chapter in the most recent edition of the *Handbook of research in second language teaching and learning* is specifically aimed at providing a resource for language teachers to help inform and improve the implementation of classroom assessment in language programs. It covers many practical applications and considerations that are involved in designing, carrying out, and using classroom assessment for readers who may not have an extensive background in assessment research and training. The chapter is broken down into sections on (a) assessment options and matching assessment to learning, (b) simple item writing strategies, (c) assessment administration and feedback, and (d) improving and analyzing test function. The accessibility of the language and the focus on practicality make this a good resource for entering into the discussion of classroom assessment.

Hill, K., & McNamara, T. (2011). Developing a comprehensive, empirically based research framework for classroom-based assessment. *Language Testing,* *29*(3), 395–420. https://doi.org/10.1177/0265532211428317

This study presents a framework for classroom-based assessment research that examines the underlying processes involved in using and interpreting assessments from both teacher and learner perspectives. The authors draw on observations of the various formal and informal assessment opportunities that arise within language classrooms to highlight the essential and common components of classroom assessment. Using two language classes as their research contexts, they observed assessment practices over 20 weeks of classes to gather data aimed at answering the following questions related to classroom assessment: (a) what is it that teachers do; (b) what do teachers look for; (c) what standards are applied; and (d) to what extent are learners aware of assessment and its uses. These questions form the basis of their final framework for researching classroom assessment, which identifies several phases and processes common in classroom assessments. Importantly, this article provides an excellent starting point for researchers and teachers interested in a closer examination of assessment opportunities in the classroom.

Turner, C. E., & Purpura, J. E. (2016). Learning-oriented assessment in second and foreign language classrooms. In D. Tsagari, & J. Banerjee (Eds.), *Handbook of second language assessment* **(pp. 255–272). Boston, MA: De Gruyter Mouton**.

This chapter from the *Handbook of second language assessment* specifically examines the past, current, and future role of learning-oriented assessment in the language classroom. The authors are guided by questions about the characteristics of assessment in the classroom and how they engender learning, what evidence of learning they can provide, and what the role of feedback is for promoting further learning. A framework is proposed that encompasses the many factors that influence how learning-oriented assessment manifests in the classroom. Included in this design is a discussion of (a) the influence of context, (b) how language is elicited, (c) the level of language, (d) language acquisition, feedback, and self-regulation, (e) the role of instruction, (f) social roles and interaction, and (g) learner affect. Taken together, these seven dimensions are given as a way to begin to understand

and explore the many possible and varied forms that learning-oriented assessments can take, concluding with several potential areas of inquiry for researchers in the area to pursue.

References

Carless, D., Joughin, G., & Liu, N. F. (2006). How assessment supports learning: Learning-oriented assessment in action (Vol. 1). Hong Kong University Press. https://doi.org/10.5790/hongkong/9789622098237.001.0001.

Cresswell, A. (2000). The role of portfolios in the assessment of student writing on an EAP course. In G. M. Blue, J. Milton, & J. Saville (Eds.), *Assessing English for academic purposes* (pp. 205–220). Peter Lang Publishing.

Goto Butler, Y., & Lee, J. (2010). The effects of self-assessment among young learners of English. *Language Testing, 27*(1), 5–31. https://doi.org/10.1177/0265532209346370

Hill, K., & McNamara, T. (2011). Developing a comprehensive, empirically based research framework for classroom-based assessment. *Language Testing, 29*(3), 395–420. https://doi.org/10.1177/0265532211428317

Poehner, M. E. (2007). Beyond the test: L2 dynamic assessment and the transcendence of mediated learning. *The Modern Language Journal, 91*(3), 323–340. https://doi.org/10.1111/j.1540-4781.2007.00583.x

Popham, W. J. (2008). Transformative assessment. Association for Supervision and Curriculum Development.

Rea-Dickins, P. (2001). Mirror, mirror on the wall: Identifying processes of classroom assessment. *Language Testing, 18*(4), 429–462. https://doi.org/10.1177/026553220101800407

Shohamy, E. (2001). Democratic assessment as an alternative. *Language Testing, 18*(4), 373–391. https://doi.org/10.1177/026553220101800404

Stoynoff, S. (2012). Looking backward and forward at classroom-based language assessment. *ELT Journal, 66*(4), 523–532. https://doi.org/10.1093/elt/ccs041

Turner, C. E., & Purpura, J. E. (2016). Learning-oriented assessment in second and foreign language classrooms. In D. Tsagari & J. Banerjee (Eds.), *Handbook of second language assessment* (pp. 255–272). De Gruyter Mouton.

Jonathan Trace has a Ph.D. in Second Language Studies and is currently an assistant professor of applied linguistics at Keio University (Kanagawa, Japan) in the Department of Environment and Information Studies. He has co-authored and presented on numerous papers on language assessment in a variety of areas including both large-scale and classroom assessment, test validation, and rater negotiation in performance assessments. In addition to interests in curriculum development, mixed-methods research, and listening and speaking pedagogy, his current research is in the area of using games as tasks for learning, teaching, and assessment purposes.

English Language Proficiency: What is it? and Where do Learners Fit into it?

James Dean Brown

Throughout my 42 years in language testing, whenever I have talked about overall English language proficiency I have always added (soto voce) whatever that is. I have come to suspect that we lack a clear understanding of ELP because: (a) we only define ELP in terms of the target language using myopic definitions and (b) we ignore the role in ELP of examinees and what they need from English.

Typically, we define ELP as proper English (whatever that is) or as the language of the native speaker (NS), or (realizing how vague that is) as the educated native speaker (whatever that is).

In terms of proper English, our definition ignores what we have learned about World Englishes. Which English(es) are we talking about? Inner-circle Englishes (e.g., the English in UK, US, Australia, etc.)? Outer-circle Englishes (e.g., the English in India, Singapore, Nigeria, etc.)? Expanding-circle Englishes (e.g., the English learned in Japan, Germany, Mexico, etc.)? And which dialect(s) of those? (See Kachru, 1986).

In terms of NS English, Davies (2011) proposed that two types of NSs figure into our definitions: "all of us" and an "idealization." He elaborated: "models, scales, and examinations that use as criterion the native speaker do not mean any or all native speakers. What they mean is 'the (idealised) native speaker'" (p. 308) (also see Leung et al., 1997).

Either way of defining ELP is largely inadequate. Worse, focusing on the target language inevitably means that we are overlooking the examinees' needs and their role in defining the ELP construct.

Ignoring the Examinees

Examinee needs. After taking one of the major ELP tests (like the TOEFL, IELTS, etc.) and being admitted to a university in one of the English-speaking countries,

J. D. Brown (✉)
Second Language Studies, University of Hawai'i at Mānoa, Honolulu, Hawai'i, USA
e-mail: brownj@hawaii.edu

© Springer Nature Switzerland AG 2021
H. Mohebbi and C. Coombe (eds.), *Research Questions in Language Education and Applied Linguistics*, Springer Texts in Education,
https://doi.org/10.1007/978-3-030-79143-8_57

students will need to read and write formal written English, which fortunately is fairly homogeneous across Englishes. However, students will also need to listen and speak, sometimes with NSs, but more often with speakers of various inner-circle Englishes (and a variety of dialects within those), speakers of outer-circle Englishes, and even more so with speakers of expanding-circle Englishes. Thus, they will spend only a small fraction of their time communicating orally with NSs from the inner-circle.

Examinee Performances. In developing standardized ELP tests, we want to use test items that require examinees to read, write, listen to, and speak English (however we define that). What we forget is that those test items are not a representative sample of the language. After all, they were piloted and selected because they worked (i.e., they separated high performing examinees from low). Hence, those items that survive in the final, revised ELP test are inevitably decided by the language learning experiences of the examinees. In other words, we think we are testing the English language as presented to the examinees in the pilot test items, but we are actually only testing that subset of the language that examinees can handle or not handle depending on their learning experiences in language classrooms. Thus, without our acknowledgement, examinees are shaping our definition of the ELP construct.

The Research Questions

1. What are the lexical, syntactic, pragmatic, etc. characteristics of English that are shared by all circles of World Englishes? In the written language? In the spoken language?
2. To what extent are tests like the TOEFL, TOEIC, and IELTS based on written and spoken idealized inner-circle NS standard English. To what extent are other inner-, outer-, and expanding-circle Englishes represented?
3. To what extent do students in English speaking universities interact in written and oral English with NS English speakers? Outer-, and expanding-circle Englishes?
4. To what degree are the ELP tests measuring literacy skills (reading and writing) as opposed to oracy skills (listening and speaking)? To what extent are the ELP tests focused on issues of accuracy, fluency, and intelligibility?
5. What is the effect on item statistics, total scores, reliability, and validity for ELP tests of presenting examinees with various inner-, outer-, and expanding-circle language samples as opposed to NS English samples for reading and listening separately.
6. What is the effect on item statistics, total scores, reliability, and validity for ELP tests of using raters from various inner-, outer-, and expanding-circle language backgrounds to rate writing and speaking samples from L2 examinees as opposed to the relatively homogeneous group of NS English speaking raters.

7. What types of items survive the piloting process (i.e., have the appropriate level of item difficulty and discrimination) during the process of developing ELP tests?

8. How are those item types that survive the piloting process related to the previous language learning experiences of the examinees?

9. Are examinees from different educational backgrounds scoring high or low on the test for different reasons? That is, what is the impact of the examinees' nationality or language background on their total scores for reading, writing, listening, speaking, and other subtests, as well as on individual item difficulty and discrimination?

10. After developing, piloting, and revising an ELP test based on any of the alternative approaches discussed in Brown (2019a & b, see Suggested Resources), what are the item characteristics, descriptive statistics, reliability estimates, and validity arguments for the resulting test?

Suggested Resources

Brown, J. D. (2008). Testing-context analysis: Assessment is just another part of language curriculum development." Language Assessment Quarterly, 5(4), 1–38.

This paper begins by defining stakeholder friendly tests, defensible testing, and testing-context analysis. It then provides a rationale for stakeholder-friendly testing and testing-context analysis (TCA) and discusses the stages and steps necessary for a TCA: (a) getting ready to do the TCA; (b) doing the TCA), and (c) using the TCA results. The paper also describes an example TCA that shows how this TCA framework can be implemented. The paper ends with a discussion of the benefits that a TCA can provide and how a TCA can be used to defend the use and validity of language assessments to all stakeholder groups.

Brown, J. D. (2014). The future of World Englishes in language testing. Language Assessment Quarterly, 11(1), 5–26.

This paper defines World Englishes (WEs) in terms of inner-, outer-, and expanding-circle English(es). Then it focuses on the issues involved in the relationship between WEs and language testing from two perspectives. From the WEs perspective, the language testing (LT) community needs to understand: (a) how the so-called English NS speaker norm is no longer viable and (b) how three aspects of English diversity need to be considered in LT. From the LT perspective, the WEs community needs to understand: (a) how LT has already added to our knowledge of English variation, (b) how LT has not entirely overlooked WEs concerns, and (c) how LT has never been only about standardized international proficiency tests. The paper finishes with suggestions for making cooperation between the WEs and LT communities more productive.

Brown, J. D. (2019a). World Englishes and international standardized English proficiency tests. In C. L. Nelson, Z. G. Proshina, and D. R. Davis (Eds.), *Handbook of World Englishes* (2nd ed.). Hoboken, NJ: Wiley-Blackwell.

This paper zeros in on the relationships among WEs, English language proficiency (ELP), and the international standardized English language proficiency tests (ISELPTs) in terms of how the TOEFL iBT, TOEIC, and IELTS present themselves to the world; what ELP is; why the examinees are important in ELP testing; how the field can foster change in the ISELPTs; what alternative approaches to ELP might look like; and how testers could actually implement the assessment of some of these alternative approaches to ELP.

Brown, J. D. (2019b). Global Englishes and the International Standardized English Language Proficiency Tests? In F. Fang & H. Widodo (Eds.), *Critical Perspectives of Global Englishes in Asia: Language Policy, Curriculum, Pedagogy and Assessment*. Clevedon, England: Multilingual Matters.

This chapter first provides background by reviewing literature on Global English (es) and language testing, including those by the author (i.e., Brown, 2014 and 2019a). Then the chapter discusses what ELP is; why the NS standard may be a thing of the past; what alternatives to the NS model for ELP might be useful; why changing the ISELPTs is so slow and difficult; and what strategies might lead to making actual changes in the ISELPTs.

McKay, S. L., & Brown, J. D. (2016). Introduction. *Teaching and assessing EIL in local contexts around the World* (pp. xiii-xx). New York: Routledge.

Global English Standard (GES) is defined here in terms of six points. GES: (a) is based on the system of English rather than an idealized NS; (b) acknowledges that a system of English exists that is taught around the world to NSs (of all classes and dialects) and non-natives alike; (c) stresses that the Grammar (with a capital-G) of written English provides a common relatively homogeneous framework in all Englishes; (d) recognizes the role of a common system around the world especially in formal written English; (e) avoids the idea that NSs own English by encouraging the notion that GES is owned by all speakers of English; and (f) can exist within all Englishes and their dialects as needed. (p. xv).

References

Davies, A. (2011). Commentary: Does language testing need the native speaker?". *Language Assessment Quarterly, 8*(3), 291–308.

Kachru, B. B. (1986). The power and politics of English. *World Englishes, 5*(2/3), 121–140.

Leung, C., Harris, R., & Rampton, B. (1997). The idealised native speaker, reified ethnicities, and classroom realities. *TESOL Quarterly, 31*(3), 543–560.

James Dean Brown is currently Professor Emeritus of Second Language Studies at the University of Hawai'i at Mānoa. He has spoken and taught in many places ranging from Albuquerque to Zagreb. He has published numerous articles and books on language testing, curriculum design, research methods, and connected speech. His most recent books: *Mixed methods research for TESOL* (2014 from Edinburgh University); *Cambridge guide to research in language teaching and learning* (2015 with Coombe, Cambridge University); *Teaching and assessing EIL in local contexts around the world* (2015 with McKay, Routledge); and *Introducing needs analysis and English for specific purposes* (2016, Routledge).

Integrated Skills Assessment

58

Lia Plakans

Since the early 2000s, assessing skills in integration has increasingly garnered interest in the field of language teaching and testing. Integrated skills tasks commonly engage learners with source material followed by performances that include source content. The benefits of this approach include authentic use of language, provision of content for test users to write or speak about, and alignment with current approaches to language teaching such as task-based language teaching (TBLT) or content and language integrated learning (CLIL). However, along with these advantages, challenges exist such as defining the construct and domain features, effective task design, and reliable or valid scoring processes.

Integrated skills assessment conceptualizes language as a composite of overlapping or shared skills. Research has sought to provide a clearer picture of this composite. For example, studies have uncovered evidence of overarching language abilities driving a model of integrated skills, such as comprehension or vocabulary, (Sawaki et al., 2009) and findings also suggest the processes of discourse synthesis —connecting, selecting, organizing—are elicited by these tasks (Delaney, 2008; Yang & Plakans, 2012). Further, evidence that the integration continues to provide insight into individual skills (Weigle et al., 2013).

Research on integrated skills assessment has burgeoned since 2005, when the large-scale Test of English as a Foreign Language (iBT TOEFL), began including integrated tasks. Studies have focused on comparing integrated with independent tasks and highlighting similarities and differences underlying them (Gebril, 2010; Huang & Hung, 2013). Current research has centered on learning more about these tasks in their own right and their potential for assessing language. This work has looked at constructs, processes, products, tasks, and the rating process (e.g. Li, 2014; Wang et al., 2017). However, much more research is needed to better

L. Plakans (✉)
Department of Teaching and Learning, The University of Iowa, Iowa City, Iowa, USA
e-mail: lia-plakans@uiowa.edu

© Springer Nature Switzerland AG 2021
H. Mohebbi and C. Coombe (eds.), *Research Questions in Language Education and Applied Linguistics*, Springer Texts in Education,
https://doi.org/10.1007/978-3-030-79143-8_58

understand the nature of skill integration, the optimal design of these tasks, and ways to overcome their challenges.

The Research Questions

1. How are skills integrated in non-academic writing and speaking (e.g. social media)?
2. What is the construct underlying integrated skills assessment?
3. How are sources used in integrated speaking?
4. What are different ways to integrate skills in assessment (beyond reading into writing)?
5. What are the task characteristics that make integrated assessment difficult?
6. How do texts affect integrated skills assessment (e.g. number, type, medium, genre, difficulty length)?
7. What supports aid second language test takers in completing integrated skills assessments (e.g. notetaking, dictionary, glosses, writing template, spell check)?
8. How do low proficiency second language writers integrate skills?
9. What are characteristics of high scoring integrated skills assessment performances?
10. Are integrated skills assessment promoting language learning (e.g. classroom use)?

Suggested Resources

Cumming, A. (2013). Assessing integrated writing tasks for academic purposes: Promises and perils. *Language Assessment Quarterly, 10*(1). 1–8.

Cummings' editorial introduces a special issue on integrated writing assessment. He cites promises and perils with these tasks. The opportunities they provide include: (1) realistic and complex engagement with literacy, (2) source-based writing, (3) direct assessments of language use, and (4) alignment with current views of literacy. The challenges he points out include a lack of clarity of the construct for integrated skills, the need for a threshold level of proficiency to complete, and unclear domain analysis to determine what integration looks like in academic settings. Scoring is an area that is also of concern, both in rubric design and in how performances blend the test taker's language and the source language. The conclusion in this editorial is that these tasks have potential and should be designed, but with encouragement to pursue research that addresses the multiple concerns.

Cho, Y., Rijmen, F., & Novák, J. (2013). Investigating the effect of prompt characteristics on the comparability of TOEFL iBT integrated writing tasks. *Language Testing, 30(4),* **513–534.**

This study explores the characteristics of prompts for an integrated reading-listening-writing task. Using a questionnaire and sample prompts given to native speakers of English, the researcher explored what made prompts different in the eyes of this population. The rationale for the study was to provide test developers guidance in designing multiple parallel forms of integrated tasks. After language differences, two additional characteristics of the source texts lead to noted variation in the prompts: passage difficulty and lecture distinctness (how clearly distinguished the main points were in the listening source material). These findings are useful in understanding the many aspects of integrated tasks that can affect the test taker.

Yu, G. (2009). The shifting sands in the effects of source text summarizability on summary writing. *Assessing Writing, 14(2),* **116–137.**

This study considered source text differences in written summaries of text for assessment uses.

The researchers identified characteristics of source texts in terms of impact on written performances of English as a foreign language test takers (in China). Three texts were used in the study, each representing a different genre—expository, narrative, and argumentation. Participants wrote summaries in English and in their native language, Chinese. The results indicated that the source text had a higher impact on the performance than writing in either a first or foreign language. With further investigation, the researchers determined that several text characteristics seemed to affect performance: (1) overall source organization, (2) familiarity of the topic, (3) familiar vocabulary, and (4) length of the source text. The argumentative task seemed to cause the most difficulty for test takers due to the propositions on conflicting viewpoints (argument to counter-argument). These findings show that genre of source texts is an important feature to consider in designing integrated tasks.

Gebril, A. & Plakans, L. (2014). Assembling validity evidence for assessing academic writing: Rater reactions to integrated tasks. *Assessing Writing, 21,* **56–73.**

To better understand how raters contend with scoring integrated writing, the researchers conducted interviews and verbal protocols with raters scoring a reading-writing task. The raters showed a high level of self-monitoring and repeated reference to the source materials. The latter was divided into three activities: locating ideas originating from the source material, checking citation mechanics, and evaluating the quality of source use. The study provides implications for rater preparation and monitoring with source-based writing such as consideration of source material integration in terms of accuracy, effectiveness, and overall quality.

Cho, Y. & Choi, I. (2018). Writing from sources: Does audience matter? *Assessing Writing, 37, 25–38.*

This study explored how test takers were affected by instructions to write for specific audiences. Using a reading-listening-writing task, the test takers were assigned to either write with no audience specified or to write for classmates who had not heard about the topic. Analysis of the summaries reflected an intention by writers to communicate with the audience specified by giving contextual background, communicating ideas accurately, and providing complete summaries. The researchers found that the differences in audience awareness occurred differentially across English proficiency score levels. The implications for this study are that integrated assessments would benefit from more recognition of the socially-bound nature of writing, even when writing from sources.

References

Delaney, Y. A. (2008). Investigating the reading-to-write construct. *Journal of English for Academic Purposes, 7,* 140–150.

Gebril, A. (2010). Brining reading-to-write and writing only assessment tasks together: A generalizability analysis. *Assessing Writing, 15,* 100–117.

Huang, H. T., & Hung, S. T. (2013). Comparing the effects of test anxiety on independent and integrated speaking test performance. *TESOL Quarterly, 47,* 244–269.

Li, J. (2014). Examining genre effects on test takers' summary writing performance. *Assessing Writing, 22,* 75–90.

Sawaki, Y., Stricker, L. J., & Oranje, A. H. (2009). Factor structure of the TOEFL Internet-based test. *Language Testing, 26*(1), 5–30.

Wang, J., Engelhard, G., Raczynski, K., Song, T., & Wolfe, E. (2017). Evaluating rater accuracy and perception for integrated writing assessments using a mixed-methods approach. *Assessing Writing, 33,* 36–47.

Weigle, S. C., Yang, W., & Montee, M. (2013). Exploring reading processes in an academic reading test using short answer questions. *Language Assessment Quarterly, 10,* 28–48.

Yang, H. C., & Plakans, L. (2012). Second language writers' strategy use and performance on an integrated reading-listening-writing task. *TESOL Quarterly, 46,* 80–103.

Lia Plakans is an professor of Multilingual Education at the University of Iowa. Her research focuses on second language learning with particular emphasis on language assessment and literacy. She has directed assessment research grants funded by Educational Testing Service (ETS), Cambridge Michigan Language Assessments, and *Language Learning* journal. She has been an associate editor for *Language Assessment Quarterly.* She has co-authored the books *Assessment Myths: Applying Second Language Research to Classroom Teaching* and *Reading and Writing for Academic Success* (University of Michigan Press). Her research has been published in academic journals such as *TESOL Quarterly, Language Testing, Language Assessment Quarterly,* and *Journal of Second Language Writing.* She was an English language teacher for over 15 years in Iowa, Texas, Ohio, and Latvia.

Language Assessment in English Medium Instruction

Slobodanka Dimova

As part of their process of internationalization, many English non-dominant universities have started implementing English medium instruction (EMI) courses and programs. Hence, the EMI reference relates to situations where, "non-language courses, in for instance medicine, physics or political science, are taught in English to students for whom it is a foreign language. As often as not, it is also taught by a lecturer who does not have English as a first language (L1)" (Hellekjær, 2010, p. 11). Given that most stakeholders involved in EMI are L2 speakers of English, concerns have been raised among university managements regarding the quality of instruction and students' academic success. To address these concerns, requirements to provide evidence of English proficiency have been established for both lecturers and students.

Following the practices at universities in the United States, the United Kingdom, and Australia, many English non-dominant universities require all students (except for L1 English speakers) to provide scores from standardized academic English proficiency (EAP) tests, like the Test of English as a Foreign Language (TOEFL) or the International English Language Testing System (IELTS), as language proficiency evidence for EMI program entry. A number of research studies have investigated the relevance, the impact, the uses, and the predictive validity of the standardized test scores at Anglophone universities (e.g., Cho & Bridgeman, 2012; Wait & Gressel, 2009), but little is known about their adequacy for the EMI context.

Many universities require the same EAP tests (e.g., TOEFL, IELTS) also for university lecturer certification to teach in EMI programs (Klaassen & Bos, 2010). Although in absence of choices, taking one of these tests may be a quick solution, their relevance regarding lecturers' language skills related to EMI as the target

S. Dimova (✉)
Centre for Internationalization and Parallel Language Use, University of Copenhagen, Copenhagen, Denmark
e-mail: slobodanka.dimova@hum.ku.dk

© Springer Nature Switzerland AG 2021
H. Mohebbi and C. Coombe (eds.), *Research Questions in Language Education and Applied Linguistics*, Springer Texts in Education,
https://doi.org/10.1007/978-3-030-79143-8_59

language use (TLU) domain have been questioned. Therefore, some universities have developed local oral English proficiency tests for certification of EMI lecturers. More research is needed, though, to examine the indigenous assessment criteria to be used in local tests as well as the assumptions we make about the minimum proficiency level needed for EMI teaching.

Finally, lack of research exists in whether and how language is assessed in content courses (e.g., in physics, medicine, political science), as well as to what degree students' English proficiency increases over the course of study in EMI.

The Research Questions

1. What are the purposes of language assessment in the context of EMI in higher education?
2. What is the relationship between university policies for internationalization and language assessment practices in EMI?
3. What factors affect decisions about what language tests should be used for student admission in English medium instruction (EMI) programs?
4. What is the relevance of existing standardized academic English tests for student admission in EMI programs?
5. What is the role of language assessment in EMI content courses?
6. What is the level of language assessment literacy among EMI content teachers?
7. What methods are relevant for assessing the English proficiency levels of non-native English-speaking EMI lecturers?
8. What characteristics of the EMI teaching domain are reflected in the language assessment?
9. To what degree do pedagogy and discipline-specific content influence the assessment of language proficiency in testing methods based on simulated lectures?
10. What is the validity of including translanguaging tasks in language assessment for lecturers and students in EMI contexts?

Suggested Resources

Dimova, S. (2017). Life after oral English certification: The consequences of the Test of Oral English Proficiency for Academic Staff for EMI lecturers. *English for Specific Purposes*, **46,** 45–58.

The article presents a study that examines the consequential validity of TOEPAS (Test of Oral English Proficiency for Academic Staff), which is a performance-based test used for oral English certification of lecturers at the University of Copenhagen. More specifically, it analyzes the consequences resulting from TOEPAS score and feedback interpretations and uses based on interviews with lecturers (n = 24) and written formative feedback for tested lecturers (n = 400). The results from the interviews suggest that the TOEPAS results (scores and feedback) were used mostly as intended by the test developers. Two important unintended consequences were identified: the stakes are higher for the lecturers who have other L1s than English and those who have temporary employment, and the written formative feedback contains technical terminology, with which the lecturers are unfamiliar. This article indicates that test consequence analysis must be conducted in order to ensure adequate uses of test results by stakeholders.

Klaassen, R. G., & Bos, M. (2010). English language screening for scientific staff at Delft University of Technology. *Hermes–Journal of Language and Communication Studies*, 45, 61–75.

Given the university policy that lecturers must have a C1 proficiency level in English to teach EMI courses, Klaassen and Bos examined the proficiency levels of lecturers across departments and job profiles (professor, associate professor, etc.) to find out whether this requirement is realistic. The authors compared lecturers' results from the Oxford Quick Placement test (QPT) an oral English proficiency test that consisted of an introductory talk, a 5-min presentation, picture description, and a role play between a student and a lecturer. The findings suggested comparable average proficiency levels across faculties and job profiles. The lecturers scored higher on the QPT than on the oral proficiency test, where a large percentage of lecturers did not reach the required C1 level. The study is important because it represents one of the first large-scale analyses of EMI lecturer proficiency despite the lack of validity discussion regarding the assessment instruments used.

Kling, J., & Stæhr, L. S. (2011). Assessment and assistance: Developing university lecturers' skills through certification feedback. In R. Cancino, L. Dam, & K. Jæger (Eds.), *Policies, principles, practices: New directions in foreign language education in the era of educational globalization* (pp. 213–245). Newcastle upon Tyne, UK: Cambridge Scholars Press.

In this chapter, Kling and Stæhr present the development and the implementation of the Test of Oral English Proficiency for Academic Staff (TOEPAS), which is an English for academic purposes test used for university lecturers' oral English certification for teaching EMI courses. In the first part of the chapter, the authors discuss the policies and mandates that governed the implementation of the certification procedure, the test content, the TEOPAS scale, and the construct it measures. The authors emphasize the formative element of TOEPAS, which includes oral and written feedback and video recording, in addition to the TOEPAS score. In the second part, the authors use a specific case to illustrate the role of TOEPAS feedback in providing individualized language support for a lecturer who was not certified. This represents one of the few published reports on the development, implementation, and use of locally-developed English proficiency tests for EMI lecturers.

Schoepp, K. (2018). Predictive validity of the IELTS in an English as a medium of instruction environment. *Higher Education Quarterly*, **72, 271–285.**

This article is based on a study that investigates the predictive validity of the International English Language Testing System (IELTS) at an EMI university in the United Arab Emirates (UAE). More specifically, based on a large sample of students (n = 953), the study examines whether the IELTS scores can predict students' academic success. Correlations and analysis of variance were used to analyse the relationship between IELTS scores and students' grade point average. Results indicate that the IELTS score is a good predictor of academic success, with an IELTS 6.0 being the key benchmark. Based on these findings, Schoepp suggests that moderate proficiency is a better fit for the EMI context, and that language support and bilingual courses should be available for lower level students. Although standardized academic English proficiency tests' predictive validity has been examined widely in English dominant university contexts, this study is among the first to use an EMI setting.

Wilkinson, R., Zegers, V., & van Leeuwen, C. (Eds.) (2006). *Bridging the assessment gap in English-medium higher education.* **Bochum: AKS-Verlag.**

This edited volume comprises chapters that deal with language assessment challenges in English medium instruction (EMI) programs in Europe (the Nordic countries, the Netherlands, the Czech Republic, Hungary, and Wales), South Africa, and Thailand. While some of the chapters focus on the adequacy of English language assessment used for student university admission, others discuss the need to implement relevant language assessment of students during their course of study and at graduation in order to measure students' language development. The volume also includes chapters that deal with the English language assessment of non-native English-speaking lecturers, the purpose of which is to make sure that the lecturers have sufficient English language proficiency to cope with the demands of EMI teaching.

References

Cho, Y., & Bridgeman, B. (2012). Relationship of TOEFL iBT® scores to academic performance: Some evidence from American universities. *Language Testing, 29*, 421–442.

Hellekjær, H. O. (2010). Lecture comprehension in English-medium higher education. *Hermes-Journal of Language and Communication Studies, 45*, 11–34.

Klaassen, R. G., & Bos, M. (2010). English language screening for scientific staff at Delft University of Technology. *Hermes-Journal of Language and Communication Studies, 45*, 61–75.

Wait, I. W., & Gressel, J. W. (2009). Relationship between TOEFL score and academic success for international engineering students. *Journal of Engineering Education, 98*, 389.

Slobodanka Dimova is an Associate Professor at the Centre for Internationalisation and Parallel Language Use at the University of Copenhagen, where she coordinates the Test of Oral English Proficiency for Academic Staff (TOEPAS). Her published work includes articles and books on language assessment and English medium instruction. She co-authored a monograph *Local Language Testing: Design, Implementation, and Development* (2020, Routledge), an edited volume *English in European Higher Education* (2015, Mouton), and an edited volume on *Integrating Content and Language in Multilingual Higher Education* (2020, Springer). She is a member of the Executive Committee of the European Association for Language Testing and Assessment (EALTA), as a Book Review Editor for the *Language Testing* journal.

Language Assessment for Professional Purposes

60

Ute Knoch

With an increasingly mobile global workforce and a rise in large multinational companies, recent years have seen an increase in the use of language assessments for professional purposes (LAPP). These assessments can at times be high-stakes as they are often implemented to uphold safety standards in professions where insufficient language skills can be seen as a risk to safety. For example, it is deemed important that an overseas-trained doctor working in an English-speaking hospital is sufficiently proficient in English to conduct his daily work. To ensure such safety standards are met, governments or professional bodies often require proof of language proficiency for registration. They also commonly regulate what types of language proficiency tests can be taken by applicants. These tests can be divided into two types: (1) general academic language tests (e.g. IELTS, TOEFL or Pearson PTE) and (2) specific purpose language tests which have been developed to mirror the language demands in the work domain.

There are a number of challenges associated with the use of both types of tests in such contexts. Firstly, the use of general academic language assessments for the purposes of providing evidence of language proficiency for specific workplace settings is controversial as these assessments were developed for entirely different purposes. It is therefore important to gather evidence to show that these assessments are in fact measuring the desired abilities. Because of this concern about the suitability of general academic language assessments in this context, it is generally considered best practice to assess language proficiency for the workplace using an assessment instrument that is developed for this purpose.

LAPPs are usually developed following a careful needs analysis in which test developers or researchers carefully examine the types of communicative tasks that occur in the workplace as well as the kind of language used in these tasks. The

U. Knoch (✉)

Language Testing Research Centre, School of Languages and Linguistics, University of Melbourne, Parkville, VIC 3015, Australia

e-mail: uknoch@unimelb.edu.au

© Springer Nature Switzerland AG 2021

H. Mohebbi and C. Coombe (eds.), *Research Questions in Language Education and Applied Linguistics*, Springer Texts in Education,

https://doi.org/10.1007/978-3-030-79143-8_60

findings from needs analyses are then used to develop a test blueprint which includes specifications for tasks that model workplace tasks. This practice is considered to increase authenticity. At the same time, it also ensures positive washback, which means that test takers engage in work-relevant test preparation processes.

The specificity of a LAPP is a further challenge to the test developer. Should the test be designed for health professionals more generally, or focus only on doctors or doctors with a specialty in neurosurgery? This increasingly specific focus can create tensions in the test design process and complicate score interpretations.

A further challenge to test developers is the involvement of domain experts in test development. Domain experts, also referred to as subject matter experts, are crucial in the test design process as language testers generally do not have sufficient insight into the target language use domain. However, what is not clear is how the insights and values of domain experts can be faithfully translated into a language test. Domain experts are not trained to focus on language ability and often find it hard to distinguish between language proficiency and professional knowledge of the discipline. Domain experts have also been key informants in the development of scoring criteria for LAPPs and have played key roles in setting standards. However, test developers and researchers have to ensure that the thought processes involved are relevant to what the test is designed to assess (also called the test construct), and at the same time ensure that the values of these key informants are adequately represented.

The Research Questions

1. How can language ability for the workplace best be modelled in language assessments?
2. What principles should guide a needs analysis for the purposes of test development?
3. How can the findings from a needs analysis best be converted into a test blueprint?
4. How can domain experts' values and insights be best drawn on in the test development process?
5. Do test takers use the same processes, knowledge and skills when completing the test tasks as they would when working in the target language use domain?
6. How can test developers best determine the specificity of a language test for the workplace?
7. How can we best conceptualise the different language codes and varieties used in workplaces to be able to more clearly define the language assessed in LAPPs?
8. How can what domain experts value in workplace communication best be represented in scoring criteria?

9. What underlying thought processes do domain experts informants use when setting standards on language assessments for the workplace?
10. What types of validity evidence should be collected to show an assessment is appropriately measuring language proficiency for workplace purposes?

Suggested Resources

Douglas, D. (2000). *Assessing languages for specific purposes.* **Cambridge: Cambridge University Press.**

Dan Douglas' book published in 2000 presents a comprehensive and accessible introduction to the area of assessing languages for specific purposes (LSP). Although this is now nearly 20 years old, this seminal work still has high currency. Douglas describes the key debates in LSP test development and provides hands on chapters describing needs analysis and test development of the four skills (reading, listening, writing and speaking) as well as the use of technology in test development.

Knoch, U., & Macqueen, S. (2020). *Assessing English for Professional Purposes: Language and the workplace.* **London: Routledge.**

Published twenty years after Douglas' seminal text on Assessing Languages for Specific Purposes, this book broadens the area of the assessment of languages for specific purposes to include assessments by domain insiders and domain outsiders. The book also presents a reconceptualization of constructs, a thorough discussion of policy in this context and a full validity argument for assessments for domain insiders. The book is written in accessible manner, and also includes chapters relating to practice, including on needs analysis and assessment development.

Knoch, U., & Macqueen, S. (2016). Language assessment for the workplace. In D. Tsagari & J. Banerjee (Eds.), *Handbook of Second Language Assessment* **(pp. 291-308). Boston/Berlin: De Gruyter Mouton.**

In this recent book chapter, Knoch and Macqueen map the area of language assessment for the workplace. They provide two useful classification systems of the assessments used in this space, focusing on specificity and test use. An entire section of the chapter explores constructs of LAPPs. Examples of workplace language assessments and policy environments are provided and key debates in assessing language for the workplace domain are presented. This chapter provides an excellent introduction to more recent thinking in this area.

Elder, C. (2016). Special Issue: Authenticity in LSP Testing. *Language Testing,* *33*(2), 147-304.

In this special issue of the journal *Language Testing*, Elder and her colleagues present a current take on the issue of authenticity in LSP testing. They approach this issue by presenting a series of connected studies on the Occupational English Test (OET), a language screening test for health professionals applying to register to practice in English-speaking countries. The papers focus on how best to elicit indigenous criteria from domain experts (Elder & McNamara), how indigenous criteria can be translated into rating criteria (Pill), how well language-trained raters can apply such criteria (O'Hagan, Pill & Zhang), and considerations in standard-setting with domain experts (Pill & McNamara, Manias & McNamara). Two more papers focus on the relevance of the test tasks to the domain (Woodward-Kron & Elder) and the relevance and impact of the OET to the real-world domain (Macqueen, Pill & Knoch).

Ute Knoch (Associate Professor) is the Director of the Language Testing Research Centre at the University of Melbourne. Her research interests are in the area of writing assessment, rating processes, assessing languages for academic and professional purposes, and placement testing. She was the Co-president of the Association for Language Testing and Assessment of Australian and New Zealand (ALTAANZ) from 2015 to 2016 and has been serving on the Executive Board of the International Language Testing Association (ILTA) from 2011 to 2014 and again since 2017. In 2014, Dr. Knoch was awarded the TOEFL Outstanding Young Scholar Award by the Educational Testing Service (Princeton, US), recognizing her contribution to language assessment. In 2016, she was awarded a Thomson Reuter Women in Research citation award.

Language Assessment Literacy

Christine Coombe and Peter Davidson

Language assessment literacy (LAL) amongst teachers, or rather the lack of it (Tsagari & Vogt, 2017), has become an area of major concern in English Language Teaching in the past decade.

Stiggins (1995) notes that teachers with a high level of assessment literacy know what they assess, why they assess, how to assess, what the possible problems with assessment are, how to prevent these problems from occurring, and they are familiar with the possible negative consequences of poor, inaccurate assessment. Assessment literate teachers can better understand their students' needs, monitor their students' learning, and diagnose their students' learning difficulties. Fulcher (2012, p. 125), adds a further dimension to LAL, namely "to evaluate the role and impact of testing on society, institutions, and individuals".

According to Coombe et al. (2012), teachers potentially spend as much as half of their time on assessment-related activities. There is also a growing recognition that good assessment can facilitate student learning (Green, 2017; Hamp-Lyons, 2017). When teachers know how to interpret test data, they can personalize their students' learning and make improvements to the way they teach (Xu & Brown, 2017). Harding and Kremmel (2016), maintain that LAL should be an integral part of a teachers' ongoing professional development.

One of the most significant obstacles to LAL, as noted by Stiggins (1995), is a possible accumulation of multiple layers of negative emotions associated with assessment. Such negative experiences may include doing poorly on tests, being asked test questions on content that was not taught, not knowing what was going to be tested, not understanding poorly written questions, being unfamiliar with question formats, not being given sufficient time to complete tests, a perceived bias

C. Coombe (✉)
General Studies, Dubai Men's College, Higher Colleges of Technology, Dubai, UAE
e-mail: ccoombe@hct.ac.ae

P. Davidson
College of Humanities and Social Sciences, Zayed University, Dubai, UAE

© Springer Nature Switzerland AG 2021
H. Mohebbi and C. Coombe (eds.), *Research Questions in Language Education and Applied Linguistics*, Springer Texts in Education,
https://doi.org/10.1007/978-3-030-79143-8_61

in the rating of subjective questions, and not knowing what is going to be done with the test results. Another potential obstacle to teachers becoming assessment literate is that language assessment appears complex with its own difficult concepts and language, and it may involve complex mathematics and statistics. Many teachers are not required to write tests as their tests are written by specialist test writers, or they could come directly from the ministry of education.

Davidson and Coombe (2019) identify a number of ways that teachers can improve their level of LAL by studying language testing at under-graduate and post-graduate level, reading key language testing books and journals, attending talks on testing at conferences, and participating on summer courses on language testing. Teachers can also attend specialized language testing conferences such as ALTE (Association of Language Testers in Europe) and LTRC (Language Testing Research Colloquium). There are also many language testing organizations that teachers can join to learn more about assessment, such as ILTA (International Language Testing Association), English Language Testing Society (ELTS) and ALTAANZ (Association of Language Testing and Assessment of Australia and New Zealand). Finally, the Teacher Assessment Literacy Enhancement (TALE) project aims to improve the assessment literacy of teachers by offering eight open-access courses that teachers can take for free, and by providing a comprehensive Handbook (Tsagari et al., 2018).

The lack of LAL amongst English language teachers is a major concern that English language testing specialists need to help address. The ongoing quest to help teachers improve their knowledge about, and experience with, different types of language assessment is a crucial one that is worthy of more in-depth research.

The Research Questions

1. What do we actually mean by assessment literacy?
2. Should language teachers be required to reach a certain level of assessment literacy?
3. How can we measure assessment literacy?
4. What specific knowledge, skills and competencies do assessment literate teachers have?
5. To what extent are language teachers assessment literate? Why? Why not?
6. To what extent do demographic factors impact on a teacher's assessment literacy?
7. What are the barriers to making language teachers assessment literate?
8. How do teacher assessment literacy levels impact student achievement?
9. How can teachers improve their level of assessment literacy?
10. How have advances in technology impacted on the nature of assessment, and consequently, what it means to be assessment literate?

Suggested Resources

Coombe, C., Davidson, P., O'Sullivan, B. & Stoynoff, S. (2012). *The Cambridge Guide to Second Language Assessment.* **Cambridge: Cambridge University Press.**

The primary purpose of this volume is to help language teachers improve their levels of assessment literacy. This collection of original articles provides language teachers with a theoretical background of key issues associated with language testing as well as practical advice on how to improve the effectiveness of the tests they develop, implement and administer. Written by internationally prominent researchers and educators, the 34 chapters are organized into five sections: key issues in the field, assessment purposes and approaches, assessment of second language skills, technology in assessment, and administrative issues. A list and/or description of further key readings or suggested resources along with discussion questions that can be used in a teacher workshop or graduate seminar round out each chapter. Chapters assume no particular background knowledge on assessment and are written in an accessible style.

British Council's How Assessment Works project (2014 to present).

The British Council's *How Language Assessment Works* project is designed to create a series of tools for people interested in the area of language testing and assessment to increase their knowledge and understanding of the area and includes:

- *Knowledge of Assessment Animated Videos*—a series of short non-technical overviews of a range of key concepts in the field. The videos can be found at https://www.britishcouncil.org/exam/aptis/research/assessment-literacy.
- *MOOC (Language Assessment in the Classroom)*—this is a four-week free course for teachers created by the British Council and launched in April 2018. It covers practical aspects of classroom test development, scoring and reporting.
- *An A to Z of Second Language Assessment* (2018, edited by Coombe, C.). Written by teachers for teachers, these 285 terms and their respective definitions represent the collective knowledge of 81 teachers from 27 countries worldwide. Every effort was made to include definitions that are readable and easy to understand, even for teachers with little or no assessment background.

Coombe, C. (2018). *The TESOL Encyclopedia of English Language Teaching,* **Vol. 8: Assessment and Evaluation. Hoboken, NJ: Wiley-Blackwell.**

The aim of this volume is to present an up-to-date guide to the central areas of assessing the second language performance of English by speakers of other languages. The 77 entries present snapshots of significant issues and trends that have shaped language assessment in the past and highlight the current state of our understanding of these issues. Each entry includes three sections which provide a key link between theory and practice. In "Framing the Issue", important definitions pertaining to the entry topic are provided, and in the "Making the Case" section, critical research and empirical perspectives are discussed. In the final section on "Pedagogical Implications" readers are introduced to important guidelines and sample activities. Every attempt has been made to keep the entries non-technical and readable, even to novice educators or those new to the field with little or no specialist knowledge in assessment.

Coombe, C., Folse, K. & Hubley, N. (2007). *A Practical Guide to Assessing English Language Learners.* **Ann Arbor, MI: University of Michigan Press.**

The purpose of this volume is to help teachers in a multitude of contexts navigate the often-confusing field of language assessment. In each chapter, readers will encounter some ways two teachers deal with assessment in their classrooms. Ms. Wright, an experienced teacher well versed in assessment, models best practice while her less-experienced colleague, Mr. Knott, tries assessment concepts and techniques that are new to him. Through their experiences, teachers will come to: understand the cornerstones of good assessment; learn useful techniques for traditional and alternative assessment; become aware of issues in assessing the skills of reading, writing, listening and speaking; discover ways to help students develop good test-taking strategies; and become familiar with the processes and procedures of assessment.

References

Coombe, C., Troudi, S., & Al-Hamly, M. (2012). Foreign and second language teacher assessment literacy: Issues, challenges and recommendations. In C. Coombe, P. Davidson, B. O'Sullivan, & S. Stoynoff, S. (Eds.), *The Cambridge guide to second language assessment* (pp. 20–29). Cambridge University Press.

Davidson, P., & Coombe, C. (2019). Language assessment literacy in the Middle East and North Africa (MENA) region. *Arab Journal of Applied Linguistics, 4*(2), 1–23.

Fulcher, G. (2012). Assessment literacy for the language classroom. *Language Assessment Quarterly, 9*(2), 113–132.

Green, A. (2017). Learning-oriented language test preparation materials: A contradiction in terms? *Papers in Language Testing and Assessment, 6*(1), 112–132.

Hamp-Lyons, L. (2017). Language assessment literacy for language learning-oriented assessment. *Papers in Language Testing and Assessment, 6*(1), 88–111.

Harding, L., & Kremmel, B. (2016). Teacher assessment literacy and professional development. In D. Tsagari & J. Banerjee (Eds.), *Handbook of second language assessment* (pp. 413–428). Walter de Gruyter Inc.

Stiggins, R. J. (1995). Assessment literacy for the 21st century. *Phi Delta Kappa, 77*(3), 238–245.

Tsagari, D., & Vogt, K. (2017). Assessment literacy of foreign language teachers around Europe: Research, challenges and future prospects. *Papers in Language Testing and Assessment, 6*(1), 41–63.

Tsagari, D., Vogt, K., Froelich, V., Csépes, I., Fekete, A., Green A., Hamp-Lyons, L., Sifakis, N., & Kordia, S. (2018). *Handbook of assessment for language teachers.* Nicosia, Cyprus. http://taleproject.eu/mod/page/view.php?id=1200

Xu, Y., & Brown, G. T. L. (2017). University English teacher assessment literacy: A survey-test report from China. *Papers in Language Testing and Assessment, 6*(1), 133–158.

Christine Coombe has a Ph.D. from The Ohio State University. She is currently an Associate Professor of General Studies at Dubai Men's College. Christine is co-author or editor of numerous volumes on assessment including *Assessment Practices* (2003, TESOL Publications); *A Practical Guide to Assessing English Language Learners* (2007, University of Michigan Press); *The Cambridge Guide to Second Language Assessment* (2012, Cambridge University Press), and *TESOL Encyclopedia of ELT* (Vol. 8) (Wiley Blackwell, 2018). She has won many awards including: the 2002 Spaan Fellowship for Research in Second/Foreign Language Assessment; and the 2013 British Council's International Assessment Award. Her most recent honors were being named to TESOL's 50@50 and being the recipient of the 2018 James E Alatis Award which recognizes exemplary service to TESOL.

Peter Davidson currently teaches at Zayed University in Dubai, having previously taught in New Zealand, Japan, the UK and Turkey. He has given over 120 conference presentations and he has also conducted assessment literacy training with teachers in 15 different countries in Europe, South East and Central Asia, the Middle East, South American and North Africa. Peter has co-edited a number of books on testing and evaluation including *Language Assessment in the Middle East and North Africa* (2017, TESOL Arabia Publications), *The Cambridge Guide to Second Language Assessment* (2012, Cambridge University Press), *The Fundamentals of Language Assessment* (2009, TESOL Arabia Publications) and *Evaluating Teacher Effectiveness in ESL/EFL Contexts* (2007, University of Michigan Press). Peter was recently made a Fellow of the Higher Education Academy (UK).

Language Testing

Glenn Fulcher

Language Testing is the practice of collecting evidence upon which to decide whether an individual can use language to communicate in a defined real-world setting. Test takers respond to closed-response items (e.g. multiple-choice questions) or open-response tasks (e.g. speaking or writing in response to a prompt) within a limited time. The responses are transformed into a number or letter score. Score users make decisions that include admissions to educational institutions, practice in a profession where lack of communicative ability may cause harm, or granting permission to integrate within a second language speaking community. These uses are referred to as "high stakes" because a decision error leads to either an unfair outcome for an individual or a failure to protect the public. When stakes are low, we often refer to language "assessment" rather than "testing". In language learning teachers often use assessment techniques to support formative feedback, or assessment for learning. Learners undertake tasks to "notice the gap" between their current ability and the learning goal. Planned feedback, peer and self-assessment, and effective questioning are key elements of formative assessment.

Effective testing or assessment begins with a statement of the purpose for which a test is used. The purpose is usually associated with the decision(s) which score users will take based on testing outcomes. Test design therefore begins with defining the criterion to which test scores are intended to make predictions in terms of contexts and content, and the knowledge, skills or abilities (often called constructs) that individuals need to have acquired to successfully communicate in the criterion domain. Demonstrating that sound inferences can be made from a score to the likely future performance of a test taker in the real world is the process of validation. Test development is therefore a research driven activity. Processes in arriving at a suitable testing model include domain analysis and definition, the design and prototyping of suitable tasks and items that result in content represen-

G. Fulcher (✉)
School of Education, University of Leicester, Leicester, Leicestershire, UK
e-mail: glenn.fulcher@leicester.ac.uk; gf39@le.ac.uk

© Springer Nature Switzerland AG 2021   349
H. Mohebbi and C. Coombe (eds.), *Research Questions in Language Education and Applied Linguistics*, Springer Texts in Education,
https://doi.org/10.1007/978-3-030-79143-8_62

tativeness of the domain, and piloting test forms to achieve stable statistical properties. The most important of these is reliability, or the consistency of scores over critical facets of test design and administration.

Testing and assessment impacts on individuals, institutions and society. The study of washback is concerned with how a test influences learning and teaching. The study of impact concerns the relationship of the test and its use to larger institutions, society, and policy where language testing plays a key role, such as immigration. Language testing research has therefore involved itself to a greater extent in the social aspects of test use, engaging with issues of fairness, ethical practice, policy and politics, the law, and how values guide test design and score use.

As the field has expanded and become more complicated, Language assessment literacy (LAL) research has emerged as an attempt to define what different stakeholders need to know about testing and assessment to fulfil their respective roles not only effectively, but with the sensitivity required to produce just and fair outcomes for test takers.

The Research Questions

1. What is "interactional competence"? Can it be defined from the analysis of performance data?
2. Do closed- or open-response tasks better predict work-based language performance?
3. How specific do we need to make test specifications to control difficulty and content of tasks?
4. Do learners perform differentially on listening tests with and without video? What factors make video tasks easier or more difficult?
5. Does allowing note-taking while taking a test lead to higher or lower scores? Does the difference vary according to (a) proficiency level, or (b) the type of notes made?
6. Do verbal protocols collected from test takers to improve test tasks suffer from veridicality or reactivity? What methodological practices can improve the usefulness of data from test takers?
7. Is human scoring more reliable when using holistic or analytic rating scales?
8. How do admissions officers use scores to make entry decisions in Universities?
9. How do politicians decide what standards to set for immigration?
10. What skills do teachers need to use assessment to improve learning?

Suggested Resources

Fulcher, G. (2010). *Practical Language Testing***. London: Hodder Education.**

This volume is organized around the test design and development process, but places it within the context of the social purpose of language testing. The explicit rationale for this approach is that language testing, unlike other fields of applied linguistics, is concerned with building tests that will provide utility in decision making. The various tools that are required for this practical activity are also described, including the techniques of classical and modern test theory and their associated statistical tools. The text is nevertheless critical, asking the reader to consider whether the assumptions underlying practices are justified in the context of a social rather than a natural science. Each chapter is supported by challenging tasks designed to illustrate the design processes described, leading to basic competence in language test design and development by the conclusion.

Bachman, L. F. (2004). *Statistical Analyses for Language Assessment***. Cambridge: Cambridge University Press.**

Bachman's treatment of the statistical tools required for the analysis of language test scores is comprehensive and accessible. Beginning with the description of scores and distributions, it progresses through the calculation of reliability for both norm- and criterion-referenced tests, and then expands into inferential statistical methods for looking at issues such as score differences and conducting validation studies. The volume is well supported with an associated workbook by Bachman and Kunnan entitled *Statistical Analyses for Language Assessment Workbook*, also from the same publisher. Together, these texts expand upon the introduction to core statistical tools introduced in Fulcher (2010).

Lazaraton, A. (2002). *A Qualitative Approach to the Validation of Oral Language Tests***. Cambridge: Cambridge University Press.**

While this text specifically concerns itself with the assessment of speaking, it is the focus on qualitative approaches to validation that is of much more general interest. The discussions of recording spoken data, transcription and coding, and establishing units of analysis, are relevant not only to spoken data within the context of testing speaking, but any interview data with raters, learners, or even policy makers. The introduction to conversation analysis is particularly useful, and the text provides references to the discourse and sociological resources where relevant. Coding and analyzing qualitative data have always proved a challenge for students of language testing, and Lazaraton is an excellent introduction to how we may find our way through the various challenges posed by complex interactional data and the various analytical options available to the researcher. Alongside the Bachman volume, Lazaraton provides further detail and insight into the qualitative tools introduced in Fulcher (2010).

Kunnan, A. J. (2018). *Evaluating Language Assessments.* **London & New York: Routledge.**

Kunnan has developed a justifiable reputation for his work on fairness and justice in language testing. While the purpose of this book is to guide the reader through the process of evaluating a language test for a stated purpose, it really builds upon previous work to bring ethical, social, legal and political concerns to how we decide whether test use is justifiable, and "just". The text also provides a very useful discussion of frameworks and guidelines that have previously been used for the evaluation of test use, including those developed by the International Language Testing Association (ILTA). It therefore provides a commentary on part of the recent history of how language testing has attempted to engage with how language tests are used by policy makers who know (and care) very little about applied linguistics or the limitations of what language tests can do.

Fulcher, G. (2015). *Re-examining Language Testing: A philosophical and social inquiry.* **London & New York: Routledge.**

This volume steps back from the processes and practices of language testing, as well as the political uses of test scores and notions of justice that Kunnan has tackled. It asks the broader question about why we do these things, what values drive our decision making, and how both practices and decisions are reflections of underlying beliefs about the structure and nature of society, and the role of individuals within the contingent environment into which they are born. The book attempts to raise the big "why?" questions which, if we can provide some kind of answer, might inform how we transform and do things. The volume is supported by a website that helps the reader ask these "why?" questions and consider the value systems that often remain unchallenged in conventional practice: http://languagetesting.info/RLT/home.html.

Glenn Fulcher is Professor of Applied Linguistics and Language Testing at the University of Leicester, UK. He taught ESOL internationally before taking up University posts in the UK, moving to Leicester in 2006. He studied Theology and Philosophy at King's College London and Education at Christ's College Cambridge followed by an M.A. in Applied Linguistics at Birmingham University, and a Ph.D. from the University of Lancaster. His books include Testing Second Language Speaking (Longman/Pearson, 2003), Language Testing and Assessment (Routledge, 2007), Practical Language Testing (Hodder, 2010), the Routledge Handbook of Language Testing (Routledge, 2012), and Language Testing Re-examined: A philosophical and social inquiry (Routledge, 2015). The 2012 and 2015 volumes were joint winners of the SAGE/ILTA Book Award for 2016. He edited the journal Language Testing from 2007 to 2016, and has served as the President of the International Language Testing Association. In 2014 he was awarded a National Teaching Fellowship for his contribution to language assessment literacy, particularly the dissemination of information through his website, http://languagetesting.info. In 2021 he received the Messick Memorial Award from Educational Testing Service.

Oral Corrective Feedback

63

Shaofeng Li

Oral corrective feedback refers to comments a teacher or an interlocutor makes on errors that occur in second language learners' speech production. In traditional pedagogy, corrective feedback is restricted to explicit correction of errors and there is no distinction between different types of feedback. In current approaches such as task-based instruction, the concept of feedback is extended to any response that is intended and/or recognized as being corrective. Therefore, feedback can be provided in various ways, and different types of feedback are viewed differently in different theories in terms of whether and how they facilitate language learning. What types of feedback occur in the classroom? Lyster and Ranta (1997) provide a clear taxonomy of feedback based on their observations of French immersion classes. They identified six major feedback types: recasts, explicit correction, elicitation, repetition, clarification request, and metalinguistic clue (refer to Li (2018) for examples). The authors divided the six corrective strategies into two categories putting recasts and explicit correction into one category and the remaining four into the other in that the former provides the correct form and the latter (labeled as 'prompts') encourages learners to self-correct. The authors found that although recasts were the most frequent feedback type, they were not as effective as prompts in leading to uptake, which refers to responses after feedback.

Subsequently, in a series of studies, Lyster and his colleagues (e.g. Lyster, 1998; Yang & Lyster, 2010) found that in classroom settings recasts not only led to less uptake but were also less effective in facilitating learning gains measured through pretests and posttests in comparison with prompts. However, other studies revealed that the effectiveness of feedback is constrained by a host of learner and contextual factors and therefore we cannot make overarching claims about the superiority of certain feedback types. For example, Ammar and Spada (2006) reported that prompts were more effective than recasts for learners with less previous knowledge

S. Li (✉)
Florida State University, Tallahassee, USA
e-mail: sli9@fsu.edu

© Springer Nature Switzerland AG 2021
H. Mohebbi and C. Coombe (eds.), *Research Questions in Language Education and Applied Linguistics*, Springer Texts in Education,
https://doi.org/10.1007/978-3-030-79143-8_63

about the target structure, but for learners with more previous knowledge, the two feedback types worked equally well. Li (2014) showed that at a higher proficiency level, the effects of recasts were more sustainable than metalinguistic correction in the learning of a complex linguistic target but at a lower proficiency level, metalinguistic correction showed consistently larger effects than recasts. In the same study, the author found that feedback had larger effects on an oral production test than a written grammaticality judgement test. Rassaei (2015) found that the effects of feedback were subject to learners' anxiety levels: low-anxiety learners benefited equally from metalinguistic feedback and recasts while high-anxiety learners benefited significantly more from recasts than metalinguistic feedback. Furthermore, given that the effects of feedback as single corrective strategies are subject to constraining factors, it seems advisable to provide a variety of feedback (Lyster & Ranta, 2013) or hybrid feedback such as the kind provided in Li et al.'s (2016) study, which consisted of a prompt followed by a recast. Alternatively, the teacher can provide a few moves of explicit feedback which overtly draws learners' attention to errors and then switch to implicit feedback after raising learners' awareness of the linguistic target (e.g. Yilmaz, 2014).

Another perspective is to examine learners' and teachers' beliefs about corrective feedback. Li (2017) aggregated the results of 26 studies and found that (1) while students were overwhelmingly supportive of feedback (89% of all respondents), teachers were hesitant (39%); (2) teachers were positive about recasts and indirect feedback and there is a lack of research on students' preferences; (3) students' beliefs about feedback could be changed by participating in communications where they provided and received corrective feedback; (4) teachers' beliefs about feedback could be changed by engaging in hands-on, experiential activities such as conducting a small-scale study, tutoring a learner, reflecting on one's own learning and teaching experience, etc.; (5) there was much inconsistency between teachers' stated beliefs about feedback and their feedback practice in the classroom. The author pointed out that most of the survey studies only investigated feedback as part of a larger-scale study on learners' or teachers' beliefs about grammar instruction or language learning in general. The author called for more research that examines feedback beliefs exclusively.

The Research Questions

1. How do teachers provide feedback in the classroom?
2. Do learners recognize the corrective force of feedback?
3. Is feedback effective?
4. Are certain feedback types more effective than others?
5. What factors may affect the effects of feedback?
6. Should errors receive immediate correction or after some delay?
7. Should feedback be provided before, during, or after a communicative task?

8. How do learners think feedback should be provided?
9. Is hybrid feedback such as the kind that consists of a prompt followed by a recast more effective than single feedback moves?
10. Do child and adult learners benefit from feedback differently?

Suggested Resources

Li, S. (2010). The effectiveness of corrective feedback in SLA: A meta-analysis. *Language Learning, 60,* **309–365.**

This is a meta-analysis that aggregated all the empirical evidence on the effectiveness of corrective feedback. The study is characterized by comprehensive coverage and methodological rigor, and it is one of the most frequently cited feedback studies. The meta-analysis showed an overall medium effect for feedback. The moderator analysis revealed that lab studies yielded larger effects than classroom studies; explicit feedback demonstrated larger immediate effects than implicit feedback but the effects of implicit feedback were more sustainable; studies conducted in foreign language settings generated larger effects than those conducted in second language settings. The findings were interpreted primarily by drawing on the methodological features of the synthesized studies.

Li, S. (2018). Data collection in the research on the effectiveness of corrective feedback: A synthetic and critical review. In A. Gudmestad & A. Edmonds (Eds.), *Critical reflections on data in second language acquisition* **(pp. 33–61). John Benjamins.**

This study provides an evidence-based review and critique of the methods of the research on the effects of corrective feedback in second language learning. It aims to inform this substantive domain by showing how the research has been conducted, identifying issues and limitations, and proposing solutions. The researcher extracted the methodological details of 34 representative studies selected based on transparent, justified criteria. The data were coded in terms of feedback treatment, feedback elicitation task, and the measurement of treatment effects. The coded features were evaluated in terms of internal validity, external validity, and construct validity. The study is the first that provides a thorough description and discussion of the methods of experimental feedback research.

Lyster, R., & Saito, K. (2010). Oral feedback in classroom SLA: A meta-analysis. *Studies in Second Language Acquisition, 32,* **265–302.**

This meta-analysis reported that in classroom settings, prompts were more effective than recasts and that younger learners benefited more from feedback than older learners. This meta-analysis was published in the same year as Li's (2010) meta-analysis. However, they were based on different selection criteria and their analyses were considerably different. Lyster and Saito's meta-analysis only included classroom studies, most of which compared the effects of recasts and prompts—a topic on which Lyster and his colleagues have conducted a large amount of research. Li's meta-analysis included both lab and classroom studies. Their meta-analysis used confidence intervals to detect significant group differences, a practice that is criticized by experts in meta-analysis (e.g. Li et al., 2012) on the grounds that while the lack of overlap between confidence intervals suggests a significant difference, the existence of an overlap does not necessarily mean there is no significant difference. In Li's meta-analysis, Q tests were performed for group comparisons. Despite the caveats, Lyster and Saito's meta-analysis generated some valuable findings, some of which may inspire the reader to carry out further research. For example, the finding that feedback was more effective for younger learners than older learners is based on synthesized results, that is, age was a coded moderator. Therefore, age needs to be examined as an independent variable in the primary research.

Mackey, A. (Ed.) (2017). *Conversational interaction in second language acquisition.* **Oxford: Oxford University Press**.

This volume concerns the role of conversational interaction in second language acquisition, but a large percentage of the articles concern feedback—a critical feature of interaction that contributes to learning gains. In fact, a major theoretical basis for the importance of corrective feedback is the Interaction Hypothesis, which claims that interaction affords opportunities for learning by making available interactionally modified input, corrective feedback, and pushed output. The Interaction Hypothesis is the guiding theory for the studies included in the book. The theory also favours recasts, which probably explains why most of the feedback studies included in the book concern recasts. The topics examined in the feedback studies include constraining factors for the effects of recasts such as language analytic ability, working memory, and the linguistic target; peer oral feedback; learners' perceptions of recasts; and measures of the effects of feedback. The book concludes with a meta-analysis of the research on second language interaction, and feedback was examined as an important variable that contributes to the effects of interaction.

Nassaji, H., & Kartchava, E. (Eds.) (2017). *Corrective feedback in second language teaching and learning.* **NY: Routledge**.

This is the first edited volume that deals exclusively with the theory, research, and practice of corrective feedback. The book includes a collection of chapters authored by leading researchers in this substantive domain and provides a comprehensive description and an in-depth, authoritarian discussion of the knowledge that has been accumulated on each topic. The book covers nearly all aspects of the topic of feedback such as oral feedback, written feedback, computerized feedback, and beliefs about feedback. It not only has a wide coverage but also addresses original topics such as the timing of feedback, peer written feedback, oral feedback to written errors, and non-verbal feedback.

References

Ammar, A., & Spada, N. (2006). One size fits all? Recasts, prompts, and L2 learning. *Studies in Second Language Acquisition, 28*, 543–574.

Li, S. (2014). The interface between feedback type, L2 proficiency, and the nature of the linguistic target. *Language Teaching Research, 18*, 373–396.

Li, S. (2017). Teacher and learner beliefs about corrective feedback. In H. Nassaji & E. Kartchava (Eds.), *Corrective feedback in second language teaching and learning* (pp. 143–157). Routledge.

Li, S. (2018). Corrective feedback in L2 speech production. In J. Liontas (Ed.), *The TESOL encyclopedia of English language teaching* (1st ed., p. 1–9). John Wiley & Sons, Inc.

Li, S., Zhu, Y., & Ellis, R. (2016). The effects of the timing of corrective feedback on the acquisition of a new linguistic structure. *The Modern Language Journal, 100*, 276–295.

Lyster, R. (1998). Recasts, repetition, and ambiguity in L2 classroom discourse. *Studies in Second Language Acquisition, 20*, 51–81.

Lyster, R., & Ranta, L. (1997). Corrective feedback and learner uptake. *Studies in Second Language Acquisition, 19*, 37–66.

Lyster, R., & Ranta, L. (2013). Counterpoint piece: The case for variety in corrective feedback research. *Studies in Second Language Acquisition, 35*, 167–184.

Rassaei, E. (2015). Oral corrective feedback, foreign language anxiety and L2 development. *System, 49*, 98–109.

Yang, Y., & Lyster, R. (2010). Effects of form-focused practice and feedback on Chinese EFL learners' acquisition of regular and irregular past tense forms. *Studies in Second Language Acquisition, 32*, 235–263.

Yilmaz, Y. (2014). The relative effectiveness of mixed, explicit and implicit feedback in the acquisition of English articles. *System, 41*, 691–705.

Shaofeng Li is an Associate Professor of Second and Foreign Language Education at Florida State University and a Yunshan Chair Professor at Guangdong University of Foreign Studies in Guangzhou, China. Before joining Florida State University, he had worked as a Senior Lecturer of Applied Language Studies at the University of Auckland, New Zealand, and an Assistant Professor of Foreign Language Education at Hebei Teachers University, China. He earned his Ph.D. in Second Language Studies from Michigan State University and his M.A. in Linguistics from Hebei Teachers University. His main research interests include language aptitude, working memory, form-focused instruction, task-based language teaching and learning, corrective feedback, and research methods (including meta-analysis). His research has primarily focused on the joint effects of learner-external (e.g. instruction) and learner-internal (e.g. cognitive aptitudes) factors on second language learning outcomes. His publications have appeared in Applied Linguistics, International Review of *Applied Linguistics, Language Learning, Language Teaching Research, The Modern Language Journal, Studies in Second Language Acquisition, System*, among others. He has been awarded a number of research grants, totaling more than $400,000, including the Marsden Funds—the most prestigious research fund in New Zealand.

Needs Analysis

64

Li-Shih Huang

Defining the term "needs" entails a complex inquiry involving a variety of viewpoints and labels. The term "language-learning needs" further encompasses various perspectives and factors in determining what, how, and why learners need to learn (e.g., Hyland, 2006; Long, 2005; Munby, 1981). As West (1994) pointed out, "needs" is often considered an umbrella term with many different interpretations. Until the 1970s, language-learning needs were mostly intuitively determined by instructors. Since the advent of learner-centered approaches to teaching and learning, various theories about language learners' needs analysis, taxonomies, models, and frameworks have emerged (e.g., Dudley-Evans & St. John, 1998). With these have come a wide array of terms associated with the concepts of needs and needs analysis (see L. Flowerdew, 2018 or Ozdemir, 2018), including *objective* and *subjective* needs (Brindley, 1989); *perceived* and *felt* (or expressed) needs (Berwick, 1989); *target-situation* (e.g., skills needed to perform competently), *learning-situation* (e.g., preferred way of learning), and *present-situation* (e.g., current skills and language use) needs analyses (Basturkmen, 2010; Hutchinson & Waters, 1987); *product-oriented* and *process-oriented* needs (Brindley, 1989); and *necessities*, *wants*, and *lacks* (Liu et al., 2011). Although Dudley-Evans and St. John's (1998) concept of needs analysis is still regarded as the most comprehensive in integrating various key factors, challenges remain in that research is still lacking for all factors and all relevant stakeholders (Chatsungnoen, 2015).

Needs analysis is important because the results are relevant for specifying objectives, procedures, content, materials, methods, and outcomes assessment at the task, course, or program level (Flowerdew & Peacock, 2001). Hyland's (2002) definition highlighted the distinctive approach of ESP (English for specific purposes) to language teaching as "identification of the specific language features, discourse practices, and communicative skills of target groups, and … teaching

L.-S. Huang (✉)
Department of Linguistics, University of Victoria, Victoria, British Columbia, Canada
e-mail: lshuang@uvic.ca

© Springer Nature Switzerland AG 2021
H. Mohebbi and C. Coombe (eds.), *Research Questions in Language Education and Applied Linguistics*, Springer Texts in Education,
https://doi.org/10.1007/978-3-030-79143-8_64

practices that recognise the particular subject-matter needs and expertise of learners" (p. 385). Researchers generally agree that collecting and applying information about learners' needs is key to task design (e.g., Malicka et al., 2019; Mochizuki, 2017) and course/program development (e.g., Basturkmen, 2010), and also important for planning English courses, especially ESP and EAP (English for academic purposes) courses (see L. Flowerdew, 2018).

The literature on language-learning needs assessment has focused most attention on ESP and EAP (e.g., Brown, 2009; J. Flowerdew, 2013; Long, 2005). As Hyland (2006) stated, needs analysis "has been the principal method for determining what to include in ESP/EAP curricula, and for providing descriptions of academic skills and genres that EAL [English as an additional language] students may encounter in future courses" (p. 181). Identifying specific language features, discourse practices, and communicative competencies of target academic groups is thus a major concern. Since the 1980s, numerous studies have examined EAL learners' needs using a wide range of methodologies (e.g., questionnaires, interviews, test or assessment results, observations, discourse/genre analysis, corpus analysis, self-assessment, expert informants, and case studies) focusing on, for example, academic literacy skills (e.g., J. Flowerdew, 2013; Leki & Carson, 1994), academic language support needs (e.g., Huang, 2010, 2011; Read, 2008), general language skills (e.g., Geoghegan, 1983; Huang, in press/2021), and writing skills (e.g., Seviour, 2015). As pointed out by Hyland (2009), "needs are not always easy to determine... because they mean different things to different participants" (p. 204). Empirical research has also revealed that language-learning needs are learner- or group-specific and context dependent (Huang, 2010; Long, 2005).

Needs analysis in the general English setting remains lacking because of the diversity and lack of specificity compared to ESP or EAP (Ozdemir, 2018). Several studies have also highlighted a mismatch between students' perceived needs and expectations and the expectations of instructors (e.g., Alkutbi, 2018; Huang, 2010, 2013; Thorp, 1991). What instructors/learners consider an important skill to possess may not be one that learners perceive they need to develop (e.g., Huang, 2010), and learners may not always perceive their own difficulties (e.g., Auerbach, 1995; Long, 2005). These findings suggest the need to examine language-learning needs from multiple perspectives and to consider various kinds of student needs. Recent needs analysis studies (e.g., Bocanegra-Valle, 2016) to identify specific English language skills across a range of professions and disciplines in multiple settings using quantitative, qualitative, and mixed methods have further underscored the complex nature of gauging needs from the data as well as from how and whom the data are collected.

The Research Questions

1. Needs analysis factors: Consider the different factors offered by Dudley-Evans and St. John (1998) and the ESP or EAP courses you have taught or envisage teaching. Which factors or types of needs-related information in your context would be feasible to collect to help you understand your students' needs?
2. Needs analysis methods: What methods would be suitable for collecting the data for examining the factors identified in Question 1? What are the strengths and limitations of the methods identified?
3. Needs for occupational purposes: If you were involved in an initiative to settle Syrian refugee learners into the workforce by providing them with the language training needed for occupational purposes, how would you go about identifying their language-learning needs for purposes of developing a program?
4. Needs for professional purposes: You have been assigned to develop an ESP course for pharmacists or physicians who are recent immigrants from Syria and who need to pass the certification examination in order to continue practicing their profession. What steps would you take to understand their English language needs in order to design this course?
5. Needs for workplace communication: When examining the needs associated with specialized discourse, one option is to gather samples of language use. Select as your aim the development of a workplace-focused ESP class. When collecting data from participants is not possible, look into other potential data sources (e.g., corpora, manuals, official documents, websites, and research articles). What existing data sources can you locate to begin your discourse/genre analysis?
6. Needs for academic purposes: Select an academic genre or a specific topic in the genre of pedagogical interests. What are the disciplinary similarities and variations in discourse across two or more disciplines? What methods could you use to compare and contrast differences in order to inform pedagogical practices?
7. Task-based needs analysis: As pointed out by Basturkmen (2010), task-based needs analyses have increasingly been used in ESP. Is the task-based approach to needs analysis applicable across English for professional purposes, English for academic purposes, and English for occupational purposes?
8. Task-based needs analysis: Using tasks as the focus of inquiry, identify some real-world tasks in English for general purposes, English for academic purposes, or English for occupational purposes that a target group of learners will encounter. As a researcher, what can you do in your analysis of language features and communication skills needed for those identified real-world, language-based tasks to inform instructors' practices?
9. English for academic purposes: EAP is often described as "needs driven" in that it aims to address the needs of students within various target contexts, which might risk promoting conformity to conventions or institutional requirements and lead to what Hyland (2018), citing Huckin (2003), called "a

teacher-centred prescriptivism and an overly rigid focus on certain genres, forms, and tasks at the expense of others" (p. 387). In conducting needs analysis in the EAP context, what deviations from institutional conventions can be explored that could enrich our understanding of language features and discourse practices and also promote more dynamic pedagogy?

10. Research replication: As argued by Huang (2010), "efforts to seek findings' generalizability may be fruitless because needs analysis is, by definition, context-dependent and context-specific, taking into account the very different linguistic cultures and the variety of institutional environments" (p. 535). Conduct a literature review to locate a needs analysis research report that, within the context of the research, is similar to your own teaching context and that would be possible to replicate. Implement your replication study in your own context to answer this question: Do your results converge with the original study or do they support the argument?

Suggested Resources

Basturkmen, H. (2010). *Developing courses in English for specific purposes.* **Palgrave Macmillan**.

This volume focuses on developing courses for English for specific purposes at both an institutional and a classroom level in a variety of contexts. It contains an informative needs analysis chapter that provides an overview of the development of the defining key terms and their complexity as well as the processes involved in examining learner needs, in addition to an overview of the aims, methods, and stages involved in needs analysis. The chapter also highlights the dynamics of needs analysis as an ongoing and evolving process during a course's implementation, and includes hypothetical scenarios with follow-up questions. The importance of needs assessment permeates the volume, and its practical coverage provides both prospective and practicing teachers and researchers an easy start on getting up to speed in grasping the fundamentals of needs analysis.

Blaj-Ward, L. (2014). *Researching contexts, practices and pedagogies in English for academic purposes.* **Palgrave Macmillan**.

Of particular relevance to readers interested in needs analysis, Chap. 3 of this volume builds on the premise that needs analysis is fundamental to EAP provision. The chapter delves into topics on teaching materials and course design, with a central focus on needs analysis dealing with target situations using, for example, discourse and corpus analysis that examine the discourse norms in academia that students are expected to maintain. Through presenting and analyzing hypothetical scenarios, the author engages readers in needs analysis in practice. Chapter 4 shifts to needs analysis in relation to students' perceived needs rather than to features of the target situations. It also discusses needs analysis studies and the need to shift the critical stance from terminology to the broader issues related to the non-neutral nature of needs analysis in evaluating perceptions, practices, and outcomes within the macro context of higher education.

Paltridge, B. & Starfield, S. (Eds.). (2014). *The handbook of English for specific purposes.* **Wiley-Blackwell.**

This 28-chapter handbook contains a wealth of resources for teaching and research. Of relevance is the chapter by Johns (pp. 5–30), who critically reviews the historical development of ESP research, within which she traces the period when ESP research and pedagogic practice broadened to include a focus on needs assessment. In dealing with the pedagogical issues of ESP, most notably, Flowerdew's chapter (pp. 325–346) on needs analysis and curriculum development presents evolving definitions, sources, and methods of needs analysis in various ESP course types (e.g., EAP and EOP [English for occupational purposes]). This coverage is followed by a discussion of the future directions of needs analyses and curriculum development in ESP.

Long, M. (2005). Methodology issues in learner needs analysis. In M. H. Long (Ed.), *Second language needs analysis* **(pp. 19–76). Cambridge University Press.**

For researchers interested in the field of needs analysis, this seminal publication on second language needs analysis presents a collection of studies with overviews of the field, design, implementation, and outcomes in a wide variety of contexts (e.g., the hotel industry, the US military, and academia) and geographical areas (the United States, Europe, and the Pacific Rim). The volume also informs readers about various data collection methods along with insights about their strengths and limitations. Underscored are Long's overview and his discussion of the importance of data triangulation, which provide readers a sense of the complexity and challenges involved in conducting needs analysis and of the issues and approaches one must be aware of.

West, R. (1994). Needs analysis in language teaching. *Language Teaching, 27,* **1–19.** https://doi.org/10.1017/S0261444800007527.

For researchers interested in needs assessment, West's state-of-the-art article is a must read. Surveying the field broadly, it provides a comprehensive review of needs analysis in English-language teaching by first describing its origins and theoretical basis. The article also covers the questions one must ask in any needs analysis procedure, namely, what (such as necessities, lacks, wants, learning strategies, and constraints), when (i.e., when needs analysis should be carried out), who (e.g., teacher-perceived, learner-perceived, or institution-perceived needs), for whom (i.e., whom will the needs analysis benefit), how (methods and procedures), and how long (i.e., the length of time required to conduct a needs analysis). It reviews different forms of needs analysis (e.g., target-situation analysis, for instance, the language requirements in ESP or EAP contexts that learners are being prepared for), deficiency analysis (e.g., learners' present needs and the requirements of the target situation analysis), strategy analysis (i.e., learners' preferred learning approaches or methods), and means analysis (e.g., logistics, constraints in implementation, and classroom cultural factors). The article concludes with a critical discussion of the limitations of needs analysis.

References

Alkutbi, D. (2018). *Bridging the gap: A study of academic language-learning needs of Saudi international students* (Ph.D. dissertation). The University of Victoria, BC, Canada.

Auerbach, E. (1995). The politics of the ESL classroom: Issues of power in pedagogical choices. In J. Tollefson (Ed.), *Power and inequality in language education* (pp. 9–33). Cambridge University Press.

Basturkmen, H. (2010). *Developing courses in English for specific purposes*. Palgrave Macmillan

Berwick, R. (1989). Needs assessment in language programming: From theory to practice. In R. L. Johnson (Ed.), *The second language curriculum*. Cambridge University Press.

Bocanegra-Valle, A. (2016). Needs analysis for curriculum design. In K. Hyland & P. Shaw (Eds.), *The Routledge handbook of English for academic purposes* (pp. 560–576). Routledge.

Brindley, G. (1989). The role of needs analysis in adult ESL program design. In R. Johnson (Ed.), *The second language curriculum* (pp. 63–78). Cambridge University Press.

Brown, J. D. (2009). Foreign and second language needs analysis. In M. H. Long & C. J.

Chatsungnoen, P. (2015). *Needs analysis for an English for specific purposes (ESP) course for Thai undergraduates in a food science and technology programme* (unpublished doctoral dissertation). Massey University, Palmerston North, New Zealand.

Dudley-Evans, T., & St John, M. J. (1998). *Developments in English for specific purposes: A multi-disciplinary approach*. Cambridge University Press.

Flowerdew, J. (2013). *Discourse in English language education*. Routledge.

Flowerdew, J., & Peacock, M. (2001). The English for academic purposes curriculum: Introduction. In J. Flowerdew & M. Peacock (Eds.), *Research perspectives on English for academic purposes* (pp. 169–176). Cambridge University Press.

Flowerdew, L. (2018). Needs analysis for the second language writing classroom. In D. D. Belcher & A. Hirvela (Eds.), *The TESOL encyclopedia of English language teaching* (pp. 2437–2442). John Wiley. https://doi.org/10.1002/9781118784235.eelt0523

Geoghegan, G. (1983*). Non-native speakers of English at Cambridge University*. Bell, Educational Trust.

Huang, L.-S. (2010). Seeing eye to eye? The academic writing needs of graduate and undergraduate students from students' and instructors' perspectives. *Language Teaching Research, 14*(4), 517–539. https://doi.org/10.1177/1362168810375372

Huang, L.-S. (2011). Are we having the effect we want? Implementing outcomes assessment in an academic English language-support unit using a multi-component approach. *The WPA Journal, 35*(1), 11–45.

Huang, L.-S. (2013). Academic English is no one's mother tongue: Graduate and undergraduate students' academic English language-learning needs from students' and instructors' perspectives. *Journal of Perspectives in Applied Academic Practice, 1*(2), 17–29. https://doi.org/10.14297/jpaap.v1i2.67

Huang, L.-S. (in press/2021). "I have big, big, BIG dream!" Realigning instruction with the language-learning needs of adult Syrians with refugee experience in Canada. *Canada's Journal on Refugees,* Refuge.

Hutchinson, T., & Waters, A. (1987). *English for specific purposes*. Cambridge University Press.

Hyland, K. (2002). Specificity revisited: How far should we go now? *English for Specific Purposes, 21*, 385–395. https://doi.org/10.1016/S0889-4906(01)00028-X

Hyland, K. (2006). *English for academic purposes: An advanced resource book*. Routledge.

Hyland, K. (2009). Specific purposes programmes. In M. H. Long & C. J. Doughty (Eds.), *The handbook of language teaching* (pp. 201–217). Wiley Blackwell.

Leki, I., & Carson, J. (1994). Students' perceptions of EAP writing instruction and writing needs across the disciplines. *TESOL Quarterly, 28*(1), 81–101. https://doi.org/10.2307/3587199

Liu, J.-Y., Chang, Y.-J., Yang, F.-Y., & Sun, Y.-C. (2011). Is what I need what I want? Reconceptualising college students' needs in English courses for general and specific/academic purposes. *Journal of English for Academic Purposes, 10*(4), 271–280. https://doi.org/10.1016/j.jeap.2011.09.002

Long, M. (2005). Methodology issues in learner needs analysis. In M. H. Long (Ed.), *Second language needs analysis* (pp. 19–76). Cambridge University Press.

Malicka, A., Gilabert Guerrero, R., & Norris, J. M. (2019). From needs analysis to task design: Insights from an English for specific purposes context. *Language Teaching Research, 23*(1), 78–106.

Mochizuki, N. (2017). Contingent needs analysis for task implementation: An activity systems analysis of group writing conferences. TESOL *Quarterly, 51*(3), 607–631.

Munby, J. (1981). *Communicative syllabus design.* Cambridge University Press.

Ozdemir, N. O. (2018). Needs analysis. In J. L. Liontas (Ed.), *The TESOL encyclopedia of English language teaching* (pp. 1–6). Wiley. https://doi.org/10.1002/9781118784235.eelt0200

Read, J. (2008). Identifying academic language needs through diagnostic assessment. *Journal of English for Academic Purposes, 7*, 180–190. https://doi.org/10.1016/j.jeap.2008.02.001

Seviour, M. (2015). Assessing academic writing on a pre-sessional EAP course: Designing assessment which supports learning. *Journal of English for Academic Purposes, 18*, 84–89. https://doi.org/10.1016/j.jeap.2015.03.007

Thorp, D. (1991). Confused encounters: Differing expectations in the EAP classroom. *ELT Journal, 45*(2), 108–118.

West, R. (1994). Needs analysis in language teaching. *Language Teaching, 27*(1), 19. https://doi.org/10.1017/S0261444800007527

Li-Shih Huang completed her Ph.D. at the Ontario Institute for Studies in Education of the University of Toronto. Currently, she is an Associate Professor of Applied Linguistics at the University of Victoria (UVic). Li-Shih has been the recipient of the UVic's Humanities Teaching Excellence Award, TESOL's Mary Finocchiaro Award for Excellence in Pedagogical Materials Development, and the Award for an Outstanding Paper on NNEST Issues. Li-Shih's scholarly interests include areas such as needs and outcomes assessment, strategic behaviours in language learning and language testing, and reflective learning. She has received numerous research grants from the Social Sciences and Humanities Research Council of Canada (SSHRC), the Educational Testing Service (ETS®), and the International English Language Testing System (IELTS™) for her work in those areas.

Peer Interaction Assessment

Noriko Iwashita

There has been an increased trend of using peer interaction in both public and classroom speaking tests. The introduction of this assessment format in both pedagogic and assessment contexts was initially motivated by its practicality in terms of the cost, time and resources (Berry, 2007; Bonk & Ockey, 2003; Ockey, 2009; Van Moere, 2006). The use of this format is considered to be economical as two or more test-takers can be assessed at one time (Folland & Robertson, 1976; Ockey, 2009) and interview training is not required (Ockey, 2009). Furthermore, the wide acceptance of the peer interaction format is attributed to the close resemblance to what learners do their classrooms (Saville & Hargreaves, 1999; Taylor, 2000) resulting in positive washback in the classroom for both students and teachers.

In communication-oriented approaches to language teaching, teachers are expected to introduce various activities such as small group discussions to prepare students for the test (Ockey, 2009) and students are encouraged to interact with one another in their classroom activities (Saville & Hargreaves, 1999). For that reason, the peer interaction format is considered to be more authentic to test-takers' real-life situations providing a closer link between the test results and the target language use situation (Bachman & Palmer, 1996) resulting in valid interpretation of the score (Ockey, 2009).

Along with the popularity of peer interaction in speaking assessment, a substantial volume of research has investigated various aspects of peer interaction through analysis of test discourse, test scores, verbal protocol during ratings and the findings have revealed strengths and limitations of this format of assessment. Benefits of using peer interaction are explained in terms of the symmetrical nature of interaction in this format in comparison with the oral proficiency interview. Unlike oral proficiency interviews, the peer interaction format is found to be more representative of normal conversation than an interview format and is less asym-

N. Iwashita (✉)
School of Languages and Cultures, The University of Queensland, Brisbane, QLD, Australia
e-mail: n.iwashita@uq.edu.au

© Springer Nature Switzerland AG 2021
H. Mohebbi and C. Coombe (eds.), *Research Questions in Language Education and Applied Linguistics*, Springer Texts in Education,
https://doi.org/10.1007/978-3-030-79143-8_65

metrical (Galaczi, 2008; van Lier, 1989). The symmetrical nature of peer interaction formats can also avoid the criticisms related to power relationships (Davis, 2009) that are typically associated with an interview format. Also, some studies reported that peer interaction is less intimidating and helps test-takers take more control over the direction of the conversation (e.g., Folland & Robertson, 1976; Fulcher, 1996; Shohamy et al., 1986). Peer interaction presents test-takers with an opportunity to show their ability to participate in interaction other than as an 'interviewee' responding to questions (Ducasse & Brown, 2009). As a result, test takers demonstrate a wider range of language functions and roles (Skehan, 2001) and also exhibit their conversation management skills (Galaczi, 2008). Building on prior work, more recent research has shifted the focus on an individualistic view of language performance to a co-constructed nature of performance exploring the assessment of interactional competence. Although the studies have provided sound justification for the widespread utilisation of this format with theoretical and methodological refinements, more research is called for especially for the construct of interactional competence and various interlocutor, task variables and task implementing conditions associated with the examination of interactional competence.

The Research Questions

1. In what way might the peer interaction format of speaking assessment be different from an oral proficiency interview?
2. Does test-taker proficiency contribute to variation in test-taker performance?
3. What other interlocutor variables should be considered for peer interaction assessment?
4. What tasks would be suitable for peer interaction assessment?
5. To what extent do interlocutor variables have an impact on the reliability of the test task?
6. To what extent do interlocutor variables have an impact on the validity of the test task?
7. What do raters attend to in features of interaction in peer interaction assessment tasks?
8. What features of interaction in peer interaction of a speaking task discriminate amongst test takers?
9. Does group dynamics have an impact on performance?
10. Does task implementation conditions (e.g., planning time) have an effect on test-taker performance?

Suggested Resources

Galaczi, E. (2014). Interactional competence across proficiency levels: How do learners manage interaction in paired speaking tests? *Applied Linguistics 35*(5), 553–574.

The study investigates the interaction co-constructed by learners at different proficiency levels in a paired speaking test with the aim of providing insights into the conceptualization of interactional competence and key distinguishing interactional features across levels. The interaction data drawn from the speaking test performance of 41 pairs with a range of proficiency was analysed first qualitatively using CA method, and the identified interactional features were further quantified to examine differences across the levels. The qualitative data analyses revealed test-takers' active interaction shown in the identified three key interactional features (i.e., topic development, listener support, and turn-taking management), but the quantitative analyses revealed variations in the frequency and types of the interactional moves across the levels. The study contributes to the understanding of interactional competence both in the classroom and in assessment contexts, and also suggests assessment scale needs to include listener support strategies and turn-taking management as well as interactional features such as topic development.

Lam, D. (2019). Interactional competence with and without extended planning time in a group oral assessment. *Language Assessment Quarterly 16*(1), 1–20.

The study investigated whether the length of planning time has any impact on features of interactional competence observed in group discussion task performance. The data for the study is drawn from two group discussion task performance of four student-candidates and students' and teacher-raters' comments on the interactions from stimulated recall interviews. The test was administered under two conditions: with extended planning time (4–5 h), and without extended planning time (10 min). Using a conversational analytic approach, audio-recorded transcribed test performance was analysed focusing on test candidates' ability/inability to spontaneously produce contingent responses to previous speakers' talk, and other features such as turn-taking, non-verbal behavior etc. It was found that extended planning time helped test-takers across the levels to produce responses contingent on previous speaker contribution, which resulting in impeding the assessment task's capacity to discriminate between stronger and weaker candidates. The paper discusses implications for the implementation of preparation time for the group interaction task.

Leeper, D. & Brawn, J. (2019). Detecting development of speaking proficiency with a group oral test: A quantitative analysis. *Language Testing 36*(2), 181–206.

The study investigated the changes in speaking proficiency over a two-year period using the group oral discussion test (GOT). Group discussion task was administered three times over the two years to 53 Japanese university English major students. Video-recorded test performances were rated with five criteria, and analysed with indices of complexity, accuracy, and fluency (CAF) as well as interactive function such as initiating, responding, developing, and collaborating functions. While some improvement with most of the CAF measures and interactive functions were observed over the three test administrations, the test-takers' scores in the five criteria only improved significantly in the second administration. The paper discusses possible reasons for this discrepancy and provide some suggestions for the GOT format and its administration.

Nitta, R & Nakatsuhara, F. (2014). A multifaceted approach to investigating pre-task planning effects on paired oral performance. *Language Testing 31*(2), 147–175.

The study investigates the effect of pre-task planning in a paired speaking test. Data were collected from 32 students who carried out two decision-making tasks in pairs under planned and unplanned conditions. The data for analyses includes test scores, test-taker discourse, and surveys conducted after the test administration. For discourse analysis, conversation analysis (CA) of test-taker discourse was employed to gain insights into co-constructing processes. The analysis of rating scores and discourse measures revealed limited effects of planning time on performance, and the analysis of the questionnaires did not indicate clear differences between the two conditions either. However, conversation analyses found a contrastive mode of discourse under the two planning conditions and the authors raised concerns about some negative effects of planning time on the opportunity to carry out the task collaboratively.

Ockey, G. J. (2014). The potential of the L2 group oral to elicit discourse with a mutual contingency pattern and afford equal speaking rights in an ESP context. *English for Specific Purposes 35*, 17–29.

The study investigated whether the group oral provides test takers with a sufficient opportunity to demonstrate their interactional competence in addition to their content knowledge in English for Specific Purposes context at an English-medium university in Japan. The group oral discourse of four groups (three members in each group) of graduate students who were studying English for international business was analysed employing a modified version of Keenen and Schieffelin's (1976) framework. The analysis includes measuring the degree to which the groups' discourse had a mutual contingency pattern as well as examining test takers' abilities to nominate and establish topics. The analyses revealed that all test-takers were able to nominate topics related to the two themes in the assigned discussion prompt, and roughly half of each group's nominated topics became established. These findings suggest that the group oral may be appropriate for assessing L2 oral ability as well as content knowledge of a particular field of study and can elicit discourse with a mutual contingency pattern. The research suggests, however, that various factors including the amount of time assigned for the discussion can impact the performance.

References

Bachman, L. F., & Palmer, A. S. (1996). *Language testing in practice*. Oxford University Press.

Berry, V. (2007). *Personality differences and oral test performance*. Peter Lang.

Bonk, W. J., & Ockey, G. J. (2003). A many-facet Rasch analysis of the second language group oral discussion task. *Language Testing, 20*(1), 89–110.

Davis, L. (2009). The influence of interlocutor proficiency in a paired oral assessment. *Language Testing, 26*(3), 367–396.

Ducasse, A. M., & Brown, A. (2009). Assessing paired orals: Raters' orientation to interaction. *Language Testing, 26*(3), 423–443.

Folland, D., & Robertson, D. (1976). Towards objectivity in group oral testing. *English Language Teaching Journal, 30*, 156–167.

Fulcher, G. (1996). Testing tasks: Issues in task design and the group oral. *Language Testing, 13*(1), 23–51.

Galaczi, E. (2008). Peer-peer interaction in a speaking test: The case of the First Certificate in English examination. *Language Assessment Quarterly, 5*(2), 89–119.

Ockey, G. J. (2009). The effects of group members' personalities on a test taker's L2 group oral discussion test scores. *Language Testing, 26*(2), 161–186.

Saville, N., & Hargreaves, P. (1999). Assessing speaking in the revised FCE. *English Language Teaching Journal, 53*(1), 42–51.

Shohamy, E., Reves, T., & Bejarano, T. (1986). Introducing a new comprehensive test of oral proficiency. *English Language Teaching Journal, 40*, 212–220.

Skehan, P. (2001). Tasks and language performance assessment. In M. Bygate, P. Skehan, & M. Swain (Eds.), *Researching pedagogic tasks, second language learning, teaching and testing* (pp. 167–185). Longman.

Taylor, L. (2000). Investigating the paired speaking test format. *Cambridge ESOL Research Notes, 2*, 14–15.

van Lier, L. (1989). Reeling, writhing, drawling, stretching and fainting in coils: Oral proficiency interviews as conversations. *TESOL Quarterly, 23*, 489–508.

Van Moere, A. (2006). Validity evidence in a university group oral test. *Language Testing, 23*, 411–440.

Noriko Iwashita is an Associate Professor in Applied Linguistics at The University of Queensland (UQ), teaching both undergraduate and postgraduate Applied Linguistics courses and supervising MA and Ph.D. students' research projects. For the past few years, Noriko has been involved in a large assessment project which aims at benchmarking assessment procedures in undergraduate foreign language courses against CEFR and a few assessment-related projects funded by IELTS and the British Council. Her research interests include the interfaces of language assessment and SLA, peer interaction in classroom-based research and task-based assessment, and cross-linguistic investigation of four major language traits. Her work has appeared in *Language Testing, Language Assessment Quarterly, Applied Linguistics, Language Learning* and *Studies in Second Language Acquisition* and many edited books.

Portfolio Assessment

Pauline Mak

Portfolio assessment has gained momentum in different educational settings in the past few decades (Burner, 2014). Defined as a purposeful and meaningful collection of students' work that documents their effort, progress and achievement in learning (Weigle, 2007), portfolio assessment is making a promising contribution as an alternative assessment method to impromptu essay testing and multiple-choice testing. In second language (L2) classroom writing contexts that implement portfolios, not only are students more meta cognitively aware of who they are as learners and engage more deeply in the writing process, they also have a stronger sense of responsibility and participation in the learning process, and a heightened level of self-determination (Nicolaidou, 2012; Yancey, 2009). Due to its ability to chronicle the students' learning progression over time and to offer a more comprehensive picture of students' writing ability, portfolios have blossomed into an alternative paradigm of writing (Davison & Leung, 2009; Hamp-Lyons, 2002).

Portfolios, according to Hamp-Lyons and Condon (2000), engage learners in the three-step process of collecting and selecting their own work as well as reflecting upon their performance. These three core components of a portfolio put learners at the heart of the learning process and encourage them to take control of their learning (Paulson et al., 1991). Another key characteristic of a portfolio is delayed evaluation, where teachers postpone the final assessment until students have had the opportunity to revise their drafts by incorporating feedback from peers and teachers before grading. Each step of the portfolio process, according to Belgrad (2013), promotes metacognition through ongoing monitoring, evaluation and reflection. In respect to the functions of assessment, a portfolio integrates summative and formative assessment (Ainsworth, 2007). Besides serving the summative function of assessing students' achievement, it enables learners to become more aware of their strengths and weaknesses as well as assume greater learner agency in the writing

P. Mak (✉)
The Education University of Hong Kong, Hong Kong, China
e-mail: pwwmak@eduhk.hk

© Springer Nature Switzerland AG 2021
H. Mohebbi and C. Coombe (eds.), *Research Questions in Language Education and Applied Linguistics*, Springer Texts in Education,
https://doi.org/10.1007/978-3-030-79143-8_66

process and allows the teacher to gain a better understanding of students' progress and to gauge their development in order to plan the next teaching steps. The portfolio thus integrates learning, teaching and assessment, and is a kind of formative assessment.

Despite the accolades found in research on portfolios, the implementation of portfolios in general has not made inroads into the L2 writing classroom context and is hamstrung by such factors as the prevalence of product-oriented writing pedagogy, the lack of assessment literacy on the part of the teachers, as well as the inadequacy of students' ability to make productive use of learning evidence from teachers, peers and themselves to make improvement in their learning (Lam, 2017; Mak & Wong, 2018). In the traditional product-oriented classroom where there is only one impromptu timed writing draft, assessment is detached from learning and does not afford students the opportunity to act on the teachers' feedback. Devoid of assessment competencies, teachers do not possess the knowledge and skills to provide appropriate guidance to students such as the provision of metacognitive instruction, which in turn results in students' impoverished knowledge in assessment. Research which taps into the alignment of these factors would be of significant value to support a wider spread of portfolio assessment.

The Research Questions

1. To what extent is portfolio assessment practised in second language writing?
2. What are the factors influencing the implementation of portfolio assessment in second language writing?
3. To what extent and how does the implementation of portfolio assessment enhance student writing motivation and engagement?
4. How does portfolio assessment promote metacognition?
5. How do teachers enable students to respond to feedback in portfolio assessment classrooms?
6. How do the different feedback types in portfolio assessment classrooms encourage text revision?
7. To what extent is portfolio assessment effective in improving students' writing performance?
8. What are the effects of portfolio assessment on teachers' attitudes towards the teaching of writing?
9. What are the effects of portfolio assessment on students' attitudes towards the learning of writing?
10. What challenges do teachers meet when integrating portfolio assessment into the writing classroom?

Suggested Resources

Carless, D. (2011). *From testing to productive student learning: Implementing formative assessment in Confucian-heritage settings.* **New York: Routledge.**

The aims of this book are to present the theoretical basis and practical application of formative assessment and its interrelationship with summative assessment, as well as the influence of socio-cultural forces on the implementation of formative assessment. Drawing upon a wide range of literature around the world, the author provides important insights into how teachers can make pragmatic adjustments to bring formative assessment into practice. As such, he discusses the way teachers can develop enhanced understanding of formative assessment and presents the constellation of factors that are at play to support them in changing their assessment practice. This book is highly recommended for readers who are interested in introducing an alternative form of assessment to improve teaching and learning in a context dominated by a summative orientation.

Hamp-Lyons, L., & Condon, W. (2000). *Assessing the portfolio: Principles for practice, theory and research.* **Cresskill, NJ: Hampton Press.**

Hamp-Lyons' book with Condon, which deals comprehensively and systematically with the topic of portfolio-based writing assessment, gives readers a sound grounding on what portfolio assessment is about, when and how they should be used. It thus provides easily accessible answers to questions on the most important areas of portfolio assessment. Situating the reader in the fundamental theoretical and practical issues of portfolio assessment, the authors include a thorough discussion of the types and characteristics of portfolios, lay out the benefits portfolios have for assessment purposes, as well as put forth the effects of portfolios on writing programmes.

Klenowski, V. (2002). *Developing portfolios for learning and assessment: Processes and principles.* **London: Routledge Falmer.**

Klenowski provides readers with an informative and practical guide to help them realize the potential of portfolios for assessment and learning purposes. Acknowledging that the alignment of assessment with curriculum, teaching and learning is the linchpin to the improvement of student learning, she discusses and explores their interrelationship with portfolio assessment, utilizing her extensive experiences in a variety of settings in Hong Kong, Australia and the US. By locating theory underpinning portfolio assessment and practice, she provides readers with practical examples of how to translate ideas into practice, identifies the problems and pitfalls and puts forward suggestions on the support needed to facilitate the successful implementation of portfolio assessment.

Lam, R. (2018). *Portfolio assessment for the teaching and learning of writing.* **Singapore: Springer.**

In this book Lam presents a comprehensive and integrated compilation of theory, research and practice on portfolio assessment. Organized around four central themes including conceptual and theoretical basis of portfolio assessment, its overarching principles, task design and approaches to scoring, as well as new directions for future research, the book provides theoretical insights into and specific pedagogical strategies for the implementation of portfolio assessment in different educational contexts. Concluding each chapter with discussion tasks, reflection tasks, evaluation tasks, mini-debate tasks, small-group activities or case studies, the author aims to provide pointers to further stimulate readers' reflection and generate discussion on the issues raised in the section, and help readers grasp the theories and practical know-how of portfolio assessment.

Lee, I. (2017). *Classroom writing assessment and feedback in L2 school contexts.* **Singapore: Springer.**

This book synthesises two intertwining key components of writing pedagogy and offers a critical examination of how classroom assessment and feedback can be utilized effectively to support student learning in the second language writing classroom. Drawing a crucial connection between assessment, learning and teaching, the author describes the key principles of effective classroom assessment and feedback practice. Linking current theories in second language writing to practice, this book offers a highly accessible, practical and valuable resource to both pre- and in-service teachers to develop effective classroom assessment and feedback in general. The practical pedagogical material such as feedback forms and assessment rubrics can be easily adapted to be used in a portfolio-based writing classroom at different education levels.

References

Ainsworth, L. (2007). Common formative assessments: The centerpiece of an integrated standards-based assessment system. In D. Reeves (Ed.), *Ahead of the curve: The power of assessment to transform teaching and learning* (pp. 79–102). Solution Tree.

Belgrad, S. F. (2013). Portfolios and e-portfolios: Student reflection, self-assessment, and global setting in the learning process. In J. H. McMillan (Ed.), *Sage handbook of research on classroom assessment* (pp. 331–346). Sage.

Burner, T. (2014). The potential formative benefits of portfolio assessment in second and foreign language writing contexts: A review of the literature. *Studies in Educational Evaluation, 43,* 139–149.

Davison, C., & Leung, C. (2009). Current issues in English language teacher-based assessment. *TESOL Quarterly, 43*(3), 393–415.

Hamp-Lyons, L. (2002). The scope of writing assessment. *Assessing Writing, 8*(1), 5–16.

Hamp-Lyons, L., & Condon, W. (2000). *Assessing the portfolio: Issues for research, theory and practice.* Hampton Press.

Lam, R. (2017). Taking stock of portfolio assessment scholarship: From research to practice. *Assessing Writing, 31,* 84–97.

Mak, P., & Wong, K. M. (2018). Self-regulation through portfolio assessment in writing classrooms. *ELT Journal, 72*(1), 49–61.

Nicolaidou, I. (2012). Can process portfolios affect students' writing self-efficacy? *International Journal of Educational Research, 56*, 10–22.

Paulson, F. L., Paulson, P. R., & Meyer, C. A. (1991). What makes a portfolio a portfolio? *Educational Leadership, 48*(5), 60–63.

Weigle, S. C. (2007). Teaching writing teachers about assessment. *Journal of Second Language Writing, 16*, 194–209.

Yancey, K. B. (2009). Electronic portfolios a decade into the twenty-first century: What we know, what we need to know. *Peer Review, 11*(1), 28–33.

Pauline Mak completed her doctoral study in English language education at the Faculty of Education of the Chinese University of Hong Kong. She is currently working as an assistant professor in the Department of English Language Education at the Education University of Hong Kong. Her research interests include language assessment, second language writing and second language teacher education. Her publications have appeared in *Canadian Modern Language Review, ELT Journal, English Teaching: Practice and Critique, International Journal of Applied Linguistics, Language Teaching Research, System, Teaching and Teacher Education, TESOL Quarterly*, as well as *The Asia–Pacific Education Researcher*.

Rachael Ruegg

Many experts have warned that providing too much constructive feedback can be overwhelming and damaging to a student's confidence (e.g. Bitchener & Ferris, 2012). However, studies of feedback on writing have involved the provision of as little as four instances of feedback on a single draft of a piece of writing. While the phrase 'too much feedback' often appears in research of feedback on writing, no one has attempted to find out how much feedback is too much.

Providing praise is another suggestion that has been made by experts in the field (e.g. Ferris, 2003; Grabe & Kaplan, 1996; Hyland, 1996). In fact, it has been suggested that feedback should consist of as much as 50% praise (Ferris & Hedgcock, 2014). On the other hand, it has also been found that too much praise can demotivate learners (Cleary, 1990; Cohen, 1987). Like constructive feedback, we need to be careful not to give too much praise so as not to demotivate learners. With praise too, there is a lack of empirical research investigating the appropriate quantity to provide to students.

It has been suggested that students have more autonomy in the feedback process by communicating their feedback preferences to the teacher through a range of different methods (Anson & Anson, 2017; Charles, 1990; Reid, 1993; Shvidko, 2015; Sommers, 1988). In practice, many writing teachers now ask their students to communicate what kind of feedback they would like to receive. Many different methods are used, such as different formats of feedback sheets and different methods of providing feedback. However, research has lagged behind pedagogical practice and there is a lack of research identifying the effects of student-led feedback processes and the effects of different formats and methods of communicating such requests and providing feedback in response to them.

R. Ruegg (✉)
School of Linguistics and Applied Language Studies, Victoria University of Wellington, Wellington, New Zealand
e-mail: rachael.ruegg@vuw.ac.nz

© Springer Nature Switzerland AG 2021
H. Mohebbi and C. Coombe (eds.), *Research Questions in Language Education and Applied Linguistics*, Springer Texts in Education, https://doi.org/10.1007/978-3-030-79143-8_67

The Research Questions

1. What is the optimum amount of constructive feedback for learners to receive on their writing?
2. What is the optimum amount of praise for learners to receive on their writing?
3. To what extent is it possible to encourage learners to become more autonomous through feedback provision?
4. How can different forms of feedback change a learner's writing processes?
5. Does the format of a feedback sheet affect the types of feedback learners request?
6. How does the format of a feedback sheet affect learners' reflective processes?
7. Does self-assessment affect the types of feedback learners request?
8. Does the method of providing feedback affect the types of feedback learners request?
9. How does the method of providing feedback affect learners' reflective processes?
10. How does self-assessment affect the affective effect of teacher feedback?

Suggested Resources

Ferris, D. (2003). *Response to Student Writing: Implications for second language students.* **Lawrence Erlbaum Associates.**

This book starts by providing an overview of the history of second language writing and the way in which the field emerged out of the L1 composition field. It provides a comprehensive review of literature on teacher feedback, error correction and peer feedback, before providing several chapters of specific pedagogical suggestions for teachers who would like to improve their practice in providing teacher feedback, providing error correction or implementing peer feedback in their classrooms. This is a very useful reference book for understanding and critical analysis of the literature in the area of providing feedback to second language writers.

Hyland, K. & Hyland, F. (2006). *Feedback in Second Language Writing: Contexts and issues.* **Cambridge University Press.**

This is an edited collection of studies on providing feedback on second language writing. It contains a number of important studies in the area, covering topics such as appropriation of student writing through feedback, electronic feedback, providing feedback through teacher student conferences, providing feedback to writing portfolios, the development of learner autonomy through feedback provision, and contextual and interpersonal variables in the provision of feedback. This book takes a deeper look at feedback than most other books in the area, considering the importance of socio-cultural and interpersonal factors and the crucial role of context rather than merely the effect of feedback on grammatical accuracy.

Crusan, D. (2010). *Assessment in the second language writing classroom.* **University of Michigan Press.**

This is a comprehensive practical sourcebook for teachers who are interested in applying sound assessment practices in their classrooms. The book starts with the history and theoretical background of the assessment of writing before introducing all the different considerations at play when we assess students' written work. The book then provides practical guidance on how to design assessment tasks and tools, as well as how to limit bias in writing assessment. Finally, large scale writing tests are introduced and current and future applications of technology in the assessment of writing are evaluated. This book offers very practical guidance on a wide range of methods of assessing writing that can be applied by classroom practitioners.

Ferris, D. & Hedgcock, J. (2014). *Teaching ESL composition: Purpose, process and practice.* **Routledge.**

This book provides a broad overview of overarching themes in the field of writing in an additional language. It describes different groups of students who often learn to write in an additional language and the different contexts in which they often study. It provides a general overview of the broad theories of learning, both cognitive and pedagogical, as well as how to plan a curriculum for a course on writing in an additional language. It provides an overview of classroom assessment practices, and the provision and facilitation of feedback on writing. The final two chapters zoom in on the micro-level of the L2 writing classroom and focus on how to provide feedback on issues related to language accuracy and how to incorporate a focus on form in a composition classroom context. In providing an overview of a large number of concepts, pedagogical ideas and practices, it is a useful introductory guide for those who do not have background in the area of teaching writing.

Bitchener, J., Storch, N. & Wette, R. (2017). *Teaching writing for academic purposes to multilingual students: Instructional approaches.* **Routledge.**

This book focusses specifically on the effective (and ineffective) instructional approaches in the context of EAP writing. The book is a collection of chapters from big names in the field of L2 writing. The areas covered include instructional approaches in EAP in the university context, instructional approaches in genre-based instruction, and instructional approaches to increasing language accuracy in writing. The book is not presented as a cohesive text to be read from cover to cover, but rather as a reference book. I personally would strongly recommend reading the two final chapters of the book: Future research in EAP and Epilogue, even if time does not allow for reading the entire volume.

References

Anson, I., & Anson, C. (2017). Assessing peer and instructor response to writing: A corpus analysis from an expert survey. *Assessing Writing, 33*, 12–24.

Bitchener, J., & Ferris, D. (2012). *Written corrective feedback in second language acquisition and writing*. Routledge.

Charles, M. (1990). Responding to problems in written English using a student self-monitoring technique. *ELT Journal, 44*(4), 286–293.

Cleary, L. (1990). The fragile inclination to write: Praise and criticism in the classroom. *English Journal, 79*(2), 22–28.

Cohen, A. (1987). Student processing of feedback on their compositions. In A. Wenden & J. Rubin (Eds.) *Learner strategies in language learning*. Prentice-Hall.

Ferris, D. (2003). *Response to student writing*. Lawrence Erlbaum Associates.

Ferris, D., & Hedgcock, J. (2014). *Teaching ESL composition: Purpose, process and practice*. Lawrence Erlbaum Associates.

Grabe, W., & Kaplan, R. (1996). *Theory and practice of writing*. Pearson Education.

Hyland, K. (1996). *Second language writing*. Cambridge.

Reid, J. (1993). *Teaching ESL writing*. Prentice Hall.

Shvidko, E. (2015). Beyond "Giver-Receiver" relationships: Facilitating an interactive revision process. *Journal of Response to Writing, 1*(2), 55–74.

Sommers, J. (1988). Behind the paper: Using the student-teacher memo. *College Composition and Communication, 39*(1), 77–80.

Rachael Ruegg has a Ph.D. in Linguistics from Macquarie University, Australia. She is currently a Senior Lecturer in the School of Linguistics and Applied Language Studies at Victoria University of Wellington, New Zealand, where she coordinates and teaches courses in the Academic and Professional Writing Programme as well as supervises doctoral candidates in Applied Linguistics. She has more than 15 years teaching experience in New Zealand, Japan, Germany and China. She has published numerous articles related to her research interests: Instruction, feedback and classroom assessment of writing, learner autonomy, English for Academic Purposes and English-medium Instruction in non-Anglophone contexts.

The Role of the Rater in Writing Assessment

Sara T. Cushing

One of the most challenging aspects of writing assessment is ensuring that raters adhere to agreed-upon standards in evaluating written work. This is true for both classroom teachers and international testing programs. For a test to be fair, it must be both reliable and valid. In terms of raters, reliability means that raters agree with each other, so that a script will receive the same or similar scores no matter who assigns those scores. Validity has to do with whether the criteria used to evaluate the writing are meaningful for the testing purpose, and whether raters actually use those criteria in assigning scores.

Much of the research on raters in writing has focused on the process of rating; that is, how raters interact with rating scales, how they balance various aspects of the scale such as language and content, and what features both within the text itself and external to the text affect this process. Textual features range from somewhat superficial features such as handwriting to more complex features such as how writers incorporate language from source texts in their writing. One area that has received a fair amount of attention, given the increase in the use of computers in education and testing, is whether raters are affected by the differences between writing done by hand or on a computer. Beyond the text itself, research has demonstrated that raters can be influenced by their expectations and biases, by the order in which texts are read, the type of scale used (holistic or analytic), and by background characteristics of raters such as first language, teaching experience, and experience as a rater (see Weigle, 2002; Shaw & Weir, 2007, for overviews of this research).

An important factor in achieving reliable and valid rating is rater training. Research in this area suggests that training can go a long way towards reducing variability among raters but that this variability is not possible to eliminate; rather

S. T. Cushing (✉)
Department of Applied Linguistics & ESL, Georgia State University, Atlanta, GA, USA
e-mail: stcushing@gsu.edu

© Springer Nature Switzerland AG 2021
H. Mohebbi and C. Coombe (eds.), *Research Questions in Language Education and Applied Linguistics*, Springer Texts in Education,
https://doi.org/10.1007/978-3-030-79143-8_68

than trying to avoid variability, then, efforts have been made to understand it and adjust for it statistically (see, for example, Eckes, 2009).

Recent advances have been made in computer scoring of writing and in comparing human ratings with computer scores (see Weigle, 2013 for an overview). This is an expanding area of research as artificial intelligence and machine learning become more widespread.

The Research Questions

1. What is more important in reliable rating—background or training?
2. What features of texts (relevant to the construct of interest, or not) do raters attend to in assigning scores?
3. What aspects of rating scales influence how raters evaluate writing?
4. What aspects of the scoring situation influence rater reliability and validity?
5. How do human ratings compare to ratings generated by automated scoring systems?
6. What background variables (e.g., first language, education, teaching experience) affect rater behavior?
7. Is there a relationship between certain background variables and tendency to prioritize one aspect of writing (e.g., content) over others (e.g., linguistic accuracy)?
8. Are consistency and severity stable traits in raters or do they change over time?
9. What are the effects of different text types (e.g., narrative, expository, independent vs source-based writing) on rater reliability?
10. What are the psychometric implications of different methods for resolving discrepant ratings?

Suggested Resources

Barkaoui, K. (2010). Variability in ESL essay rating processes: The role of the rating scale and rater experience. *Language Assessment Quarterly*, *7*(1), 54–74.

Barkaoui's paper is an example of the use of think-aloud protocols in examining how raters make scoring decisions in assessing writing. Barkaoui examined the think-aloud protocols of 11 novice and 14 experienced raters as they scored 12 essays both holistically and analytically, finding that the scale had more of an influence on raters' decision making than did rater experience. In his paper, Barkaoui reviews relevant literature on the use of think-aloud protocols in rater research, the variable of rater experience, and different scale types.

Deane, P. (2013). On the relation between automated essay scoring and modern views of the writing construct. *Assessing Writing*, *18*(1), 7–24.

This is a paper from a special issue of *Assessing Writing* on assessing writing with automated scoring systems. Deane's paper provides an excellent overview of automated essay scoring systems, outlines the relationships between automated and human scores, addresses common critiques of automated scoring, and outlines a principled way to determine when automated scoring can be appropriate and when it should be eschewed. Future directions for research on automated scoring are also provided.

Humphry, S., & Heldsinger, S. (2019). Raters' perceptions of assessment criteria relevance. *Assessing Writing*, *41*, 1–13.

This is a qualitative study of how the criteria raters used to rank order pairs of writing performances. Using a rubric consisting of ten criteria, raters recorded which criteria were relevant to making their decisions. The authors found that criteria related to authorial aspects of writing were more frequently perceived as relevant than writing conventions such as punctuation and spelling.

Schaefer, E. (2008). Rater bias patterns in an EFL writing assessment. *Language Testing*, *25*(4), 465–493.

This paper presents a useful introduction to multi-faceted Rasch measurement (MFRM), which is a statistical tool that is useful for modeling rater consistency and severity. Schaefer's study investigates a group of raters in terms of the reliability of the rating scale, differences between raters in how they rate different aspects of performance, and patterns of weighing different categories in assigning scores. The author found that raters who evaluated content and organization more strictly tended to be more lenient when rating language use and/or mechanics, and vice versa.

Shaw, S, D., & Weir, C. J. (2007). *Examining writing: Research and practice in assessing second language writing.* **Cambridge: Cambridge ESOL/Cambridge University Press.**

This volume, one in a series of books on language testing published by Cambridge University Press, outlines the approach to writing assessment taken by a major testing company. While the main focus of the book is on the Cambridge suite of tests, it provides an excellent review of research on writing assessment and presents detailed research-based practices that can be useful to anyone interested in writing assessment. A lengthy chapter on scoring validity provides a wealth of information on rating scales, rater selection and training, and the rating process.

Weigle, S. C. (2002). *Assessing Writing.* **Cambridge: Cambridge University Press.**

This highly-cited volume provides a comprehensive overview of writing assessment, with chapters devoted to the nature of writing ability, research on writing assessment, developing assessment tasks, and scoring procedures for writing assessment. The chapter on research discusses task and rater variables and their interaction, and the chapter on scoring covers types of rating scales and the process of organizing scoring sessions and monitoring raters for consistency of scoring. There are also chapters on classroom assessment of writing and portfolio assessment.

References

Eckes, T. (2009). Many-facet Rasch measurement. *Reference supplement to the manual for relating language examinations to the Common European Framework of Reference for Languages: Learning, teaching, assessment. Programs for all students: Validity, technical adequacy, and implementation* (pp. 261–287).

Shaw, S, D., & Weir, C. J. (2007). *Examining writing: Research and practice in assessing second language writing.* Cambridge ESOL/Cambridge University Press.

Weigle, S. C. (2002). *Assessing writing.* Cambridge University Press.

Weigle, S. C. (2013). English language learners and automated scoring of essays: Critical considerations. *Assessing Writing, 18*(1), 85–99.

Sara T. Cushing (also known as Sara Cushing Weigle) is Professor of Applied Linguistics and Senior Faculty Associate for the Assessment of Student Learning at Georgia State University. She has published research in the areas of assessment, second language writing, and teacher education, and is the author of *Assessing Writing* (2002, Cambridge University Press). She has been invited to speak and conduct workshops on second language writing assessment throughout the world, most recently in Norway, Thailand, Colombia, and Vietnam. Her current research focuses on assessing integrated skills and the use of automated scoring for second language writing.

Second Language Vocabulary Assessment

69

John Read

Given its long history in language education, vocabulary testing may simply be taken for granted in many contexts as an essential tool for measuring progress and achievement in the classroom. Vocabulary tests can also have a role in placing incoming students at the appropriate level in a language teaching programme and in providing diagnostic information on the adequacy of learners' vocabulary knowledge. At the school level, the tests are typically teacher-made, published in the course book, or taken from some other source. Even with such ready-made tests, there is scope for action research in schools to ensure that the test is well written, has an appropriate level of difficulty and has a positive motivating effect on the learners.

In order to consider vocabulary assessment more broadly, it is useful to adopt Read's (2000) distinction between discrete and embedded measures. A conventional vocabulary test is **discrete** in that it simply measures whether learners can link the forms of a set of L2 words and their meanings, with little if any context provided. Among the most influential tests of this kind are the Vocabulary Levels Test (VLT) (Webb et al., 2017), which uses a word—definition matching format, and the Vocabulary Size Test (VST) (Beglar, 2010), consisting of multiple-choice items. Both these tests have generated a significant amount of research, focusing on issues such as the value of using bilingual versions of the test tailored for learners with particular first languages, and the effect of guessing behaviour on test scores.

There are three dimensions of vocabulary knowledge that have not received much attention in the design of discrete vocabulary tests until recently. The first is the measurement of aspects of word knowledge other than the basic meaning. These include: multiple and extended meanings, grammatical functioning, associations and collocations with other words, and style or register. These aspects are collectively known as "depth" of knowledge. In a recent review of the research, Schmitt

J. Read (✉)

School of Cultures, Languages and Linguistics, University of Auckland, Auckland, New Zealand

e-mail: ja.read@auckland.ac.nz

© Springer Nature Switzerland AG 2021

H. Mohebbi and C. Coombe (eds.), *Research Questions in Language Education and Applied Linguistics*, Springer Texts in Education,

https://doi.org/10.1007/978-3-030-79143-8_69

(2014) found some evidence that depth represents a distinct dimension of knowledge, but he noted a lack of validated tests to measure it as a single construct. However, it is becoming standard practice in research on vocabulary learning to measure the outcomes by means of multiple post-tests, each targeting one aspect of word knowledge. The second neglected dimension is comprehension of words in their spoken form, ie, listening vocabulary tests. And the third is speed of access: measuring reaction times to discrete vocabulary items on a computer-based test. In a series of studies, Harrington (2018) has shown that speed of response adds to the predictive power of a vocabulary test designed as a measure of learners' language proficiency.

Read's other approach to the topic, **embedded** vocabulary assessment, refers to the role of lexical measures in more communicatively oriented tests. Thus, in a reading comprehension test, some test items may assess understanding of words and phrases in the context of the reading passage. In speaking and writing tasks, the test-takers' use of vocabulary is often assessed, either by means of an analytic rating scale, or by applying statistics to measure diversity, sophistication and appropriateness, taking into account all the words in the learners' output. These lexical statistics play a prominent role in the automated scoring of speaking and/or writing tasks in international tests like the Pearson Test of English and the Test of English as a Foreign Language.

The Research Questions

1. Is a particular published test useful for its intended purpose in a local school setting?
2. To what extent does guessing behaviour play a role in vocabulary tests with selected-response items, and how can its effects be minimized?
3. What are the different aspects of vocabulary knowledge that learners can acquire from participating in a vocabulary learning study?
4. What are suitable measures of particular aspects of vocabulary knowledge, such as derived forms, extended meanings, collocations and appropriate usage?
5. How can word association techniques be used effectively to evaluate learners' vocabulary knowledge?
6. How does learners' knowledge of spoken vocabulary compare with their written vocabulary knowledge?
7. What are some effective means of measuring knowledge of multi-word units, such as phrasal verbs, collocations, formulaic expressions and idioms?
8. How can we measure learners' ability to activate their receptive knowledge of words for productive use?
9. How can lexical statistics contribute to the assessment of speaking and writing tasks?
10. To what extent can measurement of learners' reaction times contribute to the ability of a vocabulary test to predict communicative performance?

Suggested Resources

Read, J. (2000). *Assessing Vocabulary.* **Cambridge: Cambridge University Press**.

This is the first and most comprehensive book on the topic. It introduced the distinction between discrete and embedded assessment of vocabulary and explored the design issues related to each of these approaches. It also takes a critical perspective on some key concepts related to vocabulary assessment. There is a review of research to that time on the use of vocabulary tests for various purposes in language teaching and second language acquisition research. The book includes case studies of several influential vocabulary tests, along with a discussion of the published evidence for their validity. It is still an essential reference for anyone undertaking research on vocabulary assessment or engaged in the development of vocabulary tests.

Schmitt, N. (2010). *Researching Vocabulary: A Vocabulary Research Manual.* **Basingstoke: Palgrave Macmillan**.

This is an invaluable resource for anyone whose research focuses on second language vocabulary knowledge and ability, written by one of the most productive researchers in the field. Its coverage is much broader than just assessment but it includes a substantial chapter on measurement. A very useful section for novice researchers is one on "prominent knowledge gaps in the field of vocabulary studies". The Resources section at the end provides a wealth of practical information about tests, corpora, statistical tools, bibliographies and websites. A little frustratingly for a reference work, the book lacks an index, but this is partly compensated for by a reasonably detailed table of contents and a "quick checklist" of questions the reader may be seeking answers to.

Nation, I.S.P., & Webb, S. (2011). *Researching and Analyzing Vocabulary.* **Boston: Heinle ELT**.

This book, by two other very prominent researchers in the field, covers much of the same ground as Schmitt's volume. It is organised into a series of chapters which each deals with one of the major topics in L2 vocabulary research, under the categories of deliberate vocabulary learning, incidental vocabulary learning and corpus-based research. The chapters include critiques of published studies and suggestions for future research. The longest section of the book comprises four chapters on testing vocabulary knowledge, which give detailed advice on the issues faced by researchers in selecting or designing appropriate assessment tools.

Meara, P. & Miralpeix, I. (2016). *Tools for Researching Vocabulary*. **Bristol: Multilingual Matters**.

For many years Paul Meara directed a successful doctoral programme and research group on vocabulary acquisition at Swansea University. His approach to L2 vocabulary studies is more psycholinguistic in its orientation than that of other scholars in the field and it has also involved the development of multiple computer-based measurement tools, drawing on Meara's interest in programming. The current versions of many of these programs are freely available on his website: www.lognostics.co.uk. This book, co-authored with Imma Miralpeix, is partly a manual on how to use the tools, but it also provides background on the research issue that each tool was designed to address, as well as a published research study in which the tool was employed. Since it is intended for use by students and other beginning researchers, the book includes practical advice and stimulating suggestions for small-scale studies that can be carried out with these tools.

Webb, S. (Ed.) (2020). *The Routledge Handbook of Vocabulary Studies*. **London: Routledge**.

Stuart Webb has assembled this impressive volume, which covers all aspects of research and professional practice in the study of second language vocabulary. It includes a survey chapter on key issues in designing discrete vocabulary tests, as well as a set of six chapters discussing how to measure particular components of vocabulary ability: depth of word knowledge, knowledge of multiword items, vocabulary learning progress, the ability to learn words, vocabulary knowledge and lexical processing, and lexical richness.

References

Beglar, D. (2010). A Rasch-based validation of the Vocabulary Size Test. *Language Testing, 27* (1), 101–118.

Harrington, M. (2018). *Lexical facility*. Palgrave Macmillan.

Read, J. (2000). *Assessing vocabulary*. Cambridge University Press.

Schmitt, N. (2014). Size and depth of vocabulary knowledge: What the research shows. *Language Learning, 64*(4), 913–951.

Webb, S., Sasao, Y., & Balance, O. (2017). The updated Vocabulary Levels Test: Developing and validating two new forms of the VLT. *ITL—International Journal of Applied Linguistics, 168* (1), 34–70.

John Read is Professor Emeritus in the School of Cultures, Languages and Linguistics at the University of Auckland, New Zealand. His PhD is from the University of New Mexico. He previously taught at Victoria University of Wellington, the SEAMEO Regional Language Centre in Singapore, the University of Texas-El Paso, and Indiana University. Throughout his career he has specialized in language testing and assessment, with a focus on vocabulary assessment and testing English for academic and professional purposes. His major publications are *Assessing Vocabulary* (Cambridge, 2000), *Assessing English Proficiency for University Study* (Palgrave Macmillan, 2015), and *Post-admission Language Assessment of University Students* (edited) (Springer, 2016). He was co-editor of *Language Testing* (2002–06) and served as President of the International Language Testing Association (ILTA) in 2011–12.

Self-assessment

Yuko Goto Butler

Self-assessment (SA) is a type of assessment that learners can use to evaluate their own knowledge and skills. As a self-directive activity that can promote learners' reflective abilities, SA is unique. The self-directive nature of SA corresponds well with modern learning theories and practice, such as learner-centered teaching, self-reflective and self-regulated learning, autonomous learning, and assessment-for-learning. Reflecting SA's growing popularity among educators, classroom learning materials increasingly include SA items. SA can be used for both summative and formative purposes. It can be used in conjunction with other types of assessment, such as portfolios, and it may also be used as an alternative to objective measurements. SA grids and can-do statements have been developed for different purposes and for different target learner groups; examples include can-do statements prepared by the American Council on the Teaching of Foreign Languages (ACTFL) and the Common European Framework of Reference (CEFR).

The subjective nature of SA can have different implications depending on the purpose of its use. If the primary purpose of SA is to consistently make accurate inferences about a learner's "true" abilities (i.e., assessment of learning), the subjectivity of SA is a potential threat to the validity and reliability of the assessment. Empirical research has shown that SA can be a valid and reliable assessment of learning, particularly among adult learners, but a number of factors influence the degree of validity and reliability. Such factors include the target language domains/skills being assessed, item wording, learning environment, and learners' personality, age, affective conditions, and past experience with SA.

If the primary purpose of SA is to inform and assist a learner's ongoing learning (i.e., assessment for learning), the self-directive nature of SA should be conceptualized differently. Validity concerns regarding SA when it is used for learning include the extent to which SA can help students to reflect on their own learning

Y. G. Butler (✉)
Graduate School of Education, University of Pennsylvania, Philadelphia, PA, USA
e-mail: ybutler@gse.upenn.edu

© Springer Nature Switzerland AG 2021
H. Mohebbi and C. Coombe (eds.), *Research Questions in Language Education and Applied Linguistics*, Springer Texts in Education,
https://doi.org/10.1007/978-3-030-79143-8_70

processes and outcomes, which in turn can promote their motivation and learning. To maximize the effective use of SA for learning, educators should (a) make sure that learners sufficiently understand the assessment criteria and purpose of conducting SA; (b) construct contextualized items for learners that focus on the process of learning itself; (c) implement SA appropriately based on learners' age, experience with SA, and instructional goals; and (d) provide students with meaningful feedback.

Compared with research on SA from the "assessment of learning" perspective, empirical investigations of SA from the "assessment for learning" perspective remain relatively limited. Suggested topics for research on SA for learning include: (a) What do learners' self-reflective processes look like during SA?; (b) How do learners and teachers use and interpret SA results?; (c) What are the long-term effects of SA on learners' motivation and learning?; (d) How do social, educational, and cultural contexts influence learners' use of SA and its effectiveness for learning?; (e) How do learners' individual differences (e.g., age, proficiency levels, experiences, personality) influence the way they use SA and the effectiveness of SA for learning?; and (f) How can SA be used in nontraditional digital-based learning (e.g., Massive open online courses, MOOCs) in order to maximize learners' motivation and learning?

The Research Questions

1. What is self-assessment (SA)? What exactly does it capture?
2. What individual factors influence a student's accuracy of SA (i.e., relations between a student's SA responses and his/her knowledge and skill levels that are externally measured)?
3. How do the implementation and procedures of SA influence its validity and reliability?
4. To what extent can young learners accurately and consistently self-assess their linguistic knowledge and skills?
5. How do teachers construct SA items in order to obtain information about their students' ongoing learning and/or learning processes?
6. What kinds of experiences and assistance do students need in order to self-assess their linguistic knowledge and skills?
7. How do teachers use SA to primarily assist their students' self-reflective abilities, autonomy, and motivation as well as language learning?
8. What kinds of feedback from teachers would be useful for student learning based on their SA responses?
9. How is SA incorporated into various types of instruction (e.g., flipped classrooms, virtual classrooms, game-based learning, etc.)?
10. How do social, cultural, and educational contexts of learning/teaching influence the use and effectiveness of SA?

Suggested Resources

Oscarson, M. (2013). Self-assessment in the classroom. In A. Kunnan (ed.), *The companion to language assessment, Vol. II: Approaches and development* **(pp. 712–729). New York: Wiley-Blackwell.**

This concise but comprehensive overview of SA focuses on the use of SA for learning in language classrooms. After locating SA in historical and theoretical contexts and identifying favorable conditions for implementing SA in language education, the chapter provides cases where SA has been successfully incorporated into instruction. Examples include the *European Language Portfolio* (ELP) based on the *Common European Framework of Reference for Languages* (CEFR) and two projects—one using web-based SA materials and the other using SA to highlight the process of writing—undertaken in Sweden. The chapter concludes with suggestions for future research.

Ross, S. (1998). Self-assessment in second language testing: A meta-analysis and analysis of experimental factors. *Language Testing, 15*(1), 1–19.

This article includes both (a) a meta-analysis of concurrent validity studies of SA and (b) an experimental study comparing the effects of two SA item types. The meta-analysis was conducted on 60 correlations between learners' SA responses and second language proficiency measures. The results reveal robust relationships between SA and criterion measures but also show substantial variability across studies. The correlations are higher in receptive skill domains (reading and listening) than in productive skill domains (speaking and writing), a finding which is contrary to general beliefs about this issue. The author attributed this result to the learners' greater experience with receptive activities. The experimental study in the second part of the paper confirms the hypothesis regarding the effect of experience. Specifically, the students were more accurate when SA items matched the tasks that they experienced (experience-based SA) than when SA items referred to more general proficiency (abstract SA). The article also addresses issues associated with conducting the meta-analyses and interpreting its results.

Little, D. (2009). Language learner autonomy and the European Language Portfolio: Two L2 English examples. *Language Teaching, 42*(2), 222–233.

This article outlines the key concept underlying the Council of Europe's European Language Portfolio (ELP): namely, language learner autonomy. After defining language learner autonomy, the author explains how this concept was realized in the ELP through goal setting and self-assessment. Two case studies among English-as-a-second language learners in Ireland (adult immigrants and primary school students) nicely illustrate how language learner autonomy was cultivated through the ELP. The author argues that SA "is not a matter of learners simply ticking off the tasks they claim they can perform" but rather "an interactive process guided by the teachers, supported by peer assessment, and validated by the evidence that learners provide in support of their claims" (p. 230).

Butler, Y. G. (2016). Self-assessment of and for young learners' foreign language learning. In M. Nikolov (ed.), *Assessing young learners of English: Global and local perspectives* **(pp. 291–315). New York: Springer.**

This chapter focuses on self-assessment for young learners (defined as children up to the end of primary school years). It discusses issues related to validity and subjectivity of self-assessment both from the *assessment of learning* and *assessment for learning* perspectives, while paying special attention to children's cognitive and social-cognitive development as well as their specific learning environments. The chapter also classifies existing self-assessment items for young learners based on the following five dimensions: "(a) domain setting; (b) scale setting; (c) goal setting; (d) focus of assessment; and (e) method of assessment" (p. 291). This classification can be a useful framework for teachers and researchers when developing self-assessment for young learners.

Black, P., Harrison, C., Lee, C., Marshall, B., & Wiliam, D. (2003). *Assessment for learning: Putting it into practice.* **Berkshire, U.K.: Open University Press.**

This book reports on a two-year case study conducted at six secondary schools involving 36 teachers in the U.K. It provides detailed descriptions of how participating teachers interpreted and implemented formative assessment in their classrooms. Although the study did not focus on self-assessment per se, self-assessment nonetheless played a critical role in their project as part of formative assessment. The teachers' trial-and-error implementation process and their reflections during the process provide rich and insightful information on the possibilities and challenges of putting formative assessment into practice. Their struggles reveal that self-assessment is not an easy task for students. As with Little (2009) above, this book makes clear that even though self-assessment is considered a self-directed activity in theory, in practice it can be very social. This is because teachers and peers play an important role in the meaningful implementation of SA, at least in the initial stages.

Yuko Goto Butler is a professor of Educational Linguistics at the Graduate School of Education at the University of Pennsylvania. She is also the director of the Teaching English to Speakers of Other Languages (TESOL) Program at Penn. Her research primarily focuses on improving second/foreign language education among young learners in the United States and Asia in response to the diverse needs of an increasingly globalizing world. She is also interested in identifying effective ways to use technology in instruction as well as in finding assessment methods that take into account the relevant linguistic and cultural contexts in which instruction takes place for young learners.

Strategic Competence: The Concept and its Role in Language Assessment

71

A. Mehdi Riazi

Ever since Canale and Swain (1980) introduced the "communicative competence" model, there has been enormous attention to this concept from researchers and practitioners. Canale and Swain initially introduced three components, namely, "linguistic competence", "sociolinguistic competence", and "strategic competence" in their model of communicative competence. However, later on, Canale (1983) added a fourth component, that of "discourse competence". In fact, Canale and Swain were the first researchers who included "strategic competence" in their model.

Canale and Swain's concept of "strategic competence" was merely focused on compensation strategies. That is, their conception of strategic competence was related to the language users' ability to recognize and repair communication breakdowns when they were involved in a communication event. They defined the concept of strategic competence as a competence "made up of verbal and nonverbal communication strategies that may be called into action to compensate for breakdowns in communication due to performance variables or to insufficient competence" (Canale & Swain, 1980, p. 30). For example, when talking to an interlocutor, a language user may not know a specific word to convey an intended meaning. In that case, they could use an "avoidance" strategy and instead use a word they knew and was close in meaning to the word they were looking for. Alternatively, they could use a "paraphrase" strategy to convey the meaning of the unknown word or concept. On the other hand, language users may use gestures, facial expressions, and intonation patterns to complete face-to-face conversations.

Later on, researchers like Bachman (1990) and Bachman and Palmer (1996) drew on Canale and Swain's model and contributed to a more advanced conceptualization of communicative competence by presenting their "communicative language abil-

A. M. Riazi (✉)
Department of Linguistics, Macquarie University, Sydney, Australia
e-mail: mehdi.riazi@mq.edu.au; ariazi@hbku.edu.qa

College of Humanities and Social Sciences, Middlebury Institute of International Studies at Monterey, Monterey, CA, USA

© Springer Nature Switzerland AG 2021
H. Mohebbi and C. Coombe (eds.), *Research Questions in Language Education and Applied Linguistics*, Springer Texts in Education,
https://doi.org/10.1007/978-3-030-79143-8_71

ity" (CLA) model. Bachman (1990) defined strategic competence to include the following three components:

- Assessment of the situation and achieving the communicative goal in that situation
- Planning for retrieving the required and relevant knowledge structures and language knowledge to act successfully in the situation, and
- Execution of the communicative event.

Bachman and Palmer (1996) further elaborated on the CLA model and the role of strategic competence. In their model, Bachman and Palmer reconceptualized "strategic competence" to include what in the literature (see, e.g., O'Malley & Chamot, 1990) is called "metacognitive strategies". In their reformulation of CLA, Bachman and Palmer (1996) considered strategic competence to consist of the following metacognitive strategies:

- Goal setting (identifying one or more tasks the language user wishes to complete)
- Assessment (assessing what is needed in terms of knowledge structures and language knowledge and how well one has done it), and
- Planning (retrieving relevant items such as grammatical, textual, illocutionary, and sociolinguistic from language competence and formulating a plan which when acted upon is expected to achieve the communicative goal).

The important point that Bachman and Palmer (1996) make is that strategic competence plays a significant mediating role among other CLA components, namely, knowledge of the world, knowledge of language, and context of the situation. It, therefore, plays a far more important role than the compensation strategies perceived in Canale and Swain's (1980) communicative competence model. This point was highlighted by Bachman (1990, p. 100) where he asserted that strategic competence is "an important part of all communicative language use, not just that in which language abilities are deficient and must be compensated for by other means."

Since Bachman (1990) and Bachman and Palmer (1996) introduced their CLA and a modified conceptualization of strategic competence, many researchers (see, e.g., McNamara, 1996; Phakiti, 2003; Purpura, 1998, 1999) have investigated the nature and function of strategic competence in different contexts and as related to different communication skills. Notwithstanding the significant contribution of Bachman and Palmer (1996) and subsequent studies on the conceptualization and understanding of strategic competence, there are still some key research questions to be addressed in future studies on this important construct. Further studies are especially crucial given other researchers such as McNamara (1996) contended that the model proposed by Bachman and Palmer is only 'preliminary' as such strategic use in their model touches on major topics in cognitive and social psychology and pragmatics. In addition, Purpura (1999) asserted that the metacognitive strategies included in Bachman and Palmer's strategic competence are not based on empirical research. Accordingly, the research questions presented in the next section are deemed crucial if we are to gain a better understanding of strategic competence.

The Research Questions

1. What evidence from empirical data and analysis can we provide to support the construct and constituents of strategic competence as related to communicative language ability?
2. To what extent can we provide evidence from empirical data and analysis in favour of a generic strategic competence related to different communication skills?
3. To what extent might the construct of strategic competence be similar or different in oral (listening and speaking) and written (reading and writing) proficiency?
4. To what extent might the construct of strategic competence be different for each of the four communication skills (listening, reading, speaking, and writing)?
5. If the role of strategic competence is to mediate between the external situational context and the internal cognitive knowledge in communicative language ability model (Bachman & Palmer, 1996), how does this mediation function?
6. How might language users' characteristics including personal attributes such as gender, age, native language and culture, and background knowledge affect their strategic competence?
7. How would other socio-psychological factors such as motivation, attitude, and level of anxiety affect language users' strategic competence?
8. How might level of language proficiency (beginning, intermediate, and advanced) affect language users' strategic competence?
9. How might context (ESL vs. EFL) affect language user's strategic competence?
10. How might other contexts (such as test vs. real-life situation) affect language users' strategic competence?

Suggested Resources

Chalhoub-Deville, M. (2003). Second language interaction: Current perspectives and future trends. *Language Testing, 20*(4), 369–383.

Chalhoub-Deville's (2003) model of "an ability-in writer-in context" model is driven by arguments presented by McNamara (1996), Young (2000), and Johnson (2001) who asserted that while Bachman's (1990) and Bachman and Palmer's (1996) model of Communicative Language Ability (CLA) "does address issues related to language use, it remains a psycholinguistic ability model"

(Chalhoub-Deville, 2003, p. 370). These researchers believe that CLA ignores the synergic interaction of language ability and the context in which language is used. Consequently, "an ability-in writer-in context" is drawn from Douglas (2000), Swain (2001), and Bachman's (2002a, b) revisions of the CLA model, and represents an interactional competence and "claims that the ability components the language user brings to the situation or context interact with situational facets to change those facets as well as to be changed by them" (Chalhoub-Deville, 2003, p. 372). Strategic competence is seen to mediate between language user's ability and situational factors.

de Milliano, I., van Gelderen, A., & Sleegers, P. (2012). Patterns of cognitive self-regulation of adolescent struggling writers. *Written Communication, 29*(3), 303–325.

These researchers investigated how struggling writers might benefit from self-regulatory strategies. They used think-aloud data from 51 adolescent struggling writers and examined the relationship between patterns of cognitive self-regulatory activities (planning, formulating, monitoring, revising, and evaluating) and the quality of texts produced. Results showed that those participants who put more effort in planning and formulation produced better texts. Since one aspect of strategic competence is how it might help language users as they are involved in oral and written communication, this study can provide some insights into the use of strategies in producing texts.

Han, F. (2018). Strategic processing of Chinese young English language learners in an international standardized English language test. *Frontiers of Psychology, 9*, Article 1020.

This study examined the nature of strategic processing in the four communication skills of 138 Chinese young English language learners when they performed on Cambridge Young Learners English Tests–Flyers test. Following the completion of the test, three questionnaires regarding strategic processing were administered to the participants. A confirmatory factor analysis verified a cognitive and a metacognitive dimension in the four skills. Both cognitive and metacognitive strategic processing was moderately related to the test performance, explaining from 7 to 31% of the variance in the total test score. The participants adopted significantly more metacognitive than cognitive strategies in the three sections of the test perhaps due to the status of the test. Results also showed that high-performing test-takers used both cognitive and metacognitive strategies more frequently than the moderate- and low-performing test-takers across the four skills. The results of the study can contribute to the current knowledge of strategic processing in language testing.

O'Malley, J. M., & Chamot, A.U. (1990). *Learning strategies in second language acquisition.* **Cambridge: Cambridge University press.**

O'Malley and Chamot proposed a classification of different types of language strategies based on information processing models of language acquisition. They classified language strategies into operative or cognitively-oriented and managerial or metacognitively oriented. They defined operative or cognitive strategies as those strategies which are directly related to the performance on individual learning tasks. These strategies entail direct manipulation or transformation of the learning materials the language learner is working with. On the other hand, metacognitive strategies involve thinking about the learning process by planning for learning, monitoring of comprehension or production while it is taking place, and self-evaluation of learning after the language activity is completed. They also introduced a third category of strategies, namely, social and affective.

Phakiti, A. (2007). *Strategic competence and EFL reading test performance.* **Frankfurt: Peter Lang Publications.**

This book is the author's Ph.D. dissertation in which the author has attempted to clarify the parameters of strategic competence. Through a multitrait-multimethod approach, the author examines the relationships of general strategic knowledge and strategic regulation in a specific EFL context. The required data are collected through reading test performance over time as well as survey questionnaires. Utilizing a structural equation modeling (SEM) approach, the researcher aims at generalizing the nature of strategic competence. The book concludes by proposing multidimensional models to assist in the investigation of strategic competence. There is also a discussion of the pedagogical models for strategic reading instruction.

References

Bachman, L. (1990). *Fundamental considerations in language testing.* Oxford University Press.

Bachman, L., & Palmer, A. (1996). *Language testing in practice.* Oxford University Press.

Bachman, L. F. (2002a). Alternative interpretations of alternative assessments: Some validity issues in educational performance assessments. *Educational measurement: Issues and practice, 21,* 5–18.

Bachman, L. F. (2002b). Some reflections on task-based language performance assessment. *Language Testing, 19,* 453–476.

Canale, M. (1983). From communicative competence to communicative language pedagogy. In J. Richards & R. Schmidt (Eds.), *Language and communication* (pp. 2–27). London Group Ltd.

Canale, M., & Swain, M. (1980). Theoretical bases of communicative approaches to second language teaching and testing. *Applied Linguistics, 1*(1), 1–47.

Chalhoub-Deville, M. (2003). Second language interaction: Current perspectives and future trends. *Language Testing, 20*(4), 369–383.

Douglas, D. (2000). *Assessing languages for specific purposes.* Cambridge: Cambridge University Press.

Johnson, M. (2001). *The art of nonconversation: A re-examination of the validity of the oral proficiency interview.* New Haven, CT: Yale University Press.

McNamara, T. F. (1996). *Measuring second language performance.* Longman.

O'Malley, J. M., & Chamot, A. U. (1990). *Learning strategies in second language acquisition.* Cambridge University Press.

Phakiti, A. (2003). A closer look at gender and strategy use in L2 reading. *Language Learning, 53,* 649–702.

Purpura, J. E. (1998). Investigating the effects of strategy use and second language test performance with high- and low-ability test-takers: A structural equation modeling approach. *Language Testing, 15,* 333–379.

Purpura, J. E. (1999). *Learner strategy use and performance on language tests: A structural equation modeling approach.* University of Cambridge Local Examinations Syndicate and Cambridge University Press.

Swain, M. (2001). Examining dialogue: Another approach to content specification and to validating inferences drawn from test scores. *Language testing, 18,* 275–302.

Young, R. F. (2000). Interactional competence: Challenges for validity. *Paper presented at the Language Testing Research Colloquium,* Vancouver, Canada, March.

A. Mehdi Riazi is Professor of Applied Linguistics in the College of Humanities and Social Sciences of Hamad Bin Khalifa University. He is also an honorary professor in the Department of Linguistics, Macquarie University in Australia. He has supervised 22 Ph.D. dissertations and 54 master's theses to completion. He is also the author of *The Routledge Encyclopedia of Research Methods in Applied Linguistics* (2016, Routledge) and *Mixed Methods Research in Language Teaching and Learning* (2017, Equinox). He was the principal investigator for three research projects granted by IELTS, Pearson, and TOEFL. In the IELTS and TOEFL-iBT projects, he has addressed aspects of test validation as related to the writing skill. In the Pearson project, he investigated the scalability of PTE-Academic through concurrent and predictive validity procedures.

Translation Assessment

Renee Jourdenais

While the translation of written texts from one language to another has been occurring around the globe for over a thousand years, the field of translation studies is ascribed largely to work that has been done in the past fifty years or so, and the subsequent focus on translation assessment is even more recent.

One of the central foci of translation assessment over the years has been on assessing the quality of completed translations. This type of assessment is tightly tied to theoretical perspectives on the goals of translation and whether a translation is expected to be a more "literal" translation, focused on paralleling the form and content of the original text, or more "functional," designed to ensure that the translated text serves the same communicative purpose as the original (e.g., Nida, 1964/2012; Reiss, 1989; Vermeer, 1989), greatly influences the assessment of the translated text. Decisions also need to be made as to how to address cultural and social assumptions of the source text (e.g., House, 2001) as well as how to address the crucial revision and editing processes which make up a quality translation (e.g., Mellinger, 2018). Considering the multitude of factors inherent in creating a translation, it has been difficult to determine what, in fact, identifies a "successful" translation and how translations should be best assessed.

Translations may also be assessed for the types of strategies employed by the translator as they translate a text (e.g., Chesterman, 1997; Newmark, 1988; Vinet & Darbelnet, 1958/1995). While strategy use is often examined by comparing original and translated texts, there is increasing interest in assessing the cognitive processes involved in translation, particularly as translators determine how best to represent the complexity of features (i.e., grammatical, syntactical, lexical, textual, pragmatic, cultural, etc.) inherent in a written text (e.g., Jaaskelainen, 1999, 2016).

R. Jourdenais (✉)
Graduate School of Translation, Interpretation, and Language Education,
Middlebury Institute of International Studies at Monterey, Monterey, CA, USA
e-mail: rjourden@middlebury.edu

© Springer Nature Switzerland AG 2021
H. Mohebbi and C. Coombe (eds.), *Research Questions in Language
Education and Applied Linguistics*, Springer Texts in Education,
https://doi.org/10.1007/978-3-030-79143-8_72

The array of competencies needed by translators is another area of great interest to the field and various competency models highlight the numerous skills beyond language fluency that are required to be a successful translator (e.g., Angelelli, 2009; Lefeber, 2012, 2013). The identification of these skills leads to the challenging need to develop assessment measures that are able to determine the skills a translator has and/or may need to develop. Closely related to this point is the validity of the many translation exams used by universities and professional institutions who are interested in training or hiring translators. Issues such as task authenticity, whether resource use is permitted, and the qualities of the source text itself, all complicate the test development process (e.g., Lefeber, 2012, 2013).

As knowledge grows about the competencies needed for translation and the skills and strategies employed by successful translators, those training translators are interested in identifying formative assessment measures that offer feedback to young translators, providing them with information about "good" translations and where their own translation skills may be lacking. Researchers are exploring such things as the use of detailed analytic criteria, corpora, systematic functional linguistics, and norm-referenced feedback (e.g., Angelleli, 2009; Bowker, 2001; Eyckmans et al, 2009; Kim, 2009) to see how these approaches might contribute to a more context-focused, meaning-based model of formative assessment than to which many current assessment tools lend themselves.

The Research Questions

1. What criteria identify a "quality" translation?
2. How can we successfully measure the quality of a translation?
3. What are the constructs of translation competence?
4. How should we assess translation competence?
5. How can we best assess the strategies/cognitive processes employed by translators?
6. What criteria should be used for the development of assessments of translators for professional readiness?
7. What criteria should be used for the development of assessments of translation aptitude for training purposes?
8. How does the selection of a source text impact the test-taking performance?
9. What does good formative assessment look like for students of translation?
10. How can we build translation assessment literacy among companies, universities, and organizations assessing translation competence?

Suggested Resources

Angelelli, C. (2009). Using a rubric to assess translation ability: Defining the construct. In C. Angelelli and H. Jacobson (Eds). *Testing and Assessment in Translation and Interpreting Studies* **(pp. 13–47). Philadelphia: John Benjamins**.

Angelelli urges the development of translation assessment tools using sound assessment development practices, including careful consideration/definition of constructs, reliability and validity. She parallels Bachman's (1990) model of communicative competence, proposing a model of translator competence which includes linguistic competence, textual competence, pragmatic competence, and strategic competence. Utilizing the tenets of these competencies, she has constructed an analytical rubric of translation ability which includes five categories: comprehension of the source text meaning, style and cohesion, situational appropriateness, grammar and mechanics, and translation skill. She encourages the testing of this rubric by professional organizations and researchers.

Colina, S. (2008). Translation Quality Evaluation. *The Translator, 14*(1), **97–134**.

Colina argues for a functionalist/componential means of assessing translations which takes into account the purposes of the translation, as articulated in the translation brief. This form of assessment utilizes a descriptive, analytic rubric for different components of the translated text. In this research study, Colina develops an assessment tool to be used on healthcare texts. Interrater reliability proves high, suggesting that the tool can be used successfully by people with different types of expertise. Colina believes that this tool could be adapted to different types of texts and priorities, and used for finer-grained analyses of texts.

Kim, M. (2009). Meaning-oriented assessment of translations: SFL and its application to formative assessment. In C. Angelelli and H. Jacobson (Eds). (2009). *Testing and Assessment in Translation and Interpreting Studies* **(pp. 123–58). Philadelphia: John Benjamins**.

Kim discusses the use of text analysis, as based on systematic functional linguistics, to offer meaning-oriented feedback to students of translation. She contrasts this with more traditional, and more subjective, error deduction assessment that offers students little meaningful input on areas needing improvement and, in fact, may make them focus inappropriately on sentence-level features of the text. Kim's model examines experiential, logical, interpersonal, and textual meaning, each for accuracy and naturalness, and at lexis, clause, and text (if appropriate) levels. Her research finds that this type of assessment is beneficial both for students' subsequent productive skills and their analytical abilities.

Lafeber, A. (2013). *The search for (the right) translators: Recruitment testing at international organizations.* **Riga, Latvia: LAP Lambert Academic Publishing**.

Lafeber investigates translator recruitment testing at intergovernmental organizations. She surveys 25 organizations in order to identify specific skills and knowledge both needed and desired in various translator positions. Based on this information, Lafeber proposes changes are needed to current recruitment testing practices in order to improve test validity and to recognize candidates who meet the "ideal translator" profile that the organizations are seeking. She reports on a pilot of a "profile-adapted" test, as compared to performance on more typical recruitment tests. Findings have implications for those seeking positions in these organizations, for translator-training programs, and for test development.

Mellinger, C. (2018). **Re-thinking Translation Quality: Revision in the Digital Age.** *Target: International Journal of Translation Studies, 30(2), 310–331*.

Mellinger highlights the role of editing and revision in translation workflows, explaining that they are critical components of translation quality, but notes that most models of translation quality assessment are product-focused and neglect these important processes of revision and editing in the translation task. In this article, he considers the nature of quality in light of computer-assisted translation tools and makes an argument for including revision and editing in translation quality assessment models, as he explores the cognitive nature of the translation task.

References

Angelelli, C. (2009). Using a rubric to assess translation ability: Defining the construct. In C. Angelelli & H. Jacobson (Eds.), *Testing and assessment in translation and interpreting studies* (pp. 13–47). John Benjamins.

Bowker, L. (2001). Towards a methodology for a corpus-based approach to translation evaluation. *Meta, 46*(2), 345–364.

Chesterman, A. (1997). *Memes of translation: The spread of ideas in translation theory.* John Benjamins.

Eyckmans, J., Anckaert, P., & Segers, W. (2009). The perks of norm-referenced translation evaluation. In C. Angelelli & H. Jacobson (Eds.), *Testing and assessment in translation and interpreting studies* (pp. 73–94). John Benjamins.

House, J. (2001). Translation quality assessment: Linguistic description versus social evaluation. *Meta, 46*(2), 243–257.

Jääskeläinen, R. (1999). *Tapping the process: An explorative study of the cognitive and affective factors involved in translating.* University of Joensuu.

Jaaskelainen, R. (2016). Think-Aloud protocols. *Handbook of Translation Studies, 1*, 371–373.

Kim, M. (2009). Meaning-oriented assessment of translations: SFL and its application to formative assessment. In C. Angelelli & H. Jacobson (Eds.), *Testing and assessment in translation and interpreting studies* (pp. 123–158). John Benjamins.

Lafeber, A. (2012) Translation at inter-governmental organizations: The set of skills and knowledge required and the implications for recruitment testing. (Unpublished doctoral dissertation.) Universitat Rovira I Virgili, Tarragona, Spain.

Lafeber, A. (2013). *The search for (the right) translators: Recruitment testing at international organizations.* LAP Lambert Academic Publishing.

Mellinger, C. (2018) Re-thinking translation quality: Revision in the digital age. *Target: International Journal of Translation Studies, 30:2,* 310–331.

Newmark, P. (1988). *A textbook of translation.* Prentice Hall.

Nida, E. (2012) Principles of correspondence. In L. Venuti (Ed.), *The translation studies reader* (pp. 153–167). Routledge. (Reprinted from *Toward a science of translating,* pp. 156–171, by E. Nida, 1964, E.J. Brill).

Reiss, K. (1989). Text types, translation types and translation assessment. In A. Chesterman (Ed and Trans) *Readings in translation theory* (pp. 105–115). Finn Lectura.

Vermeer, H. (1989). Skopos and commission in translation theory, in A. Chesterman (Ed. and Trans.), *Readings in translation theory* (pp 173–187). Finn Lectura.

Vinay, J., & Darbelnet, J. (2012). A methodology for translation. In L. Venuti (Ed.), *The translation studies reader* (pp. 84–93). Routledge. (Reprinted from *Comparative stylistics of French and English: A methodology for translation,* pp. 31–42, by J. C. Sager and M. J. Hamel (Trans. and Eds) 1995, John Benjamin).

Renee Jourdenais is a Professor of Applied Linguistics at the Middlebury Institute of International Studies at Monterey. She served as Dean of the Graduate School of Translation, Interpretation and Language Education at the Middlebury Institute for ten years, overseeing the Institute's Master's programs in TESOL/TFL; Translation, Interpretation, and Localization; Language and Intercultural Studies; and Language and Professional Programs. Her areas of specialty include teacher education, assessment, research, curriculum design, and second language acquisition and use. She has presented, published, and consulted on issues of cognitive processing of linguistic input, curriculum development, and assessment focused in the areas of language teaching, translation, and interpretation. She teaches a range of courses including language, applied linguistics, pedagogy, assessment and research methodology.

Validation of Assessment Scores and Uses

73

A. Mehdi Riazi

Tests are prevalent in today's societies. They are used for a variety of purposes including, but not limited to, the assessment of progress and mastery in educational settings, high-stakes purposes such as certification, and citizenship and naturalization purposes. The main rationale and, perhaps better said, justification for the use of tests is that through them awards, opportunities, and entitlements could be distributed rather fairly. In other words, test developers and users assumedly consider tests as means of "meritocracy" (Fulcher, 2014) in their societies. As such, we need "an optimistic agenda of expanding our knowledge and learning how to build better tests in the service of meritocratic and just decision making" (Fulcher, 2014, p. 1448). A critical and counter-argument though considers tests of any kind and purpose as means for the perpetuation of power relations (see, e.g., Shohamy, 2001, 2009). The debate over whether tests are integral to the modern societies or means of suppression is an ongoing one and beyond the scope of the current contribution. In what follows, I would like to focus more on the validation of test score interpretations and uses. That is, the plausibility of the interpretations we make from test scores to judge about individuals' abilities and the decisions and uses we make based on those interpretations. In a nutshell, the focus is on the validity of the test score interpretations and uses.

Validity is a century-old concept and relates to theories of test score interpretation and use. From a very general perspective, theories related to validity could be classified as pre-Messick and post-Messick theories. As such, Messick's (1989) theory can be considered a turning point in the theorization of validity. Pre-Messick theories of validity were componential. That is, validity was conceived and defined as separate aspects of test scores; aspects such as face validity, content validity, criterion-related validity and construct validity. In addition, reliability of the tests

A. M. Riazi (✉)
College of Humanities and Social Sciences, Hamad Bin Khalifa University (HBKU), Doha, Qatar
e-mail: mehdi.riazi@mq.edu.au; ariazi@hbku.edu.qa

Department of Linguistics, Macquarie University, Sydney, Australia

© Springer Nature Switzerland AG 2021
H. Mohebbi and C. Coombe (eds.), *Research Questions in Language Education and Applied Linguistics*, Springer Texts in Education,
https://doi.org/10.1007/978-3-030-79143-8_73

was conceived to be a separate feature of tests denoting the consistency of the tests in measuring test takers' ability. Messick proposed a unitary and complementarity conceptualisation of validity in that construct validity is proposed as the overarching validity with all the other aspects, reliability, and social consequences subsumed under it. Messick's model of validity is thus a unitary multi-faceted conception of this key term.

Validation, on the other hand, is the process of gathering evidence in support of the theory of validity. Validation involves an evaluation of evidence proposed for the interpretation (and use) of the test scores. As Kane (2016) states, if *validity* is a theory of score interpretation and use, *validation* would require an analysis of the plausibility of that interpretation and use. Since validation would require an analysis of the appropriateness of the proposed interpretations and uses, it would also require an analysis of the *consequences* of the uses. In each case, the evidence needed for validation would depend on the specific claims being made from test score and use. An Argument-based framework (Kane, 1992, 2006, 2013, 2016) is currently the predominant validation framework in testing and assessment validation studies, which draws on Messick's unitary theory of validity. In the field of language testing and assessment, Bachman (2005), Bachman and Palmer (2010), and Chapelle et al. (2008) have contributed significantly to the use of argument-based frameworks to language testing and assessment validation studies.

A century of validity theories and validation procedures has resulted in significant contributions and understanding of this concept. The following are some questions in need of further investigations related to language testing programs in different contexts.

The Research Questions

1. To what extent can test validation studies provide evidence for both test score interpretation and test score use?
2. What claims and relevant evidence could be put forward to support the validity argument if validity is to encompass both "measurement" (test score interpretation) and "decision-making" (test score use)?
3. What is different stakeholders' conception of positive and negative consequences of testing programs?
4. What sort of evidence can we provide from empirical data and analysis for the evaluation of "consequences" (decision-making) in different contexts?
5. In what ways are consequences defined and evaluated in language testing programs?
6. What sort of claims can we make from empirical data and analysis in an argument-based framework for specific test uses (e.g., admission, placement, achievement, etc.)?

7. What sort of evidence can be derived from empirical data and analysis to support each of the claims installed in the argument-based framework for specific test uses?

8. What sort of evidence from empirical data and analysis can we provide for the validity of a same when it is used for uses?

9. What is different cultural groups' (e.g., aboriginals, or immigrants) conception of a test administered to them? How might these cultural groups' conceptions be related to the construct of the test?

10. What are different stakeholders' (e.g., test takers, decision makers, policy developers, etc.) views of test score interpretation and uses and how these views are related to the test validity?

Suggested Resources

American Educational Research Association, American Psychological Association, & National Council on Measurement in Education. (2014). *Standards for educational and psychological testing*. Washington, D.C.: American Educational Research Association.

This edition of the *Standards for Educational and Psychological Testing* describes validity in terms of both test score interpretations and uses: "Validity refers to the degree to which evidence and theory support the interpretations of test scores for proposed uses of tests". However, not all testing and assessment experts agree on this definition. While some agree that both test score interpretation and use are important and in need of examination, others disagree with regard to making a distinction between supporting interpretations based on test scores and justifying test use. *Standards*, as it is known, is however currently the predominant reference among the testing experts.

Borsboom, D., Mellenbergh, G. J., & Van Heerden, J. (2004). The concept of validity. *Psychological Review, 111*, 1061–1071.

Borsboom et al. (2004, p. 1061) argue that "a test is valid for measuring an attribute if and only if (a) the attribute exists and (b) variations in the attribute causally produce variations in the outcomes of the measurement procedure". Their definition of test validity encompasses the "measurement" aspect of the tests and leaves out the "decision-making" or test use aspect. According to Borsboom et al., test developers need to have a strong theoretical understanding of the construct to be measured and how the construct is expected to be manifest in test scores.

Carney, M., Crawford, A., Siebert, C., Osguthrope, R., & Thiede, K. (2019). Comparison of two approaches to interpretive use arguments. *Applied Measurement in Education, 32,* **10–22.**

The authors present two approaches to articulating the interpretation/use argument. One approach uses the five sources of validity evidence in the Standards for Educational and Psychological Testing as a framework and the other approach uses Kane's chain of assumptions/inferences as a framework. The authors also identify aspects of these approaches that need to be further clarified for instrument developers to consistently implement either approach, identified important differences in the perspective each approach takes on validation, and highlight important questions for the measurement and mathematics education research fields to consider.

Hubley, A. M., & Zumbo, B. D. (2011). Validity and the consequences of test interpretation and use. *Social Indicators Research, 103,* **219–230.**

Hubley and Zumbo (2011) present an integrated framework for validation. They argue that at the core of the vast majority of measures, there is a purpose of personal and social change. As such, test developers and test score users usually intend to have personal and social consequences and impact accounted for by their tests and measures. It is, therefore, critical to consider the consequences, both intended and unintended, and side effects of measurement in the validation process. In fact, Hubley and Zumbo's framework for test validation draws on and expands on the concept of consequences discussed by Messick (1989) while also situating consequences in their proper place relative to other types of validity evidence. From their perspective, intended and unintended consequences and side effects form one of many sources of evidence that can be presented when evaluating the interpretation and use of test scores.

Kane, M. (2016). Explicating validity. *Assessment in Education: Principles, Policy & Practice, 23*(2), **198–211.**

Following his earlier publications on validity and validation, Kane (2016) suggests that an argument-based approach to validation involves two steps: developing an interpretation framework and evaluating the interpretation framework by a validity argument. Accordingly, test developers or test validation researchers need to firstly specify the interpretations and uses they intend to draw from a particular test and present it as an interpretation/use argument (IUA). "The IUA provides a framework for validation by specifying what is being claimed. This proposal can then be evaluated by the validity argument, using analyses that are relevant to the claims laid out in the IUA. Interpretations and uses that make sense and are supported by appropriate evidence are considered to be valid, and interpretations or uses that are not adequately supported by evidence are not considered to be valid" (p, 201).

Messick, S. (1989). Validity. In R. L. Linn (Ed.), *Educational measurement* (pp. 13–103). Washington, DC: American Council on Education and National Council on Measurement in Education.

Messick (1989) attempted to unify validity theory by proposing a unified construct-based framework that focused on construct-based interpretations of test scores. He was very concerned about the ethical responsibility of test developers and test score users and therefore felt the need to examine the consequences of testing programmes. His intention was to minimise negative consequences while maintaining the construct-based framework for validity. Messick maintained that, if evidence could be provided that the negative consequences are due to a flaw in the testing programme (e.g., construct-irrelevant variance), the adverse consequences would count against the validity of the testing programme. He provided a matrix with two columns, test score interpretation and test use requiring both theoretical and evidential support.

Newton, P. E., Shaw, S. D. (2016). Agreements and disagreements over validity. *Assessment in Education: Principles, Policy & Practice, 23*(2), 316–318.

There is a debate over whether both test score interpretation and use should be subsumed under the label 'validity'. Newton and Shaw discuss the question of how far validity should extend. They argue that "there is no distinct concept of validity because scholars of different persuasions have associated the word with all sorts of different concepts over the years and still continue to do so" (p. 316). They do not recommend leaving out different concepts because they believe many of these concepts are very useful. However, they take position with the divergent and often promiscuous usage of the word. The point of their paper is to propose "three possible routes to consensus as an alternative way of framing the debate and to help distinguish the issues which are genuinely at stake from those which are not" (p. 317). They believe that the best approach for professionals as well as researchers who wish to communicate about validity and validation is to state their conceptualization of the term up front.

References

Bachman, L. F. (2005). Building and supporting a case for test use. *Language Assessment Quarterly, 2*(1), 1–34.

Bachman, L. F., & Palmer, A. S. (2010). *Language assessment in practice.* Oxford University Press.

Chapelle, C. A., Enright, M. K., & Jamieson, J. M. (Eds.). (2008). *Building a validity argument for the test of English as a foreign language.* Routledge.

Fulcher, G. (2014). Philosophy and language testing. In A. J. Kunnan (Ed.), *The companion to language assessment* (pp. 1433–1451). Wiley Blackwell.

Kane, M. (1992). An argument-based approach to validity. *Psychological Bulletin, 112*, 527–535.

Kane, M. T. (2006). Validation. In R. L. Brennan (Ed.), *Educational measurement* (4th ed., pp. 17–64). Praeger.

Kane, M. T. (2013). Validating the interpretations and uses of test scores. *Journal of Educational Measurement, 50*, 1–73.

Kane, M. T. (2016). Explicating validity. *Assessment in Education: Principles, Policy & Practice, 23*(2), 198–211.

Messick, S. (1989). Validity. In R. L. Linn (Ed.), *Educational measurement* (3rd ed.) (pp. 13–103). American Council on Education & Macmillan.

Shohamy, E. (2001). *The power of tests: A critical perspective on the uses of language tests.* Pearson.

Shohamy, E. (2009). Language tests for immigrants: Why language? Why tests? Why citizenship? In G. Hogan-Brun, C. Mar-Molinero, & P. Stevenson (Eds.), *Discourses on language and integration: Critical perspectives on language testing regimes in Europe* (pp. 61–82). John Benjamins.

A. Mehdi Riazi is Professor in the College of Humanities and Social Sciences of Hamad Bin Khalifa University in Qatar. He is also an honorary professor of Applied Linguistics in the Department of Linguistics, Macquarie University in Australia. He has supervised 22 Ph.D. dissertations and 54 master's theses to completion. He is also the author of *The Routledge Encyclopedia of Research Methods in Applied Linguistics* (2016, Routledge) and *Mixed Methods Research in Language Teaching and Learning* (2017, Equinox). He was the principal investigator for three research projects granted by IELTS, Pearson, and TOEFL. In the IELTS and TOEFL-iBT projects, he has addressed aspects of test validation as related to the writing skill. In the Pearson project, he investigated the scalability of PTE-Academic through concurrent and predictive validity procedures.

Vocabulary, its Development over Time and Writing Quality in L2 Contexts

Lee McCallum

Vocabulary use has been a popular research area for more than half a century in both first and second language circles (Durrant, Brenchley & McCallum, 2020). However, special emphasis has been placed on how vocabulary is used by second language learners. This emphasis is often tied to the fact that learners mention specific vocabulary issues when asked to comment on the language present in their essays (Engber, 1995). Learners report having a narrow range of words at their disposal which are often register, genre and discipline inappropriate (Engber, 1995). Research into these difficulties appears to support that inadequate vocabulary use has an influence on students' academic success at university where learners strive to join their academic disciplines (Crossley & McNamara, 2012).

In establishing these difficulties, researchers have taken an interest in two interrelated areas: how vocabulary 'grows' or develops over time and how vocabulary measures are able to predict writing quality via awarded composition grades in second and foreign language contexts. This interest has more widely attempted to operationalize Read's (2000) construct of 'lexical richness' into three dimensions that are at the heart of the quantitative approach: lexical diversity, lexical sophistication and lexical density. Operationalizing these constructs has produced numerous quantitative measures and studies that inform the area with wide-ranging summaries of these measures provided in Durrant, et al., (2020).

Lexical diversity is taken to be word variation in a text whereby several amended versions of the type-token ratio (TTR) have been used to measure the number of types (different words) ÷ the number of tokens (all words). This measure taps into how varied vocabulary is whereas lexical sophistication aims to tap into vocabulary which is not merely 'everyday' vocabulary but vocabulary that is appropriate for the topic, register and discipline that students are immersed in. This has been commonly operationalized via the Lexical Frequency Profiles (LFPs) developed by

L. McCallum (✉)
Graduate School of Education, University of Exeter, Exeter, UK
e-mail: L.McCallum2@exeter.ac.uk

© Springer Nature Switzerland AG 2021
H. Mohebbi and C. Coombe (eds.), *Research Questions in Language Education and Applied Linguistics*, Springer Texts in Education,
https://doi.org/10.1007/978-3-030-79143-8_74

Laufer and Nation (1995). These profiles classify words used according to their frequency band with less frequent words viewed as more sophisticated. Therefore, learner texts containing more vocabulary in the less frequent lists are deemed more sophisticated and have often been found to receive higher grades from raters (Banerjee et al., 2007). Another operationalization of sophistication has been cross-checking learner vocabulary use with vocabulary present in academic corpora (e.g. academic sub corpora in the Corpus of Contemporary American English (COCA) via automatic tools such as the Tool for the Automatic Analysis of Lexical Sophistication (TAALES) by Kyle (2017) and lists of vocabulary such as the Academic Word List (Laufer, 1994)). Like, the use of the LFPs, these have also proved insightful with learners found to use more of these words over a period of time (Laufer, 1994). Lastly, lexical density has been operationalized under variations of counting the number of adjectives/verbs/nouns and dividing them with the number of all words. The measure of density has been consistently found to have an inconsistent relationship with writing quality (Engber, 1995) and shows little development over time (Zheng, 2016).

Despite a wealth of studies, a clear trajectory for future research lies in operationalizing Read's (2000) notion of 'appropriateness' by building in aspects of 'accurate' vocabulary use. This trajectory is a much-needed dimension that quantitative researchers should aim to investigate further to better understand how vocabulary develops and how it influences grade scores for compositions. Further to this gap, researchers should also consider moving away from an over-reliance on multiple linear regression as an analysis method to consider structural and mixed-effect models which incorporate learning context effects (e.g., see Kim & Crossley, 2018).

The Research Questions

The research questions presented below reflect key questions asked by researchers studying development over time and/or writing quality relationships.

1. Will there be a significant difference between the LFPs of learners at different language proficiency levels?
2. Does lexical variation in advanced learners' compositions change over time and if yes, how does it change?
3. How do scores on quantitative complexity metrics correlate with subjective ratings of writing quality given by experienced raters?
4. Which complexity metric(s), or combinations best predict subjective ratings of writing quality?
5. Can lexical macro-features be used to predict L2 writing proficiency?
6. How does EFL students' writing develop over time, in terms of essay length, word length, type/token ratio, argument structure, and cohesive devices?

7. What effect does task have on relationships between vocabulary and writing quality/development over time?
8. What can we learn from comparing features found in student essays and teachers' holistic assessment of these same essays?
9. How did the lexical sophistication, diversity and density measures of the participants' use of individual words change throughout an academic year?
10. Is there any effect of genre on the measures of lexical complexity?

Suggested Resources

Laufer, B. (1994). The lexical profile of second language writing: Does it change over time? *RELC Journal*, **25, 21–33.**

As a longitudinal study, this paper studes the lexical profiles exhibited over one academic year. Laufer's study uses 48 university student essays from the Language/Literature department of a university. The study measures both lexical sophistication and lexical variation/diversity with sophistication determined by the number of 'non-basic words' in the essays. Non-basic words are those which are on the University Word List and words not found on any of the computer programme word lists. The study uses essays from the start of the academic year upon placement, after one semester (fourteen weeks of teaching) and at the end of two semester (at the end of twenty-eight weeks of teaching) and analyses the essays by using paired t-tests and MANOVA tests. After one or two semesters the proportion of most frequent words decreases, the percentage of words at the 2nd 1000 words also decreases. However, words from the UWL significantly increases. The percentage of words not on the list goes up in one group of students but goes down in the other group. This paper is a key reading in quantitative measures as it tackles both diversity and sophistication and at the same time it provides a reliable example of carrying out longitudinal work.

Laufer, B., & Nation, P. (1995). Vocabulary size and use lexical richness in L2 writtenproduction. *Applied Linguistics*, **16(3), 307–322.**

In this paper, Laufer and Nation introduce the LFP as a measure of the proportion of high frequency general service and academic words in texts. Laufer and Nation analyze the development of learner writing at intermediate proficiency level. Laufer and Nation claim that the LFP is an effective measure of vocabulary size and also make clear that vocabulary in the first and second lists are more relevant to vocabulary used by lower level students whereas words from the University Word List are more appropriate a measure for advanced proficiency learners. The aim of this study was to compare the LFPs between learners at different proficiency levels. They find that there is a decrease in the number of 1,000-word list with increased proficiency level, no significant difference in the number of the 2nd 1,000 words and a significant number of words from the University Word List and words not on lists when proficiency level increases. This paper is the catalyst for several replication studies in L2 research.

Crossley, S.A., & McNamara, D.S. (2012). Predicting second language writing proficiency: The roles of cohesion and linguistic sophistication. *Journal of Research in Reading*, *35*(2), 115–135.

An essential reading in quantitatively measuring vocabulary sophistication, this paper marks one of the first of many explicit shifts to using automatic text analysis tools. The key aim of the paper was to examine relationships between lexical measures and writing grades by examining a wider range of measures than previous manual-oriented studies. This was achieved through using the automatic text analysis tool Coh-metrix. Coh-metrix can automatically calculate word frequency measures and the diversity measures: MTLD and D. MTLD and D are measures that attempt to phase out the text length effects that influence traditional TTR-based measures. The authors analyzed a sub corpus of essays from an examination taken by Hong Kong based high school students. Both MTLD and D yielded positive correlations with essay grades highlighting how higher quality texts appear to use more diverse vocabulary. This paper is an essential reading for those with an interest in automatic tools and how they have evolved.

Bulté, B., & Housen, A. (2014). Conceptualizing and measuring short-term changes in L2 writing complexity. *Journal of Second Language Writing*, *26*, 42–65.

Using of a corpus of texts written on a short-term EAP course at a U.S university, Bulté and Housen (2014) study change over time and how the lexical measures contained in the Lexical Complexity Analyzer correlate to essay grades. Over a semester they analyze 90 essays from 45 students: one essay at the start and end of a short EAP course. They found that over a single semester, unlike the Crossley and McNamara (2012) findings, lexical diversity measured by D did not significantly develop over time or have a relationship with quality ratings. However, lexical diversity measured through the Guiraud Index showed non-significant decreases over the semester and this had a positive relationship with writing quality ratings. In contrast, lexical sophistication measured by the Advanced Guiraud Index did not increase significantly over the semester and was not a significant predictor of quality in subsequent regression modeling. This paper is a useful reading for researchers who wish to study sophistication over time with traditional longitudinal methods.

Kim, M., Crossley, S.A., & Kyle, K. (2018). Lexical sophistication as a multidimensional phenomenon: Relations to second language lexical proficiency, development, and writing quality. *The Modern Language Journal*, *102* (1), 120–141.

This paper marks a shift from linear regression modeling carried out with multiple regression to incorporating different methods. The authors aim to establish how the numerous TAALES measures can be condensed into the most useful ones which are not correlated with other measures in the tool. The paper uses a corpus of essays written by Korean university students to examine how the measures identified through Principal Component Analysis (PCA) can be used to predict overall writing quality. Their analyses of argumentative essays through PCA reveals that 11 components yield significant correlations with writing proficiency. Positive significant correlations are found for academic formulaic language and word specificity as measures of sophistication. Negative significant correlations were found between content word frequency, content word properties, function word properties and function word frequency and range and writing proficiency scores. Overall, this paper is a key reading for its use of recent text analyses tools.

References

Banerjee, J., Franceschina, F., & Smith, A. M. (2007). Documenting features of written language production typical at different IELTS band score levels. *IELTS Research Report, 7*, 1–70.

Bulté, B., & Housen, A. (2014). Conceptualizing and measuring short-term changes in L2 writing complexity. *Journal of Second Language Writing, 26*, 42–65.

Crossley, S. A., & McNamara, D. S. (2012). Predicting second language writing proficiency: The roles of cohesion and linguistic sophistication. *Journal of Research in Reading, 35*(2), 115–135.

Durrant, P., Brenchley, M., & McCallum, L. (2020). *Understanding development and proficiency in writing: Quantitative corpus linguistics approaches*. Cambridge University Press.

Engber, C. A. (1995). The relationship of lexical proficiency to the quality of ESL compositions. *Journal of Second Language Writing, 4*(2), 139–155.

Kim, M., & Crossley, S. A. (2018). Modeling second language writing quality: A structural equation investigation of lexical, syntactic, and cohesive features in source-based and independent writing. *Assessing Writing, 37*, 39–56.

Kyle, K. (2017). TAALES linguistic tool. Available at: kristopherkyle.com. Last accessed July 31, 2018.

Laufer, B. (1994). The lexical profile of second language writing: Does it change over time? *RELC Journal, 25*, 21–33.

Laufer, B., & Nation, P. (1995). Vocabulary size and use lexical richness in L2 written production. *Applied Linguistics, 16*(3), 307–322.

Read, J. (2000). *Assessing vocabulary*. Cambridge University Press.

Zheng, Y. (2016). The complex, dynamic development of L2 lexical use: A longitudinal study on Chinese learners of English. *System, 56*, 40–53.

Lee McCallum holds a Doctorate in Education from the University of Exeter. She has extensive teaching experience in academic writng and EAP from the Middle East, Europe and China. Her research interests include language assessment and writing instruction with a focus on how corpus-based research methods can enhance these two areas. Her most recent work, published by Cambridge University Press in early 2020, is titled *Understanding Development and Proficiency in Writing: Quantitative Corpus Linguistics Approaches*. She has also acted as an editor and contributor on a number of publications with Palgrave Macmillan, Springer and Routledge.

Washback

Rubina Khan

The concept of washback in language assessment is a multi-faceted and complex issue which needs attention and further exploration as in most high-stakes contexts tests exert immense influence on student lives. The terms washback and backwash have been used interchangeably in the assessment literature. Both attempt to explain the effects of tests on teaching and learning.

A plethora of definitions on the washback phenomenon are available in the literature. Pearson (1988), Hughes (1989), Bailey (1996) and Alderson and Wall (1993) refer to washback as 'the influence of tests on teaching and learning'. Shohamy (1992, p.513) observes that washback has a major effect on the lives of test takers and is "the utilization of external language tests to affect and drive foreign language learning in the school context". Alderson and Wall (1993) posited 15 hypotheses regarding washback which point to the influence of tests on teachers, students, content, method, rate, sequence, degree, depth and attitudes of teaching and learning. They add that important tests have washback and unimportant tests do not.

Bailey (1996, p. 269) upholds that "washback can be either positive or nega-tiveto the extent that it either promotes or impedes the accomplishment of educational goals held by the learner and/or program personnel".Positive/beneficial washback takes place when good teaching practice is followed and learners develop their proficiency level or when course/program objectives are met. Positivewashback can be enhanced through making tests direct, cost effective, objective oriented and criterion referenced (Hughes, 1989).

Negative/harmfulwashback may occur when teachers specifically teach to the test and learners do not develop the required skills or if there is lack of alignment between curricular goals and examinations. It exerts negative effects on pedagogical practices (Cheng & Curtis, 2004).

R. Khan (✉)
Department of English, University of Dhaka, Dhaka, Bangladesh
e-mail: rkhan@agni.com; rkhan@du.ac.bd

© Springer Nature Switzerland AG 2021
H. Mohebbi and C. Coombe (eds.), *Research Questions in Language Education and Applied Linguistics*, Springer Texts in Education,
https://doi.org/10.1007/978-3-030-79143-8_75

There is a difference between the terms 'washback'and 'impact' in the field. 'Washback' has a micro focus, is narrow in scope and explores the effect of testing within the classroom. On the other hand, 'impact' has broader implications, and goes beyond the classroom boundaries. It has a macro focus and examines assessment effects on educational systems and society at large and involves a range of stakeholders. Cheng and Curtis (2012) contend that washback and impact have important bearings for psychometric and social aspects of testing.

The nature of washback is complicated and may vary for each educational setting. Currently there is a paucity of empirical studies on washback. As washback is a complex phenomenon and student lives are impacted by examination results, detailed washback research needs to be conducted.

The Research Questions

1. What do we actually understand by 'washback'? Do we need to rethink the definition of washback? Why/why not?
2. How can washback be measured?
3. To what extent and in what ways do examinations influence teaching and learning at school/college/university level?
4. How does washback impact student lives?
5. What is the influence of the public/national examinations on students and teachers perceptions towards the examination?
6. How does a new test influence teacher and student performance?
7. What strategies do the Examination Boards/authorities use to implement changes in examinations?
8. What strategies can be used to identify and combat negative backwash?
9. What was the nature and scope of the washback effect on teachers' and students' perceptions of aspects of teaching towards the new examination?
10. What are teachers' perceptions of washback, both positive and negative?

Suggested Resources

Bachman, L. & Dambock, B. (2017). *Language Assessment for Classroom Teachers.* **Oxford: Oxford University Press**.

This book focuses on classroom-based assessment and provides teachers with new approaches of using and developing classroom assessments to support classroom instruction. The aim is to provide pertinent information, knowledge and skills to equip teachers to improve their use of classroom assessment. The book is divided into four parts and discusses major concepts and procedures in the field; provides definition of terminologies; gives illustrative examples to complement previous discussion topics and gives specified examples of language assessment tasks (covering four skills and different levels of ability). The examples are useful and provide templates for classroom-based assessment which can be used for developing one'sown assessment. It also includesactivities which help to reinforce concepts. The appendices include: checklists; templates; answers to the activities and suggestions for further reading. In short the book is a complete practicalguide for teachers who aim to develop classroom-based assessments.

Brookhart, S. M. & Nitko, A. J. (2015). *Educational assessment of students.* **7th Edition. Pearson.**

This book is comprehensive in nature and presents a balanced view in dealing with traditional and alternative assessments. It emphasizes classroom assessment issues covering both formative and summative dimensions. The revised edition adds a chapter on providing formative feedback as well as presents an expanded treatment of formative assessment. There is also additional information about the role and use of technology in assessment. The book can serve as a core text for undergraduate courses on testing and assessment. Special features include examples of dealing with designing classroom assessments; checklists for assessing assessments; strategies for assessing higher-order thinking; chapter end exercises; updated websites related to assessment and appendices of statistical concepts with spreadsheet applications and tutorials. In short, it is a very useful book for teachers and can serve as required reading for undergraduate and graduate level studies on assessment.

Cheng, L., Watanabe, Y & Curtis, A. (Eds). (2004). *Washback in Language Testing: Research Contexts and Methods.* **Mahwah, NJ: Lawrence Erlbaum and Associates.**

This book is an excellent compilation of chapters on washback which serve a dual purpose. Firstly, the aim is to inform and teachers, researchers and administrators about the varied landscape of assessment and familiarize them with the complex issues surrounding washback and the impact on teaching and learning. A second aim of the book is to share a number of studies on washback from different contexts which can act as a spring board for further studies in the particular area.

The book is divided into two parts. Part one has a general focus and familiarizes the readers with an array of factors associated with testing, teaching and learning. Part two presents an assortment of empirical studies on washback conducted in different parts of the world (e.g. Washington, Australia, New Zealand, Hong Kong, and China). The book highlights important issues like test ethics and social justice. It is a very useful book and compulsory reading for teachers and researchers interested in conducting research on washback.

Coombe, C. (Ed.) (2018). *An A to Z of Second Language Assessment: How Language Teachers Understand Assessment Concepts.* **British Council.**

A valuable resource on language testing and assessment which contains more than 285 definitions of terms related to the field of language testing and assessment. The glossary is written by classroom practitioners and the language used is comprehensible and easy to understand. An indispensable and useful resource for teachers who want to develop their understanding of assessment related terminology.

Coombe, C., Davidson, P., O'Sullivan, B. & Stoynoff, S. (Eds.). (2012). *The Cambridge Guide to Second Language Assessment.* **Cambridge, UK: Cambridge University Press**.

The Cambridge Guide to Second Language Assessment consists of articles focusing on key issues in language assessment. It explores the theoretical framework of assessment-related areas and also provides practical guidelines to teachers for test development and implementation. The articles written by experts in the field cover five specific sections associated with major issues in the field: assessment purposes and approaches, assessment of second language skills, technology in assessment and administrative concerns in assessment. This book is presented in a very lucid and structured manner and is an easy read for all.

References

Alderson, J. C., & Wall, D. (1993). Does washback exist? *Applied Linguistics, 14*(2), 115–129.

Bailey, K. M. (1996). Working for washback: A review of the washback concept in language testing. *Language Testing, 13*(3), 257–279.

Cheng, L., & Curtis, A. (2004). Washback or backwash: A review of the impact of testing on teaching and learning. In L. Cheng, Y. Watanabe, &A. Curtis (Eds.), *Washback in language testing: Research contexts and methods.* Lawrence Erlbaum and Associates.

Cheng, L., & Curtis, A. (2012). Test impact and Washback: Implications for teaching and learning. In P. Davidson, S. Stoynoff, B. O'Sullivan, & C. Coombe (Eds.), *The Cambridge guide to second language assessment* (pp. 89–95). Cambridge.

Hughes, A. (1989). *Testing for language teachers.* Cambridge University Press.

Pearson, I. (1988). Tests as levers for change. In D. Chamberlain & R.J. Baumgardner (Eds.), *ESP in thecClassroom: practice and evaluation*, ELT Documents (Vol. 128, pp. 98–107). Modern English Publications.

Shohamy, E. (1992). Beyond proficiency testing: A diagnostic feedback testing model for assessing foreign language learning. *The Modern Language Journal, 76*(4), 513–521.

Rubina Khan is Professor at the Department of English, University of Dhaka. She has an MA in TESOL from the University of Northern Iowa and a Ph.D. in ELT from the University of Warwick. She has worked as an educational consultant on assessment and teacher development and has publications in professional journals at home and abroad. Her recent publications include entries on 'Assessment & Evaluation' and 'Assessing Large Classes' in Volume 8 of the *TESOL Encyclopedia of ELT* (Wiley Blackwell, 2018). She is also a contributor in the *An A to Z of Second Language Assessment: How Language Teachers Understand Assessment Concepts* (2018, British Council). She is the President of the Bangladesh English Language Teachers Association (BELTA).

Written Corrective Feedback

Icy Lee

Written corrective feedback (WCF), also known as error feedback, error correction or grammar correction (Lee, 2004; Truscott, 1996), refers to feedback on language errors for the purpose of developing students' written accuracy (Bitchener & Ferris, 2012; Bitchener & Storch, 2016).

Thanks to Truscott's (1996) landmark article that argues vehemently for the abandonment of grammar correction in writing, research on WCF has mushroomed and remained vibrant for over two decades. Much of the WCF research has focused on the amount of WCF (i.e. whether teachers should respond to all errors comprehensively or to errors selectively) and the WCF strategies that are most effective in helping students improve written accuracy (e.g. whether teachers should provide correct answers, simply indicate error location, or use error codes). Findings for these two lines of research are inconclusive.

Although research evidence is largely in favour of focused WCF (i.e. teachers responding to a number of error types), such research has predominantly taken place in experimental or quasi-experimental classrooms with a focus on one or two error types only, which is considered to lack relevance for real classroom contexts. In the absence of conclusive research evidence about the effectiveness of comprehensive WCF (Truscott & Hsu, 2008; Van Beuningen et al., 2008), also drawing on second language acquisition perspectives, researchers suggest that teachers adopt focused WCF so as not to overload students cognitively with a large number of disparate errors (Bitchener, 2008); in any event some of the grammar items covered in teacher comprehensive WCF are likely to fall outside learners' readiness (Pienemann, 1998) making uptake impossible. Bitchener and Ferris (2012) advise that comprehensive WCF is suitable for advanced learners whose writing exhibits few errors.

I. Lee (✉)
Faculty of Education, The Chinese University of Hong Kong, Shatin, Hong Kong
e-mail: icylee@cuhk.edu.hk

© Springer Nature Switzerland AG 2021
H. Mohebbi and C. Coombe (eds.), *Research Questions in Language Education and Applied Linguistics*, Springer Texts in Education,
https://doi.org/10.1007/978-3-030-79143-8_76

Research on the effectiveness of WCF strategies has similarly yielded inconclusive findings. There is evidence about the benefits of indirect WCF (i.e. indicating errors without provision of correct answers) (e.g. Ferris, 2006; Lalande, 1982), leading to the conclusion that an indirect approach to WCF can involve students in "guided learning and problem solving" (Lalande, 1982, p. 143) and promote reflection on students' existing knowledge (Bitchener & Ferris, 2012). More recent research has, however, found that direct WCF (i.e. providing correct answers) may be more beneficial than indirect WCF in the long term (Bitchener & Knoch, 2010; Van Beuningen et al., 2008, 2012), and it is especially "preferable if learners are unable to correct their own errors" (Shintani et al., 2014, p. 105). Research has also addressed the effectiveness of codes (e.g. "T" for "verb tense) in indirect WCF, again producing mixed research findings (e.g., Ferris & Roberts, 2001; Robb et al., 1986). While codes can enhance students' cognitive engagement (Ferris, 2011), they are mainly useful in classrooms that emphasize explicit grammar instruction.

Translated into classroom practice, focused WCF is likely to benefit less proficient L2 learners, indirect and direct WCF can be used with treatable/rule-governed and untreatable/non-rule-governed errors respectively, and coded WCF may best suit learners with strong explicit knowledge of grammar. Overall, the effectiveness of comprehensive versus focused WCF and of various WCF strategies cannot be determined without consideration for context-related and individual learner factors, such as the instructional context and learners' proficiency level, beliefs and attitudes (Storch, 2018).

The Research Questions

1. What are teachers' beliefs about comprehensive and focused WCF? What have shaped their beliefs?
2. Do teachers put their beliefs about comprehensive/focused WCF into practice? What discrepancies are there, if any, between their beliefs and practice, and what are the reasons for such discrepancies?
3. What are students' attitudes to comprehensive WCF? What are the reasons for their preference for/dislike of comprehensive WCF?
4. Is focused WCF more effective than comprehensive WCF in helping students improve written accuracy?
5. May a combination of focused and comprehensive WCF be effective in helping students improve their accuracy in writing?
6. How do students respond to/engage with coded WCF? Does coded WCF help students improve written accuracy better than uncoded WCF?
7. Is providing correct answers for errors (i.e. direct WCF) effective in helping students improve written accuracy?

8. Is metalinguistic explanation supplemented with direct WCF effective in enhancing students' written accuracy?
9. What problems/challenges do teachers face in giving WCF?
10. What roles does language awareness play in influencing teachers' WCF?

Suggested Resources

Bitchener, J., & Ferris, D. R. (2012). Written corrective feedback in second language acquisition and writing. New York: Routledge.

This volume, which is the first of its kind to bring together the second language acquisition and writing/composition research, augments our understanding of written corrective feedback by surveying theory, research and practice on the topic. Authored by two prominent feedback researchers in the field, the book provides a state-of-the-art review of written corrective feedback, as well as a critical analysis and comprehensive synthesis of research on oral and written corrective feedback in second language acquisition, and impact of written corrective feedback in second language writing. The book also explores practical applications of written corrective feedback theory and research, ending with a chapter that addresses how writing teachers can be prepared to give written corrective feedback in language learning and composition contexts.

Bitchener, J., & Storch, N. (2016). *Written corrective feedback for L2 development*. Bristol: Multilingual Matters.

With a focus on written corrective feedback and L2 development, this book addresses the language learning potential of written corrective feedback, advancing our understanding of the role of written corrective feedback in second language acquisition. The book brings together cognitive and sociocultural perspectives, both theoretical and empirical, and critically reviews how these two different paradigms can contribute to our understanding of key issues in the controversial topic of written corrective feedback. Specifically, the authors examine cognitive processing conditions, context-related and individual learner factors in facilitating or inhibiting the effectiveness of written corrective feedback for L2 development. The book provides useful insights for L2 writing researchers and teachers, offering them useful theoretical, methodological and pedagogical implications for research and practice.

Ferris, D. R. (2011). *Treatment of error in second language student writing* (2nd ed). Ann Arbor: University of Michigan Press.

This second edition of the book by Ferris examines the topic of error treatment for the benefit of second language teaching. Although intended mainly for writing teachers, the volume offers a balanced treatment of theory and practice, providing researchers with ideas for classroom research and practical implications for teachers to help them enhance their written corrective feedback practices. Common issues that plague novice and experienced writing teachers are examined in the book, such as whether teachers should respond to errors comprehensively or selectively, which errors teachers should respond to and when, and what strategies are most effective to help students improve written accuracy. The book also offers ideas about how teachers can be trained to treat errors in student writing in writing teacher preparation programmes. The discussion/analysis questions at the end of each chapter can provide practical ideas for teacher professional development workshops.

Lee, I. (2019). Teacher written corrective feedback: Less is more. *Language Teaching, 52, 524–536.*

This position paper addresses a central debate in the written corrective feedback literature—whether teachers should respond to all errors in student writing comprehensively, or whether they should adopt a focused approach to written corrective feedback. In the paper, Lee argues that more written corrective feedback is not better, but instead less is more. Focused written corrective feedback is recommended as "the staple approach" for L2 student writers except for proficient or advanced learners who make few errors in writing. The author begins by analyzing the problems arising from comprehensive written corrective feedback and then examines the benefits of focused written corrective feedback for teachers and students. She further scrutinizes some common arguments against focused written corrective feedback that pose impediments to its implementation and provides a critical analysis of these arguments to strengthen her case for focused written corrective feedback. The position paper concludes with suggestions about what teachers, teacher educators and researchers can do to move forward with focused written corrective feedback.

Storch, N. (2018). Written corrective feedback from sociocultural theoretical perspectives: A research agenda. *Language Teaching, 51, 262–277.*

This "Thinking allowed" paper is intended mainly for researchers as it sets out a relatively new research agenda for written corrective feedback, with concrete suggestions of research ideas for interested researchers. Storch begins by rightly indicating a lacuna in extant research on written corrective feedback, which is primarily experimental or quasi-experimental in nature, thus lacking ecological validity and pedagogical relevance. In her paper, she proposes a research agenda that is informed by sociocultural theory, drawing on three specific areas of the theory. The first area focuses on the zone of proximal development and scaffolding to ascertain the nature and appropriateness of written corrective feedback. The second area concerns the notion of mediating tools, such as computer-mediated feedback, to assess their effectiveness in helping students improve written accuracy. The final area draws on activity theory, focusing specifically on the contextual and individual learner factors that impinge on teachers' provision of written corrective feedback, as well as students' engagement with it. Each of the three areas is illustrated with examples of research tasks, with useful suggestions about research design, data collection, and data analysis.

References

Bitchener, J. (2008). Evidence in support of written corrective feedback. *Journal of Second Language Writing, 17*, 102–118.

Bitchener, J., & Ferris, D. R. (2012). *Written corrective feedback in second language acquisition and writing*. Routledge.

Bitchener, J., & Knoch, U. (2010). Raising the linguistic accuracy level of advanced L2 writers with written corrective feedback. *Journal of Second Language Writing, 19*, 207–217.

Bitchener, J., & Storch, N. (2016). *Written corrective feedback for L2 development*. Multilingual Matters.

Ferris, D. R. (2006). Does error feedback help student writers? New evidence on the short- and long-term effects of written error correction. In K. Hyland & F. Hyland (Eds.), *Feedback in second language writing: Contexts and issues* (pp. 81–104). Cambridge University Press.

Ferris, D. R. (2011). *Treatment of error in second language student writing* (2nd ed.). University of Michigan Press.

Ferris, D. R., & Roberts, B. (2001). Error feedback in L2 writing class: How explicit does it need to be? *Journal of Second Language Writing, 10*, 161–184.

Lalande, J. F. (1982). Reducing composition errors: An experiment. *The Modern Language Journal, 66*, 140–149.

Lee, I. (2004). Error correction in L2 secondary writing classrooms: The case of Hong Kong. *Journal of Second Language Writing, 13*, 285–312.

Pienemann, M. (1998). *Language processing and second language development: Processability theory*. John Benjamins.

Robb, T., Ross, S., & Shortreed, I. (1986). Salience of feedback on error and its effect on EFL writing quality. *TESOL Quarterly, 20*, 83–96.

Shintani, N., Ellis, R., & Wataru, S. (2014). Effects of written feedback and revision on learners' accuracy in using two English grammatical structures. *Language Learning, 64*, 103–131.

Storch, N. (2018). Written corrective feedback from sociocultural theoretical perspectives: A research agenda. *Language Teaching, 51*, 262–277.

Truscott, J. (1996). The case against grammar correction in L2 writing classes. *Language Learning, 46*, 327–369.

Truscott, J., & Hsu, A. Y. (2008). Error correction, revision, and learning. *Journal of Second Language Writing, 17*, 292–305.

Van Beuningen, C. G., De Jong, N. H., & Kuiken, F. (2008). The effect of direct and indirect corrective feedback on L2 learner's written accuracy. *International Journal of Applied Linguistics, 156*, 279–296.

Van Beuningen, C. G., De Jong, N. H., & Kuiken, F. (2012). Evidence on the effectiveness of comprehensive error correction in second language writing. *Language Learning, 62*, 1 41.

Icy Lee is currently a Professor in the Department of Curriculum and Instruction of the Faculty of Education, The Chinese University of Hong Kong. Her publications have appeared in international journals such as the *Journal of Second Language Writing, TESOL Quarterly, Language Teaching, System* and *Language Teaching Research*. She was former editor of the *Journal of Second Language Writing* and currently Principal Associate Editor of *The Asia–Pacific Education Researcher*. She was President of the Hong Kong Association for Applied Linguistics and Chair of the NNEST (Nonnative English Speakers in TESOL) Interest Section of the TESOL International Association. She has won several international awards, including the TESOL Award for Excellence in the Development of Pedagogical Materials (1998–1999) and the TESOL Award for Excellence in Teaching (2009–2010).

Writing Assessment Literacy

Deborah Crusan

Although classroom writing assessment is a significant responsibility for writing teachers, many instructors lack an understanding of sound and effective assessment practices in the writing classroom aka Writing Assessment Literacy (WAL). WAL can be defined as the ability of teachers to create effective assignments and their accompanying scoring tools, to understand the reasons for assessing their students' writing, to recognize the value of student self-assessment, to identify why, how, and when to use data gathered from assessments, and to carry on their assessment duties ethically and conscientiously (Crusan et al., 2016). As has been evident from past research (Crusan, 2010; Lee, 2017; Weigle, 2007) a research-practice gap exists and is a main barrier to implementation of good writing assessment practices.

The practical aspects of writing assessment literacy cannot be overlooked. Without it, teachers are left to make decisions about assessment with little theoretical and practical knowledge. Let us consider the very new writing teacher coming from a teacher education program that required no assessment component. Regardless of the lack of training, that new teacher's job centers on making decisions about her students' ability to write. What happens in her classroom when her students submit their first assignment? How did she frame that assignment? Did she provide criteria for her students? Do students know what they have to do? Does the teacher know what she wants her students to do? Teachers should consider these aspects and be prepared to implement good assessment practices such as fairness, accountability, and transparency when grading.

D. Crusan (✉)
Department of English Language and Literatures, Wright State University, Dayton, USA
e-mail: deborah.crusan@wright.edu

© Springer Nature Switzerland AG 2021
H. Mohebbi and C. Coombe (eds.), *Research Questions in Language Education and Applied Linguistics*, Springer Texts in Education,
https://doi.org/10.1007/978-3-030-79143-8_77

It is clear, then that assessment is complex; because language is not a static entity, neither can assessment be. Teachers need to be clear about what it is we are testing. Requirements must be clearly defined. One way to clearly express our criteria is through the creation of effective, ethical rubrics. Rubrics provide feedback to teachers regarding instructional effectiveness and supply benchmarks upon which to measure and document progress. They also provide feedback to students in the form of criteria—a rubric can specify exactly what is expected in the assignment.

Crusan (2010) cautions teachers to be mindful of the rubric in their heads, a set of criteria or standards that, even though they have not been overtly shared with students, often underlie all the criteria upon which students will be graded. A good rubric, therefore, is as important for the teacher as it is for the student because it forces teachers to focus on the explicit evaluation criteria. Rubrics can also be used to train students to give peer feedback and aid them in developing confidence and competence in their ability to express themselves in writing.

While it is true that creating effective and efficient assessment tools remains a labor-intensive endeavor, the benefits far outweigh the assertion. For one thing, teachers establish accountability to and credibility with their students by providing them with clear, accessible, and understandable assessment materials, which also provide necessary transparency. This kind of rapport and trust between student and teacher cannot be overestimated.

The Research Questions

1. In what ways have second language writing teachers obtained assessment knowledge?
2. What are the common beliefs held by second language writing teachers about writing assessment?
3. What are the assessment practices of second language writing teachers?
4. What is the impact of linguistic background on writing assessment knowledge, beliefs, and practices?
5. What is the impact of teaching experience on writing assessment knowledge, beliefs, and practices?
6. What skills are necessary for teachers to claim that they are literate in writing assessment?
7. How can teaching be enhanced through writing assessment literacy?
8. In what ways might teachers' work be shaped by testing policies and practices?
9. How does context affect teacher practices in writing assessment?
10. Should teachers be required to provide evidence of writing assessment literacy? If so, how?

Suggested Resources

Crusan, D., Plakans, L., & Gebril, A. (2016). Writing assessment literacy: Surveying second language teachers' knowledge, beliefs, and practices. *Assessing Writing*, *28*, 43–56. **https://doi.org/10.1016/j.asw.2016.03.001**.

Claiming a teacher knowledge gap in all aspects of writing assessment, the authors explore ways in which writing teachers have obtained writing assessment literacy. Asserting that teachers often feel un(der)prepared for the assessment tasks they face in the writing classroom, the researchers surveyed 702 writing teachers from around the globe to establish evidence for this claim; the researchers found that although teachers professed education in assessment in general and writing assessment in particular, these same teachers worried that they are less than sure of their abilities in rubric creation, written corrective feedback, and justification of grades, crucial elements in the assessment of writing. The study also uncovered interesting notions about linguistic background: NNESTs reported higher levels of writing assessment literacy.

Fernando, W. (2018). Show me your true colours: Scaffolding formative academic literacy assessment through an online learning platform. *Assessing Writing*, *36*, 63–76. https://doi.org/10.1016/j.asw.2018.03.005

In this paper, the author focuses on student writing processes and examines ways those processes are affected by students' formative academic literacy assessment. Does formative academic literacy promote more engagement with composing processes and if so, what evidence supports this proposition? To investigate, the author asked students to use an online learning platform to generate data in the form of outlines/essays with feedback, student-generated digital artefacts, and questionnaires/follow-up interviews to answer two important questions: "(1) How can formative academic literacy assessment help students engage in composing processes and improve their writing? (2) How can online technology be used to facilitate and formatively assess student engagement with composing processes?" (p. 65). Her findings offer evidence for and indicate that students benefit from understanding their composition processes; additionally, this understanding is furthered by scaffolding formative academic literacy assessment through an online platform that uncovers and overcomes students' difficulties as they learn to write.

Inbar-Lourie, O. (2017). Language Assessment Literacy. In: E. Shohamy, I. Or, & S. May (Eds.), *Language Testing and Assessment: Encyclopedia of Language and Education* **(3rd ed.). Cham, Switzerland: Springer.**

While this encyclopedia entry does not specifically address *writing* assessment literacy, it provides an excellent definition of *language* assessment literacy (LAL) and broadly informs the field of this definition and argues for the need for teachers to be assessment literate. Calling for the need to define a literacy framework in language assessment and citing as a matter still in need of resolution the divide between views of formative and dynamic assessment. Operationalization of a theoretical framework remains important, but contextualized definitions might be the more judicious way to approach this issue, since many different stakeholders (e.g. classroom teachers, students, parents, test developers) are involved.

Lam, R. (2015). Language assessment training in Hong Kong: Implications for language assessment literacy. *Language Testing, 32*(2), **169–197. https://doi. org/10.1177/0265532214554321**

Although this article is not specifically about writing assessment literacy, its author makes the same arguments for training of teachers as those who argue for writing assessment literacy for teachers. These arguments bring home the lack of teacher education in assessment in general and writing assessment in particular. Lam surveys various documents, conducts interviews, examines student assessment tasks, and five institutions in Hong Kong, targeting pre-service teachers being trained for the primary and secondary school settings. Lam uncovered five themes running through the data from which he distills three key issues: (1) local teacher education program support for further language assessment training, (2) taking care that the definition of LAL is understood from an ethical perspective, and (3) that those who administer the programs in Lam's study collaborate to assure that pre-service teachers meet compulsory standards for language assessment literacy.

Xu, Y., & Brown, G. T. L. (2016). Teacher assessment literacy in practice: A reconceptualization. *Teaching and Teacher Education, 58,* **149–162.**

The authors synthesized 100 studies concerning teacher assessment literacy (TAL) to determine what has and has not worked in the advancement of TAL. Following this and based on their findings of their comprehensive literature review, the authors developed a conceptual framework of Teacher Assessment Literacy in Practice (TALiP), which calls for a crucial knowledge base for all teachers, but which the authors call necessary but not sufficient. They then go on to categorize other aspects that need to considered before a teacher can be fully assessment literate, calling the symbiosis between and among components reciprocal. Along with the knowledge base, elements include the ways in which teachers intellectualize assessment, contexts involved especially institutional and socio-cultural, TALiP (the framework's primary notion), teacher learning, and ways (or if) in which teachers view themselves as competent assessors. The framework has implications for multiple platforms: pre-service teacher education, in-service teacher education, and teacher training challenges encountered when attempting expansion of TAL.

References

Crusan, D. (2010). *Assessment in the second language writing classroom*. University of Michigan Press.

Crusan, D., Plakans, L., & Gebril, A. (2016). Writing assessment literacy: Surveying second language teachers' knowledge, beliefs, and practices. *Assessing Writing, 28*, 43–56. https://doi.org/10.1016/j.asw.2016.03.001

Lee, I. (2017). *Classroom writing assessment and feedback in L2 school contexts*. Springer.

Weigle, S. C. (2007). Teaching writing teachers about assessment. *Journal of Second Language Writing, 16*, 194–209. https://doi.org/10.1016/j.jslw.2007.07.004

Deborah Crusan is professor of TESOL/Applied Linguistics at Wright State University where she prepares teachers for the language classroom and teaches linguistics, assessment, and pedagogical grammar in the MATESOL program and writing assessment in the English graduate program. Her work has appeared in numerous academic journals and edited collections. Her research interests include writing assessment for placement, writing teacher education, directed self-placement, and the politics of assessment. With Todd Ruecker, she recently published *The politics of English second language writing assessment in global contexts* (Routledge). Her earlier book, *Assessment in the Second Language Writing Classroom*, was published by University of Michigan Press. She serves as a member of TESOL International Association's Board of Directors (2016–2019).

Part IV
Language Skills and Subskills

Aural Vocabulary Knowledge

78

Joshua Matthews

L2 aural vocabulary knowledge (AVK) is an important yet relatively under-researched and underemphasized dimension of L2 vocabulary knowledge (Matthews, 2018; Siegel, 2016). AVK in very simple terms is knowledge of what a word 'sounds' like in speech. In more complete terms, AVK is the store of knowledge that facilitates accurate perception of the phonological form of spoken words and enables rapid mapping of those forms onto existing representations held in the mental lexicon of the listener.

Words in speech have different attributes to words presented in the written form, and these differences make the development of AVK challenging for many language learners. For example, unlike words written on a page, spoken lexis is available to the listener for only a very short period of time, and in order for meaning to be reliably extracted words need to be recognized very quickly. In short, the effective application of AVK occurs within tight time constraints. Additionally, the spaces between words on a page are explicit, but words in speech are typically produced in connected intonation units which have no acoustic 'blank space' between them, and this makes lexical segmentation challenging for the L2 listener. Further, the phonological form of a word in speech is often influenced by its surrounding acoustic context resulting in significant modification (e.g., reduced forms, assimilation, clision, resyllabification, etc. See Field, 2003, pp. 329–332). A learner may know a word when it is presented in the written form, but without adequate levels of AVK, this same word may not be recognized and understood when it is encountered in speech (Goh, 2000).

Ensuring learners have an adequate breadth of AVK appears to be important because it is strongly associated with L2 listening comprehension success, especially AVK of the most frequent 3000 words (Matthews & Cheng, 2015). However, efforts to develop the AVK of learners should proceed with an appreciation of the

J. Matthews (✉)
School of Education, University of New England, Armidale, NSW, Australia
e-mail: Joshua.Matthews@une.edu.au; jmatth28@une.edu.au

© Springer Nature Switzerland AG 2021   439
H. Mohebbi and C. Coombe (eds.), *Research Questions in Language Education and Applied Linguistics*, Springer Texts in Education,
https://doi.org/10.1007/978-3-030-79143-8_78

modality specific nature of vocabulary knowledge. Aural vocabulary and written vocabulary are best thought of as distinct constructs (Cheng & Matthews, 2018). For this reason, efforts to develop AVK should involve greatly increasing learners' meaningful engagement with spoken target language discourse (e.g., Chang & Millett, 2014), which is an element of language learning that is often lacking especially in EFL contexts. Further, systematic testing of AVK is also important, but traditional vocabulary tests are often mediated solely through the written modality and the production of a broader range of tests that measure AVK would be a useful step forward.

The Research Questions

1. Overview and synthesize the relevant literature in order to define AVK. Develop a protocol that could be used to operationalize this construct in an action research project in a classroom.
2. Undertake a small scale investigation with second language learners. Devise and implement a methodology that could be used to determine whether AVK is important for this group of language learners or not?
3. Overview and synthesize the relevant literature that describes current approaches to testing AVK. Use a theoretical framework of your choice to substantiate your criticism of the existing modes of testing AVK.
4. Design and validate a new test format that would be useful in efforts to systematically measure AVK. What improvements to existing aural vocabulary tests will this new test bring?
5. What research protocols and instruments could be used to effectively measure and track the development of AVK of a group of L2 language learners over time?
6. What pedagogical interventions are effective in developing AVK; for example, do extensive listening programs boost the AVK of learners?
7. What is the strength of association between AVK and L2 listening comprehension, and is this strength of association standard across different proficiency levels and different first language groups?
8. Does quasi-experimental investigation demonstrate that an improvement in AVK among a treatment group results in improved L2 listening comprehension performance when compared to that of a control group?
9. How can technology be used to effectively test and enhance the AVK of language learners?
10. What can qualitative investigations of groups of learners with low and high AVK tell us about the factors that facilitate and impede its development in authentic language learning contexts?

Suggested Resources

Cheng, J., & Matthews, J. (2018). The relationship between three measures of L2 vocabulary knowledge and L2 listening and reading. *Language Testing, 35* **(1), 3–25**

This research article presents the relationship between three forms of vocabulary knowledge and L2 listening and reading. Three vocabulary tests were administered among 250 tertiary level Chinese EFL students; two of the test formats were delivered solely in the written modality, whereas a third test format required test takers to process stimulus through the aural modality. Results indicated that AVK was far more predictive of L2 listening test scores than was vocabulary knowledge measured solely in the written form. Factor analysis also indicated that orthographic (written) and phonological (aural) test elements loaded onto different factors, suggesting that AVK and written vocabulary knowledge should be considered as distinct constructs. This is one of the few large studies that investigates AVK and clearly demonstrates the modality specific nature of this construct and the value it has in predicting L2 listening.

Matthews, J. (2018). Vocabulary for listening: Emerging evidence for high and mid-frequency vocabulary knowledge. *System, 72,* **23–36**

This article investigates the relationship between AVK and L2 listening comprehension among 247 tertiary level Chinese EFL students. Results indicated that measures of high and mid-frequency level AVK were able to predict over half of the variance observed in L2 listening test scores for the entire cohort. The written component and the sound file for the 63 item AVK test used in the research are available in the article's appendix. This article presents an initial picture of the strong link between AVK and L2 listening among the participants of the study, but more research, especially among learners with a range of L1 backgrounds, is required in order to confirm the generalizability of these findings to other contexts.

Matthews, J., Cheng, J., & O'Toole, J. M. (2015). Computer-mediated input, output and feedback in the development of L2 word recognition from speech. *ReCALL, 27* **(3), 321–339**

This article reports on a quasi-experimental investigation that sought to establish the effectiveness of a computer-mediated approach to the development of word knowledge mediated through the aural modality. The article describes the design features of an online computer application that provides learners with increased opportunities to engage with aural input, while also affording opportunities to produce output and receive automated feedback. A treatment group of 65 participants used the application over a period of five weeks, and their mean capacity to recognize words from the aural modality improved over that time when compared to the 30 control group participants that didn't use the application. This study presents one example of how technology can be used to develop AVK among a cohort of language learners and encourages the development and evaluation of more sophisticated technology-mediated approaches to the development of AVK, including those that can be delivered through mobile technology.

McLean, S., Kramer, B., & Beglar, D. (2015). The creation and validation of a listening vocabulary levels test. *Language Teaching Research*, *19*(6), 741–760

This article presents an initial validation of a new vocabulary test that measures test takers' aural vocabulary knowledge. The test version described in the article is specifically designed for Japanese English language learners, as there are elements of the test written in Japanese. The Listening Vocabulary Levels Test entails learners listening for target words in aural stimulus and matching them to their corresponding meaning (presented as one of four multiple choice options). Target words are drawn from the 1000 to 5000-word frequency level and there is also a section that measures AVK of academic words. The study describes the administration of the test among 214 Japanese university students and also presents a useful framework that can be applied to the validation of new tests. The study concludes with a call to produce and validate similar test formats that are suitable for use in other language learning contexts.

Siegel, J. (2016). Listening Vocabulary: Embracing Forgotten Aural Features. *RELC Journal*, *47*(3), 377–386

This article is a reflective description of a classroom-based innovation designed to improve AVK among first-year university students in Japan. The author explains that AVK is typically underemphasized in the study context, with learners often having better knowledge of lexis in written form than they do for the same words presented in speech. Examples of some of the activities that were undertaken during the intervention are described, and interview data overviewing some of the participants' impressions of the AVK development activities are presented. The article concludes with suggestions that the application of similar pedagogical approaches may be useful for learners of different ages and proficiency levels. Rigorous investigation of the efficacy of such recommendations through quantitative and qualitative approaches represents a potentially useful direction for future research.

References

Chang, A. C., & Millett, S. (2014). The effect of extensive listening on developing L2 listening fluency: Some hard evidence. *ELT Journal, 68*(1), 31–40.

Cheng, J., & Matthews, J. (2018). The relationship between three measures of L2 vocabulary knowledge and L2 listening and reading. *Language Testing, 35*(1), 3–25.

Field, J. (2003). Promoting perception: Lexical segmentation in L2 listening. *ELT Journal, 57*(4), 325–334.

Goh, C. C. (2000). A cognitive perspective on language learners' listening comprehension problems. *System, 28*, 55–75.

Matthews, J. (2018). Vocabulary for listening: Emerging evidence for high and mid-frequency vocabulary knowledge. *System, 72*, 23–36.

Matthews, J., & Cheng, J. (2015). Recognition of high frequency words from speech as a predictor of L2 listening comprehension. *System, 52*, 1–13.

Siegel, J. (2016). Listening vocabulary: Embracing forgotten aural features. *RELC Journal, 47*(3), 377–386.

Joshua Matthews has a Ph.D. in education specializing in TESOL from the University of Newcastle, Australia, and is currently a lecturer at the School of Education at the University of New England, Australia. His main research interests include the use of technology in language teaching and learning, L2 vocabulary knowledge, L2 listening, and language testing. He has undertaken TESOL research in Thailand, China, Japan and Australia, and his previous research articles have been published in journals such as *Language Testing, Computer Assisted Language Learning, ReCALL* and *Language Learning and Technology*. Dr. Matthews always welcomes correspondence from fellow researchers, including research students.

Ali Shehadeh

Although there is no clear consensus among researchers on what collaborative is, it is possible to say that there is a general agreement among researchers that collaborative writing (CW) is a situation in which two or more learners work together on producing a single piece of writing. In addition to this broad definition, researchers have put forward other, more specific definitions for CW. An early definition of CW was provided by Bruffee (1984) who defines CW in terms of what mostly characterizes it: a group intellectual activity mediated by *conversation*. He explains that "(w)hat students do when working collaboratively on their writing is not write or edit or, least of all, read or proof. What they do is converse. They talk about the subject and about the assignment. They talk through the writer's understanding of the subject" (p. 645).

Other researchers, particularly Storch, view writing in general, and CW in particular as a process rather than a product (Storch, 2005, 2011, 2013). Storch defines CW as "the joint production or the coauthoring of a text by two or more writers" (Storch, 2011, p. 275). Based on this definition, for a text to be collaboratively produced, it should be carried out through collaborative processes including all writing phases such as outlining, planning and drafting, and coming up with one final draft. Louth et al. (1993) define CW as an activity in which "group members interact during the writing process and the group is responsible for the final product" (p. 217). Reviewing the various definitions, Shehadeh (2011, pp. 293–294) defines CW as an educational strategy in which pairs or small groups of L2 learners produce or co-author a single text based on their joint effort throughout all the writing phases including brainstorming, planning and outlining, generating ideas, drafting, revising, and producing the final product. Ede and Lunsford (1990) identify three vital criteria of CW: (a) substantive interaction among students in

A. Shehadeh (✉)
Curriculum and Instruction, United Arab Emirates University, Al Ain, UAE
e-mail: Ali.Shehadeh@uaeu.ac.ae

© Springer Nature Switzerland AG 2021
H. Mohebbi and C. Coombe (eds.), *Research Questions in Language Education and Applied Linguistics*, Springer Texts in Education,
https://doi.org/10.1007/978-3-030-79143-8_79

pairs or small groups, (b) shared decision making power, and (c) the production of a single written text.

With the shift move towards learner-centered instruction (LCI) in education in general and second/foreign language (L2) teaching and learning in particular in the last 20–25 years, CW has become a favored and effective classroom strategy. What really makes CW an effective strategy in teaching L2 learners is the powerful pairing of writing and verbal interaction among learners in pairs or small groups. The role of interaction in second language learning is based on both theoretical and pedagogical foundations. Theoretically speaking, first, **cognitive theories** to language acquisition, whether first or second, view interaction as fundamentally important (Long, 1996). In second language acquisition (SLA), considering the learning potentials, tasks and activities containing writing and verbal interaction are more effective than tasks containing only speaking or writing (Weisberg, 2006). Moreover, Swain's (1985, 2000) output model emphasizes learner's pushed output in the language acquisition process because only when learners use their language, do they notice gaps in their interlanguage and test hypotheses they formed about it, which activates their cognitive internal processes, and then learning occurs. Second, the **social constructivist** approach by Vygotsky (1978) puts human development in an interactional framework. The child, as a novice member of the community, depends on adults (experts) to learn language and develop socially and cognitively. Thus, human knowledge is a social construction that occurs, and is constructed, in a social context of relationships; and consequently, conversation and social interaction are necessary for learning. Viewed from this perspective, CW is a classroom-based socially constructed activity important for L2 language and writing development.

From a pedagogical perspective, learning in pairs or small groups helps learners communicate in the second language. Communication-based approaches to L2 learning and teaching like communicative language teaching (CLT) and task-based language teaching (TBLT) enable learners to negotiate meaning and form (Long, 1998) and develop their language skills because they provide a great deal of interaction. Moreover, CW tasks are meaning oriented though they can focus on some linguistic form, which advances both learner writing and language knowledge in general. In such a CW atmosphere, where learners become responsible for their learning process by being capable of making decisions and planning writing activities, learner autonomy is significantly enhanced. Through this rich and active interaction on problem solving, analyzing and evaluating activities, students not only improve their writing skills, but also advance their L2 learning process as a whole.

In summary, based on the theoretical and pedagogical importance of CW mentioned above, it is possible to summarize the benefits of CW in the L2 classroom as follows (see also Speck, 2002; Shehadeh, 2011):

(1) CW enhances students' higher-order thinking skills such as critical thinking, analyzing and evaluating.

(2) CW allows students to enrich their learning strategies by knowing how their classmates write and develop their ideas, reasoning, and problem-solving skills.
(3) CW gives students a valuable chance to get immediate feedback on their writing whether from each other or from the teacher.
(4) CW enables students to achieve together what they cannot achieve when working alone.
(5) CW lowers the anxiety in students by working in a supportive group that provides a safe audience.
(6) CW raises students' awareness -and deepens their understanding- of their audience, which better prepares them for their future careers.

The Research Questions

1. Examine the difference between collaborative writing and cooperative writing. Which one is more conducing to L2 learning? Why?
2. To what extent do you think that CW depends on the proficiency level of the learners and/or their age group?
3. To what extent do you think CW is determined by socio-cultural factors?
4. Think of your teaching situation, do you think that CW can be applied in your context? Why? Why not?
5. How would you investigate the effectiveness of CW in your teaching situation?
6. To what extent can you utilize CW in a traditional, teacher-centered teaching situation?
7. What role does technology play in facilitating the utilization of CW in the L2 classroom?
8. In what way and to what degree do you think that task-based language teaching facilitates CW?
9. How would you investigate whether and to what degree CW enhances students' higher-order thinking skills such as critical thinking, analyzing, transfer of knowledge, and evaluating?
10. To what extent do you think that CW impacts on the other language skills like reading, speaking and listening?

Suggested Resources

Manchón, R. (Ed.). (2009). *Writing in foreign language contexts.* **Clevedon, England: Multilingual Matters.**

This collection of chapters is solely devoted to theory, research and pedagogy on L2 writing in foreign language (FL), as opposed to second language (SL) contexts. In her introductory, conceptualization chapter to the volume, Manchón states that "... mainstream pedagogical discussions have rarely debated whether or not instructional recommendations for SL contexts apply to FL settings" (p. 2). She also points out that "the SL bias of scholarly work in the field [...] means that the bounds of claims of official discourse have not been sufficiently tested across diverse contexts (much less across widely varying EFL contexts)" (pp. 16–17). The volume extends research boundaries on L2 writing from FL to SL contexts. Although the volume does not address the issue of CW in detail, it has motivated a number of researchers to investigate the potential of CW in L2 in various FL contexts.

Shehadeh, A. (2011). Effects and student perceptions of collaborative writing in L2. *Journal of Second Language Writing, 20,* **286–305.**

In part motivated by Manchón's (2009) volume above on extending research from second language (SL) to foreign language (FL) contexts, Shehadeh investigated the effectiveness and students' perceptions of CW in an EFL setting in two intact classes at a large university in the UAE. Results of the study showed that CW has had an overall significant effect on students' L2 writing; however, this effect varied from one writing skill area to the other. Specifically, the effect was significant for the components of content, organization, and vocabulary, but not for grammar or mechanics. Most students who used CW during the 16-week semester of the study found the experience enjoyable and felt that it contributed to their L2 learning. The paper discusses a number of theoretical and pedagogical implications based on the findings of the study.

Storch, N. (2013). *Collaborative writing in L2 classrooms.* **Clevedon, England: Multilingual Matters.**

This is the first book-length treatment of CW in L2 classrooms. In this book Storch, an internationally renowned scholar in the field of L2 writing, provides theoretical, pedagogical and empirical rationales for the use of CW in L2 classes, both in face-to-face settings and in online mode. The book discusses factors that impact on the nature and outcomes of CW, and examines teachers and students' beliefs about CW. The book critically reviews the existing literature on CW, obtaining theoretical and research insights from a wide range of intellectual traditions, including SLA, interaction studies, sociocultural theory, composition studies, and L2 writing. Storch concludes the book by outlining a principled and detailed research agenda on CW, thereby encouraging researchers to continue investigating CW in the L2 classroom.

Byrnes, H. and Manchón, R. (Eds.). (2014). *Task-based language learning: Insights from and for L2 writing.* **Amsterdam: John Benjamin's.**

This volume is motivated by the rationale that research within the task-based language teaching (TBLT) framework can be enriched and advanced by investigating the complex phenomenon of writing. The main purpose of the volume is to foster fuller appreciation of the construct of *task* in our understanding of learning and teaching L2 writing. The various contributions consider the relationship between TBLT and L2 writing research from a range of perspectives. Although the volume is not specifically devoted to CW per se; nonetheless, it provides important insights into CW, given that one of the main underlying principles of TBLT is students' pair/group collaborative work in the L2 classroom including CW.

Belcher, D. & Hirvela, A. (Ed.). (2018). *Teaching writing* **(Volume IV).** *The TESOL encyclopedia of English language teaching,* **First Edition. Edited by John I. Liontas (Project Editor: Margo DelliCarpini), Hoboken, USA: John Wiley & Sons, Inc.**

This encyclopedia volume is part of the largest encyclopedia project in the world to date on English language teaching. It is the Wiley Blackwell 8-volume print (14-volume online) encyclopedia titled *The TESOL encyclopedia of English language teaching.* The *Teaching writing* volume consists of five sections: Core Issues Contexts, Responding to and Assessing Writing, Writing Curricula and New Technologies, and Writing Teacher Preparation and Research. The volume places all aspects and issues relevant to L2 writing, including collaborative writing, into perspective. It considers the theory, research, pedagogy, and practice of all aspects of L2 writing from a wide range of perspectives including cognitive, socio-cultural, and interactional viewpoints.

References

Bruffee, K. (1984). Collaborative learning and the "conversation of mankind." *College English, 46*(7), 635–652.

Ede, L., & Lunsford, A. (1990). *Singular texts/plural authors.* Southern Illinois University Press.

Long, M. (1996). The role of the linguistic environment in second language acquisition. In W. C. Ritchie & T. K. Bhatia (Eds.), *Handbook of language acquisition* (Vol. 2, pp. 413–468). Academic Press.

Long, M. (1998). Focus on form in task-based language teaching. *Working Papers in ESL, 16*(2), 35–49.

Louth, R., McAllister, C., & McAllister, H. A. (1993). The effects of collaborative writing techniques on freshman writing and attitudes. *The Journal of Experimental Education, 61*(3), 215–224.

Shehadeh, A. (2011). Effects and student perceptions of collaborative writing in L2. *Journal of Second Language Writing, 20*(4), 286–305.

Speck, B. (2002). *Facilitating students' collaborative writing (Report No 6).* Wiley Periodicals Inc.

Storch, N. (2005). Collaborative writing: Product, process, and students' reflections. *Journal of Second Language Writing, 14*(3), 153–173.

Storch, N. (2011). Collaborative writing in L2 contexts: Processes, outcomes, and future directions. *Annual Review of Applied Linguistics, 31*, 275–288.

Storch, N. (2013). *Collaborative writing in L2 classrooms*. Multilingual Matters.

Swain, M. (1985). Communicative competence: Some roles of comprehensible input and comprehensible output in its development. In S. Gass & C. Madden (Eds.), *Input in second language acquisition* (pp. 235–253). Newbury House.

Swain, M. (2000). The output hypothesis: Mediating acquisition through collaborative dialogue. In J. Lantolf (Ed.), *Sociocultural theory and second language learning* (pp. 97–114). Oxford University Press.

Vygotsky, L. (1978). *Mind in society: The development of higher psychological processes.* Harvard University Press.

Weisberg, R. (2006). *Connecting speaking and writing.* University of Michigan Press.

Ali Shehadeh is Professor of Applied Linguistics and TESOL in the Department of Curriculum and Instruction, College of Education, UAE University (UAEU). He has taught under- and postgraduate courses in Applied Linguistics, Second Language Acquisition (SLA) and TESOL. He has supervised or sat on the committees of over 45 Master's and Doctoral dissertations in the region and beyond. He published in top-tier research journals in the field like *Language Learning, TESOL Quarterly, System, Journal of Applied Linguistics, Journal of Second Language Writing,* and *ELT Journal.* Dr. Shehadeh has a total of 80 + publications to his name. These include: Refereed journal articles and book chapters; Edited books; Articles in international ELT specialized magazines; Encyclopedia entries; and Book reviews.

Developing L2 Listening Fluency

80

Anna A. C.-S. Chang

Good listening skills seem to burgeon much later than good reading skills and other linguistic knowledge dimensions. This is because listening used to be considered a passive skill; its major function was to receive spoken messages and comprehend them. This view, however, has recently been reconsidered (Richards, 2005; Vandergift, 2004). Scholars suggest that L2 learners first must learn to listen, so they can use their improved listening skills to acquire more knowledge of the target language. When L2 learners can comprehend the spoken messages without difficulties, they have developed the ability to listen fluently. Listening fluency normally involves two elements: ease and speed, which means that L2 learners can comprehend oral utterances delivered at a normal speed without paying too much attention to decoding the language elements and can also restructure what is heard with what is already known (Nation & Newton, 2009).

Given the above, the importance of developing the listening fluency skill in learning an L2 is equally important as reading, which has always been the main channel that most L2 learners prioritize in acquiring linguistic elements. Although a number of L2 listening studies have focused on the activities of enhancing listening comprehension (e.g., Chang & Read, 2006), very few studies look at approaches that would benefit L2 learners' development in fluency in the long run. The main reason is that developing L2 listening fluency is not easy, and it requires thousands of hours of exposure to the comprehensible input. L2 teachers usually do not see improvement before a course ends. More recently, based on the impressive learning outcome through numerous extensive reading studies, some L2 language scholars have started to promote implementing extensive listening programs (Chang & Millett, 2016; Chang et al., 2019) in the hope that L2 listening skills can be developed through abundant aural input. Despite this, studies into the effects of extensive listening in developing listening fluency are still under-researched. In

A. A. C.-S. Chang (✉)
Department of Applied English, Hsing Wu University, New Taipei, Taiwan
e-mail: annachang@livemail.tw

© Springer Nature Switzerland AG 2021
H. Mohebbi and C. Coombe (eds.), *Research Questions in Language Education and Applied Linguistics*, Springer Texts in Education,
https://doi.org/10.1007/978-3-030-79143-8_80

addition, unlike speaking, listening fluency seems difficult to quantify because it is a very individual process, except in an interactive context.

In addition to massive listening through investing thousands of hours of time, some L2 educators suggest narrow listening, which means that listeners focus on particular topics or genres in which they are interested (Krashen, 1996). The underpinning theory, based on some corpus studies (e.g., Rogers & Webb, 2011), is that if L2 learners listen to relevant texts, they will have a better background for comprehending the input, and the vocabulary load is lighter. With these two advantages, it is likely that the listeners will be able to process the utterances more efficiently. The materials can be audio books, TV programs, or any related audio texts.

There are some other approaches for developing L2 listening fluency—simultaneous listening and reading (so-called bimodal input), repeated listening, or extended listening-focus tasks. These aforementioned approaches, however, have not been extensively researched. The advantages of adopting simultaneous reading and listening are that if listeners can confirm what they hear through the written form, they can match the aural form and the written form; above all, bimodal input improves comprehension and hence promotes motivation to listen more (Chang, 2009). As for repeated listening, which might have been derived from repeated reading, it remains unknown whether it will work well on L2 listening fluency development. The effectiveness of these approaches leaves a number of unanswered questions for L2 researchers to explore.

The Research Questions

1. Does repeated listening to the same aural input yield comparable effects as extensive listening to massive varying aural input (assuming the length of time for input is the same)?
2. Will the effects for the approaches mentioned be moderated by L2 learners of different language proficiency?
3. What are L2 learners' perceptions of varying approaches mentioned? Does the approach favoured by the L2 learners produce better effects?
4. Which approach is most effective in developing L2 listening fluency?
5. How long does it take to see the effects of developing listening fluency through extensive (wide) listening?
6. Is narrow listening more effective than wide listening for developing L2 listening fluency?
7. Can the fluency gained through narrow listening be extended to comprehending topics beyond a specific scope?
8. Will the effects of listening plus doing extended listening-focused task significantly differ from listening without listening-focused tasks?

9. Is the narrow viewing of TV programs more effective than narrow reading while listening to audio books?
10. What are the differences in selecting approaches for developing listening fluency between good listeners and poor listeners?

Suggested Resources

Nation, I. S. P. & Newton, J. (2009). *Teaching ESL/EFL Listening and Speaking*. Routledge: Taylor & Francis Group.

This book is written based on the lead author's framework—four strands in a language curriculum. The book draws on theory and research of applied linguistics and provides many useful hands-on techniques for L2 teachers. Each technique is described in detail, so it is easy to use. There is a total of 10 chapters. In Chap. 9, the authors focused particularly on developing listening fluency. Apart from providing a few listening fluency activities, the authors explain how to include listening fluency in a course, and how to link listening skills with other skills, e.g., reading and listening, listening and speaking, speaking and listening.

Field, J. (2008). *Listening in the Language Classroom*. Cambridge, UK: Cambridge University Press.

This is must-read for anyone who wants to teach listening and does listening research. The book begins with a review of the development of listening instruction, from the very beginning of the comprehension approach, which focuses on the listening product, to the later process approach, in which the author emphasizes the importance of understanding the factors that impede listeners' comprehension. This book clarifies many misconceptions about teaching listening because many L2 teachers focus on the listening product rather than the process and using reading techniques to teach listening.

Brown, S. (2011). *Listening Myths: Applying Second Language Research to Classroom Teaching*. Ann Arbor, MI: The University of Michigan Press.

Listening Myths is a very user-friendly book, and it explores eight myths that people generally believe about listening. The eight myths are that listening is the same as reading; that listening is passive; that listening equals comprehension; that acquiring L2 is the same as acquiring L1 listening; that listening means listening to conversations; that listening is an individual, inside-the-head process; that students should listen only to authentic materials; and that listening can't be taught. The organization of the book is very clear and highly interesting to read. Every chapter contains three sections for each myth: in the real world, what the research says, and what we can do. Although the author did not focus on developing listening fluency, all suggestions made are relevant to developing good listening skills. For teachers who might be bored with reading serious research papers, this book makes reading research papers more entertaining.

Chang, A. C. S., & Millett, S. (2016). Developing L2 listening fluency through extended listening-focused activities in an extensive listening program. *RELC Journal, 47*(3), 349–362.

This study attempts to answer two research questions. The first one is whether the competence gained from listening to narrative types of listening could be transferred to comprehending conversational types of input; that is to explore whether students listening to stories can improve their TOEIC scores. This is a question that is frequently asked by teachers and students. The second question regards the effect size for doing varying amounts of listening-focused activities on listening improvement. Three groups of university students read and listened to 15 audio graded readers during a fifteen-week period, then they completed varying amounts of post-listening-focused activities, quantities ranging from 0, 5, 10, and 15. The study provided interesting answers for teachers who want to improve their students' listening competence but are afraid that the content they provide students does not help students' standardized test scores. This study suggests that the quantity and quality of listening practice are equally important.

Chang, A. C. S., Millett, S., & Renandya, A.W. (2019). Developing listening fluency through supported extensive listening practice. *RELC Journal, 50*(3), 422–438.

This is a longitudinal study, aiming to examine the levels of listening support that might facilitate L2 learners' listening fluency development. Sixty-nine EFL college students completed a 39-week intervention in which student participants studied a total of 28 graded readers with their corresponding audio CDs through one of the three modes: (1) students listened to stories without reading texts, but at the same time they answered listening questions, (2) students did not listen to any of graded readers but only read them, and (3) students read the graded readers while listening to audio CDs, afterwards doing extended listening activities without supporting materials. Overall, this study shows that developing listening fluency takes time, and for lower-level students, listening requires some written support, in particular for more difficult texts.

References

Chang, A. C. S., & Millett, S. (2016). Developing L2 listening fluency through extended listening-focused activities in an extensive listening program. *RELC Journal, 47*(3), 349–362.

Chang, A. C. S., & Read, J. (2006). The effects of listening support on the listening performance of EFL learners. *TESOL Quarterly, 40*(2), 375–397.

Chang, A. C. S. (2009). Gains to L2 listeners from reading while listening versus listening only in comprehending short stories. *System, 37*(4), 652–663.

Chang, A. C. S., Millett, S., & Renandya, A. W. (2019). Developing listening fluency through supported extensive listening practice. *RELC Journal, 50*(3), 422–438.

Krashen, S. D. (1996). The case for narrow listening. *System, 24*(1), 97–100.

Nation, I. S. P., & Newton, J. (2009). *Teaching ESL/EFL Listening and Speaking*. Routledge.

Richards, J. C. (2005). Second thoughts on teaching listening. *RELC Journal, 36*(1), 85–92.

Rodgers, M., & Webb, S. (2011). Narrow viewing: The vocabulary in related television programs. *TESOL Quarterly, 45*(4), 689–717.

Vandergrift, L. (2004). Listening to learn or learning to listen. *Annual Review of Applied Linguistics, 24*, 3–25.

Anna A. C.-S. Chang has a Ph.D. in Applied Linguistics from Victoria University of Wellington, New Zealand, and is a professor of the Department of Applied English at Hsing Wu University, New Taipei, Taiwan. Her main research interests focus on the development of listening and reading fluency, and vocabulary learning. She has published many articles in international journals (e.g., SSLA, RELC, System, RFL) in the areas of developing reading and listening fluency, and also on vocabulary learning through extensive reading.

Extensive Reading

Willy A. Renandya and Yuseva Iswandari

Extensive reading is an approach to language teaching that aims to facilitate second language acquisition by immersing L2 learners with large amounts of interesting and comprehensible language. In extensive reading, students choose what they want to read, how they want to read it and what they want to do with it after they have finished reading. The key consideration is that students should understand and enjoy what they read. Research shows that students who read a great deal in the target language become more fluent (i.e., they read faster and with greater comprehension) and independent readers, acquire more vocabulary, develop more advanced grammar and improve their overall proficiency of the language. Research also shows that students who engage in extensive pleasure reading gradually develop a higher level of motivation and have more positive attitudes towards language learning.

Extensive reading draws insights from second language acquisition theories and research. The key theoretical construct behind extensive reading is the Comprehension Hypothesis (Krashen et al., 2017), which states that we learn language when we read and hear language we understand. Extensive reading, defined as reading compelling and comprehensible materials, provides L2 learners with the opportunity to be immersed in rich and comprehensible language. This type of exposure is believed to be beneficial for language learning. Two recent meta-analysis studies provide convincing empirical evidence that extensive reading can produce a positive impact on L2 language development (Jeon & Day, 2016; Nakanishi, 2015). There are numerous other studies that have investigated the

W. A. Renandya (✉)
English Language and Literature, National Institute of Education, Nanyang Technological University, Singapore, Singapore
e-mail: willy.renandya@nie.edu.sg

Y. Iswandari
English Language Education, Sanata Dharma University, Yogyakarta, Indonesia
e-mail: yuseva@usd.ac.id

© Springer Nature Switzerland AG 2021
H. Mohebbi and C. Coombe (eds.), *Research Questions in Language Education and Applied Linguistics*, Springer Texts in Education,
https://doi.org/10.1007/978-3-030-79143-8_81

relationship between extensive reading and a set of language learning variables considered to be important in language acquisition. Examples of these include studies that examined how levels of student motivation influenced frequency and amount of reading and the extent to which extensive reading facilitated the acquisition of vocabulary, grammar and other language skills.

Extensive reading is different from the more traditional approach to teaching reading called intensive reading. In intensive reading, students typically read short texts that are often linguistically too demanding, containing many unfamiliar language features (i.e., new words and complex grammatical structures). The contents are also unappealing for the majority of the students. Not surprisingly, an intensive reading lesson looks more like a language practice session where the teacher spends time explaining the meaning of new words and new grammatical constructions. Students do a lot of activities about reading, but spend little time doing actual reading in the classroom. In extensive reading, students learn to read by reading, choosing what they want to read and having an enjoyable time reading their selection.

The implementation of extensive reading should be guided by a set of principles. Day and Robb (2015), Renandya and Jacobs (2002) and others have proposed a set of key principles that should be followed: (1) Students should read in quantity, (2) Reading materials should be highly interesting and comprehensible; (3) Reading materials should cover a wide range of topics to cater for the diverse needs and interests of the students, (4) Students should be given the freedom to choose what they want to read, and (5) Simple and fun post-reading activities should be used to increase student motivation. In addition to these principles, scholars believe that the success of an extensive reading programme is dependent upon the availability of a passionate and motivating teacher, one who is an avid reader, who serves as a model of a good reader and who tirelessly nurtures a healthy and lasting reading habit in their students.

The Research Questions

1. How can a balance between extensive reading and intensive reading be achieved in a second language programme?
2. What are L2 students and teachers' beliefs and practices of extensive reading?
3. Does reading digital graded readers result in students doing more reading compared to reading non-digital graded readers?
4. What is the effect of narrow reading on reluctant readers' reading motivation?
5. What are some of the key factors that may weaken the impact of extensive reading on L2 students' overall language proficiency?
6. How can extensive reading be implemented in low resource environments?

7. Is extensive reading equally beneficial for lower and higher proficiency students?
8. How much reading is needed before students can reap the full benefit of extensive reading?
9. What's the effect of a one year extensive reading programme on L2 students' academic writing proficiency?
10. How does home literacy culture affect the practice of extensive reading in school?

Suggested Resources

Day, R. R. & Bamford, J. (1998). *Extensive reading in the second language classroom*. Cambridge: Cambridge University Press.

This is a highly recommended book for those who need a comprehensive account of extensive reading. It provides a historical account of extensive reading in the context of English as a second and foreign language, explains the theories behind extensive reading and summarizes the empirical evidence that supports its implementation in the language classroom. Day and Bamford argue convincingly for the inclusion of extensive reading in language teaching and provide a valuable and practical guide to implementing it in a L2 curriculum.

Extensive Reading Foundation website: www.erfoundation.org

The Extensive Reading Foundation website provides a wealth of online resources for language teachers and researchers. Teachers can find useful online resources on how to start an extensive reading programme, how to find relevant reading materials, how to nurture a reading culture in school and how to seek advice from extensive reading scholars. The website houses a large annotated bibliography containing abstracts of over 600 books, journal articles, book chapters, theses and dissertations related to extensive reading in second and foreign language learning contexts.

Jeon, Eun-Young., & Day, R. R. (2016). The effectiveness of ER on reading proficiency: A meta-analysis. *Reading in a Foreign Language*, 28(2), 246–265.

This is an important meta-analysis study involving more than 70 empirical research studies published from 1980 to 2014 that examined the impact of extensive reading on reading proficiency (reading rate, comprehension and vocabulary). The authors found that the effect was largely positive, ranging from small to medium effect sizes. The study also found that (1) the effect of extensive reading was more pronounced for adults than children and teenagers; (2) the effect of extensive reading was higher in EFL than in ESL contexts (3) web-based materials produced a stronger effect than print-based materials. Finally, extensive reading produced the highest impact when implemented as an integral part of a curriculum (than as an extracurricular activity or an independent reading course).

Krashen, S. (2004). *The power of reading.* **Heinemann and Libraries Unlimited (second edition).**

In this book, Krashen builds a compelling case for self-selected extensive reading by reviewing hundreds of empirical research studies conducted in the past decades. He argues that self-selected reading often has strong effects on the reading development of a wide range of language learners; children, teenagers, older adults and second language learners can benefit a great deal from narrow and wide reading. He calls for schools to relook at their literacy programmes, urging them to fill school libraries with a rich collection of high interest books that cater to the diverse needs of their students.

Nakanishi, T. (2015). A Meta-Analysis of Extensive Reading Research. *TESOL Quarterly,* **49(1), 6–37.**

This is another important meta-analysis of extensive reading research that explored the overall impact of extensive reading on language learning. The study included 34 empirical studies from 1997 to 2012, designed to answer two major research questions: whether learners' age had an impact on learning and whether length of time had an effect of test scores. The overall impact was largely positive. The effect size was medium (d = 0.46) for the group contrasts and larger (d = 0.71) for the pretest–posttest comparisons. Older participants enjoyed a higher level of language learning benefits compared to younger ones, and participants who stayed longer in the extensive reading programme. Based on the findings, the author suggested that there was sufficient evidence to include extensive reading in the L2 curriculum.

References

Day, R. R., & Robb, T. (2015). Extensive reading. In D. Nunan & J. C. Richards (Eds.), *Language learning beyond the classroom* (pp. 3–12). Routledge.

Jeon, E.-Y., & Day, R. R. (2016). The effectiveness of ER on reading proficiency: A meta-analysis. *Reading in a Foreign Language, 28*(2), 246–265.

Krashen, S. Lee, S. Y., & Lao, C. (2017). *Comprehensible and compelling: The causes and effects of free voluntary reading.* Libraries Unlimited. ABC-CLIO, LLC.

Nakanishi, T. (2015). A meta-analysis of extensive reading research. *TESOL Quarterly, 49*(1), 6–37.

Renandya, W. A., & Jacobs, G. M. (2002). Extensive reading: Why aren't we all Doing it? In J. C. Richards & W. A. Renandya (Eds.), *Methodology in language teaching: An anthology of current practice* (pp. 295–302). Cambridge University Press.

Willy A Renandya is a language teacher educator with extensive teaching experience in Asia. He currently teaches applied linguistics courses at the National Institute of Education, Nanyang Technological University, Singapore. He has given numerous plenary presentations at regional and international conferences and has published extensively in the area of second language education. He maintains an active language teacher professional development forum called Teacher Voices: https://www.facebook.com/groups/teachervoices/.

Yuseva Iswandari is an English language lecturer and language teacher educator at Sanata Dharma University, Indonesia. She holds an MA degree in language education from Arizona State University. She was Chair of IERA (2016–2020), Indonesian Extensive Reading Association (http://iera-extensivereading.id/) and has been actively promoting extensive reading in her university and also in the local schools. In 2018, she organized a week-long extensive reading roadshow, co-facilitating extensive reading workshop sessions in a number of universities in Indonesia with Dr. Willy Renandya of National Institute of Education, Nanyang Technological University, Singapore and Dr. Rob Waring of Notre Dame Seishin Women's University, Okayama, Japan.

Berna Hendriks and Frank van Meurs

In recent decades, the increasing numbers of non-native speakers of English worldwide (Crystal, 2003) has prompted researchers to investigate the effects of non-native accentedness in English for speakers with different L1 backgrounds. The English of non-native speakers is characterised by different degrees of accentedness as a result of, for example, years of language instruction received (Moyer, 1999), or learners' aptitude for mimicry (Purcell & Suter, 1980); for an overview of such factors, see Gluszek et al. (2011).

Research into the effects of degrees of non-native accentedness began as early as the 1970s and the research has been summarized in, for example, Cargile and Giles (1998, p. 341), Dragojevic et al., (2017, pp. 386–387), Hendriks et al., (2016, p. 3), and Hendriks et al., (2017, p. 47). Studies have investigated the English of a speakers with a variety of L1s (e.g., Chinese, Dutch, German, Japanese, Korean, Mandarin, Punjabi, Saudi Arabian) and for a variety of listeners: native speakers of British or American English and a variety of NNE listeners (Albanian, Algerian, Bangladeshi, Chinese, Dutch, Ethiopian, Finnish, French, German, Greek, Jordanian, Korean, Malaysian, Nigerian, Norwegian, Polish, Spanish, Saudi Arabian, Sri Lankan, and Thai) (see Van Meurs & Hendriks, 2017).

Studies investigating the effect of accentedness are typically carried out using matched guise or verbal guise methodologies. In matched guise studies, the same speaker produces recordings of the same text in all varieties under investigation (e.g. Dragojevic et al., 2017; Rubin & Smith, 1990), whereas in verbal guise studies different speakers produce recordings of the same text in the different varieties (Hendriks et al., 2016, 2017, 2018; Nejjari et al., 2012).

B. Hendriks (✉) · F. van Meurs
Language and Communication/Centre for Language Studies, Radboud University, Nijmegen, The Netherlands
e-mail: b.hendriks@let.ru.nl

F. van Meurs
e-mail: f.v.meurs@let.ru.nl

© Springer Nature Switzerland AG 2021
H. Mohebbi and C. Coombe (eds.), *Research Questions in Language Education and Applied Linguistics*, Springer Texts in Education,
https://doi.org/10.1007/978-3-030-79143-8_82

Accentedness studies have measured the effect of degrees of accentedness in terms of understanding and attitudinal evaluations of the speaker. Understanding has been evaluated with functional measures and perceptual measures. Functional measures include *intelligibility*, which involves asking listeners to orthographically transcribe what they hear (Nejjari et al., 2012; Rubin & Smith, 1990; Stibbard & Lee, 2006), *comprehensibility*, which involves testing listeners' understanding of the content of the message (Nejjari et al., 2012), and *interpretability*, which involves testing listeners' understanding of the purpose of the message (Nejjari et al., 2012). When perceptual measures are used, listeners are asked to indicate how difficult to understand they consider the speaker and recording to be (Hendriks et al., 2016, 2017, 2018; Roessel et al., 2019).

Attitudinal evaluations in accentedness studies have included *status* of the speaker (Bresnahan et al., 2002; Cargile & Giles, 1998; Dragojevic et al., 2017; Hendriks et al., 2017; Nejjari et al., 2012), *competence* of the speaker (Hendriks et al., 2016, 2017, 2018; Roessel et al., 2019), *teaching* ability (Rubin & Smith, 1990), *affect* (Dragojevic et al., 2017; Hendriks et al., 2017; Nejjari et al., 2012; Roessel et al., 2019), *dynamism* (Bresnahan et al., 2002; Cargile & Giles, 1998), and *solidarity* (Dragojevic et al., 2017).

Overall, accentedness studies have shown that both native and non-native listeners evaluated relatively strongly accented speakers more negatively than weakly accented speakers and native speakers in terms of understanding as well as attitudinal evaluations, while weakly accented speakers are evaluated as positively as native speakers on both dimensions.

The Research Questions

1. Which features (e.g. phonetic discrepancies, intonation) of non-native English pronunciation are most annoying?
2. Are there differences in evaluation of speakers with different L1 backgrounds? For instance, are Korean English speakers evaluated differently from German English speakers?
3. Which dimensions/dependent variables are affected most by foreign accent strength?
4. Is foreign accent strength evaluated differently in different contexts (e.g., informal versus formal, classroom versus business)?
5. What listener characteristics are relevant to evaluations of foreign accent strength (e.g. native versus non-native listeners, listeners with the same versus different L1 backgrounds)?
6. Does it matter which native speaker variety (e.g. British, American, Canadian) is used in accentedness research?
7. How can speakers compensate for the effect of foreign accent strength? For instance, what strategies can speakers use to improve clarity and the impression they make?

8. Can listener beliefs about foreign accent strength be changed?
9. What is the relative effect of foreign accent strength versus non-nativeness in other areas (e.g. grammar, vocabulary, style) on speaker evaluation and comprehensibility?
10. Can the effect of foreign accent strength be investigated using psychophysiological methods, such as electrodermal activity (EDA) or Electroencephalography (EEG)?

Suggested Resources

Derwing, T. M., & Munro, M. J. (2015). *Pronunciation fundamentals: Evidence-based perspectives for L2 teaching and research.* **Amsterdam/ Philadelphia: John Benjamins Publishing Company.**

This book discusses the history of pronunciation teaching with a focus on why and when pronunciation teaching may be necessary and when it should start. Written by two leading authorities in the field of pronunciation research, it offers a comprehensive overview of this research area for graduate students, language instructors and language researchers. The book includes a discussion of L2 phonetic acquisition and reviews empirical pronunciation studies with a focus on intelligibility and implications for teaching. Separate chapters are devoted to the importance of error gravity, pronunciation assessment and the ethics of accent reduction. The book also discusses social aspects of accentedness and the changing role of English pronunciation in view of the emergence of World Englishes and English as a lingua franca.

Fuertes, J. N., Gottdiener, W. H., Martin, H., Gilbert, T. C., & Giles, H. (2012). A meta-analysis of the effects of speakers' accents on interpersonal evaluations. *European Journal of Social Psychology, 42*(1), 120–133. **https://doi.org/10.1002/ ejsp.862**.

This paper is a good starting point for graduate students and researchers interested in investigating accentedness. It reports on a meta-analysis of empirical studies about the effects of accentedness on attitudinal evaluations. It provides an overview of characteristics that have been included in accentedness research about the effects of standard accents versus non-standard accents (both foreign and spoken by minorities), albeit with a strong focus on American English, rather than British English. In discussing effect sizes found in accentedness studies, the authors show that accentedness can have a powerful effect on how speakers are perceived by others. The article also outlines an agenda for future research in accentedness, which may be useful for anyone designing a research study in this area.

Jenkins, J. (2000). *The phonology of English as an international language.* **Oxford: Oxford University Press.**

Against the backdrop of the increasing numbers of non-native speakers of English, Jennifer Jenkins discusses the consequences of English as an International Language (EIL) for English Language Teaching (ELT) and pronunciation teaching in particular. She argues against the importance of native English L1 varieties as the norm against which non-native accents are evaluated. Instead, she argues in favour of establishing a phonological core of intelligibility, a so-called Lingua Franca Core. Such a Lingua Franca Core should ensure mutual intelligibility among ELF speakers and be at the basis of pronunciation teaching. The main part of the book is devoted to outlining the linguistic features of the Lingua Franca Core, followed by implications for pronunciation teachers. The book is a useful resource for anyone (teachers, researchers) interested in ELT pronunciation teaching and/or pronunciation research.

Gluszek, A., & Dovidio, J. F. (2010). The way they speak: A social psychological perspective on the stigma of nonnative accents in communication. *Personality and Social Psychology Review, 14*(2), 214–237. https://doi.org/10. 1177/1088868309359288.

This overview article discusses empirical studies on nonnative accentedness in relation to stigma as perceived by both speakers and listeners. The authors discuss studies investigating social and contextual factors that impact the effects of accentedness on speakers and listeners and their interactions. The article outlines a framework of the factors involved in the stigma of nonnative accents. It discusses possible areas of future research into the effects of accentedness as well as studies that have investigated successful interventions to deal with the effect of stigmatization caused by regional, ethnic or foreign accentedness.

Mai, R., & Hoffmann, S. (2014). Accents in Business Communication: An integrative model and propositions for future research. *Journal of Consumer Psychology, 24*(1), 137–158. https://doi.org/10.1016/j.jcps.2013.09.004

This article is useful for graduate students and researchers interested in the impact of accentedness in business contexts. It describes when and how regional or foreign accentedness can influence consumer attitudes. Using insights from social psychology and linguistics, the authors propose a model for understanding the effects of accentedness in organisational contexts. In the model, they discuss the effects of social categorization, stereotype activation, and speech processing, and factors relating to sender, receiver, and communication. The article provides extensive suggestions for further research in the area of regional and foreign accentedness in a business context.

References

Bresnahan, M. J., Ohashi, R., Nebashi, R., Liu, W. Y., & Shearman, S. M. (2002). Attitudinal and affective response toward accented English. *Language & Communication, 22*(2), 171–185. https://doi.org/10.1016/S0271-5309(01)00025-8
Cargile, A. C., & Giles, H. (1998). Language attitudes toward varieties of English: An American Japanese context. *Journal of Applied Communication Research, 26*(3), 338–356. https://doi. org/10.1080/00909889809365511
Crystal, D. (2003). *English as a global language.* Cambridge University Press.

Dragojevic, M., Giles, H., Beck, A. C., & Tatum, N. T. (2017). The fluency principle: Why foreign accent strength negatively biases language attitudes. *Communication Monographs, 84*(3), 385–405. https://doi.org/10.1080/03637751.2017.1322213

Gluszek, A., Newheiser, A.-K., & Dovidio, J. F. (2011). Social psychological orientations and accent strength. *Journal of Language and Social Psychology, 30*(1), 28–45.

Hendriks, B., van Meurs, F., & Hogervorst, N. (2016). Effects of degree of accentedness in lecturers' Dutch-English pronunciation on Dutch students' attitudes and perceptions of comprehensibility. *Dutch Journal of Applied Linguistics, 5*(1), 1–17. https://doi.org/10.1075/duja.5.1.01hen

Hendriks, B., van Meurs, F., & de Groot, E. (2017). The effects of degrees of Dutch accentedness in ELF and in French, German and Spanish. *International Journal of Applied Linguistics, 27* (1), 44–66. https://doi.org/10.1111/ijal.12101

Hendriks, B., van Meurs, F., & Reimer, A. K. (2018). The evaluation of lecturers' nonnative-accented English: Dutch and German students' evaluations of different degrees of Dutch-accented and German-accented English of lecturers in higher education. *Journal of English for Academic Purposes, 34*, 28–45. https://doi.org/10.1016/j.jeap.2018.03.001

Moyer, A. (1999). Ultimate attainment in L2 phonology: The critical factors of age, motivation and instruction. *Studies in Second Language Acquisition, 21*(1), 81–108.

Nejjari, W., Gerritsen, M., van der Haagen, M., & Korzilius, H. (2012). Responses to Dutch-accented English. *World Englishes, 31*(2), 248–267. https://doi.org/10.1111/j.1467-971X.2012.01754.x.

Purcell, E. T., & Suter, R. W. (1980). Predictors of pronunciation accuracy: A reexamination. *Language Learning, 30*(2), 271–287.

Roessel, J., Schoel, C., Zimmermann, R., & Stahlberg, D. (2019). Shedding new light on the evaluation of accented speakers: Basic mechanisms behind nonnative listeners' evaluations of nonnative accented job candidates. *Journal of Language and Social Psychology, 38*(1), 3–32. https://doi.org/10.1177/0261927x17747904.

Rubin, D. L., & Smith, K. A. (1990). Effects of accent, ethnicity, and lecture topic on undergraduates' perceptions of nonnative English-speaking teaching assistants. *International Journal of Intercultural Relations, 14*(3), 337–353.

Stibbard, R. M., & Lee, J.-I. (2006). Evidence against the mismatched interlanguage speech intelligibility benefit hypothesis. *The Journal of the Acoustical Society of America, 120*, 433–442. https://doi.org/10.1121/1.2203595

Van Meurs, F., & Hendriks, B. (2017). Native and non-native listeners' evaluation of degrees of foreign accentedness in English: A literature review. In S. Lindenburg & D. Smakman (Eds.), *Proceedings van schools tot scriptie III. Een colloquium over universitair taalvaardigheid-sonderwijs held at Leiden University on 2 December 2016* (pp. 102–111). Leiden University Repository. Retrieved January 23, 2018 from https://openaccess.leidenuniv.nl/bitstream/handle/1887/57214/Proceedings_VSTS_III_Hoofdstuk_9.pdf?sequence=1,%203.

Berna Hendriks is an Assistant Professor in the department of Language and Communication and the Centre for Language Studies at Radboud University, Nijmegen, the Netherlands. Her research focuses on aspects of the use of (B)ELF, the effects of non-native accentedness, the use of accentedness in advertising and politeness. Her work has been published in journals such as *Dutch Journal of Applied Linguistics, IEEE Transactions on Professional Communication, Intercultural Pragmatics, Journal of Business Communication, Journal of English for Academic Purposes, International Journal of Applied Linguistics, Journal of Multilingual and Multicultural Development* and *Multilingua*.

Frank van Meurs is an Assistant Professor in the department of Language and Communication and the Centre for Language Studies at Radboud University, Nijmegen, the Netherlands. His research focuses on the use and effect of English and other foreign languages in Dutch job and product advertising and on the effect of non-native accents. His work has been published in journals such as *Dutch Journal of Applied Linguistics, English for Specific Purposes, ESP across Cultures, IEEE Transactions on Professional Communication, Journal of Advertising Research, Journal of Business Communication, International Journal of Applied Linguistics, Journal of Global Marketing, Journal of Multilingual and Multicultural Development, Multilingua, Technical Communication*, and *World Englishes*.

Foreign Language Reading Fluency and Reading Fluency Methodologies

83

Greta Gorsuch and Etsuo Taguchi

One challenge for foreign language learners is getting sufficient L2 input and experience using the L2 (Gorsuch et al., 2015). Reading continues to be a reliable means for accomplishing this (Al-Homoud & Schmitt, 2009). Nation (2009) refers to extensive reading as an important tool to provide meaning-focused input in a program, where "the learners' focus is on understanding the message" (2009, p. 1). This means that learners read actual texts, and not single sentences for introducing grammar or lexis (Bernhardt, 2011; Tanaka & Stapleton, 2007). This also means that learners choose texts to read for their own self-directed purposes and needs (Kern, 2003). Fluency in lower-level reading processes is a cornerstone to successful reading comprehension (Grabe & Stoller, 2011). Without comprehension, reading cannot be input. By "reading fluency," we mean fast and accurate character and word recognition, and also basic post-lexical processes such as parsing sentences.

There are two keys to developing reading fluency. The first is to make a substantial place for reading in a foreign language curriculum (Gorsuch & Taguchi, 2009; Gorsuch et al, 2015; Taguchi & Gorsuch, 2012). A second key is to use methods to build learners' reading fluency. Poor reading fluency may persist for many learners if they do not engage in fluency building. There is an unexamined assumption in many programs that "reading" is done by having learners experience intensive reading methodologies using difficult texts. Such instructional practices or texts will not build reading fluency. Low reading fluency prevents readers from

G. Gorsuch (✉)
Classical and Modern Languages and Literatures, Texas Tech University, Lubbock, TX, USA
e-mail: greta.gorsuch@ttu.edu

E. Taguchi
Department of Japanese, Daito Bunka University, Tokyo, Japan
e-mail: taguchi@ic.daito.ac.jp

© Springer Nature Switzerland AG 2021
H. Mohebbi and C. Coombe (eds.), *Research Questions in Language Education and Applied Linguistics*, Springer Texts in Education,
https://doi.org/10.1007/978-3-030-79143-8_83

developing an enjoyment of reading independently (e.g., Grabe & Stoller, 2011; Segalowitz, 2003). Low reading fluency also impacts comprehension. Theories on information processing in reading (i.e., Automaticity Theory, LaBerge & Samuels, 1974; and Verbal Efficiency Theory, Perfetti, 1985) posit that the more attention learners need to expend on recognizing words and/or parsing basic grammar, the more their comprehension will suffer, because they have little attention available for text comprehension. By building learners' fluency, the more attention they will have for comprehending texts they read.

Extensive Reading (ER) and Repeated Reading (RR) promote L2 readers' fluency and language acquisition (Day, 2015; Nakanishi, 2015; Samuels, 1979). We believe RR can be used alone, or as a complement to conventional extensive reading (ER) programs. In RR learners read the same 300 to 500-word text multiple times with an audio version of the text.

Some new studies on RR (Chang & Millett, 2013) and meta-analyses on RR (Gutierrez, 2017) and extensive reading (ER) (Nakanishi, 2015) are encouraging. This means that RR, and other reading fluency methodologies, are being investigated and implemented. Key issues of assessing learner comprehension, and establishing and refining the relationship between reading fluency and reading comprehension, continue to propel research agendas in this area. Finally, there continues to be a need for evaluation research on methodologies used in reading fluency programs.

The Research Questions

1. When readers become more fluent, what aspects of their lower level reading processes change? How do L2 readers' skills of recognizing words, phonological processing, and orthographical processing change as their reading fluency increases? How do L2 readers' skills of grammatical parsing of texts change?
2. What would eye tracking technologies reveal about changes in learners' lower level reading processes as their fluency increased longitudinally, using new, unpracticed texts? This question is relevant to typical Extensive Reading (ER) and Repeated Reading (RR) programs.
3. What would eye tracking technologies, coupled with guided retrospective learners' reports, reveal about short-term changes in learners' lower level reading processes and comprehension as they engage in a series of reading fluency activities? This question is relevant to typical RR programs.
4. What would explain dips in learners' reading fluency as they read a new, unpracticed text? But then what would explain increasingly faster fluency rates with new, unpracticed texts when learners engage in a reading fluency program, particularly RR programs, longitudinally?

5. Do silent reading fluency methodologies affect reading fluency development and reading comprehension growth in different ways than reading fluency methodologies that provide audio models of the text?

6. What is the role of audio support in reading fluency methodologies in developing reading fluency and reading comprehension? Does it help or not help?

7. What is the relationship between reading fluency development and reading comprehension growth? What characteristics of the texts selected for fluency building affect reading comprehension growth differently? How does the length and/or intensity of fluency building programs affect reading comprehension gains? Do gains change over time?

8. What are reliable, valid, and sustainable ways to measure learners' reading fluency? Which measurement methods result in learners' motivation and self-awareness? By "sustainable," we mean methods that teachers and learners can easily use.

9. What are reliable, valid, and sustainable ways to measure learners' reading comprehension? By "sustainable," we mean testing models and methods teachers can easily and regularly use.

10. What are sustainable methods teachers can use to make a good balance between working with learners to read intensively and but also read for fluency building? There is still a need to bridge the gap between graded and authentic texts which L2 readers should cross in order to become independent readers.

Suggested Resources

Chang, C-S. & Millet, S. (2013). Improving reading rates and comprehension through timed repeated reading. *Reading in a Foreign Language, 25*(2), 126–148.

This is a well-designed 13-week quasi-experimental study that found learners in a repeated reading group read more fluently and comprehended more than a control group. This effect held even on unpracticed passages in a series of post-tests. The control group read the same number of passages as well, over 13 weeks, just not repeatedly (in other words, without a fluency building methodology), suggesting that simply reading texts in an unguided way will not have the same positive effect as treatments that have this particular methodology. The article presents an effective metanalyses of previous reading fluency studies.

Day, R.R. (2015). Extending extensive reading. *Reading in a Foreign Language, 27*(2), 294–301.

This concise article examined 44 studies out of 500 on extensive reading (ER) published since 1998. Based on the top ten principles of ER (Day, R. R. & Bamford, J. (1998). *Extensive reading in the second language classroom.* Cambridge: Cambridge University Press.) referred to in those studies, the article proposes criteria to understand various types of extensive reading programs. The criteria constitute continua grounded on the use of the top ten ER principles. On one side is the "Pure ER" using all ten principles, and on the other is the "Fringe ER" using none of them. An ER program can take various forms, and can be teacher-supervised, self-directed, or blended with intensive reading. The criteria can serve to place such programs within an extensive reading framework, allowing for principled considerations on changing or maintaining programs, and planning for resources and curricula.

Gutierrez, T. (2017). Implementing silent repeated-reading: How much can non-native readers of English be expected to develop their reading fluency? *Research Bulletin of the Institute of Humanities and Social Sciences, Nihon University, 94,* **103–125**.

This article summarizes seven studies on repeated reading (RR) in English L2 settings. It poses five questions to examine effects on L2 readers: How much RR improves L2 readers' reading rate upon each repetition, within RR treatments, and after whole RR treatments. The remaining two questions involve how RR improves L2 readers' comprehension and how RR affects L2 readers' reading behaviors. This article critically reviews seven studies using those questions, and further provides useful suggestions for future research on RR. The article will make a good starting point for researchers and teachers interested in how to develop L2 readers' fluency via RR. It also makes some recommendations on how best to implement RR based on research findings. It is an example of a significant article buried in a lesser-known research venue, that of a university-sponsored bulletin. Here is the link: https://www.chs.nihon-u.ac.jp/institute/human/kiyou/94/9.pdf

Rayner, K., Pollatsek, A., Ashby, J., & Clifton, C. E. (2012). *Psychology of reading* **(2nd ed.). London, U.K.: Psychology Press**.

This book is an excellent resource to learn about eye movement research in cognitive psychology. The book is divided into four parts, and the first two parts deal with lower-level processes of word identification. The second part, Chapters 3 to 5, make a good introduction to eye movement research in reading. Part three describes higher-level processes of reading comprehension, such as parsing and discourse comprehension. The fourth and final part deals with reading ability development. Theory-driven eye movement research using eye tracking technologies is needed to understand how L2 readers actually read, how L2 reading differs from L1 reading, and in what reading processes L2 readers are likely to encounter difficulty.

Samuels, S. J. (2004). Toward a theory of automatic information processing in reading, revisited. In R. B. Ruddell & N. J. Unrau (Eds.), *Theoretical models and processes* **(pp. 1127–1148). Newark, DE: International Reading Association.** https://doi.org/10.1598/0872075028.40.

S. J. Samuels was the first researcher who gave reading fluency its place in reading education in English L1 settings. One of the proponents of Automaticity Theory (LaBerge & Samuels, 1974), he devised a method called "repeated reading" so as to apply Automaticity Theory to instructional practice. Gorsuch, Taguchi, and their colleagues have adapted his original method to be implemented in English L2 and FL classrooms, and also to Japanese FL classrooms.

References

Al-Homoud, F., & Schmitt, N. (2009). Extensive reading in a challenging environment: A comparison of extensive and intensive reading approaches in Saudi Arabia. *Language Teaching Research, 13*, 383–401.

Bernhardt, E. (2011). *Understanding advanced second-language learning.* Routledge.

Chang, C.-S., & Millet, S. (2013). Improving reading rates and comprehension through timed repeated reading. *Reading in a Foreign Language, 25*(2), 126–148.

Day, R. R. (2015). Extending extensive reading. *Reading in a Foreign Language, 27*(2), 294–301.

Day, R., & Bamford, J. (1998). Extensive reading in the second language classroom. Cambridge University Press.

Gorsuch, G., Taguchi, E., & Umehara, H. (2015). Repeated reading for Japanese language learners: Effects on reading speed, comprehension, and comprehension strategies. *The Reading Matrix, 15*(2), 18–44.

Gorsuch, G. J. & Taguchi, E. (2009). Repeated reading and its role in an extensive Reading program. In A. Cirocki (Ed.), *Extensive reading in English language teaching* (pp. 249–271). Lincom Europa.

Grabe, W., & Stoller, F. (2011). *Teaching and researching reading* (2nd ed.). Longman.

Gutierrez, T. (2017). Implementing silent repeated-reading: How much can non-native readers of English be expected to develop their reading fluency? *Research Bulletin of the Institute of Humanities and Social Sciences, Nihon University, 94*, 103–125.

Kern, R. (2003). Literacy as a new organizing principle for foreign language education. In P. C. Patrikis (Ed.), *Reading between the lines: Perspectives on foreign language literacy* (pp. 40–59). Yale University Press.

LaBerge, D., & Samuels, S. J. (1974). Toward a theory of automatic information processing in reading. *Cognitive Psychology, 6*, 293–323.

Nakanishi, T. (2015). A meta-analysis of extensive reading research. *TESOL Quarterly, 49*, 6–37.

Nation, P. (2009). *Teaching ESL/EFL reading and writing.* Routledge.

Perfetti, C. (1985). *Reading ability.* Oxford University Press.

Rasinsky, T., Blachowicz, C., & Lems, K. (Eds.). (2012). Fluency instruction: Research-based best practices (2nd ed.). The Guilford Press

Samuels, S. J. (1979). The method of repeated readings. *The Reading Teacher, 32*, 403–408.

Segalowitz, N. (2003). Automaticity and second language. In C. Doughty & M. Long (Eds.), *The handbook of second language acquisition* (pp. 382–408). Blackwell.

Taguchi, E., & Gorsuch, G. J. (2012). Fluency instruction in reading in a second or foreign language. In T. Rasinsky, C. Blachowicz, & K. Lems (Eds.), *Fluency instruction: Research-based best practices* (2nd ed., pp. 255–288). The Guilford Press.

Tanaka, H., & Stapleton, P. (2007). Increasing reading input in Japanese high school EFL classrooms: An empirical study exploring the efficacy of extensive reading. *The Reading Matrix, 7*, 115–131.

Greta Gorsuch has been teaching English as a Foreign Language and Applied Linguistics in Japan, the United States, and Vietnam. She has published articles with Etsuo Taguchi and other research colleagues on reading and speaking fluency in journals such as *Language Teaching Research, Reading in a Second Language,* and *System;* and in books, including *Fluency*

Instruction: Research-based Best Practices (Rasinsky et al., 2012). She has written books on evaluation and second language testing with Dale T. Griffee, *Second Language Course Evaluation* (2016, Information Age Publishing) and *Second Language Testing for Student Evaluation and Classroom Research* (2018, Information Age Publishing). She wrote and edited *Tests that Second Language Teachers Make and Use* (2019, Cambridge Scholars Publishing).

Etsuo Taguchi is a Professor of Applied Linguistics at Daito Bunka University, Tokyo, Japan. He is interested in L2 reading processes, especially interactions between lower identification skills and higher comprehension skills. He is currently interested in scaffolding in L2 reading and how it benefits L2 readers. He seeks the best ways to promote fluency in L2 readers, in the hope that they will eventually help them become independent lifelong readers in their L2. He has been working with Greta Gorsuch and other colleagues on an online reading program which will be available for English L2 readers and teachers to use for free. He has co-authored articles which were published in *Reading in a Foreign Language, Reading Matrix*, and other professional journals and books.

Learner Corpora for Disciplinary Writing

84

Lynne Flowerdew

A learner corpus is generally taken to refer to non-native student output (Gilquin & Granger, 2015), although, arguably, students who are native speakers of English can also be considered as novice writers as they are undergoing acculturation into disciplinary discourses and practices (Friginal, 2013). While early studies of learner corpora of writing centred on argumentative essays, more recent studies target specific academic genres in different disciplines, e.g. dissertations in biochemistry. The majority of learner corpora of disciplinary writing are usually compiled in the local context and are relatively small, ranging from 50,000 to one-million words (Flowerdew, 2004). Many investigations target postgraduate writing and have a strong focus on examining concordance output of lexico-grammatical patterning for specific rhetorical functions.

Very recent developments in the field include the investigation of professional genres (Conrad, 2017), investigation of (quasi)-longitudinal data of learner production across different years of study (Hafner & Wang, 2018; Miller & Pessoa, 2018) and increased use of qualitative methods (interviews and close textual analysis) to aid analysis and interpretation of quantitative corpus data (Parkinson et al., 2017). More emphasis is now attached to the compilation of local learner corpora for pedagogic purposes, either for data-driven learning (DDL) or corpus-informed activities (Kwon et al., 2018). While corpus linguistic techniques have been used to analyse English as a lingua franca (ELF) and advanced learner language of disciplinary writing, there have to date been no substantial studies investigating similarities and differences between the two (Flowerdew, 2019).

L. Flowerdew (✉)
Department of Applied Linguistics and Communication,
Birkbeck, University of London, London, UK
e-mail: flowerdewlynne@gmail.com

© Springer Nature Switzerland AG 2021
H. Mohebbi and C. Coombe (eds.), *Research Questions in Language Education and Applied Linguistics*, Springer Texts in Education,
https://doi.org/10.1007/978-3-030-79143-8_84

There are a number of methodological issues to consider. One issue concerns the choice of reference corpus exemplifying expert writing for comparison purposes. Not only is the size of both the learner and expert corpus important, but whether each contains a sufficient number of texts from the genre and discipline under investigation to ensure representativeness. Other issues concern whether the corpus should be tagged (annotated) for specific features such as errors or rhetorical structures, and which corpus tools and statistical procedures are suitable for the item (s) under investigation (see Weisser, 2016 for a user-friendly overview of these issues).

The findings from corpus-based analyses of learner disciplinary writing can usefully inform needs analyses and materials development in EAP/ESP by targeting the specific language needs of a specific group of learners (see Chambers, 2015 for representative case studies) and can also be used for testing and assessment purposes (Nordrum & Eriksson, 2015). However, this important sub-field of applied corpus linguistics is a relatively under-developed area and requires more attention in teacher education programs.

The Research Questions

1. What are some of the issues for the teacher to consider in building a learner corpus of disciplinary writing for research purposes?
2. What are some of the issues for the teacher to consider in building a learner corpus of disciplinary writing for (primarily) pedagogic purposes?
3. What are the advantages and drawbacks of tagging a learner corpus?
4. What kinds of linguistic enquiry can be carried out on learner corpora of disciplinary writing?
5. What kinds of reference corpora are suitable for comparison with a learner corpus of disciplinary writing?
6. Who might the teacher interview and why to collect additional data for a learner corpus study?
7. What are the advantages and disadvantages of using learner corpora of disciplinary writing for hands-on concordancing with students?
8. What problems might students face in building self-compiled corpora for pedagogic purposes of their own disciplinary writing and expert writing?
9. Who is responsible (the teacher or student) for deciding which items to investigate in a learner corpus of disciplinary writing?
10. How can the teacher know whether the concordancing activities using learner corpora have been successful?

Suggested Resources

Charles, M. (2018). Corpus-assisted editing for doctoral students: More than just concordancing. *Journal of English for Academic Purposes*, **36, 15–25**.

The few accounts in the literature on using learner corpora with doctoral students mostly focus on lexicogrammatical and functional aspects of writing aimed at students in the early stages of writing up their theses. The DDL tasks described make use of concordancing software. In contrast, this article discusses a course which is targeted at late-stage doctoral students and illustrates how individual expert and learner corpora, compiled by the students themselves, can be used for editing purposes. The author illustrates how the affordances of individual tools in the freely-available and user-friendly software package *Antconc* (http://www.laurenceanthony.net/software) can be used to tackle editing challenges not only at the linguistic level but also in terms of organisation and content. The application of corpus tools for addressing known issues (concordance, clusters and collocates, concordance plot) as well as tools targeting issues unknown to students (n-grams, word lists, keyword lists) are illustrated with reference to individual case studies.

Cotos, E. (2014). Enhancing writing pedagogy with learner corpus data. *ReCALL*, **26(2), 202–224**.

To date, several experimental studies have been carried out to gauge the effectiveness of using expert corpora for pedagogic purposes. However, another key question to ask is whether students benefit from writing instruction using *learner* corpus data. The study reported in Cotos (2014) on linking adverbials provides promising results on this issue. The participants in this study were 31 international graduate students from a variety of disciplines who were divided into two groups. All students had access to a one-million-word NS corpus in his/her own discipline while the experimental group also had access to a local learner corpus (final term papers etc.). Pre- and post- tests were conducted on the same two writing tasks and two questionnaires completed. At the end of the semester the author also analysed students' final term papers as a delayed production component of the experiment. While there has been some criticism of exposing students to learner data on account of its erroneous nature, the results of this experiment suggest that having students notice a gap between their writing and expert writing can enhance writing pedagogy.

Flowerdew, L. (2015). Learner corpora and language for academic and specific purposes. In S. Granger, G. Gilquin & F. Meunier (Eds.). *The Cambridge Handbook of Learner Corpus Research* **(pp. 465–484). Cambridge: Cambridge University Press**.

This chapter has a strong focus on disciplinary writing. Flowerdew outlines key learner corpus studies as well as major academic reference corpora against which learner corpora are compared. She notes the difficulty in sourcing corpora which are exactly comparable to the learner corpus in terms of genre, discipline and educational context. She also outlines the main types of phraseological investigations that have been carried out (lexico-grammatical patterning of keywords, lexical-bundles approach; pattern-grammar approach). Metadiscourse and comparison with EAP vocabulary lists are other major areas of investigation. The point is made that until 2015 the majority of learner corpus studies of disciplinary writing employed bottom-up lexico-grammatical approaches, with only a few studies combining these with a more top-down Swalesian genre-analytic approach.

Granger, S. Gilquin, G. & Meunier, F. (Eds.) (2015). *The Cambridge Handbook of Learner Corpus Research.* **Cambridge: Cambridge University Press.**

This handbook is essential reading for researchers and practitioners alike. All 27 chapters follow a similar format (Introduction; Core issues; Representative studies; Critical assessment and future directions). The handbook is divided into the following five parts:

Part I: Learner corpus design and methodology.
Part II: Analysis of learner language.
Part III: Learner corpus research and second language acquisition.
Part IV: Learner corpus research and language teaching.
Part V: Learner corpus research and natural language processing.

Parts I, II and IV are of particular relevance for the analysis of learner corpora of disciplinary writing and the applications thereof. Part I deals with issues relating to compilation, annotation and statistics for learner corpus research. The focus of Part II is on the key language features examined (lexis, phraseology, grammar, discourse and pragmatics). Several of the representative studies in Part IV cover disciplinary writing.

Friginal, E. (2018). *Corpus Linguistics for English Teachers. New Tools, Online Resources and Classroom Activities.* **London: Routledge.**

This timely volume bridges theory and practice with its focus on the 'English teacher as a corpus-based researcher'. The volume comprises the following three main parts: (A) Corpus linguistics for English teachers: Overview, definitions and scope, (B) Tools, corpora and online resources, and; (C) Corpus-based lessons and activities in the classroom. While the book is a general textbook on corpus linguistics, this up-to-date volume is highly recommended for researchers/ practitioners working in the area of disciplinary writing. There is valuable information in each part which is of relevance for the use of learner corpora for disciplinary writing; for example, written learner corpora and their compilation are discussed in Part B.

References

Chambers, A. (2015). The learner corpus as a pedagogic corpus. In S. Granger, G. Gilquin, & F. Meunier (Eds.), *The Cambridge handbook of learner corpus research* (pp. 446–464). Cambridge University Press.

Conrad, S. (2017). A comparison of practitioner and student writing in civil engineering. *Journal of Engineering Education, 106*(2), 191–217.

Cotos, E. (2014). Enhancing writing pedagogy with learner corpus data. *ReCall, 26*(2), 202–224.

Flowerdew, L. (2004). The argument for using English specialised corpora to understand academic and professional language. In U. Connor & T. Upton (Eds.), *Discourse in the professions* (pp. 11–33). John Benjamins.

Flowerdew, L. (2019). English as a lingua franca and learner English in disciplinary writing: A corpus perspective. In K. Hyland & L. Wong (Eds.), *Specialised English: New directions in ESP and EAP research and practice* (pp. 79–90). Routledge.

Friginal, E. (2013). Developing research report writing skills using corpora. *English for Specific Purposes, 32*, 208–220.

Gilquin, G., & Granger, S. (2015). Learner language. In D. Biber & R. Reppen (Eds.), *The Cambridge handbook of english corpus linguistics* (pp. 418–435). Cambridge University Press.

Hafner, C., & Wang, S. (2018). Hong Kong learner corpus of legal academic writing in English. *TESOL Quarterly, 52*(3), 680–691.

Kwon, H., Partridge, R., & Staples, S. (2018). Building a local learner corpus: Construction of a first-year ESL writing corpus for research, teaching, mentoring and collaboration. *International Journal of Learner Corpus Research, 4*(1), 112–127.

Miller, R., & Pessoa, S. (2018). Corpus-driven study of information systems project reports. In V. Brezina & L. Flowerdew (Eds.), *Learner corpus research: New perspectives and applications* (pp. 112–133). Bloomsbury.

Nordrum, L., & Eriksson, A. (2015). Data commentary in science writing: Using a small specialised corpus for formative self-assessment practices. In M. Callies & S. Götz (Eds.), *Learner corpora in language testing and assessment* (pp. 59–83). John Benjamins.

Parkinson, J., et al. (2017). Writing like a builder: Acquiring a professional genre in a pedagogic setting. *English for Specific Purposes, 46*, 29–44.

Weisser, M. (2016). *Practical corpus linguistics*. Wiley-Blackwell.

Lynne Flowerdew is currently a Visiting Research Fellow in the Department of Applied Linguistics and Communication, Birkbeck, University of London. She has published widely on different aspects of (applied) corpus linguistics in several international journals, including *TESOL Quarterly, International Journal of Corpus Linguistics, English for Specific Purposes* and *Journal of English for Academic Purposes*. She has co-edited the following volumes on corpus linguistics: *Learner Corpus Research: New Perspectives and Applications* (2018, Bloomsbury); *New Trends in Corpora and Language Learning* (2011, Continuum/Bloomsbury). Her authored volumes include the following: *Corpus-based Analyses of the Problem-Solution Pattern* (2008, John Benjamins) and *Corpora and Language Education* (2012, Palgrave Macmillan).

Lexical Inferencing and Vocabulary Development

Hossein Vafadar and Hassan Mohebbi

Language acquisition researchers and practitioners are now in agreement that language comprehension and vocabulary acquisition are two intertwined issues of language learning. A text contains unfamiliar words, which often leads a reader to make informed guesses or inferences in order to derive meanings by context. A proper inferencing brings along the accuracy of text comprehension, whereas an inappropriate inferencing may lead to miscomprehension. However, most readers ignore many of these unfamiliar words when they encounter them in a text and do not attempt to infer the meanings. Readers often resort to other means to deal with unknown words or confirm their inferred meanings such as asking for help or consulting a dictionary. These means, however, are not always readily available to readers.

Lexical inferencing (LIF) is one of the most common techniques that L2 learners may employ when they come across unknown lexical items (Deschambault, 2012). LIF is defined as making informed guesses about the meaning of unknown words in a text based on available linguistic and non-linguistic cues and different aspects of the learner's knowledge (Qian, 2005). It is considered a cognitive strategy through which L2 learners draw upon contextual cues and background knowledge and unite them to find out the meaning of an unknown lexical item (Wesche & Paribakht, 2010). LIF, as they argue to be the case, involves both declarative knowledge, linguistic and nonlinguistic, and procedural knowledge, such as searching for and identifying pertinent cues in a text and combining information to arrive at a plausible meaning for an unknown lexical item in the text. Successful comprehension needs inferencing at all levels of comprehension, in particular connecting text to background knowledge, various parts of the texts to each other, and known elements to unknown ones (Nassaji, 2007). Moreover, the processes involved in LIF

H. Vafadar (✉)
School of Languages, Literacies and Translation, Universiti Sains Malaysia, Penang, Malaysia

H. Mohebbi
European Knowledge Development Institute (EUROKD), Ankara, Turkey

© Springer Nature Switzerland AG 2021
H. Mohebbi and C. Coombe (eds.), *Research Questions in Language Education and Applied Linguistics*, Springer Texts in Education,
https://doi.org/10.1007/978-3-030-79143-8_85

are not only interactive, but also compensatory. When one of the components involved is deficient, it might be compensated for by other immediately present components (Pulido, 2003). It is generally accepted that L2 reading and LIF is an interaction of reader's text-based and knowledge-based processes (Alptekin, 2006).

LIF suggests that the lexical items have to be placed on a continuum at one end and with what students employ as a knowledge source to do inferencing at the opposite end. This knowledge comes from both linguistic and non-linguistic sources (Wesche & Paribakht, 2010). The linguistic sources involve L2-based sources, namely word knowledge such as word association, word morphology, and word form, sentence knowledge, including sentence meaning and grammar, and discourse knowledge, namely discourse meaning, formal schemata, and text style and register and L1-based sources which include L1 collocation and L1 word form. World/background knowledge is the non-linguistic source which might influence LIF. Nassaji (2006) stated that successful lexical inferencing may relate not only to the use of certain strategies but also on the extent to which other sources of knowledge inside and outside the text are united and worked together.

As noted above, the two intertwined issues of comprehension and vocabulary growth are of primary urgency in language learning that is worthy of further research to extend knowledge about, particularly, the ways to help them improve such as lexical inferencing.

The Research Questions

1. What is the effect of teacher's prompt and late assessment of the lexical inferencing rate of success on better acquisition of inferred words?
2. How are knowledge sources manifested at inferencing the meaning of unknown words from reading and listening?
3. What is the cross-linguistics relationship between L1 and L2 learners' lexical inferencing ability and their knowledge sources?
4. How does declarative and procedural knowledge of learners' lexical inferencing affect their vocabulary development and long-term retention of inferred words?
5. What is the relationship between individual differences, learning styles, and cognitive and mental efforts of learners with the lexical inferencing?
6. What is the effect of computerized-dynamic or static assessment on the lexical inferencing rate of success at retention of inferred words in reading and listening?
7. What are the text-based and knowledge-based factors that negatively affect the lexical inferencing and lead to unreliable meanings?
8. What is the effect of lexical inferencing pre-task modeling and repetitions on L2 learners' lexical inferencing?

9. What are the knowledge sources of lexical inferencing for L2 learners' different language proficiency levels?
10. Do collaborative lexical listening tasks lead to more accurate lexical inferencing and L2 vocabulary gain than individual lexical inferencing tasks?

Suggested Resources

Hassanzadeh, Z., Hadidi Tamjid, N., & Ahangari, S. (2019). The effect of lexical inference strategy instruction on Iranian EFL learners' vocabulary depth and breadth. *Cogent Education*, **6, 1–16.**

The article investigates the possible effects of lexical inference strategy training on Iranian upper-intermediate EFL learners' vocabulary depth and breadth. This quasi-experimental study was conducted among 45 upper-intermediate EFL learners at Simin Language Institute, in Rasht, Iran, who were selected through convenience sampling. All learners were female, aged 18 to 40, from three intact classes who were randomly assigned to one experimental group and one control group. In the experimental group, the participants were taught how to infer the meaning of new words from the context, employing lexical inference strategies. The control group received the traditional method of teaching vocabulary.

Ebadi, S., Weisi, H., Monkaresi, H., & Bahramlou, K. (2018). Exploring lexical inferencing as a vocabulary acquisition strategy through computerized dynamic assessment and static assessment. *Computer Assisted Language Learning, 31*(7), **790–817.**

In this quasi-experimental study, the authors have adopted a dynamic assessment (DA) approach and took measures to ensure noticing of the new words. They selected 80 intermediate English as a Foreign Language (EFL) students through purposive sampling. There are two groups: computerized dynamic assessment (CDA) and static assessment (SA). Participants read five texts, one per week, and inferred the meaning of highlighted unfamiliar words. In the CDA group, through a software program, struggling learners receive graduated mediational hints for each target word which help them to infer the meaning of unfamiliar words. No mediational assistance is provided to the participants of the SA group. Acquisition and retention post-tests were administered to both groups four weeks after reading each text respectively.

Wesche, M. B., & Paribakht, T. S. (2010). *Lexical inferencing in a first and second language: Cross-linguistic dimensions.* **Toronto: Multilingual Matters.**

This book includes two closely related parts: the first, a comprehensive review of research on the topic of lexical inferencing, which has co-authored by Kirsten Haastrup, consists of two chapters that together provide an overview of the topics and introduce the empirical study reported in Part 2. The second part is a presentation of a trilingual study of first language (L1) influences in second language (L2) lexical inferencing and other cross-linguistic dimensions of L1 and L2 lexical inferencing by Persian, French, and English speakers.

Zeeland, H. V. (2014). Lexical inferencing in first and second language listening. *The Modern Language Journal, 98*(4), 1006–1021.

This article assesses listeners' success at inferencing the meaning of unknown words from listening. It explores the effects of three variables found to affect lexical inferencing success in L2 reading: background knowledge, contextual clue types, and L2 vocabulary size. It also measures to what extent L2 listeners notice unknown vocabulary in listening inasmuch as this noticing is a prerequisite for any lexical inferencing to occur. The research presented in this article is carried out with both native speakers (NSs) and nonnative speakers (NNSs) of English. The NNS data are the main focus of this study, with the NS data serving as a baseline for comparison.

Paribakht, T. S. (2005). The influence of first language lexicalization on second language lexical inferencing: A study of Farsi-speaking learners of English as a foreign language. *Language Learning, 55*(4), 701–748.

This article reports on an introspective study that examined the relationship between first language (L1, Farsi) lexicalization of the concepts represented by the second language (L2, English) target words and learners' inferencing behavior while reading English texts. Participants are 20 Farsi-speaking university students of English as a foreign language. Lexicalization in the L1 may be one of the factors influencing learners' differential success in L2 text comprehension and vocabulary development.

References

Alptekin, C. (2006). Cultural familiarity in inferential and literal comprehension in L2 reading. *System, 34*, 494–508.
Deschambault, R. (2012). Thinking-aloud as talking-in-interaction: Reinterpreting how L2 lexical inferencing gets done. *Language Learning, 62*(1), 266–301.
Nassaji, H. (2006). The relationship between depth of vocabulary knowledge and L2 learners' lexical inferencing strategy and use. *The Modern Language Journal, 90*, 387–401.
Nassaji, H. (2007). Schema theory and knowledge-based processes in second language reading comprehension: A need for alternative perspectives. *Language Learning, 57*(1), 79–113.
Pulido, D. (2003). Modeling the role of second language proficiency and topic familiarity in second language incidental vocabulary acquisition through reading. *Language Learning, 53*(2), 233–284.

Qian, D. D. (2005). Demystifying lexical inferencing: The role of aspects of vocabulary knowledge. *TESL Canada, 22*(2), 34–54.

Wesche, M. B., & Paribakht, T. S. (2010). *Lexical inferencing in a first and second language: Cross-linguistic dimensions*. Multilingual Matters.

Hossein Vafadar has a Ph.D. in Applied Linguistics from Universiti Sains Malaysia (USM), Penang. He is currently an executive committee member of Canadian Institute of Knowledge for Development (CIKD), Consulting Education Research. He is the editor of IJOL and MBR. He is the founder of "CORESEARCHER", training and research company, providing services on the areas of research analysis, editing, training, programing, web-designing, and translation. His research interests are in the areas of Applied Linguistics, Second Language Acquisition, willingness to communicate, assessment and testing.

Hassan Mohebbi His main research interests are individual differences, writing, assessment literacy, vocabulary instruction, CALL, and ESP. He is an editorial board member of Language Testing in Asia (Springer), Asian-Pacific Journal of Second and Foreign Language Education (Springer), Language Teaching Research Quarterly (EUROKD), and Australian Journal of Applied Linguistics (Book Reviews Editor).

Oral Academic Genres and Features of Student Academic Presentations

Alla Zareva

Academic genres are highly specialized and one of the main goals of research into specialized language is to uncover and describe its intricacies so that the field can move forward with useful theoretical, empirical, and practical application of its discoveries (Mauranen, 2012; Zareva, 2019). Recently, the genre/sub-register of student academic presentations has attracted a good deal of research attention as both educators and employers have started to realize that developing students' presentational skills is essential to their professionalization (Boyd, 1989; Morton & Ross, 2011; Zareva, 2011a). In other words, once college students enter their professional areas of specialization, they are expected to communicate their ideas and present their professional products effectively and convincingly, which suggests that their training in the oral genres typical of their disciplines should start early in their education (Zareva, 2015; Zareva, 2020). The need to show good presentation skills is even more pressing for English as a second/subsequent language students in English-based degree-granting programs primarily because they are expected to show familiarity and mastery of these skills as soon as they enter their disciplinary areas of study even though they may have never given an academic presentation before in their native (L1) or second language (L2) (Zareva, 2011a).

In his corpus-based study of academic language, Biber (2006) has rightly pointed out that the informational communication, at least in American universities, is accomplished through different linguistic means in speech and writing. In this regard, both Swales (2004) and Biber (2006) have commented that, in comparison to academic writing, academic speech in the U.S. tends to be more interactive and informal, perhaps, because classes tend to incorporate more interactive and communicative activities. Additionally, not only the instructors but the students as well are expected to engage in the delivery of complex informational content in a variety of ways and the academic presentation is one of the genres which fulfills that pur-

A. Zareva (✉)
Department of English, Old Dominion University, Norfolk, VA, USA
e-mail: azareva@odu.edu

© Springer Nature Switzerland AG 2021
H. Mohebbi and C. Coombe (eds.), *Research Questions in Language Education and Applied Linguistics*, Springer Texts in Education,
https://doi.org/10.1007/978-3-030-79143-8_86

487

pose. This shared responsibility of informational knowledge display is probably one of the reasons why interest in the student academic presentation has picked up in the last couple of decades. More importantly, we need to have a description of the range of linguistic features that characterize the genre/sub-register of presentations before we can determine which of them are more intuitive to students (both L1 and L2) and which may need more focused attention in ESP/EAP instructional materials.

Given that the student presentation is intricately intertwined with other oral and written academic genres college students are exposed to (e.g., lectures, seminars, discussion groups, textbooks, etc.), we can reasonably expect that it will share certain linguistic features with both academic speech and written prose (Zareva, 2016). Thus, any investigation of the language features typical of presentations should be informed by findings related to the other genres that form "the network of genres" (Swales, 2004) in which college students actively participate.

In the last couple of decades, there has been a good number of studies on oral academic discourse produced by both students and experts—for instance, corpus-based studies on academic language (Biber, 2006; Mauranen, 2012), lectures (Crawford-Camiciottoli, 2004), seminars (Rendle-Short, 2006; Weissberg, 1993), metatalk (Swales, 2001) and evaluation in academic talk (Mauranen, 2002; Zareva, 2012a, 2018), various aspects of student presentations (Boyd, 1989; Csomay, 2015; Morton & Ross, 2011; Zareva, 2009a, 2009b, 2011a, 2012b, 2013, 2020), student PowerPoint presentation designs (Zareva, 2011b) and others. Those studies have uncovered a wealth of linguistic features characteristic of oral academic speech in general and highlighted not only differences across various academic genres, sub-registers, and student populations but, equally importantly, similarities across genres, registers, and language users. The common thread that runs through all of them is the effort to shed more light on each of the oral academic genres/registers so that instructors and material designers are better prepared to address students' needs based on research findings rather than on prescriptive tips (Zareva, 2016).

The Research Questions

1. What discourse moves are typical of student presentations?
2. How do student presenters try to accommodate their listeners?
3. How do students express their stance and evaluation in their presentations?
4. How do various language features of student presentations compare across different disciplines?
5. How do various language features of student presentations compare across different languages and academic contexts?
6. What factors need to be taken into account in deciding what aspects of the presentation should be taught to a particular group of language users and what aspects can be safely ignored?
7. How do various linguistic features of student presentations compare to other oral and/or written academic genres that students are expected to participate in?

8. How should teachers develop students' presentational competence?
9. What are the effects of developing students' presentational competence on their overall academic language development?
10. Can presentations be used to increase learners' language proficiency?

Suggested Resources

Biber, D. (2006). *University language: A corpus-based study of spoken and written registers.* **Amsterdam/Philadelphia: John Benjamins.**

The discussion of various language features of the spoken and written academic registers in this book is based on a corpus of American English, which helps define and illustrate academic language as students experience it in university settings. The corpus covers a wide range of academic registers, including some instructional registers (e.g., handbooks, catalogues, web pages, etc.), spoken institutional registers (e.g., service encounters, classroom management talk, etc.), study groups, office hours, etc. The analyses Biber offers highlight a wealth of language features that not only provide a comprehensive description of the university spoken and written registers, but can also help EAP/ESP instruction and material design. Even though the book does not exclusively focus on the language features of student presentations, it offers a solid background of comparisons between oral and written academic language use which can be applied and further explored in the context of presentations.

Mauranen, A. (2012). *Exploring ELF: Academic English shaped by non-native speakers.* **Cambridge: Cambridge University Press.**

The book focuses on the use of English as a lingua franca (ELF) in academic settings. The analyses of various language features are based on the corpus of ELF in academic settings, which contains 1 million words of transcribed spoken academic ELF (e.g., lectures, presentations, seminars, thesis defenses, and conference discussions) across a variety of disciplines. In her discussion of different features of ELF communication, Mauranen offers interesting explanations about how they may have emerged and what they reveal about ELF communication in academic settings. The author draws our attention to some lexical features of ELF and lexical process (e.g., lexical searching, echoing, approximation) as well as to larger linguistic units such as grammatical constructions, phraseological issues, and multi-word items. She explores those structures not only from the point of view of their contribution to the explicitness and discourse organization of ELF communication but also from the vantage point of their facilitative effects on the interaction and comprehensibility of ELF as used in global academic settings. The book is one of the most comprehensive overviews of ELF for academic purposes and offers valuable insights into the implications this language variety may have for EAP teaching and learning.

Rendle-Short, J. (2006). *The academic presentation: Situated talk in action.* **Aldershot and Burlington, VT: Ashgate.**

The book details the complexities of giving seminar presentations by describing what presenters do in order to structure their talks, engage their listeners, maintain their attention throughout the presentation, interact simultaneously with the audience and the technology they use, and manage their transitions from talk to non-talk. The analysis is based on several videotaped computer science seminar presentations, each of which is about 40–50 min long. Johanna Rendle-Short takes mainly a conversation analysis (CA) approach to her analyses of the presentations and she also offers some interesting insights into non-CA features of academic talk such as gaze, hand gesture, and body position. A central idea that permeates her discussion of the seminar presentation is the understanding of the monologue as an unfolding interactive event where presenters interact not only with their audience but also with their environment. Being based on a small specialized corpus of presentations, the book can be of interest primarily from the point a view of CA in the area of computer science and engineering.

Zareva, A. (2020). *Speech accommodation in student presentations.* **Palgrave Macmillan.**

The book provides an accessible introduction to current theory and research in speech accommodation in relation to student academic presentations, particularly from the point of view of linguistic features (e.g., lexical uses, choice of certain types of collocations, etc.) that reveal presenters' attempts to accommodate their listeners. The analyses are based on a corpus of university students' presentations (over 100,000 words) from a range of disciplinary areas and show how several aspects of speech accommodation have been implemented in actual, successful student-produced academic discourse. Zareva links theory, language use, and practice in ways that illustrate how the findings of research can be implemented in textbooks and materials, designed to teach oral communication for academic purposes. She also offers a critical evaluation of practices included in textbooks and manuals designed to teach students in higher education how to give effective academic presentations. The book can be of interest to several reading audiences (e.g., students, teachers, researchers, and material designers) as it relates practical concerns of listeners' accommodation to the research and findings which underlie them.

References

Biber, D. (2006). *University language: A corpus-based study of spoken and written registers.* John Benjamins.

Boyd, F. A. (1989). Developing presentation skills: A perspective derived from professional education. *English for Specific Purposes, 8,* 195–203.

Crawford-Camiciottoli, B. (2004). Interactive discourse structuring in L2 guest lectures: Some insights from a comparative corpus-based study. *Journal of English for Academic Purposes, 3*, 39–54.

Csomay, E. (2015). A corpus-based analysis of linguistic variation in teacher and student presentations in university settings. In V. Cortes & E. Csomay (Eds.), *Corpus-based research in applied linguistics: Studies in honor of Doug Biber* (pp. 1–23). John Benjamins.

Mauranen, A. (2012). *Exploring ELF: Academic English shaped by non-native speakers.* Cambridge University Press.

Mauranen, A. (2002). 'A good question': Expressing evaluation in academic speech. In G. Cortese, G. & P. Riley (Eds.), *Domain-specific English: Textual practices across communities and classrooms* (pp. 115–140). Peter Lang.

Morton, J., & Rosse, M. (2011). Persuasive presentations in engineering spoken discourse. *Australasian Journal of Engineering Education, 17*(2), 55–64.

Rendle-Short, J. (2006). *The academic presentation: Situated talk in action.* Ashgate.

Swales, J. M. (2001). Metatalk in American academic talk. *Journal of English Linguistics, 29*, 34–54.

Swales, J. M. (2004). *Research genres: Explorations and applications.* Cambridge University Press.

Weissberg, B. (1993). The graduate seminar: Another research-process genre. *English for Specific Purposes, 12*, 23–36.

Zareva, A. (2009a). Informational packaging, level of formality, and the use of circumstance adverbials in L1 and L2 student academic presentations. *Journal of English for Academic Purposes, 8*, 55–68.

Zareva, A. (2009b). Student academic presentations: The processing side of interactiveness. *English Text Construction, 2*(2), 265–288.

Zareva, A. (2011b). L2 graduate student PowerPoint presentation designs: A reality check. *International Journal of Innovation and Learning, 9*(2), 127–144.

Zareva, A. (2011a). "*And so that was it*": Linking adverbials in student academic presentations. *RELC Journal, 42*(1), 5–15.

Zareva, A. (2012a). Expression of stance and persuasion in student academic presentations. In G. Mininni & A. Manuti (Eds.), *Applied psycholinguistics* (vol. II, pp. 316–323). Franco Angeli.

Zareva, A. (2012b). Lexical composition of effective L1 and L2 student academic presentations. *Journal of Applied Linguistics, 6*(1), 91–110.

Zareva, A. (2013). Self-mention and the projection of multiple identity roles in TESOL graduate student presentations: The influence of the written academic genres. *English for Specific Purposes, 32*, 72–83.

Zareva, A. (2015). "*I think I wanna talk about the reasons why I chose my topic*": Discourse functions of self-mention in Asian graduate student academic presentations. *Journal of Asia TEFL, 12*(1), 141–168.

Zareva, A. (2016). Multi-word verbs in students' academic presentations. *Journal of English for Academic Purposes, 23*, 83–98.

Zareva, A. (2018). Evaluation in moderation: Evaluative adjectives in student academic presentations. *Journal of Academic Language and Learning, 12*(2), 149–162.

Zareva, A. (2019). Lexical complexity of academic presentations: Similarities despite situational differences. *Journal of Second Language Studies, 2*(1), 72–93.

Zareva, A. (2020). *Speech accommodation in student presentations.* Palgrave Macmillan.

Alla Zareva is a Professor in the Department of English at Old Dominion University (USA). She teaches courses in linguistics and applied linguistics, including corpus-based language analysis, research methods, language acquisition, methods for teaching English to speakers of other languages, etc. Her research interests spread over a variety of topics such as the organization of the mental lexicon, linguistic features of academic presentations, and the intersection between oral and written academic genres. She has held teaching appointments and carried out research at several universities in the USA and abroad and has published and presented her work nationally and internationally. She is also the recipient of grants, scholarships, and fellowships from the George Soros Foundation, the British Council, the U.S. Department of Education, and several universities.

Speech Fluency

Xun Yan, Yuyun Lei, and Hyunji (Hayley) Park

Speech fluency has been extensively researched as a core construct in oral language proficiency development. Fluency has been conceptualized in both broad and narrow senses. In the broad sense, fluency, synonymous with overall proficiency, is an all-encompassing term covering a range of speech features such as rapidity, accuracy, complexity, coherence, and even idiomaticity (Fillmore, 1979). In contrast, the narrow approach limits fluency to temporal characteristics of speech, i.e., rapidity and smoothness (Lennon, 1990). Tavakoli and Skehan (2005) further classified temporal fluency into three dimensions: speed, breakdown, and repair fluency, where speed fluency focuses on the rate features of speech, breakdown fluency refers to the nature of disfluencies, and repair fluency deals with effort and strategies used to overcome disfluencies.

When it comes to operationalizing fluency, applied linguistics research tends to use macro-level temporal features that are computed by counting the number of syllables or pauses produced in speech (e.g., speech rate, number of pauses). These features can be easily automated and are often regarded as proxies of overall proficiency (e.g., Ginther et al., 2010; Kormos & Denes, 2004). In contrast, research in cognitive sciences tends to focus on micro-level disfluency features that reflect where and why pauses occur and how they are repaired (e.g., pause position and repair). These features can provide evidence for the cognitive processes of speech

X. Yan (✉) · H. (Hayley) Park
Department of Linguistics, University of Illinois at Urbana-Champaign, Illinois, USA
e-mail: xunyan@illinois.edu

H. (Hayley) Park
e-mail: hpark129@illinois.edu

Y. Lei
East Asian Languages and Cultures, Wake Forest University, Winston-Salem, USA
e-mail: leiy@wfu.edu

© Springer Nature Switzerland AG 2021
H. Mohebbi and C. Coombe (eds.), *Research Questions in Language Education and Applied Linguistics*, Springer Texts in Education,
https://doi.org/10.1007/978-3-030-79143-8_87

production, enhancing our understanding of how language is comprehended and produced (e.g., Clark & Tree, 2002).

In language acquisition, fluency is a crucial construct for learners acquiring a new language. However, fluency does not necessarily develop in a linear, consistently progressive fashion. As overall proficiency increases, there is often a trade-off among fluency, complexity, and accuracy (Skehan, 2009). Fluency development is not simply a matter of increasing speed or speaking non-stop, but rather a matter of developing procedural linguistic knowledge that results in the perception of fluency (Towell et al., 1996). When the procedualization of linguistic knowledge is achieved, temporal fluency will emerge as a natural outcome.

The Research Questions

1. What do we mean by fluency?
2. What temporal features are reliable indicators of fluency?
3. What is the relationship between fluency and language proficiency?
4. What are the relationships among the subdimensions of speech fluency?
5. What are the relationships between speech fluency and other components of language proficiency (e.g., linguistic complexity and accuracy)?
6. What strategies do second language speakers use to develop speech fluency?
7. What strategies do first and second language speakers use to overcome disfluencies in speech?
8. How does the speech fluency of second language speakers develop over time?
9. What factors can influence the development of speech fluency of second language speakers?
10. How do first and second language speakers process disfluencies in speech?

Suggested Resources

Clark, H. H., & Tree, J. E. F. (2002). Using uh and um in spontaneous speaking. *Cognition, 84*(1), 73–111.

Clark and Tree explored the use of fillers *uh* and *um* in several large corpora of spontaneous speech of native English speakers. They examined *uh* and *um* in terms of their preceding and following delays, their locations, and their prosodic features. Their analysis showed that native English speakers use *uh* and *um* to signal that they are going to have disfluency (pause or hesitation) in speech. If the pause is expected to be short, they will formulate *uh*, and if long, *um*. Based on where they initiate the hesitation, they decide whether to attach the filler as a clitic onto the previous word (e.g. and-uh) or prolong it. Listeners can use these signals, in turn, to implicate if the speaker encounters planning problems or wants the next turn. This article provides insights into where, when and how disfluencies occur.

Ginther, A., Dimova, S., & Yang, R. (2010). Conceptual and empirical relationships between temporal measures of fluency and oral English proficiency with implication for automated scoring. *Language Testing*, *27*(3), 377–399.

Ginther et al.'s paper examined the relationship among temporal measures of fluency and holistic scores assigned by raters on a local oral English proficiency test. While previous studies are usually concerned with a small number of samples and deal only with one proficiency level, their study has a large sample of L1 and L2 speakers, covering a full range of proficiency levels specified on the rating scale. Their results showed that a number of fluency measures (e.g. speech rate, mean length of run, the number, and length of silent pauses) had moderate to strong correlations with the holistic score, suggesting that these variables can be selected as reasonable proxies of overall language proficiency for the development of automated scoring systems for speech. However, temporal measures of fluency alone could not distinguish adjacent levels on the rating scale, so the authors call for further inquiries into the broader sense of fluency to understand the meaning of test scores.

Lennon, P. (1990). Investigating fluency in EFL: A Quantitative Approach. *Language Learning*, *40*(3), 387–417.

In this well-cited article, Lennon defines fluency in two different senses. Fluency, in the broad sense, is a cover term for global oral proficiency, while in the narrow sense, it refers to "native-like rapidity". Concerning the narrow sense of fluency, he conducted an empirical study to investigate what variables contribute to perceived oral fluency and how these variables change over time. Fluency measures were taken for speech samples of four EFL learners in a study abroad program over a six-month period. His results showed that even though all participants were perceived as more fluent after studying abroad, their performances varied in the two subcomponents of fluency Lennon identified. That is, while learners tended to improve on "the temporal component", individual differences existed in the "vocal dysfluency marker component". Lennon suggested that among fluency variables, some are "core" and some are "peripheral".

Riggenbach, H. (2000). *Perspectives on fluency*. **Ann Arbor, MI: University of Michigan Press.**

This edited volume covers different perspectives on fluency from linguistics, psychology, language education, and speech pathology. It begins with a survey of different notions of fluency, including articles from Lennon, Fillmore, Koponen and Riggenbach, and others. In the second section, essential components of fluency are examined, such as nonverbal behaviors (Bavelas), intonation (Wennerstrom), time associated with negotiating turns (Fiksdal), and speaker's perception of sense of self (Doutrich). Later, the book discusses hypotheses regarding what cognitive processes may underlie fluency, including attentional skills (Segalowitz), encoding capacity (Pawley and Syder), or neural and conceptual network (Oppenheim). The last section of the book provides several empirical studies on factors affecting the impression of a speaker's fluency or ratings on a fluency assessment scale. Those factors are study abroad experience (Freed), conversational skills or strategies (Morales- López), and task type, or genre of talk (Ejzeberg).

Segalowitz, N. (2010). *Cognitive bases of second language fluency.* **New York, NY: Routledge.**

Segalowitz's book suggests a conceptual framework for thinking about L2 fluency from a cognitive science perspective. Each chapter provides a detailed survey of the relevant literature by answering and expanding on five anchor questions on L2 fluency. Such questions cover reliable indicators of L2 utterance fluency, the relationship between general cognitive processing fluency and L2 fluency and social factors influencing L2 fluency. The resulting framework summarized in the final chapter places L2 fluency in a dynamic system, where L2 speech production is influenced by at least four interacting components, namely cognitive fluency (or processing efficiency), motivation to communicate, social context and relevant experiences (e.g. exposure or practice). By initiating a cognitive science approach to L2 fluency, the author opens up opportunities to study L2 fluency from a broader, interdisciplinary perspective. The volume concludes with implications for teaching and learning and an annotated bibliography for recommended reading.

References

Clark, H. H., & Tree, J. E. F. (2002). Using uh and um in spontaneous speaking. *Cognition, 84*(1), 73–111.

Fillmore, C. J. (1979). On fluency. In C. J. Fillmore, D. Kempler, & W. S-Y. Wang (Eds.), *Individual differences in language ability and language behavior.* Academic Press.

Ginther, A., Dimova, S., & Yang, R. (2010). Conceptual and empirical relationships between temporal measures of fluency and oral English proficiency with implication for automated scoring. *Language Testing, 27*(3), 377–399.

Kormos, J., & Dénes, M. (2004). Exploring measures and perceptions of fluency in the speech of second language learners. *System, 32*, 146–164.

Lennon, P. (1990). Investigating fluency in EFL: A quantitative approach. *Language Learning, 40* (3), 387–417.

Skehan, P. (2009). Modeling second language performance: Investigating complexity, accuracy, fluency and lexis. *Applied Linguistics, 30*(4), 510–532.

Tavakoli, P., & Skehan, P. (2005). Strategic planning, task structure, and performance testing. *Planning and task performance in a second language, 239273.*

Towell, R., Hawkins, R., & Bazergui, N. (1996). The development of fluency in advanced learners of French. *Applied Linguistics, 17*(1), 84–119.

Xun Yan is an associate professor of Linguistics, Second Language Acquisition and Teacher Education (SLATE), and Educational Psychology at the University of Illinois at Urbana-Champaign. At UIUC, he is also the director of the university-level English Placement Test (EPT), designed to assess international students' writing and speaking skills for academic purposes. His research interests include speaking and writing assessment, scale development and validation, psycholinguistic approaches to language testing, rater behavior and cognition, and language assessment literacy. His work has been published in *Language Testing, TESOL Quarterly, Assessing Writing, Journal of Second Language Writing, System,* and *Asian-Pacific Education Researchers.*

Yuyun Lei is a visiting assistant professor of Chinese at Wake Forest University. She has been working as a language instructor for the Chinese language program, and also as a content developer and rater for the university-level English placement test. Her research interests include second language development and assessment, second language speech production, and computer-assisted language learning. She has published papers in the *Foreign Language Annals, Journal of Technology and Chinese Language Teaching,* and *Chinese Language Education and Research.*

Hyunji (Hayley) Park is a Ph.D. student in the Linguistics Department at the University of Illinois at Urbana-Champaign. She has been working as a research assistant for the in-house ESL placement test, EPT, and has contributed to test development, test administration, rater training and related research projects for the local test. Her research interests lie in language testing and computational and corpus linguistic approaches to language development and assessment. She has made several conference presentations including those at the American Association for Applied Linguistics (AAAL) and Midwest Association of Language Testers (MwALT).

Teaching and Learning Vocabulary

88

Suhad Sonbul and Anna Siyanova-Chanturia

Acquiring second language (L2) vocabulary can be a daunting experience. Even after years of exposure, L2 learners' vocabulary size is often limited, which makes it nearly impossible to use language effectively. According to recent estimates, in order to reach the acceptable 98% coverage of authentic texts, L2 users need to know at least 6000–7000 word families (i.e., the word and its inflected/derivational forms) for listening comprehension and 8000–9000 word families for reading comprehension (Nation, 2006).

What makes the task even more challenging is that L2 learners need to focus not only on the breadth of vocabulary being acquired (the number of words/word families) but also on the depth of the vocabulary items in question. While there are various views as to what vocabulary depth entails (see Schmitt, 2014 for an overview), the most influential view is Nation's (2013, p. 49) dimensions approach. According to Nation (2013), knowing a lexical item does not only involve linking it to the meaning; rather, the lexical repertoire is a complex multi-dimensional construct encompassing the form, meaning, and use of words both at the receptive and productive levels of mastery.

Given this complex view of vocabulary knowledge, language teachers face non-trivial challenges when teaching vocabulary in the language classroom. The first, and most difficult of these, is how best to assist beginners in learning the most frequent words in the language in order to reach the acceptable 98% coverage of

S. Sonbul (✉)
English Language Centre, Umm Al-Qura University, Makkah, Saudi Arabia
e-mail: sssonbul@uqu.edu.sa

A. Siyanova-Chanturia
School of Linguistics and Applied Language Studies, Te Herenga Waka—Victoria University of Wellington, Wellington, New Zealand
e-mail: anna.siyanova@vuw.ac.nz

A. Siyanova-Chanturia
College of Foreign Languages, Ocean University of China, Qingdao, China

© Springer Nature Switzerland AG 2021
H. Mohebbi and C. Coombe (eds.), *Research Questions in Language Education and Applied Linguistics*, Springer Texts in Education,
https://doi.org/10.1007/978-3-030-79143-8_88

easy texts. Teachers might be able to teach some vocabulary items explicitly, but it is not possible to teach all the words in the language and all aspects of word knowledge. Second, teachers need to make efficient cost/benefit decisions regarding what to teach explicitly. They further need to accept the fact that what is evident in the answers to discrete-point vocabulary exercises does not necessarily reflect fluency in using these vocabulary items in meaningful contexts, the ultimate goal of language learning.

In an attempt to address these challenges, Nation (2013) developed a balanced four-strand vocabulary framework: meaning-focused input, meaning-focused output, language-focused practice, and fluency development. Each one of these strands is meant to receive an equal share of classroom time. Thus, while the widespread classroom practice of explicit vocabulary teaching is important, in particular, for beginners to acquire the most frequent words in the language, it should not constitute more than 25% of the course. Much of the teaching time (50%), Nation (2013) argues, should be directed to contextualized practice in both the receptive (input) and productive (output) modes. This type of exposure is often referred to as 'incidental', in the sense that it happens as a by-product of language activities. This means that teachers need to maximize exposure to the language in a variety of listening and reading activities and endeavour to provide sufficient opportunities for speaking and writing practice. Finally, the often-disregarded fluency development practice should receive the remaining 25% of the classroom time, whereby L2 learners use known vocabulary items effortlessly in a range of meaningful contexts.

The Research Questions

1. How and in what order are the various aspects of vocabulary knowledge developed?
2. How can teachers help learners start building their vocabulary repertoire effectively?
3. How can teachers help learners enlarge their vocabulary repertoire to cope with the four language skills?
4. How effective are the intentional/incidental approaches to vocabulary learning in developing various aspects of lexical knowledge?
5. What lexical coverage is needed to achieve acceptable reading and listening comprehension levels?
6. Does the minimal level of lexical coverage vary according to the purpose of reading/listening activity?
7. How much exposure is needed to learn a lexical item incidentally from context?
8. How can teachers maximize language exposure to allow for incidental vocabulary learning?

9. What strategies should learners develop to become autonomous in vocabulary learning?

10. How can teachers help L2 learners develop fluency using known vocabulary?

Suggested Resources

Cobb, T. (2008). The Compleat Lexical Tutor (Lextutor), http://www.lextutor.ca/

This is an essential and freely available tool for vocabulary research and teaching. It has a variety of functions and exercises useful for language teachers and vocabulary researchers. Developed by Tom Cobb, the tests and tools available are continuously updated. The most popular tool is VocabProfile used to determine lexical coverage. The website also offers free (interactive and paper-based) versions of various standardized vocabulary tests, including the *Vocabulary Levels Test* and the *Vocabulary Size Test*. Together, these tools can be used by language teachers and researchers to determine whether a given text is suitable for a given group of learners. The website further provides tools for developing cloze tests and flashcards, and a range of other functions.

Schmitt, N. (2010). *Researching vocabulary: A vocabulary research manual.* **Cham, Switzerland: Springer.**

This is a valuable resource for researchers which provides guidelines for conducting vocabulary studies. Following an overview of ten key lexical issues, Schmitt devotes a section to major lexical topics and how they might be addressed in research: vocabulary acquisition and use, formulaic language, vocabulary research methodology, and measuring vocabulary. The final section of the book provides useful resources, including standardized vocabulary tests, corpora, vocabulary lists, and websites. One noteworthy part of the book—intended in particular for novice researchers—is a section detailing and commenting on ten examples of vocabulary research projects. Each sample project includes goals, methodology, and a useful set of research questions to consider.

Nation, I.S.P., & Webb, S. (2011). *Researching and Analyzing Vocabulary.* **Boston, MA: Heinle.**

This volume aims at providing relevant information and guidelines for researchers and teachers in the field of vocabulary acquisition. Each chapter covers one specific area of vocabulary research containing: background, literature review, research steps with critique of available designs, research issues, areas for further research, and a sample study design. The book includes 14 chapters which are grouped into four main sections: deliberate vocabulary learning, incidental vocabulary learning, corpus-based research, and testing vocabulary knowledge. Thus, the book provides readers with both theoretical and practical background on each topic. Structured in this way, the book is a valuable resource for novice and more experienced vocabulary enthusiasts alike.

Boers, F. (Ed.) (2017). Special issue: Vocabulary. *Language Teaching Research, 21*(1).

This special issue in *Language Teaching Research* is one of several recent issues dedicated to vocabulary. The volume includes empirical studies focusing on three of Nation's (2013) strands. Within the language-focused practice strand, Deconinck, Boers, and Eyckmans look at the effect of mapping the word form to its meaning on vocabulary gains. Within the meaning-focused output strand, Zou explores the relative effectiveness of three types of output assessment types: cloze task, sentence writing, and essay writing. Lee and Pulido investigate meaning-focused input (reading) activities and the various factors that can affect incidental vocabulary learning. Two further studies—by Rassaei and Sun, respectively—investigate the effect of combining meaning-focused input (reading) with meaning-focused output activities (summarizing, asking and answering questions, predicting succeeding context, and collaborative output tasks) on vocabulary acquisition.

Webb, S., & Nation, P. (2017). *How Vocabulary is Learned.* **Oxford: Oxford University Press.**

The book overviews recent research findings in the area of vocabulary learning. A key strength of the book is its focus on practical procedures for vocabulary teaching. After reviewing available evidence on the nature of vocabulary knowledge and the ways in which it can be taught/learnt, the book shifts its attention to practical topics in vocabulary teaching and learning. These include examples of popular lexical activities, factors that may affect vocabulary learning (e.g., age, context, proficiency), vocabulary learning strategies, vocabulary programme development within the four-strand framework (Nation, 2013), and useful vocabulary learning resources. Each of the book's ten chapters is followed by evaluative activities, reflection questions, and suggested readings. Of note is that the book has a companion website for additional resources (https://elt.oup.com/teachers/hvil). It is a must-read for teachers and researchers who are new to teaching and researching vocabulary.

References

Nation, I. S. P. (2006). How large a vocabulary is needed for reading and listening? *Canadian Modern Language Review, 63*(1), 59–82.

Nation, I. S. P. (2013). *Learning vocabulary in another language* (2nd ed.). Cambridge University Press.

Schmitt, N. (2014). Size and depth of vocabulary knowledge: What the research shows. *Language Learning, 64*(4), 913–951.

Suhad Sonbul is Assistant Professor in the English Language Centre at Umm Al-Qura University (Saudi Arabia). Her research interests include vocabulary learning, formulaic language, and psycholinguistic measures. She has published in several refereed journals including *Language Learning* and *Bilingualism: Language and Cognition.*

Anna Siyanova-Chanturia is Senior Lecturer in Applied Linguistics at Victoria University of Wellington (New Zealand), and Guest Professor in Linguistics and Applied Linguistics at Ocean University of China (China). Anna's research interests include second language acquisition, psycholinguistics, vocabulary and formulaic language. She has published in applied linguistics and psycholinguistics journals, such as *Applied Linguistics, Language Learning, Studies in Second Language Acquisition, Journal of Experimental Psychology: Learning, Memory and Cognition, Brain and Language,* and others.

Part V
Teachers and Teacher Education

Eric Friginal and Justin Taylor

Corpus Linguistics (CL) is a research approach to the empirical investigation of language variation and use, utilizing a quantifiable collection of "texts" known as a *corpus* (corpora, plural) and various computer-based tools and applications. The CL approach produces real-world data, patterns, and results that have, perhaps, much greater generalizability and validity and subsequent efficacy than would be feasible using traditional linguistic and discourse analytic approaches (Biber et al., 2010). The process of using corpora in the classroom is aligned with Computer-Assisted Language Learning (CALL) principles, directly related to: (1) automatic searching, sorting, and scoring of spoken and written texts; (2) promoting a learner-centered approach; (3) providing an open-ended supply of language data; and (4) enabling the learning process to be tailored (Chapelle & Jamieson, 2009; Leech, 1997). The corpus approach, therefore, merges innovations in second language acquisition, instructional technology, educational computing, and various online resources that promote the inclusion of different perspectives on language learning inside and outside of the classroom. Mobile technology, individualized instruction, and big data visualization, as integral parts of CL, all contribute to how digital learners may, in fact, fully adapt and appreciate corpus-based approaches in their learning of English or other languages (Flowerdew, 2012; Friginal, 2018).

The number of teachers incorporating CL approaches in their language classrooms has grown exponentially from the mid-1990s to the present. Teachers have utilized CL perspectives to show students the common vocabulary and lexico-grammatical features of academic writing (e.g., Coxhead, 2011; Gray, 2013; Nesi & Gardner, 2012), actual distributions of multi-word units (e.g., n-grams, lexical bundles, and p-frames) in academic and professional writing (e.g., Cortes,

E. Friginal (✉)
Department of Applied Linguistics and ESL, Georgia State University, Atlanta, GA, USA
e-mail: efriginal@gsu.edu

J. Taylor
School of Foreign Languages, Bahçeşehir University, Istanbul, Turkey

© Springer Nature Switzerland AG 2021
H. Mohebbi and C. Coombe (eds.), *Research Questions in Language
Education and Applied Linguistics*, Springer Texts in Education,
https://doi.org/10.1007/978-3-030-79143-8_89

507

2004; Römer & Wulff, 2010), or historical and semantic shifts in vocabulary usage across time periods (e.g., Davies, 2017; Friginal et al., 2014).Teachers may want to apply a CL approach to better understand how their students' conceptual understanding of grammar is progressing and also to further developed teaching materials that potentially address their students' unique language learning contexts. However, teachers may want to use corpora, their presence in teacher preparation and in the classroom has significantly increased, as can be seen through various projects of a growing number of international organizations such as the Learner Corpus Association (www.learnercorpusassociation.org), the Centre for English Corpus Linguistics at UC Louvain in Belgium, or freely-available corpus databases from the University of Michigan: MICASE (Michigan Corpus of Academic Spoken English) on university spoken discourse or MICUSP (Michigan Corpus of Upper-Level Student Papers) on A-graded student writing. In addition, several teacher training programs have incorporated corpora and computational tools into their curriculum.

Online CL resources have now been available for teachers to use for free, including web-based software that searches across hundreds of thousands of websites (iWeb), large corpora attempting to capture entire dialects of English (e.g., the Corpus of Contemporary American English or COCA or the British National Corpus or BNC), or stand-alone websites that immediately allow teachers and students to access and process corpora for various applications, e.g., *Compleat Lexical Tutor* (www.lextutor.ca) or *WordandPhrase.info* (www.wordandphrase.info). Corpus tools such as concordancers and linguistic taggers or parsers are also now easily accessible and freely shared online, e.g., *AntConc* (www.laurenceanthony.net/ software) or *Coh-Metrix*, which focuses on the automatic analysis of text on cohesion and language (Graesser et al., 2004). Finally, an increasing number of books and articles with suggestions on how to use corpora in the classroom have recently been or are currently being published (see annotated bibliography below).

The rapid development in corpora and CL in the classroom does not come without challenges. Many teachers have expressed that as soon as they begin to use a corpus, it is subject to change unexpectedly; others have lamented the limited information on how to use corpora and corpus tools that is available outside of programs designed to teach them. While many corpora can be and are user-friendly, the possibilities may initially be overwhelming for individuals who are using them for the first time. Proficient teachers and scholars should continue to investigate how corpora can be used in the classroom and attempt to make resources easily available for other language teachers.

The Research Questions

1. How has the history of corpus (and also computational) linguistics influenced the current use, understanding, and practical application of corpora in the classroom?
2. What are best ways to design and compile corpora for teaching purposes?

3. How can freely available corpus-based resources and tools be used to process and analyze corpora for teaching purposes?
4. What is the best way (approach, method, technique, etc.) to use corpora in the classroom and what are empirical ways to test for learning gains in corpus-based classrooms?
5. What aspects of language (vocabulary, grammar, forms, functions, etc.) are best taught or learned by using corpora in the classroom?
6. What factors or situations prevent teachers from using corpora in the classroom and what training may be implemented to overcome these challenges?
7. How can corpora be used to prepare future teachers for students' language learning challenges?
8. How can teachers conduct and publish their own classroom-based research using corpora?
9. What are the limitations and future directors of using corpora in classrooms?
10. What are emerging applications of CL in language teaching across platforms, contexts, and cultural settings?

Suggested Resources

Charles, M. (2012). 'Proper vocabulary and juicy collocations:' EAP students evaluate do-it-yourself corpus-building. *English for Specific Purposes, 31*(2), **93–102.**

Charles explores the feasibility of a student-collected corpus in multidisciplinary classes of advanced-level students. The course consists of six weekly, 2-h sessions focusing on academic writing, with feedback data from 50 participants presented and discussed in the paper. Over 90% of study participants found it easy to build DIY corpora and most succeeded in constructing a corpus of 10–15 research articles. Students in general were enthusiastic about working with their own corpora and about 90% of them agreed that their corpus helped them improve their writing. Most of them mentioned that they intended to use it in the future. Students view corpora as a useful resource in writing effective discipline-specific texts. Participants' attitudes and experiences are also discussed in the paper and Charles also presents the issues and problems that arise in connection with DIY corpus-building.

Conrad, S. & Biber, D. (2009). *Real grammar: A corpus-based approach to English.* **New York, NY: Pearson-Longman.**

Conrad and Biber's (2009) *Real Grammar: A Corpus-Based Approach to Language* uses corpus data to show how grammatical structures could be 'easily' developed and taught in many classroom settings. The book focuses on a select set of 50 features such as "simple past tense in polite offers," "meanings of take + noun phrase," "action verbs with inanimate subjects," and "adjective clauses that modify sentences" developed as pull-out lessons that a teacher can simply assign to students for hands-on activity in class or for work outside the classroom. Each unit starts with a review of what traditional grammar textbooks typically define or emphasize compared to actual data from corpora. This instructional part is then followed by various activities often about noticing contexts, analyzing discourse, or practice using patterns.

Friginal, E. (2018). *Corpus Linguistics for English Teachers: New Tools, Online Resources, and Classroom Activities.* **New York, USA: Routledge: Taylor & Francis Group.**

Corpus Linguistics for English Teachers: New Tools, Online Resources, and Classroom Activities describes CL and its many relevant, creative, and engaging applications to language teaching and learning for teachers and practitioners in TESOL and ESL/EFL, and graduate students in applied linguistics. English language teachers, both novice and experienced, may be able to benefit from the list of new tools, sample lessons, and resources as well as the introduction of topics and themes that connect CL constructs to established theories in language teaching and second language acquisition. Key topics discussed include, (1) CL and the teaching of English vocabulary, grammar, and spoken-written academic discourse; (2) new tools, online resources, and classroom activities; and (3) focus on the "English teacher as a corpus-based researcher.

Liu, D. & Lei, L. (2017). *Using Corpora for Language Learning and Teaching.* **Annapolis Junction. MD: TESOL Press.**

Liu and Lei asks readers, "How Can You Use Corpora in Your Classroom?" As one of the newest additions to CL in the classroom literature, this book addresses the needs of English teachers for a "step-by-step hands-on introduction to the use of corpora for teaching a variety of English language skills such as grammar, vocabulary, and English academic writing." The authors provide discussions of basic essential corpus search and teaching procedures and activities, including instructions on how to compile corpora for language instruction and research purposes.

Reppen, R. (2010). *Using corpora in the language classroom.* **Cambridge: Cambridge University Press.**

This book is one of the formative publications on corpora and language teaching written specifically for the classroom teacher. Reppen explains and illustrates how teachers can use corpora to create classroom materials and activities to address various classroom needs. Her goal was to "demystify" CL by providing clear and simple explanations, instructions, and examples. The book provides the essential knowledge, tools, and skills teachers need to enable students to discover how language is actually used in context.

References

Biber, D., Reppen, R., & Friginal, E. (2010). Research in corpus linguistics. In R. B. Kaplan (Ed.), *The Oxford handbook of applied linguistics* (2nd ed., pp. 548–570). Oxford University Press.

Chapelle, C., & Jamieson, J. (2009). *Tips for teaching with CALL: Practical approaches to computer-assisted language learning*. Pearson Education.

Cortes, V. (2004). Lexical bundles in published and student disciplinary writing: Examples from history and biology. *English for Specific Purposes, 23*, 397–423.

Coxhead, A. (2011). The academic word list 10 years on: Research and teaching implications. *TESOL Quarterly, 45*(2), 355–361.

Davies, M. (2017). Using large online corpora to examine lexical, semantic, and cultural variation in different dialects and time periods. In E. Friginal (Ed.), *Studies in corpus-based sociolinguistics* (pp. 19–82). Routledge.

Flowerdew, L. (2012). *Corpora and language education*. Palgrave Macmillan.

Friginal, E. (2018). *Corpus linguistics for English teachers: New tools, online resources, and classroom activities*. Routledge.

Friginal, E., Walker, M., & Randall, J. (2014). Exploring mega-corpora: Google Ngram viewer and the corpus of historical American English. *E-JournALL, 1*(1), 132–151.

Graesser, A. C., McNamara, D. S., Louwerse, M. M., & Cai, Z. (2004). Coh-Metrix: Analysis of text on cohesion and language. *Behavior Research Methods, Instruments & Computers, 36*(2), 193–202.

Gray, B. (2013). More than discipline: Uncovering multi-dimensional patterns of variation in academic research articles. *Corpora, 8*(2), 153–181.

Leech, G. (1997). Teaching and language corpora: A convergence. In A. Wichmann, S. Fligelstone, T. McEnery, & G. Knowles (Eds.), *Teaching and language corpora* (pp. 1–24). Longman.

Nesi, H., & Gardner, S. (2012). *Genres across the disciplines: Student writing in higher education*. Cambridge University Press.

Römer, U., & Wulff, S. (2010). Applying corpus methods to written academic texts: Explorations of MICUSP. *Journal of Writing Research, 2*(2), 99–127.

Eric Friginal is professor of applied linguistics and director of international programs at the College of Arts and Sciences, Georgia State University. He specializes in applied corpus linguistics, sociolinguistics, cross-cultural communication, distance learning, discipline-specific writing, bilingual education, and the analysis of spoken professional discourse. He makes use of corpus and computational tools as well as qualitative and quantitative research approaches in analyzing and interpreting linguistic patterning from corpora. His recent books include *Corpus Linguistics for English Teachers: New Tools, Online Resources, and Classroom Activities* (Routledge, 2018), and *English for Global Aviation: Context, Research, and Pedagogy* (Bloomsbury, 2019) with Elizabeth Mathews and Jennifer Roberts.

Justin Taylor received his master's degree in Applied Linguistics from Georgia State University and is currently an English lecturer in the School of Foreign Languages at Bahçeşehir University in Istanbul, Turkey. He has experience teaching students of all ages in a variety of settings, including young learners, university students, and adults in China, Mexico, Turkey, and the USA. Prior publications have focused on the ESL/EFL teaching experience, such as the effects of pre-service teacher training, factors influencing teacher burnout, and the effectiveness of critical pedagogy in ESL. His primary research interests are sociolinguistics, critical studies, intercultural communication, and ESL/EFL pedagogy.

EAP Teacher Education

Mahmood Reza Atai

The English for Academic Purposes (EAP) literature has tended to focus on the analysis of specialist discourse and genre of academic sub/disciplines and learners' needs. Quite recently, research has addressed the expanding conceptualizations and practice of EAP education in diverse contexts. This, in turn, has foregrounded greater demands for EAP practitioners who can assume multiple roles and responsibilities and construct new professional identities (Campion, 2016). However, to date, research on EAP teacher development and the provision of systematic formal teacher education programs has been scant (Ding & Bruce, 2017; Ding & Campion, 2016).

The early studies of EAP pedagogy highlighted the qualifications of EAP teachers compared with their ELT counterparts (Hall, 2013). EAP teachers need additional assets such as disciplinary content and language knowledge, managerial and collaborative skills, and a willingness to engage in professional development. In reality, however, background qualifications of EAP teachers may range from no formal ESL/EAP teacher education to official academic degrees and professional certificates in applied linguistics, TESOL, SLA, and EAP teaching. With the exception of the UK where master's programs and postgraduate certificates in teaching EAP are offered (Ding & Campion, 2016), EAP practitioners are content teachers or English instructors who teach the courses collaboratively or independently in institutional contexts including universities.

Although the current research on EAP teacher education is not comprehensive, some themes have recently been introduced or explored. The themes include: the challenge of specialized disciplinary content knowledge and the strategies teachers adopt to handle it (Atai & Nejadghanbar, 2017), the necessity of researching EAP practice (Hamp-Lyons, 2018), actual teaching practices and cognitions of teachers and their engagement in research-based practice (Atai & Fatahi-Majd, 2014;

M. R. Atai (✉)
Department of Foreign Languages, Kharazmi University, Tehran, Iran
e-mail: atai@khu.ac.ir

© Springer Nature Switzerland AG 2021

513

H. Mohebbi and C. Coombe (eds.), *Research Questions in Language Education and Applied Linguistics*, Springer Texts in Education,
https://doi.org/10.1007/978-3-030-79143-8_90

Bahrami et al., 2019), effective content modules for teacher education programs, models of EAP teacher education and development, reflective approaches to on-going professional development (Campion, 2016), patterns of collaboration between content teachers and EAP instructors in order to build and maintain collegiality, evaluation and renewal of EAP teacher education programs, operationalization of EAP teachers' qualifications, and EAP teachers' ideologies regarding effective EAP pedagogy in diverse sociocultural contexts (Ding & Campion, 2016).

EAP teacher education currently acknowledges teachers' roles as researchers and needs analysts, course designers, classroom teachers, materials developers, and evaluators. Currently, systematic contributions to EAP teacher education and development are associated with the British Association of Lecturers in English for Academic Purposes (BALEAP). As a pioneering step, BALEAP has developed a Competency Framework for Teachers of English for Academic Purposes (CFTEAP) which outlines and describes knowledge and skills required of EAP practitioners. The four main areas of competencies that are further subcategorized into eleven specific teacher competencies and described in the form of 'can do' statements include academic practice, EAP students, curriculum development, and program implementation (Ding & Campion, 2016). CFTEAP is currently considered as a platform for the general orientation of research and practice in EAP teacher development. The framework has further been considered as a basis for EAP course design and accreditation and teacher observation/evaluation.

Future research may investigate creative, reflective, and critical means for fostering teacher agency in EAP teacher education and development through synthesizing the new developments in the field of EAP and the broader fields of applied linguistics and Second Language Teacher Education (SLTE) with parameters of the local educational settings, as investigated through ethnographic studies.

The Research Questions

1. What are the perceptions of ELT scholars with regard to the major contrasts between ESL teacher education and EAP teacher education in terms of underlying theories and approaches, goals, design, and procedure?
2. What competency requirements may be set as prerequisite criteria for entry of the pre-service teacher candidates to formal EAP teacher education programs?
3. How can we adapt the current learner-centered and reflective models of SLTE to EAP teacher education and development across contexts?
4. What are the pros and cons of adherence to a fixed competency framework (e.g. CFTEAP) for educating and certifying prospective EAP teachers and evaluating the current practitioners across contexts?
5. What barriers may impede EAP practitioners' engagement in on-going professional development and teacher learning?

6. What research and practice trajectories do novice and experienced EAP practitioners, in various institutional contexts, follow during their teaching career and to what extent are their practices research-informed?
7. To what extent do local and international professional associations of teachers of English for Academic Purposes promote teacher agency and networking among professional practitioners, teacher educators, and policy makers?
8. What are the pedagogical content knowledge levels and research cognitions of EAP practitioners (i.e. content teachers and ELT instructors) who teach advanced skills-based EAP courses at universities? How can in-service teacher education programs change their cognitions?
9. How can we determine the optimal content modules for an EAP teacher education program in a given context and according to CFTEAP?
10. How can Critical English for Academic Purposes (CEAP) be applied to the analysis of teacher candidate needs, and planning, implementing, and evaluating of teacher education and development in local contexts?

Suggested Resources

Hyland, K. & Shaw, P. (Eds.). *The Routledge Handbook of English for academic purposes*. **New York: Routledge.**

In this volume, Hyland and Shaw expose advanced post graduate students and experts of the field to a comprehensive, rich, and balanced body of theoretical and empirical literature on highly representative themes and issues organized under 8 sections and 45 chapters. The chapters, authored by established international authors, provide the readers with well-organized and concise state-of-the-art reviews each beginning with a fluent introduction of fundamental concepts and controversies in the field followed by more contextual, technical, and critical accounts of how EAP issues and challenges are approached in different settings across the world. The volume also includes very informative sections and chapters on EAP and language skills, perspectives on pedagogical and research genres, and EAP pedagogy across institutional settings. Overall, it is a must-read book and the chapters satisfy the basic and professional needs of prospective EAP teachers in current EAP teacher education programs as well as those of in-service EAP practitioners. The chapters under the concluding section of the book are directly relevant and useful to those interested in EAP pedagogy and teacher education.

Ding, A., & I. Bruce (2017). *The English for academic purposes practitioner: Operating on the edge of academia*. **Cham, Switzerland: Springer.**

This book is one of the most coherent and critical sources on themes and issues of concern to current and prospective EAP practitioners. The authors define EAP as an established research-based field of study and elaborate on how the larger educational concepts of education and economic and political factors have shaped the roles of higher education and universities as well as EAP education. The book opens with a brief history of EAP and presents the major areas of knowledge that EAP practitioners draw upon. The authors discuss the teachers' transition from their knowledge base of mainstream TESOL to EAP education and encourage teachers to engage in research and communication with communities of practice and EAP teacher associations in order to develop their professionalism in EAP instruction. Throughout the book, the authors address practitioners as researchers and describe the process of teacher development as socialization and advise EAP practitioners to reflect on their practice and engage in on-going research.

Basturkmen, H. (2014). LSP teacher education: Review of literature and suggestions for the research agenda. *Ibérica*, *28*, 17–33.

In her critical review paper, Basturkmen holds that although the many varied circumstances where Language for Specific Purposes (LSP) instruction occurs may impose challenges on practitioners, the literature on teacher education is thin and limited. The paper presents a timely synopsis of the published literature on LSP teacher education up to 2014 and expands on the major needs of LSP practitioners (including ESP/EAP teachers). LSP teachers are generally involved in research on specialist discourses and learners' needs, course design, classroom teaching, and materials development. She reports the results of her detailed analysis of the major themes that featured in a representative sample of textbooks and papers and classifies them under 'role of specialized knowledge' and 'content for teacher education'. Furthermore, She reviews the models of language teacher education critically and argues in favor of the reflective model for in-service LSP teacher education programs. I feel confident that EAP practitioners and postgraduate students of EAP will find highly creative topics for further research if they read her concluding suggestions for future research.

Ding, A., & Campion, G. (2016). EAP teacher development. In K Hyland, P Shaw (Eds.), *The Routledge handbook of English for academic purposes* (pp. 547–559). New York: Routledge.

Chapter 41 in *The Routledge handbook of English for academic purposes* (Hyland & Shaw, 2016), co-authored by Ding & Campion presents an informative, well-referenced, professional, thought provoking and critical review of literature on EAP teacher development. The authors argue that the sophisticated conceptualizations of EAP and the diverse needs of EAP practitioners in different contexts call for a reconsideration of the goals and content of EAP teacher education. Ding and Campion brief who EAP practitioners are and introduce the current official, institutional, and informal paths for practititioners' access to professional knowledge and research in teacher education across the world. Then they thematize BALEAP as a typical example of systematic organizational experience in teacher education for EAP in the UK and introduce a wide range of postgraduate university-affiliated programs and professional pre-service courses in the UK context. The authors discuss the details of the content of the competency framework developed by BALEAP and acknowledg its contributions to the field. Finally, the authors analyze the framework critically and stress the need for recognition of the position of the wider international EAP community in setting standards for teacher qualification.

Hyland, K. (2006). *English for academic purposes.* **London: Routledge.**

Hyland (2006) introduces this book as an advanced resource book for readers interested in the field of language teaching as well as those researching and teaching English for Academic Purposes. Although the book is not intended to be a technical theme-based source on teacher education for EAP, it can be very resourceful and informative for prospective EAP practitioners, with an extensive coverage of major themes and controversies on theory and practice of EAP. What adds to the pedagogical value of the book for EAP readers is the reflective presentation of themes in a task-based and research-supported framework. This motivates the EAP practitioners to develop a solid and multidimensional understanding of the field so that they may connect the theories to the design and delivery of their local EAP courses. Ken Hyland's positive attitude toward critical EAP echoes throughout the book and the author leaves generous spaces for eliciting the readers' voices through open-ended questions well-embedded in the content of the text and research paper extracts.

References

Atai, M. R., & Fatahi-Majd, M. (2014). Exploring practices and cognitions of Iranian ELT instructors and subject teachers in teaching EAP reading comprehension. *English for Specific Purposes, 33*(1), 27–38.

Atai, M. R., & Nejadghanbar, H. (2017). Exploring Iranian ESP teachers' subject-related critical incidents. *Journal of English for Academic Purposes, 29*, 43–54.

Bahrami, V., Hosseini, M., & Atai, M. R. (2019). Exploring research-informed practice in English for Academic Purposes: A narrative study. *English for Specific Purposes, 54*, 152–165.

Campion, G. C. (2016). 'The learning never ends': Exploring teachers' views on the transition from General English to EAP. *Journal of English for Academic Purposes, 23*, 59–70.

Ding, A., & Bruce, I. (2017). *The English for academic purposes practitioner: Operating on the edge of academia.* Springer.

Ding, A., & Campion, G. (2016). EAP teacher development. In K. Hyland & P. Shaw (Eds.), *The Routledge handbook of English for academic purposes* (pp. 547–559). Routledge.

Hall, D. R. (2013). Teacher education for languages for specific purposes. In C. A. Chapelle (Ed.), *Encyclopedia of applied linguistics* (pp. 5537–5542). Blackwell.

Hamp-Lyons, L. (2018). Why researching EAP practice? *Journal of English for Academic Purposes, 31*, A3–A4.

Mahmood Reza Atai is professor of applied linguistics at Kharazmi University, Tehran, Iran. He is editor of the *Iranian Journal of Applied Linguistics* and has been a member of editorial board for some international journals. Furthermore, he has served as a member of scientific committee of some international conferences. His publications include five co/authored EAP textbooks for university students and several articles on ESP/EAP themes including needs analysis, genre analysis, course design, teacher education, and program evaluation. His recent articles appear in *English for Specific Purposes, Journal of English for Academic Purposes, System, RELC Journal*, and *Teacher Development*. Most recently, his 'National Curriculum' entry appeared in the *TESOL Encyclopedia of English Language Teaching* (NJ: Wiley-Blackwell, 2018).

Emotionality in TESOL and Teacher Education

91

Juan de Dios Martínez Agudo

> *'The heart has its reasons which reason knows nothing of... We know the truth not only by the reason, but by the heart'*—Blaise Pascal

For a long time, the overemphasis on rationality has certainly eclipsed the consideration of human emotionality (Uitto et al., 2015), mainly due to the highly subjective, irrational and hard to capture nature of emotions (Benesch, 2012), despite the fact that cognitions and emotions are closely interconnected in the complex reality of language learning and teaching. Although the cognitive perspective has historically dominated applied linguistics research, an affective turn may certainly be underway in applied linguistics (Pavlenko, 2012) as teacher emotionality is recently emerging as a potentially promising research area (Benesch, 2012, 2016, 2017). Since the advent of the critical turn in Applied Linguistics and TESOL, emotions in ELT, which have been discussed from different approaches, have been theorised from a critical theoretical perspective (Benesch, 2016). Although teacher emotionality still remains a relatively unexplored and unrecognised research area in the TESOL literature (Benesch, 2012, 2016, 2017; Martínez, 2018; Gkonou et al., 2020) and, above all, in TESOL teacher education (Golombek & Doran, 2014; Martínez, 2018; Gkonou et al., 2020), the truth is that the multifaceted nature and critical impact of teacher emotions in educational settings call for further exploration as without emotions that unexpectedly arise from everyday classroom communications and interactions, very little teaching and learning would certainly take place (Dewaele, 2015).

J. de D. Martínez Agudo (✉)
Department of Didactics of Social Sciences, Languages and Literatures, Faculty of Education, University of Extremadura, Badajoz, Spain
e-mail: jdmtinez@unex.es

© Springer Nature Switzerland AG 2021
H. Mohebbi and C. Coombe (eds.), *Research Questions in Language Education and Applied Linguistics*, Springer Texts in Education,
https://doi.org/10.1007/978-3-030-79143-8_91

Based on the extremely complex and multifaceted nature of teaching viewed not only as a rational activity but also as an emotionally intense practice, the fact of addressing the impact of teacher emotionality within educational contexts is deemed essential to be able to understand how and under what conditions teachers actually teach in emotionally demanding classroom contexts and, accordingly, how their students actually perceive and respond to such emotions and, consequently, learn (Day & Lee, 2011). L2 teaching, like all teaching, thus requires an in-depth understanding of the emotional workload involved in language learning and teaching, with a specific focus on "what teachers feel about what they think, know, believe and do" (Golombek & Doran, 2014: 103). To date, the limited research on this area is mostly concerned with the emotional stresses or anxieties resulting from non-native teachers' self-perceived English competence (Horwitz, 1996), language teachers' emotional burnout (Crandall, 2000) and the emotions experienced as a result of the relationships and interactions with students, colleagues and institutions (Cowie, 2011). In short, the largely ignored but also potentially promising research area of teacher emotionality in TESOL and teacher education certainly calls for further exploration, with a particular emphasis on the complexity and contradictions of those emotions associated with L2 instructional practices and emerging professional identities in emotionally demanding working conditions and environments (Yazan & Peercy, 2016).

Academic emotions should always be present in any discussion about L2 teacher education. Specifically, the role of emotions in student teachers' professional learning, which has been largely ignored by teacher educators, has recently been viewed as a critical functional component of language teacher professional preparation (Golombek & Doran, 2014). Indeed, academic emotions help to shape prospective teachers' emerging professional identities. Thus, teacher education programmes must promote emotional competence training in terms of developing effective strategies to competently face and manage the emotional demands associated with professional practice (Corcoran & Tormey, 2012). In short, ESL teachers need to understand the emotional workload of their job, becoming more aware of their own emotions and those of their students' so as to create a suitable emotional climate for the teaching and learning process (Chen, 2016).

The Research Questions

1. Starting from the idea of "what teachers feel about what they think, know, believe and do" as suggested by Golombek and Doran (2014: 103), how do beliefs and emotions actually interact with each other, influencing teachers' instructional actions and decisions in varied ways in the complex reality of teaching?

2. What are the main potential sources or factors influencing EFL teachers' emotions and, accordingly, their professional identity and growth? To what

extent do such sources emanate from individuals (personality characteristics, self-perceived language competence…) or external influences (educational reforms, working relationships…?

3. How does the emotionality of teacher discourse influence student language learning through classroom communications and interactions and how must teacher education programmes deal with this area?

4. Based on the idea that emotions in language teaching are socially and inter-actively constructed, together with the subjectivity of the emotional climate, how do EFL teachers emotionally face and respond to the new challenges of educational/curricular reforms?

5. Since the ecological nature of classroom emotions which are situated in specific sociocultural contexts, how do ESL teacher emotions emerge from and within professional relationships and interactions with the school community (learners, colleagues and parents) and how do teachers emotionally respond to such challenges, as suggested by Gkonou and Mercer (2017)?

6. Which academic emotions arise from collaborative experiences and working relationships between non-native speaker teachers (NNSTs) and native speaker teachers (NSTs) in EFL classrooms and how are such emotions communicated in different workplaces?

7. Given that emotions change over time because of their transitional nature, how do EFL student teachers' emotions emerge and evolve during the practicum process and their subsequent professional development?

8. How could L2 teachers' emotional competences be effectively developed through teacher education to mitigate teachers' emotional stress and, accordingly, prevent teacher burnout? What areas in particular should such formal training focus on?

9. In what way(s) are teacher emotions linked with teaching quality, as stated by Frenzel et al. (2016)?

10. Which is the best research design and instrument (questionnaires, narratives, diaries, observation-based longitudinal studies, stimulated-recall interviews…) for gathering a complete perspective on the emotional lives of EFL teachers? Why?

Suggested Resources

Benesch, S. (2012). *Considering Emotions in Critical English Language Teaching: Theories and Praxis*. New York: Routledge.

This is the first publication devoted specifically to emotions in English language teaching. This ground-breaking book provides a useful framework for understanding the emotional dimension of communication and interaction in ELT from a critical perspective. This thought-provoking book discusses, not just theoretically but also practically, emotions in the EFL classroom, both from students' and teachers' perspectives, examining identity issues faced by immigrant students learning English in higher education institutions and also offering practical ideas for teachers as a means of developing their critical language teaching.

Gkonou, C., & Mercer, S. (2017). *Understanding Emotional and Social Intelligence among English Language Teachers*. **London: British Council.**

Based on the assumption that emotional and social competences are important in ELT as well as critical components of TESOL teacher education programmes as emotions in language teaching are socially and interactively constructed, this mixed-methods empirical study examines the central role played by socio-emotional competences in language education, the characteristics underlying quality relationships in ESL teaching, and the strategies for promoting quality interpersonal relationships in the language classroom. As the authors themselves conclude, results reveal considerable diversity and individuality of teacher expertise in terms of socio-emotional competences in action in the language classroom.

Wolff, D., & Costa, P. I. (2017). Expanding the language teacher identity landscape: An investigation of the emotions and strategies of a NNEST. *The Modern Language Journal*, **101(S1), 76–90.** https://doi.org/10.1111/modl.12370.

This narrative-based study investigates the relationship between teacher professional identity and teacher emotions by tracing the trajectory of a NNEST over an academic year in a U.S. MA TESOL programme. By focusing on the student's reflexivity, the authors illustrate how their participant managed her emotions in a positive way by deploying her teaching strategies when working with her students. Drawing on varied data sources, the article highlights the reflexive relationship between the participant's emotions and her subsequent professional identity development. According to the authors, this paper calls for a new pedagogical model that helps teachers develop reflexivity and negotiate emotion-related challenges.

Martínez, J. D. (Ed.) (2018). *Emotions in Second Language Teaching: Theory, Research and Teacher Education*. **Cham: Springer.**

This edited collection sheds some light on a still largely unexplored but also highly promising research area in TESOL and teacher education by presenting the current state of theory and research on teacher emotions from different perspectives. This book specifically examines what contribution emotions make to the professional lives of EFL teachers, exploring diverse aspects of the emotional nature of L2 teaching that have been totally overlooked in the research literature so far. The issues raised in this book will be of great value and interest not only to researchers interested in a deeper understanding of the emotional dimension of L2 teaching but also to L2 teachers from all over the world who need to be aware of how to manage not only their own emotions but also their students' so as to improve the quality of language education.

Gkonou, C., Dewaele, J-M., & King, J. (Eds.). (2020). *The Emotional Roller-coaster of Language Teaching*, **Bristol: Multilingual Matters.**

This collection explores the emotional dimension of language teaching and specifically the emotional complexity and challenges affecting language teachers' pedagogical practices and professional experiences and lives from both theoretical and empirical perspectives in a wide variety of educational contexts, covering relevant topics such as emotional labour, burnout, emotion regulation, resilience, emotional intelligence and wellbeing. The crucial role that emotions play in language teachers' professional lives is thoroughly discussed. Accordingly, this book is a must read for all those concerned with understanding the affective realities that shape language teachers' professional practices and lives.

References

Benesch, S. (2012). *Considering emotions in critical English language teaching: Theories and praxis.* Routledge.

Benesch, S. (2016). Critical approaches to the study of emotions in English language teaching and learning. In C. A. Chapelle (Ed.), *The encyclopedia of applied linguistics* (pp. 1–6). John Wiley Sons.

Benesch, S. (2017). *Emotions and English language teaching: Exploring teachers' emotion labor.* Routledge.

Chen, J. (2016). Understanding teacher emotions: The development of a teacher emotion inventory. *Teaching and Teacher Education, 55,* 68–77.

Corcoran, R. P., & Tormey, R. (2012). *Developing emotionally competent teachers. Emotional intelligence and pre-service teacher education.* Peter Lang.

Cowie, N. (2011). Emotions that experienced English as a Foreign Language (EFL) teachers feel about their students, their colleagues and their work. *Teaching and Teacher Education, 27,* 235–242.

Crandall, J. (2000). Language teacher education. *Annual Review of Applied Linguistics, 20,* 34–55.

Day, C., & Lee, J. (Eds.). (2011). *New understandings of teacher's work: Emotions and educational change.* Springer.

Dewaele, J.-M. (2015). On emotions in foreign language learning and use. *The Language Teacher, 39*(3), 13–15.

Frenzel, A. C., Pekrun, R., Goetz, T., Daniels, L. M., Durksen, T. L., Becker-Kurz, B., & Klassen, R. M. (2016). Measuring teachers' enjoyment, anger, and anxiety: The teacher emotions scales (TES). *Contemporary Educational Psychology, 46,* 148–163. https://doi.org/10.1016/j.cedpsych.2016.05.003

Gkonou, C., & Mercer, S. (2017). *Understanding emotional and social intelligence among English language teachers.* British Council.

Gkonou, C., Dewaele, J-M., & King, J. (Eds.). (2020). *The emotional rollercoaster of language teaching.* Multilingual Matters.

Golombek, P., & Doran, M. (2014). Unifying cognition, emotion, and activity in language teacher professional development. *Teaching and Teacher Education, 39,* 102–111.

Horwitz, E. (1996). Even teachers get the blues: Recognizing and alleviating language teachers' feelings of foreign language anxiety. *Foreign Language Annals, 29*(3), 365–372.

Martinez, J. D. (Ed.). (2018). *Emotions in second language teaching: Theory, research and teacher education.* Springer.

Pavlenko, A. (2012). The affective turn in SLA: From 'affective factors' to 'language desire' and 'commodification of affect.' In D. Gabrys-Barker & J. Bielska (Eds.), *The affective dimension in second language acquisition* (pp. 3–28). Multilingual Matters.

Uitto, M., Jokikokko, K., & Estola, E. (2015). Virtual special issue on teachers and emotions in Teaching and Teacher Education (TATE) in 1985–2014. *Teaching and Teacher Education, 50*, 124–135.

Yazan, B., & Peercy, M. M. (2016). ESOL teacher candidates' emotions and identity development. In J. Crandall & M. Christison (Eds.), *Teacher education and professional development in TESOL. Global perspectives* (pp. 53–67). Routledge.

Juan de Dios Martínez Agudo is Associate Professor of TESOL and Teacher Education at the Faculty of Education of the University of Extremadura (Spain). His research interests lie at the interface of SLA research, L2 pedagogy and L2 teacher education, with a focus on bilingualism (CLIL), teacher learning and thinking in SLTE, classroom discourse analysis (teacher talk), and affective aspects of L2 teaching and learning. His publications have appeared in *Linguistics and Education, Language and Education, International Journal of Bilingual Education and Bilingualism, Language, Culture and Curriculum, The Language Learning Journal, Southern African Linguistics and Applied Language Studies, Porta Linguarum,* and *Australian Journal of Teacher Education,* among others. His latest edited books are *Native and Non-Native Teachers in English Language Classrooms* (2017, De Gruyter), *Emotions in Second Language Teaching* (2018, Springer) and *Quality in TESOL and Teacher Education* (2019, Routledge).

Krishna K. Dixit and Amol Padwad

Teacher motivation (TM) is undoubtedly one of the decisive factors of the success of educational ventures. Teacher motivation, as Dörnyei and Ushioda (2011) note, has received inadequate attention in educational psychology in general and in discourses of educational reform in particular. However, in the recent past, the issue of teacher motivation has come under the research-lens leading to publications (a few focusing exclusively on language teacher motivation) such as Dörnyei (2001), Dörnyei and Ushioda (2011), Lamb and Wedell (2013), Reeve and Sue (2014), Pelletier and Rocche (2016), Han and Yin (2016), and Hiver et al. (2018).

TM is often defined with reference to motivation of people to join the teaching profession and sustain over time. In the present age of rapid changes in social, economic, and knowledge domains, teachers need to be life-long learners (Day & Sachs, 2004: 3). Concerns about teacher quality are not only limited to teacher qualifications, skills and knowledge, but also touch upon their motivation for continuous learning and developing professionally.

In the general education discourse, TM has been explored using a variety of frameworks, such as flow analysis (Csikszentmihaly, 1997), self-efficacy, work motivation theory (Blackburn & Lawrence, 1995), future time perspective (FTP) (Huseman et al., 2014), Feminism (Glazer, 1997), self-determination theory (Deci et al., 1997) to mention a few. However, (English) language teacher motivation (ELTM) has remained a severely under-researched area within Dörnyei (2001) and Dörnyei and Ushioda (2011), one of the few studies in ELTM, conceive teaching as a professional activity with certain unique motivational properties, such as:

K. K. Dixit (✉) · A. Padwad
Centre for English Language Education (CELE), Dr. B. R. Ambedkar University, Delhi, India
e-mail: krishnakdixit@aud.ac.in

A. Padwad
e-mail: amol@aud.ac.in

© Springer Nature Switzerland AG 2021
H. Mohebbi and C. Coombe (eds.), *Research Questions in Language Education and Applied Linguistics*, Springer Texts in Education,
https://doi.org/10.1007/978-3-030-79143-8_92

- Prominent intrinsic component as a main constituent
- Close link with contextual factors
- Unmistakable temporal dimension
- Fragile in nature, i.e. exposed to several powerful negative influences.

Studies like Dörnyei (2001), Dörnyei and Ushioda (2011) and Pennington (1995) point out how themes such as 'moral values' and 'social service' fit nicely in the intrinsic motivation discourse of TM. Doyle and Kim (1999) build on critical language pedagogy discourse and identify various reasons centred around teachers' wellbeing for demotivation of teachers. While Shoaib (2004) attempts to map the ELTM terrain in the Saudi Arabian context, Kubanyiova (2006) investigates the nexus between TM and teacher development. Drawing on the work of Dörnyei (2009) in which he proposes three concepts, namely 'Ideal language Teacher Self', 'Ought-to Language Teacher Self', and 'Ought-to Language Teacher Self' 'Feared language teacher self' to conceptualise ELTM. Lastly, Dörnyei and Kubanyiova (2014) discuss ELTM through the notion of 'vision' focused on future visualization.

ELTM is an emergent area in language education and it invites more studies drawing from general psychology, social psychology, and educational research on teacher development and student learning outcomes.

The Research Questions

1. How do current conceptualizations of teacher motivation apply to English language teacher motivation?
2. How do education policies and pre-service and in-service teacher education influence and promote English language teacher motivation?
3. What is the relationship between English language teacher motivation and student learning outcomes?
4. In what ways does student motivation impact English language teacher motivation?
5. Given the distinct socio-cultural and politico-economic dimensions of the status of English in some contexts, what factors may particularly affect English language teacher motivation, as distinct from language teacher motivation and teacher motivation in general?
6. How does language teacher motivation change at different stages of the teacher's career? What differences, if any, are there in the factors shaping language teacher motivation at early, mid and advanced stages of the career?
7. How do different stakeholders' perceptions of the English language seem to affect English language teacher motivation?

8. Does the motivation of native English language teachers need to be conceptualised differently from that of non-native English language teachers? If yes, how?
9. What are the distinctive features and issues of English language teacher motivation at primary, secondary and tertiary levels?
10. What are the similarities and differences in English language teacher motivation in terms of gender, location (urban and rural), work contexts (state sector or private sector, EMI and Non-EMI)?

Suggested Resources

Bess, J. L. (1997) (Ed.). *Teaching Well and Liking It: Motivating Faculty to Teach Well.* **Baltimore, Maryland: John Hopkins University Press.**

The key themes explored in this book include what makes someone a good teacher, why a few teachers are motivated to teach more than others, strategies for cultivating motivation of teachers, feminist perspectives on teaching motivation, application of motivation theories, flow analysis, dynamics of organizational culture and faculty motivation, leadership and faculty motivation, politics of motivation, public policy and motivation to mention a few. The issues are developed and presented drawing on the experience of teachers working in the field. Editor James L Bess emphasizes that the effectiveness of education is determined by the quality of teaching. The book highlights that motivation of faculty is at the core of effective learning outcomes.

Dörnyei, Z. & Kubanyiova, M. (2014). *Motivating Learners, Motivating Teachers.* **Cambridge: Cambridge University Press.**

In this book a new approach for exploring and enhancing motivation—vision as a tool—is presented linking it closely with teaching-and-learning English. The authors draw on visualization research in sports, psychology and education and elaborate on the impact of powerful visualization of the future on motivation to perform. The book offers a variety of strategies to help students to visualize themselves as competent users of language. The key issues discussed in the book include vision, motivation, mental imagery, strategies to construct vision, vision focused programme design, transforming vision into action, cultivating vision are a few among many crucial topics.

Ozcan, M. (1996). Improving performance: Toward a theory of teacher motivation. A Paper presented at the Annual Meeting of the American Educational Research Association, New York.

In this article the author proposes that to develop a construct of teacher motivation teachers need to be considered as human beings with attitudes, values, and beliefs. It is stated that to construct a theory of teacher motivation the foremost thing required is to consider teachers as human beings, employees with material interests, and decision-making professionals. The author contends that teachers are naturally motivated to survive, utilize their potential, and realize that to achieve their ends they need materials and resources. Accordingly, a theory of teacher motivation is developed centred around 'ideas' (knowledge, beliefs, values etc.) and 'interests' (resources and rewards).

Richardson, P. W., Karabenick, S. A. & Watt, H. M. G. (2014). (Eds.) *Teacher Motivation: Theory and Practice.* **New York: Routledge.**

This is first book-length discussion on teacher motivation with reference to theories and practices in varied contexts. It offers an in-depth introduction to TM and outlines future directions of research. In it the authors draw on a decade of work of psychological theorists exploring people's motivation for choosing teaching as a career, the impacts of extrinsic and intrinsic forces on teaching career, and variation in motivational profile at different stages of a career. In this book TM is discussed from three distinct perspectives: theoretical approaches, motivation related processes, and motivation and teacher career trajectories.

Al-Hoorie, A. H. MacIntyre, P. D. (2019). *Contemporary Language Motivation Theory: 60 Years since Gardner and Lambert.* **Bristol: Multilingual Matters.**

This book offers a detailed discussion on varied aspects of motivation in language education focusing on the pivotal work of Robert. C. Gardner and Wallace E. Lambert. The chapters exemplify the fundamental value of Gardener and Lambert's contributions to psychology of second language acquisition, social psychology, sociology, and language teaching methodology. Through a critical and dialogic engagement this book offers theoretical, empirical and methodological insights. This is a valuable resource for exploring the motivational domain in language education.

References

Blackburn, R. T., & Lawrence, J. H. (1995). *Faculty at work: Motivation, expectation, satisfaction.* John Hopkins University Press.

Csikszentmihaly, M. (1997). Flow analysis. In J. L. Bess (Ed.), *Teaching well and liking it. Motivating faculty to teach effectively.* John Hopkins University Press.

Day, C. & Sachs, J. (2004). (Eds.) Professionalism, performativity and empowerment: Discourse in the politics, policies and purposes of continuing professional development. In C. Day & J. Sachs (Eds.), *International handbook on continuing professional development of teachers.* Open University Press.

Deci, E., Kasser, L. T. & Ryan, R. M. (1997). Self-determined teaching: Opportunities and obstacles. In J. L. Bess (Ed.), *Teaching well and liking it. Motivating faculty to teach effectively.* John Hopkins University Press.

Dörnyei, Z. (2001). *Teaching and researching motivation.* Pearson.

Dörnyei, Z. (2009). The L2 motivational self system. In Dörnyei, Z & E. Ushioda (Eds.), *Motivation, language identity and the L2 self* (pp. 9–42). Multilingual Matters.

Dörnyei, Z., & Ushioda, E. (2011). *Teaching and researching motivation* (2nd ed.). Pearson.

Dörnyei, Z., & Kubanyiova, M. (2014). *Motivating learners, motivating teachers*. Cambridge University Press.

Doyle, T., & Kim, Y. M. (1999). Teacher motivation and satisfaction in the United States and Korea. *MEXTESOL Journal, 23*(2), 35–48.

Glazer, J. S. (1997). Beyond male theory: A feminist perspective on teaching motivation. In J. L. Bess (Ed.), *Teaching well and liking it. Motivating faculty to teach effectively*. John Hopkins University Press.

Han, J., & Yin, H. (2016). Teacher motivation: Definition, research development and implications for teachers. *Cogent Education, 3*.

Hiver, P., Kim, T. -Y., & Kim, Y. (2018). Language teacher motivation. In S. Mercer & A. Kostoulas (Eds.), *Language teacher psychology*. Multilingual Matters.

Huseman, J., Duggan, M. A. & Fishman, E. (2014). The teacher time bubble: Expanding teachers' imaginings of the future to support learning. In P. W. Richardson, S. A. Karabenick, & H. M. G. Watt (Eds.), *Teacher motivation: Theory and practice*. Routledge.

Kubanyiova, M. (2006). Developing a motivational teaching practice in EFL teachers in Slovakia: Challenges of promoting teacher change in EFL contexts. *TESL- EJ* 10/2. Available online at http://www-writing.berkley.edu/TESL-EJ/ej38/a5.html.

Lamb, M., & Wedell, M. (2013). *Inspiring English teachers: A comparative study of learner perceptions of inspirational teaching*. British Council.

Pelletier, L. G., & Rocche, M. (2016). Teacher motivation in the classroom. In L. C. Wun, J. C. K. Wang, & R. M. Ryan (Eds.), *Building Autonomous Learners: Perspectives from research and practice using self-determination theory*. Springer.

Pennington, M. C. (1995). *Work satisfaction, motivation and commitment in teaching English as a second language*. ERIC Document ED404850.

Reeve, J., &, Sue, Y. -L. (2014). Teacher motivation. In M. Gagné (Ed.), *The oxford handbook of work engagement, motivation, and self-determination theory*. Oxford University Press.

Shoaib, A. (2004). *What Motivates and demotivates English teachers in Saudi Arabia: A qualitative perspective*. Unpublished Ph.D. dissertation, University of Nottingham, School of English Studies.

Krishna K. Dixit is associate professor in the Centre for English Language Education (CELE), Ambedkar University, New Delhi. He has completed his Ph.D. on English language Teacher Motivation for Professional Development in the Indian context. His areas of interest are teacher motivation, teachers' continuing professional development, history of English language in India, and modern critical theory.

Amol Padwad is Professor and Director, Centre for English Language Education, Ambedkar University Delhi. He is also the Secretary of Ainet Association of English Teachers (AINET-India). He has been actively engaged in promoting teacher development, teacher networking and associations and teacher research, and has carried out studies in these areas. He pioneered the English Teachers' Clubs—self-help teacher development groups—in rural towns of central India, some of which have been running for over fifteen years. His recent publications include *Continuing professional development* (with Rod Bolitho) and *Teaching in low-resource classrooms: Voices of experience* (with Richard Smith and Deborah Bullock).

Foreign Language Teacher Education

Friederike Klippel

Today several formats of foreign language teacher education (FLTE) are in place worldwide, and each of these—depending on local contexts and educational systems—foregrounds different aspects. Conceptualisations of FLTE can be traced back nearly 200 years, e.g. in Germany (cf. Klippel, 2012), when schools introduced modern languages; everywhere teacher education is linked to the development of higher education institutions and university modern languages departments.

The basic questions of FLTE, however, apply to any time or context. If we want instruction in languages to be efficient, (1) what do teachers need to know in order to achieve this, (2) what do teachers need to be able to do in the classroom, and (3) how can they successfully acquire the necessary knowledge, skills and attitudes? Teacher education in general can be seen to have the "accomplished teacher" as its goal, who "is a member of a professional community, who is ready, willing, and able to teach and to learn from his or her teaching experiences" (Shulman & Shulman, 2004). This concept of teaching proficiency combines knowledge, motivation, skills, experiential learning and the identification with a profession.

There is some debate whether language teachers are different from teachers of other subjects, due to the functions of the language to be learnt acting both as the content of learning and as the medium of instruction; a further difference may originate in the language teachers' identification with and use of another language, as is the case for non-native speaker teachers. Like teachers of music or art, language teachers have to combine teaching facts about their subject with fostering learners' skills and motivation, thus aiming at declarative as well as procedural knowledge and a desire to learn. Consequently, foreign language teachers have to be highly competent in the language they are teaching and motivated to continue improving their own language skills.

F. Klippel (✉)
Department of English and American Studies, Ludwig-Maximilians-University, Munich, Germany
e-mail: klippel@lmu.de

© Springer Nature Switzerland AG 2021
H. Mohebbi and C. Coombe (eds.), *Research Questions in Language Education and Applied Linguistics*, Springer Texts in Education,
https://doi.org/10.1007/978-3-030-79143-8_93

Both theory and practice play a part in teacher education. How much weight is given to each aspect and at what stage of the teacher development process it is emphasized, varies considerably. The craft model of teacher education stresses learning from a master practitioner, the applied science model relies on the application of research results, and the reflective approach concentrates on learning through experience (Wallace, 1991). In any case, teachers need to be learners themselves throughout their professional lives. To this end, in-service courses, sabbaticals and a wide range of support materials need to be made available.

In conjunction with the current output-orientation of education, various frameworks and standards of foreign language teacher competences have been developed in recent years. These reflect the predominant objectives of language teaching regarding communicative—and in some regions also intercultural or transcultural—competences. Because teaching is always context-based as well as dependent on current thinking in education and linguistics, neither standards nor any teacher education program can ever claim to be perfect.

The Research Questions

1. What should be the essential contents and components of a foreign language teacher education program in your country?
2. How could theory and practice be profitably combined in a teacher education program?
3. In which ways should foreign language teacher education programs for non-native speakers and native speakers differ? Why?
4. How do the standards for foreign language teacher competences in different parts of the world compare and what are their underlying theoretical assumptions?
5. Looking back, what do experienced FL practitioners consider to have been the most important elements of their teacher education program?
6. In what way did the format and the content of foreign language teacher education change in one country/region during a particular time span?
7. Which role can mentors play during teaching practice? What tasks do they need to be prepared for?
8. What are the benefits of being an assistant teacher in a target country?
9. What do student teachers consider to be the necessary qualifications of teacher educators?
10. Which are the individual prerequisites of becoming a foreign language teacher that need to be given, and what can be learnt in terms of knowledge, skills and attitudes?

Suggested Resources

Appel, J. (1995). *Diary of a Language Teacher.* **Oxford: Heinemann.**

In this book Appel reports on six years of teaching English as a foreign language in a German secondary school based on the diaries he kept. This may not sound relevant to language teachers elsewhere. But in his honest, reflective and well-structured book he touches on so many universal and timeless situations in language classrooms that teachers everywhere will find his experience and reflective analyses inspiring. The book has three sections, which are roughly based on his own professional development from "survival" as a novice teacher to "change" and "routine". Within each section two or three aspects are in focus, e.g. teacher's work, relevant reading and writing, exams. The first part of each chapter consists of diary entries; these are analyzed in a second part where the author refers to a rich stream of literature, not just from the field of applied linguistics. This book documents the intertwined cognitive, social and emotional strands of foreign language teacher development in a thought-provoking and laconic style.

Barkhuizen, G. (ed.) (2019). *Qualitative Research Topics in Language Teacher Education.* **New York and London: Routledge.**

This recent book edited by Barkhuizen is a multi-faceted guide to finding a research question for a qualitative study in the field of language teacher education. It contains a plethora of sound advice by many different scholars on a wide range of topics relating to the particular expertise and experience of each author. The 35 chapters range from language teacher psychology and emotions to English as an international language and action research. Some are thematically compact, e.g. strategy instruction, others touch on the fundamental questions in teacher education, i.e. the relationship between teaching and learning or learning how to teach. Each short chapter presents a few strategies for finding a research topic in this particular area, sketches current thinking on this area, lists some salient research questions as examples and a few relevant publications. Some chapters are focused on particular contexts, others have a more global reach. Although this is not a comprehensive overview of current teacher education research, this book is helpful in thinking about which research questions still need to be asked.

Benitt, N. (2015). *Becoming a (Better) Language Teacher. Classroom Action Research and Teacher Learning.* **Tuebingen: Narr.**

Benitt's qualitative interpretative case study charts the professional development of twelve teachers of English during a two-year blended learning M.A. program of FLTE, which integrates cooperative action research modules, thus fostering inquiry-based teacher education and knitting together practice and theory. Benitt gathers data from a very diverse group of teachers, i.e. diverse in their first languages, teaching experience, working contexts and backgrounds, through interviews, observations, portfolios and informal conversations. The study is worth reading for three reasons: (a) It shows that teachers develop along individual trajectories where cognitive, affective and social aspects have a different impact at different points in time. (b) Each teacher recalls "critical teaching incidents", when something suddenly makes sense, be it theoretical, practical or personal. (c) It is well-written and a very good example of qualitative research.

Freeman, D. (2016). *Educating Second Language Teachers.* **Oxford: Oxford University Press.**

In this book Freeman presents the sum of his thinking and research on (language) teacher education of more than 40 years. Thus, the book touches on a wide range of issues, positions itself within the large body of available literature in this field and culminates in a design theory in the last two chapters. It is impossible to do justice to this book in a short summary. Every chapter deals with core issues in theory and practice (with examples) and makes the arguments accessible by condensing them into diagrams and tables. Freeman considers teacher education to be a social process, by which language teachers become part of a professional community. Though he focuses on second language teacher education many of his theories apply to teacher education in general and breathe—at least to me—the wisdom of a lifetime of thinking about goals, processes and structures of becoming and being a teacher.

Johnson, K. E. (2009). *Second Language Teacher Education. A Sociocultural Perspective.* **New York: Routledge.**

This book presents an overview of the theories underlying a sociocultural perspective of teacher education. Approaching her topic from five different viewpoints, i.e. teachers as learners of teaching, language as social practice, L2 teaching as "dialogic mediation", social, cultural, and historical macro-structures which inform teacher education, and L2 teachers' professional development, Johnson argues both for awareness of the concepts which inform teacher educators' approaches and for using inquiry-based approaches in teacher education. The author includes numerous examples from her own practice as a teacher educator; this makes this book both intellectually stimulating and helpful.

References

Klippel, F. (2012). English language teacher education. *Anglistik: International Journal of English Studies, 23*(1), 153–163.

Shulman, L. S., & Shulman, J. H. (2004). How and what teachers learn: A shifting perspective. *Curriculum Studies, 36*(2), 257–271.

Wallace, M. J. (1991). *Training foreign language teachers* Cambridge: CUP.

Friederike Klippel is professor emerita at Munich University in Germany. After working as a teacher of English at secondary schools, she has been involved in English language teacher education since the mid-1970s. Her research areas comprise the history of language teaching and learning, methodology, classroom research, intercultural education, teacher education and professional development. Her many publications include *Keep Talking* (CUP 1984), a comprehensive historical study of learning and teaching English in eighteenth and nineteenth century Germany (*Englischlernen im 18. und 19. Jahrhundert.* 1994) and an ELT handbook (*Englischdidaktik.* 2007). She currently serves on the editorial boards of the journals *Language Teaching* (CUP) and *Zeitschrift fuer Fremdsprachenforschung* and is an active member of professional organisations like IATEFL, DGFF, Henry Sweet Society and Anglistenverband.

Identity in SLA and Second Language Teacher Education

Peter I. De Costa and Curtis Green-Eneix

Identity research in second language acquisition (SLA) and second language teacher education (SLTE) attempts to (1) understand how, through language, an individual achieves a sense of belonging within a sociocultural context, and (2) how relationships change over time and space (De Costa, 2016; Norton, 2013) as individuals traverse physical and cultural borders. Much of the SLA identity research has taken on a poststructuralist approach which conceives of identity as being shaped by structural forces, while also recognizing the ability of individuals to exercise some degree of agency and positioning. In addition, many identity scholars have started to explore how different identity aspects often intersect with each other (De Costa & Norton, 2016) and with ideologies (De Costa, 2016). An Asian female teacher working within an urban school setting, for example, would have to negotiate a gendered, ethnic, and classed identity as she negotiates a standard English ideology. Relatedly, there has been a growing interest in teacher identities (De Costa & Norton, 2017), which increasingly constitutes a key part of SLTE.

In terms of domain-specific research, the field has seen an expanded interested in study abroad (De Costa & Norton, 2016) and digital (Wargo & De Costa, 2017) contexts. Crucially, these new lines of research underscore how the traditional brick and mortar classroom is evolving as learning and teaching occur against a larger backdrop of transnationalism, globalization, and neoliberalism. Another new and exciting development, and in the spirit of transdisciplinarity, is that researchers have begun to explore how learner and teachers' identities are inextricably linked to

P. I. De Costa (✉)
Department of Linguistics, Languages & Cultures and Department of Teacher Education, Michigan State University, East Lansing, MI, USA
e-mail: pdecosta@msu.edu

C. Green-Eneix
Department of Linguistics, Languages & Cultures, Michigan State University, East Lansing, MI, USA
e-mail: greenen5@msu.edu

© Springer Nature Switzerland AG 2021
H. Mohebbi and C. Coombe (eds.), *Research Questions in Language Education and Applied Linguistics*, Springer Texts in Education,
https://doi.org/10.1007/978-3-030-79143-8_94

learner (De Costa, 2015) and teacher (Wolff & De Costa, 2017) emotions, respectively. These theoretical and topical developments have fortunately been accompanied by a discussion of how to go about conducting systematic identity research (Norton & De Costa, 2018) in order to ensure that rigorous identity research is carried out with a view to improving learning and teaching outcomes.

The Research Questions

1. How do in-service teachers navigate and develop their identity in a globalized classroom?
2. How do learners and teachers enact agency and engage in acts of positioning within their classrooms?
3. In what ways do language education policies shape and inform learner and teacher identities?
4. How are the identities of learners and teachers influenced by their ideologies?
5. How are the identities of learners and teachers influenced by their emotions?
6. In what ways do learners and teachers enact their agency in multilingual and multicultural classrooms?
7. How do individuals enact, perform, and negotiate their identities within online communities?
8. How do learners enact, perform, and negotiate their identities when studying abroad?
9. To what extent does a learner's social class limit or afford opportunities to acquire an additional language?
10. To what extent does a learner's ethnicity limit or afford opportunities to acquire an additional language?

Suggested Resources

De Costa, P. I. (2016). *The power of identity and ideology in language learning: Designer immigrants learning English in Singapore*. **Dordrecht: Springer.**

This monograph examines the language learning experiences of five Grade 9 students in an English-medium secondary school in Singapore. This year-long ethnographic study tracked their English language development as well as the challenges these students had to grapple with over the course of a school year. What is unique about this study is that it demonstrates how language ideologies are inextricably linked with the identities (linguistic and otherwise) in shaping the learning trajectories of students. In particular, De Costa illustrates how his focal participants had to manage a standard English language ideology and a circulating ideology that constructed as high performing students over the course of a year. The book also investigates the structural inequalities immigrant learners often encounter and the ethical issues surrounding work on immigrant communities.

Gray, J., & Morton, T. (2018). *Social interaction and English language teacher identity.* **Edinburgh: Edinburgh University Press.**

Building on the growing interest in language teacher identity research, this book explores the different identities to which teacher orient as they embark on acquiring new skills and knowledge in the profession. Foregrounding how social interaction influences teacher identity development, the fine-grained analyses Gray and Morton provide enables readers to see how identity work is a dynamic process, one that is shaped in and through interactions with those around them. The authors also situate language teacher identity development against a wider neoliberal turn that has engulfed education. While such global forces inevitably do influence the identities of teachers, the book also highlights how teachers are also able to successfully enact their own agency in surreptitious ways, thereby bringing to the fore the post-structural interface of structure and agency that underpin language education.

Kayi-Aydar, H. (2018). *Positioning theory in applied linguistics: Research design & applications.* **London: Palgrave MacMillan.**

Kayi-Aydar introduces a new analytical and methodological framework—Positioning theory—to investigate identity-based questions that focus on social and poststructural constructs such as agency and power. This book is a helpful resource for graduate students, language teachers, and faculty who want to examine how power dynamics inform second/foreign language learning and teaching in an empirical manner. In addition to providing a clear, concise, and accessible overview of Positioning theory, Kayi-Aydar also elaborates on Positioning theory's relevance within second language acquisition. Readers are also guided on how to collect and analyze their data through the helpful examples discussed in the book.

Norton, B. (2013). *Identity and language learning: Extending the conversation.* **Bristol: Multilingual Matters.**

In the second edition of her earlier seminal work, *Identity and Language Learning* (2000), Norton revisits and reframes developments within language identity research. Adopting a poststructuralist understanding of identity, which conceives of identity as being a fluid, power-inflected entity and a site of struggle, Norton develops the construct of identity through the narratives of five immigrant women in Canada. The notions of investment, capital, and imagined communities are also discussed in the book as she illustrates how her five female participants had different levels of access to resources and relationships that ultimately determined their varied levels of English language development.

Preece, S. (2016) *The Routledge handbook of language and identity*. **New York, NY: Routledge.**

This handbook provides a comprehensive overview of identity and how it is "related to a variety of 'real world problems in which language is a central issue'" (p. 1). Written in an accessible manner, the volume is a valuable resource for graduate students, language teachers, and experienced researchers who want to investigate identity through the lens of language. The 37 chapters are divided into five sections: perspectives on language and identity, categories and dimensions of identity, researching on language and identity, case studies of language and identity, and future directions on language and identity. Each chapter ends with a list of further readings to help readers develop their understanding of different identity aspects.

References

De Costa, P. I. (2015). Re-envisioning language anxiety in the globalized classroom through a social imaginary lens. *Language Learning, 65*(3), 504–532.

De Costa, P. I. (2016). *The power of identity and ideology in language learning: Designer immigrants learning English in Singapore*. Springer.

De Costa, P. I., & Norton, B. (2016). Identity in language learning and teaching: Research agendas for the future. In S. Preece (Ed.), *The Routledge handbook of language and identity* (pp. 586–601). Routledge.

De Costa, P. I., & Norton, B. (2017). Identity, transdisciplinarity, and the good language teacher. *The Modern Language Journal, 101-S*, 3–14.

Norton, B. (2013). *Identity and language learning: Extending the conversation*. Multilingual Matters.

Norton, B., & De Costa, P. I. (2018). Research tasks on identity in language learning and teaching. *Language Teaching, 51*(1), 90–112.

Wargo, J. M., & De Costa, P. I. (2017). Tracing academic literacies across contemporary literacy sponsorscapes: Mobilities, ideologies, identities, and technologies. *London Review of Education, 15*(1), 101–114.

Wolff, D., & De Costa, P. I. (2017). Expanding the language teacher identity landscape: An investigation of the emotions and strategies of a NNEST. *The Modern Language Journal 101-S*, 76–90.

Peter I. De Costa is currently an Associate Professor in the Department of Linguistics, Languages, & Cultures and the Department of Teacher Education at Michigan State University. His primary areas of research are identity and ideology in second language acquisition and second language teacher education. His work has appeared in *AILA Review, Applied Linguistics Review, International Journal of Applied Linguistics, Language Learning, Language Policy, Language Teaching, Linguistics and Education Research in the Teaching of English, System, TESOL Quarterly*, and *The Modern Language Journal*. He is the second Vice-President of the American Association for Applied Linguistics and co-editor of *TESOL Quarterly*.

Curtis Green-Eneix is a doctoral candidate in the Second Language Studies Program at Michigan State University where he was awarded the Academic Achievement Graduate Assistantship. He attained his Masters in TESOL at the University of Arizona where he also taught academic English writing to both native and international students. His work has appeared in *TESOL Journal*. Currently, his research interest includes teacher development, identity and ideology, social class and SLA, language policy, online classroom interaction, and critical discourse analysis.

Akram Nayernia

Burnout is a psychological syndrome which entails a long-term response to work stressors (Maslach, 2003). The construct was first established in psychology by Freudenberger (1974) as a state of exhaustion that emerges from working too hard without paying attention to one's own needs (Byrne, 1999). Later, Maslach and Jackson (1986) defined it as "a syndrome of emotional exhaustion, depersonalization, and reduced personal accomplishment that can occur among individuals who do 'people work' of some kind" (p. 1). However, Pines and Aronson (1988) define it as a state of physical, emotional, and mental exhaustion which can emerge because of prolonged exposure to emotionally demanding situations. Furthermore, burnout can be regarded as the result of coping with work-related stress unsuccessfully for a long time (Jennett et al., 2003). In teacher burnout, emotional exhaustion refers to when teachers feel emotionally exhausted and depleted. Depersonalization or cynicism occurs when teachers become callous and indifferent towards their students and their job. Eventually, reduced personal accomplishment is when teachers feel that they are ineffective or incompetent in helping their students learn (Maslach & Jackson, 1981; Maslach et al., 2001; Maslach, Jackson, & Leiter, 1996).

Burnout is regarded as a symptom of lack of professional well-being (Klusmann et al., 2008) of individuals who do people-oriented professions such as teaching (Byrne, 1999; Maslach & Leiter, 1999). Furthermore, teacher burnout as an experience of depletion of emotional resources, depersonalization of students, and lack of personal accomplishment has substantial impact on teachers' effective professional functioning (Butler & Shibaz, 2015).

From a theoretical perspective, burnout emerges because of a misfit between job demands and individual resources to cope with those demands (Maslach, 2003; Maslach et al., 2001). Correspondingly, different scholars have studied not only

A. Nayernia (✉)
Faculty of Foreign Languages, Iran University of Science and Technology, Tehran, Iran
e-mail: A_nayernia@iust.ac.ir

© Springer Nature Switzerland AG 2021
H. Mohebbi and C. Coombe (eds.), *Research Questions in Language Education and Applied Linguistics*, Springer Texts in Education,
https://doi.org/10.1007/978-3-030-79143-8_95

situational factors, such as misbehavior of students and supervisory support, but also teachers' individual factors, such as their sense of self-efficacy and professional knowledge, which can expose them to or buffer them from psychological pressure, stress, and burnout (Lauermann & König, 2016; Skaalvik & Skaalvik, 2010). In other words, the more individual resources and competence (e.g., professional knowledge), the more teachers overcome the difficulties of the teaching profession, they are less probable to experience the psychological strain of burnout.

Research has indicated that environmental and individual factors can lead to the emergence of burnout among teachers. Skaalvik and Skaalvik (2010) reported self-efficacy, external control, job satisfaction, and contextual factors as contributing to burnout. They also found parents and time pressure as the strongest predictors of depersonalization and emotional depletion respectively. In another study, Skaalvik and Skaalvik (2009) disclosed that teacher autonomy and supervisory support are negatively related to all three dimensions of burnout. The situation becomes more complex when one considers burnout among EFL teachers. One challenging issue regarding these teachers is their language proficiency as one of their personal resources. The significant role of EFL teachers in the educational system highlights the need to study factors contributing to teachers' well-being, among which the construct of burnout that has a direct relation with teachers' and students' performance.

The Research Questions

1. What are the factors contributing to burnout among EFL teachers?
2. What can teachers and teacher education programs do to reduce burnout levels among EFL learners?
3. What is the role of language proficiency and pedagogical knowledge in EFL teacher burnout?
4. What components of language proficiency are predictors of low burnout levels?
5. What contextual and cultural factors can lead to burnout among EFL learners?
6. What is the impact of EFL teacher burnout on students' performance?
7. Is there any relationship between teacher-student rapport and teacher burnout?
8. What is the role of teachers' assessment-related beliefs and their experience of burnout?
9. What is the role of newly-introduced educational technologies and EFL teachers' burnout?
10. Which dimension(s) of burnout is/are more prominent among EFL teachers and what can be done to reduce them?

Suggested Resources

Byrne, B. M. (1993). Burnout: Testing for the validity, replication, and invariance of causal structure across elementary, intermediate, and secondary teachers. *American Educational Research Journal 31*(3), 645–673.

The study investigated the impact of organizational (role ambiguity, role conflict, work overload, classroom climate, decision making, superior support, peer support) and personality (self-esteem, external locus of control) factors on three facets of burnout—Emotional Exhaustion, Depersonalization, and reduced Personal Accomplishment within one conceptual framework. Participants were full-time elementary (n = 1203), intermediate (n = 410), and secondary teachers (n = 1431). A hypothesized model of burnout was first tested and cross validated for each teaching panel; common causal paths were then tested for group-invariance. Results were consistent across groups in revealing the importance of (a) role conflict, work overload, classroom climate, decision making, and peer support as organizational determinants of teacher burnout, (b) self-esteem and external locus of control as important mediators of teacher burnout, and (c) the absence of role ambiguity and superior support in the causal process. Findings demonstrated that interpretations of burnout as a undimensional construct are not meaningful.

Cano-Garcia, F. J., Padilla-Munoz, E. M. & Carrasco-Ortiz, M. A. (2005). Personality and contextual variables in teacher burnout. *Personality and Individual Differences,* **38**, 929–940.

Although several papers have shown the importance of personality structure in the disposition to burnout, its role remains controversial, especially in relation to contextual variables of an organizational and environmental type. In this sense, the authors have first considered describing and then predicting the burnout levels of 99 teachers in the province of Seville (Spain). In addition to a structured, self-applied interview, they used the Spanish adaptation of the reduced version of NEO-PI-R (NEO-FFI) (Costa & McCrae, 1999). Homogeneity Analysis and Multiple Linear Regression (SPSS 11) were used. The results indicate the important role of personality structure in combination with some of the selected contextual variables, both in the description and prediction of teacher burnout. Most results confirm what has been achieved in similar research, and they especially emphasize the role of agreeableness as a protective factor (high scores) and, at the same time, as a vulnerability factor (low scores). These results are discussed from the perspective of interaction between disposition and contextual variables.

Schaufeli, W. B., Leiter, M. P. & Maslach, C. (2009). Burnout: 35 years of research and Practice. *Career Development International. 14(3)*, 204–220.

The purpose of this paper is to focus on the concept of burnout concept itself, rather than reviewing research findings on burnout. The paper presents an overview of the concept of burnout. The roots of the burnout concept seem to be embedded within broad social, economic, and cultural developments that took place in the last quarter of the past century and signify the rapid and profound transformation from an industrial society into a service economy. This social transformation goes along with psychological pressures that may translate into burnout. After the turn of the century, burnout is increasingly considered as an erosion of a positive psychological state. Although burnout seems to be a global phenomenon, the meaning of the concept differs between countries. For instance, in some countries burnout is used as a medical diagnosis, whereas in other countries it is a non-medical, socially accepted label that carries a minimum stigma in terms of a psychiatric diagnosis. The paper documents that the exact meaning of the concept of burnout varies with its context and the intentions of those using the term.

Maslach. C. & Leiter, M. P. (2008) Early Predictors of Job Burnout and Engagement. *Journal of Applied Psychology*, **93, 3, 498–512.**

A longitudinal study predicted changes in burnout or engagement a year later by identifying 2 types of early indicators at the initial assessment. Organizational employees (N_- 466) completed measures of burnout and 6 areas of work life at 2 times with a 1-year interval. Those people who showed an inconsistent pattern at Time 1 were more likely to change over the year than were those who did not. Among this group, those who also displayed a workplace incongruity in the area of fairness moved to burnout at Time 2, while those without this incongruity moved toward engagement. The implications of these 2 predictive indicators are discussed in terms of the enhanced ability to customize interventions for targeted groups within the workplace.

Nayernia, A. & Babayan, Z. (2019). EFL teacher burnout and self-assessed language proficiency: exploring possible relationships. *Language Testing in Asia,* **9. 3.**

Although teacher burnout has drawn the attention of many researchers, there is little empirical evidence for the contribution of non-native English language teachers' language proficiency level to their experience of burnout. To address this significant gap, the present study examined the relationship between English as a foreign language (EFL) teachers' self-assessed language proficiency and their experience of burnout. Research has indicated that personal resources of teachers can function as protectors against their experience of burnout. Thus, it was assumed that investigating how EFL teachers' level of burnout can be reduced through language proficiency as a personal resource can cast a new light on the role of personal resources in reducing teachers' experience of burnout. To this end, data were collected from 110 Iranian EFL teachers who were teaching in private language institutes through the Maslach Burnout Inventory—Educator Survey and Iranian EFL Teacher Self-Reported Language Proficiency Scale. The correlational analysis revealed that language proficiency had a significant negative relationship with the emotional exhaustion and depersonalization dimensions and a significant positive relationship with the personal accomplishment dimension of burnout. The results of regression analysis also indicated that, except for the reading subskill, all the other proficiency subskills were the best predictors of the different dimensions of burnout. Based on the findings of the current study, some pedagogical implications and research suggestions were also proposed.

References

Butler, R., & Shibaz, L. (2015). *Achievement goals for teaching: Implications for teacher burnout and classroom behaviors*. In Paper presented at the American educational research association.
Byrne, B. (1999). The nomological network of teacher burnout: A literature review and empirically validated model. In R. Vandenberghe & A. M. Huberman (Eds.), *Understanding and preventing teacher burnout: A sourcebook of international research and practice* (pp. 15–37). Cambridge University Press.
Costa, P. T., & McCrae, R. R. (1999). A five-factor theory of personality. *The Five-Factor Model of Personality: Theoretical Perspectives, 2,* 51–87.
Freudenberger, H. J. (1974). Staff burnout. *Journal of Social Issues, 30*(1), 159–166.
Jennett, H. K., Harris, S. L., & Mesibov, G. B. (2003). Commitment to philosophy, teacher efficacy, and burnout among teachers of children with autism. *Journal of Autism and Developmental Disorders, 33,* 583–593.
Klusmann, U., Kunter, M., Trautwein, U., Lüdtke, O., & Baumert, J. (2008). Teachers' occupational well-being and quality of instruction: The important role of self-regulatory patterns. *Journal of Educational Psychology, 100*(3), 702–715.
Lauerman, F., & König, J. (2016). Teachers' professional competence and well-being: Understanding the links between general pedagogical knowledge, self-efficacy and burnout. *Learning and Instruction, 45,* 9–19.
Maslach, C. (2003). Job burnout: New directions in research and intervention. *Current Directions in Psychological Strain, 12,* 189–192.
Maslach, C., & Jackson, S. E. (1981). The measurement of experienced burnout. *Journal of Occupational Behavior, 2,* 99–113.
Maslach, C., & Jackson, S. E. (1986). *MBI: Maslach Burnout Inventory manual* (2nd ed.). Consulting Psychologists Press.
Maslach, C., Jackson, S. E., & Leiter, M. P. (1996). *MBI: The Maslach Burnout inventory manual* (3rd ed.). Consulting Psychologists Press.
Maslach, C., & Leiter, M. P. (1999). Teacher burnout: A research agenda. In R. Vandenberghe & A. M. Huberman (Eds.), *Understanding and preventing teacher burnout: A sourcebook of international research and practice* (pp. 295–303). Cambridge University Press.
Maslach, C., Schaufeli, W. B., & Leiter, M. (2001). Job burnout. *Annual Review of Psychology, 52*(1), 397–422.
Pines, A., & Aronson, E. (1988). *Career burnout: Causes and cures*. The Free Press.
Skaalvik, E. M., & Skaalvik, S. (2009). Does school context matter? Relations with teacher burnout and job satisfaction. *Teaching and Teacher Education, 25,* 518–524.
Skaalvik, E. M., & Skaalvik, S. (2010). Teacher self-efficacy and teacher burnout: A study of relations. *Teaching and Teacher Education, 26,* 1059–1069.

Akram Nayernia is an assistant professor of Applied Linguistics in the Language Department at Iran University of Science and Technology, Tehran, Iran. She is currently teaching research methodology, testing and assessment, and materials development courses at M.A. and Ph.D. level. She has published articles and books on ESP, EAP, and testing and assessment, and teacher education in prestigious journals. Her main research interests are language testing and assessment, teacher education, materials development, and English for Specific Purposes (ESP).

Language Teacher Identity

96

Gary Barkhuizen

Language teacher identity (LTI) refers to the way language teachers see themselves and understand who they are in relation to the work they do. It is also the way others, including their colleagues and students and institutions, see them. As Gee (2000) says, identity is "being recognized as a certain 'kind of person', in a given context" (p. 99). In recent decades it has been accepted that teachers are thinking, feeling, moral human beings who make decisions about what they do in classrooms, schools, and communities. Therefore, it is important to learn about what 'kind of people' they are. As Varghese et al. (2005) say: "In order to understand language teaching and learning we need to understand teachers; and in order to understand teachers, we need to have a clearer sense of who they are: the professional, cultural, political, and individual identities which they claim or which are assigned to them" (p. 22).

Knowing who teachers are includes understanding—through research, teacher reflection, and teacher research—the many aspects of language teachers' lives that contribute to the construction of their identities. One of the more obvious aspects is the variety of roles and associated functions that teachers perform in their relational work with others. Other aspects include teachers' beliefs, their theories of language teaching, moral stance, and their emotions. Perhaps the most obvious connection with LTI is teachers' former experiences and their histories, which refer to their experiences of language learning, becoming and being a language teacher (Trent, 2012), and their imagined experiences of language teaching in other (future) contexts (Barkhuizen, 2016). Another facet is the actual practice of teaching, what teachers do as teachers—how they perform their roles in sociocultural contexts. During the social process of practice, identities are negotiated and constructed in interaction with others—teachers, learners, managers. Teachers also interact with

G. Barkhuizen (✉)

School of Cultures, Languages and Linguistics, University of Auckland, Auckland, New Zealand

e-mail: g.barkhuizen@auckland.ac.nz

© Springer Nature Switzerland AG 2021

H. Mohebbi and C. Coombe (eds.), *Research Questions in Language Education and Applied Linguistics*, Springer Texts in Education,

https://doi.org/10.1007/978-3-030-79143-8_96

non-human material objects in physical places, such as technological hardware and furniture in classrooms.

Research on LTI has drawn on a variety of different theoretical perspectives and employed mostly qualitative and narrative methodologies. From one theoretical perspective "language teacher identity is seen to be constituted by the practices in relation to a group and the process of individual identification or nonidentification with the group" (Varghese et al., 2005, p. 39). In Morgan's (2017) notion of *identity-as-pedagogy*, teachers' identities are understood to be a form of pedagogy; that is, their identities are pedagogical resources, intertextually interwoven within lessons. In *identity-in-discourse*, identity is discursively constructed and thus agency is discursively constituted, mainly through language. There could therefore be no singular definition of language teacher identity. De Costa and Norton (2017) draw on the work of the Douglas Fir Group (2016) to propose an (all-encompassing) transdisciplinarity approach to LTI.

The Research Questions

1. How can research on language teacher identity be transformative—how can it bring about change in a particular educational system?
2. How do teachers' emotions, beliefs and identities interconnect during the implementation of a curriculum innovation?
3. Are individual teachers part of a departmental or institutional collective identity, and if so, what are the consequences for those teachers' identities?
4. How are teachers' and their learners' identities produced (negotiated, imposed) in schools and classrooms in relation to the identity categories of race and ethnicity?
5. How does teachers' engagement with classroom materials (e.g., textbooks, technology, facilities) relate to the construction of their identities?
6. How do teachers in a particular school/institution (e.g., rural, urban, well-resourced, under-resourced) imagine their future identities in that workplace and in that community?
7. How do teachers construct their identities with their learners on a class social media platform (e.g., a closed Facebook page, a WhatsApp group)?
8. How do teachers negotiate their teacher and leader identities in working contexts where they function in both these interconnected roles?
9. How has the #metoo movement changed the way language teachers negotiate their identities in classrooms and schools?
10. What effect do neoliberal school policies have on teacher identities within particular working contexts of inequitable schooling practices?

Suggested Resources

Cheung, Y. L., Said, S. B., & Park, K. (2014). *Advances and current trends in language teacher identity*. **New York: Routledge.**

This book includes a section on theoretical orientations to language teacher identity (LTI) and then a number of empirical studies follow. It covers quite a bit of ground, demonstrating recent thinking and research in LTI. The 17 chapters include topics such as: the effects of apprenticeship in doctoral training on novice teacher identity; challenges faced by teachers in the construction of their professional identities; the emerging professional identity of pre-service teachers; teacher identity development of beginning teachers; the role of emotions in the professional identities of non-native English speaking teachers; a review of current LTI research; and the negotiation of professional identities by female academics.

Varghese, M. M, Motha, S., Park, G., Reeves, J., & Trent, J. (Eds.) (2016). Special-topic issue: Language teacher identity in (multi)lingual educational contexts. *TESOL Quarterly*, *50*(3), 541–783.

This special-topic issue of *TESOL Quarterly* includes six full-length articles and a number of shorter articles. Much interest was generated when this topic was announced, with over 120 proposals submitted internationally. The issue pushes boundaries both theoretically and methodologically in LTI research, but also grounds this work in familiar research and debates in TESOL and multilingual education. The introductory article by the issue editors, in which they offer commentary on the articles contextualized by relevant literature, is divided into the following sections: new ways of theorizing LTI; expanding the methodological and analytical lens in LTI work; LTI in transforming teacher education and curriculum; and further directions in LTI work.

Barkhuizen, G. (Ed.) (2017) *Reflections on language teacher identity research*. **New York: Routledge.**

This book explores current understandings of LTI grounded in a range of relevant research fields from the perspective of 41 experienced scholars and researchers. Drawing on their personal research experience, each contributor locates LTI within their respective area of expertise and research activity by considering their conceptual understanding of LTI and the methodological approaches used to investigate it. The chapters are narrative in nature, with authors embedding their discussions within biographical accounts of their professional lives and research work. The book attempts to take stock of current thinking and research on LTI from the perspective of experienced researchers. It also looks *forward*—to future directions in LTI research, which includes making suggestions for research topics and methodological approaches. The chapters are short, focused, personal and readable. All end with concrete suggestions for research topics and related methodologies.

De Costa, P. I., & Norton, B. (Eds.) (2017). Special-topic issue: Transdisciplinarity and language teacher identity. *The Modern Language Journal, 101* **(S1), 1–105.**

This special issue includes six contributions that cover topics such as how teacher identity intersects with the multilingual and translingual realities of contemporary classrooms, the investment of teachers in developing the semiotic repertoires of learners and a socially inclusive learning environment, and the emotions and ethical practices of teachers. Following a transdisciplinarity agenda and drawing on a range of different theories in conceptualising LTI, the studies take into account the highly inter-related macro, meso, and micro level dimensions of language teaching and learning. Respectively, these refer to ideological structures at the societal level, sociocultural institutions and communities, and social activity in micro spaces such as classrooms. The issue as a whole makes an important and productive contribution to our understanding of LTI by extending, as De Costa and Norton (2017) note, "an important ongoing conversation about language teacher identity, transdisciplinarity, and social change" (p. 11).

Gray, J., & Morton, T. (2018). *Social interaction and English language teacher identity.* **Edinburgh: Edinburgh University Press.**

This book provides a very readable and extensive coverage of the LTI field as a whole, both theoretically and methodologically, although the focus in its data-driven chapters is very much on the examination of social interaction in various language teaching contexts. It demonstrates through analysis how different English language teacher identities and power relationships are oriented to and made relevant in social interaction. The book shows how professional identities are established and negotiated through talk-in-interaction in different pre- and in-service ELT settings. Chapter topics include: knowledge, power and identity in trainer-trainee interaction in pre-service English language teacher education; positioning analysis of ESOL teachers' small stories about Individual Learning Plans (ILPs) in research interviews; the construction of language-related identity by non-native teachers in group discussion; and Queering the research interview.

References

Barkhuizen, G. (2016). A short story approach to analyzing teacher (imagined) identities over time. *TESOL Quarterly, 50*(3), 655–683.

De Costa, P. I., & Norton, B. (2017). Introduction: Identity, transdisciplinarity, and the good language teacher. *The Modern Language Journal, 101*(S), 3–14.

Douglas Fir Group. (2016). A transdisciplinary framework for SLA in a multilingual world. *The Modern Language Journal, 100*(S), 19–47.

Gee, J. P. (2000). Identity as an analytic lens for research in education. *Review of Research in Education, 25*, 99–125.

Morgan, B. (2017). Language teacher identity as critical social practice. In G. Barkhuizen (Ed.), *Reflections on Language Teacher Identity Research* (pp. 203–209). Routledge.

Trent, J. (2012). The discursive positioning of teachers: Native-speaking English teachers and educational discourse in Hong Kong. *TESOL Quarterly, 46*(1), 104–126.

Varghese, M., Morgan, B., Johnston, B., & Johnson, K. (2005). Theorizing language teacher identity: Three perspectives and beyond. *Journal of Language, Identity, and Education, 4*, 21–44.

Gary Barkhuizen is professor of applied linguistics at the University of Auckland, New Zealand. His research and teaching interests are in the areas of language teacher education, teacher identity, study abroad, and narrative inquiry. He has published widely on these topics in a range of international journals. His latest book is *Language Teacher Educator Identity* (Cambridge University Press, 2021). Gary has taught ESL at high school and at college level and has been involved in teacher education in South Africa, New Zealand and the United States. He is the winner of TESOL's 2017 Award for Distinguished Research.

Language Teacher Professional Development

97

Victoria Tuzlukova

The concept of language teacher professional development encapsulates a wide range of sector-wide, institutional and personal perspectives, experiences and practices (Hayes, 2014). It refers to continuous processes that extend, update and improve teachers' job-related knowledge, skills, beliefs and attitudes, and leads to their professional growth (Al-Seyabi, 2013). It also relates to different types of programs and practices, such as associations, forums, committees, organizations, research projects, teachers' resource centers, that can bring excellence and ensure visible improvements in language teaching and learning practices (Al-Busaidi & Tuzlukova, 2014). Professional development, deeply perceived, enables teachers to develop new insights into language teaching and pedagogy, and achieve high standards of professionalism and high-quality education (Scribner, 2003). It gives them means to gain various perspectives on their own teaching experience and on what has been successfully implemented in other educational scenarios and settings (Elias & Merriam, 2005). According to Clair and Adger (1999), powerful professional development considers teachers' personal and professional needs, fosters critical reflection and meaningful collaboration. In their view, to be effective, teacher professional development should be internally coherent, rigorous and sustainable. As global and local language teaching communities come to assume the importance of professional development and its operational role in achieving quality education and high standards of professionalism, teachers are able to see the benefits of a variety of professional development dimensions that range from formal and informal ways of collegial learning to small-scale individual initiatives focusing on personal development (Elsheikh et al., 2018; Hayes, 2014). However, there is a number of concerns and posed questions. One of the concerns is how to design teacher professional development that can become a critical factor in teaching rather

V. Tuzlukova (✉)
English for Humanities Department, Centre for Preparatory Studies, Sultan Qaboos University, Sultanate of Oman, Muscat, Oman
e-mail: victoria@squ.edu.om

© Springer Nature Switzerland AG 2021
H. Mohebbi and C. Coombe (eds.), *Research Questions in Language Education and Applied Linguistics*, Springer Texts in Education,
https://doi.org/10.1007/978-3-030-79143-8_97

than a shoddy and limited issue in educational settings (Scribner, 1999). For many language teachers, as Diaz-Maggioli (2003) asserts, professional development is "an elusive term" (p. 1). Some language teachers grab any developmental opportunities that can substantially deepen their content knowledge and enhance their teaching practice (Porter et al., 2000). Others are not easily involved. They often choose to take part in some of them and not to become engaged in the others in spite of the content of the offered opportunities. Another concern is related to the fact that professional development may look and be different in diverse settings (Scribner, 1999). Meaningful integration of general and specific ideas of language teacher developmental training with ground realities of the socio-cultural context of teaching (Bybee & Loucks-Housley, 2000), as well as maintaining a balanced approach that acknowledges both students' native language and culture and teachers' experiences, educational, cultural, social and linguistic histories (Clair & Adger, 1999) are among unresolved controversies related to stimulating language teacher professional development. Also, in spite of positive attitude to professional development, there are concerns related to certain complexities of evaluating the direct effects of language teacher professional development programs (Wayne et al., 2008) that call for innovations in professional development programs' implementation and assessment (Hayes, 2014). The suggested innovations focus on certain characteristics of effective teacher professional development, such as intensity, duration, collective participation, active learning, coherence, content and solutions (Desimone, 2009; Tuzlukova & Hall, 2017).

The Research Questions

1. How can professional development evolve philosophically, pedagogically and organizationally to most effectively respond to language teachers' needs and serve as an efficient tool for enhancing their knowledge, skills, attitudes and professional beliefs?
2. What efforts should be undertaken for professional development to become a critical factor in teaching rather than a shoddy and limited issue in educational setting (Scribner, 1999)?
3. What are the attitudes of teachers towards professional development?
4. What is the impact of professional development on teaching and learning? What are the variations of this impact?
5. What is the impact of professional development on teachers' ability to reflect?
6. What are the best solutions for identifying and monitoring professional development impact?
7. Can different types of professional development, for example, forums, associations, committees, organizations, projects, teachers' resource centers, have a visible influence on the educational process and eventually lead to an increase in the achievements of the students?

8. What are the relevant instruments, which can be most effectively used for monitoring and describing effective developmental training that leads to successful teaching practice and enhancement of students' achievement?
9. Are different teachers affected by professional development programs in different ways? If yes, is it essential for effective professional development to understand background, content knowledge, previous experiences and current teaching practices of the teachers?
10. What instruments can be used for measurement purposes and to link professional development to student achievement?

Suggested Resources

Hayes, D. (Ed.) (2014). *Innovations in the continuing professional development of English language teachers.* **UK, London: British Council.**

This is a very interesting collection of papers that gives a global view of innovations in teachers' continuing professional development. It shares examples and developments in practice around the world and gives valuable insight into ways to assist teachers to get involved, share, network and learn. It also provides insight into particular ways of the professional development programs' design and impact and stimulates debate on the effectiveness of teacher professional development to contemporary local and global educational settings.

Elsheikh, A., Coombe, C. & Effiong, O. (Eds.) (2018). *The role of language teacher associations in professional development.* **Cham, Switzerland: Springer.**

This volume approaches teacher professional development from the perspective of teacher involvement in professional associations and serves as a valuable resource and a reference guide. It affords the opportunity to build upon experiences, practices and approaches of teacher associations from all over the world as their significance in the overall system of language teacher professional development is too important to ignore. The papers in this volume present a diversity of contexts and perspectives and provide insight into how participation in teacher associations can benefit local teaching communities and individual teachers in their professional growth.

Al-Busaidi, S. & Tuzlukova, V. (2014). Local perspectives on teacher professional development: Targeting policy and practice. *Asian Journal of Management Sciences & Education,* **3(4), 74–84.**

This paper discusses the issues of interconnectedness of teachers' interests and motivation with their active engagement with professional development as a requirement for sustainable continuing professional development in local educational settings. Using the example of the professional development program at Sultan Qaboos University in Oman, authors also elaborate on the importance of providing a framework for identifying required content, types and aspects of professional development programs for language educators in higher education contexts.

Al Seyabi, F. (2013). Institutionalizing professional development at the Language Centre of SQU: Meeting the needs of the new general foundation programme. In S. Al-Busaidi. & V. Tuzlukova (Eds.), *General foundation programmes in higher education in the Sultanate of Oman: Experiences, challenges and considerations for the future* **(pp. 239–250). Muscat: Mazoon Publishing House.**

This chapter reports on the history of institutionalizing teachers' professional development in the context of a Gulf university. It connects the increased importance of language teacher professional development with language education reforms and initiatives and emphasizes the importance of careful examination of the experience of professional development to equip teachers with the necessary skills that can help them meet new demands and overcome challenges.

Tuzlukova, V. & Hall, A. (2017). A virtual professional development model: Bringing innovation to language teaching practice. *Journal of Teaching English for Specific and Academic Purposes*, **4(3), 603–614.**

Rooted in the belief that professional development has a visible influence on the educational process and eventually leads to student achievements, this paper discusses in-service professional development in the context of a language institution in the Sultanate of Oman with a particular focus on the benefits of virtual environments for designing and implementing professional development and training programs that will enable teachers to bring innovation and creativity to their teaching practice. It also discusses barriers and challenges to professional development in the virtual context.

References

Al Seyabi, F. (2013). Institutionalizing professional development at the Language Centre of SQU: Meeting the needs of the new general foundation programme. In S. Al-Busaidi. & V. Tuzlukova (Eds.), *General foundation programmes in higher education in the Sultanate of Oman: Experiences, challenges and considerations for the future* (pp. 239–250). Mazoon Publishing House.

Al-Busaidi, S. & Tuzlukova, V. (2014). Local perspectives on teacher professional development: Targeting policy and practice. *Asian Journal of Management Sciences and Education, 3*(4), 74–84. Retrieved October 12, 2018 from http://ajmse.leena-luna.co.jp/ajmsevol3n4.php

Bybee, R. W., & Loucks- Horsley, S. (2000). Advancing technology education: The role of professional development. *The Technology Teacher, 60*(2), 31–34. Retrieved October 20, 2018, from http://www.iteaconnect.org/TAA/linkedfiles/articles/

Clair, N., & Adger, C. (1999). *Professional development for teachers in culturally diverse schools.* ERIC Clearinghouse on Languages and Linguistics. Retrieved October 24, 2018 from http://www.ericdigests.org/2000-3/diverse.htm

Desimone, L. (2009). Improving impact studies of teachers' professional development: Toward better conceptualizations and measures. *Educational Researcher, 38*(3), 181–199.

Diaz-Maggioli, G. H. (2003). *Professional development for language teachers.* Eric Digest. EDO-FL-03–03. Retrieved June 05, 2018 from http://www.cal.org/resources/digest/0303diaz.html

Elias, J., & Merriam, S. (2005). *Philosophical foundations of adult education.* Krieger.

Elsheikh, A., Coombe, C., & Effiong, O. (Eds.). (2018). *The role of language teacher associations in professional development.* Springer.

Hayes, D. (Ed.) (2014). *Innovations in the continuing professional development of English language teachers.* British Council.

Porter, A. C., Garet, M. S., Desimone, L., Birman, B. F., & Suk Yoon, K. (2000). *Does professional development change teaching practice? Results from a three-year study.* U.S. Department of Education.

Scribner, J. (2003). Teacher learning in context: The special case of rural high school teachers. *Education Policy Analysis Archives, 11*(12). Retrieved July 9, 2018, from http://epaa.asu.edu/epaa/v11n12/

Scribner, J. (1999). Professional development: Untangling the influence of work context on teacher learning. *Educational Administration Quarterly, 36*(2), 238–266.

Tuzlukova, V., & Hall, A. (2017). A virtual professional development model: Bringing innovation to language teaching practice. *Journal of Teaching English for Specific and Academic Purposes, 4*(3), 603–614.

Wayne, A. J., Yoon, K. S., Zhu, P., Cronen, S., & Garet, M. S. (2008). Experimenting with teacher professional development: Motives and methods. *Educational Researcher, 37*(8), 469–479.

Victoria Tuzlukova has a Ph.D. in Comparative Linguistics from Moscow State University. She is currently on the English faculty of the Centre for Preparatory Studies at Sultan Qaboos University in Oman. Victoria is a co-editor of General Foundation Programmes in Higher Education in the Sultanate of Oman: Experiences, Challenges and Considerations for the Future (2013), Language, Learning and Teaching (2011), The Omani ELT Symphony: Maintaining Linguistic and Socio-Cultural Equilibrium (2010), Language of Professional Communication in Focus of Linguistics and Cultural Studies (2009)). Victoria has participated in a number of large-scale projects in Oman. Her forthcoming publications are on socio-cultural aspects of language and language pedagogy, and skills training and community-based projects in English language teaching and learning.

Language Teacher Professionalism

Britta Viebrock and Carina Kaufmann

Language teacher professionalism is a complex construct, aspects of which have concerned the academic discourse for decades (cf. e.g. Hallet, 2010; Hattie, 2011; Leung, 2009, 2013; Moskowitz, 1976; Richards, 2012; Shulman, 1986; Viebrock, 2014, 2018). In view of continuous social and technological challenges (most recently, for example, the massive migration flows and large-scale digital transformation) it is also a very dynamic concept that might encompass different competences over time. Not only do teachers need specific competences to master these challenges professionally, they also need a fundamental understanding of the vitality of the profession, which requires teachers to take on an active role as 'agents of change' (cf. Viebrock, 2018).

There is an extensive debate within the academic discourse on to what extent teachers can be considered as professionals, although the terms 'professionalism' and 'profession' are not used consistently. In a broader sense 'profession' means "an occupation whose members are expected to possess high levels of specialist knowledge, expertise, commitment and trustworthiness" (Leung, 2013: 13). This definition applies to well-established professions, e.g. physicians or lawyers. Within the educational field, the framework for characterising a profession is influenced by various perspectives such as sociological, psychological or by recent research on occupational biographies. Thus, being professional in the latter sense means to constantly adapt/expand one's own occupational biography and to engage in a process of lifelong learning. Therefore, 'professionalism' in a narrower sense comprises competences that enable teachers to professionally fulfill the demands of their everyday working life.

B. Viebrock (✉) · C. Kaufmann
Institute of English and American Studies, Goethe University Frankfurt, Frankfurt am Main/Hesse, Germany
e-mail: viebrock@em.uni-frankfurt.de

C. Kaufmann
e-mail: c.leonhardt@em.uni-frankfurt.de

© Springer Nature Switzerland AG 2021
H. Mohebbi and C. Coombe (eds.), *Research Questions in Language Education and Applied Linguistics*, Springer Texts in Education,
https://doi.org/10.1007/978-3-030-79143-8_98

The question of what defines a professional language teacher cannot be separated from considerations on teachers' professional competences and specific domains of expertise. Baumert and Kunter (2006) have developed a heuristic model of teachers' professional competences based on previous research (Shulman, 1986, 1987; Terhart, 2004). According to them, professional competences consist of aspects such as (1) knowledge, (2) beliefs, values and subjective theories, (3) motivational orientations and (4) self-regulating competences. These aspects, in turn, can be subdivided into competence areas such as (a) content knowledge, (b) pedagogical content knowledge, (c) general pedagogic knowledge, (d) orientational knowledge and (e) counselling knowledge.

That teachers' professional competences are closely connected with the quality of teaching, has been established by Helmke (2015). Based on extensive empirical research, he has developed a set of characteristics of good teaching practice. These consist of efficient classroom-management, a productive atmosphere, learner orientation or variation in methods and social constellations. These rather general characteristics partially overlap with Richards' (2012) core dimensions of good language teaching practice that 'more explicitly focus on the peculiarities of the language teaching profession' (cf. Viebrock, 2018). Examples of these dimensions are language proficiency, content knowledge, learner-focused teaching and language teacher's identity.

To capture the different dimensions of (language) teacher professionalism, Leung (2009) has proposed a distinction of what we call 'prescribed' (Leung uses the term 'sponsored') and 'independent professionalism'. Prescribed professionalism as a top-down-process "denotes the managerial competences needed by teachers to deal with the formal requirements and standards of regulatory bodies" (cf. Viebrock, 2018: 49), for example the implementation of the Common European Framework of Reference for Languages (CEFR) and its appropriation in national or federal curricula. Independent professionalism is a bottom-up process "triggered by the teacher's individual desire for change and improvement" (ibid.), for example the grassroots development of many Content and Language Integrated Learning (CLIL) programmes. Therefore, it is closely related to a reflective teaching practice that requires teachers to continuously reflect on their competences, teaching experiences, values and beliefs. Language teacher professionalism, in that sense, means to constantly develop one's own professional competences, engage in advanced teacher training and lifelong learning and act as 'agent of change'.

The Research Questions

1. What are the prerequisites for professional behavior/action in foreign language teaching contexts?
2. When can language teachers be considered (as) professional(s)?
3. What role does self-efficacy play for language teacher professionalism?

4. What kind of knowledge, skills and competences does a professional language teacher possess?
5. Which aspects of teachers' professional competences relate to which dimensions of good language teaching practice?
6. Which aspects of language teachers' professional competences can be measured and how?
7. What are the relations between teacher professionalism and the way pre-service and in-service teacher training is organised?
8. Which competences do teachers as 'agents of global change' possess in order to actively respond to the demands posed by multilingualism, globalisation or digitalisation?
9. How are reflective teaching practice and language teacher professionalism linked?
10. How are language teachers' professional competences and students' language learning linked?

Suggested Resources

Farrell, T. S. C. (2015). *Language Teacher Professional Development.* **Alexandria, VA: TESOL Press**.

This book is part of the English Language Teacher Development Series (ELTD) and aims at providing short and comprehensible resources for all types of English language teachers. The ELTD series offer a theory-to-practice approach to second language teaching as they include a wide variety of practical approaches and methods as well as reflective sections.

Farrell focuses on the professional development of language teachers and discusses questions like 'What is professional development?', 'Why develop?', 'What are different approaches to professional development?' or 'How to sustain professional development?'. By raising these questions, he also introduces strategics of planning and visualising professional development. Every chapter comprises reflective breaks which invite the readers to reflect on their experiences, attitudes, beliefs or opinions on various topics.

Leung, C. (2009). Second Language Teacher Professionalism. In Burns, A. & Richards, J.C. (eds.), *The Cambridge Guide to Second Language Teacher Education.* **(pp. 49–58). Cambridge, UK: Cambridge University Press**.

This Guide to Second Language Teacher Education provides an overview of recent research and debates within the field of second language teaching and teacher education. The book comprises 30 chapters by researchers, educators and scholars working and researching in the field. These chapters are subdivided into seven sections which focus on topics such as 'The Landscape of Second Language

Teacher Education', 'Professionalism and the Language Teaching Profession', 'Pedagogical Knowledge in Second Language Teacher Education' or 'Identity, Cognition and Experience in Teacher Learning'.

Leung's chapter on 'Second Language Teacher Professionalism' discusses the processes of second language teachers' professional development and in particular how it is defined differently by different professional or political authorities in different contexts. He proposes a distinction between 'sponsored' and 'independent professionalism', which offer top-down and bottom-up, or collective and individual perspectives on the concept respectively. While these perspectives might cause tension, Leung also suggests how teacher education programmes may contribute to develop an integrated sense of professionalism.

Viebrock, B. (2018). Teachers of English as a Foreign Language—Experience and Professional Development. In Surkamp, C. & Viebrock, B. (eds.). *Teaching English as a Foreign Language*. (pp. 39–55). Stuttgart: Metzler.

This book on Teaching English as a Foreign Language consists of fourteen chapters that deal with fundamental issues regarding the teaching and learning of English as a foreign language. The book touches on a broad variety of relevant and important principles of modern language teaching and links theory with practical issues of classroom teaching.

Britta Viebrock's chapter addresses the prerequisites of being an English as a foreign language teacher by having a closer look at the initial conditions of teacher trainees and their professional development. Furthermore, it deals with characteristics of professional (foreign) language teachers and critically discusses how far these characteristics can be acquired. Viebrock concludes by taking the future challenges of the teaching profession into consideration and highlights the importance for teachers of taking on a role as 'agents of global change'.

References

Baumert, J., & Kunter, M. (2006). Stichwort: Professionelle Kompetenz von Lehrkräften. *Zeitschrift Für Erziehungswissenschaften, 9*(4), 469–520.

Hallet, W. (2010). Didaktische Kompetenzen von Fremdsprachenlehrern. In W. Hallet & F. Königs (Eds.), *Handbuch Fremdsprachendidaktik* (pp. 350–353). Seelze-Velber.

Hattie, J. A. C. (2011). *Visible learning for teachers: Maximising impact on learning*. Routledge.

Helmke, A. (2015). *Unterrichtsqualität und Lehrerprofessionalität. Diagnose, Evaluation und Verbesserung des Unterrichts* (6th ed.). Klett-Kallmeyer.

Leung, C. (2009). Second language teacher professionalism. In A. Burns & J. C. Richards, (Eds.), *The Cambridge guide to second language teacher education* (pp. 49–58). Cambridge University Press.

Leung, C. (2013). Second/additional language teacher professionalism: What is it? In M. Olofsson (Ed.), *Symposium 2012: Lärarrollen I svenska som andrapräk* (N/A ed., Vol. N/A). Stockholms universitets förlag.

Moskowitz, G. (1976). The classroom interaction of outstanding foreign language teachers. *Foreign Language Annals, 9*(2), 135–157.

Richards, J. C. (2012). Competence and performance in language teaching. In A. Burns & J. C. Richards (Eds.), *The Cambridge guide to pedagogy and practice in second language teaching* (pp. 46–56). Cambridge University Press.

Shulman, L. S. (1987). Knowledge and teaching. Foundations of the new reform. *The Harvard Educational Review, 57*(1), 1–23.

Shulman, L. S. (1986). Those who understand. Knowledge growth in teaching. *Educational Researcher, 15*(2), 4–14.

Terhart, E. (2004). *Standards für die Lehrerbildung. Eine Expertise für die Kultusministerkonferenz.* Universität Münster: Zentrale Koordination Lehrerbildung (ZKL-Texte Nr. 24). Münster.

Viebrock, B. (2014). Zur Professionalisierung von Lehrkräften im bilingualen Erdkundeunterricht. *Zeitschrift Für Interpretative Schul- Und Unterrichtsforschung, 3*(1), 72–85.

Viebrock, B. (2018). Teachers of English as a foreign language – experience and professional development. In C. Surkamp & B. Viebrock (Eds.), *Teaching English as a foreign language* (pp. 39–55). Metzler.

Britta Viebrock, Dr. Phil., is professor of TEFL Theory and Methodology at the University of Frankfurt/Main, Germany, and was the Dean of the Faculty of Modern Languages from 2016 to 2019. Her research interests include Content and Language Integrated Learning (CLIL), digital und multimodal literacies, film in English language teaching, teacher education and teacher professionalism, qualitative research methodology as well as research ethics. She has published several books and articles on these topics.

Carina Kaufmann studied English and History to become a secondary school teacher and achieved her First State Examination in 2017. Currently, she is a research assistant and Ph.D. student on the team of Prof. Dr. Viebrock at the Department of England and American Studies at the University of Frankfurt/Main, Germany. Her research interests are multilingualism in the context of EFL, teacher education and teacher professionalism, multiliteracies as well as blended learning.

Language Teacher Well-being

Kyle Read Talbot and Sarah Mercer

Despite the centrality of language teachers to students, classrooms, and to language education more generally, a relative paucity of empirical studies exist on the psychology of these teachers and the specific factors that promote or limit their professional well-being, albeit with some exceptions in the specific areas of teacher identities and cognition (Mercer & Kostoulas, 2018). What is clear from research in general education is that teachers are more effective in their professional roles when they are motivated, have a positive sense of professional identity, feel efficacious, and when they find meaning in their work (Barber & Mourshed, 2007; Sammons et al., 2007; Zee & Koomen, 2016). As teachers are more effective when they experience high well-being, this also positively impacts their learners' well-being (Frenzel et al., 2009) and academic achievement (Sammons et al., 2007).

With links to both learner well-being and learner achievement, one might assume that teacher well-being would be of primary concern to educational stakeholders and policy makers, yet language teachers and their psychological worlds are still often neglected as the subjects of empirical research or interventions. This is true despite the fact that the teaching is undergoing rapid changes that are increasing its' complexity and commensurate stress (Day & Gu, 2010). These changes, even when well-intentioned, often have unintended consequences for teachers' relationships with students, colleagues, pedagogy, job satisfaction, and sense of professional well-being and identity (Valli & Buese, 2007). In fact, teaching has been consistently cited as one of the most stressful professions (Johnson et al., 2005) with some of the highest rates of burnout (Kieschke & Scharrschmidt, 2008; Unterbrink et al., 2007).

Language teaching certainly is no exception to this trend (Hiver & Dörnyei, 2015). In addition to the stressors that all teachers face, language educators also face

K. R. Talbot (✉) · S. Mercer
ELT Research and Methodology, University of Graz, Graz, Austria
e-mail: sarah.mercer@uni-graz.at

© Springer Nature Switzerland AG 2021
H. Mohebbi and C. Coombe (eds.), *Research Questions in Language Education and Applied Linguistics*, Springer Texts in Education,
https://doi.org/10.1007/978-3-030-79143-8_99

challenges unique to the language teaching profession such as language anxiety (Horwitz, 1996). The intercultural or culture-laden content may also be particularly salient in the language teaching profession. For instance, King and Ng (2018) argue that the culture-laden content in language teaching may generate a higher frequency and greater range of emotions than mainstream subject teaching and more emotional understanding and emotional regulation on the part of the language teacher. Those living and working in unfamiliar environments may also face increased emotional challenges or threats to their identities or senses of selves due to the nature of working in foreign cultural contexts (Cowie, 2011). A further challenge that may be unique to the language teaching profession is the skills-based and ever-shifting nature of its content. For example, Talbot and Mercer (2018) found that a challenge entrenched within the language teacher profession, is the evolving nature of language itself; teaching language, is like shooting at a "moving target".

Given the centrality of teacher well-being to effective practice and learner achievement, it is a critical omission in our body of knowledge that key stakeholders in the field know so little about language teacher psychology and, in particular, their well-being. We feel that it is long overdue that we develop a more nuanced understanding of language teacher well-being and ways in which our teachers may further enjoy it, for their sake, but also for the sake of their students.

The Research Questions

We have split this into five key areas that we think need addressing in respect to teacher well-being but given the virtual complete absence of any work in this field, the potential topics and methodological approaches are vast.

1. Ecologies of language teacher well-being

   a. In what ways is language teacher well-being connected to the teachers' personal and professional ecologies?
   b. What kind of systemic factors at the institutional and national levels contribute to language teacher well-being?

2. Dynamics of language teacher well-being

   a. To what extent does teacher well-being fluctuate across macro and micro time-scales?
   b. What factors help language teachers recover most quickly from high periods of stress and help to prolong periods of positivity?

3. Language teacher well-being and link to language learners' psychology and well-being

   a. In what ways are language teacher well-being and language learner psychological factors and/or well-being connected?
   b. What effect does language teacher well-being have on their rapport with learners and group dynamics?

4. Language teacher well-being and teaching efficacy

   a. In what ways is language teacher well-being related to language learner achievement?
   b. In what ways is language teacher well-being related to good teaching practices?

5. Language teacher well-being and individual differences

   a. What personality factors are linked with levels of language teacher well-being?
   b. To what extent does language teacher well-being vary according to age, years of experience, gender, and or family status and other socio-contextual factors?

Suggested Resources

We have also ordered our suggested resources to reflect the five main themes we identified and used as our organizing framework for the research questions.

Ecologies of language teacher well-being

McIntyre, T. M., McIntyre, S. E., & Francis, D. J. (Eds.). (2017). *Educator stress: An occupational health perspective.* **Cham: Springer International Publishing.** https://doi.org/10.1007/978-3-319-53053-6

The authors argue that there is a critical disconnect between the exponential growth of teacher stress research and the actual efforts to use this information practically to improve the profession for its' teachers. Teachers often report problems taking time off, having to work second jobs, high workload demands, working from home and on the weekends, and insufficient pay. This volume addresses both the internal and systemic factors that can lead to teacher stress. It defines educator stress in the context of the current educational climate and suggests an occupational health framework as a useful lens through which to view it. Further, this volume also suggests ways in which to manage or reduce educator stress and outlines practical implications for practice, educational policy, and further research.

Dynamics of language teacher well-being

Sonnentag, S. (2015). Dynamics of Well-Being. *Annual Review of Organizational Psychology and Organizational Behavior*, *2*(1), 261–293. https://doi.org/10.1146/annurev-orgpsych-032414-111347

Sabine Sonnentag comprehensively reviews literature related to the dynamics of well-being through the lens of organizational psychology. Though the review does not pertain to teachers specifically, it may act as an initial entry point for those interested in the dynamic nature of well-being and its' relationship to the workplace. She describes how well-being constantly fluctuates on multiple times scales simultaneously, and how this varies both within and between individuals. Specifically, she provides evidence that variability in well-being predicts variability in workplace performance. To conclude, she raises research questions, provides practical implications, and outlines both empirical and conceptual challenges that those interested in the dynamic nature of well-being and the workplace will likely face.

Language teacher well-being and link to learners' psychology and well-being

Frenzel, A. C., Goetz, T., Lüdtke, O., Pekrun, R., & Sutton, R. E. (2009). Emotional transmission in the classroom: Exploring the relationship between teacher and student enjoyment. *Journal of Educational Psychology*, *101*(3), 705–716. https://doi.org/10.1037/a0014695

The authors argue that both teacher and student enjoyment are deserving of more research attention because of their critical importance to the quality of instruction and quality of learning. They hypothesized that teacher and student enjoyment in the classroom are positively related and that a teacher's displayed enthusiasm can mediate the relationship between student and teacher enjoyment. Evidence for both hypotheses are supported by the data which consists of secondary students' self-reported enjoyment of mathematics classes (n = 1542), and teachers' reported enjoyment of teaching (n = 71). This study is of critical importance as it implies that teachers, as central figures in the classroom, make an impact on students' emotions in the classroom through contagion. The authors conclude that teacher enthusiasm could in fact be enacted as a strategy in the classroom.

Language teacher well-being and teacher efficacy

Sammons, P., Day, C., Kington, A., Gu, Q., Stobart, G., & Smees, R. (2007). Exploring variations in teachers' work, lives and their effects on pupils: Key findings and implications from a longitudinal mixed-method study. *British Educational Research Journal*, *33*(5), 681–701. https://doi.org/10.1080/01411920701582264

This important longitudinal study aimed "to describe and analyse influences on teachers' professional and personal lives, their identities and effectiveness, and explore their interconnections" (p. 682). Further, it also examined these connections in relation to the contexts in which these teachers worked. The authors argue that teachers' work is emotionally charged, complex, often intense, and clearly deserving of further study. They find that teachers' sense of professional identity is linked with their well-being and also an important factor in their effectiveness as teachers. Secondly, they find that the learners of teachers who exhibit commitment and resilience are more likely to exceed learners of teachers who do not exhibit these same qualities.

Language teacher well-being and individual differences

MacIntyre, P. D., Ross, J., Talbot, K., Mercer, S., Gregersen, T., & Banga, C. A. (2019). Stressors, personality and wellbeing among language teachers. *System,* **82, 26–38.** https://doi.org/10.1016/j.system.2019.02.013

This paper comprises the first part of a larger study exploring language teacher stress and well-being. It is one of the first empirical papers with an explicit focus on the well-being of language teachers. Drawing on data from a diverse sample of language teachers teaching in a variety of contexts across the globe, this paper examines correlations among teachers' personalities (extraversion, agreeableness, conscientiousness, emotional stability, and openness) and perceptions of well-being (positive emotion, engagement, relationships, meaning, and accomplishments) and stressors (chronic stress and life event stressors). Results of the study suggest that personality and stress are both consistently correlated to teacher-well-being, but that personality and stress were not found to correlate. The paper has important implications for teacher education and the kinds of socio-emotional strategies that can be taught to help manage stress and regulate emotions. It also raises key questions for further research.

References

Barber, M., & Mourshed, M. (2007). *How the world's best-performing school systems come out on top.* McKinsey & Company.

Cowie, N. (2011). Emotions that experienced English as a foreign language (EFL) teachers feel about their students, their colleagues and their work. *Teaching and Teacher Education, 27*(1), 235–242. https://doi.org/10.1016/j.tate.2010.08.006

Day, C., & Gu, Q. (Eds.). (2010). *The new lives of teachers.* Routledge.

Frenzel, A. C., Goetz, T., Lüdtke, O., Pekrun, R., & Sutton, R. E. (2009). Emotional transmission in the classroom: Exploring the relationship between teacher and student enjoyment. *Journal of Educational Psychology, 101*(3), 705–716. https://doi.org/10.1037/a0014695

Hiver, P., & Dörnyei, Z. (2015). Language teacher immunity: A double-edged sword. *Applied Linguistics,* 1–20. https://doi.org/10.1093/applin/amv034

Horwitz, E. K. (1996). Even teachers get the blues: Recognizing and alleviating language teachers' feelings of foreign language anxiety. *Foreign Language Annals, 29*(3), 365–372. https://doi.org/10.1111/j.1944-9720.1996.tb01248.x

Johnson, S., Cooper, C., Cartwright, S., Donald, I., Taylor, P., & Millet, C. (2005). The experience of work-related stress across occupations. *Journal of Managerial Psychology, 20*(2), 178–187. https://doi.org/10.1108/02683940510579803

Kieschke, U., & Schaarschmidt, U. (2008). Professional commitment and health among teachers in Germany: A typological approach. *Learning and Instruction, 18*(5), 429–437. https://doi.org/10.1016/j.learninstruc.2008.06.005

King, J., & Ng, K.-Y.S. (2018). Teacher emotions and the emotional labour of second language teaching. In S. Mercer & A. Kostoulas (Eds.), *Language teacher psychology* (pp. 141–157). Multilingual Matters.

Mercer, S., & Kostoulas, A. (Eds.). (2018). *Language teacher psychology*. Multilingual Matters.

Sammons, P., Day, C., Kington, A., Gu, Q., Stobart, G., & Smees, R. (2007). Exploring variations in teachers' work, lives and their effects on pupils: Key findings and implications from a longitudinal mixed-method study. *British Educational Research Journal, 33*(5), 681–701. https://doi.org/10.1080/01411920701582264

Talbot, K., & Mercer, S. (2018). Exploring university ESL/EFL teachers' emotional well-being and emotional regulation in the United States, Japan and Austria. *Chinese Journal of Applied Linguistics, 41*(4), 410–432. https://doi.org/10.1515/cjal-2018-0031

Unterbrink, T., Hack, A., Pfeifer, R., Buhl-Grießhaber, V., Müller, U., Wesche, H., & Bauer, J. (2007). Burnout and effort–reward-imbalance in a sample of 949 German teachers. *International Archives of Occupational and Environmental Health, 80*(5), 433–441. https://doi.org/10.1007/s00420-007-0169-0

Valli, L., & Buese, D. (2007). The changing roles of teachers in an era of high-stakes accountability. *American Educational Research Journal, 44*(3), 519–558. https://doi.org/10.3102/0002831207306859

Zee, M., & Koomen, H. M. Y. (2016). Teacher self-efficacy and its effects on classroom processes, student academic adjustment, and teacher well-being: A synthesis of 40 years of research. *Review of Educational Research, 86*(4), 981–1015. https://doi.org/10.3102/0034654315626801

Kyle Read Talbot is a language teacher and researcher in Applied Linguistics. He taught ESL at the University of Iowa in the United States before enrolling as a PhD student at the University of Graz in Austria. He holds an MA in TESOL/Applied Linguistics from the University of Northern Iowa. His current research and thinking interests include the psychology of language learning and teaching, well-being, bilingual and multilingual education, and applied complexity science. He is the co-editor of '*The Psychological Experience of Integrating Content and Language*'. Kyle can be reached at kylereadtalbot@gmail.com.

Sarah Mercer is Professor of Foreign Language Teaching at the University of Graz, Austria, where she is Head of ELT methodology. Her research interests include all aspects of the psychology surrounding the foreign language learning experience. She is the author, co-author and co-editor of several books in this area including, '*Towards an Understanding of Language Learner Self-Concept*', '*Psychology for Language Learning*', '*Multiple Perspectives on the Self in SLA*', '*New Directions in Language Learning Psychology*', '*Positive Psychology in SLA*', '*Exploring Psychology for Language Teachers*' (Winner of the IH Ben Warren Prize), and '*Language Teacher Psychology*'. Sarah can be reached at sarah.mercer@uni-graz.at.

Language Teachers' Self-efficacy Beliefs

100

Mark Wyatt

If teachers lack self-confidence in performing specific tasks that they feel will benefit their students' learning, tasks such as answering questions about grammar, using motivational strategies or setting up communicative group work activities, then their language teachers' self-efficacy (LTSE) beliefs for these particular tasks can be described as 'low'. Conversely, if they feel great self-confidence for performing tasks of questionable pedagogical value, such as attempting to address learners' reading difficulties by orchestrating reading aloud of previously unseen texts around the class (while remaining impervious to the humiliation and boredom this can cause), their LTSE beliefs can be seen as dangerously 'high'.

Research into language teachers' self-efficacy (LTSE) beliefs, which are their beliefs in their abilities to support language learning in various task-, domain- and context-specific ways (Wyatt, 2018), emerged in the first decade of the twenty-first century. This development followed Bandura's original (1977) psychological research being extended into various fields, including education (e.g. Tschannen-Moran & Woolfolk Hoy, 2001). Together with outcome expectations, which are beliefs about the likely results of actions, self-efficacy beliefs are crucial, according to Bandura (1977), in shaping the quality and quantity of effort put into any given task.

M. Wyatt (✉)
Department of English, Khalifa University, PO Box 127788, Abu Dhabi, United Arab Emirates
e-mail: mark.wyatt@ku.ac.ae

© Springer Nature Switzerland AG 2021
H. Mohebbi and C. Coombe (eds.), *Research Questions in Language Education and Applied Linguistics*, Springer Texts in Education,
https://doi.org/10.1007/978-3-030-79143-8_100

LTSE beliefs may have various sources. Personal experiences of succeeding or failing in previous tasks influence LTSE beliefs, as do experiences of observing or listening to others. Physiological experiences, such as butterflies in the stomach or a dry throat, can also be influential. These sources of efficacy information may interact in various ways and are not always attended to. LTSE beliefs might fluctuate over time as aspects of the task or context change, and can also be generalized across tasks (Wyatt, 2018).

LTSE beliefs may be of most interest to researchers when most under threat, as consequences may include burn-out. Groups vulnerable to low LTSE beliefs include beginning teachers struggling to develop their professional identities, teachers being redeployed to very different teaching contexts, teachers working in difficult circumstances. Non-native speakers' LTSE beliefs may be threatened by widespread discrimination, in terms of pay and employment, relative lack of interest amongst learners in some contexts for language as opposed to science learning, and self-consciousness about their own language proficiency. Consequences of such negative factors intersecting with low LTSE beliefs can include a very limited amount of target language used in class (Choi & Lee, 2016) and an avoidance of communicative language teaching. Native-speakers may have issues of their own, for example possibly low LTSE beliefs in explaining grammar (Wyatt, 2018).

The Research Questions

1. How do language teachers' self-efficacy beliefs interact with other self-beliefs central to feelings of competence, for example self-concept and self-esteem, in shaping teachers' development?
2. To what extent do language teachers' self-efficacy beliefs in specific domains, such as grammar teaching, appear to influence their teaching behavior in the same domains?
3. To what extent do learning outcomes vary, according to language teachers' self-efficacy beliefs?
4. To what extent do language teachers' self-efficacy beliefs appear to reflect these teachers' levels of pedagogical content knowledge and linguistic competence?
5. Which kinds of efficacy-building experiences do language teachers in different contexts and at different stages of development ascribe as most influential in shaping their development?
6. To what extent do environmental factors, including cultural and social factors and opportunities for collaboration, shape the development of language teachers' self-efficacy beliefs?
7. In what ways and to what extent do language teachers' self-efficacy beliefs appear to fluctuate during pre-service teacher education?

8. What impact do different forms of teacher education appear to have on the development of language teachers' self-efficacy beliefs?
9. To what extent do language teachers' self-efficacy beliefs vary, according to the status of the language taught?
10. To what extent are practitioner-researcher teacher-educators able to draw on research into language teachers' self-efficacy beliefs to enhance their pedagogical practices?

Suggested Resources

Wyatt, M. (2018). Language teachers' self-efficacy beliefs: An introduction. In S. Mercer and A. Kostoulas (eds.), *Language Teacher Psychology.* **Bristol: Multilingual Matters, pp. 122-140.** http://www.multilingual-matters.com/display.asp?K=9781783099450

Aimed at a target audience of beginning doctoral researchers, this chapter commences by contextualizing self-efficacy beliefs, and then compares these beliefs to outcome expectations; it uses scenarios drawn from language teaching to illustrate how these different kinds of beliefs interact. The chapter then highlights confusion historically in the study of teachers' self-efficacy beliefs, provides a brief overview of studies specifically focused on the self-efficacy beliefs of language teachers (LTSE beliefs), and indicates why these beliefs may be of particular interest to researchers. It then illustrates what we know to date about LTSE beliefs, examining in detail selected studies from around the world. These include studies from Venezuela and Korea (mixed methods and quantitative) that explored the interaction of LTSE beliefs, language proficiency and pedagogy, and those exploring changes in LTSE beliefs: during pre-service teacher education in Turkey and in-service teacher education in Oman. Trends in the research literature are highlighted.

Thompson, G. (2020). *Exploring Language Teacher Efficacy in Japan.* **Bristol: Multilingual   Matters.**   http://www.multilingual-matters.com/display.asp?m=2&dc=162&sort=sort_date/d&mw=1&stem=True&natural=False&sqf=/1:25&st_01=ref_no&sf_01=keyword

Centered on mixed methods research conducted with Japanese high school teachers of English and considering their collective as well as individual language teacher efficacy (LTE) beliefs, this volume both reports on the findings of a study that drew on questionnaires subjected to factor analysis and in-depth interviews, and contextualizes these findings within a comprehensive discussion of the LTE beliefs research field. Strengths of this discussion include a detailed and well-balanced historical overview of developments in the research area, and perceptive suggestions for further research. Striking LTE beliefs findings from the research at the heart of the volume include those that relate to second language (L2) capability, instructional L2 efficacy (with two different dimensions of this identified, related to developing communicative competence and preparing students for university entrance exams), and collective capability towards collaboration; there is a clear implication that context-sensitive collaborative professional development initiatives are needed to strengthen LTE beliefs.

Cabaroglu, N. (2014). Professional development through action research: Impact on self-efficacy. *System, 44*, 79–88. https://www.sciencedirect.com/science/article/pii/S0346251X14000645

Set in the context of a pre-service teacher education practicum in Turkey, in which the teacher educator/researcher was encouraging participants to engage in action research to support their own professional development, this study investigates the impact of this innovation on the beginning teachers' LTSE beliefs. The self-directed goals of most of the pre-service teachers investigated were found to relate to better managing student misbehavior, and findings then indicate how LTSE beliefs changed over ten weeks in relation to achieving such a goal. It seems that engaging in action research supported the development of problem-solving skills with regards to finding creative ways of dealing with misbehaving students. Data from the mixed methods employed, both quantitative from surveys and qualitative from reflective diaries and course evaluations, highlight that taking charge of their own professional learning positively impacted these beginners' LTSE beliefs. The study concludes that action research can really strengthen such beliefs.

Karimi, M. N., Abdullahi, K., & Haghighi, J. K. (2016). English as a foreign language teachers' self-efficacy as a determinant of correspondence between their professed orientations towards reading and their reading instructional practices. *Innovation in Language Learning and Teaching*, **10(3), 155-170.** http://www.tandfonline.com/doi/abs/10.1080/17501229.2014.920847

Drawing on research with English teachers working at private language schools in Iran, this study sets out to explore LTSE beliefs in relation to teaching reading. Specifically, it examines teachers' theoretical orientations (text- or competence-based) towards teaching reading; unlike text-based orientations, which are more focused on text than learners, competence-based orientations relate quite closely to communicative language teaching. The study compares data relating to these orientations with actual reading instructional practices and LTSE beliefs. The first stage in the research was administering an LTSE beliefs survey, and then identifying smaller samples of teachers who scored particularly high and low. The most and least efficacious teachers were then observed and interviewed (through video stimulated recall). An important finding was that only the highly efficacious teachers "showed strong evidence of competence-based orientations to reading instruction in their actual classroom practices" (p. 165). There are implications for strengthening LTSE beliefs through teacher education.

Phan, N. T. T. & Locke, T. (2015). Sources of self-efficacy of Vietnamese EFL teachers: A qualitative study. *Teaching and Teacher Education, 52,* **73-82.**
https://www.sciencedirect.com/science/article/pii/S0742051X15300068

Set in a technical university in Vietnam, this qualitative case study explores the sources of information most influential in shaping participants' LTSE beliefs. A striking finding from the data, drawn from semi-structured interviews, observations and teacher journals, was that the social persuasion that comes from listening to others was a more important source of information to these teachers than other sources, for example the mastery experiences that come from personally experienced success. Possible reasons for this finding include cultural factors, and in particular the importance of the collective in Vietnam. Contextual factors may also have contributed as well, though, in that limited professional development opportunities within the university did not encourage the vicarious experiences that come from observing others nor the mastery experiences that hands-on workshops can provide. The most inefficacious teachers, struggling to deal with unmotivated students, really needed the support that can come from contextually-attuned professional development.

References

Bandura, A. (1977). Self-efficacy: Toward a unifying theory of behavioral change. *Psychological Review, 84*(2), 191–215.

Choi, E., & Lee, J. (2016). Investigating the relationship of target language proficiency and self-efficacy among nonnative EFL teachers. *System, 58,* 49–63.

Tschannen-Moran, M., & Woolfolk Hoy, A. (2001). Teacher efficacy: Capturing an elusive construct. *Teaching and Teacher Education, 17*(7), 783–805.

Wyatt, M. (2018). Language teachers' self-efficacy beliefs: An introduction. In S. Mercer & A. Kostoulas (Eds.), *Language teacher psychology* (pp. 122–140). Multilingual Matters.

Mark Wyatt is Associate Professor of English at Khalifa University in the United Arab Emirates. He previously worked at the Universities of Leeds (on a BA TESOL project in Oman) and Portsmouth. His research into language teachers' self-efficacy beliefs has been published in various journals: *System, International Journal of Qualitative Studies in Education, International Journal of Research and Method in Education, Australian Journal of Teacher Education, Educational Review, Educational Action Research, The Language Learning Journal and TESOL Quarterly.* He is currently co-editing a book on mentoring in English language education for Palgrave MacMillan.

Mary Ann Christison and Denise E. Murray

The British Council (2013) estimated that there are about two billion people using English in the world today and that by the year 2020 about one in every four persons will be doing so. The rapid spread of English as a lingua franca for education, trade, and employment (King, 2017) has resulted in the need for more qualified teachers in order to provide instruction for the growing number of English learners. As a result, more English language teachers are seeking credentials and opportunities for professional development.

At the same time as the growth of English worldwide, there has been a dramatic increase in the use of computer technologies and the Internet, thereby, making it possible for both preservice and practicing English language teachers to obtain credentials online without attending brick and mortar institutions, and this option is particularly attractive for English language teachers who live in rural, remote, and underdeveloped areas of the world or who have restricted or limited time because of family or work obligations and need the flexibility that online learning affords. The changes relative to technological access have resulted in a proliferation of online language teacher education (OLTE) courses. Hall and Knox (2009) reported that there were 23 programs offering OLTE in the mid-1990s, and the number increased to 120 programs by 2009. In (2013) Murray identified 186 programs, which took the form of workshops, courses, and programs with many of them offering credentials of some type, from certificates of completion to undergraduate and graduate degrees.

M. A. Christison
Department of Linguistics, University of Utah, Salt Lake City, UT, USA
e-mail: ma.christison@utah.edu

D. E. Murray (✉)
Department of Linguistics, Macquarie University, Sydney, NSW, Australia
e-mail: denise.murray@mq.edu.au

D. E. Murray
San José State University, San Jose, CA, USA

© Springer Nature Switzerland AG 2021
H. Mohebbi and C. Coombe (eds.), *Research Questions in Language Education and Applied Linguistics*, Springer Texts in Education, https://doi.org/10.1007/978-3-030-79143-8_101

Along with this recent proliferation of OLTE programs has come the concern about quality in OLTE. There is no specific accrediting body for OLTE, and, in addition, there is a dearth of research specifically directed to OLTE, thereby making it difficult to determine indicators of efficacy for course and curriculum design, implementation, and pedagogical practices, especially practices that are based on learner outcomes. Fortunately, there is a rather robust literature available on computer assisted language learning (CALL) and computer mediated communication (CMC) on which OLTE researchers and teacher educators can draw (see Hockly, 2015; Pawan et al., 2016) to understand better the factors that may affect quality in online learning.

Shin and Kang (2017) and Murray and Christison (2018) have offered reviews of the extant research on OLTE; identified critical issues, emerging patterns and trends; and suggested possible areas of focus for future research. These areas of focus include the following: defining and classifying OLTE, preparing teacher educators to teach online, balancing social interaction and learner autonomy, providing feedback on teaching during the practicum and/or field experience, building community and collaboration, designing OLTE for the purposes of producing reflective practitioners, exploiting and using a wide range of online tools, and defining and measuring quality. OLTE is not exactly the same as teaching in a face-to-face (f2f) environment; nevertheless, the goals of OLTE are consistent with Wright's (2010) notions about the primary goal of teacher education, which is to produce reflective practitioners. More research on OLTE needs to be undertaken to understand the factors that influence quality in OLTE and promote reflection in language teachers.

The Research Questions

1. What strategies do instructors use to engage OLTE learners in a community of practice (CoP)? Which strategies do learners consider to be effective? Which strategies do instructors consider to be effective?
2. To what extent do learners apply the teaching knowledge and skills that they acquire in an online environment (e.g., OLTE) in their own teaching in face-to-face (f2f) classrooms?
3. What teaching practice/practicum opportunities are provided in OLTE? How do learners and their supervisors navigate these experiences virtually?
4. What are employers' perceptions of the effectiveness of OLTE courses and programs for preparing teachers for the reality of English language teaching? How do their perceptions of OLTE courses and programs compare to f2f teacher education courses and programs?
5. How is quality in OLTE defined and measured?
6. How do OLTE courses and programs address students' prior learning and real-world experiences in their curricular goals?

7. How does OLTE affect the roles of teacher educators and the roles of their students?
8. What types of online tasks and activities are used to promote reflective practices and produce reflective English language teaching practitioners?
9. What materials and types of tasks does an OLTE course or program entail? How are materials and tasks implemented throughout the course?
10. How is learner autonomy vs. social interaction across different countries and contexts dealt with in OLTE?

Suggested Resources

Edmett, A. W. (2018). *Online professional development of English teachers: An analysis of cognitive presence* **via** *the community of inquiry framework* **(Unpublished doctoral dissertation), University of Bath, Bath, England**.

Edmett uses the community of inquiry (CoI) framework, which has been used extensively to study online learning in higher education. CoI posits three essential components of teaching: teaching presence, cognitive presence, and social presence. Students develop deep understandings of the core content of a course when engaged in meaningful communication of intellectually challenging material with a supportive instructor. Edmett's study is important because it is one of only a few that have investigated cognitive presence in OLTE. He focused on different task types in online forum discussions and found that, while lower level exploratory thought was dominant, task design affects discussion and can stimulate deeper critical thought.

England, L. (Ed.). (2012). *Online teacher education: TESOL perspectives*. **New York, NY: Routledge**.

This volume was the first comprehensive examination on OLTE. England and the contributors ground the volume in distance education. The 15 chapters cover a wide range of different OLTE configurations across a diversity of contexts. Some are focused primary research of specific classes; others are personal reflections; still others are essays on specific aspects of OLTE. The volume is divided into the three areas of learning, teaching, and administration in order to address both the affordances and challenges of and online delivery of teacher education. Several themes emerge from the contributions: the importance (and difficulty) of community building, the convenience of studying (and teaching) at one's own pace and in one's own time, changing roles for students and teachers, and the complexities of assessment online. In addition, the volume provides a variety of different research tools that can be used to explore OLTE.

Murray, D. E. (2013). *A case for online language teacher education.* **Retrieved from** http://www.tirfonline.org/wp-content/uploads/2013/05/TIRF_OLTE_Two-PageSpread_May2013.pdf.

Murray's study examines OLTE from three sets of data: extant literature on distance learning, online learning, and computer-assisted language learning (CALL); an extensive and intensive global web search on the 186 existing programs; and 18 in-depth case reports of a range of different OLTE configurations and contexts. The web search demonstrated the diversity of OLTE-from single courses or workshops, to certificate programs to doctoral degrees. However, most were university based and headquartered in English dominant countries. The three sets of data identified several issues: who are the most appropriate candidates; how to develop communities of practice; the alignment or misalignment between technology and pedagogy; how to determine the quality of OLTE programs. Programs are often opaque concerning the types of technologies and pedagogies used. Students come from many different contexts and may not understand their local contexts within this new global class. Technological choices can constrain or expand the instructor's pedagogical choices. Different OLTE providers privileging different aspects of quality.

Murray, D. E., & Christison, M. A. (2017). *Online language teacher education: Participants' perceptions and experiences.* **Retrieved from** https://www.tirfonline.org/wp-content/uploads/2017/03/TIRF_OLTE_2017_Report_Final.pdf.

From 185 OLTE programs that were contacted, 137 teacher educator questionnaires and 309 teacher student questionnaires were returned. These questionnaires sought to discover who is participating in OLTE courses/programs and why; the types of OLTE courses and programs available; the configurations of these courses/programs, including activities and technologies; participants' preferences for OLTE activities and technologies; and participants' perceptions of the effectiveness of OLTE courses and the applications for the delivery of the course. Experiences and opinions of teacher educators and students differed considerably on many key factors. While teacher educators chose a variety of different ways to engage students in participation, discussion, and group work, students were more interested in the flexibility and autonomy afforded by learning online. The data show a disparity between the age and technical expertise of the teacher educators and the students. Experiences were mostly with the configuration of courses offered totally online with no synchronous component and with exams for assessment.

Rodriquez, M. E. (2016). *Effective pedagogical practice in online English language teacher education.* **Unpublished doctoral dissertation. University of Arizona. Retrieved from** https://repository.arizona.edu/bitstream/handle/10150/613241/azu_etd_14601_sip1_m.pdf?sequence=1

Using surveys, Rodriquez examined the perceptions of effective OLTE pedagogical practices of 18 instructors and 125 former students. Survey data was supplemented by interviews with 20 students, eight instructors, and two program coordinators. The component of teacher presence from the Community of Inquiry

(CoI) framework was used to examine student satisfaction. The study found positive perceptions of current pedagogical practices, but that they could be improved. Specifically, there was a desire for pedagogical practices to build community, the use new technology affordances that provide a more engaging instruction, effective feedback on all tasks, modeling of effective instruction, and the integration of student contexts and cultures into instruction.

References

British Council. (2013). *The English effect: The impact of English, what it's worth to the UK and why it matters to the world*. British Council.

Hall, D., & Knox, J. (2009). Issues in the education of TESOL teachers by distance education. *Distance Education, 30*(1), 63–85.

Hockly, N. (2015). Developments in online language learning. *ELT Journal, 69*(3), 308–313.

King, L. (2017). *The impact of multilingualism on global education and language learning*. Cambridge English. Retrieved from https://assets.cambridgeenglish.org/research/perspectives-multilingualism.pdf

Murray, D. E. (2013). *A case for online language teacher education*. Retrieved from http://www.tirfonline.org/wp-content/uploads/2013/05/TIRF_OLTE_Two-PageSpread_May2013.pdf

Murray, D. E., & Christison, M. A. (2018). Online language teacher education: A review of the literature. A commissioned research report for the Association of Quality Education and Training Online (AQUEDUTO). Retrieved from http://aqueduto.com/wp-content/uploads/2018/12/Aqueduto-Murray-Christison.pdf

Pawan, F., Wiechart, K., Warren, A., & Park, J. (2016). *Pedagogy and practice for online English language teacher education*. TESOL Press.

Shin, D.-s, & Kang, H.-S. (2017). Online language teacher education: Practices and possibilities. *RELC Journal, 00*, 1–12. https://doi.org/10.1177/0033688217716535

Wright, T. (2010). Second language teacher education: Review of recent research on practice. *Language Teaching, 43*(3), 259–296.

Mary Ann Christison is a professor in the Department of Linguistics at the University of Utah. She served on the Board of Directors for TESOL International Association for seven years, including a term as President in 1997–1998. In 2012, she received the James E. Alatis Award from TESOL International Association and in 2016 a "TESOL 50@50 Award." She currently serves on the Board of Trustees for The International Research Foundation (TIRF) for English language education. Her research interests include second language teacher education (SLTE), online language teacher education (OLTE), and neurolinguistics. She has published 20 books and over 100 journal articles and book chapters. She has worked with English language teachers in over 35 countries.

Denise E. Murray is Professor Emeritus at Macquarie University in Sydney and at San José State University in California. She has a long history as a language teacher educator and lifetime commitment to distance education for those unable to attend brick-and-mortar institutions. She was the Executive Director of the Adult Migrant English Program Research Centre and of the National Centre for English Language Teaching and Research at Macquarie University. Prior to the Macquarie appointment, she was founding chair of the Department of Linguistics and Language Development at San José. Her research interests include the intersection of language, society, and technology; OLTE; language education policy; and leadership in language education. She has published her work in seventeen books and more than 100 articles.

Reflective Practice in Language Education

102

Thomas S. C. Farrell

Reflective practice has become popular in most teaching English to speakers of other languages (TESOL) teacher education and development programs; the general consensus is that teachers who are encouraged to engage in reflective practice can gain new insight of their practice and become even become better teachers (Richards & Lockhard, 1994). With this popularity however, several issues need to be addressed such as what is reflective practice and what frameworks best facilitate reflection?

Most of the definitions can be contained within two main stances to reflective teaching, one that emphasizes reflection only on classroom actions, while the other also includes reflections on matters outside the classroom. Concerning the former approach, reflection happens when a teacher thinks about what happened in a lesson, and why it happened and what he or she has learned as a result of reflection, while the other stance also links reflection on teaching to the larger community and this is called critical reflection (Farrell, 2018a, b). Farrell (2015: 123) defines reflective practice to include both stances: "A cognitive process accompanied by a set of attitudes in which teachers systematically collect data about their practice, and while engaging in dialogue with others use the data to make informed decisions about their practice both inside and outside the classroom."

In addition to the definitions of reflective practice above, teachers must consider how they will reflect. Again, two different stances have emerged, one that suggests that teachers can informally evaluate various aspects of their teaching, or common-sense reflection. The other suggests that teachers systematically reflect on their teaching by collecting data, or data-driven reflections (Mann & Walsh, 2017) and use the information gained to make informed decisions about their teaching (Farrell, 2015). In a review of such data-driven approaches to reflective practice in

T. S. C. Farrell (✉)
Applied Linguistics, Brock University, St. Catharines, ON, Canada
e-mail: tfarrell@brocku.ca

© Springer Nature Switzerland AG 2021
H. Mohebbi and C. Coombe (eds.), *Research Questions in Language Education and Applied Linguistics*, Springer Texts in Education,
https://doi.org/10.1007/978-3-030-79143-8_102

TESOL, Farrell (2018a, b) discovered that most studies focused on case studies and non-qualitative methods with very few focused on quantitative methods.

Many different frameworks, and tools have been used to promote reflection, but most have been adopted from different professions. While most models and frameworks have admirably provided different types of structured reflection for practitioners by offering probing questions that stimulate reflection, they have mostly guided teachers on how to tackle technical issues without looking at the person who is reflecting. Within the field of TESOL, however, Farrell (2015) has recently developed a framework for reflective practice for language teachers that includes the person who is reflecting as well as what the person is reflecting on. Thus Farrell (2015) has attempted to move the concept of reflective practice to this more holistic approach by providing an overall framework for teachers to reflect on their philosophy, beliefs, values, theories, principles, classroom practices and beyond the classroom. Different tools have also been suggested that can promote reflective practice such as dialogue, writing, classroom observations, cases, portfolios, team teaching, peer coaching, and critical friends (Mann & Walsh, 2017). Overall, the research indicates that both preservice and in-service TESOL teachers are interested in, and feel they benefit from, reflecting on various aspects of their practice both inside and outside the classroom (Edge, 2011).

The Research Questions

1. How should reflective practice be defined in the field of TESOL?
2. Do you think mere participation in a study group, or keeping a journal, for example, qualify as reflection?
3. If a teacher wants to think reflectively about or inquire into her practice, what does she do first? How does she know if she is getting better at it? To what should she aspire?
4. How would you define data-led research on reflective practice?
5. Should TESOL teachers only reflect on their practice inside the classroom?
6. Should TESOL teachers reflect on practice inside the classroom as well as what they do outside the classroom (critical reflection)?
7. How can reflecting on their philosophy, principles, theory, practice and beyond practice/critical reflection heighten TESOL teachers' awareness more than just reflecting on practice inside and outside the classroom?
8. What are the strengths and weaknesses of quantitative, qualitative, and mixed-methods when it comes to designing research on the practices that encourage TESOL teachers to reflect on their practice?
9. What is the preferred reflective practice combination of instruments that best facilitates reflective practice?
10. How can we evaluate reflective practice?

Suggested Resources

Farrell, T. S. C. (2015). *Promoting teacher reflection in second language education: A framework for TESOL professionals.* **New York: Routledge.**

Taking the concept and the practice of reflective teaching forward, this book introduces a well-structured, flexible framework for use by teachers at all levels of development, from pre-service to novice to the most experienced. The framework outlines five levels of reflective practice—Philosophy; Principles; Theory-of-Practice; Practice; Beyond Practice—and provides specific techniques for teachers to implement each level of reflection in their work. Designed to allow readers to take either a deductive approach, moving from theory-into-practice, or an inductive approach where they start from a practice-into-theory position, the framework can be used by teachers alone, in pairs, or in a group.

Farrell, T. S. C. (2018a). *Research on reflective practice in TESOL.* **New York: Routledge.**

In this comprehensive and detailed analysis of recent research on encouraging reflective practices in TESOL, Farrell demonstrates how this practice has been embraced within TESOL and how it continues to impact the field. Examining a vast array of studies through his own framework for reflecting on practice, Farrell's analysis comprises not only the intellectual and cognitive but also the spiritual, moral, and emotional aspects of reflection. Reflection questions at the end of each chapter provide a jumping-off point for researchers, scholars, and teachers to further consider and reflect on the future of the field. Providing a holistic picture of reflection, this book is an original compendium of essential research on philosophy and principles, instruments used in studies, and theory and practice.

Barnard, R. & Ryan, J. (Eds.). (2017). *Reflective Practice: Voices from the Field.* **New York: Routledge.**

Barnard and Ryan's (2017) collection contains reflective practice studies of TESOL teachers (preservice and inservice) on topics such as (collaborative) lesson planning, classroom observation, lesson transcripts, post-lesson discussions, journal writing, reflection on action, reflection in action, critical friends, and focus groups. The aim of the book is to explain a range of options for implementing the reflective practice cycle in educational settings in various international contexts. Written by international academics, these studies show how reflection can be interpreted in different cultural contexts.

Mann, S. & Walsh, S. (2017). *Reflective practice in English language teaching.* **New York: Routledge.**

Mann and Walsh's (2017) book outlines an empirical, data-led approach to reflective practice and uses excellent examples of real data along with reflexive vignettes from a range of contexts in order to help teachers to reflect on their practices. Mann and Walsh also note the importance of dialogue as crucial for reflection as it allows for clarification, questioning and enhanced understanding. This is by far the best book available on RP.

Watanabe, A. (2016). *Reflective Practice as Professional Development Experiences of Teachers of English in Japan.* **Bristol, UK: Multilingual Matters**.

Atsuko Watanabe's (2016) book outlines a study of the reflective practices of seven inservice TESOL teachers in a high school setting in Japan. Beginning with a series of uncomfortable teacher training sessions delivered to unwilling participants, the book charts the author's development of new methods of engaging her participants and making use of their own experiences and knowledge. Both an in-depth examination of reflective practice in the context of Japanese cultural conventions and a narrative account of the researcher's reflexivity in her engagement with the study, the book introduces the concept of 'the reflective continuum'—a non-linear journey that mirrors the way reflection develops in unpredictable and individual ways.

References

Edge, J. (2011). *The reflexive teacher educator in TESOL*. Routledge.
Farrell, T. S. C. (2015). *Promoting teacher reflection in second language education: A framework for TESOL professionals*. Routledge.
Farrell, T. S. C. (2018b). *Reflective language teaching: Practical applications for TESOL teachers*. Bloomsbury.
Mann, S., & Walsh, S. (2017). *Reflective practice in English language teaching*. Routledge.
Richards, J. C., & Lockhard, C. (1994). *Reflective teaching*. Cambridge University Press.

Thomas S. C. Farrell is Professor of Applied Linguistics at Brock University, Canada. Professor Farrell's professional interests include Reflective Practice, and Language Teacher Education & Development. Professor Farrell has published widely in academic journals and has presented at major conferences worldwide on these topics. A selection of his books include *Reflective Practice in ESL Teacher Development Groups: From Practices to Principles* (Palgrave Macmillan, UK, 2014); *Promoting teacher reflection in language education: a framework for TESOL professionals* (Routledge, 2015), *Reflecting on Critical Incidents in Language Education* (With L. Baecher, Bloomsbury, 2017); Preservice Teacher Education. (TESOL publications, 2017); Sociolinguistics and Language Teaching. (TESOL publications, 2017); Research on Reflective Practice in TESOL (Routledge, 2018a); *Reflective Language Teaching: Practical Applications for TESOL Teachers* (Bloomsbury, 2018b). His webpage is: www.reflectiveinquiry.ca.

Second Language Teacher Education Curricula

Nikki Ashcraft

The global expansion of English language teaching, and the subsequent demand for more English teachers, have stimulated interest in analyzing the curricula of second language teacher education (SLTE) programs and evaluating the relevance of those curricula to teachers' day-to-day classroom experiences. Surveys of SLTE programs, particularly those at the graduate level, have highlighted the strong emphasis traditionally given in curricula to knowledge of language teaching methodology and linguistics (Stapleton & Shao, 2018). The prevalence of course work in specific areas like pedagogical grammar (Wang, 2003), phonology (Murphy, 1997), pragmatics (Vásquez & Sharpless, 2009), and intercultural communication (Nelson, 1998) has also been documented. Furthermore, current discourse in the field promotes a sociocultural perspective on language teaching and SLTE. This has resulted in the development of a greater number of teacher education courses related to diversity, multilingualism, and sociolinguistics (Nero, 2017; Stapleton & Shao, 2018).

Practicum courses are also well established in SLTE, especially in programs leading to K-12 teacher certification (Stapleton & Shao, 2018); however, the practicum experience is often isolated from other components of the SLTE curriculum (Baecher, 2012). Other field experiences sometimes take the form of service-learning projects, like that described in Uzám et al. (2014). Additionally, there are opportunities for student teachers to participate in study abroad or teach abroad programs (see, for example, Tomaš et al., 2008).

While some SLTE programs require students to carry out a capstone project or write a thesis at the end of their studies (Stapleton & Shao, 2018), this is not a requirement across the board. Therefore, students may receive varying levels of research training depending on which SLTE program they select.

N. Ashcraft (✉)
Learning, Teaching & Curriculum-TESOL, University of Missouri, Columbia, MO, USA
e-mail: ashcraftn@missouri.edu

© Springer Nature Switzerland AG 2021   589
H. Mohebbi and C. Coombe (eds.), *Research Questions in Language Education and Applied Linguistics*, Springer Texts in Education,
https://doi.org/10.1007/978-3-030-79143-8_103

SLTE programs face several challenges in ensuring that their curricula remain relevant in dynamic educational contexts. First, more general education teachers are being expected to teach English language learners both the content of academic subjects, like science and math, and the language and discourse of that discipline. A growing number of these teachers are entering SLTE programs to obtain ESL credentials. Second, SLTE programs need to prepare students who aspire to be language teachers how to build collaborative relationships with their general education peers. Third, new standards for K-12 education, like the Common Core State Standards in the U.S., as well as changing requirements for teacher licensure and teacher education program accreditation, can make designing SLTE curricula a reactive process. Fourth, while teachers are encouraged, and sometimes required to, incorporate educational technology into their instruction, courses in educational technology are not as common in SLTE programs as one might expect (Nero, 2017). This is problematic since teacher candidates may be adept at using technology for social interaction, but not know how to evaluate and use technology to achieve educational objectives. Finally, the rise of online teacher education has created a new environment for teacher learning (Murray, 2013) and can bring diverse teachers from a wide variety of teaching contexts together in one virtual space. It remains to be seen how SLTE curricula may need to evolve as teacher education programs reach a global teacher population.

The Research Questions

1. How are SLTE curricula shaped by the requirements of governmental agencies, the demands of accrediting bodies, and the content of licensing exams?
2. How, when, where, and to what extent is applied linguistics content being integrated into initial teacher certification coursework for general education and content-area teachers?
3. How are the curricula of SLTE programs being adapted to meet the needs of diverse teacher-learners (e.g., native English speakers, non-native English speakers, experienced teachers, inexperienced teachers, content teachers, teachers preparing to teach in ESL versus EFL contexts, teachers preparing to work at different levels of education)?
4. How prevalent are study or teach abroad programs for preservice ESL teachers, and what role do they serve in the SLTE curricula?
5. In what ways do SLTE programs prepare students to be both consumers and producers of research?
6. What relationship, if any, exists between technology integration in a teacher's SLTE program and that teacher's use of technology in the classroom?
7. What do SLTE curricula look like in different cultural contexts?
8. What criteria should be used to evaluate the efficacy of SLTE programs?
9. What affordances and challenges does online teacher education offer for designing or implementing the SLTE curriculum?

10. How are SLTE programs adapting their curricula to prepare teachers to face emerging challenges (e.g., working with refugees with interrupted formal schooling)?

Suggested Resources

Burns, A. & Richards, J. C. (Eds.) (2009). *The Cambridge guide to second language teacher education.* **Cambridge University Press**.

The 30 chapters in this volume provide an overview of second language teacher education (SLTE) and highlight issues and debates in the field. The first section conceptualizes SLTE and describes trends and approaches. The second section focuses on professionalism and covers issues such as certification, standards, and teacher assessment. Section 3 deals with the knowledge base of SLTE and discusses the SLTE curriculum more generally, as well as knowledge of language, second language acquisition, and discourse conventions, specifically. Section 4 acquaints the reader with teacher identity, teacher cognition, and the role of experience in teacher learning. Sections 5 and 6 present the different contexts in which teachers learn and the different types of relationships which facilitate teacher learning. The final section introduces teacher research and reflective practice.

Christison, M. A. & Murray, D. (2011–2014). *What English language teachers need to know* **(Vols. I–III). Routledge**.

The three volumes in this series are meant to provide a foundation for teachers new to the field of English language teaching. Examples are drawn from a variety of ESL and EFL settings so as to be relevant to teachers in diverse teaching contexts. Volume I covers issues around language use, language systems, and language learning, as well as professionalism. Volume II deals with lesson and curriculum planning, instructional methods for different learner populations and contexts (including children, adolescent, and adults), assessment of learning, and program evaluation. Volume III focuses entirely on curriculum design. It describes the curriculum design process and reviews 14 approaches to curriculum design, from the traditional structural approach to more current approaches, such as task-based and standards-based curricula. Each chapter in the three volumes opens with a vignette about a learner or a classroom scenario. The chapters contain tasks for the reader as well as discussion questions, making these volumes suitable for use in teacher education courses.

Soneson, D. & Tarone, E. (with Chamot, A. U., Mahajan, A., & Malone, M.) (Eds.). (2012). Expanding our horizons: Language teacher education in the 21st century: *Selected papers from the 6th and 7th International Language Teacher Education Conferences* (CARLA Working Paper Series). University of Minnesota, The Center for Advanced Research on Language Acquisition.

The International Conference on Language Teacher Education is a biannual conference organized by the Center for Advanced Research on Language Acquisition (CARLA). The papers selected for these refereed proceedings reflect teacher education issues for teachers of second, foreign, and heritage languages. The conference is consistently organized around the following four themes: The knowledge base of language teacher education; social, cultural, and political contexts of language teacher education; collaborations in language teacher education; and practices of language teacher education. Proceedings from previous conferences are available without cost at http://carla.umn.edu/resources/working-papers/index.html.

Temple Adger, C., Snow, C. E., & Christian, D. (Eds.). (2018). *What teachers need to know about language* **(2nd ed.). Multilingual Matters.**

The theme of this edited volume is that teachers in U.S. K-12 schools can better meet the needs of culturally and linguistically diverse students if teachers have knowledge of educational linguistics. In the first chapter, which forms the core of the book, Wong Fillmore and Snow lay out the domains of linguistic knowledge that teachers should have. These include knowledge of oral language and language structure (i.e., phonetics/phonology, morphology, vocabulary development, as well as sentence and discourse patterns), written language and the development of literacy skills, the features of academic language and text analysis, language and culture, sociolinguistics, and first and second language acquisition. The authors of the following chapters elaborate on these domains and discuss implications for classroom practice and teacher training. Special emphasis is given in the volume to the development of academic language and the role of the Common Core State Standards.

TESOL International Association (TESOL). (2019). *Standards for initial TESOL Pre-K–12 teacher preparation programs.* https://www.tesol.org/docs/default-source/books/2018-tesol-teacher-prep-standards-final.pdf?sfvrsn=23f3ffdc_6.

The TESOL International Association developed this set of standards for teacher education programs in the United States which prepare Pre-K-12 teachers who seek to earn their initial TESOL credential. These performance-based standards are meant to reflect the content knowledge as well as the pedagogical knowledge and skills that teachers need to effectively work with English language learners. The standards have been used by the Council for Accreditation of Educator Preparation (CAEP) to assess, and potentially accredit, U.S. teacher education programs. The standards are divided into five domains: knowledge about language; ELLs in the sociocultural context; planning and implementing instruction; assessment and evaluation; and professionalism and leadership. For each standard, there are four to five components. The document describes the types of assessments that have been required by CAEP to demonstrate that preservice teachers have met the standards, and there is a chart at the end which suggests the types of assessments which best align with each standard.

References

Baecher, L. (2012). Integrating clinical experiences in a TESOL teacher education program: Curriculum mapping as process. *TESOL Journal, 3*(4), 537–551.

Murphy, J. M. (1997). Phonology courses offered by MATESOL programs in the U.S. *TESOL Quarterly, 31*(4), 741–764.

Murray, D. E. (2013). *A case for online English language teacher education.* The International Research Foundation for English Language Education (TIRF). https://www.tirfonline.org/wp-content/uploads/2013/05/TIRF_OLTE_One-PageSpread_May20131.pdf

Nelson, G. L. (1998). Intercultural communication and related courses taught in TESOL masters' degree programs. *International Journal of Intercultural Relations, 22*(1), 17–33.

Nero, S. (2017, March). *Analyzing TESOL programs: Teacher preparation in changing times* [Paper presentation]. TESOL 2017 International Convention, Seattle, WA, United States.

Stapleton, P., & Shao, Q. (2018). A worldwide survey of MATESOL programs in 2014: Patterns and perspectives. *Language Teaching Research, 22*(1), 10–28.

Tomaš, Z., Farrelly, R. & Haslam, M. (2008). Designing and implementing the TESOL teaching practicum abroad: Focus on interaction. *TESOL Quarterly, 42*(4), 660–664.

Uzám, B., Petrón, M., & Berg, H. (2014). Pre-service teachers' first foray into the ESL classroom: Reflective practice in a service learning project. *TESL-EJ, 18*(3), 1–15. http://tesl-ej.org/pdf/ej71/a3.pdf

Vásquez, C. & Sharpless, D. (2009). The role of pragmatics in the master's TESOL curriculum: Findings from a nationwide survey. *TESOL Quarterly, 43*(1), 5–28.

Wang, W. (2003). How is pedagogical grammar defined in current TESOL training practice? *TESL Canada Journal/Revue TESL du Canada, 21*(1), 64–78.

Nikki Ashcraft is an Associate Teaching Professor in the online M.Ed. TESOL program at the University of Missouri, where she enjoys working virtually with teachers around the world. Dr. Ashcraft holds an M.S. in Applied Linguistics/TESOL from Georgia State University and a Ph.D. in Adult Education from the University of Georgia. During her TESOL career, Dr. Ashcraft has taught English as a second/foreign language and trained teachers in the U.S., Mexico, Chile, Kuwait, and the United Arab Emirates. Dr. Ashcraft is the author of *Lesson Planning* (TESOL Press, 2014) and formerly served as Chair of the TESOL International Association's Teacher Education Interest Section.

Teacher Knowledge Development

Phil Quirke

Contemporary literature on knowledge all points to a review of traditional and cognitive concepts of learning. From teacher studies (Darling-Hammond, 2016) and knowledge management (Serenko & Dumay, 2015) to biological and neurological studies (Maturana, 2012), social constructivists now suggest that our construction of knowledge is not only dependent on the environment that surrounds us and clearly includes the people within that environment and our communication with them but is held by the community and constructed by those within the community. These social constructivist theories view knowledge as a collective, communicative process fully dependent on the community and their interaction. These theories are based on the premises that we construct meaning out of our experience and that we are part of the knowledge constructing community; that knowledge is constructed in a social world.

According to Beattie (1997, p. 126) learning to teach "requires experiences and settings which support reflection, collaboration, relational learning and the creation of communities of inquiry", and a conviction that "a professional knowledge of teaching has many dimensions - cognitive, social, organizational, practical, moral, aesthetic, personal, political and interpersonal".

Tsui (2003) brought together the proliferation of teacher knowledge terminology into a coherent whole, which Quirke (2009) further developed into an extended model of teacher knowledge development.

The recognition of the importance of professional self-knowledge has been demonstrated continually in both the literature (Bailey et al, 2001; Elbaz, 2016), with the increase of teacher narratives and case studies (Johnson & Golombek, 2002; Tsui, 2003), and teacher education programmes that focus on the individual's knowledge at the start of their courses.

P. Quirke (✉)
Department of Education, Higher Colleges of Technology,
Abu Dhabi, United Arab Emirates
e-mail: pquirke@hct.ac.ae

© Springer Nature Switzerland AG 2021

595

H. Mohebbi and C. Coombe (eds.), *Research Questions in Language Education and Applied Linguistics*, Springer Texts in Education,
https://doi.org/10.1007/978-3-030-79143-8_104

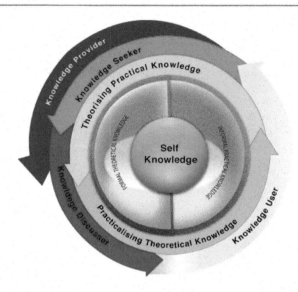

Fig. 104.1 Model of teacher knowledge development (Quirke, 2009).

The informal practical knowledge area represents the practical, experiential knowledge of teachers based on their classroom experiences in their local contexts. The formal theoretical knowledge area represents the theoretical and empirical knowledge of content and pedagogy that is widely accepted by professional bodies within English Language Teaching. 'Theorising practical knowledge' represents the teacher's search for the formal theoretical knowledge that they can align to their experience. It is the process whereby teacher's knowledge expands as they learn how to theorize their practice. 'Practicalising theoretical knowledge' represents the teacher's search for new classroom practices that mirror their often newly articulated theories or their developing and expanding formal theoretical knowledge. It is the process whereby teacher's knowledge can expand as they learn to practically apply theories often through research of their classroom practice. It is this continual cycle of theorizing practical knowledge and practicalising theoretical knowledge that creates the cycle of individual teacher knowledge. This acknowledges the complexity of teacher knowledge, the circularity of knowledge growth through practice and theoretical input and the centrality of the local situation.

The knowledge-seeker category mirrors the theorizing of practical knowledge. We have an understanding of ourselves, our situation and teaching context, and we begin to explore how we can deepen that understanding through reading, professional workshops and further study. We are in effect beginning to theorize our existing practice and by seeking new knowledge we gain a better understanding of what we are doing in the classroom through research and reflection. The changes to our existing knowledge schema triggered by reflection on newly acquired knowledge are seldom complete until we have involved others. As we shift our schemata, we need confirmation from those professional colleagues around us whom we respect as represented by the knowledge-discusser category. So, we discuss how this new knowledge maps onto our existing cognitive knowledge map and decide whether or not the change we are considering for our schema is in fact compatible to our professional context. One of the key phases in the transformation of our knowledge structure is the knowledge-user category, which mirrors the practicalising of new knowledge as we confirm our beliefs in practice. Eventually, as our knowledge grows, we begin to realise we have something to offer the professional community and begin to act as knowledge-providers. The cycle does not end here, since a natural continuation of knowledge provision is a realization of how much more we can add to our knowledge, so we begin to seek new knowledge in a process of lifelong learning. The cycle continues and grows. The knowledge-provider category is the final phase in the cyclical model of teacher knowledge and is the key reporting element, which often strengthens our knowledge structure and teacher beliefs, perhaps moving them to the central core of our professional selves.

The Research Questions

1. **Self knowledge**: How would you describe your identity as a professional language teacher and researcher? How is your identity influenced by your professional self knowledge?
2. **Informal Practical Knowledge**: How has your classroom experience shaped your professional knowledge? How can you begin to research this tacit knowledge and link it to theories of teaching and learning?
3. **Formal Theoretical Knowledge**: How would you describe your content and pedagogical knowledge and how have you attained this formal knowledge? How has your formal theoretical knowledge informed your teaching and approaches to student learning?
4. **Theorising Practical Knowledge**: What formal theoretical knowledge are you currently interested in studying? How do you expect this to impact your current teaching?
5. **Practicalising Theoretical Knowledge**: What new classroom practices are you currently interested in trying out? Where did you learn about these new practices? Why do you expect them to have an impact on your teaching and/or your students' learning?
6. **Knowledge Seeker**: How do you reflect on your practice? How do these reflections impact your teaching?
7. **Knowledge Discusser**: What professional communities of inquiry do you rely on most? Why are these communities of practice/learning communities so important to you? How could you make better use of them?
8. **Knowledge User**: As you implement new classroom practices, how do you analyse, interpret and research their success? How could you better record the results of this implementation / intervention?

9. **Knowledge Provider**: How do you report on your classroom practice? How do you give to others in the profession? In what ways are you a knowledge provider?

10. As you reflect on your reading of this entry and your responses to the above questions, what would you now like to begin researching in your classroom? How are you planning to launch this new research?

Suggested Resources

Barkhuizen, G. (Ed.). (2017). *Reflections on Language Teacher Identity Research*. **Abingdon, UK: Routledge**.

In this fascinating volume, Gary Barkhuizen has collated the reflections of forty-one experienced researchers and scholars in the fields of applied linguistics and TESOL on their personal understandings of language teacher identity. Each contributor locates their conceptual understanding of language teacher identity within a biographical narrative of their professional lives and research work. The editor has successfully woven these accounts into a guided reflective structure that takes stock of the current thinking on language teacher identity and looks towards future directions in language teacher identity research giving the reader concrete suggestions for research topics. With contributions from some of the most respected names in the field, including Bonny Norton, Simon Borg, Anne Burns, Jack C. Richards, Paula Golombek, David Nunan and Tom Farrell to name just seven, the reader is guaranteed an inspiring journey through teacher identity and how it impacts everything we do in our classrooms.

Elbaz, F. (2016). *Teacher Thinking: A Study of Practical Knowledge*. **Abingdon, UK: Routledge**.

In this book Freema Elbaz directly confronts the ways in which teaching, curriculum development and teacher growth and change are viewed by scholars and policy-makers in education today. Elbaz reports in detail an analysis of the ideas and insights of one teacher focusing on her thoughts and concerns over a series of long interviews. In doing so, she echoes how many teachers feel about their identities as professional language teachers, excited to be in the classroom creating new learning opportunities for their students and not wanting advancement but professional growth, development and change. Elbaz paints a vivid picture of what happens behind the classroom door both theoretically and methodologically and provides the reader with multiple insights that will resonate in the battle between hostile pressures and creative teaching. A book that will inspire you to reflect on how your identity and context can provide opportunities for research, conversations and collaboration.

Farrell, T. (2018). *Reflective Language Teaching: Practical Applications for TESOL Teachers* **(Second Edition). London, UK: Bloomsbury**.

This is a revised version of Farrell's 2008 Reflective Language Teaching: From Research to Practice with a clearer focus on the "how to" practical applications of reflection and reflective writing. This edition still gives the reader ample reference to the relevant research literature and includes three new chapters on the concept of reflective practice, online reflection and effective teaching. The renaming of chapter 12 to "Collegial Friendships" from the original "Critical Friendships" captures the essence of this new edition, and the new case studies clearly demonstrate that this is a book written by a colleague who reflects deeply on his practice and how it ties to his theories, beliefs and values. It is a book that will encourage everyone to deepen their reflective practice, and then research the way in which their reflections and the language they use in those reflections can provide insights into both their practice and the often hidden professional identity behind that practice.

Borg, S. (2013). *Teacher Research in Language Teaching: A Critical Analysis.* **Cambridge, UK: Cambridge University Press**.

I consider this book essential reading for all teachers undertaking research in their classrooms. The author draws upon six years of research covering four studies and over 1,700 language teaching professionals from around the world, so the reader immediately feels they are not alone. I would recommend reading the concluding Chapter 9 first as the author suggests in his introduction. This chapter reviews the key findings that emerge from the previous chapters in the form of practical responses to them, and I found it triggered multiple research ideas for my own classrooms and deepened my reading of the other chapters when I returned to them. The checklist provided to assess the feasibility of teacher research projects is also very useful in helping the reader narrow their research focus from the multitude of ideas we all have. The chapter strikes an enviable balance between the theoretical and the practical role that research can play in the classroom and how this is linked to the increasing demand for evidence-based teaching, as does the whole book.

Quirke, P. (Ed.). (2017). *Adult Education. TESOL Voices: Insider accounts of classroom life*. **Alexandria, VA: TESOL Press**.

This book is one in the TESOL Voices series edited by Tim Stewart which "aims to fill the need for expanding practical knowledge through participant research in the field." Both the editor and series editor believe that the most enduring theories in TESOL are most likely to be those that emerge from or are supported by teacher inquiry that happens in the classroom. This volume on adult education is divided into three sections based on topical spheres of influence in relation to teaching and learning interaction in the classroom. The first section on community discusses factors outside the classroom that have impacted the author's teaching and their students' learning. The second section on course planning and structure reviews factors as diverse as laughter and authentic dialogue. The final section focuses on language learning and linguistics. The book, and all the books in this motivational series, speak to the reader as a teacher searching for research inspiration, and the authors' voices resonate with us all and motivate us to research our classrooms and tell our stories and those of our learners.

References

Bailey, K., Curtis, A., & Nunan, D. (2001). *Pursuing professional development: The self as source*. Heinle & Heinle.

Beattie, M. (1997). Fostering reflective practice in teacher education: Inquiry as a framework for the construction of professional knowledge in teaching. *Asia-Pacific Journal of Teacher Education, 25*(2), 111–128.

Darling-Hammond, L. (2016). Research on teaching and teacher education and its influences on policy and practice. *Educational Researcher, 45*(2), 83–91.

Elbaz, F. (2016). *Teacher thinking: A study of practical knowledge*. Routledge.

Johnson, K., & Golombek, P. (2002). *Teachers' narrative inquiry as professional development*. Cambridge University Press.

Maturana, H. (2012). Reflections on my collaboration with Francisco Varela. *Constructivist Foundations, 7*(3), 155–164.

Quirke, P. (2009). *An exploration of teacher knowledge*. VDM Publishers.

Serenko, A., & Dumay, J. (2015). Citation classics published in knowledge management journals. Part I: Articles and their characteristics. *Journal of Knowledge Management, 19*(2), 410–431.

Tsui, A. (2003). *Understanding expertise in teaching: Case studies of second language teachers*. Cambridge University Press.

Phil Quirke has been in ELT Leadership positions for fifteen years and has published on areas as diverse as face, action research, appraisal and journaling. He has recently contributed three articles to the Wiley TESOL Encyclopedia of English Language Teaching on Observations, Journals and Classroom Management, and his book on Reflective Writing with Jill Burton, Joy Peyton and Carla Reichmann is available online at http://www.tesl-ej.org/wordpress/books/. Phil's doctorate research was on the Exploration of Teacher Knowledge and formed the basis of the publications above and the foundation of this contribution. Over the last ten years Phil has developed an educational management philosophy, DREAM Management, that places students and staff at the core of the institution and he has published widely on this approach.

Teacher Research

105

Anne Burns

The idea of research conducted by teachers emerged in the field of applied linguistics from the late 1980s. The concept that there was a role for language teachers as investigators of their own classrooms was part of a new interest in examining what should constitute teacher education for second language teaching and what kinds of knowledge, skills, attitudes and behaviours teachers needed to acquire (Richards & Nunan, 1990). Wallace (1991) argued that the training of teachers should not only involve 'received' knowledge gained through scientific research, but also 'experiential' knowledge related to ongoing professional experience. He advocated a 'reflective' model that would provide a balance between these two needs.

Teacher research is both a way of gaining and deepening experiential knowledge of teaching and furthering one's professional learning. It involves intentional and systematic processes of inquiring into teaching and learning issues identified in one's own classroom through experimentation, observation, information gathering, and reflection. Both teachers and students may be participants as well as researchers in the investigations that are carried out. Various forms of teacher research have been put forward, including (collaborative) action research (Burns, 1999, 2010), exploratory practice (Allwright & Bailey, 1991; Allwright & Hanks, 2009), reflective practice (Farrell, 2007) and exploratory action research (Smith & Rebolledo, 2018). While there are some differences among these various approaches, they share the fundamental idea of teachers exploring, preferably in collaboration with their colleagues and students, their own professional concerns and issues to understand and improve their teaching practices and their students' learning.

Various benefits of teacher research have been identified, including a reduction of teacher isolation, development of more reflective, critical and analytical

A. Burns (✉)
School of Education, University of New South Wales, Sydney, Australia
e-mail: anne.burns@unsw.edu.au

© Springer Nature Switzerland AG 2021
H. Mohebbi and C. Coombe (eds.), *Research Questions in Language Education and Applied Linguistics*, Springer Texts in Education,
https://doi.org/10.1007/978-3-030-79143-8_105

approaches to teaching, greater understanding of learners and learning, development of a greater sense of status, professionalism, autonomy and agency, decrease in dependence on external answers to professional challenges, increase in innovation and experimentation, and acquisition of research skills (Borg, 2013; Burns, 1999, 2010). On the other hand, teacher researchers also experience barriers such as limited or no training in conducting research, lack of funding and material and human support, little time and few resources, unsupportive leadership, and little academic recognition for their research (Borg, 2013; Burns, 2011).

While the concept may still be unfamiliar or alien to many language teachers, since the early 1990s there has been an undeniable increase in the spread of teacher research and increasing support for it through initiatives from organisations such as the British Council, Cambridge Assessment English, and Cambridge University Press, and professional bodies such as IATEFL and TESOL International (see Burns, 2019). In the last two decades there has also been an upsurge in the number of publications seeking to provide empirical research on the factors that promote and limit teacher engagement in research and to explore the experiences of teachers who involve themselves in researching their classrooms. There has also been a body of research exploring the ways in which action research can be facilitated by teacher educators. Nevertheless, much still remains to be done to expand the emerging field of language teacher research in order to understand these issues in greater depth.

The Research Questions

1. Who should participate in teacher research? Experienced teachers? Novice teachers? Teachers in training? What are the views of these various groups on becoming teacher researchers?
2. What motivates teachers to become researchers? What demotivates them?
3. What knowledge and skills do teachers acquire when they do teacher research?
4. What barriers exist for teachers in writing and publishing their research? What kinds of support do they value?
5. What emotional factors do teachers experience in doing research?
6. What impact does teacher research have on student achievement?
7. To what extent does teacher research contribute to ongoing professional learning?
8. What factors promote successful facilitation of teacher research?
9. What kinds of support do teachers experience when they conduct research in their institutions?
10. What institutional factors promote action research? What impedes it?

Suggested Resources

Allwright, D., & Hanks, J. (2009). *The developing language learner: An introduction to exploratory practice.* **Basingstoke: Palgrave Macmillan.**

Allwright and Hanks place emphasis on 'quality of life' in the classroom. By this they mean that putting learners at the centre of classroom life as 'key developing practitioners' (p. 2) is not only desirable but indispensible to enhanced classroom practice. They define exploratory practice as 'inclusive practitioner research [...] where teachers and learners are co-practitioners, and where learners investigate their own puzzles about their own learning lives' (p. 5). They contrast this kind of 'first person' approach to the 'third party' perspective that has characterised much research in second language acquisition, which they argue, has had limited impact on classroom practice. Instead they advocate a form of research where teachers and learners work together as research practitioners. This approach, they argue, is the more appropriate if deeper understanding of language learners and their learning is to be achieved. The book includes many practical ideas and case studies to illustrate how exploratory practice can be carried out.

Burns. A. (2010). *Doing action research in English language teaching: A guide for practitioners.* **New York: Routledge.**

This volume provides an accessible step-by-step guide for teachers wishing to do action research in their teaching programs, either individually or collaboratively with their colleagues. It draws on Kemmis and McTaggart's (1988) 'classic' stages of action research: plan, act, observe, reflect. After an introduction to the concepts and processes of action research, each chapter then describes each of these stages. 'Plan' involves identifying an issue or focus and developing questions to investigate, while 'Act' shows what tools can be used for information gathering as the plan is put in place. 'Observe' deals with analysing information qualitatively and quantitatively, while 'Reflect' considers what lessons the teacher has learned from the overall processes of conducting research and how new understandings and insights about practice could be communicated to others. The book contains many examples from teachers' research as well as action and reflection points to aid the process of learning about research.

Farrell, T. S. C. (2015). *Promoting teacher reflection in second language education: A framework for TESOL professionals.* **New York: Routledge.**

Farrell defines reflective practice as 'a cognitive process accompanied by a set of attitudes in which teachers systematically collect data about their practice, and, while engaging in dialogue with others, use the data to make informed decisions about their practice both inside and outside the classroom' (Farrell, 2015, p. 123). Beginning with chapters that outline the concepts of reflective practice, the book then goes on to provide practical suggestions for teachers wishing to enhance their teaching and develop themselves professionally through this approach. The book draws on research findings on the benefits of reflective practice and provides many case studies to illustrate reflective language teaching in action. It also discusses how reflective practice can be an effective tool to promote broader improvement at an institutional level.

Smith, R, & Rebolledo, P. (2018). *A handbook for exploratory action research.* **London: The British Council.**

This volume builds on the work of the British Council Champion Teachers program for secondary school teachers, initiated in Chile and since offered to teachers in India, Nepal and Peru. The authors explain the concept of exploratory action research, a form of practitioner research which aims to contribute to professional development targeted at school teachers working in relatively difficult circumstances. The authors describe exploratory action research as a way to 'explore, understand and improve our practice as teachers' (p. 20) and emphasise the importance of an initial stage of exploration for teachers who may be unsure about how to get started with research. The book outlines the key steps of exploratory action research, such as identifying areas to explore, developing questions, collecting information (data) and analysing and interpreting data, and provides extensive illustrations and case studies from the teachers' actual experiences of exploring their classrooms to guide the reader.

References

Allwright, D., & Bailey, K. M. (1991). *Focus on the language learner.* Cambridge University Press.

Allwright, D., & Hanks, J. (2009). *The developing language learner: An introduction to exploratory practice.* Palgrave Macmillan.

Borg, S. (2013). *Teacher research in language teaching.* Cambridge University Press.

Burns, A. (1999). *Collaborative action research for English language teachers.* Cambridge University Press.

Burns, A. (2010). *Doing action research in English language teaching: A guide for practitioners.* Routledge.

Burns, A. (2011). Action research in the field of second language teaching and learning. In E. Hinkel (Ed.), *Handbook of research in second language teaching and learning* (Vol. II, pp. 237–253). Routledge.

Burns, A. (2019). Action research: Developments, characteristics, and future directions. In A. Benati & J. W. Schweiter (Eds.), *The Cambridge handbook of language learning* (pp.166–185). Cambridge University Press.

Farrell, T. S. C. (2007). *Reflective language teaching: From research to practice.* Continuum Press.

Richards, J. C., & Nunan, D. (1990). *Second language teacher education.* Cambridge University Press.

Smith, R., & Rebolledo, P. (2018). *A handbook for exploratory action research.* British Council.

Wallace, M. (1991). *Training foreign language teachers. A reflective approach.* Cambridge University Press.

Anne Burns is an Honorary Professor of TESOL (University of New South Wales), Professor Emerita (Aston University) and Honorary Professor (University of Sydney, and The Education University, Hong Kong). She publishes extensively on action research, teacher education, and teaching speaking. Publications include The Cambridge guide to second language teacher education (2009, with Jack Richards), Researching language teacher cognition and practice: International case studies (2012, with Roger Barnard), and The Cambridge guide to learning English as a second language (2018, with Jack Richards). She is series editor with Jill Hadfield for Routledge's Research and Resources Series, and an Academic Adviser for Oxford University Press' Applied Linguistics Series. In 2017, Anne was recognised by TESOL International as one of 50@50 who had 'made significant contributions to the TESOL profession'.

The Native/Nonnative Conundrum

Péter Medgyes

The idea of separating speakers of English and, by implication, *teachers* of English, into two distinct groups is often met with objections. Linguists reject it on grounds of definitional difficulties (Davies, 1991), countering that although the majority of speakers of English fall into either the native or nonnative category, there are millions of people who may be considered 'in-between cases.' The emergence of the 'English as a Lingua Franca' movement has given fuel to opponents of the separation, too (Jenkins, 2000; Seidlhofer, 2011).

Applied linguists tend to narrow down their focus to the teaching profession. With reference to the term 'native speaker fallacy', Phillipson (1992) challenges the assumption that native speakers are born to be better teachers thanks to their native language competence. In a similar vein, Holliday (2014) draws attention to the risks of 'native speakerism', because it leads to 'othering' teachers from their peers instead of fostering collegial bonding amongst them.

At the same time, nonnative advocacy groups protest against the use of the prefix 'non' in the epithet 'nonnative', contending that on the pretext of linguistic imperfections nonnative teachers are relegated to playing second fiddle in the ELT world (Selvi, 2014). As a hint at the inappropriate use of 'non', the labels 'native speakers' and 'nonnative speakers' are occasionally put in inverted commas. Another strong argument against the separation is that it fuels discriminatory practices against nonnative teachers on the job market (Selvi, 2010).

In an effort to eliminate the two antagonistic terms, alternative labels have been offered, but none of them seems to have taken root in academic or classroom discourse. Pacek may be right in saying that the native/nonnative distinction, in spite of its shortcomings, 'cannot be simply "magicked-away" (2005, p. 243).' Paradoxically, even the most outspoken critics abide by the distinction, as a rule (Moussu & Llurda, 2008).

P. Medgyes (✉)
Department of Language Pedagogy, Eötvös Loránd University, Budapest, Hungary

© Springer Nature Switzerland AG 2021   607
H. Mohebbi and C. Coombe (eds.), *Research Questions in Language Education and Applied Linguistics*, Springer Texts in Education, https://doi.org/10.1007/978-3-030-79143-8_106

Medgyes (1994, 2017) forcefully argues that nonnative English-speaking teachers (non-NESTs) may well offset their 'linguistic deficit' with attributes of which native English-speaking teachers (NESTs) are short. On the basis of empirical studies, he contends that non-NESTs can provide a better model, teach language learning strategies more effectively, supply more information about the English language, anticipate and prevent language difficulties more successfully, show more empathy towards their learners, and benefit from the native language in monolingual classrooms. Using essentially the same research methods, scores of studies have confirmed the above assumptions. Medgyes' conclusion is that professionalism is a multi-variable and highly complex construct, in which linguistic competence is just one, albeit a crucial, component.

Strangely enough, far fewer studies investigated the challenges and difficulties faced by NESTs, especially by those working in foreign countries (Johnston, 1999; Kiss & Medgyes, 2019; Medgyes & Kiss, 2020). Suffice it to say, unfair treatment may work both ways. Therefore, it is of utmost importance that discrimination against either group be abolished and, instead, effective forms of collaboration between the two groups be explored and then implemented.

The Research Questions

1. Speakers of English may be divided into two distinct groups: native speakers and nonnative speakers of English. Are there any 'in-between cases'?
2. Moussu and Llurda claim that 'many so-called native speakers can be far less intelligible in global settings than well-educated proficient [nonnative] speakers'. What do the authors mean?
3. 'Learners are well advised to follow some standard form of native English, such as British, American or Australian.' Does this statement hold true?
4. What special learning strategies and techniques may help non-NESTs improve their English-language proficiency?
5. 'Nonnative teachers should expect their native colleagues to correct them in case they make a language error.' Is this desirable?
6. What are the major professional strengths and weaknesses of non-NESTs in comparison to their native peers?
7. Are there any differences between NESTs and non-NESTs in the way they teach? If there are, what are they?
8 In many school settings, non-NESTs are expected to teach grammar and vocabulary while NESTs are usually assigned pronunciation and conversation classes. Why?
9. Who is better, the NEST or the non-NEST?
10. In what forms can NESTs and non-NESTs work together to complement and support each other?

Suggested Resources

Braine, G. (2010). *Nonnative speaker English teachers: Research, pedagogy, and professional growth.* **New York and London: Routledge.**

A staunch supporter of the 'non-native speaker movement', the author gives a thorough overview of research on non-NESTs, weaving together the different perspectives of the teacher, teacher educator and researcher. He exemplifies his arguments with two case studies: those of a Malaysian teacher from the outer circle and a Chinese from the expanding circle. By juxtaposing the ups and downs of their personal and professional lives, the author aims to 'add depth to the research base on English language teaching' (page 61). He advocates that non-NESTs should engage in collaborative efforts, enhance their language proficiency and make the most of professional organisations. The volume is intermittently turned up by surges of emotion, but the author invariably succeeds in treading a fine line.

Mahboob, A. (Ed.). (2010). *The NNEST lens: Non native English speakers in TESOL.* **Newcastle: Cambridge Scholars Publishing.**

This edited volume examines the NEST/non-NEST conundrum through the lens of multilingualism, multinationalism and multiculturalism. The editor makes no bones about his allegiance to the non-NEST cause when he criticizes the native speaker fallacy, the deficit discourse, as well as the ideological undercurrents of interlanguage and fossilization theories. The credibility of the research included is warranted by the most diverse backgrounds represented by the 21 contributors, both NESTs and non-NESTs. Whereas the volume offers enormous variety in terms of the topics discussed and the approaches adopted, it remains coherent by examining all facets of being a non-NEST through a single lens.

Medgyes, P. (2017). *The non-native teacher (3rd edition).* **Callander: Swan Communication.**

When the first edition of the book was published in 1994, it thrust into the limelight the non-NEST, who had been hidden under the cloak of invisibility despite the fact that at that time, just as today, they were in overwhelming majority in the ELT world. Whereas the book highlighted the problems which derived from the non-NEST's 'less-than-perfect' command of the English language, it sharply focused on the advantages non-NESTs had over their NEST peers in an attempt to raise their self-esteem. This updated and revised edition has the full text of the original edition but added margin notes to give an insight into recent developments and stimulate critical reflection and further debate on the subject.

Moussu, L., & Llurda, E. (2008). Non-native English-speaking English language teachers: History and research. *Language Teaching 41*(3), 315–348.

This is the most comprehensive report on research conducted on the subject of the NEST/non-NEST conundrum, an area of study largely neglected until the early 1990s. The article begins by referring to research that argues against regarding native and nonnative speakers as two clearly distinguishable constituencies. The article then shifts its attention to non-NESTs in particular, reporting on the advantages they are supposed to enjoy over their NEST colleagues in the EFL/ESL classroom. Special chapters are devoted to revealing the attitudes of learners and programme administrators towards non-NESTs, as well as the ways in which their status could be elevated. The final parts of the article describe the diversity of research methods adopted to investigate the subject, and highlight certain areas waiting to be explored in more depth.

Riordan, E. (2018). *Language for teaching purposes: Bilingual classroom discourse and the non-native speaker language teacher.* London: Palgrave Macmillan.

The book discusses issues pertaining to the discourse in which language teachers engage in conducting their classes. It lays special emphasis on non-native speaker teachers of foreign languages, who need added support to offset their potential shortcomings in the foreign language they are destined to teach. Riordan analyses these needs with the aim of informing language teacher training programmes and encouraging further research on the subject. Built on solid empirical base comprising document analysis, teacher trainer interviews, teacher questionnaires and classroom observations, the book is a unique contribution to the field in that it targets non-native speaker teachers of *German* (and not English, as is usually the case), thus broadening the scope of applied linguistic research relating to foreign language education.

References

Davies, A. (1991). *The native speaker in applied linguistics*. University of Edinburgh.
Holliday, A. (2014). 'Native speakerism'. Available at https://www.google.hu/search?q=Holliday+Native+speakerism+2014&oq=holliday+native+speakerism+&aqs=chrome.0. 69i59j69i57j69i60.10203j0j7&sourceid=chrome&ie=UTF-8. Accessed on November 24, 2018.
Jenkins, J. (2000). *The phonology of English as an international language*. Oxford University Press.
Johnston, B. (1999). The expatriate teacher as postmodern paladin. *Research in the Teaching of English, 34*(2), 255–280.
Kiss, T., & Medgyes, P. (2019). The other side of the coin: Native expatriate teachers in focus. *Language Teaching Research Quarterly, 11*, 1–11.
Medgyes, P. (1994). *The non-native teacher*. Macmillan.
Medgyes, P. (2017). *The non-native teacher* (3rd ed.). Swan Communication.

Medgyes, P., & Kiss, T. (2020). Quality assurance and the expatriate native speaker teacher. In J. D. Martinez Agudo (Ed.), *Quality in TESOL and teacher education* (pp. 94–102). Routledge.

Moussu, L., & Llurda, E. (2008). Non-native English-speaking English language teachers: History and research. *Language Teaching, 41*(3), 315–348.

Pacek, D. (2005). Personality not nationality: Foreign students' perceptions of a non-native lecturer of English at a British university. In E. Llurda (Ed.), *Non-native language teachers: Perceptions, challenges and contributions to the profession* (pp. 243–62). Springer.

Phillipson, R. (1992). *Linguistic imperialism*. Oxford University Press.

Seidlhofer, B. (2011). *Understanding English as a lingua franca*. Oxford University Press.

Selvi, A. F. (2010). All teachers are equal, but some teachers are more equal than others: Trend analysis of job advertisements in English language teaching. *WATESOL NNEST Caucus Annual Review, I*, 156–181.

Selvi, A. F. (2014). Myths and misconceptions about the non-native English speakers in TESOL (NNEST) movement. *TESOL Journal, 5*, 573–611.

Péter Medgyes, CBE, is Professor Emeritus of Applied Linguistics and Language Pedagogy at Eötvös Loránd University Budapest. During his career he has been a schoolteacher, teacher trainer, vice president of IATEFL, vice rector, deputy state secretary, and ambassador of Hungary. He has been a plenary speaker in over fifty countries and is the author of numerous articles and books, including *The non-native teacher* (Macmillan, 1994, winner of the Duke of Edinburgh Book Competition), *Laughing matters* (Cambridge University Press, 2002), and *Reflections on foreign language education* (Eötvös Publishing House, 2015). His most recent book is the 3rd edition of *The non-native teacher* (Swan Communication, 2017, shortlisted for the Ben Warren Prize). His main professional interests lie in language policy, teacher education and humour research.

Mónica S. Cárdenas-Claros

Within the research on Computer Assisted Language Learning, studies on Computer-Based Second Language Listening (CBL2L) examine specifically the use of digital applications that take advantage of the computer's ability to provide enhanced input.

In classroom situations, input enhancements are made by the teacher through word translations, definitions, pictures, and scripts of the aural text that are used before or after a listening episode. In multimedia contexts, these enhancements are operationalized as help options or embedded resources of programs that assist learners in performing computing operations and/or support language learning.

CBL2L promotes student-centered learning. In classroom-based listening, language teachers decide the number of times a text should be played, select words students may not be familiar with, and predict particular segments students may find problematic. The potential of CBL2L lies in the control afforded to second language listeners to decide if, when, and how to approach oral texts as they replay, stop, and pause segments; read along from transcripts, subtitles, and captioned materials; access cultural notes; and receive feedback.

Research in CBL2L has evolved from a comparative focus to an examination of features of multimedia that promote listening comprehension, with particular interest given to help options. Research has investigated help option use/non-use, listener attitude towards help option use, frequency of help option use and performance, and help option use and listener variables.

CBL2L research lacks theorizing grounded in L2 acquisition and human–computer-interaction theories. One attempt to address this issue has been the "CoDe" framework, a theoretically—and empirically-based framework for the conceptualization and design of help options. The conceptualization component

M. S. Cárdenas-Claros (✉)
Instituto de Literatura y Ciencias del Lenguaje, Pontificia Universidad Católica de Valparaíso, Viña del Mar, Chile
e-mail: monica.cardenas@pucv.cl

© Springer Nature Switzerland AG 2021   615
H. Mohebbi and C. Coombe (eds.), *Research Questions in Language Education and Applied Linguistics*, Springer Texts in Education,
https://doi.org/10.1007/978-3-030-79143-8_107

("Co") distinguishes four types of help options: operational, regulatory, compensatory, and explanatory. Briefly, operational help options assist the user with the functions of the program (user manual, training modules). Regulatory options afford opportunities for listeners to regulate their learning. They can be used before the listening tasks (listening tips) or after task completion (feedback). With compensatory options, input is modified to make it more accessible to the learner: aural-to-visual (transcript, captions), visual-to-visual (transcripts to translations), and aural-to-aural (rewind-pause-forward buttons). The explanatory options prompt learners' attention to key linguistic features of the input (hyperlinked elements) and provide enriched input (dictionaries, concordancers). The design component ("De") describes design criteria in which help options are easy to use, promote learner control, support guidance, and stimulate learning.

There are many issues with CBL2L that need to be addressed. Teachers' long-lasting fears about listeners' developing entrenching strategies as a result of working in CBL2L are increasingly being dispelled, but we still need to find pedagogical ways to progressively reduce help option support. Another problem concerns learner variables. Although research shows that listeners use help options because they find them relevant for task completion, text comprehension, language learning, and real-life language use, we lack understanding of how learner variables affect CBL2L and how that use translates into improved comprehension and vocabulary acquisition. Another area of concern is CBL2L theorizing. More work establishing links between L2 listening theory and help option research is needed.

The Research Questions

1. How does task design affect listener-computer interaction in computer-based listening activities?
2. How effective is learner training in computer-based listening environments?
3. How do listeners from different language backgrounds use help options in computer-based L2 listening?
4. What patterns of interaction with help options in computer-based L2 listening translate into improved comprehension?
5. Do patterns of interaction with help options in computer-based listening vary across task, text types, or proficiency levels?
6. Is there any correlation between progressive reduction of help options and improved computer-based L2 listening comprehension?
7. Can help option effectiveness be enhanced through collaborative listening activities?
8. How effective is the use of computer-based listening materials in on-line extensive listening projects?

9. How can listening theory from a metacognitive standpoint be linked to help option research?
10. How can help options be conceptualized from a socio-cultural perspective?

Suggested Resources

Cárdenas-Claros, M. S., Campos-Ibaceta, A & Vera-Saavedra, J. (2021). Listeners' patterns of interactions with help options: towards empirically based pedagogy. *Language Learning & Technology*, **25**(2), 111–134.

Using a multiple case study design, in this paper Cárdenas-Claros et al., (2021) identify the patterns of L2 listener interactions with help options presented in the form of listening tips, culture/technology/biology notes, transcripts, glossary, keywords, audio/video control bars, and an online dictionary. The patterns of interaction are identified per section (pre, while and post), type of exercise (vocabulary activation, multiple-choice, dictation-cloze, sentence completion, and extension activity) and per session (1–6). The authors also record student reasons for using these identified patterns and introduce a set of guidelines to inform computer-based L2 listening instruction. The relevance of this work is that it is a first attempt to inform instruction on computer-based listening drawn from empirical research and it responds to multiple calls to link listening theory to computer-based listening.

Hubbard, P. (2017). Technologies for teaching and learning L2 listening. In C. A. Chapelle & S. Sauro (Eds.), *The Handbook of Technology and Second Language Teaching and Learning* **(pp. 93–106). Hoboken, NJ: Wiley Blackwell.**

This up-to-date review by Hubbard (2017) introduces the reader to the field of L2 listening with technologies. It provides a historical overview of how advances in technological affordances for listening have triggered a change in listener behaviors with regards to their comprehension goals. He links SLA theory to help options and explains how such theories have grounded work in computer-based L2 listening. He also remarks on the renewed need of a mindset shift away from questions about the efficacy of affordances and toward a focus on a deeper inquiry about how most to exploit such affordances. The relevance of this work is that it highlights the importance of reflection, encourages training initiatives on help option use, and invites researchers to establish stronger links between listening theory to computer-based L2 listening.

Cross, J. (2017). Help options for L2 listening in CALL: A research agenda. *Language Teaching*, **50**(4), 544–560.

In this paper, Cross (2017) sets out a research agenda for help options in Computer-based L2 listening. He encourages novice researchers to renew interest in help option examinations given the plethora of opportunities in the field as most language learners increasingly rely on online and self-regulated materials. Cross (2017) provides detailed guidelines on how to conduct replication research to expand our research base to understand better if and how listener variables influence comprehension and language learning. This work invites researchers to establish links between metacognition and listening theories, an area ripe for study.

Cárdenas-Claros, M. S., & Gruba, P. A. (2013). Decoding the "CoDe": a framework for conceptualizing and designing help options in computer-based second language listening. *ReCALL*, **25(2), 250–271**.

In this paper, Cárdenas-Claros and Gruba (2013) lay out the "CoDe", a comprehensive framework for the conceptualization and design of help options in computer-based L2 listening. In the conceptualization part of the framework, they present a novel four-part classification of help options grounded in empirical data that explain the help option use/non-use phenomena as viewed from the perspective of language learners. In the design section they discuss how findings relied on participatory design methodologies with language learners, language teachers, and software designers. They present four guidelines to encourage the design of help options that are easy to use, promote learner control, frame guidance, and stimulate language learning. This paper is relevant as baseline research that can be used to expand our understanding of under which conditions help options are more effective.

Montero-Perez, M. M., Van Den Noortgate, W., & Desmet, P. (2013). Captioned video for L2 listening and vocabulary learning: A meta-analysis. *System*, **41(3), 720–739**.

A prolific area of research in computer-based L2 listening has examined the effects of captions for listening comprehension and vocabulary acquisition. In this work, Montero-Perez and colleagues present a solid meta-analysis conducted of 13 journal articles and five doctoral dissertations. The goal of this study, as posited by the authors, was to identify overall caption effectiveness regarding listening comprehension and vocabulary learning as well as to identify the relationship between captioning effectiveness, test type (receptive and productive), and proficiency level. The authors concluded that captioning is a powerful tool for [reinforcing] comprehension of video learning materials and vocabulary learning. They also report that proficiency level was found not to be a moderator of listening comprehension and vocabulary learning.

Mónica S. Cárdenas-Claros has a Ph.D. in Applied Linguistics from the University of Melbourne. She currently works as an Associate Professor at the Instituto de Literatura y Ciencias del Lenguaje at *Pontificia Universidad Católica de Valparaíso* in Chile. Mónica is co-author of a number of articles on help options in computer-based L2 listening, technology integration and blended learning that are published in top-tier CALL journals. She has presented at CALL-research conferences worldwide. Mónica is also the co-author of the book *Blended Language Program Evaluation* (Routledge, 2016) and co-author of a chapter on the flipped classroom in the Routledge Handbook of English Language Teaching. She was recently appointed secretary of the LatinCALL association.

Zohreh R. Eslami and Mahjabin Chowdhury

Game-based learning (GBL) has gained an enormous amount of attention from researchers and practitioners. GBL defines an environment where game content and game play enhance knowledge and skills acquisition, and where game activities include problem solving spaces and challenges that provide learners with a sense of achievement (Qian & Clark, 2016). A number of review studies have researched the effectiveness of game-based learning in various content areas (e.g., Boyle et al., 2014; Connolly et al., 2012; Qian & Clark, 2016). The findings of these reviews indicate GBL can facilitate knowledge acquisition, problem solving skills, critical thinking, creativity, collaboration, and communication.

The intervening variables affecting the success of GBL include academic topic, learner preferences and participant age (Qian & Clark, 2016). Furthermore, the design complexity of the game influences learning and engagement (Young et al., 2012). Educational games with simple designs are narrowly focused on academic content, target low-level literacy, provide drill and practice methods similar to worksheets, and stress memorization of facts, and thus fail to enhance students' motivation and engagement. However, research has revealed that entertainment games are able to promote meaningful learning through providing players with adaptive challenge, inquisitiveness, self-expression, innovation, immediate feedback, clear goals, player control, immersion, collaboration, competition, variable rewards, and low-stakes failure (e.g., Boyle et al., 2014, 2016; Squire, 2011).

Effective game design elements are well aligned with learning theories such as social constructivism (e.g., the sociocultural theory of learning) and can provide situated learning, promote social interactions, increase motivation and engagement, and afford opportunities to develop skills such as collaboration, creativity, com-

Z. R. Eslami (✉) · M. Chowdhury
Educational Psychology, Texas A&M University, College Station, TX, USA
e-mail: zeslami@tamu.edu

Z. R. Eslami
Teaching, Learning, and Culture, Texas A&M University, College Station, TX, USA

© Springer Nature Switzerland AG 2021
H. Mohebbi and C. Coombe (eds.), *Research Questions in Language Education and Applied Linguistics*, Springer Texts in Education,
https://doi.org/10.1007/978-3-030-79143-8_108

munication, and critical thinking (Qian & Clark, 2016; Young et al., 2012). Game designs which feature a blending of established learning theories with game design elements aligned with entertainment games design features, are most likely to lead to effective learning (Qian & Clark, 2016). With regard to game genres, design-based games tend to work better than simply having students play educational or entertainment games.

Games are categorized into different genres including educational (e.g. serious games, simulations, edutainment), entertainment and mobile games. A wide range of learning outcomes (e.g., creativity, critical thinking, collaboration and communication) and age range (pre-elementary-adult) are examined in research on GBL.

Research and review studies on GBL provide sufficient reason to be optimistic about the potential of using a game-based learning approach to promote the skills needed in twenty-first century learning (e.g., creativity, communication, collaboration, critical thinking).

The Research Questions

1. How is GBL different from traditional instructional methods?
2. What learning skills are typically promoted by GBL?
3. What theoretical approaches are used in designing GBL?
4. What are the different types of games and which type has shown to be more effective for skill development? Why?
5. To what extent are effective game designs conducive to developing learners' critical thinking, collaboration, and communication skills?
6. What variables should be considered for the game design to be successful?
7. What are some differences between serious games and entertainment games?
8. How can teachers scaffold GBL to support students' development?
9. What factors should be considered in choosing appropriate games for learners to foster twenty-first century skill development?
10. What do teachers need to know to become a classroom game designer? How can we help teachers to develop such expertise?

Suggested Resources

Jabbari, N., & Eslami, Z. (2019). Second language learning in the context of massively. multiplayer online games: A scoping review. *ReCALL*, *31*(1), 92–113. https://doi.org/10.1017/S0958344018000058.

This scoping review examines the second language acquisition (SLA) literature with regard to the role of "massively multiplayer online games" (MMOGs) in second language (L2) learning. The review mainly focuses on commercially developed off-the-shelf MMOGs. The study reviews the current empirical research to determine which aspects of L2 learning have been examined, how they were investigated, and what the findings propose in relation to L2 learning opportunities and outcomes within and beyond MMOG contexts. The authors synthesized the findings of 31 empirical studies examining the role of MMOGs in L2 learning. Their findings revealed that the empirical research in this area was mainly qualitative and that motivational and affective factors, L2 vocabulary, and learners' communicative competence were the most widely investigated topics. The authors used the findings to present a model that illustrates hypothetical interrelationships among (a) MMOG designed settings, (b) the social and affective affordances present in these settings, (c) L2 learning opportunities, and (d) L2 learning outcomes achieved. The authors conclude that MMOGs offer socially supportive and emotionally safe (i.e. low-language anxiety) environments that offer multiple opportunities for L2 learning and socialization, facilitating L2 learners' enhancement of their L2 vocabulary repertoire and promotion of their communicative competence in the target language.

Boller, S., & Kapp, K. (2017). *Play to learn: Everything You Need to Know About Designing Effective Learning Games*. **Alexandria, VA: ATD Press**.

This book ventures to connect between instructional design and game design. The book presents relevant terminologies, key concepts and strategies from a designer's point of view. The authors guide the reader by explaining instructional and learning goals, creating player identities, and defining the hurdles of the games. Also, the authors exemplify how to align the learning objectives with the game design, mechanics, theme and story. It provides great examples and step-by step advice on creating effective learning games that capture the learners' attention. They provide detailed explanation on three phases of game testing and provide practitioners with strategies to collect crucial feedback from players. The book is full of useful tools for studying commercial games and for designing your own games. The book includes several worksheets to help teachers plan the goal and rules for an educational game.

Farber, M. (2017). *Gamify Your Classroom: A Field Guide to Game-Based Learning (New Literacies and Digital Epistemologies)*. **New York: Peter Lang Publishing Inc**.

This book provides guidelines on how to apply game-based learning in everyday classrooms. It gives an outline of the current theories of gamification, the history of the movement, future predictions, and some new learning platforms developed by leading tech companies. Moreover, the author provides the readers with a plethora of tips, ideas, knowledge, lesson plans, and resources beneficial for both teachers and teacher educators at the end of each chapter. This book presents a highly accessible model for implementing new instructional frameworks using game-based learning.

Becker, K. (2016). *Choosing and using digital games in the classroom: A practical guide.* **Cham, Switzerland: Springer.**

This book displays an in-depth synopsis of the uses of digital games in education, from K-12 up through post-secondary classroom. It begins with a glance at the history of games in education and the setting for the digital games. It provides an overview about the different methods of serious game implementation, including the Magic Bullet Model, which focuses on the player's perspectives of the game experience. This book also discusses how to measure the effects of game-based learning in education and provides guidelines about how to create digital-game based lesson plans. It is a highly useful resource for teachers and practitioners.

De Freitas, S. (2006). *Learning in Immersive Worlds: A review of Game-based Studies.* **London, UK: JISC e-Learning Program.**

This report was produced to inform practitioners who are considering using games and simulations in their practice. The report includes a review of the literature and a series of case studies to illustrate the wide array of uses of games and synthesizes key issues and themes to be considered when learning in immersive worlds. A useful list of findings from the case studies is included in the executive summary at the beginning of the report. Furthermore, this comprehensive report includes productions from a consultation with experts in the field.

References

Boyle, E. A., Hainey, T., Connolly, T. M., Gray, G., Earp, J., Ott, M., & Pereira, J. (2016). An update to the systematic literature review of empirical evidence of the impacts and outcomes of computer games and serious games. *Computers & Education, 94,* 178–192. https://doi.org/10.1016/j.compedu.2015.11.003

Boyle, E. A., MacArthur, E. W., Connolly, T. M., Hainey, T., Manea, M., Karki, A., et al. (2014). A narrative literature review of games, animations and simulations to teach research methods and statistics. *Computers & Education, 74,* 1–14.

Connolly, T. M., Boyle, E. A., MacArthur, E., Hainey, T., & Boyle, J. M. (2012). A systematic literature review of empirical evidence on computer games and serious games. *Computers & Education, 59*(2), 661–686.

Qian, M., & Clark, K. R. (2016). Game-based Learning and 21st century skills: A review of recent research. *Computers in Human Behavior, 63,* 50–58.

Squire, K. (2011). *Video games and learning: Teaching and participatory culture in the digital age.* Teachers College Press.

Young, M. F., Slota, S., Cutter, A. B., Jalette, G., Mullin, G., Lai, B., et al. (2012). Our princess is in another castle: A review of trends in serious gaming for education. *Review of Educational Research, 82,* 61–89.

Zohreh R. Eslami is a Professor at the Department of at Texas A&M University in College Station and currently serves as the Liberal Arts Program Chair at Texas A&M University at Qatar. Her research has examined intercultural and cross-cultural communication, English as an International language, sociocultural perspectives of teaching, acquisition of, and English-medium instruction. Her publications include over one hundred journal papers, book chapters and conference proceedings.

Mahjabin Chowdhury is a Ph.D. student at Texas A&M University in the Department of Teaching, Learning, and Culture (TLAC). Her research interests lie in game-based learning, language learning and technology, and literacy. She currently works as an instructor of record and a teaching assistant for the department. She has presented nationally and internationally and has several publications. Recently she was awarded the Former Students Pooler Scholar (2018–2019) at Texas A&M University.

Digital Genres and Teaching English for Academic Purposes

María José Luzón

In the last decades new technologies have been integrated in the communication practices of disciplinary communities and academics are increasingly using digital genres to conduct research, share their research data and outcomes, interact and discuss knowledge and information, and engage diverse audiences (including public audiences). Since digital genres are changing radically the way academics communicate, the ability to understand and produce the digital genres used by disciplinary communities in an important component of academic literacies.

Digital genres are significantly different from genres existing in other media due to their functionality or technological affordances (Askehave & Nielsen, 2005; Herring, 2013; Shepherd & Watters, 1999). These affordances include, among others, hyperlinking, heightened multimodality, global reach, ease of reusing and remixing textual and visual elements, modularity, interactivity (i.e. audiences' ability to comment and contribute). The affordances of new technologies allow for new production and consumption practices (e.g. they facilitate knowledge co-construction) and enable academics to compose for a diversified audience, blurring the boundaries between experts and lay publics.

Digital genres differ in their origin and the degree to which they exploit technological affordances (Crowston & Williams, 2000; Herring, 2013; Shepherd & Watters, 1999). Some genres result from the migration to the Web of conventional genres and their progressive evolution to adapt to the new medium (e.g. journal articles, digital notebooks); others are web-native genres that exploit Internet affordances more fully to respond to new rhetorical needs. However, all these genres exist on a cline, with no clear boundary between reproduced, adapted and

M. J. Luzón (✉)
Department of English Studies, University of Zaragoza, Zaragoza, Spain
e-mail: mjluzon@unizar.es

© Springer Nature Switzerland AG 2021
H. Mohebbi and C. Coombe (eds.), *Research Questions in Language
Education and Applied Linguistics*, Springer Texts in Education,
https://doi.org/10.1007/978-3-030-79143-8_109

web-native genres, since in the web all genres tend to evolve quickly to adapt to changing contexts: they merge and blend with other genres, incorporate new features, are reformulated, repurposed or reframed in the new medium, and interact with each other and with the repertoire of genres used by disciplinary communities in complex new ways.

Given the dynamism and fluidity of digital genres, they are not amenable to characterization in terms of their linguistic features. However, many of the digital genres used by academics share features that distinguish them from traditional forms of academic communication: more complex interactions between various semiotic modes, prominence of narrative elements, more informal, personal and conversational style, higher engagement with the reader (Rowley-Jolivet & Campagna, 2011).

Digital genres imply, therefore, new academic literacy practices, which should be addressed in English for Academic Purposes (EAP) courses (Hyland & Hamp-Lyons, 2002). This involves covering digital literacy practices, moving beyond the teaching of single genres to focus on multimodality, hybridity and synergies between genres, and making students aware of the web-afforded composition and reception properties of digital genres and of how the use of digital media impacts language use.

The Research Questions

1. How can digital genres for academic communication be characterized and described?
2. How are digital genres related to conventional academic genres and how do they improve them?
3. How do academic genres evolve in the digital medium to respond to new social needs?
4. How do academics compose digital genres to accommodate public audiences and facilitate public participation in science?
5. How is the repertoire of genres used by disciplinary communities changing due to the integration of new technologies?
6. How do various modalities interact to produce meaning in digital genres for academic communication?
7. How do digital genres used by academics interact with each other and with genres in other media?
8. What are the implications that new forms of text production and reception afforded by the Internet have for academic literacy practices and for the teaching of academic genres?
9. What (sets of) digital genres should be focused on in EAP courses?
10. How can EAP teachers raise students' awareness of the purposes and discursive features of digital genres?

Suggested Resources

Campagna, S., Garzone, G., Ilie, C. & Rowley-Jolivet, E. (eds.) (2012). *Evolving Genres in Web-mediated Communication*. **Peter Lang.**

The authors in this volume challenge assumptions about the nature of genre and emphasize the need to extend existing theories and analytical tools to account for the new forms of communication on the Internet. Digital genres are analyzed here taking into account their dynamic, hypertextual, multimodal and participatory nature. The chapters are organized into three sections: the first dealing with websites and other Web 1.0 applications, the second devoted to more participatory Web 2.0 applications (e.g. online laboratory protocols, wikis, memes, and newsgroups) and the last one focusing on blogging and microblogging. The various chapters explore the migration of print genres to the Internet and the connection between these traditional genres and digital genres in various discourse communities, including academia. Two chapters deal with academic genres and are therefore of particular interest for EAP: the chapter by Rowley-Jolivet, which describes the changes in structure, purpose and linguistic expression undergone by the lab protocol when migrating to the web, and the chapter by Sokół, which analyzes how identity is constructed in academic blogs.

Georgakopoulou, A. & Spilioti, T. (eds.) (2015). *The Routledge Handbook of Language and Digital Communication*. **London and New York: Routledge.**

As the editors claim in the introduction, this volume "bring[s] together a collection of state-of-the-art chapters that provide an overview of key issues and current advances in language-focused research on digital communication" (p. 1) and thus shows avenues for research on digital genres. The chapters are organized into seven sections, all of them dealing with topics and issues highly relevant for EAP research and teaching in the twenty-first century, e.g. genres, digital literacies, communication with public audiences, communities, identity construction. The volume showcases different methods to analyze language online and covers various approaches to Computer-Mediated Communication (sociolinguistics, network analysis, digital ethnography, multimodal discourse analysis). In chapter 5, Heyd provides an overview of digital genre analysis and discusses topics that are key to understanding these genres. The other chapters are also useful for EAP researchers, because they deal with important concepts for EAP (e.g. multilingual practices), discuss genres and tools that are increasingly used by academics (e.g. Twitter) or reveal how academic digital genres can be analyzed by using mixed methods and interdisciplinary approaches.

Gross, A. & Buehl, J. (eds.) (2016). *Science and the Internet: Communicating Knowledge in a Digital Age.* **Amityville, New York: Baywood's Technical Communications.**

This is the first book to focus on digital genres for science communications, revealing pathways for research in this field. It consists of 13 chapters, written by leading scholars of rhetoric, which report on case studies illustrating how new technologies are bringing about radical changes in how scientific knowledge is constructed and disseminated. The chapters show how digital genres have transformed communication with peers (e.g. Web-enhanced research articles, new procedures of peer review) and have eroded the boundaries between expert and public audiences, offering new possibilities for public engagement with science and participation in research. By examining how scholars are using new genres to respond to new exigences and reach new audiences, the book offers insights into the new literacy skills that EAP students will need to communicate in the digital era.

Kuteeva, M. & Mauranen, A. (guest editors) (2018). *Discourse, Context & Media: Digital Academic Discourse: Texts and Contexts,* **24,** **1–150.**

This Special Issue brings together two lines of research: genre analysis of academic discourse and literacies research. The five papers in the issue analyze the function and features of digital genres in academic and research settings by focusing on the rhetorical and lexico-grammatical features of such genres and on the literacy practices involved in the production of academic texts with the support of digital media. The articles address how the use of digital technologies shapes academic writing, including collaborative research writing practices, the use of English as a Lingua Franca by multilingual scholars in digital genres, the extended participatory framework afforded by digital media, and the impact of situation and medium factors on the communicative purpose, rhetorical organization and interpersonality resources in digital genres.

Luzón, M. J. & Pérez-Llantada, C. (eds.) (2019). *Science Communication on the Internet: Old Genres Meet New Genres.* **Amsterdam-Philadelphia: John Benjamin Publishing Company.**

Science Communication on the Internet is an edited collection of articles which focus on an essential aspect to understand digital genres for science exchange and communication: their relations and interaction with other genres used by a community. The articles explore the synergies among digital genres and the relationships between digital genres and their printed predecessors. The different chapters, which analyze a variety of digital genres (e.g. the online scientific article, the graphical abstract, hypermodal articles in science magazines, audiovisual genres, peer review genres, citizen science genres), discuss issues central to the fields of academic and scientific communication, which should be considered in the teaching of EAP: multimodality in the communication of scientific knowledge, digital genres for public communication of science, genre remediation and hybridity in digital contexts, the blurring of boundaries between the scientific community and the public, changes in the practices of peer review.

References

Askehave, I., & Nielsen, A. E. (2005). Digital genres: A challenge to traditional genre theory. *Information, Technology & People, 18*, 120–141.

Crowston, K., & Williams, M. (2000). Reproduced and emergent genres of communication on the world wide web. *Information Society, 16*(3), 201–215.

Herring, S. C. (2013). Discourse in Web 2.0: Familiar, reconfigured, and emergent. In D. Tannen & A. M. Tresler (Eds.). *Discourse 2.0: Language and new media* (pp. 1–25). Georgetown University Press.

Hyland, K., & Hamp-Lyons, L. (2002). EAP: Issues and directions. *Journal of English for Academic Purposes, 1*, 1–12.

Rowley-Jolivet, E., & Campagna, S. (2011). From print to Web 2.0: The changing face of discourse for Special Purposes. *LSP Journal, 2*(2), 44–51.

Shepherd, M., & Watters, C. (1999). The functionality attribute of cybergenres. In R. H. Sprague (Ed.), *Proceedings of the Thirty-Second Annual Hawaii International Conference on System Sciences*. Los Alamitos, CA: IEEE Computer Society. http://www.computer.org/cspress/CATALOG/procb.htm

María José Luzón is a Senior Lecturer of English at the University of Zaragoza, Spain, where she teaches courses on academic discourse and language teaching. She has a Ph.D. in English Linguistics and has published papers on academic and professional discourse and on English for Specific Purposes in various internationally refereed journals. She has co-edited books on corpus analysis and digital genres, including *Science Communication on the Internet* (John Benjamins), and has been co-editor of the journal *Miscelánea: A Journal of English and American Studies.* Her current research interests include genre analysis, especially the analysis of online academic genres, English for Academic Purposes and academic literacies. At present she is investigating digital genres used by academics to disseminate their research to diverse audiences.

Nicky Hockly

The last few decades have seen an increased emphasis on the development of 'twenty-first century skills' in education. These include digital literacies, 'the individual and social skills needed to effectively interpret, manage, share and create meaning in the growing range of digital communication channels' (Dudeney et al., 2013: 3). A number of frameworks have been proposed to describe digital literacies. Three frameworks that have particular potential for framing research into digital literacies in second language classrooms are described below.

Gillen (2014) draws on cultural psychology, education, sociology and internet linguistics, and positions digital literacies as dialogic practice. She suggests that digital literacies are socially situated and result from dialogic practices influenced by the wider sociocultural context in which online and offline communication takes place. For Gillen, digital literacies are not a fixed list of skills, but are constantly in flux, 'grounded in people's activities as they participate in diverse kinds of cultural practices' (2014: 31); they develop through individual meaning-making and the creation of identity in online spaces.

Walker and White (2013) propose a framework of 'digital competence' based on Canale and Swain's (1980) model of communicative competence, thus explicitly linking digital literacies to second language acquisition. Their framework consists of four elements: procedural competence (the ability to effectively use hardware and software); socio-digital competence (the ability to use technology and language in online contexts and domains); digital discourse competence (the ability to deploy skills and knowledge to produce digital artefacts); and strategic competence (the ability to repair online communications).

Dudeney et al. (2013, 2018, 2022) suggest a framework for digital literacies with four overlapping areas: communication, information, collaboration and (re-)design. They propose a number of literacies within each area; for example, the focus on

N. Hockly (✉)
The Consultants-E, Swansea, United Kingdom
e-mail: nicky.hockly@theconsultants-e.com

© Springer Nature Switzerland AG 2021
H. Mohebbi and C. Coombe (eds.), *Research Questions in Language Education and Applied Linguistics*, Springer Texts in Education,
https://doi.org/10.1007/978-3-030-79143-8_110

information includes tagging and hashtag literacy, search literacy, information and data literacy, and filtering literacy. Dudeney, Hockly and Pegrum's framework is the most granular of the three discussed here and aims to help language teachers operationalize digital literacies in the classroom by suggesting language teaching activities that support and foreground a range of literacies while focusing on language acquisition. A number of researchers have used this framework to investigate digital literacies within ELT, for example the DigiLanguages project funded by the Irish National Forum for the Enhancement of Teaching and Learning (www.digi-languages.ie), and Swedish pre-service and in-service teacher development programmes (Allen, 2015; Berggren & Allen, 2017).

Critics point to the tendency of research into digital literacies to focus on well-resourced contexts (e.g. Walton, 2007), or the potential negative or 'toxic' effects of ever more technologies in the classroom (e.g. Palmer, 2006). However, it is widely accepted that digital literacies need to be overtly taught, and that learners who grow up with digital technologies are not automatically effective users of these technologies. For example, a large-scale comparative study into digital literacies around the world, involving sixty thousand 13- to 14-year-old students in 21 countries and education systems, found low levels of digital competence across the board (Fraillon et al., 2013).

The Research Questions

1. What are the key digital literacies for learners in your context?
2. What are the key digital literacies for teachers in your context?
3. How digitally literate are teachers in your context?
4. How digitally literate are learners in your context?
5. How important are teachers' digital literacies in supporting the development of learners' digital literacies?
6. How are digital literacies curricula developed by education ministries operationalised in classrooms in your context? Is there a gap between theory and practice, and if so, what are the effects of this?
7. What approach(es) are most effective in assessing learners' digital literacies in your context?
8. How effective is Dudeney et al. (2018) revised framework of digital literacies in developing learners' digital literacies in your context?
9. What effect(s) do learners' ages have on the teaching and/or learning of digital literacies in schools?
10. What effect(s) do learners' out of school digital practices have on the teaching and/or learning of digital literacies in schools?

Suggested Resources

Dudeney, G., Hockly, N., & Pegrum, M. (2013, 2022). *Digital Literacies.* **London: Routledge.**

This volume reviews the educational and media theory that informs current understandings of digital literacies and provides a detailed theoretical framework for operationalizing digital literacies in the second language classroom. The book provides a rationale for integrating these skills into classroom practice as well as the background for a deeper understanding of these key twenty-first century skills. It includes practical activities to help learners and teacher develop digital literacies in tandem with key language skills, as well as a consideration of how to integrate digital literacies into the English language syllabus in a principled manner, and how to assess them. It can provide a framework for researchers wishing to investigate this topic with learners in the language classroom.

Dudeney, G., Hockly, N., & Pegrum, M. (2018). Digital literacies revisited. *The European Journal of Applied Linguistics and TEFL, 7 (2),* 3–24.

This paper reviews and updates the original digital literacies framework described in Dudeney, Hockly and Pegrum's *Digital Literacies* (2013). The original framework was revised in light of ongoing technological developments such as the continued rise of mobile technologies, augmented reality and virtual reality interfaces, coding and robotics, big data and learning analytics. In addition, the revised framework is informed by sociopolitical developments such as increasing superdiversity coupled with a countertrend of resistance to globalisation, and the need in this context for a more critical perspective on our technologies and the information and communication channels they offer. The article further substantiates the original framework in light of recent developments, while extending its existing categories to take into account our evolving contexts.

Fraillon, J., Ainley, J., Schulz, W., Friedman, T., & Gebhardt, E. (2013). Preparing for life in a digital age. *The IEA International Computer and Information Literacy Study International Report.* **Springer Open: Springer International Publishing AG Switzerland.**

This paper describes a large-scale study into the state of learners' digital literacies around the world. Carried out by the International Association for the Evaluation of Educational Achievement (IEA), an independent consortium of national research agencies, sixty thousand 13 to 14-year-old students in 3300 schools in 21 education systems or countries were surveyed, with additional data collected from 25,000 teachers, school principals, and school ICT coordinators. The study included a focus on using technology to investigate, create and communicate. The study also considered the impact of student characteristics, and home and school context, on levels of computer literacy. Results showed relatively low levels of digital literacy, and additional factors (e.g. students' expected educational attainment, parents' educational level and profession, among others) affected results across most education systems. The study is significant for its scope, investigate approach and robust methodology.

Gillen, J. (2014). *Digital literacies.* **London: Routledge.**

Gillen's view of digital literacies as emerging dialogic practice is laid out in this book. Adopting a sociocultural ethnographic perspective, she suggested literacies are socially situated, and posits a theoretical framework for understanding digital literacies that takes into account the idea that knowledge is built through activity, and that meaning-making is achieved within and through digital practices. Key to her conceptualisation of digital literacies is the importance of individual agency, how agency is created and performed online, and how digital environments can provide spaces for ongoing learning. In this book, she analyses language in a number of communicative digital environments through a case study approach. Her theoretical framework provides a useful starting point for researchers wishing to investigate digital literacies through case studies.

Walker, A., & White, G. (2013). *Technology enhanced language learning: Connecting theory and practice.* **Oxford: Oxford University Press.**

Walker and White's framing of digital competence within Canale and Swain's (1980) model of communicative competence provides a useful link between digital literacies and second language acquisition. The four elements of their framework (procedural competence, socio-digital competence, digital discourse competence, and strategic competence) provide another framework for researchers to test, with opportunities to align the framework to specific communicative linguistic competences.

References

Allen, C. (2015). Marriages of convenience? Teachers and coursebooks in the digital age. *ELT Journal, 69*, 249–263.

Berggren, J., & Allen, C. (2017). The assessment of digital project work in the EFL classroom. Paper presented at *EuroCALL,* Southhampton, Aug. 23–26.

Canale, M., & Swain, M. (1980). Theoretical bases of communicative approaches to second language teaching and testing. *Applied Linguistics, 1*(1), 1–47.

Dudeney, G., Hockly, N., & Pegrum, M. (2013, 2022). *Digital literacies.* Routledge.

Dudeney, G., Hockly, N., & Pegrum, M. (2018). Digital literacies revisited. *The European Journal of Applied Linguistics and TEFL, 7*(2), 3–24.

Fraillon, J., Ainley, J., Schulz, W., Friedman, T., & Gebhardt, E. (2013). Preparing for life in a digital age. *The IEA International Computer and Information Literacy Study International Report.* Springer Open: Springer International Publishing AG Switzerland.

Gillen, J. (2014). *Digital literacies.* Routledge.

Palmer, S. (2006). *Toxic childhood: How the modern world is damaging our children and what we can do about it.* Orion Books.

Walker, A., & White, G. (2013). *Technology enhanced language learning: Connecting theory and practice*. Oxford University Press.

Walton, M. (2007). Cheating literacy: The limitations of simulated classroom discourse in educational software for children. *Language and Education, 21*(3), 197–215.

Nicky Hockly is Director of Pedagogy of The Consultants-E (www.theconsultants-e.com), an award-winning online training and development organisation. She is an educational consultant, teacher, trainer and international plenary speaker, and she gives workshops and training courses for teachers all over the world. Nicky writes regular columns on technology for teachers' magazines and journals, and she has also written many articles and several prize-winning methodology books about digital technologies in language teaching. Her most recent books include *Digital Literacies* (2013), *Going Mobile* (2014), *Focus on Learning Technologies* (2016), and *ETPedia Technology* (2017). Her research interests include blended and online learning, as well as the integration of learning technologies in the face-to-face English language classroom.

Exploring the Potential of Social Media in SLA: Issues, Affordances and Incentives

Liam Murray and Marta Giralt

Technology in the form of Social Media (SM) is reinventing how humans interact with and learn from one another. Given the presence and important role that SM plays in our lives, the use of this Internet-based application has been used for learning purposes and its application is increasing extensively. There is a growing body of research on SM in the area of CALL with multiple examples and research evidence of how the use of SM can enhance language learning (Lamy & Zorou, 2013), and in related research fields, such as virtual games (Murray et al., 2018). We understand SM as "a group of Internet-based applications that build on the ideological and technological foundations of Web 2.0, which allows the creation and exchange of user-generated content" (Kaplan & Haenlein, 2012: 61).

The use of SM among language learners becomes very relevant when we take into account that SM is userg-enerated content, creating a space for the learner to produce in the target language as well as to share, interact and create content collaboratively with other users/language learners. Echoing some socio-constructivist theories (Mondahl & Razmerita, 2014; Vygotsky, 1978), platforms such as *Facebook* may be a clear example on how SM enhances language learning as it prompts interaction between users, benefits relationship building and establishes a sense of belonging (Kabilan et al., 2010).

Other examples of how SM promotes SLA are blogs, which have been used for many years with language learning purposes (Hourigan & Murray, 2010), *Twitter*, *Wechat* (Zhang, 2018) or *Instagram*. Research suggests that SM may also contribute to the development of sociolinguistic and intercultural competences which may be improved via communication and collaboration (Borau et al., 2009).

L. Murray (✉) · M. Giralt
School of Modern Languages & Applied Linguistics, University of Limerick,
Limerick, Ireland
e-mail: Liam.Murray@ul.ie

M. Giralt
e-mail: Marta.Giralt@ul.ie

© Springer Nature Switzerland AG 2021
H. Mohebbi and C. Coombe (eds.), *Research Questions in Language Education and Applied Linguistics*, Springer Texts in Education,
https://doi.org/10.1007/978-3-030-79143-8_111

On the negative front, the use of SM may produce some challenges. Wise et al. (2011) claim that *Facebook* has very limited potential, if any, to engage students on an academic level, as well as raising privacy issues. Others point out that SM is inherently distractive (Benini et al., 2018), a focus disruptor (Rosen et al., 2013) and heavily interferes with student study time (Giralt et al., 2017). In sum, SM carries much potential both inside and outside the classroom setting, and if embraced, then the teacher should be sufficiently digitally literate (Dudeney & Hockly, 2016) to manage the issues and exploit the affordances.

The Research Questions

1. How do you define the current elements that make up Social Media?
2. What criteria do you include when evaluating Social Media for language learning purposes?
3. What disadvantages exist in using Social Media for language learning?
4. Which Social Media suit better the practice of the different intralingual skills?
5. To what extent are language teachers digitally literate?
6. How can SM promote the development of sociolinguistic competence?
7. How can SM promote the development of intercultural skills?
8. What is the role of the teacher when using SM in the language classroom?
9. What challenges do teachers face in using Social Media in their language teaching?
10. How much peer to peer and teacher-learner collaboration is involved in employing Social Media in language learning environments?

Suggested Resources

Rosell-Aguilar, F. (2018). Twitter as a formal and informal language learning tool: from potential to evidence. In F. Rosell-Aguilar, T. Beaven, & M. Fuertes Gutiérrez (Eds), *Innovative language teaching and learning at university: integrating informal learning into formal language education* **(pp. 99–106). Research-publishing.net.** https://doi.org/10.14705/rpnet.2018.22.780.

This researcher has a long history in CALL research and his chapter here offers a wide overview of the evidence-based potential of *Twitter* as a language learning tool and discusses a number of various studies in support of using *Twitter* in different language learning environments. Rosell-Aguilar correctly stresses the multimodal qualities of *Twitter* as it is typically and erroneously perceived as being a text-driven medium. He shows how *Twitter* can be used to livestream videos and make links available to audio and video resources, be they produced by learners or teachers alike. He presents examples of *Twitter* use for language acquisition as input (both linguistic and cultural), output (writing and speaking) and interaction with peers, native speakers, teachers and chatbots or virtual assistants. He concludes by recognising the proven potential of *Twitter* in formal contexts and calls for additional research into how *Twitter* may be used in more informal settings.

Dudeney, G., & Hockly, N. (2016). Literacies, technology and language teaching in Farr, F. & Murray, L (Eds), *The Routledge handbook of language learning and technology*, **Oxford, UK, pp. 115–121**.

Dudeney and Hockly explore the concepts behind digital literacies and their application in the language learning classroom. They begin with a short overview of the history of digital literacies and go on to offer a taxonomy of these new literacies. In their highly practical and applied exploration of these 'twenty-first century skills', they elaborate on traditional understandings of digital literacies to include an awareness of social practices in an expanded classification which is directly relevant to the classroom. They examine how teachers might introduce digital literacies into their pedagogic practice and demonstrate this with a number of practical classroom activities. It is well worth considering this important chapter and investigating how essential these digital literacies are and how they will need further expansion and updating as technologies, and thus inevitably, language learner practices evolve and change.

Al-Ali, S. (2014). Embracing the Selfie Craze: Exploring the Possible Use of Instagram as a Language mLearning Tool. *Issues and Trends in Educational Technology*, **2(2), University of Arizona Libraries**.

Beginning with a brief history and examples of Social Media, Al-Ali shows how *Instagram* rapidly became hugely popular around the entire world even though it has only existed since 2010. The researcher's article describes an action research methodology that attempted to integrate *Instagram* as a successful mobile learning tool in a language bridge programme. He asked learners in two pre-intermediate/intermediate ESL classes to use the various functions of *Instagram* in order to produce a holiday project and two writing activities. Quite interestingly, his results from the study indicate that although students were not enthusiastic with the initiative at the very beginning of the project, they eventually warmed to the idea and were actively encouraged to be creative in completing their writing tasks. In his conclusions, the researcher offers some sound guidelines for improving the integration of *Instagram* as a learning tool in language classrooms.

James, R. (2012). '*Social Media: Brilliant Tool or Distraction?***' [online] Available at:** https://edtechdigest.wordpress.com/2012/12/18/social-media-brilliant-tool-or-distraction/ **[Accessed 31st Oct 2018]**.

In this short, informative and balanced article, James (a secondary school teacher and technophile) argues that because Social Media has now become an integral part of nearly everyone's daily life, there exists a huge potential for distraction, difficulty in switching off from Social Media (a form of addiction) and low productivity. He highlights, in particular, the dangers for younger generations in becoming incapable of maintaining a decent level of concentration. On the other hand, he also points out several advantages to using social media in teaching and learning scenarios. He lists studies that show how the brain's ability to create new social relationships and boost interaction is improved. As with everything, he cautions for moderation in use and underlines how we should be teaching the practical uses of social media as well as "its cultural significance, rather than just demonising it as a distracting source of pleasure".

Lamy, M., & Zourou, K. (Eds.). (2013). *Social networking for language education***. Cham: Springer.**

Editors Lamy and Zourou have put together ten chapters from a range of notable researchers in a volume that seeks to examine if and how social networking may promote language learning. The different chapters focus on a number of insightful theoretical insights and they also offer empirical data gleaned from a variety of methodological approaches. This highly informative and diverse book raises important issues such as the relationship between social networking, language learning and teaching, and how socialisation (see James's article above) within social media may contribute to language acquisition. The complete volume is made up of four sections, entitled 'The Wider Ecology of Language Learning with SNS [Social Networking Sites]', 'Pedagogies and Practitioners', 'Learning Benefits and Challenges', and 'Overview'.

References

Benini, S., Giralt, M., & Murray, L. (2018). RTE Brainstorm, *Just how much Social Media is enough?* https://www.rte.ie/eile/brainstorm/2018/0601/967562-just-how-much-of-social-media-is-enough/

Borau, K., Ullrich, C., Feng, J., & Shen, R. (2009). 'Microblogging for language learning: Using twitter to train communicative and cultural competence.' In *International Conference on Web-based Learning* (pp. 78–87). Springer.

Dudeney, G., & Hockly, N. (2016). Literacies, technology and language teaching. In F. Farr, L. Murray (Eds.), *The Routledge handbook of language learning and technology* (pp. 115–121). Routledge.

Giralt, M., Benini, S., & Murray, L. (2017). Is attractive the new distractive? Distractive technologies and student performance: an investigation of language learners experiences, perceptions and awareness. *EUROCALL 2017. CALL in a climate of change*, Southampton, UK, 23-Aug-17 to 26-Aug-17.

Hourigan, T., & Murray, L. (2010). Using blogs to help language students to develop reflective learning strategies: Towards a pedagogical framework. *Australasian Journal of Educational Technology, 26*(2), 209–225.

Kabilan, M. K., Ahmad, N., & Abidin, M. J. Z. (2010). Facebook: An online environment for learning of English in institutions of higher education? *The Internet and Higher Education, 13*(4), 179–187.

Kaplan, A. M., & Haenlein, M. (2012). Social media: Back to the roots and back to the future. *Journal of Systems and Information Technology, 14*(2), 101–104.

Lamy, M., & Zourou, K. (Eds.). (2013). *Social networking for language education*. Springer.

Mondahl, M., & Razmerita, L. (2014). Social media, collaboration and social learning: A case-study of foreign language learning. *Electronic Journal of e-Learning, 12*(4), 339–352.

Murray, L., Buckley, J., DeWille, T., Exton, C., & Exton, G. (2018). A Gamification–motivation design framework for educational software developers. *Journal of Educational Technology Systems*, 0047239518783153.

Rosen, L. D., Carrier, L. M., & Cheever, N. A. (2013). Facebook and texting made me do it: Media-induced task-switching while studying. *Computers in Human Behavior, 29*(3), 948–958.

Vygotsky, L. S. (1978). *Mind in society: The development of higher psychological processes.* Harvard University Press.

Wise, L. Z., Skues, J., & Williams, B. (2011). Facebook in higher education promotes social but not academic engagement. In *Changing demands, changing directions* (pp. 1332–1342). *Proceedings Ascilite Hobart.*

Zhang, D. (2018). *Exploring language learning via social media beyond the classroom: A case for WeChat.* https://ollren.org/ld.php?content_id=44788661

Liam Murray is a Senior Lecturer in French and Language Technologies in the School of Modern Languages and Applied Linguistics at the University of Limerick, Ireland and teaches courses on CALL, digital games-based language learning, French civilization, e-learning and evaluation at both undergraduate and postgraduate levels. Areas of research interest include CALL, Games-Based Learning and the application of Social Media and blog writing to second language acquisition. Since 1991, he has contributed many articles and book chapters on these research areas, publishing in journals such as *AJET, System, Eludamos, Educational Media International, Recall,* and *Learning, Media and Technology.* Academic homepage: https://ulsites.ul.ie/mlal/node/8101.

Marta Giralt has been a lecturer in Applied Linguistics and Spanish at the University of Limerick since 2015. She teaches ICT and Languages, Intercultural Communication and Spanish. Her research interests are in Applied Linguistics, in particular, Second Language Acquisition and Oral Language, ICT and Language Learning, and Intercultural Communication. In 2007 she was awarded first prize in the II Premio Cristobal de Villalón for Pedagogic Innovation at the Universidad de Valladolid, Spain. She has participated in several projects involving ICT and is currently researching the pedagogic potential Virtual Exchanges in Second Language Acquisition. Academic homepage: https://ulsites.ul.ie/mlal/dr-marta-giralt-0.

Genre-based Automated Writing Evaluation

Elena Cotos

Genre-based automated writing evaluation (GBAWE) is an emergent domain of inquiry and praxis motivated by the need to assist students in advanced writing contexts to acquire the specialized discourses of their target disciplinary communities. It involves the design and pedagogical use of digital writing tools that analyze and generate automated feedback on texts based on the communicative conventions of the genre they pertain to. Unlike traditional AWE (See Cotos, 2018), GBAWE feedback is generally operationalized to reflect the formal characteristics of genres as theorized in the field of English for Specific Purposes (ESP) (Bhatia, 2004; Swales, 1990). In other words, the feedback focuses on communicative goals called 'moves' and functional strategies called 'steps,' which are conventionalized rhetorical forms that both constitute and reproduce genres.

Pioneering examples of GBAWE were developed for the abstracts (Anthony & Lashkia, 2003) and introductions (Cotos, 2011) of the research article genre. Automated analysis of these part-genres was based on the create-a-research-space (CARS) moves—establishing a territory, establishing a niche, and occupying the niche (Swales, 1981, 1990, 2004). The CARS moves, validated in ESP genre studies and widely adopted by teachers, continued to serve as the foundation for new developments. For example, a cross-disciplinary framework for Introduction, Methods, Results, and Discussion/Conclusions was applied to generate automated move and step-level feedback on individual sentences as well as discipline-specific, goal-orienting feedback on a student's entire draft (Cotos, 2016; Cotos et al., 2015). In a similar vein, rhetorically salient sentences are highlighted for feedback on analytical, argumentative, reflective essay genres (Gibson et al., 2017; Knight et al., 2018).

While essentially grounded in ESP, GBAWE crosses disciplinary boundaries within applied linguistics and beyond. Theoretically, it intersects with perspectives

E. Cotos (✉)
English/Applied Linguistics and Technology, Iowa State University, Ames, IA, USA
e-mail: ecotos@iastate.edu

© Springer Nature Switzerland AG 2021
H. Mohebbi and C. Coombe (eds.), *Research Questions in Language
Education and Applied Linguistics*, Springer Texts in Education,
https://doi.org/10.1007/978-3-030-79143-8_112

on genre in systemic functional linguistics and rhetoric. When designed for use by language learners, it accounts for theoretical tenets in second language acquisition. Operationally, the feedback affordances are possible due to methods in computational linguistics, natural language processing, and machine learning. In terms of practical uses, connections extend to writing pedagogy, computer-assisted language learning, and more broadly to writing and learning analytics.

Considering that it builds on scholarship and praxis in different fields, the advancement of GBAWE thus calls for an interdisciplinary research agenda. Studies providing comprehensive descriptions of the rhetorical, functional, linguistic, and content realizations of a wider range of genres and discourse communities (e.g., Cotos, 2019) still need to feed into the design of new systems. Computational models for automated analysis and feedback need to be trained, evaluated, and augmented for improved accuracy (e.g., Cotos, forthcoming; Fiacco et al., 2019). Most importantly, practical uses of GBAWE (e.g., Cotos et al., 2017; Shibani et al., 2019) need to be investigated to understand the factors that may enhance or inhibit the development of genre writing competence, and to generate guidelines for effective pedagogical implementation. Few GBAWE exemplars are available to date; therefore, this is an area ripe for investigation and scalability. The general directions that need to be pursued as points of departure include principled design, feedback generation and optimization, usefulness for genre-based writing pedagogy, and impact on genre knowledge and writing competence.

The Research Questions

1. To what extent can GBAWE feedback accurately reflect students' genre writing competence?
2. How helpful is GBAWE for revision practice and genre writing improvement?
3. How do students use GBAWE, and what strategies are most effective?
4. What kind of and how much training do students and teachers need to use GBAWE effectively?
5. How can teachers assess the effectiveness of GBAWE implementations in their classrooms?
6. What are the strengths and limitations of GBAWE compared to other digital writing technologies, and how can different strands of research on feedback, usefulness, and impact address limitations and further inform the advancement of GBAWE?
7. How can we most appropriately operationalize genre constructs to design 'actionable' GBAWE feedback; i.e., feedback that provides the guidance needed for improvement in genre writing?
8. How can the functionality and output of GBAWE engines be evaluated and interpreted in meaningful ways for teachers and students?

9. How can different theories, research results, and practical needs be best integrated in the design of GBAWE for a range of target contexts?
10. What principles should be developed to scale GBAWE from individual genres to genre systems spanning different contexts and discourse communities?

Suggested Resources

Anthony, L., & Lashkia, G. (2003). Mover: A machine learning tool to assist in the reading and writing of technical papers. *IEEE Transactions on Professional Communication*, **46(3), 185–193**.

This paper describes the approach to developing the first genre-based automated analysis tool called the Mover. While not conceptualized as a feedback tool, it was intended to assist novices with their reading and writing in science and engineering related fields by presenting the move structure of texts based on a modified *create-a-research-space (CARS)* model. Explicitly linking to the interdisciplinary field of machine learning, Anthony and Lashkia comprehensibly and accessibly describe the process of designing the Mover as a learning system. In short, the Mover was trained to 'learn' the moves from a collection of abstracts, to apply the information learned to the automatic identification of moves in a new text, and then to display the moves associated with each sentence to the user. To determine the degree to which the Mover could be confidently used in the classroom, it was evaluated in terms of accuracy of automated analysis and usefulness for reading and writing tasks in a classroom context. This work served as proof-of-concept for automated genre analysis and laid the foundation for GBAWE.

Cotos, E. (2014). *Genre-based automated writing evaluation for L2 research writing: From design to evaluation and enhancement.* **Basingstoke, UK: Palgrave Macmillan**.

This book launches the notion of GBAWE, proposing it as a novel approach to enhancing academic writing pedagogy for second language (L2) writers. Cotos argues for the importance of connecting teaching and learning needs with theoretical premises and research findings and introduces a new conceptual model for GBAWE design grounded in theoretical and operational frameworks. The theoretical framework includes genre theory, systemic functional linguistics, second language acquisition and skill acquisition theories. The operational framework allows for the integration and actualization of the different theoretical tenets drawing on research in formative assessment, intelligent computer-assisted learning, and evidence-centered design. Showcasing how this model guided the development, implementation, and evaluation of a prototype tool, Cotos further explains how empirical evidence derived from a study with mixed and triangulated methods informed scaling up from the prototype to a full-fledged system—the Research Writing Tutor (RWT). Apart from demonstrating how specific needs can be attended to through GBAWE, this book offers critical reviews of genre-based pedagogies, cognitive and socio-disciplinary dimensions of research writing competence, and state-of-the art of automated writing evaluation technology.

Cotos, E. (2016). Computer-assisted research writing in the disciplines. In S. A. Crossley & D. S. McNamara (Eds.), *Adaptive educational technologies for literacy instruction* **(pp. 225–242). NY: Taylor & Francis, Routledge**.

The chapter in this volume has three main foci: theoretical, descriptive, and evaluative. In the first part, GBAWE is situated within a theoretical landscape where ESP genre theory and cognitive writing theories are presented in a symbiotic relationship with regard to research writing competence. From the perspective of cognitive writing models, novice writers need to practice and improve their revision skills in order to move from knowledge-telling *to* expert-like knowledge-transformation in their writing. Considering that, the second part of the chapter elaborates on how GBAWE can create conditions for revision practice through the example of RWT. Here, this system is described as integrating genre and disciplinary conventions in a platform for independent writing and revision practice enabled by its interactive modules with feedback and corpus-based scaffolding affordances. The third part shifts to a review of studies investigating implementations of RWT in English for academic purposes contexts. Research results indicate the potential of the feedback to activate novice researchers' higher-order thinking processes and strategies during revision, foster their knowledge of rhetorical conventions, improve genre writing quality, and have a positive impact on their motivation.

Cotos, E., & Pendar, N. (2016). Discourse classification into rhetorical functions for AWE feedback. *CALICO Journal*, **33(1), 92–116**.

This article will be useful to those interested in knowing how GBAWE feedback is generated by combining genre analysis and machine learning. The authors present an accessible description of the approach adopted in the development of the automated analysis engine of RWT. The readers are first acquainted with natural language processing and machine learning approaches to automated discourse categorization as well as with implementations in computer-assisted writing tools. Following this overview, the method by which RWT categorizes sentences in student texts into rhetorical moves is described. First, a corpus was manually annotated with moves and steps. Then, linguistic features indicative of rhetorical functions were extracted. Sentences were represented as vectors in two-dimensional planes, and supervised vector machine models were trained to classify sentences into moves and steps. The authors report measures of accuracy for all the moves and steps, discussing the challenges of the genre classification task and proposing techniques for improving the performance of the analytic models that generate feedback.

Knight, S., Buckingham Shum, S., Ryan, P., Sándor, Á., & Wang, X. (2018). Designing academic writing analytics for civil law student self-assessment. *International Journal of Artificial Intelligence in Education*, **28(1), 1–28**.

This is a classic example of interdisciplinary work by collaborators in learning analytics, linguistics, natural language processing, software development, and the target discipline. The team describes the process of designing and evaluating the Academic Writing Analytics (AWA) tool intended to provide formative feedback to undergraduate students. While not explicitly positioned in relation to GBAWE, AWA was developed to assist students in an English for specific purposes context who need to master a civil law genre. Also, its feedback is generated based on parsing students' drafts into rhetorically-salient sentences, which are closely associated with Swales' (1990) rhetorical moves. After a comprehensive description of the participatory design process through which the parsing engine was tested and refined, the authors report student data that substantiates the usefulness of AWA and also reveal limitations to be addressed in future work. Importantly, they emphasize the need to make writing analytics transparent to different stakeholders.

References

Anthony, L., & Lashkia, G. (2003). Mover: A machine learning tool to assist in the reading and writing of technical papers. *IEEE Transactions on Professional Communication, 46*(3), 185–193.

Bhatia, V. K. (2004). *Worlds of written discourse: A genre-based view*. London: Continuum.

Cotos, E. (2011). Potential of automated writing evaluation feedback. *CALICO Journal, 28*(2), 420–459.

Cotos, E. (2016). Computer-assisted research writing in the disciplines. In S. A. Crossley & D. S. McNamara (Eds.), *Adaptive educational technologies for literacy instruction* (pp. 225–242). Taylor & Francis, Routledge.

Cotos, E. (2018). Automated writing evaluation. In J. I. Liontas (Ed.), *The TESOL Encyclopedia of English language teaching*. Wiley.

Cotos, E. (2019). Articulating societal benefits in grant proposals: Move analysis of broader impacts. *English for Specific Purposes Journal, 54*, 15–34.

Cotos, E. (forthcoming). Towards a validity argument for genre-based AWE. In J. Xu & G. Yu (Eds.), *Language test validation in a digital age*. Cambridge Assessment English and Cambridge University Press.

Cotos, E., Huffman, S., & Link, S. (2015). Furthering and applying move/step constructs: Technology-driven marshalling of Swalesian genre theory for EAP pedagogy. *Journal of English for Academic Purposes, 19*, 52–72.

Cotos, E., Link, S., & Huffman, S. (2017). Effects of DDL technology on genre learning. *Language Learning and Technology Journal, 21*(3), 104–130.

Fiacco, J., Cotos, E., & Rose, C. (2019). Towards enabling feedback on rhetorical structure with neural sequence models. In *Proceedings of the 9th International Conference on Learning Analytics & Knowledge* (pp. 310–319). ACM Press.

Gibson, A., Aitken, A., Sándor, Á., Buckingham Shum, S., Tsingos-Lucas, C. & Knight, S. (2017). Reflective writing analytics for actionable feedback. In *Proceedings of the 7th International Conference on Learning Analytics & Knowledge* (pp. 153–162). ACM Press.

Knight, S., Buckingham Shum, S., Ryan, P., Sándor, Á., & Wang, X. (2018). Designing academic writing analytics for civil law student self-assessment. *International Journal of Artificial Intelligence in Education, 28*(1), 1–28.

Shibani, A., Knight, S., & Buckingham Shum, S. (2019). Contextualizable learning analytics design: A generic model, and writing analytics evaluations. In *Proceedings of the 9th International Conference on Learning Analytics & Knowledge* (pp. 210–219). ACM Press.

Swales, J. M. (1981). *Aspects of articles introductions* (p. 1). The University of Aston in Birmingham.

Swales, J. M. (1990). *Genre analysis: English in academic and research settings.* Cambridge University Press.

Swales, J. M. (2004). *Research genres.* Cambridge University Press.

Elena Cotos is an Associate Professor of Applied Linguistics and the Director of the Center for Communication Excellence at Iowa State University, USA. Her scholarship focuses on genre-based automated writing evaluation, corpus-based genre analysis and pedagogy, and computer-assisted language learning and assessment. She authored *Genre-based automated writing evaluation for L2 research writing* (2014). Her contributions appeared in different journals (e.g., *ESPJ, JEAP, LLT, ReCALL, CALICO, IJCALLT, Writing & Pedagogy*) and edited volumes (e.g., C. A. Chapelle (Ed.), *The Encyclopedia of Applied Linguistics* (2018), J. I. Liontas (Ed.); *The TESOL Encyclopedia of English Language Teaching* (2018); C. Chapelle & S. Sauro (Eds.), *The Handbook of Technology in Second Language Teaching* (2017, Wiley Blackwell); S. A. Crossley & D. S. McNamara (Eds.), *Adaptive educational technologies for literacy instruction* (2016)).

Jacqueline S. Stephen

Institutions of higher education have maintained that offering online courses is critical to their long-term strategy and continuous growth (Allen et al., 2016). Moreover, the Babson Survey Research Group's 2018 report revealed that enrollment in online courses is on the rise and the number of U.S. students enrolled in at least one online course has increased by 5.6% (Seaman, Allen, & Seaman, 2018). As a result of this increase in enrollment and anticipated growth, there is a need for online instructors at higher education institutions to teach online (Allen & Seaman, 2015). Despite the demand in online courses, instructors who have traditionally taught face-to-face may not be ready to embrace this change. A challenge that higher education institutions may face is the readiness, preparedness, and overall motivation of individual instructors to undergo the transformation from teaching face-to-face to the online learning environment. While some faculty professional development programs emphasize technical skills, it is imperative that an attempt is made to further understand other needs instructors may have to better prepare them for the online teaching environment. The rapid proliferation of online courses at higher education institutions necessitates a better understanding of instructor readiness to transform traditional teaching practices into effective methods for online course design and delivery. A greater understanding of what inspires traditional face-to-face instructors to acquire the knowledge and skills necessary for online course design and delivery and migrate to online teaching is fundamental.

In addition to its aforementioned findings about growth in online learning, the Babson Survey Research Group's 2016 survey also revealed that many instructors are resistant to online teaching and skeptical of it altogether (Allen et al., 2016).

J. S. Stephen (✉)
College of Professional Advancement, Mercer University Instructional Designer & Director of the Office of Distance Learning Assistant Professor, Mercer University, Atlanta, GA, USA

J. S. Stephen
Department of Leadership Studies, Human Resources Administration and Development, Mercer University, Atlanta, GA, USA

© Springer Nature Switzerland AG 2021
H. Mohebbi and C. Coombe (eds.), *Research Questions in Language Education and Applied Linguistics*, Springer Texts in Education,
https://doi.org/10.1007/978-3-030-79143-8_113

Thus, an understanding of the sources of this resistance and skepticism is fundamental to instructor preparedness for online teaching. Consequently, this understanding can be incorporated into the design of professional development programs to address instructor resistance and skepticism.

The Research Questions

1. Which face-to-face teaching practices effectively transfer to the online learning environment?
2. In what ways does teacher perception of online teaching influence their motivation to transition to an online teacher?
3. In what ways can perception impact failure and success of a first-time online teacher?
4. What differences exist between face-to-face teachers and online teachers in their perception of online teaching?
5. What strategies are used to encourage teacher participation and engagement in professional development to prepare for online teaching?
6. Which incentives encourage instructor transformation to online teaching?
7. In what ways does the perception of workload impact teacher's decision to transform to online teaching?
8. How does technology self-efficacy impact a teacher's decision to transform to online teaching?
9. What impact does the growth in online education programs impact a teacher's choice to transition to online teaching?
10. What are teachers' perceptions of differences in quality between online and face-to-face instruction?

Suggested Resources

Gosselin, K. P., Northcote, M., Reynaud, D., Kilgour, P., Anderson, M., & Boddey, C. (2016). Development of an evidence-based professional learning program informed by online teachers' self-efficacy and threshold concepts. *Online Learning Journal, 20*(3), 178–194.

The continued growth in online course offerings has created a demand for professional development programs to prepare teachers for the design, development, and implementation of online instructional materials. Gosselin et al. (2016) conducted a study to identify the threshold concepts that teachers encounter while learning about teaching online and determine if there is a difference in how experienced and inexperienced teachers face these concepts. Additionally, the researchers sought to identify ways in which the identified threshold concepts can be used to inform future professional development for online teachers. The study found confidence and self-efficacy to be pivotal in developing a teacher for online teaching. Additionally, the authors found that confidence and self-efficacy are developed though skills, understanding about the online environment, pedagogical knowledge, mentoring, and developing a personal history of success.

Horvitz, B., Beach, A., Anderson, M., & Xia, J. (2015). Examination of faculty self-efficacy related to online teaching. *Innovative Higher Education, 40*(4), **305–316**.

The authors sought to better understand the challenges faced by instructors as they transitioned to online teaching. This study aimed to identify the different levels of teaching self-efficacies exhibited by online instructors, including the degree to which demographic and attitudinal variables impacted self-efficacy, including its relationship to online learner engagement, instructional strategies, classroom management, and computer use. The results of the study confirmed that participants who had previously taught online had higher self-efficacy in the use of online instructional strategies and classroom management than in fostering student engagement. In regard to gender, male instructors reported a lower self-efficacy in employing online instruction strategies. Satisfaction with online teaching, perception of student learning, and professional schools were found to be significant predictors of overall self-efficacy.

Meyer, K., & Murrell, V. (2014). A national study of training content and activities for faculty development for online teaching. *Journal of Asynchronous Learning Networks, 18*(1).

The aim of the study was to identify topics and delivery format, and to determine if these differed by the Carnegie type of the institution. Assessment of student learning, creating community, and CMS (student learning styles, instructional design models) were identified as the top three topics at 45 of the surveyed institutions. Workshops, one-on-one training sessions, and hands-on training were identified as the top three delivery formats at 44 of the surveyed institutions. However, differences by Carnegie classification type were common, with a stronger emphasis on creating community, assessment of student learning, student learning styles, and instructional design models. As for training content, topics dealing with pedagogies were identified as having the highest value. The most favored training delivery formats were the short sessions, workshops, one-on-one training and hands-on training.

Stephen, J. S. (2021). Transforming yourself into an online educator. *In Professionalizing your English language teaching.* **Springer**.

This resource examines teacher assumptions and beliefs of online teaching and the impact of these perceptions on the transformation from a face-to-face to online teacher. The pedagogical, social, managerial, and technical roles of an online teacher are described and accompanied by examples that illustrate the teacher tasks aligned to each role. Strategies teachers can employ to fulfill each of the aforementioned roles are also presented, along with the knowledge, skills, and attributes/abilities necessary for an online teacher to meet the requirements of each role. Opportunities and recommendations for continuous teacher professional development are also presented in this resource, along with resources that teachers can use to self-assess readiness and preparedness to teach online.

Stephen, J. S., Tawfik, A. A. (2022). Self-efficacy sources and impact on readiness to teach online. *In Routledge encyclopedia of education.* **Routledge.**

This resource examines sources of self-efficacy that can support face-to-face teachers in their acquisition of knowledge and skills necessary for transitioning to online teaching. The significance of social cognitive theory to the transition process is examined to determine the impact of self-efficacy and perception on teacher readiness to teach online. Fears and assumptions, as well as perceptions, can negatively impact a teacher's confidence in their ability to successfully transition to the online teaching environment. As such, teacher professional development programs need to consider the process of transition and implement initiatives to support and guide teachers as they confront fears and address assumptions of online teaching.

References

Allen, I. E., & Seaman, J. (2015). *Grade level: Tracking online education in the United States.* Babson Survey Research Group and Quahog Research Group, LLC. http://www.onlinelearningsurvey.com/reports/gradelevel.pdf

Allen, I., Seaman, J., Poulin, R., & Taylor Straut, T. (2016). *Online report card. Tracking online education in the United States.* Babson Survey Research Group and Quahog Research Group, LLC.

Seaman, J., Allen, I., & Seaman, J. (2018). *Grade increase: Tracking distance education in the United States.* Retrieved from Online Learning Consortium website: https://onlinelearningconsortium.org/

Jacqueline S. Stephen is an assistant professor in the Department of Leadership Studies in the College of Professional Advancement at Mercer University in Atlanta, Georgia, USA. She also serves as the college's Instructional Designer and the Director of The Office of Distance Learning. Her research interests include online learner persistence, women and underrepresented populations in STEM, instructional design, and faculty professional development in the use and integration of technology to support teaching and learning. Jacqueline holds a bachelor's degree in Elementary Education, a master's degree in Instructional Technology, and a doctoral degree in Instruction and Curricular Leadership.

Intelligent Computer Assisted Language Learning

Trude Heift

Intelligent Computer Assisted Language Learning (ICALL) is a field within Computer Assisted Language Learning (CALL) that applies concepts, techniques, algorithms, and technologies from artificial intelligence to CALL. One of the branches of AI most relevant to CALL is research in Natural Language Processing (NLP). NLP studies the problems of automated understanding and generation of natural human languages. In natural language understanding, the computer takes written or spoken language input and turns it into a formal representation that captures phonological, graphological, grammatical, semantic, and pragmatic features. In contrast, natural language generation is the reverse process of going from a formal representation to natural language output.

In ICALL, the treatment of grammatical errors has received the most attention. Identifying and describing errors in written learner language has played an essential role in research and development and, independent of the computational framework used, the common goal has been to assist language learners with their written language by providing feedback on their language output. Two main ICALL environments designed to assist language learners with their written language are Tutorial CALL and systems for Automatic Writing Evaluation (AWE).

Tutorial CALL follows a deductive teaching approach by presenting explicit explanations of grammatical concepts and by focusing language practice on graded and discrete grammatical points. The grammar learning activities mainly consist of short sentence-based practice and cover isolated grammatical forms which are presented as multiple choice, fill-in-the-blank, matching or ranking, and reassemble or translate small chunks of text items. One of the main differences among Tutorial CALL programs lies in the ways in which learner responses are processed and evaluated. To a large extent, these computational algorithms determine the different types and levels of specificity of the corrective feedback the CALL program pro-

T. Heift (✉)
Linguistics Department, Simon Fraser University, Burnaby, BC, Canada
e-mail: heift@sfu.ca

© Springer Nature Switzerland AG 2021   655
H. Mohebbi and C. Coombe (eds.), *Research Questions in Language Education and Applied Linguistics*, Springer Texts in Education,
https://doi.org/10.1007/978-3-030-79143-8_114

vides. In its simplest form of error processing, the computer application is based on monolithic string-matching algorithms and binary knowledge of answer processing that compare the learner input with a pre-stored, correct answer. As a result of this computationally limited error-processing technique, the feedback is very general in that it does not identify or explain the source of error. In contrast, Intelligent Language Tutoring Systems (ILTSs) which rely on NLP techniques can detect a wide variety of learner errors and thus provide contextual learner feedback and instructional guidance. Yet, while the detection of errors has much advanced also due to more recent statistical and machine learning approaches to language understanding, questions that center around learner feedback and learner profiling with the goal to individualize the learner process still need to be answered.

Unlike Tutorial CALL, which emphasizes form-focused instruction at the sentence level for mainly grammar teaching, AWE systems evaluate word-processed essays. As with Tutorial CALL, the feedback in AWE programs focuses primarily on error correction but these systems also include summative scoring as well as a range of formative assessment features. Pre-writing tools in the form of graphic organizers, for instance, also make available an emphasis on idea development. The impact of automated feedback in AWE on improving student writing is limited but growing. While AWE systems provide a type of feedback that might complement a larger, comprehensive approach, much still has to be learned, however, about the context in which these programs are best employed and the types of learners who best benefit from feedback strategies that mostly rely on learner autonomy.

The Research Questions

1. What is Intelligent Computer Assisted Language Learning?
2. What are the computational challenges that ICALL faces?
3. What kind of pedagogical tasks/exercise types should an ILTS provide?
4. How can an ILTS or AWE system be most effectively used by L2 learners?
5. What kind of feedback should an ICALL system provide?
6. What are the factors that determine the type of feedback of an ICALL system?
7. What is the best timing of feedback in an ICALL system?
8. How can the tasks and exercise types in an ICALL system be used to assess learners' progress?
9. What are the learner variables and strategies that should be part of a learner profile?
10. In what ways can or should a learner profile determine the interaction between a learner and the ICALL system?

Suggested Resources

Heift, T. & Schulze, M. (2007). *Errors and intelligence in CALL. Parsers and pedagogues.* **New York: Routledge.**

This book provides the first comprehensive overview of theoretical issues, historical developments and trends in ICALL, a field that has also been referred to as NLP in CALL, or parser-based CALL. It draws on methods developed within computational linguistics with the goal to provide more contextual feedback to the user. The five chapters of the book focus on NLP, spell and grammar checkers, feedback, student models, and future directions of ICALL by surveying the literature and discussing the challenges as well as the benefits of an ICALL system. The book assumes a basic familiarity with SLA theory and teaching, CALL, and linguistics and is geared at upper undergraduate and/or graduate students as well as researchers interested in CALL, SLA, language pedagogy, applied linguistics, computational linguistics or artificial intelligence.

Heift, T. & Schulze, M. (2015). Research Timeline: Tutorial CALL. *Language Teaching,* **48(4), 1–20.**

This article presents a timeline (1968–2013) of survey and review articles that summarize the state of the art at that time and focus on research questions, processes and challenges pertinent to Tutorial CALL. It also describes articles that deal with language pedagogy by focusing on general aspects of second language development and language teaching methodology. Two important specific aspects are considered: (1) Corrective Feedback which subsumes form-focused feedback on individual items of practice activities, written texts and dialogues, and generally the recognition and processing of learner errors; and (2) Language Awareness which encompasses scaffolding resources for students' perceptive activities and guidance that focuses their attention, facilitates noticing, and generally helps learners to sequence the necessary steps in a complex problem-solving process. The timeline also considers ICALL and Tutorial CALL research and development projects. The article is a useful resource for an overview of the research that was conducted during those years.

Shermis, M. & Burstein, J. (2013). *Handbook of Automated Essay Evaluation: Current Applications and New Directions.* **New York: Routledge.**

This comprehensive, interdisciplinary handbook reviews methods and technologies used in automated essay evaluation (AEE), also referred to as automated writing evaluation (AWE). Highlights include the latest in the evaluation of performance-based writing assessments and recent advances in the teaching of writing, language testing, cognitive psychology, and computational linguistics. It is aimed at educators, researchers and administrators responsible for developing writing programs or distance learning curricula or those who teach using AWE technologies. The book also serves as a reference for graduate courses on automated essay evaluation taught in education, computer science, language, linguistics, and cognitive psychology.

Hegelheimer, V., Dursun, A. & Li, Z. (Eds) (2016). Automated writing evaluation in language teaching: Theory, development and application. *CALICO Special Issue, 33.1.*

This special issue includes conceptual and empirical research on AWE tool development, AWE tool classroom implementation, and resulting pedagogical implications. It is an informative resource for AWE designers and developers, applied-linguistics researchers, and language teachers and practitioners alike. With an emphasis on AWE development for classroom use and its implementation, the issue is a good complement to existing books on AWE. In total, six research articles that include a theoretical discussion and/or empirical research on the promise, challenges, and issues related to the development, implementation, or evaluation of AWE tools are presented. (see also the Special Issue in *Language Testing* on 'Automated Scoring and Feedback Systems for Language Assessment and Learning,' 27(3), July 2010)).

Dickinson, M., Brew C. & Meurers, D. (2012). *Language and Computers.* **Hoboken, NJ: Wiley-Blackwell.**

In this book, the authors provide an introduction to the fundamentals of how computers are used to represent, process, and organize textual and spoken information by introducing them to key concepts from computational linguistics. Concepts are grounded in real-world examples with which students can identify, using these to explore the technology and how it works. The authors cover a broad spectrum of language-related applications and issues, including major computer applications involving natural language and the social and ethical implications of these new developments. The book is written specifically for the undergraduate audience but offers additional sections that give greater detail on selected advanced topics, rendering the book appropriate for more advanced courses, or for independent study.

Trude Heift is Professor of Linguistics in the Department of Linguistics at Simon Fraser University, Canada. Her main research areas focus on the design as well as the evaluation of CALL systems. From an SLA perspective, her work examines learner-computer interactions (e.g., navigation patterns, learner strategies and responses within intelligent systems, learner and task variables), corrective feedback and error analysis. From a computational point of view, she is interested in the automatic analysis of learner language and learner modeling. She is the author of *E-Tutor*, an ILTS for L2 learners of German and is currently (Co-)editor of *Language Learning & Technology*.

Flora Debora Floris

,

The broad perception of CPD considers teacher development as "a planned, continuous and lifelong process whereby teachers try to develop their personal and professional qualities, and to improve their knowledge, skills and practice, leading to their empowerment, the improvement of their agency and the development of their organizations and their pupils" (Padwad & Dixit, 2001, p. 7). It may be either initiated by school administrators, educational authorities, or by the individual teacher. It is believed that CPD is crucial to promote student achievement and improve learning outcomes (Powell & Bodur, 2016). Furthermore, Borg (2013) states that CPD can achieve a positive and sustained impact on teachers, learners, and organizations when it is seen by teachers to be relevant to their needs and those of their students.

One of the most significant changes in CPD over the past years has been the shift from face-to-face CPD to online CPD. Today teachers are fortunate to have a wide range of opportunities for online professional development at their fingertips. Below is a list of nine common types of online professional development programs available to teachers today.

1. Professional Learning Network (PLN) or Professional Learning Community (PLC)
2. Massive Open Online Courses (MOOC)
3. Traditional online courses
4. Online graduate programs
5. Corporate-sponsored training programs
6. Webinars
7. Video Tutorials

F. D. Floris (✉)
English Department, Petra Christian University, Surabaya, Indonesia
e-mail: debora@petra.ac.id

© Springer Nature Switzerland AG 2021
H. Mohebbi and C. Coombe (eds.), *Research Questions in Language Education and Applied Linguistics*, Springer Texts in Education,
https://doi.org/10.1007/978-3-030-79143-8_115

8. Online Conference/Seminars
9. Learning via social media (Facebook, Twitter, etc.).

Online CPD offers many potential benefits. Here are a few to consider:

1. *Affordable Cost*: Technology reduces the cost of attending off-site professional development activities.
2. *Flexibility*: Teachers can work at their own pace, access CPD materials any time of the day from the comfort of their home, office, or when working remotely.
3. *Experience in using online technology*: Teachers taking online CPD will enhance their technology skills.
4. *Potential Network*: Through online CPD, teachers have a chance to learn, connect and work with reputable scholars and other teachers outside of their school district in real time or asynchronously.
5. *Increased Accountability*: In some online CPD programs, the accountability is high because all assignments, activities, and participant progress can be monitored online easily.
6. *Tailored to specific needs or interests*: Countless amounts of online CPD programs or activities in various formats and styles ranging from broad subjects to specific topics of interest are available. Teachers can choose the programs based on their needs, ensuring the best possible learning experience.

Along with its potential benefits, online CPD has some potential barriers to its effective implementation:

1. *Lack of knowledge and skills related to the use of computers*: Many teachers are aware of the existence of online CPD activities, but they probably do not know where to find or how to join them. Some teachers also might have problems related to their technical skills in using computers the internet, or required applications.
2. *Limited access to technology*: Some teachers might not have a computer or internet connection that works well to access the online CPD activities.
3. *Lack of support from administrators*: Some administrators might remain skeptical about the potential of online CPD; and others might think that online professional development should be done away from the school.
4. *Teachers' traditional beliefs and practices*: Some teachers might be skeptical about online CPD and some might fail to understand their own learning needs and implement autonomous learning strategies. Some teachers might feel isolated because they feel that they have no real classmates, while others do not really have the skills to communicate in online settings and may appear rude or demanding in their emails or postings.

As teachers sail through the 21st century, the use of technology in their professional development should not be seen as a gimmick. Instead, effective and meaningful support systems for the ongoing growth and development of teachers should be created to reach the potential advantages of online CPD programs.

The Research Questions

1. What online professional opportunities do teachers participate in?
2. What factors need to be taken into account in deciding what online programs to attend?
3. What changes in teaching practices, if any, do teachers report after participating in an online professional development program?
4. How do online professional development programs compare with face-to-face programs regarding the pedagogical effects on teachers?
5. What do teachers think before and after taking an online CPD program?
6. What are the teachers' attitudes, opinions, and concerns regarding the integration of technology in their online CPD program?
7. What high quality online CPD features are voiced by teachers as participants?
8. What interactions sustain the online CPD communities?
9. How does the use of online CPD reflect teachers' professional identity?
10. Is there any significant relationship between teachers' online CPD and their self-efficacy?

Suggested Resources

Curtis, A. (2018). Online professional development. In J.I. Liontas (Ed.) *The TESOL encyclopedia of English language teaching* **(pp. 1–7). New York: John Wiley & Sons, Inc.**

In this article, the author reviewed the major characteristics of online and off-site CPD programs. He then suggested that teachers carefully choose their online professional programs to match their needs and the time available.

Erkmann, M., Petersen, A. K., & Christensen, P. L. (2019). The three spaces model for online CPD. *Designs for Learning, 11*(1), 118–126.

In this article, the authors proposed a new model for designing assignments for online CPD courses. The model was developed based on the evaluation of two widely used models for course design, i.e., Salmon's five-stage model and Ryan & Ryan's TARL model.

Fancera, S. F. (2019). School leadership for professional development: The role of social media and networks. *Professional Development in Education*, **1–13**.

This article presented the results of a study that aimed to find out how school leaders in the United States used social media and networking for CPD, and which platforms were considered the most effective for CPD. The key finding revealed that the school leaders employed social media and networking, particularly Twitter, in a multi-faceted approach to provide teachers opportunities to enhance their professionalism.

Muls, J., Triquet, K., Vlieghe, J., De Backer, F., Zhu, C., & Lombaerts, K. (2019). Facebook group dynamics: an ethnographic study of the teaching and learning potential for secondary school teachers. *Learning, Media and Technology*, **44(2), 162–179**.

This ethnography study explored the role of Facebook on secondary school teachers' professional development, learning and teaching practices. The researchers found that Facebook addressed limitations faced by teachers in the current education system and promoted a new source of learning processes and reflection.

Parsons, S.A., Hutchison, A.C., Hall, L.A., Parsons, A.W., Ives, S.T. & Leggett, A.B. (2019). U.S. teachers' perceptions of online professional development. *Teaching and Teacher Education: An International Journal of Research and Studies*, **82(1), 33–42**.

This study focused on how teachers viewed their online CPD experiences, how they used what they had learned, and which experiences that they liked. The findings confirmed that teachers in the United States tended to find online CPD beneficial, and that online PD might take many different formats.

References

Borg, S. (2013). *Teacher research in language teaching: A critical analysis*. Cambridge University Press.

Padwad, A., & Dixit, K. (2001). *Continuing professional development: An annotated bibliography*. British Council India.

Powell, C. G., & Bodur, Y. (2016). Professional development for quality teaching and learning: A focus on student learning outcomes. In C. G. Powell & Y. Bodur (Eds.) *Handbook of research on professional development for quality teaching and learning* (pp. 652–677). IGI Global.

Flora Debora Floris is a lecturer at Petra Christian University, Surabaya, Indonesia where she teaches general/business English and language teaching methodology courses. Her publications include *Mining Online L2 Learning Resources: From SLA Principles to Innovative Task Design* with Willy A. Renandya and Bao Dat (Multilingual Matters, 2018), *Promoting the Value of Non-Native English-Speaking Teachers* with Willy A. Renandya (PASAA, 2020), and *Inspirational Stories from English Language Classrooms* with Willy A. Renandya (TEFLIN, 2020).

Ruth Trinder

Informal out-of-class language learning is a phenomenon that has always existed—and is even regarded a sine-qua-no of successful acquisition by many—yet was long neglected by research at the expense of instructed SLA. Now, as reflected in the increasing number of contributions to the literature (e.g. Benson & Reinders, 2011; Nunan & Richards, 2015), educational as well as technological changes have triggered a shift in emphasis to the world beyond the classroom (Benson, 2017).

In the last decade, opportunities for out-of-class language use have multiplied mainly due to the ready availability of affordable Web 2.0 technologies, and the skills young people acquire more or less inadvertently by engaging in everyday Internet-based activities have started to baffle teachers and to interest SLA researchers. As noted by Isbell (2018) and others, today more language learning happens in online environments than in institutional settings.

This has sparked interest in a specific form of learning beyond the classroom, namely online informal language learning (OILL). OILL takes place exclusively at the learner's initiative and through the affordances of digital applications more commonly associated with leisure than with learning (e.g. gaming, online TV, social media). As English is not only the dominant language of much web-based communication, but also holds a unique position concerning popular culture, it is naturally the target of the large majority of studies in this emergent field.

In the influential investigations conducted by Sockett and associates, informal learning refers to the basket of "internet-based communicative leisure activities" (Kusyk & Sockett, 2012, p. 46) students participate in, with popular activities including listening to music, viewing American/British TV series, and battling in virtual worlds. These studies set out to quantify use of various online resources and measure its impact on aspects of proficiency. Research outcomes of these and

R. Trinder (✉)
Department of Foreign Language Business Communication,
Vienna University of Economics and Business, Vienna, Austria
e-mail: rtrinder@wu.ac.at; bizcomm@wu.ac.at

© Springer Nature Switzerland AG 2021
H. Mohebbi and C. Coombe (eds.), *Research Questions in Language Education and Applied Linguistics*, Springer Texts in Education,
https://doi.org/10.1007/978-3-030-79143-8_116

similarly organized studies indicate that exposure to massive amounts of personally relevant input and/or the opportunities for interaction in online communities, coupled with users' motivation and inherent interest, indeed facilitate language development; in Cole and Vandeplank's (2016) investigation to such an extent that exclusively self-instructed online learners outperformed classroom-instructed ones.

Yet informal online learning is not just about fun and games. Researching adults' everyday online practices, Stevens (2010) and Trinder (2016) documented the diversity of online activities in naturalistic contexts and found that more mundane Web applications such as news sites and email were experienced as extremely valuable tools for the acquisition of work-related language skills.

Finally, while OILL is usually conceptualized as a form of incidental, unintentional learning, it is becoming increasingly clear that at least some learners are aware of the affordances of informal activities and consciously employ strategies to exploit them. In this case, though language acquisition is still a by-product of interest-driven language use, it constitutes a consciously sought after, valued secondary objective. At times, as shown for instance by Lin and Siyanova-Chanturia (2015), improving language skills can even be the main reason for participating in online activities. The dynamic interplay between deliberate and incidental use of the naturalistic learning opportunities provided by digital media as well as the challenge of integrating them into instructed contexts represent two fascinating new areas of inquiry.

The Research Questions

1. What activities, conducted via which technologies, should be included in the concept of 'online informal language learning (OILL)'?
2. What kind of learners—with what profile—benefit most from OILL activities?
3. What kind of attention is necessary for acquisition to take place in OILL?
4. What skills and competencies benefit most from OILL activities?
5. To what extent, and under which circumstances, do learners engage in OILL activities with the intention of learning?
6. What is the role of motivation and intrinsic interest in the activity?
7. Can we teach strategies to improve the uptake from OILL input, and to increase output?
8. How can we help less autonomous and reflective learners become aware of the learning opportunities offered by informal online activities?
9. What are the barriers to integrating OILL activities into instructed environments?
10. How important is OILL in languages other than English?

Suggested Resources

Sockett, G. (2014). *The Online Informal Learning of English.* **Basingstoke: Palgrave Macmillan.**

The first and so far the only monograph on informal online learning, this book has played an important role in positioning OILL as a research subject. Associating the nature of Internet-based learning with dynamic systems theory, Sockett's accounts of the OILL practices of non-English majors at a French university empirically document the unusual trajectories of individual learners' developments as well as the breadth and depth of informal learning. A large majority of his respondents participate productively or receptively in Internet communication, picking up target language structures along the way. The comparison of frequent and irregular viewers of popular TV series, for instance—one of the quantitative studies presented—provides evidence for the hypothesized potential of online leisure activities. Sockett further explores the often uneasy relationship between formal and informal environments and addresses the ambivalent feelings teachers have concerning the impact of informal learning on 'their' domain. This comprehensive, theoretically anchored and very readable introduction to the subject succeeds in what it sets out to do—"bringing the wild into focus" (p.161).

Sundqvist, P. & Sylvén, K. L. (2016). *Extramural English in teaching and learning: From theory and research to practice.* **London: Palgrave Macmillan.**

This volume brings together theory, research, and practice concerning English encountered outside the classroom, demonstrating how extramural activities lead to learning—and how they can be integrated into teaching. Sundqvist and Sylvén offer insights into ways in which school-age learners successfully develop their language skills through exposure to extramural English. Though the focus is not entirely on online language use, much of the empirical evidence cited shows the dominance of music, film and gaming as the preferred leisure activities of this age group. True to the subtitle of the book, the authors also provide hands-on tools for teachers to evaluate the popularity of informal activities amongst their own students and suggest ways of involving learners in the exploitation of their interests for classroom activities.

Cole, J. & Vanderplank, R. (2016). Comparing autonomous and class-based learners in Brazil: Evidence for the present-day advantages of informal, out-of-class learning. *System 61*, 31–42.

It is widely accepted that in order to be truly successful, learners need to step outside the classroom and find opportunities for authentic language use for themselves. Cole and Vanderplank's investigation goes one step further, establishing that high levels of proficiency can be achieved completely autonomously and without any classroom instruction. The study compares two groups of high-level Brazilian learners. In the battery of seven language tests administered, the "fully autonomous self-instructed learners" (FASILs), who had acquired English exclusively via informal Internet-based activities, outperformed classroom-trained learners on every single measure. Perhaps most intriguing is the conclusion that fossilization of errors and transfer mistakes are not, as suggested in the mainstream SLA literature, a by-product of naturalistic learning, but rather persist in classroom settings. The authors suggest that the superiority of autonomous learning is due to self-determined instrumental motivation characterizing FASILs, as well as a mode of learning that provides "authentic communication for authentic purposes" (p. 40), rather than the "systematized and impoverished language" (p. 33) of the classroom context.

Nunan, D. & Richards, J. (Eds.). (2015). *Language learning beyond the classroom*. London: Routledge.

This edited volume spans a wide range of learning environments, resources and pedagogies, displaying the many guises learning outside the classroom can take. However, since it is primarily aimed at teachers, it puts a certain emphasis on approaches that complement formal curricula, with most chapters addressing the question of how educators can support students in their efforts to make use of out-of-class learning opportunities. Of the five parts—(i) involving the learner in out-of-class learning; (ii) using technology and the internet; (iii) learning through television; (iv) out-of-class projects; and (v) interacting with native speakers—the first three are particularly relevant for those interested in researching or applying OILL. Each of the 28 chapters is organized in the same way, offering an introduction, a vignette about a learner, principles for use, extended applications, payoffs and pitfalls, and concludes with discussion questions and links to resources.

Benson, P. & Reinders, H. (Eds.). (2011). *Beyond the language classroom*. London: Palgrave Macmillan.

This collection of 13 especially written papers has a stronger emphasis on theory and research than the similarly entitled volume above. The introductory chapter by Benson provides a useful theoretical framework according to which the various settings beyond the classroom can be analyzed. Addressing the obsolescence of simple dichotomies such as in-class versus out-of-class learning, he proposes the dimensions location, formality, pedagogy, and locus of control, and the distinction between settings and modes of practice to characterize the various contexts for learning. The twelve contributions that follow adopt a variety of theoretical perspectives. Some of the chapters deal with 'core-OILL' topics such as self-directed use of technology and its effects in terms of SLA (e.g. Sundqvist's study of Swedish learners of English). Others look at institutional initiatives to provide virtual and offline spaces for language learning beyond the classroom. Indeed, the role of teachers and educational institutions in co-constructing less conventional learning spaces and supporting less experienced or autonomous learners is a recurring theme of the volume, as highlighted by Reinders' concluding chapter entitled 'Materials Development for Learning Beyond the Classroom'.

References

Benson, P. (2017). Language learning beyond the classroom: Access all areas. *Studies in Self-Access Learning Journal, 8*(2), 135–146.

Benson, P., & Reinders, H. (Eds.). (2011). *Beyond the language classroom*. Palgrave Macmillan.

Cole, J., & Vanderplank, R. (2016). Comparing autonomous and class-based learners in Brazil: Evidence for the present-day advantages of informal, out-of-class learning. *System, 61*, 31–42.

Isbell, D. (2018). Online informal language learning: Insights from a Korean learning community. *Language Learning & Technology, 22*(3), 82–102.

Kusyk, M., & Sockett, G. (2012). From informal resource usage to incidental language acquisition: Language uptake from online television viewing in English. *Asp, 62*, 45–65.

Lin, P. M. S., & Siyanova-Chanturia, A. (2015). Internet television for vocabulary learning. In D. Nunan & J. Richards (Eds.), *Language learning beyond the classroom* (pp. 149–158). London, UK: Routledge.

Nunan, D., & Richards, J. (Eds.). (2015). *Language learning beyond the classroom*. Routledge.

Stevens, A. (2010). *Study on the impact of information and communication technology (ICT) and new media on language learning*. European Commission. https://digital-strategy.ec.europa.eu/en/library/report-impact-information-and-communication-technology-ictand-new-media-language-learning.

Trinder, R. (2016). Blending technology and face-to-face: Advanced students' choices. *ReCALL, 28*, 1–20.

Ruth Trinder is Associate Professor at the Department of Foreign Business Communication at Vienna University of Business and Economics. She wrote her doctoral dissertation on new media in language learning and teaching at the University of Vienna. Her areas of research include technology in teaching and learning, individual differences theory, and online informal language learning. As project leader, she has been involved in the development and evaluation of online learning materials at her university. She has written a monograph focusing on students' attitudes towards online/blended learning in the context of individual learner differences. Her recent research has addressed the informal language learning practices of Austrian business students.

Phuong Tran

Social networking tools have evolved into various different forms such as Twitter, Facebook, Messenger, WhatsApp, and WeChat which have gained rapid popularity over the past ten years. Different tools have come to be used in different ways depending on the demographics of the users, such as their age, location, and personal preferences (Hattem & Lomicka, 2016; Roblyer et al., 2010; Tran, 2016). Regardless of the variations, these tools have various functions that have resulted in millions of users using them to communicate and share ideas, views, and information with each other. With the advances in technology, social networking is not merely a means of communicating, but has become an essential part of the daily routine and practices of many around the world. Social networking enables users to create various connections with other users with whom they can choose what they share, either publicly or with a limited network of friends and family (see Boyd & Ellison, 2008).

It is not altogether surprising that social networking has attracted the attention of second language educators as well (e.g., Bosch, 2009; Boyd & Ellison, 2008; Hamid et al., 2015; Meskill, 2013). Computer-mediated communication (CMC), which may be seen in some ways as a predecessor to social networking tools, dominated much of the research in language teaching and learning in the early 2000s (Stockwell, 2007). Functions of CMC (i.e., text-based, audio-based, and video-based communication) are still an integral part of social networking, but the audience may be far more open, in that participants may find themselves as a part of varied real or imagined communities (Kanno & Norton, 2003; Norton & Kamal, 2003). Communication still has the potential to take place on a one-to-one basis, but the tools also open up possibilities for communication with one-to-many (cf., Levy & Stockwell, 2006) with members of various online communities.

P. Tran (✉)
School of International Liberal Studies, Waseda University, Tokyo, Japan
e-mail: phuongtran@aoni.waseda.jp

© Springer Nature Switzerland AG 2021   669
H. Mohebbi and C. Coombe (eds.), *Research Questions in Language
Education and Applied Linguistics*, Springer Texts in Education,
https://doi.org/10.1007/978-3-030-79143-8_117

By its very nature, social networking entails interaction between participants involved in the communication context, and there has been an extensive amount of work that has been carried out over the past several years to investigate various elements of this interaction (e.g., Amichai-Hamburger, 2005). For example, wikis may boost an L2 writer's confidence (Mark & Coniam, 2008); blogging tools have been used to develop connective writing (Richardson, 2006), and online interaction on Facebook has built a sense of community which is thought to have enhanced the classroom atmosphere (Leier, 2012).

In educational settings, social networking may be thought as being closely related to concepts such of teaching presence, social presence, and cognitive presence as a part of communities of inquiry (CoI) (see Garrison et al., 2000, 2010; Swan & Shea, 2004), and how these relate to learner engagement in both the community itself and in tasks and activities that are the object of discussion in the community. What remains as a key area for making the most of the potential of social networking for language teaching and learning is furthering our understanding of the roles that teachers and learners play in these communities, and how these can be related to better practice.

The Research Questions

1. What is the nature of the discussions carried out by participants in a social networking community?
2. How can social networking be used as a support for learning outside of the classroom?
3. How can an online learning community be built through social networking?
4. How can an online learning community be built and used to support for teaching and learning?
5. What is the role of the teacher in facilitating interaction in an online community?
6. What problems do teachers face when teaching through social networking?
7. What are learner preferences for individual and group social interaction when using social networking tools?
8. How do learners perceive online social interaction as a support for language learning outside of class?
9. How do the learners perceive teaching presence, cognitive presence, and social presence in the interactions through social networking learning?
10. Can an online community be used to enhance out-of-class task engagement?

Suggested Resources

Pasfield-Neofitou, S. E. (2012). *Online communication in a second language: Social interaction, language use and learning Japanese.* **Bristol: Multilingual Matters.**

This is an interesting book based on the author's PhD dissertation. Pasfield-Neofitou covers relevant issues including the linguistic backgrounds of the learners, how to manage the communication, the features of the interactions themselves, and the use of other external resources to facilitate their communication. The author has written this based on her study of Australian learners of Japanese, most of whom were highly motivated to engage in communication which does provide insights into a particular type of learner but is still of interest to read. Smart phones were just starting to come into widespread use at the time of writing, however, so the implications of social interaction through mobile devices (which is now thought to be one of the most common ways of accessing social media) are rather limited.

Lomicka, L. & Lord, G. (Eds.). (2009). *The next generation: Social networking and online collaboration in foreign language learning.* **Austin: CALICO.**

This edited book from Lomicka and Lord is an excellent example of how social networking has been used in language teaching and learning, covering a wide range of contexts. There are examples of mobile technologies being used, such as podcasting, and social technologies that are still popular today (e.g., Twitter), but it is clearly starting to be a little dated given the enormous developments in social networking tools over the past decade. The volume looks at various projects that are pedagogically oriented, which provides examples of how social networking can be used for language teaching.

Lamy, Marie-Noëlle & Zourou, K. (Eds.). (2013). *The Palgrave Macmillan handbook of social networking for language education.* **Hillsdale: Palgrave Macmillan.**

The book starts with an overview of the wider "ecology" of language learning with SNS. Then it moves on to what they term as "pedagogies and practitioners" which looks at some specific examples of how social networking has been used in language teaching and learning contexts. The three chapters in this part cover quite different types of approaches to using social networking in specific contexts, but this is obviously a rather narrow view of the possibilities. The last part entitled "overview" contains a single chapter that aims to show insights from research and practice.

Lee, M. S. (2014). The relationships between higher order thinking skills, cognitive density, and social presence in online learning. *Internet & Higher Education,* **21, 41–52.**

This study looked at college students who communicated using an online discussion board. The author sought to investigate social and cognitive presence in the interactions and concluded that even if there was a greater cognitive presence evident in the interactions, it did not necessarily equate with higher order thinking skills. She found also that social presence was necessary to enhance cognitive presence in the interactions. The study is interesting as it looks at the interplay between the different types of presences and challenges the superiority of cognitive presence for enhancing learning.

Akbari, E., Pilot, A. & P. Robert-Jan Simons. (2015). Autonomy, competence, and relatedness in foreign language learning through Facebook. *Computers in Human Behavior*, **48, 126–134**.

This is an ambitious study that seeks to look at learners' perceptions of their autonomy in engaging in out-of-class learning, comparing one group that interacted through Facebook and another that interacted through face-to-face interaction. An interesting result of the study was that while there was very little difference in actual outcomes of learning outside of class, the students in the Facebook group felt that they were more autonomous. This study is an important one in that it sheds light on the differences between real and perceived autonomous behavior, and how this may link to efficient task engagement.

References

Amichai-Hamburger, Y. (Ed.). (2005). *The social net: Human behaviour in cyberspace*. Oxford University Press.

Bosch, T. E. (2009). Using online social networking for teaching and learning: Facebook use at the University of Cape Town. *Communication: South African Journal for Communication Theory and Research, 3*(2), 185–200.

Boyd, D. M., & Ellison, N. B. (2008). Social networking sites: Definition, history, and scholarship. *Journal of Computer-Mediated Communication, 13*(1), 210–230.

Garrison, D. R., Anderson, T., & Archer, W. (2000). Critical inquiry in a text-based environment: Computer conferencing in higher education. *Internet and Higher Education, 2*(2–3), 87–105.

Garrison, D. R., Cleveland-Innes, M., & Fung, T. S. (2010). Exploring causal relationships among teaching, cognitive and social presence: Student perceptions of the community of inquiry framework. *Internet and Higher Education, 13*, 31–35.

Hamid, S., Waycott, J., Kurnia, S., & Chang, S. (2015). Understanding students' perceptions of the benefits of online social networking use for teaching and learning. *Internet and Higher Education, 26*, 1–9.

Hattem, D., & Lomicka, L. (2016). What the Tweets say: A critical analysis of Twitter research in language learning from 2009 to 2016. *E-Learning and Digital Media, 13*(1–2), 5–23.

Kanno, Y., & Norton, B. (Eds.). (2003). *Imagined Communities and educational possibilities*. Routledge.

Leier, V. (2012). Facebook used in a German film project. In *The EUROCALL review. Proceedings of the EUROCALL 2011 conference* (Vol. 20, pp. 95–99). Nottingham, UK: Eurocall. Retrieved January 9, 2019, from https://files.eric.ed.gov/fulltext/ED542419.pdf.

Levy, M., & Stockwell, G. (2006). *CALL dimensions: Options & issues in computer-assisted language learning*. Lawrence Erlbaum Associates.

Meskill, C. (Ed.). (2013). *Online teaching and learning: Sociocultural perspectives*. Bloomsbury Publishing.

Mark, B., & Coniam, D. (2008). Using wikis to enhance and develop writing skills among secondary school students in Hong Kong. *System, 36*(3), 437–455.

Norton, B., & Kamal, F. (2003). The imagined communities of English language learners in a Pakistani school. *Journal of Language, Identity, and Education, 2*(4), 301–317.

Richardson, W. (2006). *Blogs, wikis, podcasts, and other powerful web tools for classrooms.* Corwin Press.

Roblyer, M. D., McDaniel, M., Webb, M., Herman, J., & Witty, J. V. (2010). Findings on Facebook in higher education: A comparison of college faculty and student uses and perceptions of social networking sites. *Internet and Higher Education, 13*, 134–140.

Stockwell, G. (2007). A review of technology choice for teaching language skills in the CALL literature. *ReCALL, 19*(2), 105–120.

Swan, K., & Shea, P. (2004). The development of virtual learner communities. In S. R. Hiltz & R. Goldman (Eds.), *Learning together online: Research on asynchronous learning networks* (pp. 239–260). Lawrence Erlbaum Associates.

Tran, P. (2016). Training learners to use Quizlet vocabulary activities on mobile phones in Vietnam. *The JALT CALL Journal, 12*(1), 43–56.

Phuong Tran is Assistant Professor at Waseda University, Tokyo, Japan. She has taught in Vietnam and Japan for nearly nine years. Since 2014, she has been conducting research about the role that social networking plays in language learning. She has already written a number of academic articles investigating the development of learner autonomy through social interaction and networking in language learning settings. She has extensive research experience in the field of social networking for language teaching and learning, currently carrying out research with language learners in Asia including Vietnam, China, South Korea, and Japan.

Part VII
Politics, Policies and Practices in Language Education

Bilingualism

Gillian Wigglesworth and Carmel O'Shannessy

Even though more people in the world are bilingual than monolingual, bilingualism remains one of the least-well understood areas of human language development and use. Approaches to studying bilingualism are varied, but tend to fall into either social-interactional aspects of language-in-use, including discourse analysis, or psycholinguistic aspects, e.g. models of speech production, lexical retrieval and storage, sentence interpretation and linguistic interaction.

Bilingualism is an extremely complex topic and defining it is fundamental. What is it that constitutes being 'bilingual'? How much knowledge of the two (or more) languages must a person have for them to be called 'bilingual'? The definition itself has been extensively contested, but in recent years researchers have tended to take Grosjean's (2008) view of the regular use of two or more languages in everyday life as the default. In many countries in the world, everyone is bilingual—as in much of Africa and Asia where children are born into communities in which multiple languages are spoken—parents may speak different languages; the local community language may differ from the 'official' language of the country which is used in education and government. In other contexts, people become bilingual in myriad different ways. Valdes and Figueroa (1994) divide the ways of becoming bilingual into two categories: *circumstantial* bilinguals who learn another language because it is required by life circumstances—migration being the most common—and *elective* bilinguals who choose to learn another language.

A long-standing topic related to bilingual acquisition has addressed the extent to which there are cognitive benefits to being bilingual, with some recent research suggesting that bilingualism can delay the onset of dementia (see, e.g. Bialystok &

G. Wigglesworth (✉)
University of Melbourne, Melbourne, Australia
e-mail: g.wigglesworth@unimelb.edu.au; gillianw@unimelb.edu.au

C. O'Shannessy
Australian National University, Canberra, Australia
e-mail: Carmel.OShannessy@anu.edu.au

© Springer Nature Switzerland AG 2021
H. Mohebbi and C. Coombe (eds.), *Research Questions in Language Education and Applied Linguistics*, Springer Texts in Education,
https://doi.org/10.1007/978-3-030-79143-8_118

Sullivan, 2017). A major focus of much bilingual research centres on education which includes a wide range of questions including the extent to which early learning is enhanced when it is in the child's first language, and the extent to which immersion education results in fully bilingual adults. In the context of, among other things, bilingual education, we need to consider how to measure the acquisition of bilingualism, and with increasing migrant populations, how fair it is to measure children's school performance in a language in which they may not yet be fully competent, given this takes between five and seven years to achieve (Cummins, 2017). The increasing reliance on standardised tests to determine progress in many educational systems makes this a highly topical issue.

Questions about how children acquire two or more languages from birth, or soon after, are relevant to researchers, educators and families. Major questions include whether, and how, very young children use their languages differently in different contexts, suggesting that they are operating with two linguistic systems. The question is applied to speech production and processing, where ingenious experiments tap into how babies and young children respond to stimuli with different patterns. A growing area of research is how speakers make use of two languages when one is a sign language and one is a spoken language, also examining both production and language processing.

The Research Questions

1. How do speaker ideologies of multilingual language use differ (or not) across types of speaker communities?
2. How and when do very young bilingual children develop the understanding that they are hearing and speaking two languages?
3. How is bilingual development cognitively similar to, and different from, that of monolingual development?
4. How do the characteristics of the input to children influence their bilingual development?
5. What evidence is there for the influence of bilingualism vs monolingualism on human cognition?
6. What are the sociolinguistic environments which most favor active bilingualism?
7. How do bilingual and multilingual speakers use their languages in interactions?
8. Are there universal constraints on code-switching?
9. How does bimodal bilingualism (i.e. signed and spoken languages) compare to unimodal bilingualism, interactionally and cognitively?
10. How do people's attitudes toward the languages they speak influence their sense of identity and their language use?

Suggested Resources

De Houwer, A. & L. Ortega (Eds.) (2018). *The Cambridge handbook of bilingualism.* **Cambridge: Cambridge University Press**.

With 27 chapters from experts in their fields, this handbook provides a comprehensive overview of bilingualism across the lifespan, detailing learning from childhood through to older adulthood, exploring the social aspects of bilingualism in relation to the law, planning, policy and economics. Different approaches to bilingual learning are discussed in several chapters, as is bilingualism in relation to different disciplines including clinical linguistics, education and cognitive science. The final section of the handbook focuses on areas of bilingualism which have tended to be under-researched including bilingualism and modality (e.g. sign languages), bilingualism and dialectal variation, how bilingualism and language contact relate, as well as multilingualism.

García, O. (2011). Bilingual Education in the 21st Century: A Global Perspective. London: Wiley Blackwell.

Education is a central concern in bilingualism and a substantial number of different models of bilingual education exist. Bilingual education uses language as the medium of instruction by teaching content through two languages, or through a language which is additional to the child's first language. Its goals differ from those of foreign language instruction since bilingual education ultimately aims to educate children to live, work and function in different cultural contexts. This monograph explores bilingual education from socio-political perspectives, the benefits of bilingualism, the range of different models and theoretical approaches that can be adopted, and how different variables may impact on bilingual education. The book also provides a detailed overview introducing approaches to pedagogy and practice, as well as approaches to assessment.

Ng, B. C., & G. Wigglesworth. (2007). *Bilingualism: An advanced resource book.* **London: Routledge**.

Designed to expand the knowledge of those interested in all aspects of bilingualism, this volume is in three parts. The first section provides an easily accessible introduction to the range of issues related to bilingualism, moving from acquisition to attrition, from description to measurement, and including discussions of the role of cognition, education and attitudes. The second part expands the discussion of each of these topics through incorporating and contextualising excerpts from key publications in the field and discussing their contributions. Following a discussion of ethical issues related to data collection and research, the final part of the volume details a variety of empirical projects which can be conducted by individuals or groups in relation to each of the topics explored in the book, which can be used either for assessment purposes or for general interest.

Grosjean, F., & Li, P. (2013). *The psycholinguistics of bilingualism.* **Hoboken, NJ: John Wiley & Sons.**

With chapters written by experts in each topic, this volume collates research examining several key aspects of bilingualism and language processing, showing how studies of bilingualism enhance our understandings of the human mind. Research on spoken and written language processing, including both production and comprehension, are synthesised and explained in an accessible way. Elements of two types of bilingual language acquisition are examined, simultaneous and successive. The final section gives an overview of research on the cognitive effects of bilingualism, bilingual memory, and how the rapidly growing area of neurolinguistics can shed light on bilingual processing.

De Houwer, A. (2009). *Bilingual first language acquisition.* **Multilingual Matters.**

This book contains comprehensive, accessible descriptions and analyses of the language development of children in a variety of Bilingual First Language Acquisition (BFLA) settings, meaning settings where children hear two languages from birth, or soon after. It presents a significant amount of bilingual child speech data by way of illustrating concepts, from many different pairs of languages. It examines questions such as how children are socialized into using their two languages, and the cognitive relationship between their two languages. It presents research on perspectives from very early comprehension of sounds, through to production of sounds, words and larger constructions. It also includes a section on research methods in bilingual acquisition.

References

Bialystok, E., & Sullivan, M. D. (2017). The importance of bilingualism for the aging brain. In E. Bialystok & M. Sullivan (Eds.), *Growing old with two languages: Effects of bilingualism on cognitive aging*. Amsterdam/Philadelphia: John Benjamins.

Cummins, J. (2017). BICS and CALP: Empirical and theoretical status of the distinction. *Literacies and Language Education*, 59–71.

Grosjean, F. (2008). *Studying bilinguals*. Oxford: Oxford University Press.

Valdes, G. & R. Figueroa. (1994). *Bilingualism and testing: A special case of bias*. Norwood, New Jersey, Ablex.

Gillian Wigglesworth is Redmond Barry Distinguished Professor in the School of Languages and Linguistics at the University of Melbourne and chief investigator in the ARC Centre of Excellence for the Dynamics of Language. She has published extensively in first and second language acquisition and bilingualism. Collaborating with Indigenous and non-Indigenous teachers, her research focusses on the languages Australian Indigenous children are learning in the complex language ecologies they grow up in, and on the resulting linguistic challenges the children face as they enter the formal, usually English-based, school system. Her most recent co-edited book *From Home to School: Language Practices of Indigenous Children and Youth* (Palgrave Macmillan), documents much of this work.

Carmel O'Shannessy is a Senior Lecturer in the School of Literature, Languages and Linguistics at the Australian National University. Her research is in language contact and acquisition, including the emergence of Light Warlpiri, a new Australian mixed language, and children's development of Light Warlpiri and Warlpiri. She is especially interested in the roles of children and adults in contact-induced language change. She has been involved with languages and education in remote Indigenous communities in Australia since 1996, in the areas of bilingual education and her current research.

C. J. Denman

The relationship between English language teaching (ELT) and international development is one that has received relatively little direct investigative attention. English and ELT have remained important parts of the public and private education systems of many "developing" countries across the world, even after decolonisation and the formal achievement of independence (Erling et al., 2013).

The use of English in former British colonies as a marker of socio-economic status and/or middle class mobility may have historically lent itself to the desirability of learning the language among local communities. The development and expansion of local education systems by retreating colonial powers to help maintain post-independence influence also played an important part in this. However, today desire to learn in and about English is more typically associated with its role as the language of globalisation (Pennycook, 2017). It is within this context that English's ties with social and economic development have been strengthened in the eyes of many (Seargeant & Erling, 2013), with the language subsequently assuming a central role in numerous international development programs and initiatives.

English in a number of developing nations is closely associated with access to education and employment, knowledge and information, travel opportunities, and technological advancement. As a result, ELT continues to be promoted as a driver of international development initiatives that move beyond a more traditional, narrow focus on economics, and seek to improve the overall quality of life of people in local communities (Erling et al., 2013).

Appleby (2010, p. 4) highlights the importance of locating ELT in its "diverse social, cultural, and political contexts", and warns that, without engaging in collaboration, participation, and the inclusion of local knowledges, ELT as part of international development initiatives risks privileging developed nations over

C. J. Denman (✉)
Office of Deputy Vice-Chancellor for Postgrasduate Studies and Research,
Sultan Qaboos University, Muscat, Oman
e-mail: denman@squ.edu.om

© Springer Nature Switzerland AG 2021
H. Mohebbi and C. Coombe (eds.), *Research Questions in Language
Education and Applied Linguistics*, Springer Texts in Education,
https://doi.org/10.1007/978-3-030-79143-8_119

developing ones, and perpetuating patriarchal, cultural-linguistic hierarchies. Moreover, the privileged position English has assumed as the world's lingua franca means that international development programs supporting ELT largely determine who has the opportunity to participate in the global economy, and who does not. Here, Seargeant and Erling (2013) describe how education can reproduce social inequalities, especially when Western education models and cultural assumptions and practices are introduced uncritically to recipient nations.

The Research Questions

1. What assumptions promote the place of ELT in international development initiatives in local and national contexts?
2. In what ways can ELT support national development initiatives in recipient nations?
3. How can community English language learning needs be accurately identified to ensure that ELT initiatives are appropriate for the socio-linguistic realities of targeted communities?
4. How can the relationships between ELT, unequal power relations, and global inequality be transformed?
5. What socio-cultural issues impact upon the effectiveness of ELT initiatives for international development in developing contexts?
6. How can issues of cultural deracination and linguistic imperialism be addressed when promoting ELT for international development?
7. What is the relationship between access to English-language education and local and national social and economic development?
8. How can ELT support access to information, technology, employment, and education opportunities in developing contexts?
9. What are the key considerations in aligning ELT with local community needs?
10. How effective is assigning ELT similar status in international development initiatives to the provision of basic services (including access to clean food, water, electricity etc.)?

Suggested Resources

Appleby, R. (2010). *ELT, gender and international development: Myths of progress in a neocolonial world.* **Bristol: Multilingual Matters**.

Appleby describes how studies exploring the link between ELT and development traditionally focus on the "success" of "modern" education methods and expertise in bringing social and economic benefits to developing countries. These studies are noted as highlighting the instrumental connection between ELT and international development in the framework of modernisation. Appleby's book, which features empirically-informed critical perspectives on ELT in international development contexts, however, moves away from this approach by exploring the ways in which ELT, through its place in international development processes, can perpetuate social inequality. In addition to examining gender dynamics in ELT, Appleby details attempts by ELT practitioners in East Timor and Indonesia to understand and transform the relationship between ELT, international development, wider power relations and global inequality.

Erling, E. J., & Seargeant, P. (Eds.). (2013). *English and development: Policy, pedagogy and globalization.* **Bristol: Multilingual Matters.**

The editors begin by acknowledging English's status as a global language that is viewed by individuals and governments around the world as fundamental to full participation in twenty-first century societies. They pose, among many others, the question of why English and ELT should be considered important resources for international development at a time when so many people lack access to basic necessities, including water, health care, and basic education. Having problematized the issue, the book presents a series of edited chapters featuring examinations and case studies that explore the connections between English proficiency and individual and national development, in addition to the potential impact ELT can have on local languages and learners' cultural identities.

Phillipson, R. (1992). *Linguistic imperialism.* **Oxford: Oxford University Press.**

Phillipson's (1992) seminal volume is an important starting point for those seeking to understand the historical antecedents of ELT for international development. *Linguistic Imperialism* outlines the roots of English's current status as the world's dominant international language in the following terms: as rulers of the lion's share of the globe, the British imposed English upon their foreign subjects as a means of diluting local beliefs and allegiances and valorising the metropolis. Phillipson argues that English is still today promoted by Anglophonic Western nations as a means of maintaining economic, if not social and cultural, control, and that this linguistic imperialism is one of the means through which Western nations ensure the global inequalities on which modern economies have been built are maintained. Phillipson's work, though the subject of much debate, forms a strong foundation for understanding contemporary links between ELT and international development, especially in former British colonies.

Erling, E. J., Seargeant, P., Solly, M., Chowdhury, Q. H., & Rahman, S. (2013). Attitudes to English as a language for international development in rural Bangladesh. In S. Sheehan (Ed.), *British Council ELT research papers: Volume 1* **(pp. 183–212). London: British Council.**

Erling et al. explore attitudes towards ELT as part of international development initiatives in rural Bangladesh. The authors contextualise the research by stating evidence of the positive relationship between English and development is, in fact, hard to come by. The paper presents participant case studies based on data collected through an ethnographically-based approach from two rural regions. Findings indicate a strong desire to learn English among rural communities due to the language's associations with modernity, social status, and access to information and employment opportunities. English was not viewed as presenting a threat to participants' use of local languages or socio-cultural identity. The authors conclude that there is a strong link between English and development. However, they offer the caveat that, "What is perceived as a need for English may also indicate a need for further access to literacy in general" (p. 206)—an important consideration for those designing education development programs.

Shamim, F. (2017). English as the language for development in Pakistan: Issues, challenges and possible solutions. In H. Coleman (Ed.), *Dreams and realities: Developing countries and the English language* **(pp. 2–21). London: British Council**.

Shamim details how English is often viewed as playing a multi-faceted role in international development, including in increasing employment opportunities, offering access to research and information, facilitating mobility, and acting as a "neutral" language in contexts of disharmony. It is for these reasons that English is often considered the "de facto language for development in developing countries" (p. 3), including in Pakistan where it is largely accepted as the language of individual and national development. The research featured in this paper, however, indicates tension between local languages in Pakistan as an expression of traditional values and the need to identify with global culture through English. Shamim also notes how the impact and sustainability of ELT-directed development programs can be limited due to a lack of local stakeholder engagement. The author argues that planning English language projects as part of development processes needs to take into account local capacity building and the development of local learning materials and resources.

References

Appleby, R. (2010). *ELT, gender and international development: Myths of progress in a neocolonial world.* Multilingual Matters.

Erling, E. J., Seargeant, P., Solly, M., Chowdhury, Q. H., & Rahman, S. (2013). Attitudes to English as a language for international development in rural Bangladesh. In S. Sheehan (Ed.), *British Council ELT research papers* (Vol. 1, pp. 183–212). British Council.

Pennycook, A. (2017). *The cultural politics of English as an international language.* Routledge.

Seargeant, P., & Erling, E. J. (2013). Introduction: English and development. In E. J. Erling & P. Seargeant (Eds.), *English and development* (pp. 1–20). Multilingual Matters.

C. J. Denman is a researcher at the Office of the Deputy Vice-Chancellor for Postgraduate Studies and Research at Sultan Qaboos University, Oman. He was previously affiliated with the university's Humanities Research Centre and was also an instructor at its Language Centre, following from ELT experience at the secondary and tertiary levels in Australia, South Korea, and Japan. He has published in international journals and edited books, in addition to being co-editor of several volumes concerned with various aspects of English language instruction in the Arab world and internationally.

ELT Textbook Ideology

Esmat Babaii

Critical discourse analysis tells us that no text is innocent and neutral, as far as advocating a particular ideology is concerned (see Weiss & Wodak, 2003). This main doctrine of critical discourse analysis is also true for textbooks, whatever the subject matter. Textbooks, as noted by Apple and Christian-Smith (1991, p. 2), are "the result of political, economic, and cultural activities, battles and compromises". In fact, they are meant to influence their audience's perceptions and orientations in accordance with the macro-level policy adopted in a given community. Considering the historical link between ELT and colonialism, on the one hand, and the contemporary concerns with the role of English in the globalization process, on the other, it is not difficult to see why the critical study of ideological import of English language teaching materials has become an attractive area of research, especially for those with a critical orientation toward English as an international language.

ELT textbook ideology research to date has unearthed certain ethically-challenged attitudes such as sexism, racism, and ethno-centrism in both verbal and pictorial materials which serve as input to language learners at different stages of second language development (Babaii et al., 2016; Gray, 2010; Lee & Collins, 2009; Pashmforoosh & Babaii, 2015; Porreca, 1984; Poulou, 1997, to mention but a few). Whether and to what extent these ideologies can influence the learners' attitude, life style and their native societies are yet to be investigated. However, we can argue against such practices in terms of the EFL/ESL learners' right to be educated through non-imposing, non-inculcating linguistic input, a right which is hardly taken seriously in the majority of educational systems.

Apple (2004), as a notable critic of textbook-based curricula, suggests implementing a "negotiated curriculum" as its democratic alternative, one in which "the materials are built by teachers and students in direct response to local community problems" (p. 195). Though it seems quite fascinating at first glance, the fact is that

E. Babaii (✉)
Department of Foreign Languages, Kharazmi University, Tehran, Iran
e-mail: babai@ku.ac.ir

© Springer Nature Switzerland AG 2021
H. Mohebbi and C. Coombe (eds.), *Research Questions in Language Education and Applied Linguistics*, Springer Texts in Education,
https://doi.org/10.1007/978-3-030-79143-8_120

689

such an idealistic, radical option may not be available in many EFL/ESL settings. Besides, it tends to presuppose a great deal of educational sophistication and familiarity with tenets of materials development on the part of both teachers and learners. Nevertheless, the reality of language classes does not need to be so desperate. We should not throw up our hands in despair when we are expected to teach a predetermined set of instructional materials. The role of teachers as mediators between the EFL/ESL materials and the learners should not be underestimated. Research has documented that things happening inside the classroom as a result of interactions between teacher and learners tend to have a long-lasting effect on the learners' attitude and achievement (Gray, 2000; Wright, 1999). This means that teachers do not need to be passive with regard to the overt and covert ideologies in the materials they are teaching. They can, and in fact should, raise learners' awareness and equip them with the critical thinking skills necessary to handle the flood of information they receive through exposure to textbooks, media and any other linguistics and/or multimodal input.

The Research Questions

1. Do ELT textbook writers follow a personal and/or institutional agenda in promoting certain ideologies?
2. Are EFL learners affected by the ideologies advocated in ELT textbooks? Which ideologies tend to affect them most?
3. Do teachers challenge English-centrist ideologies in EFL materials?
4. Can sexist, racist and ethno-centrist ideologies in ELT materials act as de-motivating factors in language learning?
5. What happens when teachers and learners are not aligned with the ideologies presented in teaching materials?
6. Can critical pedagogy help teachers and learners detect and challenge textbook ideologies?
7. What are dominant ideologies in the materials teaching other languages (e.g., materials teaching Chinese, Arabic, German, Persian, etc. as a foreign language)?
8. Why can't locally-produced EFL materials compete with international materials produced by Western organizations?
9. Can we produce interactive ELT materials capable of giving more options and voice to the teachers and learners?
10. How can we enhance the role of teachers and learners in handling ELT materials?

Suggested Resources

Apple, M. (2004). *Ideology and curriculum* **(3rd ed.). New York: Routledge**.

In the third edition of *Ideology and Curriculum,* Michael Apple argues how education contributes to maintaining and justifying unequal power relations in human societies. Throughout the nine chapters of the book, he deals with some relevant core concepts such as hegemony, cultural and economic reproduction through education, ideology of social control, and hidden curriculum. Chapter ten contains Apple's interview in which he talks about new hegemonic relations. Although the book does not directly address language ideology, it introduces the core concepts needed for the researcher interested in investigating ideology in English language teaching materials. It provides a bird's- eye view through which one can find the link between language policy, hegemony and international trends such as globalization.

Babaii, E., & Sheikhi, M. (2018). Traces of neoliberalism in English teaching materials: a critical discourse analysis. *Critical Discourse Studies*, **15(3), 247–264**.

In this article, the researchers apply Fairclough's (2001) model of Critical Discourse Analysis (CDA) to uncover traces of neoliberalism, as the dominant socio-economic principle in the West, in popular ELT materials taught to a considerably large group of Iranian learners of English. The analysis reveals that certain neoliberal ideas, such as focus on the market, consumerism, branding and individualism are advocated in the studied corpus. Besides, a great number of themes and social relations introduced in the analyzed textbooks are market-led. In their treatment of multiculturalism, the materials are found to highlight positive characteristics of the West while they tend to present a stereotypically undesirable picture of non-Western places and people. The authors argue against this kind of ideologically-loaded materials and call for awareness-raising for teachers and learners who are dealing with them.

Bori, P. (2018). *Language textbook in the era of neoliberalism.* **New York: Routledge**.

The current book discusses the ways neoliberalism is instantiated in language textbooks. The book starts with a history of language education in Europe examining the interaction among political, social and economical factors. Through a review of critical research on language textbooks, the author discusses how diversity is problematized. Adopting a more local perspective, he reviews the case of Catalan textbooks for non-Catalan speakers and demonstrates the contribution of contextual factors to their development. The next chapters are devoted to the results of language textbooks analysis investigating the representation of social class and some relevant neoliberal values such as celebrating house ownership. At the end, the author emphasizes the necessity of critical analysis of textbooks from political economy perspective. The book seems to be a timely contribution to language textbook ideology research as it extends the scope of research to non-English language materials.

Gray, J. (2010). *The construction of English: Culture, consumerism and promotion in the ELT global course book.* **New York: Palgrave Macmillan.**

In this book, which consists of eight chapters, the author offers a critical evaluation of global English teaching materials as a significant ingredient of ELT enterprise. To make a compelling case, he starts by narrating a number of anecdotes which are later discussed in light of global trends and issues. The next chapter is devoted to the relation between language and culture. Later, a detailed report of several ELT textbooks analysis is presented where the texts are examined in terms of features such as representation of race, gender and different accents. The findings are supplemented by the publishers' viewpoints and dilemmas. The book ends with discussing future directions for global ELT textbooks. Overall, the book seems to provide a good mixture of theoretical arguments and empirical findings for a critical state-of-art assessment of English as an international language.

Hartman, P., & Judd, E. (1978). Sexism and TESOL materials. *TESOL Quarterly,* **12(4), 383–393**.

This is an oft-cited paper which can be considered a pioneering work in textbook ideology research. The study explores portrayal of men and women in a series of ESL materials. The findings indicate explicit linguistic and pictorial bias against women, manifested through allocating less visibility for women as well as assigning stereotypical roles and emotional reactions to them. The authors proceed to discuss sexism in the English language by examining certain linguistic features like generic 'he' and the titles used for men and women. They set forth some suggestions to reduce sexism in language teaching materials. For the interested reader, this paper can provide an opportunity to compare the status of textbooks in the 1970s with that of current ones in terms of morally-challenged linguistic and pictorial features.

References

Apple, M. (2004). *Ideology and curriculum* (3rd ed.). Routledge Falmer.

Apple, M., & Christian-Smith, L. (1991). *The politics of the textbook*. Routledge.

Babaii, E., Atai, M., & Kafshgarsoute, M. (2016). A social semiotic analysis of social actors in English learning software applications. *Journal of Teaching Language Skills (JTLS), 35*(3), 1–40.

Gray, J. (2000). The ELT coursebook as cultural artefact: How teachers censor and adapt. *ELT Journal, 54*(3), 274–283.

Gray, J. (2010). *The construction of English: Culture, consumerism and promotion in the ELT global coursebook*. Palgrave Macmillan.

Lee, F., & Collins, P. (2009). Australian English-language textbooks: The gender issues. *Gender and Education, 21*(4), 353–370.

Pashmforoosh, R., & Babaii, E. (2015). Whose culture and how far? Culture presentation in current business English textbook series. *Journal of Teaching in International Business, 26*(3), 216–236.

Porreca, K. (1984). Sexism in current ESL textbooks. *TESOL Quarterly, 18*(4), 705–724.

Poulou, S. (1997). Sexism in the discourse roles of textbook dialogues. *The LanguageLearning Journal, 15*(1), 68–73.

Weis, G., & Wodak, R. (Eds.). (2003). *Critical discourse analysis: Theory and interdisciplinarity.* New York: Palgrave Macmillan.

Wright, M. (1999). Influences on learner attitudes towards foreign language and culture. *Educational Research, 41*(2), 197–208.

Esmat Babaii is Professor of Applied Linguistics at Kharazmi University, Iran where she teaches research methodology, discourse analysis, contrastive rhetoric and language testing to graduate students of applied linguistics. She has published articles and book chapters dealing with issues in Systemic Functional Linguistics, Appraisal theory, test-taking processes, discursive analysis of textbooks, and critical approaches to the study of culture and language. She has served on the editorial boards and review panels of several Iranian and international professional journals. In her most recent work, (to appear in McCallum & Coombe's (2020) edited volume on L2 writing assessment), she examines the promises and problems of World Englishes in assessing writing. She is quite critical of the uncritical ELT pedagogy commonly practiced in many periphery, non-English speaking countries.

Embedding Academic Literacy in Degree Curricula

Neil Murray

In recent years, there has been growing interest in the notion of embedding academic literacy in university degree course curricula (e.g. Arkoudis & Starfield, 2007; McWilliams & Allen, 2014) rather than teaching it as an extra-curricular activity typically delivered via English language teaching units or cognate departments (e.g. TESOL and Applied Linguistics). This interest has arisen largely from a recognition of academic literacy as a pluralistic concept inasmuch as each and every academic discipline has associated with it a particular set of literacy practices through which it is expressed, explored, analysed, and contested. In this respect it embodies Halliday's idea, central to Systemic Functional Linguistics, that language develops to serve the particular purposes for which its users choose to employ it (Halliday, 1985). Thus the academic literacies a Nursing student will need to learn will differ from those of a Business student, for example, and this argues against the kind of centralized generic academic English model often adopted in universities and which assumes that literacy practices are transferable between different disciplinary contexts. In their seminal 1998 paper on academic literacies, Lea and Street spoke of 'the requirement to switch practices between one setting and another, to deploy a repertoire of linguistic practices appropriate to each setting, and to handle the social meanings and identities that each evokes' (1998, p. 159). These practices encompass

> … not just concepts and associated vocabulary, but also rhetorical structures, the patterns of action, that are part of any tradition of meaning-making. They include characteristic ways of reaching consensus and expressing disagreement, of formulating arguments, of providing evidence, as well as characteristic genres for organizing thought and conversational action. (Rex & McEachen., 1999, p. 69).

A discipline is effectively defined and differentiated by its literacy practices and it is through becoming conversant in those practices and learning how to be 'par-

N. Murray (✉)
Department of Applied Linguistics, University of Warwick, Coventry, UK
e-mail: N.L.Murray@warwick.ac.uk

© Springer Nature Switzerland AG 2021
H. Mohebbi and C. Coombe (eds.), *Research Questions in Language Education and Applied Linguistics*, Springer Texts in Education,
https://doi.org/10.1007/978-3-030-79143-8_121

ticular kinds of people: that is to write "as academics", "as geographers", "as social scientists"' (Curry & Lillis., 2003, p. 11) that students become socialized into the discipline and thus bona fide members of its community of practice.

The argument for embedding academic literacy within the curriculum is not only a response to disciplinary variation in literacy practices but also to the realization that all students—home and overseas, native and non-native speakers—stand to benefit from academic literacy tuition: given the diverse student demographic in most universities today, few assumptions can be made regarding their knowledge, upon commencing their degree studies, of those academic literacies pertinent to their discipline, particularly in the case of subjects not taught in secondary education. Furthermore, it supports the idea that language is best learned authentically, in precisely those contexts in which it is to be employed.

While there are sound arguments for embedding academic literacy, the process of doing so can be challenging. Firstly, it requires buy in from various stakeholders including university senior management, Deans of Teaching and Learning, academic departments, and English language providers. These stakeholders need to understand the rationale and what 'academic literacies' means. Secondly, academics need to be able to identify the literacies of their disciplines, and the evidence suggests that making explicit what is largely implicit knowledge that they manifest procedurally every day in the course of their professional lives can be problematic. Thirdly, finding space in the curriculum can be difficult, especially where curricula are heavily prescribed and under pressure from other agendas such as, inclusiveness and employability. Finally, getting academics to understand that academic literacy is fundamental to the discipline and not an 'optional extra' can present major obstacles, not least because the natural corollary of this is that academic staff should be imparting the relevant literacies to students, with English language teachers contributing in a support role. However, while academics are best-placed to do so on the grounds they are most familiar with what is required (even if they require help in articulating it), they may regard language development as outside of their remit and area of expertise. This means that professional development may need to be a part of any initiative to embed academic literacies in the curriculum.

The Research Questions

1. What is academic literacy and how is it a pluralistic concept?
2. How can universities and their staff be persuaded of the need for and benefits of embedding academic literacy in the curriculum?
3. What particular literacies might you expect to need teaching to students studying (a) Nursing, (b) Engineering, and (c) Management?
4. What challenges do academic staff face in their attempts to embed academic literacies?

5. In what ways can English language teachers collaborate with academic staff most effectively to embed academic literacies in the curriculum?
6. How does one decide where in the curriculum different literacies are positioned?
7. How do academic staff feel about embedding and teaching academic literacy? Why?
8. How can English language teachers and academic developers support academic staff in their teaching of academic literacies?
9. What are the advantages and disadvantages of embedded academic literacies being taught (a) by academic staff (b), by English language teachers, (c) jointly by academic staff and English language teachers?
10. What benefits does the decentralised/devolved model of teaching academic literacy within the department/discipline have over a centralized model where it is taught by an English language unit?

Suggested Resources

Curnow, T. J., & Liddicoat, A. J. (2008). Assessment as learning: Engaging students in academic literacy in their first semester. In *Proceedings of the ATN assessment conference 2008: Engaging students in assessment*, **eds. A. Duff, D. Quinn, M. Green, K. Andre, T. Ferris and S. Copland [Online]. Available from:** http://www.ojs.unisa.edu.au/index.php/atna/issue/view/ISBN%20978-0-646-504421/showToc.

In this article, the authors describe in detail the process of embedding academic literacies within the core courses of an applied linguistics undergraduate pro-gramme in an Australian university. Their starting point is the observation that while academic literacy has a 'core role' in the construction of knowledge in university settings, it tends to get ignored in teaching and assessment approaches in favour of a narrower focus on content. They argue that the first stage of embedding involves determining the academic literacy practices students would be expected to have developed upon completion of a programme and then distributing these practices between the different assessment items across those core courses in which they arise most naturally in terms of being a prerequisite to engaging with their content. In so doing, recognition is given to the symbiotic relationship between academic literacy and discipline content in course delivery and assessment. The article provides a clear articulation of the rationale at each stage of the embedding process and makes for interesting reading.

Murray, N., & Nallaya, S. (2014). Embedding academic literacies in university programme curricula: a case study. *Studies in Higher Education*, **41(7), 1296–1312**.

While there is a growing body of literature focused on the idea of embedding academic literacies in degree course curricula, there are relatively few that report on case studies and describe in detail the actual process of embedding This article provides such an account and records the authors' experience in terms of the collaborative process, the resources employed to support academic staff through the process, and the difficulties encountered along the way. It focuses on an embedding initiative undertaken as a pilot study in an institutional context where the vision was to embed academic literacies in all programme curricula. The pilot was conducted in two first-year university programmes offered in the Division of Education, Arts and Social Sciences, namely, the Bachelor of Teaching degree, located within the School of Education, and the Bachelor of Arts degree.

Murray, N. (2016). *Standards of English in higher education.* **Cambridge: Cambridge University Press**.

This book places the issue of embedding literacies in the curriculum within the broader context of English language policy and provision within higher education. Specifically, it discusses it in relation to (a) the problematic notion of proficiency and the implications of how one deconstructs 'proficiency for determining which students need access to particular kind(s) of language development; (b) English language assessment pre- and post-enrolment; and (c) the notion of decentralization in the provision of English language services. While it makes a detailed case for embedding academic literacies within the curriculum, it considers some of the political, logistical and other challenges involved in doing so.

Nesi, H., & Garner, S. (2012). *Genres across the disciplines: Student writing in higher education.* **Cambridge: Cambridge University Press**.

In this book, using the Sydney School's approach to genre, the authors draw on faculty and student interview data and the British Academic Written English (BAWE) corpus of nearly 3000 positively-evaluated student papers across over 30 academic disciplines to categorize into 13 families the genres students are expected to engage in during their studies. These genres are grouped and then discussed in relation to the five social functions of university education as reflected in national (UK) education guidelines; namely, demonstrating knowledge and understanding, developing powers of independent reasoning, building research skills, preparing for professional practice and writing for oneself and others. The book makes very concrete and gives pedagogical currency to the notion of discipline-specific literacy by taking this approach and including authentic examples of assignment tasks, macrostructures, concordances and keywords, all of which can be used to inform course design, regardless of whether or not academic literacy is delivered via an embedded model.

Wingate, U. (2018). Academic literacy across the curriculum: Towards a collaborative instructional approach. *Language Teaching,* **51(3), 349–364**.

This article describes an alternative, non-embedded model of discipline-specific language provision and teaching methodology, and its theoretical underpinnings (genre analysis, systemic functional linguistics/social constructivist theory)— aspects often missing from other accounts. Lecturers from four disciplines identified a genre for which they felt teaching support was needed, and provided text examples that were assessed and accompanied by feedback. Students received three high-scoring text examples with commentary; one high-scoring text example for which they had to write a commentary; a 'Notes' section in which to list their observations of expected features of successful writing; two low-scoring text examples with commentary, and a reflection section. Students then used what they had learnt from this process to edit peers' essays and subsequently their own assignments. Feedback on the model was very positive but lack of subject lecturer engagement suggested that top-down policies are needed if initiatives are to be truly collaborative. The author discusses some of the disadvantages of this kind of non-embedded discipline-specific approach and provides some useful suggestions for how to utilise Postgraduate Certificate of Academic Practice (PGCAP)-type programmes as mechanisms for developing lecturers' ability to deliver academic literacy tuition within their subject.

References

Arkoudis, S., & Starfield, S. (2007, August). In-course language development and support. In *Paper presented at the national symposium: English Language competence of international students*, Sydney.

Curry, M. J., & Lillis, T. M. (2003). Issues in academic writing in higher education. In C. Coffin, M. J. Curry, S. Goodman, A. Hewings, T. Lillis, & J. Swann (Eds.), *Teaching academic writing: A toolkit for higher education* (pp. 1–18). Routledge.

Halliday, M. A. K. (1985). *Introduction to functional grammar*. Edward Arnold.

Lea, M. R., & Street, B. (1998). Student writing in higher education: An academic literacies approach. *Studies in Higher Education, 23*(2), 157–172.

McWilliams, R., & Allen, Q. (2014). Embedding academic literacy skills: Towards a best practice model. *Journal of University Learning and Teaching Practice, 11*(3), 1–20.

Rex, L. A., & McEachen, D. (1999). If anything is odd, inappropriate, confusing, or boring, it's probably important: The emergence of inclusive academic literacy through English classroom discussion practices. *Research in the Teaching of English, 24*, 65–129.

Neil Murray is Professor in the Department of Applied Linguistics, University of Warwick, UK and was previously Head of Language and Literacy at the University of South Australia. He has published widely on language assessment, academic literacy and pragmatics. His current research interests include English language policy and regulation in higher education, and English as a medium of instruction. While in Australia, he engaged with government-driven initiatives around English language provision in the tertiary sector, serving as consultant to a number of universities seeking to respond to such initiatives. His book publications include *Standards of English in higher education: Issues, challenges and strategies* (Cambridge University Press) and *Dynamic ecologies: A relational perspective on languages education in the Asia-Pacific region* (with Angela Scarino, Springer).

English Language Education Policy

Robert Kirkpatrick and M. Obaidul Hamid

English language education policy is a subset of language in education policy, also known as language acquisition planning (Kaplan & Baldauf, 1997). Language in education policy refers to the deployment of language in education contexts, shaping the character, processes and outcomes of education for different linguistic and social groups (Johnson & Pratt, 2014; Menken & Garcia, 2010). The choice of language in education sites—whether as a medium for teaching and learning or curriculum content—is ideological, that seeks to pursue national interests and ideologies.

English language education policy is linked to the spread of English worldwide. British and American colonization of Asia and Africa, which brought English to these parts of the world, provided the initial context for English language policy in education. As globalization has turned English into a global lingua franca in the key domains of information and communication, science and technology, education and knowledge and trade and commerce, teaching and learning of English has dominated education systems in emerging English-using nations. Recent English language policy in these polities reflects two major global trends: the earlier introduction of English in the curriculum, and the growing use of English as a medium of instruction (Hamid, 2016). English as a medium of instruction (EMI) policy seeks to develop students' English proficiency through their exposure to English-medium content teaching without explicit instruction in language. EMI has been favoured in Asia and Africa and is increasingly being used in higher education (Fenton-Smith et al, 2017). An approach that has an explicit instructional focus on both continent and language is called Content and Language Integrated Learning (CLIL), which has become popular particularly in Europe (Diaz Perez

R. Kirkpatrick (✉)
Gulf University for Science and Technology, Mubarak Al-Abdullah, Kuwait

M. Obaidul Hamid
The University of Queensland, Brisbane, Australia
e-mail: m.hamid@uq.edu.au

© Springer Nature Switzerland AG 2021
H. Mohebbi and C. Coombe (eds.), *Research Questions in Language Education and Applied Linguistics*, Springer Texts in Education,
https://doi.org/10.1007/978-3-030-79143-8_122

et al, 2018). Thus, English language policy may have to replace local/national languages in education in some polities; in others, the policy has become part of bilingual/multilingual education seeking to ensure the co-existence of global and local languages in the education space. The other trend of using English earlier in the curriculum has led to significant policy and pedagogical efforts in teaching English to young learners (Garton & Copland, 2018) to give children a head start, also for instrumentalist outcomes.

The intensified use of English in education is motivated by the development of human capital which is widely believed to lead to individual mobility and national economic development. This human capital is also considered essential for nations to stay competitive in a competitive globalized environment.

English language education policy in many of the polities is initiated at the macro level, typically by national policy makers. The education sector is then trusted with the task of implementing policy and producing policy outcomes, often with limited resources. While the agency of educator actors is critical in this policy translation, some policies including EMI and CLIL may also have more local origins. Thus, understating the process of policy initiation and enactment calls for ethnographic approaches which can present a holistic view of the multilayered policy cycle. English language policy in education also tells us that the education space is an essential mechanism for implementing policies for the entire society.

The Research Questions

1. How does English language education policy relate to national identity and nation building in a globalized world?
2. What are the drivers of EMI in at different levels of education across polities?
3. Who are the actors of English language policy in education and how do they exercise their agency?
4. What are the challenges in the implementation of early English language in the curriculum?
5. How does English language education policy affect local languages?
6. How does EMI relate to social justice and equity issues?
7. What is the role of English language proficiency in employability in developing society?
8. What is the relationship between English language and national development in a globalized economic environment?
9. What are the effects of neoliberalism on English language education policy?
10. How does translanguaging relate to English language education policy?

Suggested Resources

Kirkpatrick, A., & Liddicoat, A. J. (Eds.). (2019). *The Routledge international handbook of language education policy in Asia*. **London; New York: Routledge**.

This latest handbook provides a comprehensive overview of language education policy in Asia. The book is divided into five parts. The first part is an overview and includes three chapters. The first introduces the handbook, while the other two discuss minority languages in education and multilingual education respectively. The remaining 29 chapters of the book constitute the other four parts, each of which focuses on one region of the vast continent including East Asia, South-East Asia, South Asia and Central Asia. These chapters cover language education policy issues in 32 polities. Although these chapters are not necessarily about English language education policy, English occupies a significant space in each.

Kirkpatrick, R. (Ed.) (2016). *English language education policy in Asia*. **Netherlands: Springer**.

This volume gives an in-depth study of educational policies concerning the teaching of English in a 16 Asian countries. It includes assessments of top-down government implemented polices and looks at the implementation of policy in schools and on the wider population. Topics include the sometimes fraught relationship between English education and national language(s) and also highlights economic, political, and cultural issues related to the learning of English. There is a sister volume which covers the Middle East and North Africa, also by Kirkpatrick.

Hamid, M. O. (2016). The politics of language in education in a global polity. In K. Mundy, A. Green, B. Lingard, & A. Verger (Eds.), *The handbook of global education policy* **(pp. 259–274). London: Wiley Blackwell**.

This chapter explicates the nature of the politics of language that has informed education policymaking in different social contexts. The author discusses how the term politics has been understood by different scholars. He points out that it should be understood in the sense of discourses or ideologies of language that have underpinned the educational use of English and other languages. The author discusses five examples of language policy of global relevance including English in the national curriculum, English and higher education, language and migration, minority languages, and foreign languages other than English.

Walter, S. J., & Benson, C. (2012). Language policy and medium of instruction in formal education. In B. Spolsky (Ed.), *The Cambridge handbook of language policy* **(pp. 278–300). Cambridge: Cambridge University Press**.

This chapter provides a comprehensive overview of medium of instruction policy as practiced in different parts of the world at the primary level and of the consequences of this policy. The authors start with a picture of the linguistic diversity of the world. This is an important reading for a critical understanding of some of the key issues in language in education planning. The chapter provides empirical evidence which would help to address many of the contentious issues about mediums of instruction policy.

Shohamy, E. (2006). *Language Policy: Hidden Agendas and New Approaches.* **London: Routledge.**

Although written over a decade ago the book gives an important perspective to researchers who want to see beyond the most obvious elements of explicit language policy, using examples from the USA and the UK. Divided into 3 sections, Part I discuses language, manipulations, and policy, Part II the mechanisms affecting de facto language policies, and Part III the consequences and reactions. In Chap. 6 Shohamy shows how the backwash from language testing is in effect itself a de facto language policy. Overall, a fascinating read that has had an influence on research ever since its publication.

References

Diaz Perez, W., Fields, D. L., & Marsh, D. (2018). Innovations and challenges: Conceptualizing CLIL challenges. *Theory into Practice, 57*(3), 177–184.

Fenton-Smith, B., Humphreys, P., & Walkinshaw, I. (Eds.). (2017). *English medium instruction in higher education in Asia-Pacific: From policy to pedagogy.* Springer.

Garton, S., & Copland, F. (Eds.). (2018). *The Routledge handbook of teaching English to young learners.* New York: Routledge.

Hamid, M. O. (2016). The politics of language in education in a global polity. In K. Mundy, A. Green, B. Lingard, & A. Verger (Eds.), *The handbook of global education policy* (pp. 259–274). London: Wiley Blackwell.

Johnson, D. C., & Pratt, K. L. (2014). Educational language policy and planning. In C. A. Chapelle (Ed.), *The Encyclopedia of applied linguistics* (pp. 1–7): Wiley. https://doi.org/10.1002/9781405198431.wbeal1416

Kaplan, R. B., & Baldauf, R. B., Jr. (1997). *Language planning: From practice to theory.* Multilingual Matters.

Menken, K., & Garcia, O. (Eds.). (2010). *Negotiating language policies in schools: Educators as policymakers.* Routledge.

Robert Kirkpatrick has taught English and applied linguistics at universities in Japan and Thailand and is now a member of the English faculty at Gulf University for Science and Technology in Kuwait. He is Editor-in-Chief of *Language Testing in Asia*, an open access SCOPUS indexed journal by SpringerNature. His latest edited volume is *English Language Education Policy in the Middle East and North Africa* a sister volume to the well-received *English language education policy in Asia*, both volumes in the Springer *Language Policy* series.

M. Obaidul Hamid Ph.D. is Senior Lecturer in TESOL Education at the University of Queensland, Australia. Previously he worked at the University of Dhaka, Bangladesh. His research focuses on the policy and practice of TESOL education in developing societies. He is Co-editor of *Language planning for medium of instruction in Asia* (Routledge, 2014). He is on the editorial board of *Current Issues in Language PlanningEnglish Teaching: Practice & Critique* and the *Journal of Asia TEFL*.

Nicola Galloway and Jim McKinley

Internationalization has become a priority for universities around the globe. Many efforts are being made to internationalize curricula, establish and extend international partnerships, publish internationally and conduct collaborative research with international partners to raise international profiles. In non-Anglophone settings, this internationalization has led to an increased focus on teaching content subjects in English, as higher education institutions come under increased pressure to offer programmes that use English medium instruction (EMI) to draw international students and staff (Kirkpatrick, 2011). This *Englishization* is found in programmes in both the secondary and tertiary sector.

EMI is defined here as "an educational system where content is taught through English in contexts where English is not used as the primary, first, or official language" (Rose & McKinley, 2018, p. 114). There has been a growing apprehension regarding social justice issues concerning both students who have not had much exposure to English, and academic staff where an ability to teach in English is increasingly a major criterion in faculty hiring decisions. Indeed, Englishization can be seen as either a "threat or opportunity" in internationalized higher education. Phillipson (2015, p. 39) argues, "Universities need to be committed to articulating policies that can achieve greater social justice, for instance ensuring that any threat from English is converted into an opportunity that does not impact negatively on the vitality of other languages."

Furthermore, rather unfairly, the number of EMI courses on offer is often used to determine the quality of an institution's educational provision and is used to determine government funding and rankings. There is also increased pressure on

N. Galloway (✉)
School of Education, University of Glasgow, Glasgow, UK
e-mail: nicola.galloway@glasgow.ac.uk

J. McKinley (✉)
UCL Institute of Education, London, UK
e-mail: j.mckinley@ucl.ac.uk

© Springer Nature Switzerland AG 2021
H. Mohebbi and C. Coombe (eds.), *Research Questions in Language Education and Applied Linguistics*, Springer Texts in Education,
https://doi.org/10.1007/978-3-030-79143-8_123

faculty to publish in international journals; many universities mandate that newly hired staff teach at least some of their classes in English and require students to take at least some EMI classes to graduate.

This rapidly expanding provision, however, has not been matched with an extensive body of empirical research. Research has reported the lack of monitoring systems or clear outcomes, which makes it difficult to measure the effectiveness of EMI programmes (Galloway et al., 2017; McKinley, 2018; Rose & Galloway, 2019). Internationalization education policy decisions need to be matched with research into the complexities of such rapid developments. Such research is needed to inform effective policy implementation in context sensitive ways. Thus, we outline research questions to prompt urgently needed research to address the broad range of relevant social, theoretical and practical issues, to conduct a needs analysis and facilitate curriculum development. The prompts concern the following calls for research and monitoring systems to investigate the effectiveness of EMI, including the impact on students' learning, staff experiences, university reputation; as well as a response to recent calls for an examination of the challenges faced by students in EMI contexts (see Macaro et al., 2018). Also in need of investigation is one of the main driving forces behind Englishization of higher education: to attract students and funding through international student fees.

The Research Questions

1. How did the main driving forces lead to the Englishization of higher education?
2. To what extent is EMI a major part of the internationalization agenda? (and in different departments).
3. What are key stakeholders' opinions towards the transition to EMI?
4. What monitoring systems have been put in place? What outcomes? Learning objectives?
5. How is policy being implemented? How is EMI approached in different contexts and disciplines?
6. What is the impact on students' learning, staff experiences, university reputation?
7. What challenges does it present?
8. What are the key motivating factors behind student enrolment?
9. What support is in place? Collaboration between content and English for Academic Purposes teachers?
10. How is it linked to developments in applied linguistics/ what is the impact on English Language Teaching?

Suggested Resources

Galloway, N., Kriukow, J., & Numajiri, T. (2017). Internationalisation, higher education and the growing demand for English: an investigation into the English medium of instruction (EMI) movement in China and Japan. *British Council.* **Retrieved 27 November 2017, from** https://www.teachingenglish.org.uk/article/internationalisation-higher-education-growing-demand-english-investigation-english-medium.

This study explored the EMI phenomenon in higher education in Japan and China. Questionnaires, interviews and focus groups with staff and students were used to examine the differing approaches to, driving forces behind, and attitudes towards EMI. Approaches to EMI entry requirements varied, particularly in relation to the provision of English language support. Findings showed that staff and students' attitudes towards this differed. Students saw EMI as a tool for learning English and indicated a belief in 'native' English ownership of the language. Academic staff believe EMI programmes should only use English, many also believe that the mother tongue can be a useful pedagogical tool. Students, however, do not favour the use of the mother tongue in class. The study raised questions as to whether approaching EMI monolingually is the best way forward. The report concluded with some practical suggestions for different stakeholders, including staff, students, materials writers and policymakers.

Macaro, E., Curle, S., Pun, J., An, J., & Dearden, J. (2018). A Systematic Review of English Medium Instruction in Higher Education. *Language Teaching,* **51(1), 36–76.**

This timely systematic review by a project team at the University of Oxford covers research in English medium instruction (EMI) in higher education (HE). They highlight the rapid growth of EMI positioning in the broader context of content and language research. They conducted an in-depth review of 83 EMI studies in HE in different parts of the world. The studies reviewed first cover university teachers' and students' beliefs before then considering the evidence of the benefits of EMI regarding English proficiency versus a potential detrimental effect on content learning. The team held serious concerns about the implementation of EMI despite its inevitable introduction in HE, concluding that the extant research is insufficient to argue whether EMI is beneficial to language learning or detrimental to content learning.

Phillipson, R. (2015). English as threat or opportunity in European higher education. In S. Dimova, A. K. Hultgren & C. Jensen (Eds.). *English-medium instruction in European higher education,* **3, 19–42.**

This book chapter positions English as key to globalization in a joint effort by the US and UK to dominate capitalism world-wide. The author, known for his position on English linguistic imperialism, considers the idea of English serving all people equally to be a myth. The increased use of English in higher education is discussed in relation to efforts from Nordic countries and Germany to avoid marginalization of local languages. While investment in increasing English usage is inevitable, these efforts are targeting the potential limitations of national languages and their democratic functions. Academic discourse, particularly British, is blamed for playing down the power of English linguistic imperialism, failing to position the expansion of English in relation to the forces behind its increased use. The author makes a call for the development of language policies that better balance English with other languages.

Rose, H., & McKinley, J. (2018). Japan's English-medium instruction initiatives and the globalization of higher education. *Higher Education,* **75, 111–129.**

This article analyses Japan's "Top Global University Project" (TGUP), an initiative that aims to internationalize higher education in Japan, targeting the creation of globally oriented universities, increased role of foreign languages, and fostering of global human resources. The project funded 37 universities: 13 designated for competition in the top 100 university world rankings and 24 to serve as models of internationalized higher education. This study addresses the lack of research on the TGUP, considering changes from previous internationalization policies. An analysis is presented of documents regarding the policy, found on the 37 participant universities' websites. The TGUP was found to be an improvement on older policies, taking on board flexible, new approaches to English language education.

Wächter, B. & Maiworm, F. (2015). *English-Taught Programmes in European Higher Education: The state of Play in 2014.* **ACA Papers on International Cooperation in Education.**

This report published online presents the third study by a collaboration between the Academic Cooperation Association, the Gesellschaft für Empirische Studien, and Study Portals BV, designed to map and analyse English-Taught Programmes (ETPs) in Europe. The first two studies were published in 2002 and 2008. The total number of ETPs in Europe was 725 in 2001; 2389 in 2007; and to 8089 in this study, indicating an exponential growth of ETPs being offered across non-English-speaking Europe. In addition to volume and country distribution, the report also addressed institutional contexts, operational aspects of ETPs, language concerns, and impact of ETPs. The methods for the study involved four surveys—two large and two small—targeting institutional and programme levels. The findings revealed that English language proficiency has become less of a problem since their 2007 and 2001 surveys.

References

Galloway, N., Kriukow, J., & Numajiri, T. (2017). Internationalisation, higher education and the growing demand for English: an investigation into the English medium of instruction (EMI) movement in China and Japan. British Council. Retrieved 27, November, 2017, from https://www.teachingenglish.org.uk/article/internationalisation-higher-education-growing-demand-english-investigation-english-medium

Kirkpatrick, A. (2011). Internationalization or Englishization: Medium of instruction in today's universities. *CGC Working Papers Series 2011/003.*

Macaro, E., Curle, S., Pun, J., An, J., & Dearden, J. (2018). A systematic review of English medium instruction in higher education. *Language Teaching, 51*(1).

McKinley, J. (2018). Making the EFL to ELF transition at a global traction university. In A. Bradford & H. Brown (Eds.), *English-medium Instruction at Universities in Japan: Policy, challenges and outcomes* (pp. 238–249). Multilingual Matters.

Phillipson, R. (2015). English as threat or opportunity in European higher education. In S. Dimova, A. K. Hultgren, & C. Jensen (Eds.). *English-medium instruction in European higher education* (Vol. 3, pp. 19–42).

Rose, H., & Galloway, N. (2019). *Global Englishes for language teaching.* Cambridge University Press.

Rose, H., & McKinley, J. (2018). Japan's English-medium instruction initiatives and the globalization of higher education. *Higher Education, 75,* 111–129.

Nicola Galloway is a senior lecturer in TESOL at The University of Glasgow. She is author of *Global Englishes and Change in English Language Teaching: Attitudes and Impact* (2017) and co-author of *Introducing Global Englishes* (2015) and *Global Englishes for Language Teaching* (2019). She has published on both Global Englishes- and EMI-related research and is currently involved in a follow-on British Council funded project in the Southeast Asian context.

Jim McKinley is an associate professor of applied linguistics and TESOL at UCL Institute of Education, University of London. He is an author and editor of several books on research methods in applied linguistics. He also publishes on EMI, higher education, and second language writing in book chapters and journals such as the *Journal of Second Language Writing, Applied Linguistics,* and *Higher Education.* He is a co-editor of the journal *System.*

Linguistic Barriers in Foreign Language Education

124

Heiko Motschenbacher

"Linguistic barrier" (Motschenbacher, 2016a) is a cover term that captures all language- and communication-related aspects that may pose obstacles to language learning, communicative success or the social inclusion of certain (groups of) individuals, often in educational contexts (see Motschenbacher, 2019). As opposed to the notion of a language barrier, which more specifically refers to communication difficulties that arise from speakers not possessing sufficient skills in a certain language, the term "linguistic barrier" covers a much broader range of language-related aspects, including differences between learners' native language and the target language, cross-cultural communication differences, discourses, language ideologies and language attitudes that may have negative effects on learning and inclusion, as well as exclusionary mechanisms of linguistic and multimodal representation.

Various social dimensions are potentially relevant when it is our aim to raise inclusivity levels in the foreign language classroom. Among them are disability and learning difficulties, high talent, gender, sexuality, ethnicity and L1 background, refugee populations, race, non-nativeness, social class, and religion. This entry concentrates on four of these dimensions: gender, sexuality, non-nativeness, and ethnicity/L1 background. The various types of linguistic barriers outlined above do not affect all of these dimensions in the same way and to the same extent. Instead, the four aspects show certain centers of gravity concerning the linguistic barriers that prevail in their discursive construction.

Sexuality as a linguistic barrier mainly affects the level of linguistic representation in teaching materials and classroom talk, where a negative, stereotypical or non-representation of non-heterosexual identities, relationships, families and desires may cause language learning to become a less personally relevant business for

H. Motschenbacher (✉)
Departmnt of Language, Literature, Mathematics and Interpreting,
Western Norway University of Applied Sciences, Bergen, Norway
e-mail: heim@hvl.no

© Springer Nature Switzerland AG 2021
H. Mohebbi and C. Coombe (eds.), *Research Questions in Language Education and Applied Linguistics*, Springer Texts in Education,
https://doi.org/10.1007/978-3-030-79143-8_124

certain learners, which in turn is likely to result in drawbacks in terms of language learning motivation (Motschenbacher, 2021; Sauntson, 2018, 2019).

Gender is also often connected to representational linguistic barriers, for example, when female and male social actors are represented in gender-stereotypical or asymmetrical ways that may clash significantly with the self-identification especially of younger learners (Motschenbacher, 2016b) or when gender non-conforming aspects and transgender experiences are not made visible. Besides this, another barrier may arise at the level of language ideologies and attitudes. Female learners are, for example, widely believed to be better language learners, while good foreign language skills may be perceived to clash with male learners' masculinity concepts (Carr & Pauwels, 2006; Sunderland, 2019).

Non-nativeness is a dimension of inclusion that has major repercussions on the level of representation, too, with EFL textbooks often showing a strong preponderance of native-speaker and native-culture representation to the detriment of the representation of second language identities, foreign language identities, translanguaging or the use of English as an international lingua franca, in short, identifications and language uses that are likely to be most directly relevant for English language learners (Motschenbacher, 2019). Another relevant level is that of the evaluation of language skills, where communicative efficiency represents a learning goal that is more relevant and more realistic for many learners than native-likeness or grammatical correctness.

Finally, linguistic barriers that affect the inclusion of learners from ethnic backgrounds and with L1s other than those of the dominant population in a given society may surface at a wide variety of levels, ranging from contrasts between learners' native language/culture and the target language/culture, the (non-)representation of ethnic groups in teaching materials and classroom interactions, restrictive national language policies, and negative discourses associated with certain ethnic groups (Starr & Hiramoto, 2019; Yu & Hsia, 2019).

The research questions listed below target exclusive mechanisms more generally as well as specific social dimensions of exclusion and are meant to facilitate the finding of solutions to the problems caused by linguistic barriers. Such barriers can be empirically approached drawing on a wide range of language data (teaching materials, classroom interactions, interviews or questionnaires with teachers, learners or parents as informants, curriculum and educational policy documents, learner output, language structures) and linguistic methods (including those of sociolinguistics, pragmatics, critical discourse studies, linguistic ethnography, conversation analysis, corpus linguistics, contrastive linguistics and second language acquisition).

Research Questions

1. Which language- and communication-related aspects can be observed that may constitute linguistic barriers to successful learning, communication and inclusion for certain (groups of) learners in a particular foreign language learning context (identification of linguistic barriers)?
2. How can the identified linguistic barriers be overcome (proposing of linguistic inclusion strategies)?
3. Which linguistic barriers may prevent the successful inclusion of female and male learners, or of trans-identified learners in the foreign language classroom?
4. How can the negative effects of such gender-related linguistic barriers be countered or avoided?
5. Are there aspects of the linguistic and multimodal representation of social actors in the foreign language classroom that put the personal relevance and learning motivation of non-heterosexually identified students or students in close contact with non-heterosexual families and friends at risk?
6. How can these aspects be changed in order to cater for the needs of students in whose lives non-heterosexuality plays a role?
7. Which linguistic barriers can be found that suggest that non-native language users are not legitimate users of a language and that non-native language use is unacceptable, even though it may be communicatively successful?
8. How can these linguistic barriers be eliminated, to grant foreign language learners and non-native language teachers a more self-confident and motivation-enhancing view on their own use of linguistic resources?
9. Which linguistic barriers pose challenges for the inclusion of learners from ethnic backgrounds and with native languages other than those that predominate in a given society?
10. How can these linguistic barriers be lowered, to ensure that these students can learn, communicate, understand and participate successfully?

Suggested Resources

Motschenbacher, H. (2016). Inclusion and foreign language education: What linguistics can contribute. *ITL—International Journal of Applied Linguistics* 167(2), 159–189.

This article serves as a useful theoretical entrance point for those who are planning to conduct research on inclusion in foreign language education from a linguistic point of view. It outlines the narrower and broader senses of educational inclusion, introduces the notion of "linguistic barrier", and identifies various ways in which exclusion may manifest itself in language and communicative practices. It is argued that purely cognitivist approaches to second language acquisition are insufficient for achieving higher levels of inclusivity, as they do not cater for the social and contextual aspects that shape practices of exclusion and inclusion. Alternative approaches such as sociocultural theory are shown to be better equipped for this purpose. Various prominent exclusion-related dimensions in relation to language and linguistic practices are discussed, among them exclusion related to learners with special needs, ethnicity, gender, sexuality and non-native language users. Suggestions are made of how to proceed methodologically in linguistic investigations of exclusionary practices, with the aim of creating effective, linguistically based inclusion strategies.

Motschenbacher, H. (2019). Non-nativeness as a dimension of inclusion: A multimodal representational analysis of EFL textbooks. *International Journal of Applied Linguistics* **29 (3), 285–307**.

This article discusses key aspects of inclusion and applies them to the realms of language, communication and language learning. The concept of "linguistic barrier" is discussed. Against this theoretical backdrop, the article hones in on non-nativeness as a dimension of inclusion in foreign language teaching. Processes of exclusion and inclusion are illustrated through a multimodal critical discourse analysis of representational practices in units from a German EFL textbook series. The main focus of analysis lies on verbal and visual cultural indexes that allow for conclusions on the representation of native and non-native social actors from ENL, ESL and EFL cultures. Based on the finding that the material shows a strong predominance of native language user representation, it is argued that a mainstreaming of second language identities and English as an international lingua franca in ELT can foster higher levels of inclusion that are likely to have positive, empowering effects for learners of English and non-native English language teachers alike.

Sauntson, H. (2018). *Language, Sexuality and Education.* **Cambridge: Cambridge University Press**.

This book on queer applied linguistics is an excellent resource for scholars conducting research on sexuality as a dimension of linguistic inclusion in educational contexts more generally and in foreign language education more specifically. The author argues that sexuality-related discrimination, bullying and normativity do not just affect non-heterosexually identified learners but potentially all learners. These issues are the outcome of influential sexuality discourses whose traces often surface in communicative practices and can therefore fruitfully be studied using linguistic types of analysis. The book presents evidence for the current salience of the issue in UK and US contexts, a theoretical overview of language and sexuality studies and, more specifically, of the field of language, sexuality and education. Against this background, it documents research-based evidence for practices of sexuality-related linguistic exclusion, drawing on a remarkable range of data types (interviews with young people and teachers, curriculum documents, classroom interactions) and linguistic methodologies (appraisal analysis, critical discourse analysis, corpus linguistics).

Sunderland, J. (2019). Inclusion and exclusion in foreign language education: A critical overview, with illustrations from studies of a German classroom for young secondary learners and of five Polish textbooks. *International Journal of Applied Linguistics* **29 (3): 308–321**.

This article discusses central mechanisms of gender-based linguistic exclusion in foreign language education, taking a critical stance at earlier work on this issue. Central aspects outlined include the discursive construction of the foreign language classroom as a stereotypically feminine and heteronormative space, the dominance of boys in classroom interactions, and a lower representational visibility of female social actors in teaching materials. The impact of gender is further illustrated adducing data from two empirical studies on classroom interactions and gender representations in textbooks.

Yu, B. & Hsia, S. (2019). Inclusion of heritage language learners on the autism spectrum: Lessons from second-generation parents. *International Journal of Applied Linguistics* **29 (3): 356–369**.

This research paper provides a unique account of linguistically mediated processes of exclusion in the education of heritage language learners on the autism spectrum. The study concentrates on learners who are children of second-generation Chinese-Americans, and thus advances our understanding of the complexities that inclusive language pedagogy has to face at the intersection of ethnicity and disability. Drawing on questionnaire and interview data, the authors show that the identification of a disability induces shifts in educational practices from heritage language enrichment to remediation and thus has detrimental effects on heritage language learning.

References

Carr, J., & Pauwels, A. (2006). *Boys and foreign language learning: Real boys don't do languages*. Palgrave Macmillan.

Motschenbacher, H. (2016a). Inclusion and foreign language education: What linguistics can contribute. *ITL—International Journal of Applied Linguistics, 167*(2), 159–189.

Motschenbacher, H. (2016b). Gender, inclusion and English language teaching: A linguistic perspective. In D. Elsner & V. Lohe (Eds.). *Gender and language learning: Research and practice* (pp. 97–112). Tübingen: Narr.

Motschenbacher, H. (Ed.). (2019). Linguistic dimensions of inclusion in language teaching and multilingual contexts [special issue: International Journal of Applied Linguistics, 29(3)]. New York: Wiley-Blackwell.

Motschenbacher, H. (2019). Non-nativeness as a dimension of inclusion: A multimodal representational analysis of EFL textbooks. *International Journal of Applied Linguistics, 29* (3), 285–307.

Motschenbacher, H. (2021). Foreign language learning and sexuality-related inclusion: A multimodal analysis of representational practices in the German textbook series Navi Englisch. In Ł. Pakuła (Ed.). *Linguistic perspectives on sexuality in education* (pp. 51–75). Cham: Palgrave Macmillan.

Sauntson, H. (2018). *Language, sexuality and education*. Cambridge University Press.

Sauntson, H. (2019). Language, sexuality and inclusive pedagogy. *International Journal of Applied Linguistics, 29*(3), 322–340.

Starr, R. L., & Hiramoto, M. (2019). Inclusion, exclusion, and racial identity in Singapore's language education system. *International Journal of Applied Linguistics, 29*(3), 341–355.

Sunderland, J. (2019). Inclusion and exclusion in foreign language education: A critical overview, with illustrations from studies of a German classroom for young secondary learners and of five Polish textbooks. *International Journal of Applied Linguistics, 29*(3), 308–321.

Yu, B., & Hsia, S. (2019). Inclusion of heritage language learners on the autism spectrum: Lessons from second-generation parents. *International Journal of Applied Linguistics, 29*(3), 356–369.

Heiko Motschenbacher is Full Professor of ESL/EFL at Western Norway University of Applied Sciences, Bergen. He is principal investigator of an EU-funded research project on *Linguistic Dimensions of Sexual Normativity*, carried out at Florida Atlantic University and Goethe-University Frankfurt, and co-editor of the *Journal of Language and Sexuality*. Recent publications include *New Perspectives on English as a European Lingua Franca* (2013), *Language, Normativity and Europeanisation* (2016), *Gender Across Languages, Vol. 4* (2015, with Marlis Hellinger), and special journal issues on *Queer Linguistic Approaches to Discourse* (2013, with Martin Stegu), *Corpus Linguistics in Language and Sexuality Studies* (2018) and *Linguistic Dimensions of Inclusion in Educational and Multilingual Contexts* (2019). His research interests include language, gender and sexuality, critical discourse analysis, corpus linguistics, English as a lingua franca, language, nationalism and Europeanisation, and linguistic inclusion in ELT.

Policy Enactment for Effective Leadership in English Language Program Management

Kashif Raza

For the efficient delivery of English courses and effective language skills development, language programs around the world need leaders that can manage their respective English language programs (ELPs) to ensure quality and proficiency. Since the effectiveness of leadership in an ELP directly influences excellence in language education, program success, and learner-educator contentment (Gordon et al., 2016), it is necessary that leaders in language programs prepare themselves for the expected and unexpected challenges and issues that are generally faced in these positions. An adequate strategy to do so will be the continuous development of leadership skills through courses, workshops and trainings that not only refresh previously learnt knowledge but also provide opportunities to synthesize the previous management experience with advanced leadership training (Knights, Grant & Young, 2018).

Development of the field of English language teaching and learning (ELTL) after its recognition as a lingua franca has expanded the profession in different directions and has increased the number of English language learners as well as teachers across the globe. Though this recognition and growth has developed the field in general, it has also posed serious questions for our leaders, policy makers, and researchers on how to meet the changing needs and demands of the profession through effective leadership (Pennington & Hoekje, 2010). One major concern in this regard is to understand the factors that contribute to effective leadership in ELP management. This will help the future leaders to: (a) continue to develop the field in different contexts (Anderson, 2005); (b) ensure the provision of quality English education; (c) train and prepare educators to meet diverse learner needs (Anderson, 2005; Mazurkiewicz, 2011); (d) promote and manage innovation into (English) language teaching and learning (Gordon et al., 2016; Heyworth, 2003); and (e) keep the progress and the development of the field steady and constant (Anderson, 2005).

K. Raza (✉)
Werklund School of Education, University of Calgary, Calgary, Canada

© Springer Nature Switzerland AG 2021
H. Mohebbi and C. Coombe (eds.), *Research Questions in Language Education and Applied Linguistics*, Springer Texts in Education,
https://doi.org/10.1007/978-3-030-79143-8_125

Borg (2006) investigated the job language teachers have to do in contrast to other disciplines and concluded that the distinctiveness of the field of language teaching drives its roots from the uniqueness of the subject, content, methodology, student–teacher rapport and dissimilarities between native-non-native English speakers. Since language teachers play distinctive roles as compared to others, the nature of challenges and their management in ELPs must also be different from other disciplines. Stolen (2015) disapproves the notion of universal characteristics of effective leaders and argues that they are rather context specific. Developing on these findings, one area of concern is investigating the nature of the job(s) done by leaders in ELPs and setting the parameters when choosing a person to lead a language program or a department.

Future research should focus on the distinctive roles played by the leadership in ELPs and how an assessment criteria can be developed to assess the effectiveness of a leader for ELPs in different contexts. This should help understand the characteristics leadership in English language teaching (ELT) needs and the strategies to perceive and respond to situations that particularly exhibit themselves in this context.

The Research Questions

1. What is the role of social categorizations such as gender, class, and race in the construction of leadership practices in different ELT contexts?
2. What specific knowledge, skills and competencies do leaders in the field of English language teaching need to have to become effective?
3. Does an ELT context define the characteristics and the qualities of an effective leader?
4. Is it necessary for an effective leader to be an effective English language teacher? Why? Why not?
5. Is there a need to develop assessment criteria for effective leaders in ELT? How can we develop these benchmarks?
6. To what extent do good leaders in English language programs (ELPs) become good trainers for novice leaders? What training models are available?
7. Does continuous professional development affect the efficiency of leadership in ELT?
8. What are the barriers to making effective leadership in English language teaching?
9. To what extent does leadership in ELT affect teacher and student performance?
10. What areas do researchers in the field of TESOL need to direct their investigation to prepare the leadership for the challenges of the twenty-first century?

Suggested Resources

Wilkinson, J., & Bristol, L. (2018). *Educational leadership as a culturally-constructed practice: New directions and possibilities.* **New York, NY: Routledge**.

This book challenges the conventional approaches to leadership as being uni-dimensional and decontextualized phenomenon and presents it as a multi-dimensional practice that is informed by cultural construct at practice and research levels. Furthering the debate on leadership as a culturally situated practice, the book raises three significant questions about current approaches to leadership. First, theories that patronize the development of culturally inclusive leadership practices (e.g., white masculine leadership) without scrutiny are debated. Secondly, the book highlights theories that employ a unitary approach to observe the relationship between leadership and different social categories such as ethnicity, gender and race but fail to recognize the interconnected nature of these social categorizations as they apply to leadership enactment and its practices. The last set of questions relate to approaches that inform the selection of certain theoretical frameworks used in the examination of leadership practices and their validity in observing the effectiveness of leadership in specific contexts. The book comprises 12 chapters that extend these three questions at different levels of leadership as well as in different contexts and settings.

Pennington, M. C., & Hoekje, B. J. (2010). *Language program leadership in a changing world: An ecological model.* **UK: Emerald Group Publishing Limited**.

This book presents an ecological model for language program management in different contexts. Considering language program structure as an ecology where all the parts are interconnected, the authors address the nature of work leaders in language programs do, the challenges in managing these programs and their interacting parts, and the strategies to balance between different roles they have to play in these leadership positions. The three distinct parts of the book are efficiently designed to provide useful information about the context of leadership in language programs in a changing world, the stakeholders involved in this leadership, and the possibilities effective leadership can achieve in terms of curriculum and program development. The theories and concepts presented in this book are substantiated with the provision of case studies, thus, creating a balance between theory and practice.

Christison, M. A., & Murray, D. E. (2009). *Leadership in English language education: Theoretical foundations and practical skills for changing times.* **New York, NY: Routledge**.

This volume is intended for a wide readership including people that are currently working as leaders, individuals that are interested in assuming leadership positions in the future, and students studying in leadership and administration programs. The volume is divided into three distinct parts and each part is focused on a central theme. The first part of the book discusses the roles, characteristics, skills, and foundations that define an effective leader and provides examples of how successful leaders can perform in different contexts. The second part consists of six chapters that focus on the strategies for skills development that are necessary for effective leaders. The last part of the volume presents practical examples of effective leaders that perform in different situations and environments. The three chapters in this part report findings of the studies that have investigated IQ development of English language educators and the expansion of their skills through their experiences as leaders. Each chapter includes interactive tasks that not only help readers understand the concepts presented in the chapters but also reflect upon their understanding of the content by answering follow-up questions given at the end of the chapter.

Coombe, C., McCloskey, M. L., Stephenson, L., & Anderson, N. L. (2008). *Leadership in English language teaching and learning*. Ann Arbor, MI: University of Michigan Press.

This book consists of contributions from experienced and knowledgeable professionals from the field of TESOL and is divided into five parts. In the first part of the book, Lauren Stephenson and Neil J. Anderson discuss concepts and theories related to the notion of leadership. Part 2, 3 and 4 consist of fourteen chapters that focus on the interpersonal, communication, and organizational skills and strategies that are necessary for effective leadership in ELT. What makes this section more interesting is that the authors of each chapter emphasize the development of a specific skill. For instance, in part two, Christine Coombe, Liz England and John Schmidt highlight the importance of public speaking and presentation skills in ELT leadership. Similarly, Brock Bradly discusses fundraising as a quality of a leader and Andy Curtis enlists the principles of professional development for effective leadership in part three. The last part of the book has two chapters that discuss the issues ELT leadership faces in public schools and present strategies to deal with these challenges. The significance and the importance of the contents of this book lies in the fact that the contributions come from the authors that have first-hand, extensive leadership experience in the field of TESOL and have played pivotal roles in the development and progress of the ELT profession in different capacities.

English, F. W. (2006). *Encyclopedia of educational leadership and administration* (Vols. 1–2). USA: Sage.

This 2-volume encyclopedia on educational leadership and administration consists of high quality and comprehensive contributions on current philosophies, research, ideas, terminologies, and accounts of educational leadership and administration from more than two hundred stakeholders that are educators, students, specialists, and members of different associations and come from different disciplines and backgrounds. With around 600 A–Z entries, this encyclopedia aims to provide an all-inclusive knowledge base for current school administrators and future educational leaders by covering a wide range of topics including but not limited to administration, biographies, curriculum, law and policy, leadership, organizations, teacher and teaching, and testing. Each entry provides practical information about an aspect of educational administration and covers the dynamic field of educational administration by including examples from the content taught at training programs and practices at different educational institutions. The extensive experience and knowledge of the contributors like Ellwood Cubberley, Andrew Halpin, and William Torrey Harris, and the variety of topics covered in this Encyclopedia make it a very valuable reference book for both beginners and experienced educational leaders.

References

Anderson, N. J. (2005). Leadership is not about position: Leading from behind. In *A TESOL symposium on leadership: Initiating and managing changes in English language teaching*. TESOL International Association. Retrieved from. http://www.tesol.org/docs/default-source/new-resource-library/symposium-on-leadership-5.pdf?sfvrsn=0

Borg, S. (2006). The distinctive characteristics of foreign language teachers. *Language Teaching Research, 10*(1), 3–31.

Gordon, S. P., Oliver, J., & Solis, R. (2016). Successful innovations in educational leadership preparation. *International Journal of Educational Leadership Preparation, 11*(2), 51–70.

Heyworth, F. (2003). *The organization of innovation in language education: A set of studies*. Council of Europe Publishing.

Knights, J., Grant, D., & Young, G. (2018). *Leading beyond the ego: How to become a transpersonal leader*. New York, NY: Routledge.

Mazurkiewicz, G. (2011). Educational leadership: Key elements supporting teaching and learning. *International Journal of Contemporary Management, 2*, 84–98.

Pennington, M. C., & Hoekje, B. J. (2010). *Language program leadership in a changing world: An ecological model*. Emerald Group Publishing Limited.

Stolen, D. W. (2015). Distributing leadership in English sixth form colleges: Liberation or another form of managerial control? *International Journal of Educational Management, 29*(5), 522–538.

Kashif Raza is currently a lecturer in English at Qatar University's Foundation Program, and has previously taught in the USA and Pakistan. He has served on various leadership positions as well as Faculty Senate. With his knowledge and experience in curriculum development, Kashif has actively participated in a large-scale project of restructuring all the English language courses in the Foundation Program, and has developed, delivered and administered the first ever ESP Law course at QU. His research interests include language policy development, educational leadership, expectations and perceptions in education, and second language writing. Kashif presents frequently at international and regional conferences, and serves on the editorial board of *Language Teaching Research Quarterly* and *English Language Teaching: Theory, Research and Pedagogy* (book series).

Ruanni Tupas

"It is a pity," according to Pennycook (2017), that so much work has focused on putative varieties of English from a world Englishes perspective, when what we really need to address are the questions of unequal Englishes" (p. xiv).

For more than five decades now, research on the pluralities and pluralization of English has helped provide evidence and sound arguments for the legitimacy of the different ways people use English around the world (Kachru, 1990). Scholars celebrate the idea that users of English around that world have not simply passively or naively used English as an imperial or colonial language but, more crucially, they have also transformed (even 'destroyed') the English language to suit their own cultural realities and ideological systems. Therefore, English*es*—more than English —appropriately describes the nature of English today as it has undergone the twin processes of globalization and localization.

Consequently, the notion of Englishes has dramatically deconstructed most if not all of the so-called sacred cows (Kachru, 1988) or fallacies (Phillipson, 1992) in applied linguistics and language education, which includes the belief that only 'native speaker' norms are legitimate and should be taught, and the 'English-only' policies and practices in multilingual classrooms. It has opened up new and constructive possibilities for different Englishes to be recognized and used in classrooms around the world (Matsuda, 2019).

Unequal Englishes pushes the conversations further by alerting us to the reality that the globalization/localization/pluralization of the English language continues to promote harmful ideologies and perpetuate unequal relations between speakers through the use of different unequal Englishes (Sabaté-Dalmau, 2018), as well as

R. Tupas (✉)
Institute of Education, University College London, London, UK
e-mail: r.tupas@ucl.ac.uk

© Springer Nature Switzerland AG 2021
H. Mohebbi and C. Coombe (eds.), *Research Questions in Language Education and Applied Linguistics*, Springer Texts in Education,
https://doi.org/10.1007/978-3-030-79143-8_126

has created new unequal relationships due to dominant social phenomena such as neoliberal globalization, mobilities and the super diversification of societies (Salonga, 2015; Tupas & Salonga, 2016). Much has been written about native speakerism and accent discrimination, but *Unequal Englishes* is strategically positioned to investigate the politics of Englishes today because of the following fundamental assumptions:

- Central to the study of the globalization/localization/plural of Englishes today is the idea of 'inequality.' We cannot simply describe Englishes without locating them within contexts of unequal relations and ideologies (Lee & Jenks, 2018; Tupas, 2015).
- It is not enough to describe inequalities between speakers and their Englishes without locating them within the 'enduring conditions of coloniality' in the world today (Tupas, 2019). Despite our celebration of Englishes, they continue to impact speakers' lives unequally (Kubota, 2015), including the lives of teachers and students in the classroom (Henry, 2015).
- Resistance to linguistic inequalities does not erase the 'centrality of enduring and emerging ideologies and practices' associated with different forms of social and linguistic inequalities (Dovchin et al., 2016).
- Unequal Englishes is 'the study of the unequal lives of speakers of Englishes' (Darvin, 2017; Lorente, 2017).

Thus, *Unequal Englishes* counts pluralization as a highly political, historical and stratifying phenomenon which shapes—but not completely determines—speakers' life chances, identities, and relationships with other speakers. The circulation of unequal Englishes in the classroom shapes not only the identities and practices of teachers and students, but also students' success (or lack of it) in school. Because of "educational structures that breed unequal Englishes" (Canilao, 2019, p. 91), there is now a need to investigate the "effects of *unequal Englishes*" (Pennycook, 2017, p. ix, italics as original).

The Research Questions

1. What are the *effects* of unequal Englishes on the lives of students, teachers, users of English, etc.?
2. How does the use of 'non-standard' varieties to teach the 'standard' variety in the classroom improve the academic performance of students who are dominant in such 'non-standard' varieties?

3. Do non-standard varieties of English have a role to play in the teaching of English in the classroom? If yes, what strategies may be used?
4. What do students, teachers, users of English, language policies, etc., do to resist or transform unequal Englishes?
5. How are unequal Englishes produced and sustained in language tests and assessments?
6. How do unequal Englishes play out at home, in the workplace, or in the linguistic landscape of a particular community or society?
7. What is the role of language policy (including language-in-education policy) in the making of unequal Englishes?
8. How do unequal Englishes today continue to work under conditions of coloniality?
9. How are structures of feeling (English speakers' attitudes and feelings about English) formed in specific contexts of English language use?
10. What language ideologies do speakers (teachers, for example) invoke to sustain or breakdown unequal Englishes?

Suggested Resources

Dovchin, S., Sultana, S., & Pennycook, A. (2016). Unequal translingual Englishes in the Asian peripheries. *Asian Englishes*, *18*(2), 92–108.

The paper examines 'translingual Englishes' among young students in Mongolia and Bangladesh. However, instead of simply conceptualizing translingual Englishes as creative, playful and performative—a general tendency in studies on mixed, hybrid language practices—the paper aims to expand the theoretical reach of its analysis by incorporating the notion of *Unequal Englishes* into its framework. According to the authors, *Unequal Englishes* is critical in understanding the nature of translingual Englishes by locating language practices within issues of access, distribution and social class. There is no doubt, the authors have found, that young people in Mongolia and Bangladesh are invested in local uses of English and, in fact, are radically transforming them, but their social standing (for example in relation to social class) either limits or opens up their access to particular privileged configurations of English language use. Thus, with the theoretical help from *Unequal Englishes*, the authors describe young speakers' English-shaped language practices as unequal translingual Englishes.

Henry, E. S. (2015). Just an Old Joke': Chinglish, narrative, and linguistic. inequality in the Chinese English Classroom. In R. Tupas (ed.), *Unequal Englishes: The politics of Englishes today* (pp. 95–110). Basingstoke: Palgrave.

This paper invokes *Unequal Englishes* in Chinese English classrooms, more specifically in terms of how joke narratives about *Dongbei English*—a non-standard form of English inflected with local and rural connotations—help construct linguistic inequality in classrooms in China. By mocking local uses of English, however, one also invokes a seemingly unequal relation between Chinese learners of English and 'native' speakers of English, with the former inscribed with un-modern, inward-looking identities. Teachers who use such joke stories in the classroom participate in the legitimization of so-called native speaker norms which, as part of the narrative, open up opportunities to Chinese speakers of English in terms of socioeconomic and cross-national mobilities, especially with China's march towards modernization and capitalist globalization. In the process, regional identities and local practices are mocked and marginalized as Dongbei English supposedly 'fails' to help its speakers to transcend their regional affiliations and participate in practices of the global and cosmopolitan culture.

Park, J. S. Y. (2015). Structures of feeling in unequal Englishes. In R. Tupas (ed.), *Unequal Englishes: The politics of Englishes today* (pp. 59–73). Basingstoke: Palgrave.

In this paper, the author demonstrates, in the context of Korea's historical association with the English language, how Koreans' anxieties about speaking English are deeply personal but also much linked to larger structural inequalities in society. In other words, the paper configures people's emotional or affective experience with speaking English (where Koreans freeze, get nervous, become insecure, and so on, when faced with the need to speak English) as one of the mechanisms of *Unequal Englishes* in Korean society. The paper clearly shows the link between these seemingly mundane feelings about English—feelings of insecurity or *junuk*–and Korea's historical engagement with modernity and its associated values like enlightenment and moral ascendancy. The ability to speak 'good' or 'standard' English has been packaged ideologically as one's moral responsibility to the nation. Moreover, one's experience of being immobilized by the presence of a powerful, dominant 'Westerner' is likewise indicative of Korea's uneasy historical relationship with the so-called Western world.

Sabaté-Dalmau, M. (2018). 'I speak small': unequal Englishes and transnational identities among Ghanaian migrants. *International Journal of Multilingualism*, 15(4), 365–382.

The paper examines unequal Englishes and transnational identities among migrants in Barcelona. In particular, the research upon which the paper is based is a multi-site ethnography of three homeless Ghanaian migrant men whose historical trajectories are complex and conflicted despite their marginalized positioning in Spain, having come from Ghana with some form of cultural and linguistic capital.

The paper describes how shifting identities of the migrant men are indexed by their deployment of unequal Englishes embedded in their much larger multilingual practices, sometimes invoking their inability to use English—'small' or 'no' English—linked to African stereotypes of being uneducated or uncouth, but also sometimes mobilizing their proficiency in the language in order to position themselves as 'better English' speakers than local people. Mobilizations of unequal Englishes, according to the paper, showcase the situated forms of marginalized conditions under which the migrants live and (co)construct their varied and complex identities.

Tupas, R. (2015). *Unequal Englishes: The politics of Englishes today.* **Basingstoke: Palgrave**.

This edited volume brings together chapters which operationalize and unpack the notion of *Unequal Englishes* under four research concerns: Approaches to Unequal Englishes, Englishes in Nexuses of Power and Inequality, Englishes in Changing Multilingual Spaces, and Englishes in Unequal Learning Spaces. All chapters assume that Englishes and their speakers are implicated in forms and practices of social and educational inequality, and the role of researchers and scholars is to surface or expose them in order to find spaces within which we may be able to alter and transform inequitable policies and practices. The volume features examples from a wide variety of contexts, including the spread and the perpetuation of unequal Englishes in a linguistic landscape and a classroom in China, the performance of gayness and English across unequal spaces in call centers in the Philippines, and the construction of unequal Englishes through imagined ('native' and 'non-native') intercultural interactions among international students in Malaysia.

References

Canilao, M. L. E. N. (2019). Looking through the eyes of global Englishes: Enhancing English language teaching in multicultural classrooms. In F. Fang & H. P. Widodo (Eds.), *Critical perspectives on global Englishes in Asia: Language policy, curriculum, pedagogy and assessment* (pp. 84–103). Multilingual Matters.

Darvin, R. (2017). Social class and the inequality of English speakers in a globalized world. *Journal of English as a Lingua Franca, 6*(2), 287–311.

Dovchin, S., Sultana, S., & Pennycook, A. (2016). Unequal translingual Englishes in the Asian peripheries. *Asian Englishes, 18*(2), 92–108.

Henry, E. S. (2015). Just an old joke: Chinglish, narrative, and linguistic inequality in the Chinese English classroom. In R. Tupas (ed.), *Unequal Englishes: The politics of Englishes today* (pp. 95–110). Palgrave.

Kachru, B. (1990). *The Alchemy of English: The spread, functions and models of non-native Englishes.* University of Illinois Press.

Kachru, B. B. (1988). The sacred cows of English. *English Today, 4*(4), 3–8.

Kubota, R. (2015). Inequalities of Englishes, English speakers, and languages: A critical perspective on pluralist approaches to English. In R. Tupas (Ed.), *Unequal Englishes: The politics of Englishes today* (pp. 21–41). Basingstoke: Palgrave.

Lee, J. W., & Jenks, C. J. (2018). Aestheticizing language: Metapragmatic distance and unequal Englishes in Hong Kong. *Asian Englishes, 21*(2), 128–141.

Lorente, B. P. (2017). *Scripts of servitude: Language, labor migration and transnational domestic work.* Multilingual Matters.

Matsuda, A. (2019). World Englishes in English language teaching: Kachru's six fallacies and the TEIL paradigm. *World Englishes, 38*(1–2), 144–154.

Park, J. S. Y. (2015). Structures of feeling in unequal Englishes. In R. Tupas (Ed.), *Unequal Englishes* (pp. 59–73). Palgrave Macmillan.

Pennycook, A. (2017). *The cultural politics of English as an international language (first published in 1994).* Routledge.

Pennycook, A., Kubota, R., & Morgan, B. (2017). Preface. In B. Lorente (author), *Scripts of servitude: Language, labor migration and transnational domestic work* (pp. xi–xv). Multilingual Matters.

Phillipson, R. (1992). *Linguistic imperialism.* Oxford University Press.

Sabaté-Dalmau, M. (2018). 'I speak small': Unequal Englishes and transnational identities among Ghanaian migrants. *International Journal of Multilingualism, 15*(4), 365–382.

Salonga, A. (2015). Performing gayness and English in an offshore call center industry. In R. Tupas (ed.), *Unequal Englishes: The politics of Englishes today* (pp. 130–144). Basingstoke: Palgrave.

Tupas, R. (2019). Entanglements of colonialism, social class, and unequal Englishes. *Journal of Sociolinguistics, 23*(5), 529–542.

Tupas, R. (2015). *Unequal Englishes: The politics of Englishes today.* Basingstoke: Palgrave.

Tupas, R., & Salonga, A. (2016). Unequal Englishes in the Philippines. *Journal of Sociolinguistics, 20*(3), 367–381.

Ruanni Tupas teaches Sociolinguistics in Education at the Institute of Education, University College London. He is an Associate Editor of the *International Journal of the Sociology of Language,* and is also a multi-awarded educator having received several excellent teaching awards from the National University of Singapore and National Institute of Education, Singapore. The Linguistic Society of the Philippines has honoured him with honorary and lifetime membership for his contributions to language studies.

Values in the Language Classroom

Graham Hall

Language teaching is a 'profoundly value-laden activity' (Johnston, 2003, p. 1). Teachers make decisions based on values, and students and teachers often express particular values during lessons (Menard-Warwick et al., 2016). Beyond the classroom, values also permeate, for example, national language policies, curriculum design, language testing, and materials development (Hall, 2017).

Johnston (2003, p. 6) defines *values* as 'that set of a person's beliefs that are evaluative in nature … [and] which concern what is good and bad, what is right and wrong'; Johnston regards *morality* as essentially synonymous with *values*. Values are both 'personal' and 'cultural' (Buzzelli and Johnston, 2003, p. 3), that is, individual and social; values are mediated by individuals who are subject to strong socio-cultural influences. Thus, values 'are played out in social settings—when our inner beliefs are converted into actions which affect others' (Johnston, 2003, p. 6). As Hall (2017) notes, therefore, the language classroom is an inherently value-laden environment social setting, where teachers make decisions which they believe are right for individual learners, for the whole class, and, indeed, for themselves.

Menard-Warwick et al. (2016) differentiate between *values about* and *values within*, the former referring to the evaluation of topics during classroom discussions, the latter to beliefs enacted through classroom interaction, behaviours and policies. For example, a classroom discussion of the role of women in the workplace reveals values *about* gender, while interaction and turn-taking patterns which encourage or deny women the opportunity to speak out in class demonstrate values *within* the classroom (ibid.).

According to Menard-Warwick et al. (2016), talking *about* values during lessons can often motivate learners to speak more expansively than they would otherwise. Yet talking about values itself reflects a value-laden perspective associated with

G. Hall (✉)
English Language and Linguistics, Department of Humanities, Northumbria University, Newcastle upon Tyne, UK
e-mail: g.hall@northumbria.ac.uk

© Springer Nature Switzerland AG 2021
H. Mohebbi and C. Coombe (eds.), *Research Questions in Language Education and Applied Linguistics*, Springer Texts in Education,
https://doi.org/10.1007/978-3-030-79143-8_127

Communicative Language Teaching (ibid.). Meanwhile, both topic selection and the place of the teacher's own opinions in such discussions remain complex. The appropriateness of talking about politics, sexuality, and religion, for example, varies according to context, learners' age etc., and although teachers might aim for *committed impartiality* within the classroom (in which they state their own view, then allow competing perspectives to be freely aired and fairly heard (Kelly, 1986; Menard-Warwick et al., 2016)), their status and authority in class might potentially silence those students who fear to disagree (Miller-Lane et al., 2006).

Values are reflected *within* classroom practices in a number of ways. Johnston et al. (1998) highlight the explicit rules and regulations that maintain teacher and institutional discipline in class (e.g. concerning cheating, lateness etc.), while Hafernik et al. (2002) focus on the dilemmas posed by poor learner attendance and non-completion of homework, issues that potentially challenge teacher authority and may also reduce the learning opportunities of other students in class. Hansen (1993), meanwhile, focuses on the ways in which hand-raising in class not only establishes order and turn-taking, but also reinforces the values of learner patience and teacher authority. Values also underpin the ways in which classroom talk and interaction are managed. For example, how might teachers balance the widely-held principle of relatively equal learner turn-taking in class with an individual's right to be silent if they choose, i.e., 'voluntary silence' versus 'enforced speech' (Johnston, 2003, p. 35)?

Ultimately, although many language teachers would not consider that they explicitly teach values, values infuse teacher decision-making as, in our specific contexts, we try to 'do the right thing' for our students.

The Research Questions

Focusing on a particular language classroom or classrooms:

1. What rules and regulations operate in a/the language classroom (for example, about learner lateness, cheating, chatting, and even school uniform)? What values are conveyed by these rules?
2. To what extent, and how, do the teachers teach values explicitly in the classroom? What values are taught?
3. To what extent, and how, are particular values conveyed to learners implicitly in the classroom? What values are conveyed?
4. To what extent are the values that 'learners should participate relatively equally in class' and 'learners have the right not to speak ('the right to silence')' evident in the classroom? How is this tension resolved, if at all, and why does the teacher (and/or learners) take this approach?
5. To what extent, and how, do teachers express their own views during values-based class discussions, for example, about aspects of politics or gender? Why, according to the teachers, do they take this approach?

6. In what ways do values play out in a language classroom of younger learners compared to a classroom of adult learners? How does the age of the learners affect value-based issues in the classrooms?

7. To what extent do teachers (and/or learners) report holding values which are contradictory (e.g., 'honesty' and 'tact' and 'diplomacy'), and how are such contradictions managed in practice in the classroom?

8. Identify a 'critical incident' in a classroom in which a conflict between learners has emerged, for example, a disagreement during a value-based discussion (i.e., 'values about'), or learners not working well together (e.g., interrupting, not listening, or not wishing to work together; i.e., 'values within'). To what extent, and how, is the conflict dealt with in a way which attends both to the values of the learners involved and to the values and norms of the class more generally?

9. How far do teachers believe they should attend to the needs or wishes of an individual learner if they run counter (a) to the teacher's own beliefs about what is right or appropriate in class, and (b) the teacher's perceptions of the needs of the whole class? How are any differences resolved in practice in the classroom?

10. To what extent do the reported values of the teacher, learners and the school/institution coincide or differ? How are any differences resolved in practice in the classroom?

Research methodologies might include classroom observation, field notes and/or audio and video-recording; interviews and focus groups with teachers, learners and school/institutional managers; questionnaires and surveys; and the collation of relevant documentary evidence. Differing data sources might be triangulated to compare and contrast perspectives, and to build a more complete picture of values in the language classroom.

Suggested Resources

Buzzelli, C. and Johnston, B. (2002). *The Moral Dimensions of Teaching*. New York: Routledge.

This accessible book focuses on what the authors term 'the moral dimensions of classroom interaction' (co-author Bill Johnston (2003) subsequently equates with 'morality' with 'values'; see 'Overview' and reference below). It analyses classroom interaction transcripts to reveal 'moral meaning' in incidents and episodes where values are not, at least at first glance, obvious. The book focuses on three main issues: teachers' (and learners') use of language, and how this supports or hinders learners' participation in class; how power relationships are mediated in teaching, particularly with regard to testing and assessment, the physical organisation of teaching, and the notion of learners' 'voice'; and the ways in which differing cultural values might come together in classrooms. The volume conveys a sense of the value-based complexities and ambiguities which are part of teaching and highlights the importance of context and the importance of teachers' knowledge of their own classrooms.

Crookes, G. (2013). *Critical ELT in Action.* **New York: Routledge**.

Bringing together theory and practice, this volume aims to introduce teachers to second language critical pedagogy, that is, a perspective on language teaching, learning and curricula that critiques the status quo, creates alternative forms of practice, and seeks social justice for all. The book is an exploration of key issues, offering prompts to teachers who wish to develop the possibility of critical ELT in their own professional context. It consequently examines the ways in which values might underpin curricula and materials, classroom discourse, the ways in which we understand language and learning, and the institutional and administrative concerns which surround ELT programmes. Central to the discussion is the relationship between theory and values-in-theory on the one hand, and what happens in classrooms in practice on the other. In some ways, therefore, the book (deliberately!) asks as many questions of teachers as it answers.

Hall, G. (2016). *The Routledge Handbook of English Language Teaching.* **New York: Routledge**.

A substantial number of chapters in this handbook explore value-related issues in English Language Teaching. The opening five chapters examine the global context of ELT. They discuss how the emergence and recognition of varieties of English around the world, and of English as a Lingua Franca (ELF), poses value-based questions about what English should be taught and tested; how differing values might 'flow' and 'compete' within the politics and power relationships of global ELT; the ways in which English carries discourses, identities, memories, cultures and values at a global and local scale; changing perspectives, challenges and values around the 'traditional' distinction between so-called 'native' and 'non-native' speakers; and the implications of differing educational traditions—indigenous, progressive and critical—on ELT. Elsewhere, the volume examines how ELT materials represent both language for pedagogical purposes (and the simplifications and distortions this might entail) and the world and its inhabitants (and the failure to recognise some stigmatised social groups). Meanwhile, chapters focusing on English for academic purposes (EAP), English for specific purposes (ESP), language education and migration, bilingual education in a multilingual world, appropriate methodology, and the use of the learners' own language(s) in class all reflect upon the ways in which *what* and *how* we teach draws on and reflects particular perspectives on the world around us, viewpoints which are infused with values. Each chapter concludes with *Discussion questions* to prompt further reader reflection, and a short annotated list of *Further readings*.

Johnston, B. (2003). *Values in English Language Teaching.* **New York: Routledge.**

This book provides an in-depth and wide-ranging exploration of the ways in which language teaching is 'shot through with values' (p 1). It argues that the morality of teaching is 'highly complex, paradoxical, and saturated with important and difficult dilemmas' (ibid.) and presents readers with practical value-related conundrums to prompt reflection. Following an introduction which defines key terms and emphasises the interplay between 'the social' and 'the individual' as values play out in practice, subsequent chapters focus on: the value-based complexities and dilemmas of classroom interaction (see also Buzzelli & Johnston, 2002); the politics of ELT in the world (including perspectives on Critical Pedagogy); the moral dilemmas which underlie language testing and assessment; value-based issues within language teacher identity (including teacher-student relationships, professionalism, and teachers' religious beliefs); and the values, and indeed clashes of values, that underlie teacher development.

Menard-Warwick, J. (2013). *English Language Teachers on the Discursive Faultlines: Identities, ideologies, pedagogies.* **Bristol, UK: Multilingual Matters.**

This book explores the language ideologies, linguistic and cultural identities and cultural pedagogies of teachers from Chile and from California, drawing on the perspectives of the teachers themselves. The discussion takes as its starting point the idea that socio-historical and cultural contexts influence the linguistic and cultural identities of teachers. This affects they ways in which language teachers engage with competing discourses, summarised by the author as 'ways of referring to and evaluating particular topics, such as sexuality, celebrity and the legal system —or ELT ... realised through language' (p 2). As teachers increase their own awareness of the interconnections between language, ideology, culture, and identity, they will be better able to make informed decisions about locally appropriate English language pedagogies.

References

Buzzelli, C., & Johnston, B. (2002). *The Moral Dimensions of Teaching*. Routledge.

Hansen, D. (1993). From role to person: The moral layeredness of classroom teaching. *American Educational Research Journal, 30*(4), 651–674.

Hafernik, J., Messerschmitt, D., & Vandrick, S. (2002). *Ethical issues for ESL faculty*. Routledge.

Hall, G. (2017). *Exploring English Language Teaching: Language in action* (2nd ed.). Routledge.

Johnston, B. (2003). *Values in English Language Teaching*. Routledge.

Johnston, B., Juhász, A., Marken, J., & Rolfs Ruiz, B. (1998). The ESL teacher as moral agent. *Research in the Teaching of English, 32*(2), 161–181.

Kelly, T. (1986). Discussing controversial issues: Four perspectives on the teacher's role. *Theory and Research in Social Education, 14*(2), 113–138.

Menard-Warwick, J., Mori, M., Reznik, A., & Moglen, D. (2016). Values in the ELT classroom. In G. Hall (Ed.), *The Routledge handbook of English Language Teaching* (pp. 556–570). Routledge.

Miller-Lane, J., Denton, E., & May, A. (2006). Social studies teachers' views on committed impartiality and discussion. *Social Studies Research and Practice, 1*(1), 30–44.

Graham Hall is Professor of Applied Linguistics/TESOL at Northumbria University, UK, where he teaches on the university's Applied Linguistics and TESOL programmes. He has been involved in English language teaching/TESOL for over twenty-five years, working in Poland, Hungary, Saudi Arabia and the UK, first as a teacher, then as a teacher educator and researcher. He is the author of *Exploring English Language Teaching: language in action* (Routledge, 2011; 2nd edition, 2017), winner of the 2012 British Association for Applied Linguistics (BAAL) book prize. He also edited the *Routledge Handbook of English Language Teaching* (2016) and was editor of *ELT Journal* from 2013–17. His professional and research interests range from classroom discourse and language teaching methodology to the cultural politics of English language teaching.

Part VIII
Research and Research-related Topics

Tineke Brunfaut

Eye-tracking, which involves the recording of people's eye movements, has only recently been adopted as a research method in the fields of second language learning and testing. Its use is based on the assumption that there is a strong association between what our eyes are fixating on and what the focus of our attention is at that same point in time. Following this logic, the fixations (the points at which our eyes rest or 'pause') and the movements of our eyes (also called 'saccades') can give an indication of the information we are processing, in what sequence we are processing that information, and at what pace.

Eye-tracking methodology has been used quite extensively in the field of psychology in the past few decades (see e.g., the work by Keith Rayner and colleagues), for example, to gain insights into how readers process words, phrases and sentences in their first language. While this existing literature has been pivotal to setting up eye-tracking experiments in language testing research, differences in the types of research questions asked and language issues studied mean that the established methodological procedures and measures are not necessarily fully transferrable or comprehensive enough for research in language testing. An important difference, for example, is that language tests do not just present an input stimulus but also require test-takers to complete a specific task related to the input. For instance, research on the testing of reading is not only concerned with the processing of a text but also the task associated with it, and the interaction between the text and the task. Therefore, we cannot simply assume that all existing eye-tracking measures are suitable or valid for the context of language testing, and it may be necessary to adapt them or develop new measures to be able to answer research questions in language testing (see e.g., McCray & Brunfaut, 2018).

Nevertheless, the introduction of eye-tracking as a research method in language testing seems fruitful, with the first sets of studies having primarily explored

T. Brunfaut (✉)
Department of Linguistics and English Language, Lancaster University, Lancaster, UK
e-mail: t.brunfaut@lancaster.ac.uk

© Springer Nature Switzerland AG 2021
H. Mohebbi and C. Coombe (eds.), *Research Questions in Language Education and Applied Linguistics*, Springer Texts in Education,
https://doi.org/10.1007/978-3-030-79143-8_128

test-takers' cognitive processing while completing reading tests (see e.g., Bax, 2013; Brunfaut & McCray, 2015; Brunfaut, 2016). A particularly productive approach entails the combination of eye-tracking with other methods such as post-test interviews. Brunfaut and McCray (2015), for example, traced test-takers' eye movements, and also used the eye movement recordings as stimulus material to help test-takers recall their thought processes after completing a reading task. They found that eye-tracking gave comparatively more useful insights into lower-level reading processes (e.g., word- or sentence-level processing), whereas the stimulated recalls provided more insights into higher-level processes such as inferencing. Together, however, the two methods offered a comprehensive view on reading test processing, including of test-takers' overal reading approaches (e.g., careful versus expeditious reading, or local versus global reading of a text).

Since the use of eye-tracking is novel in language testing, scholars are only starting to discover its potential (as well as its challenges) as a research method that can help further language test theory, development, and validation. Recently, for example, eye-tracking has also been incorporated in the methodology of studies on the testing of writing (e.g., Révész, Michel, & Lee, 2017; Yu, He, & Isaacs, 2017), the testing of listening (e.g., Holzknecht et al., 2017; Suvorov, 2015), and on raters' use of rating scales (e.g., Winke & Lim, 2013).

The Research Questions

Questions on eye-tracking as a research method:

1. How can eye-tracking be used to gain insights into the validity of language tests?
2. What eye-tracking measures are useful for researching language tests?
3. What are the strengths/advantages of using eye-tracking as a research method in language testing?
4. What are the limitations/disadvantages of using eye-tracking as a research method in language testing?
5. What insights can eye-tracking provide into the interaction between the task input and task output while completing language tests?

Questions on language testing for which eye-tracking could be used as a research method:

6. What are test-takers' cognitive processes while completing a language test (reading, listening, writing, vocabulary, grammar, integrated skills,...)?
7. In what ways do the cognitive processes of test-takers at different levels of language proficiency differ?
8. What aspects of the task input (e.g. instructions, visuals, texts, answer options) do test-takers pay attention to while completing a language test, and when?

9. What aspects of a test-taker's writing test performance do raters pay attention to?

10. How do raters use a rating scale while marking written or spoken test performances?

Suggested Resources

Winke, P. (2013). Eye-tracking technology for reading. In. A. J. Kunnan (Ed.), *The companion to language assessment* **(pp. 1029–1046). Hoboken, NJ: Wiley-Blackwell.**

This book chapter is a useful first read for those who are not yet familiar with eye-tracking. Although written for the context of reading research, the condensed overview of fundamentals in eye-tracking is equally useful for research on other language skills or in language testing. The chapter opens with examples of the range of topics in first and second language reading (and the testing of reading) investigated through eye-tracking methodology at the time of publication. The author then explains the underlying theoretical rationale and assumptions of eye-tracking for research into reading and language processing. The chapter also lists key eye-tracking concepts and their meaning. A particularly useful feature of this chapter is its review of different types of eye-tracker machines, and the implications of different eye-trackers' technical specifications for their suitability to investigate specific topics. The chapter ends with suggestions on research issues in language testing that could potentially be investigated by means of eye-tracking.

Conklin, K., & Pellicer-Sánchez, A. (2016). Using eye-tracking in applied linguistics and second language research. *Second Language Research, 32*(3), **453–467.** https://doi.org/10.1177/0267658316637401

With this article, Conklin and Pellicer-Sánchez aim to raise second language researchers' awareness of what underlies innovative tools such as eye-trackers, what they can measure, what they are useful for, and what researchers need to keep in mind when adopting eye-tracking as a research method. By means of eight 'how to' instructions, the authors guide researchers through a set of considerations that are indispensable for anyone who intends to use eye-tracking. The tips include information on: (1) checking the eye-tracker's technical specifications, (2) familiarising oneself with the eye-tracker hard- and software, (3) carefully designing the presentation of the eye-tracking stimulus, 4) controlling for other input variables, (5) determining meaningful areas for data capturing, (6) establishing relevant eye-tracking measures for analyses, (7) cleaning the data, and (8) identifying the limitations of eye-tracking. Adhering to this advice will enable a valid and sound use of eye-tracking in relation to one's specific research aims and purposes.

Holmqvist, K., Nyström, M., Anderson, R., Dewhurst, R., Jarodzka, H., & van de Weijer, J. (2011). *Eye Tracking*. **Oxford: Oxford University Press.**

Homqvist et al. (2011) is an essential guide and reference text for anyone who wants to use eye-tracking in their research. It offers a solid introduction on the nature of the human eye and eye movements, on equipment that is used to track eye movements, and on the process of recording eye movements. Importantly, it provides clear and detailed definitions of terminology associated with this research methodology, such as *fixation duration* and *dwell time*, which can otherwise be quite obscure for a novice eye-tracking researcher. Recommendations are also made on how to determine which equipment and eye-tracking measures to use for your specific research aims, and how to analyse the resulting data. Essentially, Holmqvist et al. guide the reader through establishing an effective experimental design, and include many valuable "DOs" and "DON'Ts". The volume also describes in more detail how to work with the large amount of output from the eye-tracker and turn it into interpretable data. Furthermore, the available range of quantitative measures are illustrated through concrete examples of experimental questions.

McCray, G., & Brunfaut, T. (2018). Investigating the construct measured by banked gap-fill items: evidence from eye-tracking. *Language Testing, 35*(1), **51–73.** https://doi.org/10.1177/0265532216677105

This open access article provides an example of an empirical study that used eye-tracking technology to gain insights into what is being tested by a particular task type—namely, banked gap-fill tasks designed for the testing of second language reading proficiency. Readers may find it helpful to see how a theoretical construct (in this case, Khalifa and Weir's (2009) reading model) can be translated into a set of hypotheses, and how these, in turn, can be operationalised through a set of eye-tracking measures. The article furthermore shows how statistical results from eye-tracking analyses can be used to countercheck the originally formulated hypotheses (in this case, on test-takers' processing while completing banked-gap fill tasks). The findings led to a refinement of the original reading model, describing proportional processing differences between test-takers with different performance levels. The study illustrates how the use of eye-tracking methodology can help advance second language reading theory, as well as result in advice for valid test task design.

Brunfaut, T., & McCray, G. (2015). *Looking into test-takers' cognitive processing whilst completing reading tasks: A mixed-methods eye-tracking and stimulated recall study.* **ARAGs Research Reports Online, AR/2015/01. London: British Council. ISSN 2057–5203.** https://www.britishcouncil.org/sites/default/files/brunfaut_and_mccray_report_final.pdf

Brunfaut, T. (2016). *Looking into reading II: A follow-up study on test-takers' cognitive processes while completing Aptis B1 reading tasks.* **British Council Validation Series, VS/2016/01. London: British Council.** https://www. britishcouncil.org/sites/default/files/brunfaut_final_with_hyperlinks_3.pdf

These two freely accessible publications report on one of the first studies in the field of language testing that combined eye-tracking with stimulated recall methodology. The studies explore test-takers' cognitive processing while completing a total of five different types of tasks from a large-scale second language reading test. The findings from the mixed-methods study were then compared with the intended reading processes as set out by the test developers. This provided insights into the test's cognitive validity.

The two reports are particularly interesting to read in combination. They demonstrate how the findings from the first study (Brunfaut & McCray, 2015) were followed up in the second study (Brunfaut, 2016), and therefore also how eye-tracking can be integrated into and contribute to a test development and validation cycle. The studies also show how the combination of the two research methods—eye-tracking and stimulated recalls—led to a very rich dataset whereby the two methods compensated for each other's limitations and allowed for data triangulation. This methodology has since been adopted by other scholars, using eye-tracking for research into the testing of reading, as well as the testing of listening and writing.

References

Bax, S. (2013). The cognitive processing of candidates during reading tests: Evidence from eye-tracking. *Language Testing, 30*(4), 441–465. https://doi.org/10.1177/0265532212473244

Brunfaut, T. (2016). *Looking into reading II: A follow-up study on test-takers' cognitive processes while completing Aptis B1 reading tasks.* British Council Validation Series, VS/2016/01. London: British Council. https://www.britishcouncil.org/sites/default/files/brunfaut_final_with_hyperlinks_3.pdf

Brunfaut, T., & McCray, G. (2015). *Looking into test-takers' cognitive processing whilst completing reading tasks: A mixed-methods eye-tracking and stimulated recall study.* ARAGs Research Reports Online, AR/2015/01. London: British Council. https://www.britishcouncil.org/sites/default/files/brunfaut_and_mccray_report_final.pdf

Holzknecht, F., Eberharter, K., Kremmel, B., Zehentner, M., McCray, G., Konrad, E., & Spöttl, C. (2017). *Looking into listening: Using eye-tracking to establish the cognitive validity of the Aptis listening test.* ARAGs Research Reports Online, AR-G/2017/3. London: British Council. https://www.britishcouncil.org/sites/default/files/looking_into_listening.pdf

McCray, G., & Brunfaut, T. (2018). Investigating the construct measured by banked gap-fill items: Evidence from eye-tracking. *Language Testing, 35*(1), 51–73. https://doi.org/10.1177/0265532216677105

Révész, A., Michel, M., & Lee, M. (2017). *Investigating IELTS Academic Writing Task 2: Relationships between cognitive writing processes, text quality and working memory.* IELTS Research Reports Online Series, 2017/3. The IELTS Partners: British Council, Cambridge English Language Assessment and IDP: IELTS Australia. https://www.ielts.org/-/media/research-reports/ielts_online_rr_2017-3.ashx

Suvorov, R. (2015). The use of eye tracking in research on video-based second language (L2) listening assessment: A comparison of context videos and content videos. *Language Testing, 32*(4), 463–483. https://doi.org/10.1177/0265532214562099

Winke, P., & Lim, H. (2015). ESL essay raters' cognitive processes in applying the Jacobs et al. rubric: An eye-movement study. *Assessing Writing, 25*, 37-53. https://doi.org/10.1016/j.asw. 2015.05.002

Yu, G., He, L., & Isaacs, T. (2017). *The cognitive processes of taking IELTS Academic Writing Task 1: An eye-tracking study*. IELTS Research Reports Online Series, 2017/2. The IELTS Partners: British Council, Cambridge English Language Assessment and IDP: IELTS Australia. https://www.ielts.org/-/media/research-reports/ielts_online_rr_2017-2.ashx

Tineke Brunfaut is a Professor in Linguistics and English Language at Lancaster University (UK). Her main research interests are in language testing, and reading and listening in a second/foreign language. She has focused on, for example, diagnostic assessment, the role of task and test-taker characteristics in L2 reading and listening, and the use of eye-tracking in language testing research. Her work has been published in journals such as *Applied Linguistics, Studies in Second Language Acquisition, TESOL Quarterly, Language Assessment Quarterly and Language Testing*. She is a recipient of the *ILTA Best Article Award*, the *e-Assessment Award for Best Research and the TOEFL Outstanding Young Scholar Award*. She regularly conducts language test development, training, and consultancy work for professional and educational bodies around the world.

Richard Smith

Stern (1983) offers a good review and summary of early studies of the history of language teaching. He also sets out reasons why, in his view, historical research is essential to the development of language teaching theory. He states as a primary reason that a historical approach 'is needed if language teaching is not to fall victim to a succession of passing fashions' (p. 517) and he presents a more positive corollary of this elsewhere in the same book: 'Through studying the history of language teaching we can gain perspective on present-day thought and trends and find directions for future growth' (p. 76). Smith (2016) recaps and adds to these arguments, suggesting that 'developing "historical sense" is an important aspect of language teacher education' and that 'historical evidence is needed as a basis on which to build appropriate reform efforts' (p. 76).

Thirty years after Stern's review, McLelland and Smith (2014) brought together updated overviews of historical research into the teaching of English, French, German and Spanish in a special issue of the journal *Language & History*. As they note in their introduction, research relating to the history of learning/teaching specific languages is still comparatively rare, making the history of language teaching a rich area for potential doctoral and other primary research-based explorations.

Applied linguistics itself now has a 70-year history as a properly constituted field and is also ripe for historical treatment, both of relatively recent work (cf. de Bot, 2015) and of longer-term developments (cf. Linn et al., 2011; Smith, 2009, 2016). Most applied linguistic topics can be explored historically, and this can place present-day conceptions in perspective, revealing historically constituted limitations and indicating possible alternatives.

A positive development in recent years has been the construction of a mutually supporting community of researchers (HoLLT.net n.d), enabling comparisons to be

R. Smith (✉)
Department of Applied Linguistics, University of Warwick, Coventry, UK
e-mail: R.C.Smith@warwick.ac.uk

© Springer Nature Switzerland AG 2021
H. Mohebbi and C. Coombe (eds.), *Research Questions in Language Education and Applied Linguistics*, Springer Texts in Education,
https://doi.org/10.1007/978-3-030-79143-8_129

drawn between different language-based and regional traditions which have hitherto been considered in separation. Building on the *Language & History* special issue, Smith and McLelland (2018) brought together overviews of language teaching history in different regions of Europe, while their three-volume edited collection. *The History of Language Learning and Teaching* (McLelland & Smith, 2018) offers many examples of the kind of 'in-depth studies of […] restricted scope, treating specific problems, settings or periods, or […] events and persons' which Stern (1983, p. 83) identified as necessary for the development of the field. In their introduction to these volumes (freely available online via the publisher's website: http://www.mhra.org.uk/pdf/HoLLT-Introduction.pdf), McLelland and Smith sum up the progress that has been made, characterizing History of Language Learning and Teaching (HoLLT) as a 'newly emerging interdisciplinary, intercultural and plurilinguistic field of enquiry' (p. 1), while highlighting also that many areas— including histories of language learning and teaching practice beyond Europe— remain to be researched.

Smith (2016) provides further guidance for researchers new to the field. In particular, drawing a distinction with Linguistic Historiography, he calls for a greater focus—in Applied Linguistic Historiography—on contexts for production and reception of ideas, in other words on 'histories of practice' as well as ideas.

The Research Questions

1. What do local histories of practice in different contexts contribute to an understanding of the nature of appropriate innovation?
2. What traditions of language teaching are dominant and can be built upon in different contexts?
3. In what ways can histories of practice grounded in particular contexts counteract received notions and contribute to revised conceptions of language learning and teaching?
4. What can we recover of value from forgotten or neglected practices or ideas, and why have they been ignored?
5. When and why have monolingual ideologies and bilingual practices been dominant in the history of language learning and teaching?
6. When and why have notions of learning through communication and learning through focus on form (s) been dominant in the history of language learning and teaching, and with what effects?
7. What have different traditions of language teaching shared and how have they differed in different contexts and languages, and what can be learnt from such comparisons?

8. What different conceptions of the roles of theory, research and practice have there been in the history of applied linguistics, and what could this contribute to current understandings?

9. What can historical research into (neo) colonial ideologies and practices contribute to current understandings in the fields of applied linguistics and language teaching?

10. How can 'historical sense' (critical perspectives and teacher autonomy which come from an awareness of history) be developed via an emphasis on history in language teacher education programmers?

Suggested Resources

Linn, A., Candel, D. & Léon, J. (Eds). (2011). *Linguistique appliquée et disciplinarisation*. **Special issue of** *Histoire-Epistémologie-Langage, 33 (1)*. **Open Access:** http://www.persee.fr/issue/hel_0750-8069_2011_num_33_1?sectionId= hel_0750-8069_2011_num_33_1_3206.

A ground-breaking collection of articles on the post-World War II history of applied linguistics in various countries including Britain, France, Germany and the USA, with contributions also on its 'pre-history' (eg. the late-19th-century European Reform Movement and the work of Harold E. Palmer (1877–1949) in Britain and Japan). Varying conceptions are revealed regarding the links between practice and background disciplines, and new information is presented regarding the institutionalization and 'disciplinarization' of applied linguistics in different countries. The collection also contains several articles on the history of teaching English in Scandinavia and the introduction provides details of archives which can be consulted by historians of applied linguistics.

McLelland, N. & Smith, R. (Eds). (2014). Building the history of language learning and teaching. Special issue of *Language & History, 57 (1)*. **Open Access:** https://www.tandfonline.com/toc/ylhi20/57/1?nav=tocList.

This is a collection of historical overviews of second/foreign language teaching in Europe. Separate articles consider the parallel overall histories of French, German, Spanish and English learning and teaching, and survey research into these different language traditions. The four papers here by Henri Besse (research on the history of teaching and learning French), Helmut Glück (German), Aquilino Sánchez (Spanish), and Howatt and Smith (English) are by the leading authorities in their respective language disciplines, each written in response to the request to provide an 'overview of the field'. An introduction by the special issue editors reviews previous research into the history of language learning and teaching overall and indicates points of comparison between different language traditions.

McLelland, N. & Smith, R. (Eds.) (2018). *The history of language learning and teaching*, 3 volumes (Vol. I: *16th–18th century Europe;* Vol. II: *19th–20th century Europe;* Vol. III: *Across cultures*). **Oxford: Legenda (Modern Humanities Research Association).**

This three-volume set brings together current research in the history of language learning and teaching. Volume I presents the history of how languages were learnt and taught across Europe, from Russia and Scandinavia to the Iberian peninsula, up to about 1800. Case studies deal with the teaching and learning of French, Italian, German and Portuguese, as well as Latin, still the first 'foreign language' for many learners in this period. The chapters in Volume II consider 19th-century innovations in Europe including the Reform Movement and its precursors, as well as developments in policy and practice in the twentieth century. Volume III specifically examines the history of how 'foreign cultures' have been presented and it also contains studies of the history of language learning and teaching beyond Europe, including in the Middle East, China, Japan, India and New Zealand. The overall introduction to the three volumes is downloadable here: http://www.mhra.org.uk/pdf/HoLLT-Introduction.pdf.

Smith, R. (2016). Building 'Applied Linguistic Historiography'. *Applied Linguistics, 37 (1)*, **71–87. Open Access:** https://academic.oup.com/applij/article/37/1/71/1741459.

This article argues for the establishment of 'Applied Linguistic Historiography' (ALH), that is, a new domain of enquiry within applied linguistics involving a rigorous, scholarly, and self-reflexive approach to historical research. Considering issues of rationale, scope and methods in turn, the article provides reasons why ALH is needed and argues that, while this new field can borrow from *Linguistic* Historiography, it should also distinguish itself, for example by paying more attention to histories of practice as well as ideas, with corresponding methodological emphases and challenges. Making specific reference to the histories of applied linguistics and language learning and teaching, the article identifies ways in which theories, theory–practice links, and practices themselves can be investigated historically in a more rigorous and ultimately useful manner.

Smith, R. & McLelland, N. (Eds.) (2018). Histories of language learning and teaching in Europe. Special issue of *The Language Learning Journal, 46 (1)*. **Open Access:** https://www.tandfonline.com/toc/rllj20/46/1.

The articles in this Open Access special issue consider the history of learning and teaching languages within particular European countries or regions. The papers provide accessible, state-of-the-art overviews which cover similar facets of history, enabling comparisons to be usefully drawn and interconnections to be identified. The collection is a counterpart to the *Language & History* special issue above, 'cutting the cake' of the European history of language learning and teaching in a different, more situated, socio-cultural and multilingual way, viewing history according to geographical location of the learners, classrooms and teachers, rather than according to specific target language. Thus, it contains separate historical overviews of language teaching in Britain (going back to the Norman conquest), the Netherlands (1500–2000), the German-speaking parts of Central Europe (Middle Ages to the present day), France and francophone Switzerland (1740–1940), Spain (sixteenth–eighteenth centuries) and Portugal (eighteenth–nineteenth centuries).

References

de Bot, K. (2015). *A history of applied linguistics: From 1980 to the present*. Routledge.

HoLLT,.net. (n.d). AILA research network on history of language learning and teaching website: http://hollt.net

Linn, A., Candel, D., & Léon, J. (Eds.). (2011). Linguistique appliquée et disciplinarisation. Special issue *of Histoire-Epistémologie-Langage, 33*(1), Open Access: https://www.persee.fr/issue/hel_0750-8069_2011_num_33_1?sectionId=

McLelland, N., & Smith, R. (Eds.). (2014). Building the history of language learning and teaching. Special issue of *Language & History, 57*(1), Open Access: https://www.tandfonline.com/toc/ylhi20/57/1?nav=tocList

McLelland, N., & Smith, R. (Eds.). (2018). *The history of language learning and teaching, 3 volumes*. Legenda (Modern Humanities Research Association).

Smith, R. (2009). Claude Marcel (1793–1876): A neglected applied linguist? *Language & History, 52*(2), 171–181.

Smith, R., & McLelland, N. (Eds.). (2018). Histories of language learning and teaching in Europe. Special Issue of *The Language Learning Journal, 46*(1), Open Access: https://www.tandfonline.com/toc/rllj20/46/1

Smith, R. (2016). Building applied linguistic historiography. *Applied Linguistics, 37*(1), 71–87. https://academic.oup.com/applij/article/37/1/71/1741459

Stern, H. H. (1983). *Fundamental concepts of language teaching*. Oxford University Press.

Richard Smith is Professor of ELT and Applied Linguistics at the University of Warwick, UK. Founder of the Warwick ELT Archive (www.warwick.ac.uk/elt_archive) and the AILA Research Network on History of Language Learning and Teaching (http://hollt.net), he has been active in the fields of historical research, learner autonomy, teaching in difficult circumstances, and teacher-research in language education. In 2008, he co-founded TELCnet (the Teaching English in Large Classes research and development network: http://bit.ly/telcnet-home). In recent years, he has been involved in projects with teachers from Chile, India, Peru and Nepal and has produced open access books for teachers in difficult circumstances including *A handbook for exploratory action research* (with Paula Rebolledo) and *Teaching in low-resource classrooms: Voices of experience* (with Amol Padwad and Deborah Bullock).

Luke Plonsky

Quantitative research methods in applied linguistics are currently undergoing a period of reform. There are several causes or conditions that have led us here. For one, as the field began to apply meta-analysis in the last two decades as a means to understand empirical evidence in its aggregate form, many syntheses uncovered—whether by design or more incidentally—methodological challenges facing individual substantive domains. Developing alongside such observations was a growing sense of the importance of 'study quality' (see Plonsky, 2013), which had hitherto been largely assumed or de-emphasized in favor of theoretical and/or practical concerns. An enhanced awareness of methodological practices could also, rather simply, be argued to be a natural consequence of our maturity as an academic discipline (e.g., Marsden & Plonsky, 2018; Ortega, 2005).

Evidence of this movement can be observed in many different settings and venues. As we might expect, important steps have been taken by academic journals in the form of editorials (e.g., Trofimovich & Ellis, 2015), revised author guidelines (e.g., Norris et al., 2015), and new procedures for and indicators of 'open science' practices (Marsden et al., 2018). The movement is also manifesting itself through a variety of other activities. These include (a) workshops and methodologically oriented symposia, (b) studies of methodological literacy/training (e.g., Gonulal et al., 2017), (c) methodological syntheses seeking to describe and evaluate research and reporting practices (e.g., Marsden, Thompson, & Plonsky, 2018; Plonsky, 2013), (d) a newly added Research Methods strand at AAAL, and, (e) the introduction of novel analytical techniques (e.g., bootstrapping in Larson-Hall & Herrington, 2010; Bayesian data analysis in Norouzian et al., 2018).

Despite these and other advances, there is still much room for improvement and for the development of a full-fledged agenda of methodological work in applied linguistics as suggested in the Research Questions provided below.

L. Plonsky (✉)
English Department, Northern Arizona University, Flagstaff, AZ, USA

© Springer Nature Switzerland AG 2021
H. Mohebbi and C. Coombe (eds.), *Research Questions in Language Education and Applied Linguistics*, Springer Texts in Education,
https://doi.org/10.1007/978-3-030-79143-8_130

The Research Questions

1. To what extent have open science practices been integrated in applied linguistics research?
2. To what extent do seminal, well-established findings in quantitative applied linguistics research replicate?
3. To what extent are applied linguists willing to share data with other researchers for the purpose of re-analysis and secondary data analysis?
4. What is the relationship between choice of data collection instrument and study outcome?
5. To what extent do self-reported measures of methodological and/or statistical literacy correlate with performance/task-based measures of the same? Put differently, how valid are self-report measures of methodological literacy?
6. To what extent have less commonly applied statistical procedures (eg., logistic regression, structural equation modelling) been applied and reported on appropriately in published applied linguistics research?
7. To what extent do researchers omit, suppress, or choose not to publish results that do not align with their expectations, theoretical orientation, or that simply fail to yield a statistically significant result?
8. To what extent do statistical analyses based on violated assumptions affect the results of published findings in applied linguistics?
9. Building on recent reviews of the use of self-paced reading (Marsden et al., 2018) and judgment tasks (Plonsky, Marsden, Crowther, Gass, & Spinner, 2020), to what extent are other data collection tools such as questionnaires and observation protocols employed and reported on appropriately?
10. Building on Plonsky and Oswald's (2014) synthesis of and resulting guidelines for interpreting correlation coefficients (r) and standardized mean differences (d), what is the distribution of eta^2 values in L2 research?

Suggested Resources

Gudmestad, A., & Edmonds, A. (Eds.). (2018). *Critical reflections on data in second language acquisition.* **Amsterdam: John Benjamins**.

The only book in this set of suggested readings, as stated in the title, this text exemplifies the kind of 'critical reflection' that is so badly needed among applied linguists. The focus in the chapters of this volume, which draw on empirical work spanning substantive domains that range from pragmatics to pronunciation and from CALL to corpora, is largely on instrumentation and the collection of data more generally. Rather than making methodological decisions based on convenience or convention, the work in this book highlights in a very deliberate way the value in reflecting on and discussing the trade-offs inherent in these choices.

Ioannidis, J. P. A., Fanelli, D., Dunne, D., Goodman, S. N. (2015). Meta-research: Evaluation and improvement of research methods and practices. *PLoS One Biology*, *13*, e1002264.

As scholars in a relatively young discipline, it is often helpful or even necessary to draw on works from other more established or mature disciplines. This article was published in a biology journal, but the ideas it presents are as relevant and timely for applied linguistics as any field in the natural or social sciences. The authors lay out a systematic framework for "meta-research"—that is, research that takes research itself as its primary object of investigation. This work is not limited to methodological syntheses. Meta-research includes a number of other types of activities and topics related to the reproducibility, publication processes, evaluation of, and incentives for engaging in research. Meta-research in these and other areas have the potential to provide a great service to our field.

Loewen, S., Lavolette, E., Spino, L. A., Papi, M., Schmidtke, J., Sterling, S., & Wolff, D. (2014). Statistical literacy among applied linguists and second language acquisition researchers. *TESOL Quarterly*, *48*, 360–388.

Loewen et al. is a replication of Lazaraton, Riggenbach, and Ediger (1987), who sought to assess the statistical literacy in the field. Loewen et al. adapted the original survey which they administered to 331 researchers. This instrument asked participants to evaluate their ability to interpret a variety of statistical concepts and terms such as mean, reliability, regression, and Rasch analysis. Among other analyses, the authors used factor analysis to group participant responses, the variation of which was also examined as a function of demographic variables. The view this study provides into self-assessed researcher knowledge is complementary to findings obtained in methodological syntheses. This study has also been influential in spurring further studies into researcher knowledge, training, and development.

Marsden, E. J., Morgan-Short, K., Thompson, S., & Abugaber, D. (2018). Replication in second language research: Narrative and systematic reviews, and recommendations for the field. *Language Learning*, *68*, 321–391.

As I see it, this article accomplishes at least three major objectives. First, the authors make an extremely compelling case for the place and importance of replication research and reproducibility more generally. Second, they conduct and present a systematic review of self-labeled replications. The results of this synthesis are cause for concern on the grounds of both the scarcity and what we might refer to as idiosyncrasy of replication efforts. For example, multiple variables are often altered from the initial to the replication study thus obscuring our ability to pinpoint the source of any differences between the two. As part of this review, the authors also examine variables predictive of 'agreement' between initial and replication studies such as collaboration. Finally, as is fitting to the duty of methodological reviews, the article concludes with an empirically-grounded set of 16 recommendations for improving future replication efforts in the field.

Plonsky, L. (2013). Study quality in SLA: An assessment of designs, analyses, and reporting practices in quantitative L2 research. *Studies in Second Language Acquisition, 35,* **655–687.**

This study presents a methodological synthesis of designs, analyses, and reporting practices in a sample of 606 quantitative studies published in *Language Learning* and *Studies in Second Language Acquisition*. The results provide empirical evidence for some strengths, yes, but more often for widespread weaknesses in the field's research and reporting practices. The Literature Review and the Discussion sections also raise a number of issues, tying the results to broader themes and concerns that merit the attention of quantitative researchers. A follow up to this study, Plonsky (2014), is based on the same data set. The purposes of that study are, however, to explore changes taking place over time and to provide a clear and specific set of recommendations to researchers, editors, and other stakeholders. To be sure, the goal in these works, as in other methodological syntheses, was not solely to look back or to criticize but, rather, to aid future studies.

References

Gonulal, T., Loewen, S., & Plonsky, L. (2017). The development of statistical literacy in applied linguistics graduate students. *International Journal of Applied Linguistics, 168,* 4–32.

Larson-Hall, J., & Herrington, R. (2010). Improving data analysis in second language acquisition by utilizing modern developments in applied statistics. *Applied Linguistics, 31,* 368–390.

Lazaraton, A., Riggenbach, H., & Ediger, A. (1987). Forming a discipline: Applied linguists' literacy in research methodology and statistics. *T ESOL Quarterly, 21,* 263–277.

Luke, P. E., Dustin, M., Crowther Susan, M., Patti, G., & Spinner. (2020). A methodological synthesis and meta-analysis of judgment tasks in second language research. *Second Language Research 36*(4), 583–621. https://doi.org/10.1177/0267658319828413

Marsden, E., & Plonsky, L. (2018). Data, open science, and methodological reform in second language acquisition research. In A. Gudmestad, & A. Edmonds (Eds.), *Critical reflections on data in second language acquisition*: *Philadelphia PA* (pp. 219–228). John Benjamins.

Marsden, E., Morgan-Short, K., Trofimovich, P., & Ellis, N. (2018). Introducing registered reports at language learning: Promoting transparency, replication, and a synthetic ethic in the language sciences [Editorial]. *Language Learning, 68,* 309–320.

Marsden, E., Thompson, S., & Plonsky, L. (2018). A methodological synthesis of self-paced reading in second language research. *Applied Psycholinguistics, 39,* 861–904.

Norouzian, R., de Miranda, M. A., & Plonsky, L. (2018). The Bayesian revolution in second language research: An applied approach. *Language Learning, 68,* 1032–1075.

Norris, J. M., Plonsky, L., Ross, S. J., & Schoonen, R. (2015). Guidelines for reporting quantitative methods and results in primary research. *Language Learning, 65,* 470–476.

Ortega, L. (2005). Methodology, epistemology, and ethics in instructed SLA research: An introduction. *The Modern Language Journal, 89,* 317–327.

Plonsky, L. (2013). Study quality in SLA: An assessment of designs, analyses, and reporting practices in quantitative L2 research. *Studies in Second Language Acquisition, 35,* 655–687.

Plonsky, L. (2014). Study quality in quantitative L2 research (1990–2010): A methodological synthesis and call for reform. *The Modern Language Journal, 98,* 450–470.

Plonsky, L., & Oswald, F. L. (2014). How big is 'big'? Interpreting effect sizes in L2 research. *Language Learning, 64*, 878–912.

Trofimovich, P., & Ellis, N. (2015). Open science badges [Editorial]. *Language Learning, 65*, v–vi.

Luke Plonsky is Associate Professor of Applied Linguistics at Northern Arizona University, where he teaches courses in SLA and research methods. Recent and forthcoming publications in these and other areas can be found in *Applied Linguistics, Language Learning*, and *The Modern Language Journal*, among other journals and volumes. He has also written and edited several books. Luke is Senior Associate Editor of *Studies in Second Language Acquisition*, Managing Editor of *Foreign Language Annals*, Co-Editor of the de Gruyter Mouton Series on Language Acquisition, and Co-Director of the IRIS (iris-database.org). Luke held previous faculty appointments at Georgetown University and University College London. He has also taught in China, Japan, The Netherlands, Poland, Puerto Rico, and Spain. Luke received his Ph.D. in Second Language Studies from Michigan State University.

Ali H. Al-Hoorie

A cursory look at the literature is enough to convince the reader that motivation research is an increasingly flourishing area in applied linguistics. More and more researchers are showing interest in understanding learner (and teacher) motivation, in theory and in practice. This may be because of the perception that motivation has more direct applications (and perhaps less dry) than some other areas of applied linguistics.

However, a closer look at this growing literature will also show the reader that the majority of studies follow one pattern: The researcher approaches the participants (e.g., learners, teachers, etc.) and asks them about their motivation. This could be in the form of an open-ended qualitative interview or in a more quantified form using questionnaire surveys—especially those drawing from Likert-type items (Al-Hoorie, 2017).

This self-report approach makes at least two assumptions. First, it assumes that the participant is aware of their motives and what drives their behavior. Second, it additionally assumes that participants are equally able to articulate these motives and communicate them to others. While hardly anyone would claim that these two assumptions are always false, many would also entertain the possibility that there might be other, unconscious motives and processes of which the individual is unaware (Al-Hoorie, 2015). If this is the case, then asking our research participants about such unconscious aspects of their motivation and behavior may not be very fruitful.

This recognition has led some researchers to complement self-reports with other methods that do not rely on direct questions to the participant. One early method is the matched-guise technique (see Al-Hoorie, 2019). Here, the participant listens to speakers in two languages (or accents) reading the same text. The participant's job

A. H. Al-Hoorie (✉)
Jubail English Language and Preparatory Year Institute,
Royal Commission for Jubail and Yanbu, Jubail Industrial City, Saudi Arabia
e-mail: hoorie_a@jic.edu.sa

© Springer Nature Switzerland AG 2021   755
H. Mohebbi and C. Coombe (eds.), *Research Questions in Language
Education and Applied Linguistics*, Springer Texts in Education,
https://doi.org/10.1007/978-3-030-79143-8_131

would be to judge the personality of each speaker, something like how one makes an impression about someone on the phone or on the radio. The tricky part, however, is that the people speaking in the two languages are actually one person fluent in them. If the participant judges the personality of the two speakers differently, this might reflect unconscious/implicit attitudes about the target language or its speakers.

More recently, a number of new instruments have been devised by psychologists in an attempt to measure implicit attitudes. One popular instrument is the Implicit Association Test (Greenwald et al., 1998). Here, the participant is asked to perform a special task that involves classifying a series of words to the right or left on a computer screen. The participant's implicit attitudes are deduced from the speed at which s/he responds to these stimuli (see, e.g. Al-Hoorie, 2016a, b). Several other instruments and variations are available for researchers.

Importantly, researchers interested in the unconscious aspect of motivation do not claim that conscious motivation should be downplayed or replaced by unconscious motivation. Instead, these two perspectives complement each other in order to come up with a more complete picture of human motivation. This idea is sometimes referred to as a dual-process theory of cognition (Sherman et al., 2014). It is likely that the language motivation field would benefit from paying more attention to unconscious processes involved in language learning and teaching.

The Research Questions

1. To what extent do unconscious factors influence language motivation, learning, and teaching? What can unconscious factors contribute to our knowledge over and above the contribution of conscious factors?
2. How do conscious and unconscious factors and processes interact? How can we investigate their dynamic interaction?
3. How do language-related implicit attitudes develop? What links are there to evolution theory and evolutionary psychology?
4. Do these implicit attitudes change over time? What factors lead to this change?
5. To what extent can we intervene to modify unconscious factors to make language learning and teaching more productive?
6. Which of the different implicit measures are more suitable to the different problems in the language motivation field? Can we devise new implicit instruments specifically for the context of language motivation?
7. Other than language motivation, how can the different subdisciplines of language education and applied linguistics benefit from implicit measures?
8. Using qualitative methods, do individuals with positive implicit attitudes perceive and approach language learning/teaching any differently from those with negative implicit attitudes?

9. What effect does awareness of one's own implicit attitudes have?
10. Apart from learners and teachers, how is the topic of implicit attitudes relevant to other stakeholders including parents, school administrators, and future employers?

Suggested Resources

Gawronski, B., & Payne, B. K. (Eds.). (2010). *Handbook of implicit social cognition: Measurement, theory, and applications*. New York: Guilford Press.

This book, just like most of the other items in this annotated bibliography, comes from psychology. This is because psychologists are the pioneers in this area. In fact, most language motivation theories originated from psychology and were then adapted to our purposes in one way or another. Therefore, the language motivation field owes a lot to psychology. In this edited volume, the contributors shed light on various topics and issues related to implicit social cognition. This book would provide the uninitiated reader with a wealth of information about this active area of research.

Wittenbrink, B., & Schwarz, N. (Eds.). (2007). *Implicit measures of attitudes: Procedures and controversies*. **New York: Guilford Press**.

This book focuses specifically on implicit measures. The contributors discuss and raise important conceptual questions regarding implicit attitudes and their measurement. An important and highly cited chapter in this volume is the one by Lane, Banaji, Nosek, and Greenwald titled "Understanding and using the Implicit Association Test: IV. What we know (so far) about the method". This is the fourth installment of a series of papers on the Implicit Association Test, detailing evidence on its reliability and validity as well as how to design one suitable for a specific purpose. This chapter is essential reading for anyone planning to use the Implicit Association Test.

Banaji, M. R., & Greenwald, A. G. (2013). *Blindspot: Hidden biases of good people*. **New York: Delacorte**.

This is a very readable introduction to implicit attitudes and their role in our daily lives. The authors present complex ideas in plain (and entertaining) English. The authors argue that anyone can have hidden biases and prejudges, even if they feel disgusted by such biases at the explicit/conscious level. Examples of domains where biases can creep in include age, gender, race, ethnicity, religion, social class, disability status, and nationality. The authors use the term "blindspot" to describe the idea that such biases can exist in one's mind without their awareness of it. The authors also founded the Implicit Project (currently hosted at Harvard University website: www.implicit.harvard.edu), where anyone can try different implicit tests to get a glimpse of their own potential biases free of charge.

Schultheiss, O. C., & Brunstein, J. C. (Eds.). (2010). *Implicit motives.* **Oxford, UK: Oxford University Press.**

This book is on another area of unconscious motivation, namely implicit motives. Research in this area has a long history dating as far back as the 1940s. This line of research has shown that individuals can be high or low on three main motives: achievement, power and, affiliation. The primary instrument used in this line of research is the Picture Story Exercise. The participant is presented with an ambiguous picture (e.g., a young male staring blankly into the window and a female figure standing in the background) and is asked to make up story about what might be happening. The story is then coded to determine the underlying motives. The rationale of the Picture Story Exercise is that the individual is going to project his/her own motives on that ambiguous picture. The contributors to this volume discuss various topics and developments in this area.

Weinberger, J. L., & Stoycheva, V. (2020). *The unconscious: Theory, research, and clinical implications.* **New York: Guilford Press.**

In this book, the authors present a state-of-the-art analysis of various domains related to unconscious processes. The book starts with important philosophical and historical aspects of the unconscious, and then provides an overview of each of the major areas in unconscious research. These areas include heuristics, implicit memory, implicit learning, implicit motivation, automaticity, misattribution, affective primacy, and embodied cognition. The final part of the book deals with the neuroscientific underpinnings of the unconscious. This part discusses topics like computations models of the mind, modularity, and parallel distributed processing. Considering its wide scope, this book is an up-to-date and relatively concise treatment for readers interested in the unconscious.

References

Al-Hoorie, A. H. (2015). Human agency: Does the beach ball have free will? In Z. Dörnyei, P. MacIntyre, & A. Henry (Eds.), *Motivational dynamics in language learning* (pp. 55–72). Multilingual Matters.

Al-Hoorie, A. H. (2016a). Unconscious motivation. Part I: Implicit attitudes toward L2 speakers. *Studies in Second Language Learning and Teaching, 6*(3), 423–454. https://doi.org/10.14746/ssllt.2016.6.3.4

Al-Hoorie, A. H. (2016b). Unconscious motivation. Part II: Implicit attitudes and L2 achievement. *Studies in Second Language Learning and Teaching, 6*(4), 619–649. https://doi.org/10.14746/ssllt.2016.6.4.4

Al-Hoorie, A. H. (2017). Implicit attitudes in language learning. Unpublished Ph.D. thesis, University of Nottingham, UK.

Al-Hoorie, A. H. (2019). Motivation and the unconscious. In M. Lamb, K. Csizér, A. Henry, & S. Ryan (Eds.), *The Palgrave handbook of motivation for language learning* (pp. 561–578). Palgrave Macmillan.

Greenwald, A. G., McGhee, D. E., & Schwartz, J. L. (1998). Measuring individual differences in implicit cognition: The implicit association test. *Journal of Personality and Social Psychology, 74*(6), 1464–1480. https://doi.org/10.1037/0022-3514.74.6.1464

Sherman, J. W., Gawronski, B., & Trope, Y. (Eds.). (2014). *Dual-process theories of the social mind.* Guilford Press.

Ali H. Al-Hoorie is an assistant professor at the Jubail English Language and Preparatory Year Institute, Royal Commission for Jubail and Yanbu, Saudi Arabia. He completed his Ph.D. in Applied Linguistics at the University of Nottingham under the supervision of Professors Zoltán Dörnyei and Norbert Schmitt. He also holds an MA in Social Science Data Analysis from Essex University. His research interests include motivation theory, research methodology, and complexity. He has published in various journals including *Language Learning, The Modern Language Journal, Studies in Second Language Acquisition, ELT J, Language Teaching Research, and Learning and Individual Differences.* He is also the co-author of the book *Research Methods for Complexity in Applied Linguistics and a co-editor of Contemporary Language Motivation Theory: 60 Years Since Gardner and Lambert (1959).*

Salah Troudi

In conducting and evaluating research in the areas of applied linguistics, teaching English to speakers of other languages (TESOL) or language education in general it is common practice to focus on the content and methodology of the study. Content locates a research study in a particular area such as writing, assessment, professional development or curriculum evaluation whereas methodology addresses issues of research design, sampling, data collection instruments, data analysis and ethical dimensions. In fact, most research manuals and publications in the areas of TESOL and applied linguistics focus on methodological and practical considerations of how to develop research questions, design a study and analyse data. The major polarity or division in research between qualitative and quantitative traditions still exists and it still characterises the majority of research output in the field. There are of course studies that have crossed the divide in favour of bridging the gap and mixing what seems to be opposing approaches to research. Literature and research manuals on mixed methods and mixed-design studies in TESOL (Brown, 2014) have started to find their way into the field.

What needs to be stated is that research in TESOL and language education, like research in other fields, is informed by different philosophical perspectives or theoretical frameworks that reflect the researchers' views on the nature of educational reality and how learners learn. These views on reality and learning are known in philosophy as ontology and epistemology. When conducting research, researchers are led by assumptions or definitions they have on what constitutes the reality or realities of the area they are studying. For example, when investigating professional development of English language teachers or English speaking proficiency, a researcher will have her views on what constitutes professional development and how teachers continue learning on the job. For English speaking proficiency, she is likely to have a definition or a particular understanding of what it

S. Troudi (✉)
Graduate School of Education, University of Exeter, Exeter, England
e-mail: s.troudi@exeter.ac.uk

© Springer Nature Switzerland AG 2021
H. Mohebbi and C. Coombe (eds.), *Research Questions in Language Education and Applied Linguistics*, Springer Texts in Education,
https://doi.org/10.1007/978-3-030-79143-8_132

means to be proficient and how learners of English as a foreign language use different strategies to improve their speaking performances. These views on the nature of reality, i.e. ontology, and views on the nature of learning and how we learn, i.e. epistemology, form the theoretical elements of what is known as a paradigm of inquiry. These theoretical elements have impacts on the other two elements of a paradigm, namely methodology and methods of data collection (Crotty, 1998; Howell, 2013; Pring, 2015). TESOL researchers are encouraged to become familiar with the discourses of paradigms, different and competing philosophical positions and the array of terminologies that are associated with various research traditions.

Research paradigms such as positivism, interpretivism, critical theory, pragmatism and postmodernism assume different positions on the nature of reality and learning and often use different methodologies. A positivist or a post positivist researcher in TESOL is likely to have a different research agenda from someone informed by interpretive theory. While the former is interested in reaching generalizable conclusions or results based on a confirmatory methodology, the latter is interested in studying a particular phenomenon and how participants in a school setting construct meaning and define their learning. In this case, the researcher is likely to use an exploratory research methodology to understand the multiple realities represented by the participants. TESOL researchers need also to be aware that paradigms cannot also be seen in complete separation from one another as there are levels of compatibilities between them and possibilities of mixing methodologies (Tashakkori & Teddlie, 2010).

The Research Questions

1. Why does research in TESOL need to be informed by philosophical perspectives?
2. Do you think researchers in TESOL will benefit from the discourses of research paradigms? How?
3. Which particular research paradigm, if any, do you think represents your views on reality and knowledge? And why?
4. Can one be informed by more than one paradigm at the same time?
5. Which area in philosophy deals with the nature of reality?
6. Which area in philosophy deals with the nature of knowledge and learning?
7. With which research paradigm or approach would you associate confirmatory methodology? Why?
8. For what research purpose will you use an exploratory methodology?
9. Do researchers state what paradigms inform their studies when publishing their research?
10. When reading a published research study how can you tell which ontological and epistemological positions inform the study?

Suggested Resources

Pring, R. (2015). *Philosophy of educational research* **(3rd ed.). London: Bloomsbury**.

The third edition of this book introduces readers to key theoretical concepts in educational research as well as a number of practical considerations such as methods of data collection. Perhaps the most salient feature of this book is the way it explains philosophical concepts and terms in an accessible way. Chapter two stresses the importance of thinking philosophically about key concepts in education as learning, teaching, personal development, human flourishing, and educational discourse. Pring acknowledges that there is poor educational research out there when compared to research in other fields and that a fair amount of research in education is seen as worthless because of its irrelevance to practice, inaccessibility or the inability of schools to use results of studies in their decision-making processes. The sections on the different research paradigms, methodologies and associated terminologies are based on a premise stated by the author on page 9 explaining that in order to produce worthwhile research we need to "start by getting clear the nature of what is to be researched into".

Crotty, M. (1989). *The foundations of social research: Meaning and perspective in the research process.* **London: Sage**.

In this book Crotty provides a substantial description and analysis of a number of major research perspectives in education. If the reader is new to the discourse of paradigms then perhaps a shorter and lighter publication on the topic is advisable. By introducing the research process in the first chapter the author delineates key terms that need to be understood in order to be able to navigate through the philosophical discourses of each research perspectives. Crotty uses the term "perspective" rather than paradigm. Epistemology, ontology, methodology, and methods are explained and Fig. 1 on page 4 shows the relationship between these terms and how one informs the other. Of particular use to those new to this discourse is Table 1 on page 5 which takes each of these terms and associates it with corresponding or appropriate terms. For example, under epistemology, the term objectivism is associated with positivism and post-positivism. Ethnography and phenomenological research are in the column of methodology and are associated with constructivism as an epistemology. Starting with the second chapter Crotty traces the historical development of each major theoretical perspective, explains the nature of its epistemological and ontological assumptions and refers to major works of philosophers associated with that perspective. For example, readers are introduced to August Comte and Carl Popper with positivism. Max Weber and Herbert Mead are associated with interpretivism, Charles Peirce and John Dewey with Pragmatism and Jurgen Habermas with critical enquiry.

Howell, K. E. (2013). *The philosophy of methodology: An introduction.* **London: Sage**.

One of the main features of this book is that each chapter includes a definition box to provide an explanation of the main concepts being addressed by the chapter. A reflection box is also provided to engage the reader in thinking about some theoretical and methodological concepts and how they can be applied to understand human action, interaction and learning. Some of the 14 chapters also come with a question section. This is another interactive feature of the book whereby the reader is invited to read the text again with a specific purpose in mind. The questions serve also as a comprehension check opportunity which is a useful exercise, especially for novice researchers and readers who are new to the literature on educational and research philosophy. On page 42, readers are asked to "identify the difficulties for social sciences when dealing with immutable laws, prediction and objectivity". These are important issues for TESOL researchers whether at the level of design or the application of research findings in classrooms. Howell also provides a good number of tables which present the main concepts and associated authors in a clear and accessible way. The first five chapters are rich with theoretical explanations while the rest of the chapters provide a good link between theories and research methodologies.

Paltridge, B. & Phakiti, A. (2010) (Eds.). *Continuum to research methods in applied linguistics.* **London: Continuum**.

Researchers in applied linguistics, TESOL and language education will find this volume useful and practical. While the three above books deal with the theories informing research traditions, this book is mainly practical in nature. The chapters are written by very established researchers in the field. As stated by Paltridge and Phakiti at the start of the book, the chapters are meant for beginning researchers and students such as those embarking on doctoral studies. The eight chapters of the first part represent positivism, interpretive research and critical enquiry. In each chapter the authors start by explaining the philosophical assumptions behind their study then move to a description of the specifics of their chosen methodology such as experimental design, case study, ethnography or critical research. A particularly useful feature is the section of *a sample study* which illustrates to the reader how a study in a particular methodology is designed. This section is short and does not report on the study in its entirety, so readers are encouraged to read the full version of the study. In the second part of the book, 13 chapters are dedicated to different research areas in applied linguistics covering a wide range of topics such as grammar, vocabulary, pragmatics, assessment and language and identity. The chapters are more or less organised in the same way as in the first part. They all include a section on resources for further readings which introduces the reader to relevant publications about the topic of the chapter.

Brown, J.D. (2014). *Mixed methods research for TESOL.* **Edinburgh: Edinburgh University Press.**

For researchers interested in mixed methods research (MMR) in TESOL Brown's book is clearly an essential resource. The book is not heavy on theoretical explanations, but it does provide a rationale for using mixed methods designs in the first chapter. Divided into three sections the 10 chapters of the book take the reader through the major phases of a MMR design. In the first section, Brown starts with a focus on balancing the quantitative and qualitative elements, on avoiding misconceptions about triangulation and on writing good research questions. The second section is dedicated to analysing quantitative, qualitative and MMR data. The last section deals with presenting the research results, writing the reports and disseminating research. Guided readings are offered throughout the book to help the reader understand research concepts, techniques and procedures through extracts from published MMR studies in the field of TESOL.

Gournelos, T. Hammonds, J. R. & Wilson, M. A. (2019). (1st ed.). *Doing academic research: A Practical guide to research methods and analysis.* **New York: Routledge.**

This is a useful research reference and a practical guide to how to plan, design and conduct research. For early researchers in disciplines such as education and social sciences in general. The book offers practical tips and strategies on successfully completing research projects. It also demystifies research and presents it in an encouraging way. For those interested in publishing their research, the authors provide straightforward and accessible information on presenting academic research and the skill of persuasion. The book comes in twelve chapters covering both quantitative and qualitative research, and all the steps and procedures involved, along with many examples and illustrations. A useful glossary is also provided at the end of the book.

References

Brown, J. D. (2014). *Mixed methods research for TESOL*. Edinburgh University Press.
Crotty, M. (1998). *The foundations of social research: Meaning and perspective in the research process*. Sage.
Howell, K. E. (2013). *The philosophy of methodology: An introduction*. Sage.
Pring, R. (2015). *Philosophy of educational research* (3rd ed.). Bloomsbury.
Tashakkori, A., & Teddlie, C. (2010). *Sage handbook of mixed methods in social & behavioral research*. Sage Publications.

Salah Troudi is an academic at the Graduate School of Education of the University of Exeter. He supervises doctoral students and also teaches on the M.Ed., Ed.D. and Ph.D. TESOL programmes. His teaching and research interests include language teacher education, critical issues in TESOL and language education, language policy, curriculum development and evaluation, and classroom-based research. He has published articles in several TESOL and language education journals and edited a number of books. He is an international consultant and speaker in the areas of language education, programme evaluation, critical research and TESOL. He has taught at Florida State University, The University of Tunis, and the United Arab Emirates University.

Teacher Research Engagement

Daniel Xerri

Research engagement on the part of teachers consists of two main activities. Teachers engage *with* research when they critically read, listen to, and discuss the research published by academics or other teachers. They engage *in* research when they plan, undertake and reflect upon research projects in their own contexts. Both forms of research engagement contribute to teachers' professional development and help to transform the teaching and learning environment (Xerri & Pioquinto, 2018); however, the act of engaging in research is recognised as being especially significant. Teacher research enables classroom practitioners to reflect on their practices in a systematic manner and it can empower them to free themselves from the precepts imposed by trainers and inspectors because they are able to discover which methods and materials are most effective for their context (Field, 1997).

Teacher research has the potential to enhance the status of teaching in society because it generates knowledge that can be considered useful for a variety of stakeholders, including policy makers, academics and teacher educators (Atay, 2008). However, the main beneficiaries of teacher research are the practitioners that engage in it, and their students and colleagues. Teacher research allows the professionals who have first-hand experience of the classroom to problematize issues concerning teaching and learning. As Gao and Chow (2012) point out, "While many pedagogical problems can be successfully addressed through research, we also hope to see that teachers could see research as a critical means to deepen teachers' understanding of particular problems in teaching, rather than solve them" (p. 231). In this sense, teachers' engagement in research is not only significant for their professional development and classroom practices but also has an impact on the learners' experience and on the wider educational milieu.

Despite the benefits associated with teacher research, there exist a number of challenges that prevent teachers from engaging in research. One of these is the fact

D. Xerri (✉)
University of Malta, Centre for English Language Proficiency, Msida, Malta
e-mail: daniel.xerri@um.edu.mt

© Springer Nature Switzerland AG 2021
H. Mohebbi and C. Coombe (eds.), *Research Questions in Language Education and Applied Linguistics*, Springer Texts in Education,
https://doi.org/10.1007/978-3-030-79143-8_133

that most published research in language education and applied linguistics is not conducted by teachers but rather by academics that are provided with plenty of support for them to carry out their work. In fact, Borg (2013) asserts that despite there being "a substantial amount of theoretical support for the notion that research engagement can be beneficial for teachers and their schools … globally speaking it remains an activity which only a minority of language teaching professionals participate in" (p. 22). Unless teachers are provided with the support required for them to engage in research, they are likely to feel disheartened or to see research as alien to their professional identity. Support takes a myriad of forms, including providing teachers with the time in which to do research, developing their research literacy, recognising that research can be part of their professional duties, and trusting them as professionals who can generate knowledge for the advancement of the field (Xerri & Pioquinto, 2018).

Developing a research culture amongst teachers in a context where teacher research is not valued and hence not supported is highly challenging. Most often cultivating such a culture entails developing teachers' beliefs about research and equipping them with the necessary knowledge and skills to be able to engage in research beyond formal training and in their own classrooms (Borg, 2013). If teachers are not provided with support, they are likely to consider the task of conducting research as being too onerous for it to be sustained for long.

The Research Questions

1. What do teachers understand by 'research'?
2. What level of research literacy do teachers possess?
3. How can teachers improve their level of research literacy?
4. What specific knowledge, skills, attitudes and beliefs do research literate teachers have?
5. Why do some teachers engage in research? How?
6. What impact does teacher research have on student achievement?
7. What are the obstacles hindering teachers from doing research?
8. What forms of support do teachers require for them to do research?
9. What are the attitudes of school leaders toward teacher research?
10. What are the benefits and challenges of research collaboration between teachers and professional researchers?

Suggested Resources

Borg, S. (2013). *Teacher research in language teaching: A critical analysis.* **Cambridge: Cambridge University Press**.

Based on four studies involving more than 1700 language teaching professionals from around the globe, this book is a seminal work on the subject of teacher research. The book evaluates different conceptualizations of teacher research in order to establish a definition for this activity. It reviews the origins of teacher research, and considers its benefits and critiques. Besides investigating the conceptions of research held by language teaching professionals, the book discusses the two main forms of teacher research engagement: reading and doing research. The book also examines the relationship between research engagement and teaching quality, as well as the influence of the teaching context on one's research engagement. In addition to its empirical dimension, the book provides an insight into Borg's thoughts and experiences with respect to how language teacher research projects can be facilitated. The book seeks to indicate how research can be promoted effectively if it is deemed desirable and feasible for teachers to engage in it in their own contexts.

Mackay, J., Birello, M., & Xerri, D. (Eds.). (2018). *ELT research in action: Bridging the gap between research and classroom practice.* **Faversham: IATEFL**.

For some teachers, research is an activity that is somewhat alien to their professional concerns. This means that the research produced by academics is not always considered relevant to classroom practice, especially since teachers might not play a similarly active role in generating knowledge. This edited collection is an attempt to illustrate how the gap between research and classroom practice can be bridged. The book's first section is made up of chapters that engage in reflection and debate on the key issues that unite and divide research and practice. The next section considers how research can inform practice through the relation, testing and application of theory to classroom settings. The book's final section consists of chapters that explore some of the practical issues and questions that teachers might have and how research can help them to seek useful solutions and answers. The book makes a case for teacher research engagement, whether in the form of engaging *with* or *in* research.

Pinter, A., & Mathew, R. (2016). *Children and teachers as co-researchers: A handbook of activities.* **London: British Council**.

Teacher research need not be an isolating activity; collaboration with colleagues and students can make the experience far more enriching. This innovative book consists of a series of activities that teachers in India used in their classrooms in order to involve young children as co-researchers. Through these activities, children were given a say in what they would like to do in class and worked together with their teachers to investigate different dimensions of their learning. Despite the possible lack of research experience of both teachers and learners, the book demonstrates how they can become co-researchers through the acts of questioning, hypothesizing, gathering and analyzing people's views, and developing an understanding of a classroom event. The 45 activities in the book are organized in six sections: trying out something new; children making choices; teachers handing over control to children; building positive relationships; designing research tools and analyzing empirical data; and feedback and self/peer-assessment. Even though there is a description of how every activity was conducted by real teachers and learners, readers are free to modify an activity to suit the needs of their students and lessons.

Smith, R., & Rebolledo, P. (2018). *A handbook for exploratory action research.* **London: British Council.**

This book aims to demonstrate how teachers can engage in research for professional development purposes and to enhance students' learning experiences. Addressing the needs of primary and secondary school teachers working in relatively difficult circumstances, the book is informed by insights developed in the course of teacher research projects held in Peru, India, Nepal and Chile. Exploratory Action Research is described as an effective means of dealing with difficult circumstances because it allows teachers to improve their understanding of the classroom and to develop suitable forms of teaching that are not dependent on external solutions. The book shows how the exploratory phase of one's research is as important as the action phase. Featuring real examples provided by teachers working in difficult circumstances, the book invites readers to complete practical tasks that enable them to reflect on their own teaching experiences and to consider the value of researching their professional contexts.

Xerri, D., & Pioquinto, C. (Eds.). (2018). *Becoming research literate: Supporting teacher research in English language teaching.* **Sursee: ETAS.**

The aim of this volume is to bring together a wide range of contributions on how teacher research can be supported. The development of research literacy is deemed to play a fundamental role in providing teachers with support. Some of the contributors consider how research literacy does not only involve equipping teachers with the relevant knowledge and skills for them to do research, but it also entails developing their conceptions of research and their attitudes and beliefs with respect to the value that research has for teachers' professional identity. The book is divided into four parts, each one containing articles and interviews that showcase the views of teachers, academics, teacher educators, and teacher association leaders from around the world. Part 1 discusses some of the key issues of teacher research in language teaching, while Part 2 consists of chapters that review the different forms of support that teachers might require in order to do research. Part 3 considers how research can be embedded into professional practice via activities like action research and narrative inquiry, while Part 4 highlights the thoughts of classroom practitioners on the act of engaging in research.

References

Atay, D. (2008). Teacher research for professional development. *ELT Journal, 62*(2), 139–147.

Borg, S. (2013). *Teacher research in language teaching: A critical analysis.* Cambridge University Press.

Field, J. (1997). Key concepts in ELT: Classroom research. *ELT Journal, 51*(2), 192–193.

Gao, X., & Chow, A. W. K. (2012). Primary school English teachers' research engagement. *ELT Journal, 66*(2), 224–232.

Xerri, D., & Pioquinto, C. (Eds.). (2018). *Becoming research literate: Supporting teacher research in English language teaching.* ETAS.

Daniel Xerri is a Lecturer in TESOL at the University of Malta. He holds postgraduate degrees in English and Applied Linguistics, as well as a Ph.D. in Education from the University of York. He is the author of many publications on different areas of education and TESOL. His most recent co-edited books are *The Image in English Language Teaching* (2017, ELT Council), *ELT Research in Action: Bridging the Gap between Research and Classroom Practice* (2018, IATEFL), *Teacher Involvement in High-stakes Language Testing* (2018, Springer), *Becoming Research Literate: Supporting Teacher Research in English Language Teaching* (2018, ETAS), and *English for 21st Century Skills* (2020, Express Publishing). Further details about his talks and publications can be found at: http://www.danielxerri.com.

Part IX

Applied Linguistics and Second Language Acquisition

Bilingual Code-mixing and Code-switching

134

Tej K. Bhatia

Bilingualism and Multilingualism is an interdisciplinary and complex field. As is self-evident from the prefixes (bi- and multi-), the bilingualism and multilingualism phenomena are devoted to the study of production, processing, and comprehension of two (or more) languages, respectively.

Defining and measuring bilingualism is a very complex and uphill task due to the number and types of input conditions. For instance, while a monolingual child receives input from their parents only in one language in all settings, a bilingual child is provided input in at least two separate languages (e.g. one-parent one-language input; one-place one-language input) in addition to a code-mixed input in a variety of environments. In addition, biological (age of acquisition), socio-psychological and other non-linguistic factors lead to varying degrees of bilingual language competencies. Therefore, it is natural that no widely-accepted definition or measure of bilingualism exists. Instead, a rich range of scales, dichotomies, and categories are employed to describe bilingualism, which pose serious conceptual and methodological challenges for research in the bilingual language acquisition and bilingual verbal behavior (see Bhatia, 2018; Weinreich, 1953).

Is a bilingual a composite of two monolinguals? Does the bilingual brain comprise two monolinguals crowded into a limited space? For some researchers, the answer to these questions has traditionally been affirmative. Such a view of bilingualism is termed, the 'fractional view.' According to this view monolingualism holds the key to the understanding of bilingualism. However, a more balanced and accurate picture of bilingualism emerges from the 'holistic' view of

T. K. Bhatia (✉)
Department of Linguistics (LLL), Syracuse University, Syracuse, NY 13244, USA
e-mail: tkbhatia@syr.edu

© Springer Nature Switzerland AG 2021
H. Mohebbi and C. Coombe (eds.), *Research Questions in Language Education and Applied Linguistics*, Springer Texts in Education,
https://doi.org/10.1007/978-3-030-79143-8_134

bilingualism. According to this view, a bilingual person is neither a mere sum of two monolinguals nor is the bilingual brain a composite of two monolingual brains. The reason for this position is that the cooperation, competition and coexistence of the bilingual's two languages make a bilingual a very complex and colorful individual (see Grosjean, 2010).

Language separation and language integration are the two most salient characteristics of bilinguals and thus, of the bilingual brain. Whenever deemed appropriate, bilinguals can turn-off one language and turn-on the other language. This enables them to switch from one language to another with an ease like a driver of a stick-shift car shifting into different gears whenever necessary. The 'fractional' view of bilingualism can account for such a verbal behavior of bilinguals. In addition to keeping the two linguistic systems separate, bilingualism, however, can integrate the two systems by mixing two languages. Language mixing is a far more complex cognitive ability than language separation. The 'holistic' view of bilingualism can account for these two types of competencies. Language mixing is very natural to bilinguals. Therefore, it is not surprising that mixed languages such as Spanglish, Hinglish, Japlish, and Germlish are emerging around the globe. Contrary to the claims of earlier research, the grammar of language mixing is very complex and yet systematic (see MacSwan, 2014; Gardner-Chloros, 2009).

The Research Questions

1   Are bilinguals just a composite of two monolinguals in a single individual? Why? Why not?
2. Is language mixing (Code-mixing and Code-switching) a random or a systematic phenomenon? Why?
3. Is there a grammar of Code-mixing and Code-switching?
4. What motivates bilinguals to mix and alternate two languages? Do language educators use language mixing in classrooms?
5. How is a matrix language distinguished from embedded language in a code-mixed utterance?
6. What is the social evaluation of language mixing and language alternation?
7. What is the difference between code-mixing/code-switching and other related phenomena—borrowings, pidgin and creole languages and diglossia?
8. What are the two salient characteristics of the bilingual brain?
9. Is childhood language mixing different from adult language mixing?
10. Unlike monolinguals, a decision to speak multiple languages requires a complex unconscious process on the part of bilinguals. What factors determine language choice by bilinguals?

Suggested Resources

Bhatia, T., & Ritchie, W. (Eds.). (2013). *The handbook of bilingualism and multilingualism.* **Oxford: Blackwell Publishing Ltd.**

This handbook provides state-of-the art overviews of central issues of bilingualism and plurilingualism. The work represents a new integration of interdisciplinary research by a team of internationally-renowned scholars. The handbook is organized into four parts and comprises thirty-six chapters, covering neurolinguistics, psycholinguistics, sociolinguistics, and educational aspects of bilingualism. It covers of a wide variety of topics, ranging from neuro- and psycho-linguistic research to studies of media and role of language in psychological counseling.

Included in the handbook is the latest assessment of the global linguistic situation with particular emphasis on those geographical areas which are centers of global conflict and commerce. New topics such as global media and mobile and electronic language learning are also included. Chapter 13, devoted to methodology, is particularly useful for researchers interested in multidisciplinary research methodological approaches to bilingualism/multilingualism, while Chap. 15 underscores the social-psychological basis of bilingual language mixing. Other topics of interests are: Multilingualism and forensic linguistics; Bilingualism and writing systems; Bilingual education; and Endangered languages. This volume was the recipient of the Choice Outstanding Academic Award.

Gardner-Chloros, P. (2009). *Code-switching.* **Cambridge, UK: Cambridge University Press.**

It is quite common for bilingual speakers to use two or more languages, dialects or varieties in the same conversation, without any apparent effort. This book explores how, when, why, and where aspects of Code Switching (CS) and Code Mixing (CM), using rich and diverse sources of data sets. Structurally diverse patterns of CS and CM across a wide-variety of language-pairs are presented. The phenomenon, known as CM and CS (aka, translanguaging), has become a major focus of attention in linguistics, language pedagogy and language policies. This concise and original study explores how, when and where code-switching occurs. Drawing on a diverse range of examples from medieval manuscripts to rap music, novels to advertisements, emails to political speeches, and above all everyday conversation, it argues that CS and CM can only be properly understood if we study it from a variety of interdisciplinary perspectives such as sociolinguistic, psycholinguistic, grammatical, and language developmental aspects of the two phenomena.

Kroll, J., & De Groot, A. M. B. (Eds.). (2005). *Handbook of bilingualism: psycholinguistic approaches.* **Oxford: Oxford University Press.**

This handbook fills an important gap by exploring the psycholinguistics, neuro- and cognitive linguistic basis of bilingualism. Methodological and experimental issues are also explored. Like the other handbooks in the field, it is aimed at scholarly and cross disciplinary audiences.

This handbook explores the following central questions of bilingual/multiingual language development:

- How is language acquired when infants are exposed to multiple language input from birth and when adults are required to learn a second language after early childhood?
- How do adult bilinguals comprehend and produce words and sentences when their two languages are potentially always active and in competition with one another?
- What are the neural mechanisms that underlie proficient bilingualism?
- What are the effects of bilingualism for cognition and for language and thought?

In addition, it sheds light on the complex dimensions of additive and subtractive bilingualism.

Phakiti A., De Costa, P., Plonsky, L., Starfield, S. (Eds). (2018). *The Palgrave handbook of applied linguistic research methodology.* **London: Palgrave Macmillan.**

This Handbook provides a comprehensive treatment of basic and advanced research methodologies in applied linguistics and offers a state-of-the-art review of methods particular to a variety of subfields including ELT/TESOL. The handbook is organized in four parts and is comprised of forty-one chapters. It covers a range of research approaches, presents current perspectives, and addresses key issues in different research methods, such as designing and implementing research instruments and techniques, and analyzing different types of applied linguistics data. As such, it offers an up-to-date and highly accessible entry point into both established and emerging approaches that offer new possibilities and perspectives as well as thorough consideration of best practices. This wide-ranging volume is an invaluable resource to applied linguists at all levels, including scholars in related fields such as language learning and teaching, multilingualism, corpus linguistics, critical discourse analysis, discourse analysis and pragmatics, language assessment, language policy and planning, multimodal communication, and translation.

Weinreich, U. (1953). Languages in contact: findings and problems. The Hague: Mouton.

This pioneering work represents a classic in bilingualism. It presents a comprehensive study of grammars in contact, underpinning the mechanism and structural factors in the language development of bilinguals. The role of non-linguistic factors also receives substantive treatment in this book. The book was the first to draw attention to language mixing by bilinguals. Code Mixing and Code Switching, interference, borrowing among other related phenomena such as interference, borrowing, pidgin-creoles. Weinreich laid out the concepts, principles and issues that govern theoretical and empirical issues and challenges in the field of bilingualism and multilingualism. Chapter 3 is noteworthy for its synthesis of the psychological and linguistic deficiency theories of individual bilingualism. This work views bilingualism as a life-long phenomenon, which makes the task of defining and measuring bilingualism a formidable challenge.

References

Bhatia, T. K., et al. (2018). Bilingualism and multilingualism. In A. Phakiti (Ed.), *The Palgrave handbook of applied linguistic research methodology* (pp. 681–701). Palgrave Macmillan.
Gardner-Chloros, P. (2009). *Code-switching*. Cambridge University Press.
Grosjean, F. (2010). *Bilingual: Life and reality*. Harvard University Press.
MacSwan, J. (ed.) (2014). *Grammatical theory and bilingual codeswitching*. Language and Linguistics series. MIT Press. ISBN 978-0-262-02789-2. Viii+326 pages.
Weinreich, U. (1953). *Languages in contact: Findings and problems*. Mouton.

Tej K. Bhatia is a Professor of Linguistics and Director of South Asian Languages at Syracuse University, Syracuse, New York. He has published a number of books (16), articles and book chapters in the areas of bilingualism, multiculturalism, media (advertising) discourse, socio- and psycho-linguistics, and the structure and typology of English and South Asian languages (particularly Hindi, Urdu, Punjabi). His publications include five handbooks with William C. Ritchie—*Handbook of Bilingualism and Multilingualism* (2013; Oxford: Wiley-Blackwell); *A New Handbook of Second Language Acquisition* (2009); *Handbook of Bilingualism* (2006); *Handbook of Child Language Acquisition* (1999); and *Handbook of Second Language Acquisition* (1996). He has been the recipient of a number of grants from the National Science Foundation, US Department of Education, American Council of Learned Societies.

Mark D. Johnson

Recent second language (L2) writing research on cognitive task complexity has sought to bring together models of working memory in first language (L1) writing (Kellogg, 1996) with the predictions of task-based language teaching and learning or TBLT (Ellis, this volume), particularly the predictions of (a) the limited attentional capacity model (Skehan, 1998) and/or (b) the cognition hypothesis (Robinson, 2011). The limited attentional capacity model predicts that increasing the complexity of a language task will cause the learner to focus on conveying a message. Thus, the learner will favor the fluent production of language, resulting in decreased complexity and/or accuracy. In contrast, decreasing the complexity of a language task will cause the learner to focus on the production of more complex and/or more accurate—though less fluent—language. The cognition hypothesis theorizes two dimensions of task complexity: (a) resource-directing features of task complexity are predicted to focus learners' attention on the production of complex, accurate language (though fluency will suffer), whereas (b) resource-dispersing features of task complexity are thought to distract learners' attention from language production, resulting in reduced complexity, accuracy, and fluency.

In L2 writing research, evidence for the two hypotheses is inconclusive (Kormos, 2011; Tavakoli, 2014; Yuan, 2001) or contradictory (Kuiken & Vedder, 2008), leading some researchers to doubt the ability of either hypothesis to explain the effects of cognitive task complexity on L2 writing (Johnson et al., 2012). Adding to the difficulty in making comparisons across studies is the nature of the writing process itself. Kellogg's model of working memory in L1 writing is based on the early work of Flower and Hayes (1980), which identified three primary writing systems: (a) formulation (comprised of planning and translation), (b) execution (the coordination of muscle movements to encode language on the page), and (c) monitoring (comparing the developing text to goals and objectives).

M. D. Johnson (✉)
Department of English, East Carolina University, Greenville, NC, USA
e-mail: johnsonmark@ecu.edu

© Springer Nature Switzerland AG 2021
H. Mohebbi and C. Coombe (eds.), *Research Questions in Language Education and Applied Linguistics*, Springer Texts in Education,
https://doi.org/10.1007/978-3-030-79143-8_135

Formulation is thought to place the greatest burden on working memory capacity, whereas, monitoring is thought to place the second greatest burden on working memory capacity.

The results of a recent research synthesis and meta-analysis of cognitive task complexity in L2 writing (Johnson, 2017) found no conclusive support for the limited attentional capacity model or the cognition hypothesis. However, the results point to consistent effects of task complexity features on written L2 production. Additionally, the results of the research synthesis and meta-analysis suggest that L2 writers may consciously direct their attention to either the formulation or the monitoring system of writing regardless of task complexity features. Thus, increases in the complexity, accuracy, and fluency of L2 written production may be influenced by a combination of task complexity features and learner focus on the formulation system or the monitoring system.

The results of Johnson's meta-analysis provide a good deal of evidence to support Manchón's (2014) call for a greater understanding of learners' interpretations and representations of the writing task and, more generally, the role of writing in TBLT.

The Research Questions

1. How does the cognitive complexity of a task influence L2 written performance?
2. Does cognitive task complexity affect oral and written L2 performance differently? If so, how?
3. How do learners interpret the demands of a writing task? Do their interpretations match theoretical conceptions of the task's complexity?
4. What, if any, is the relationship between the complexity of a writing task and the L2 writer's interpretation of the task?
5. How can cognitive complexity of tasks be used to sequence tasks in order to promote L2 writing performance and/or general L2 development?
6. In what ways does genre knowledge constitute a feature of cognitive task complexity?
7. How do features of cognitive task complexity affect the writing systems (i.e., formulation, execution, and monitoring) and writing processes (i.e. planning, translating, reading, and editing) of L2 writers?
8. How do cognitive task complexity features interact with general L2 proficiency, instruction, and/or genre knowledge to affect L2 writing development/ performance?
9. How does cognitive task complexity promote "deep, meaningful language processing" (Byrnes & Manchón, 2014, p. 7)?
10. How do cognitive task complexity and writer collaboration (Manchón, 2014) interact to affect L2 writing development/performance?

Suggested Resources

Byrnes, H., & Manchón, R. M. (2014). Task-based language learning: Insights from and for L2 writing, an introduction. In H. Byrnes & R. M. Manchón (Eds.), *Task-based language learning: Insights from and for L2 writing* **(pp. 1-23). Amsterdam: John Benjamins**.

In the introduction to this edited volume, Byrnes and Manchón first outline the historic focus of TBLT research on oral language production, arguing that the view of writing in such research is as "a culture-dependent secondary manifestation of human language" (p. 2). The authors then argue that writing and task can (and should) be viewed as a tool for language learning due to the greater availability of time to focus on language, the visibility/permanence of written output as well as feedback on that output, and the nature of writing as a problem-solving activity. The authors then argue for a view of writing as "a meaning-filled event" (p. 7) which allows an expanded view of task: (a) as an opportunity for deep, meaningful language processing and (b) as a means of motivating literacy development.

Johnson, M. D. (forthcoming). Task complexity studies. In R. M. Manchón, & C. Polio (Eds.), *Handbook of second language acquisition and writing*. **New York, NY: Routledge**.

Focused on writing as a locus for second language acquisition, this chapter provides an overview of theoretical and methodological issues in the research of cognitive task complexity in second language writing and provides a discussion of future directions for researchers. In particular, Johnson calls for future research to examine (a) the relationship(s) among working memory capacity, L2 writing systems (i.e., formulation, execution, and monitoring), and L2 writing processes (i.e., translation and planning); (b) the effect of cognitive task complexity on the propositional complexity of L2 writing as well a the relationship(s) among propositional complexity, syntactic complexity, and lexical complexity; and (c) the role of genre familiarity as a resource-dispersing feature of cognitive task complexity.

Johnson, M. D. (2017). Cognitive task complexity and L2 written syntactic complexity, lexical complexity, accuracy, and fluency: A research synthesis and meta-analysis. *Journal of Second Language Writing*, *37*, **13-38.** https://doi.org/10.1016/j.jslw.2017.06.001.

In this systematic review of L2 writing research on TBLT, Johnson uses Robinson's triadic componential framework to code cognitive task complexity features. Using meta-analytic techniques, Johnson compares the effect of cognitive task complexity manipulation on the syntactic complexity, accuracy, lexical complexity, and fluency of L2 written production. Although the results of the study offer no conclusive support for the cognition hypothesis, a number of trends suggest consistent effects of certain task complexity features on L2 written production. However, the results also suggest that L2 writers react to complex task features by directing their attention to various writing systems and processes.

Manchón, R. M. (2014). The internal dimension of tasks: The interaction between task factors and learner factors in bringing about learning through writing. In H. Byrnes & R. M. Manchón (Eds.), *Task-based language learning: Insights from and for L2 writing* (pp. 27-52). Amsterdam: John Benjamins.

Manchón examines the cognition hypothesis and its application to L2 writing, arguing for a greater need to examine more complex, more varied, tasks completed under more varied conditions (timed and untimed, individually and collaboratively). Key to this examination is Manchón's articulation of the role of task engagement from various theoretical viewpoints as well as an articulation of task representation—the interaction of the writer's understanding of rhetorical concerns with the writer's goals and strategies for completion of the writing task. From this examination, Manchón sets forth several priorities for future L2 writing research from a TBLT perspective: (a) a better understanding of individual and collaborative writing tasks and task execution/performance, (b) a better understanding of how tasks contribute to language development, and (c) an understanding of how feedback contributes to language learning in a TBLT framework.

Robinson, P. (2011). Second language task complexity, the cognition hypothesis, language learning, and performance. In P. Robinson. (Ed.), *Second language task complexity: Researching the cognition hypothesis on language learning and performance* (pp. 3-37). Amsterdam: John Benjamins.

In this, the introduction to an edited volume, Robinson argues for tasks as the central focus of L2 teaching and learning. Task complexity is proposed as the driver of linguistic complexity as more complex language is needed to encode more complex propositions. Situating the cognition hypothesis in broader theories of pedagogy and assessment, Robinson presents a taxonomy for describing the complexity of language tasks and ordering such tasks to promote language development and/or language performance. In this taxonomy, the cognitive complexity of tasks can be described along a resource-directing dimension of task complexity and a resource-dispersing dimension of task complexity. Resource-directing features of task complexity are hypothesized to focus learner attention on complex, accurate language production. In contrast, resource-dispersing features of task complexity are hypothesized to interfere with language production.

References

Byrnes, H., & Manchón, R. M. (2014). Task-based language learning: Insights from and for L2 writing, an introduction. In H. Byrnes & R. M. Manchón (Eds.), Task-based language learning: Insights fromand for L2 writing (pp. 1–23). Amsterdam: John Benjamins.

Flower, L. S., & Hayes, J. R. (1980). The dynamics of composing: Making plans and juggling constraints. In L. W. Gregg & E. R. Steinberg (Eds.), *Cognitive processes in writing* (pp. 31–50). Lawrence Erlbaum.

Johnson, M. D. (2017). Cognitive task complexity and L2 written syntactic complexity, lexical complexity, accuracy, and fluency: A research synthesis and meta-analysis. *Journal of Second Language Writing, 37*, 13–38. https://doi.org/10.1016/j.jslw.2017.06.001

Johnson, M. D., Mercado, L., & Acevedo, A. (2012). The effect of planning sub-processes on L2 writing fluency, grammatical complexity, and lexical complexity. *Journal of Second Language Writing, 21*, 264–282. https://doi.org/10.1016/j.jslw.2012.05.011

Kellogg, R. T. (1996). A model of working memory in writing. In C. M. Levy & S. Ransdell (Eds.), *The science of writing* (pp. 57–71). Lawrence Erlbaum Associates.

Kormos, J. (2011). Task complexity and linguistic and discourse features of narrative writing performance. *Journal of Second Language Writing, 20*, 148–161. https://doi.org/10.1016/j.jslw.2011.02.001

Kuiken, F., & Vedder, I. (2008). Cognitive task complexity and written output in Italian and French as a foreign language. *Journal of Second Language Writing, 17*, 48–60. https://doi.org/10.1016/j.jslw.2007.08.003

Manchón, R. M. (2014). The internal dimension of tasks: The interaction between task factors and learner factors in bringing about learning through writing. In H. Byrnes & R. M. Manchón (Eds.), *Task-based language learning: Insights from and for L2 writing* (pp. 27–52). John Benjamins.

Robinson, P. (Ed.). (2011). *Second language task complexity: Researching the cognition hypothesis of language learning and performance.* John Benjamins.

Skehan, P. (1998). *A cognitive approach to language learning.* Oxford University Press.

Tavakoli, P. (2014). Storyline complexity and syntactic complexity in writing and speaking tasks. In H. Byrnes & R. M. Manchón (Eds.), *Task-based language learning: Insights from and for L2 writing* (pp. 217–236). John Benjamins.

Yuan, F. (2001). *The effects of planning on language production in task-based language teaching.* Unpublished doctoral dissertation. Temple University.

Mark D. Johnson Ph.D., is associate professor of TESOL and Applied Linguistics at East Carolina University, where he teaches second language acquisition, research methods, and language assessment courses for teachers of English as a second language. His research interests focus on how teachers may improve students' second language writing performance and include task-based language teaching and second language writing; the effect of planning on second language writing; and the range and development of vocabulary in second language writing performance.

Complexity, Accuracy and Fluency (CAF)

Alex Housen

In applied linguistics, second language acquisition (SLA) and language education research, complexity, accuracy and fluency (henceforth CAF) have been considered as major components and basic dimensions of performance, proficiency and development in a second or foreign language. The origins of the CAF triad lie in the search for a developmental index of second language (L2) development in the 1970s, by which researchers could "expediently and reliably gauge proficiency and development in a L2" (Larsen-Freeman, 1978, p. 440) in an objective, verifiable and quantitative way. At the same time, a distinction was made in L2 pedagogy between *fluent* versus *accurate* L2 use to investigate the development of communicative L2 proficiency in classroom contexts (e.g. Brumfit, 1984). Skehan (1989) was the first to propose a model of L2 proficiency and development that included all three dimensions—accuracy, fluency *and* complexity. In the 1990s, complexity, accuracy and fluency were given their traditional working definitions, which are still widely used today. *Complexity* is thus characterized as the *range of forms* (i.e. items, structures, patterns, rules) available to an L2 learner and the *degree of elaboration and sophistication* of these forms, *accuracy* as the ability to produce *target-like and error-free L2 speech and writing*, and fluency as the ability to produce L2 speech or writing with *target-like rapidity, pausing, hesitation, or reformulation* (Wolfe-Quintero et al., 1998).

In the last 30 years, CAF have appeared prominently in research on applied linguistics, SLA, language education and language testing, mainly as dependent variables, that is, as properties of L2 learners' L2 performance which are evaluated to investigate the effect of other factors. Thus, CAF have been used as indices of L2 proficiency and development to examine, for example, the effects of age on L2 attainment, the effects of different types of instruction, of individual learner dif-

A. Housen (✉)
Department of Linguistics & Literary Studies, Vrije Universiteit Brussel (VUB), Brussel, Brussels, Belgium
e-mail: ahousen@vub.ac.be

© Springer Nature Switzerland AG 2021
H. Mohebbi and C. Coombe (eds.), *Research Questions in Language Education and Applied Linguistics*, Springer Texts in Education,
https://doi.org/10.1007/978-3-030-79143-8_136

ferences, or the effects of different learning context or of task designs (e.g. Bygate, 1999; Robinson, 2001; Yuan & Ellis, 2003). More recently, CAF have also figured as primary or independent variables (e.g. De Jong, 2018; Larsen-Freeman, 2006; Norris & Ortega, 2009; Polio & Shea, 2014).

CAF have been measured by means of (subjective) ratings and, more typically, (objective) quantitative measures, of which there are many (see reviews in Wolfe-Quintero et al., 1998; Ellis & Barkhuizen, 2005).

Complexity, accuracy and fluency have been shown to be conceptually distinct and empirically separable basic dimensions of L2 performance, proficiency and development, indicating that all three components should be considered in order to make valid claims about learners' L2 performance, proficiency or development (Housen & Kuiken, 2009; Norris & Ortega, 2009). Theoretically, CAF have been linked to major developmental changes in learners' underlying L2 systems, that is, to the *internalisation* of new L2 elements (or greater complexity, as more elaborate and more sophisticated L2 knowledge systems are developed), to the *modification* of L2 knowledge (as learners restructure and fine-tune their L2 knowledge, including the deviant or non-targetlike aspects of their interlanguage (IL) so that they become not only more complex but also more accurate L2 users), and to the *consolidation* and *proceduralisation* of L2 knowledge (i.e. fluency, through routinisation, lexicalisation and automatisation of L2 elements, leading to greater performance control over the L2 system) (Housen et al., 2012).

The Research Questions

1. How can complexity, accuracy and fluency be defined as scientific constructs?
2. Are the three CAF components themselves monolithic or, rather, multi-componential and multi-layered constructs? If the latter, what are the relevant subcomponents?
3. Do CAF exhaustively capture all relevant aspects and dimensions of L2 performance, proficiency and development, or are there other aspects that should be considered (e.g. functional or communicative adequacy or maturity)?
4. How do CAF manifest themselves at the various linguistic domains and layers of language (phonology, lexis, morphology, syntax) and their respective interfaces?
5. How can the three constructs best be operationalized and adequately (i.e. validly, reliably and practically) measured, and how do subjective ratings (cor-) relate with objective quantitative measures of CAF?
6. Which measures of CAF best index L2 proficiency and L2 development? Which CAF measures best discriminate between different L2 proficiency levels and stages of L2 development?
7. To what extent are the three CAF dimensions in(ter)dependent in L2 performance, L2 proficiency and L2 development, and are there trade-offs between the three dimensions, both in their synchronic manifestation in specific

instances of language use as well as in the diachronic process of L2 development?

8. What are the underlying linguistic, cognitive and psycholinguistic correlates of CAF, and how does each component relate to theoretical models of L2 competence, L2 proficiency, L2 processing and L2 development? For instance, how does CAF relate to the L2 proficiency levels distinguished by the Common European Framework of Reference (CEFR) for languages?

9. Which factors (can) influence the manifestation and development of CAF in L2 learning and use, with particular attention to effects of the specific target language, task characteristics (e.g. type and amount of planning, task complexity), text types and genres (e.g. descriptive, narrative, argumentative), language mode (writing vs. speech) and L2 learner characteristics (e.g. degree of extraversion, language anxiety, motivation, language aptitude)?

10. How can each of the three CAF dimensions be developed in an educational setting (e.g. a foreign language classroom) and which instructional or pedagogical approaches are (most) effective for developing L2 learners' complexity, accuracy and fluency?

Suggested Resources

Wolfe-Quintero, K., Inagaki, S. & Kim, H-Y. (1998). Second Language Development in Writing: Measures of Fluency, Accuracy and Complexity (Technical Report 17). Honolulu: University of Hawai'i, Second Language Teaching and Curriculum Center.

This technical report is still one of the most comprehensive publications devoted to CAF. It analyzes over 100 quantitative measures from 39 empirical studies on L2 writing to identify features of learners' L2 writing performances that situate the interlanguages on a developmental spectrum. The report consists of six chapters. The introductory chapter presents working definitions of the three constructs. Chapters 2–5 present detailed critiques of measures of, respectively, fluency, accuracy, grammatical complexity (structural variety and sophistication) and lexical complexity measures (lexical variety and sophistication). Chapter 6 concludes with evaluations of the best developmental measures and suggests new measures as well as directions for new future research, many of which are still relevant today.

Ellis, R. & Barkhuizen, G. (2005). *Analysing Learner Language*. Oxford: Oxford University Press.

This book offers a 'hands-on' approach to different methods for analysing learner language. Chapter 7 is devoted to '*Analysing accuracy, complexity and fluency*', with a special focus on analysing oral learner data produced in the frame of task-based language teaching (TBLT; see Ellis, this volume). The chapter opens with a number of useful working definitions of complexity, accuracy and fluency, followed by a sketch of the historical and theoretical context in which CAF research has been embedded. Next a range of 22 measures of accuracy (6), fluency (8) and complexity (8) are critically examined and applied to transcriptions of two short oral narratives. Interestingly, the range of complexity measures not only includes purely linguistic complexity measures (by far the most frequent type of complexity measures used) but also measures of what the authors call 'interactional', 'functional' and 'propositional' complexity.

Applied Linguistics, 30, 4. Special Issue: Complexity, Accuracy and Fluency (CAF) in Second Language Acquisition Research.

This special issue on CAF in SLA research consists of seven articles. The article by Housen and Kuiken summarizes the state of the art of CAF research in SLA. The article by Rod Ellis addresses the role and effects of planning on CAF in task-based L2 performance and L2 acquisition. In the third article, Skehan claims that CAF measures need to be supplemented by measures of lexical use because lexis constitutes a separate aspect of L2 performance. Robinson, Cadierno and Shirai investigate the effects of increasing task complexity on CAF dimensions in L2 performance, using specific rather than general measures of CAF. The remaining three articles by Norris and Ortega, Larsen-Freeman, and Pallotti all critically examine current conceptions of CAF and CAF measurement practices. These authors emphasize the multidimensional nature of CAF as a dynamic and inter-related set of constantly changing sub-systems which develop in a non-linear fashion, and the need for more 'organic' measurement practices to capture such CAF phenomena. Pallotti also argues that communicative adequacy should be considered both as a separate performance dimension in addition to CAF and as a way of interpreting CAF measures.

Housen, A., Kuiken, V. & Vedder, I. (Eds). (2012). *Dimensions of L2 Performance and Proficiency—Investigating Complexity, Accuracy and Fluency in SLA*. **Amsterdam: John Benjamins**.

This edited volume showcases the diversity of current research on complexity, accuracy and fluency as a part of Benjamins' *Language Learning and Language Teaching* series. The book contains 12 chapters divided into two sections, the first addressing theoretical and methodological issues (Chaps. 2–5 and 12), and the second reporting empirical studies (Chaps. 6–11). Chapter 1, and its companion Chapter 12, provide a brief history of CAF as research variables, discuss the current status, scope and goals of CAF research, and identify a number of challenges for future CAF studies. Chapter 2, by Bulté and Housen, is devoted to complexity, arguably the most complex and problematic dimension of the CAF triad, both in terms of definition and in terms of measurement. Chapters 3 (by Towell) and 4 (by Myles) address the definition of CAF and its cognitive and linguistic underpinnings from a theoretical and linguistic-acquisitionist perspective. The remaining chapters report on empirical cross-sectional (Chaps. 6–9) and longitudinal (Chaps. 10 and 11) studies, examining L2 performance with regard to CAF by learners from a variety of L1 backgrounds and in a variety of educational contexts. The target languages under study include English, Dutch, French, and Italian.

Larsen-Freeman, D. (2006). The Emergence of Complexity, Fluency, and Accuracy in the Oral and Written Production of Five Chinese Learners of English. *Applied Linguistics*, **27/4: 590–619**.

This empirical study is the first to approach CAF as dimensions of L2 performance, proficiency and development from a Dynamic Systems Theory (DST) perspective, which underlines the inherent variability and the nonlinearity of language learning and "the interdependence, [social] situatedness and dynamic interaction of dimensions of CAF" (p. 587). This longitudinal study was the first to identify the competition ('trade-offs') between complexity, accuracy and fluency in the course of L2 development as well as the supportive influence that one dimension may exert on the others. As such, this publication served as an inspiration for a spade of other DST-inspired CAF studies in SLA.

References

Brumfit, C. (1984). *Communicative methodology in language teaching.* Cambridge University Press.

Bygate, M. (1999). Quality of language and purpose of task: Pattern of learners' language on two oral communication tasks. *Language Teaching Research, 3*(3), 185–214.

De Jong, N. (2018). Fluency in Second language testing: Insights from different disciplines. *Language Assessment Quarterly, 15*(3), 237–254.

Ellis, R., & Barkhuizen, G. (2005). *Analysing learner language.* Oxford University Press.

Housen, A., & Kuiken, F. (2009). Complexity, accuracy and fluency in second language acquisition. *Applied Linguistics, 30*(4), 461–473.

Housen, A., Kuiken, V. & Vedder, I. (2012). Complexity, accuracy and fluency: Definitions, measurement and research. In A. Housen, F. Kuiken, & I. Vedder (Eds.), *Dimensions of L2 performance and proficiency—Investigating complexity, accuracy and fluency in SLA* (pp. 1–20). John Benjamins.

Larsen-Freeman, D. (1978). An ESL index of development. *TESOL Quarterly, 12*(4), 439–448.

Larsen-Freeman, D. (2006). The emergence of complexity, fluency, and accuracy in the oral and written production of five Chinese learners of English. *Applied Linguistics, 27*(4), 590–619.

Norris, J., & Ortega, L. (2009). Towards an organic approach to investigating CAF in instructed SLA: The case of complexity. *Applied Linguistics, 30*(4), 555–578.

Polio, C., & Shea, M. (2014). Another look at accuracy in second language writing development. *Journal of Second Language Writing, 23*, 10–27.

Robinson, P. (2001). Task complexity, task difficulty, and task production: Exploring interactions in a componential framework. *Applied Linguistics, 22*(1), 27–57.

Skehan, P. (1989). *Individual differences in second language learning*. Edward Arnold.

Wolfe-Quintero, K., Inagaki, S., & Kim, H.-Y. (1998). *Second language development in writing: Measures of fluency, accuracy, and complexity*. University of Hawaii, Second Language Teaching & Curriculum Center.

Yuan, F., & Ellis, R. (2003). The effects of pre-task planning and on-line planning on fluency, complexity and accuracy in L2 oral production. *Applied Linguistics, 24*(1), 1–27.

Alex Housen is Professor of English Linguistics and Applied Linguistics at the Vrije Universiteit Brussel (VUB). His research focus on linguistic, social and cognitive factors in second/foreign language acquisition and teaching, bilingualism and bilingual education. He co-authored and co-edited several volumes, including *Investigations in Instructed Second Language Acquisition* (de Gruyter, 2005), *Dimensions of L2 Performance and Proficiency—Investigating Complexity, Accuracy and Fluency in SLA* (John Benjamins, 2012). He also guest-edited several special journal issues on the topic of CAF, including the 2009 Special Issue of *Applied Linguistics* on *Complexity, Accuracy and Fluency in SLA Research* and the 2019 Special Issue of *Second Language Research* on *Multiple approaches to L2 Complexity*.

Diane Larsen-Freeman

Complexity Theory, now referred to in the field of second language development as Complex Dynamic Systems Theory (CDST), originated in the physical sciences, but has had widespread influence on many other disciplines, including those in the social sciences and the humanities. CDST is a relational systems theory, a transdisciplinary theory that attempts to account for processual phenomena from an ecological holistic perspective. CDST insists that one cannot understand a system unless one understands how its parts interrelate. As the parts interconnect, new patterns and new complex regimes of order emerge, ones that could not have been anticipated from examining the parts independently (Larsen-Freeman, 2017). A second important consideration is the dimension of time. This is because how the parts relate changes over time (e.g., de Bot et al., 2007). A third is space: complex systems are situated in particular contexts, which shape the patterns that result.

In the case of the language classroom system, the "parts" are not only the teacher and the students (and all of their accompanying thoughts, embodied actions, emotions, behaviors, dispositions, identities, social capital, etc.), but they also include how the teacher and students relate to the properties of the physical and temporal context. For instance, the size and configuration of the room, the desks, their orientation, the temperature, the time of the day/week/year at which the lesson is conducted, and so on, all potentially influence teaching and learning (Larsen-Freeman, 2016). Additionally, because systems operate at different levels of scale, i.e., the classroom is within a school, which may be part of a school district, and so on, the systems above and below the focal system also need to be taken into account (Lemke & Sabelli, 2008).

D. Larsen-Freeman (✉)
Linguistics Department/School of Education, University of Michigan, Ann Arbor, Michigan, USA
e-mail: dianelf@umich.edu

© Springer Nature Switzerland AG 2021
H. Mohebbi and C. Coombe (eds.), *Research Questions in Language Education and Applied Linguistics*, Springer Texts in Education,
https://doi.org/10.1007/978-3-030-79143-8_137

Adaptation plays an important role in complex systems. Agents in language classrooms co-adapt with other agents. Stabilized, but not static, patterns emerge from co-adaptation on various timescales (Larsen-Freeman & Cameron, 2008). Furthermore, since all learners perceive different affordances (Larsen-Freeman, 2020) and have different experiences, there will be a great deal of inter-individual variability in the patterns over time. CDST thus ascribes more agency to learners in how they configure their own learning trajectories (Lowie & Verspoor, 2015) rather than seeing them as mere consumers of input (Larsen-Freeman, 2019). Moreover, the learning trajectories are also characterized by intra-individual variability and nonlinearity, with phase shifts demarcating shifts in the learner's language repertoire.

If researching language classroom dynamics seems like a tall order, well, it is. However, to do otherwise, e.g., to conduct a conventional experiment, in which an attempt is made to control all variables except one, is to remove the "pattern that connects" (Bateson, 1988) and to run the risk of producing ecologically invalid findings. Happily, there is assistance available in coping with the complexity (See, for example Hiver & Al-Hoorie, 2016, 2020; Larsen-Freeman & Cameron, 2008; Verspoor, de Bot, & Lowie, 2011).

The Research Questions

1. When students use language corpora, constructed based on their own interests, does it help them to perceive more affordances for learning?
2. What are ways that a teacher can help learners cultivate a relationship between the ambient language and what they perceive as affordances for learning?
3. Does increased variability of language use by a language learner signal an imminent phase shift in the learner's language repertoire?
4. Granted that each learner is unique, can certain general learner profiles be established?
5. Adaptation is critically important to learning. We do it naturally in languages in which we are proficient. Can students be taught to adapt their L2 language repertoires?
6. If adaptability can be taught, what are some efficacious ways of doing so?
7. If the learning process is non-linear, how can a state-imposed syllabus be made to work?
8. If the learning process is non-linear, how can progress be assessed, particularly when progress is not assessed with regard to native speaker norms?
9. How do levels above and below a focal level of a system determine constraints on the dynamics at the focal level?
10. How does a change of context transform the dynamic patterns that result?

Suggested Resources

Hiver, P., & Al-Hoorie, A. H. (2016). Putting complexity into practice. A dynamic ensemble for second language research. *The Modern Language Journal,* *100*(4), 741–756.

Observing that Complex Dynamic Systems Theory (CDST) has influenced many areas in Applied Linguistics to date and that it is likely here to stay, the authors introduce a "dynamic ensemble," methodological considerations for conducting research from a CDST perspective. Building on Larsen-Freeman and Cameron's (2008) "complexity thought modeling," the authors' 9 considerations fall into 4 categories: operational, contextual, macro-system and micro-structure. After discussing each category, the authors explain what implementing a research study would entail.

Concurring with Larsen-Freeman that CDST is a meta-theory, the authors suggest that many different research methods may be utilized, particularly if they are repurposed to fit a CDST framework. "Putting complexity into practice," the authors conclude with a review of 5 case-based methods that are widely used in the social sciences and that are congruent with CDST: qualitative comparative analysis, process-tracing, concept mapping, social network methods, and agent-based modeling.

Larsen-Freeman, D. (2006). The emergence of complexity, fluency and accuracy in the oral and written production of five Chinese learners of English. *Applied Linguistics, 27*(4), 590–619.

This article reports on research conducted with five female Chinese participants who speak English at an intermediate level. The women studied English in the same course at an English Language Institute in a mid-Western university in the U.S. At four different times, separated by six weeks, over a 6-month period, the participants were asked to tell and then write a "story" of their own choosing.

Each retelling of the same story was analyzed for its accuracy, fluency, grammatical complexity and lexical complexity. The data were laid out in idea units. At the group level, the women made clear progress on all four measures. However, group means only tell part of the story. At a lower level of granularity, i.e., the individual level, a great deal of inter– and intra individual variability was detected.

In addition, this study provided evidence that development is not discrete and stage-like but more like the waxing and waning of patterns, in which the language repertoires of each individual are uniquely transformed through use.

Larsen-Freeman, D. (2016). Classroom-oriented research from a complex systems perspective. *Studies in Second Language Learning and Teaching, 6*(3), **377–393.**

Bringing a CDST perspective to bear on classroom-oriented research, the author enumerates characteristics of complex systems as they apply to second language classrooms. For instance, the perspective calls for seeing the classroom ecology as one dynamic system nested in a hierarchy of such systems at different levels of scale, all of which are spatially and temporally situated. This is important because it is obvious that the classroom is shaped by larger systems in which it is embedded.

In addition, conducting educational research from the viewpoint of complex systems calls for a departure from standard epistemological assumptions. For instance, CDST questions the value of randomized control experiments for classroom-oriented research, even though such experiments have often been considered "the gold standard." CDST challenges the idea that a single cause will give rise (in a linear fashion) to a complex event. Furthermore, CDST gives import to the history of a system, which randomized controlled trial experiments ignore. Moreover, attempts to control all aspects in the enactment of an experimental intervention in a classroom make the circumstances of the treatment artificial and ecologically suspect.

However, there are research methods that are more compatible with CDST. Among these are microdevelopment, idiodynamic approaches, social network analysis, formative experiments, design-based, ethnographic and action research, and relational model building. Above all, CDST gives us a new way to think about teaching, learning, language, and classrooms.

Larsen-Freeman, D. (2017). Complexity theory: The lessons continue. In L. Ortega & Z.-H. Han (Eds.), *Complexity Theory and Language Development: In Celebration of Diane Larsen-Freeman* **(pp. 11 − 50). Amsterdam and Philadelphia: John Benjamins.**

In this chapter, the author offers a genealogy of complexity theory. While it has many progenitors, it shares with post-structuralism a rejection of reductionism, and with it, recognizes that our understandings can only be partial and provisional. After recapitulating the main qualities of the theory, Larsen-Freeman goes on to explain her investment in grappling with the complex, nonlinear, dynamic quality of the world and the systems within it while explaining how a theory that originated in the physical sciences enhances our understanding of human behavior and development.

Next, she inventories the many contributors in Applied Linguistics who have contributed insights from CDST, and then proposes thirty aphorisms regarding language, learners, learning, and teaching that draw inspiration from CDST. While these aphorisms have becoming increasingly accepted, they represent innovative thinking as compared with two decades ago when CDST was first introduced. The remainder of the chapter is devoted to addressing three additional "lessons" in SLD, namely the need to interrogate dichotomies, solving the boundary problem, and concern for generalizability.

Lowie, W. M., & Verspoor, M. H. (2018). Individual differences and the ergodicity Problem. *Language Learning*, **early view, pp. 1–23.**

The ergodicity problem has loomed large in second language development from a CDST perspective. Stated simply, the ergodicity principle insists that findings from the study of group behavior cannot be generalized to individuals and vice versa, unless two conditions are met: the group must be homogeneous, and any data must be stable across measurements over time. Because these conditions are rarely met in studies of L2 development, the principle has serious consequences for studies of individual differences among second language learners. This is so because traditionally, "individual" differences, such as motivation and attitude, have been studied using groups of second language learners.

Another contribution of CDST is to underscore the fact that individual differences are dynamic; furthermore, they may be differentially influential over time. Because of the large number of individual differences, the fact that they are difficult to measure, are dynamic and interact nonlinearly, results in a great deal of variability. For these reasons, the authors concur with others in observing that developmental trajectories of individuals are unique. They demonstrate that this is the case by investigating the role of motivation and aptitude in a group study and in 22 longitudinal case studies of adolescent Dutch learners of English. While studies of groups have their place, longitudinal studies of individual learners are needed to understand the learning processes of individuals.

References

Bateson, G. (1988). *Mind and nature: A necessary unity*. Hampton Press.

de Bot, K., Lowie, W., &Verspoor, M. (2007). A dynamic systems approach to second language acquisition. *Bilingualism: Language and Cognition, 10*, 7–21, 51–55.

Hiver, P., & Al-Hoorie, A. H. (2016). Putting complexity into practice. A dynamic ensemble for second language research. *The Modern Language Journal, 100*(4), 741–756.

Hiver, P., & Al-Hoorie, A. H. (2020). *Research methods for complexity theory in applied linguistics*. Multilingual Matters.

Larsen-Freeman, D. (2016). Classroom-oriented research from a complex systems perspective. *Studies in Second Language Learning and Teaching, 6*(3), 377–393.

Larsen-Freeman, D. (2017). Complexity theory: The lessons continue. In L. Ortega & Z-H. Han (Eds.), *Complexity theory and language development: In celebration of Diane Larsen-Freeman* (pp.11–50). John Benjamins.

Larsen-Freeman, D. (2019). On language learner agency: A complex dynamic systems perspective. *The Modern Language Journal, 103*(Special Issue), 61–79.

Larsen-Freeman, D. (2020). Complex dynamic systems theory. In B. VanPatten, G., Keating, & S. Wulff (Eds.). *Theories in second language acquisition* (3rd ed.). Routledge.

Larsen-Freeman, D., & Cameron, L. (2008). *Complex systems and applied linguistics*. Oxford University Press.

Lemke, J. L., & Sabelli, N. H. (2008). Complex systems and educational change: Towards a new research agenda. *Educational Philosophy and Theory, 40*(1), 118–129.

Lowie, W., & Verspoor, M. (2015). Variability and variation in second language acquisition orders: A dynamic reevaluation. *Language Learning, 65*, 63–88.

Verspoor, M. H., de Bot, K., & Lowie, W. (2011). (Eds.) A dynamic approach to second language development: Methods and techniques. John Benjamins.

Diane Larsen-Freeman holds a Ph.D. in Linguistics from the University of Michigan. She is currently Professor Emerita of Education and of Linguistics, and Research Scientist Emerita at the University of Michigan, Ann Arbor. In addition, she is a Professor Emerita at the SIT Graduate Institute in Brattleboro, Vermont and a Visiting Faculty Member at the University of Pennsylvania. She has co-authored *An Introduction to Second Language Acquisition Research* (Longman Publishing, 1991, with Michael Long), edited a book on discourse analysis, and co-authored (With Marianne Celce-Murcia) the third edition of *The Grammar Book: Form, Meaning, and Use for English Language Teachers* (Cengage/National Geographic Learning, 2015). She has directed the popular grammar series *Grammar Dimensions: Form, Meaning, and Use*. She has written *Techniques and Principles in Language Teaching* (Oxford University Press, 2011, this third edition co-authored with Marti Anderson). In 2003, she published *Teaching Language: From Grammar to Grammaring*. Another book, entitled *Complex Systems and Applied Linguistics* (Oxford University Press, 2008), co-authored with Lynne Cameron, was a winner of the Kenneth Mildenberger Book Prize, awarded by the Modern Language Association. Dr. Larsen-Freeman edited the journal *Language Learning* for five years and served as Chair of its Board of Directors. In 2009, she received an Honorary Doctoral Degree in Humanities from the Hellenic American University, and in 2011 the American Association for Applied Linguistics bestowed upon her its highest honor: The Distinguished Scholarship and Service Award.

Complex Dynamic Systems Theory and Second Language Development

Marjolijn Verspoor and Wander Lowie

The field of Applied Linguistics was first introduced to Complex Dynamic Systems Theory by Larsen Freeman (1997), later followed by De Bot et al. (2007). Today, CDST is known as a powerful framework to study the actual developmental processes in second language (L2) learners. A CDST approach holds that (second) language development is not pre-programmed in the mind but emerges as an individual interacts with other individuals in his or her environment and is therefore non-linear because of the following general principles:

1. *Sensitive dependence on initial conditions*

   When a system starts to develop, the conditions that are initially already in place are very important in that they affect the further course of development. This means that an L2 learner's first language, age or maturity, proficiency in the L2, previous experience in learning additional languages, aptitude, motivation, and so on will affect the course of development.
2. *Dependence on internal and external resources*
   To learn an L2, an individual operates in a context, bringing his/her own initial conditions (i.e. internal resources) to the classroom or environment (i.e. external resources) in which s/he learns the language. For example, the greatest external resource required for L2 development may be meaningful exposure to the L2.
3. *Iteration and emergence*

M. Verspoor · W. Lowie (✉)
Department of Applied Linguistics, University of Groningen, Groningen, The Netherlands
e-mail: w.m.lowie@rug.nl

M. Verspoor
e-mail: m.h.verspoor@rug.nl

M. Verspoor
Department of Applied Linguistics, University of Pannonia, Veszprem, Hungary

© Springer Nature Switzerland AG 2021   799
H. Mohebbi and C. Coombe (eds.), *Research Questions in Language
Education and Applied Linguistics*, Springer Texts in Education,
https://doi.org/10.1007/978-3-030-79143-8_138

Iteration—the basic process in a dynamic system—is related to emergence. Iteration stands for the notion that the first state produces the second, and the second state to produce the third, and so on. This means, for example, that for an L2 learner hearing the "same" utterances is never quite the same as he may notice something new every time.

4. *Complete interconnectedness*
   Complete interconnectedness means that a change in one element affects all other elements in the system. In other words, if new words are learned these will affect the syntactic constructions that can be made.

5. *Interacting variables*
   In development, various behaviors may first develop rather independently, then perhaps compete, and then eventually coalesce to create a coordinated new behavior. For instance, L2 learners may need to first develop their lexicon before they can work on their syntactic development.

6. *Self-organization*
   Self-organization refers to the process of changing relationships of the elements in a subsystem over time. For example, after a learner has developed sufficiently in the lexicon, s/he may work on syntactic constructions at the expense of the lexicon. However, once having mastered sufficiently in syntax, both may develop simultaneously.

7. *Variability*
   Within a CDST perspective, variability is seen as a prerequisite of development and therefore it takes a central role in the analyses of single variables. The reason is that learners are not assumed to have a pre-determined developmental path, but simply try out new strategies or modes of behavior that are not always successful and may therefore alternate with old strategies or modes of behavior.

8. *Nonlinearity in development*
   Because of the seven previous principles, development is not linear and cannot be entirely predicted. Moreover, because each individual has to discover his own path in the L2 learners are not likely to be exactly the same so it is important to study individuals over time.

The Research Questions

1. From the literature, find 3 initial conditions (such as age, motivation, aptitude, willingness to communicate, and so on) that have shown to influence an L2 learner's development positively. Report on the empirical evidence.

2. From the literature, find 3 external resources (such as meaningful exposure, teacher, interaction, explicit instruction, and so on) that have shown to influence an L2 learner's development positively over time. Report on the empirical evidence.

3. In the literature, frequency of exposure has been mentioned as one of the best predictors of L2 development. Find out more about CDST and explain how iteration and frequency of exposure can be related.
4. Complete interconnectedness in language means that in the L2 all linguistic elements such as vocabulary, phrases and grammar are interdependent and also interact with pronunciation and intonation and even gestures. Assuming this is true, find in the literature an instructional approach that recognizes these interactions and argue why it would be an approach in line with CDST.
5. Based on the literature and the information in question 4, discuss which three interacting linguistic variables would be interesting to study if you were to trace the development of an L2 learner over the course of one year (with weekly writings or recordings).
6. Taking the variables mentioned in question 4 and 5, what kinds of self-organization patterns would you expect. Based on the literature, argue that some variables may need to develop before others.
7. In the following examples taken from an authentic data set of beginner learners of English, identify some variability (hit and miss behavior)? Based on the variability literature, argue why a teacher should not correct the "misses".

   1. We learn good English, but ist's very difficelt. I mean, it's a really diffecelt language.
   2. Sometimes a girlfrend rides with me, and some times I ride with her.
   3. My new school ar verry fun. I have alot new friends maekt. the teachers are oke haha it was a joke she ar verey fun. you kan have fun with them.

8. In the following figure, we traced the development of one beginner-level Dutch learner of English in terms of Mean Length of Utterance (MLTU), which is supposed to be a general sentence complexity measure and Guiraud, which is a measure of lexical variety. Based on the literature, what can you conclude from the learner's development? (Fig. 138.1).

Suggested Resources

Hiver, P., & Al-Hoorie, A. H. (2016). A dynamic ensemble for second language research: Putting complexity theory into practice. *The Modern Language Journal, 100*(4), 741–756.

This article introduces a template of methodological considerations, termed "the dynamic ensemble," for scholars doing or evaluating empirical second language development (SLD) research within a complexity/dynamic systems theory (CDST) framework. It presents a practical catalog of 9 considerations intended to inform

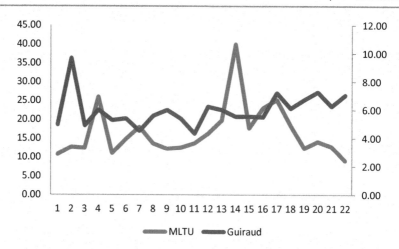

Fig. 138.1 Syntactic development in terms of Mean Length of T Unit (MLTU-left axis), and lexical development terms of type token ratio (Guiraud)

research design at multiple stages and contextualizes them by discussing how these have been framed and addressed within one previous CDST study.

Larsen-Freeman, D. (1997). Chaos/complexity science and second language acquisition. *Applied linguistics*, *18*(2), 141–165.

This seminal paper is an essential reading for anyone interested in CDST as it first introduced the new science of chaos/complexity to the field of second language acquisition (SLA) in which it is argued that the study of dynamic, complex non-linear systems is meaningful in SLA as well.

Lowie, W. M., & Verspoor, M. H. (2018). Individual differences and the ergodicity problem. *Language Learning*. Online pre-publication (25 September 2018), retrieved from https://onlinelibrary.wiley.com/doi/abs/10.1111/lang.12324.

This article gives a good overview of how different initial conditions (individual differences) may affect development and shows that even though learners may be very similar to each other they all show different developmental paths. It is argued that longitudinal studies of individuals are necessary to complement findings of group studies to really understand the developmental trajectories.

Verspoor, M., de Bot, K. & Lowie, W. (Eds.). (2011). *A dynamic approach to second language development: Methods and techniques*. Amsterdam: John Benjamins Publishing Company.

This book is the most comprehensive introduction so far on the general principles of a CDST approach to L2 development as it shows how research can be conducted from a CDST perspective and presents a great number of practical examples on methodological CDST issues.

References

De Bot, K., Lowie, W., & Verspoor, M. (2007). A dynamic systems theory approach to second language acquisition. *Bilingualism: Language and Cognition, 10*(1), 7–21.

Hiver, P., & Al Hoorie, A. H. (2016). A dynamic ensemble for second language research: Putting complexity theory into practice. *The Modern Language Journal, 100*(4), 741–756.

Larsen-Freeman, D. (1997). Chaos/complexity science and second language acquisition. *Applied Linguistics, 18*(2), 141–165.

Lowie, W. M., & Verspoor, M. H. (2019). Individual differences and the ergodicity problem. *Language Learning, 69,* 184–206.

Verspoor, M., de Bot, K., & Lowie, W. (Eds.). (2011). *A dynamic approach to second language development: Methods and techniques.* John Benjamins Publishing Company.

Marjolijn Verspoor is Professor of English Language and English as a Second Language at the University of Groningen, Netherlands and at the University of Pannonia, Hungary. Her main research interests are second language development from a dynamic usage based perspective and instructional approaches in foreign language teaching.

Wander Lowie holds a Ph.D. in Applied Linguistics from the University of Groningen and is chair of Applied Linguistics at this university. He is a research associate of the University of the Free State in South Africa and is associate editor of *The Modern Language Journal.* His main research interest lies in the application of Dynamic Systems Theory to second language development (learning and teaching). He has published more than 50 articles and book chapters and (co-)authored five books in field of Applied Linguistics.

Corpora in Applied Linguistics

Sandra C. Deshors

Over the past forty years, corpora (singular, *corpus*) have played an increasingly important role in Applied Linguistics (AL). As large carefully structured datasets, corpora are electronic collections of naturally occurring spoken or written text, designed to represent a language, a language variety or a specific domain of language use. As such, they are important both as research tools and pedagogical resources. As research tools, their large scale allows scholars to better understand the linguistic processes involved in second language acquisition based on how systematically learners use individual linguistic items. As classroom resources, they facilitate both the teaching and learning of a target language by providing authentic material and linguistic context that both instructors and learners can exploit.

Depending on their applications (i.e. research or teaching/learning), different corpora serve different purposes. For instance, learner corpus researchers tend to use specialized corpora such as, amongst others, the *International Corpus of Learner English* and the *Louvain International Database of Spoken English Interlanguage* that are representative of non-native language varieties. These corpora allow for large-scale comparisons of learner data against native data to capture differences in linguistic patterns across native and learner language. Ultimately, observed differences can tell us something about learners' systematic knowledge of the target language (i.e. their interlanguage), the extent to which their native language influences their interlanguage and the type of forces that trigger cross-linguistic transfer during second language production.

Beyond research, general corpora of native language such as, in the case of English, the Brown; Lancaster, Oslo, Bergen corpus; the British National Corpus; the Corpus of Contemporary American English, and the International Corpus of English tend to be widely exploited as teaching/learning resources. For learners,

S. C. Deshors (✉)
Department of Linguistics, Languages, and Cultures, Michigan State University,
East Lansing, MI, USA
e-mail: deshorss@msu.edu

© Springer Nature Switzerland AG 2021
H. Mohebbi and C. Coombe (eds.), *Research Questions in Language Education and Applied Linguistics*, Springer Texts in Education,
https://doi.org/10.1007/978-3-030-79143-8_139

these corpora facilitate a better understanding of grammar by providing valuable information about how frequently native speakers use certain words and linguistic patterns, how they combine words together and how they use certain linguistic items differently across speech and writing. For instructors, corpora serve as the basis for the development of corpus-informed classroom activities that typically include word lists and concordance lines with real examples of language in use. Because corpus-informed classroom activities are engaging, they help learners use the target language and retain new information longer (Reppen, 2011). The pedagogical benefits of corpora have increasingly inspired textbook designers to use the usage frequency information corpora provided to prepare grammar and vocabulary books. Ultimately, this type of information is helpful to select the linguistic features that should be included in the textbooks (Meunier & Reppen, 2015).

Looking forward towards maximizing even more the usefulness of corpora in AL, (learner) corpus compilers are starting to design new corpora that include more metadata in the form of detailed speaker-specific information such as personality, language aptitude, motivation, proficiency, and others (e.g. the Trinity Lancaster Corpus). Research increasingly shows that these characteristics may affect L2 learners' uses of a target language. While these new corpora are in their infancy, more generalized access to this information on a large scale will undoubtedly lead to a deeper understanding of the linguistic patterns that shape interlanguage varieties.

The Research Questions

1. What criteria need to be taken into account in deciding which (learner) corpus to use?
2. How do you decide what corpus tool(s) to use in order to dig into corpus data?
3. Why would you choose to take a qualitative or a quantitative approach to explore corpus data?
4. What are the benefits of using learner corpora for language testing and assessment?
5. What theoretical models of second language acquisition and use are compatible with and useful for corpus-based approaches to learner language?
6. What role do learner corpora play in the pedagogy of English for specific purposes?
7. How do the following approaches to corpora differ from one another: corpus-informed, corpus-based and corpus-driven?
8. To what extent do existing (learner) corpora provide the necessary data to test Second Language Acquisition theories rigorously?
9. To what extent can a learner corpus be considered and used as a pedagogic corpus?
10. What are the practicalities of integrating corpora in teaching?

Suggested Resources

Meunier, F., De Cock, S., Gilquin, G & Paquot, M. (2011). *A taste for corpora: In honour of Sylviane Granger*. **Amsterdam & Philadelphia: Benjamins**.

This book is a collection of eleven articles that, altogether, show the important and multifaceted role that corpora play in the field of Applied Linguistics. Specifically, these articles illustrate, through the lens of cutting-edge research, the numerous benefits of using corpora to explore the linguistic patterns that characterize learner language and enhance second/foreign language instruction and acquisition. Throughout the volume, corpora are discussed in relation to a variety of perspectives such as (i) the range of corpora currently available (e.g. learner and native corpora, expert users corpora, parallel corpora and corpora of New Englishes), (ii) language learning; (iii) methodological frameworks (e.g. Contrastive Interlanguage Analysis); (iv) the different types of non-native English varieties (learner vs. new Englishes);(v) methodological issues related to error tagging and the detection of L1 interference with learners' interlanguage and (vi) the usefulness of corpora to better understand learners' uses of specific linguistic items such as lexical bundles and phrasal verbs.

Granger, S., Gilquin, G. & Meunier, F. (2015). *The Cambridge Handbook of Learner Corpus Research*. **Cambridge: Cambridge University Press**.

Almost twenty years after the release of the first large-scale corpus of learner English (the *International Corpus of Learner English*) and the emergence of Learner Corpus Research (LCR) as its own research field, this volume takes stock of the many developments that LCR has undergone since its inception. For that purpose, this volume offers a comprehensive overview of the field and the diverse applications of learner corpora. Throughout the volume, these corpora are discussed from a variety of perspectives including the procedural steps involved in the compilation of learner corpora, issues related to the annotation of learner data (e.g. the annotation of spoken data, error annotation schemes) and methodological issues related to quantitative and statistical approaches to learner data. The volume also covers more theoretical aspects related to second language acquisition such as cross-linguistic transfer, formulaic language, learning contexts, language teaching (e.g. language testing, pedagogic corpora) and natural language processing.

Hunston, S. (2002). *Corpora in Applied Linguistics*. **Cambridge: Cambridge University Press**.

This volume is a must-read for students and young scholars interested in achieving in-depth understanding of the impact of corpora on AL. After a general introduction on corpora, what they have to offer as datasets, how they are used and the different forms they come into, this volume delves into methodological and analytical considerations central to corpus linguistics. Specifically, the author guides the reader through the analysis of concordance lines (i.e. how to search, present and interpret concordance lines and how to handle linguistic contextual information). In addition, attention is paid to other methodological aspects of dealing with corpus data, namely frequency, key-word lists, collocations, tagging and parsing. The author then focuses on the relevance of these issues for applied linguistics by discussing how they relate to areas such as grammar, translation, stylistics and forensic linguistics. Finally, the author turns to the specific area of language teaching to discuss how corpora relate to data-driven learning and syllabus design.

Reppen, R. (2010). *Using corpora in the language classroom.* **Cambridge: Cambridge University Press.**

This book is a practical, hands-on guide to using corpora for language teaching and learning purposes. The volume begins with an explanation of (i) why and how language learners can benefit from using corpora to support their learning experience and (ii) what pedagogical corpus-based material looks like. The author then turns to language teaching by presenting an overview of the corpus-based materials currently available to instructors. Further, the author provides valuable information to language teachers on how to connect effectively corpus research and pedagogy; that is, how to make the best of corpus research to enhance language learning in the classroom environment. In addition, attention is dedicated to how to create corpora for use in the classroom using internet data and how, practically, internet corpora can be used for classroom activities. Finally, throughout the volume, ample examples of corpus-informed classroom activities are provided to guide and inspire the reader into developing their own teaching and learning material.

Deshors, S. C. (2016). *Multidimensional perspectives on interlanguage: Exploring may and can across learner corpora. Corpora and Language in Use.* **Louvain: Presses Universitaires de Louvain.**

This book is the first large-scale corpus-based multifactorial study of a lexical alternation (*may* vs. *can*) in learner language (specifically French–English and Chinese-English interlanguage varieties). Using a comprehensive approach to corpus annotation (i.e., one that incorporates semantic and morpho-syntactic contextual information) along with state-of-the-art statistical modeling techniques (specifically logistic regression, cluster and collexeme analyses), the author investigates how the interaction of semantic and morpho-syntactic features co-determine the uses of *may* and can in the learner varieties she investigates. Empirical findings are discussed within the usage-based theoretical framework with regard to their cognitive implications and, ultimately, processes such as resorting to the default term can where grammatical environments become too complex were hypothesized to explain the different linguistic structures observed in written native and learner English. Ultimately, this book speaks to the usefulness of corpora to explore variation across learner language varieties in a systematic and cognitively-inspired.

References

Meunier, F. & Reppen, R. (2015). Corpus vs. non-corpus informed pedagogical materials: Grammar as the focus. In D. Biber & R. Reppen (Eds.), *The Cambridge handbook of English corpus linguistics* (pp. 498–514). Cambridge University Press.

Reppen, R. (2011). *Using corpora in the language classroom*. Cambridge University Press.

Sandra C. Deshors is Associate Professor in the Second Language Studies Ph.D. program at Michigan State University. Her research, which specializes in quantitative corpus-based approaches to non-native language, contrasts EFL, ESL and World Englishes at large. Theoretically, her work is anchored in the usage-based theoretical framework and recognizes a correlation between speakers' mental knowledge of linguistic items and their uses in grammatical contexts. Recent book publications include *Modeling World Englishes: Assessing the interplay of emancipation and globalization of ESL varieties* (published in Benjamins' Varieties of English around the World book series), *Rethinking linguistic creativity in non-native Englishes* (published in Benjamin's Current Topics book series) and *Multidimensional perspectives of interlanguage: Exploring may and can across learner corpora* (published with Presses Universitaires de Louvain).

Xiaofei Lu, J. Elliott Casal, and Yingying Liu

Corpus-based genre analysis is an emerging approach to the analysis of academic writing practices that considers the recurring linguistic patterns of academic genres in terms of the rhetorical goals that writers employ them to realize. Ideally, it entails manual rhetorical move-step annotation of each text in a corpus and identification of recurring linguistic features (e.g., lexical, phraseological, and syntactic), which are then mapped to each other. In contrast, much past English for Specific/Academic Purposes (ESP/EAP) research has either emphasized the conventionalized linguistic forms associated with particular genres through corpus-driven approaches or the rhetorical structures through move-step analysis, and the impacts that these approaches have had on our understanding of disciplinary knowledge making practices are considerable. Nonetheless, in spite of calls for the "integration of genre analysis and corpus-based investigations" (Flowerdew, 2005, p. 5), and Moreno and Swales' (2018) recent efforts to address this "function-form gap" (p. 41) in EAP research, a still limited body of corpus-based genre analysis exists (e.g., Cortes, 2013; Durrant & Mathews-Aydınlı, 2011; Le & Harrington, 2015; Lu et al., 2020; Omidian et al., 2018).

Closely associated with the ESP/EAP traditions and the work of Swales (1990), such research has a strong pedagogical orientation, with the aim of raising student-writers' genre awareness and developing genre competence. Therefore, it is in part motivated by the practical pedagogical understanding that second language student writers often struggle both in incorporating linguistic features into their

X. Lu (✉) · J. E. Casal · Y. Liu
Department of Applied Linguistics, The Pennsylvania State University,
University Park, PA, USA
e-mail: xxL13@psu.edu

Y. Liu
e-mail: yzl222@psu.edu

J. E. Casal
Department of Cognitive Science, Case Western Reserve University, Cleveland, OH, USA

© Springer Nature Switzerland AG 2021
H. Mohebbi and C. Coombe (eds.), *Research Questions in Language Education and Applied Linguistics*, Springer Texts in Education,
https://doi.org/10.1007/978-3-030-79143-8_140

writing in functionally appropriate ways and in finding suitable linguistic forms to accomplish their rhetorical goals. At the same time, corpus-based genre analysis can be supported by recent theoretical advances in the field, including Tardy's (2009) four-dimensional model of genre knowledge that entails the steady integration of formal, rhetorical, process, and subject knowledge, and usage-based views of learners' function driven developmental trajectories from formula-like chunks to flexible constructions (e.g., Ellis & Cadierno, 2009). The integration of corpus-based methodologies and genre-analysis has important pedagogical implications, including in the potential creation of rhetorical move-step specific lists of linguistic features (to complement the academic word and phrase list tradition), and in informing integrated corpus and discourse analysis-based pedagogies (e.g., Charles, 2007). It can also potentially have important implications for automated writing evaluation, as many current approaches rely on the presence/absence or the co-occurrence of linguistic features, rather than the use of particular features in rhetorically appropriate ways.

Of course, corpus-based genre analysis faces a number of methodological challenges, many of which are closely related to genre analysis itself. Rhetorical move-step annotation is a time consuming and labor-intensive qualitative coding process, and as such it entails difficulties related to resources and intercoder reliability. Some early efforts to conduct corpus-based genre analysis have attempted to address the time concern by assigning rhetorical move-step codes to extracted linguistic features, rather than the entire corpus, but such analysis is problematically decontextualized. In addition, there exist a number of approaches to segmenting texts into rhetorical moves and steps, with some scholars adopting linguistic boundaries (e.g., phrase, sentence), and others adopting a rhetorical definition of variable length linguistically. A final, practical concern is that such analyses often produce vast amounts of data that can be opaque and unwieldy for non-researcher teachers.

The Research Questions

1. What level of intercoder reliability can be achieved in rhetorical move-step annotation of a corpus of academic writing and what methodological practices can help maximize such intercoder reliability?
2. What language features distinguish or correlate strongly with different rhetorical moves and steps?
3. How do expert writers vary their use of items and structures at different linguistic levels (e.g., lexical, phraseological, and syntactic) to achieve their rhetorical goals?
4. Are academic writing learners adequately aware of the importance of the mappings between rhetorical functions and language forms?
5. Do academic writing teachers pay adequate attention to the mappings between rhetorical functions and language forms in pedagogy?

6. How might corpora of academic writing annotated for rhetorical moves and steps and their associated language features be used in genre-based writing pedagogy to improve L2 learners' genre competence?
7. How will learning outcomes be affected by presenting rhetorical and linguistic structures in isolation or in tandem in academic writing pedagogy?
8. Do raters pay adequate attention to the mappings between rhetorical functions and language forms?
9. How can we reliably assess the appropriateness and effectiveness of the mappings between rhetorical functions and language forms in learner writing?
10. What is the quantitative relationship of form-function mappings to human ratings of writing quality?

Suggested Resources

Biber, D., Connor, U., & Upton, T. A. (2007). *Discourse on the move: Using corpus analysis to describe discourse structure*. Amsterdam/Philadelphia: John Benjamins.

Based on the introductory chapter, the term "discourse analysis" in this book is used in the broad sense of *analyzing discourse,* as the authors divide "discourse analysis" into three branches: study of structural organization of texts, study of language use, and study of social practices and ideological assumptions. This work focuses on the first two major lines of research with the aim of merging the top-down perspective adopted in the study of structural organization (e.g., genre analysis) and the bottom-up perspective in the study of language use (e.g., corpus analysis). After the introductory chapter, the main body of this book is divided into two main parts. The first part is dedicated to the top-down approach (Chaps. 2–5) and centers on Swalesian move analysis, while the second part is dedicated to the bottom-up approach (Chaps. 6–8) and emphasizes Multi-Dimensional Analysis of lexico-grammatical features, which is based on the TextTiling procedure. Chapter 9 illustrates the differences between the two approaches by comparing their respective descriptions of biology research articles.

Tardy, C. M. (2009). *Building genre knowledge*. West Lafayette, IN: Parlor Press.

This work traces the development of genre knowledge of four multilingual graduate students through their learning and practices in an ESL writing class, disciplinary subject courses and disciplinary research. The author presents a four-dimensional model of genre knowledge (formal, rhetorical, process, and subject-matter), which develops toward the integration of initially isolated components. The first chapter lays the groundwork by discussing foundational concepts used in the follow-up analysis. Chapter 2 introduces the research context and participants. Chapters 3 and 4 examine the students' genre knowledge development through their engagement in an ESL writing class, focusing on the class assignments of writing job application cover letters and conducting genre analysis. Chapter 5 analyzes the four participants' exposure, production and development of their knowledge of the multimodal *presentation slides* genre across different learning contexts. Chapter 6 shifts to disciplinary content courses with a focus on the genres of lab reports and reviews. Chapter 7 traces one participant's master's thesis writing process during which his advisor's feedback on the drafts plays a central role in the development of his knowledge of the master's thesis genre. Chapter 8 analyzes the sole doctoral student among the four focal participants and considers his learning process in writing conference-related research papers. Chapter 9 examines the development of genre knowledge building and offers pedagogical suggestions. By reading this book, academic writing instructors and researchers can gain insights into how individual students in different disciplines and in various learning contexts develop academic literacy and genre knowledge through engaging in general English language classes, disciplinary content courses, as well as other tasks and interactions.

Charles, M., Pecorari, D., & Hunston, S. (Eds.) (2010). *Academic writing: At the interface of corpus and discourse.* **London: Continuum**.

This edited collection represents an effort to explore the interface between corpus linguistics and discourse analysis. The two approaches are not regarded as opposing, as some scholars have argued, but rather serve as two ends of a continuum. This idea is outlined in the editors' preface. The main body of this book includes 14 studies of academic writing organized in three foci: genre and disciplinary discourse, interpersonal discourse, and learner discourse. Each study represents an author's perspective of academic writing research, situated on either end of the corpus-discourse analysis continuum. Collectively, these studies cover a wide diversity of genres, disciplines, methods and linguistic features. In addition to the preface and main chapters, the afterword written by John Swales is also worth reading. He begins with a brief discussion of the preface and afterword genres themselves, and then presents his own reflections on some of the studies included in this volume. Swales concludes with a noteworthy reflection on the extent to which researchers can incorporate aspects of the other side of the continuum, stating that "we will often see that it is typically somewhat easier for discourse analysts to incorporate corpus linguistics than for corpus linguists to expand their textual horizons to encompass the discoursal plane".

Swales, J. M., & Feak, C. B. (2012). *Academic writing for graduate students* **(3rd ed.). Ann Arbor, MI: University of Michigan Press**.

Now in its third edition, this popular EAP textbook targets both first and second language English graduate student writers. Considering the diversity of academic genres that target readers face in academia, the authors construct their course book with the aim of raising genre awareness of graduate student writers by guiding them through a series of analytical and writing tasks. The tasks draw on corpus and genre-based approaches to writing analysis, integrating them for pedagogical purposes. The first of the book's eight chapters presents basic concepts of genre theory that are essential for the following material and for considering writing as a series of choices in relation to community expectations. The second and third chapters outline two broad structural patterns of academic writing: the general-to-specific pattern and the problem–solution pattern. Chapters 4–6 deal with three largely pedagogical genre families, including data interpretation and discussion, summaries, and critiques. The last two chapters tie these skills and writing purposes together in an overview of research article writing for publication. The design and arrangement of the tasks in each chapter align well with the authors' strong belief in the "rhetorical consciousness raising" cycle (i.e., *analysis-awareness-acquisition-achievement*), with each chapter entailing comprehension and production tasks, conceptual genre discussion as well as language preparation for particular genres. This book can be used as a textbook in a general EAP program or as a reference book for apprentice academic writers in any discipline.

Whitt, R. J. (Ed.) (2018). *Diachronic corpora, genre, and language change.* **Amsterdam/Philadelphia: John Benjamins**.

With the collective position that genre both affects language change and constitutes a locus of language change, the studies in this volume examine the interplay between language change and genre using diachronic corpora, showcasing the effectiveness of corpus-based methodologies as well as highlighting the issues and challenges in this line of research. The volume consists of three parts. Part I includes three chapters that focus on methods, resources and tools in diachronic corpus linguistics. Niehaus and Elspass describe the composition of the *Nineteenth-Century German Corpus* and illustrate the benefits of integrating texts of diverse registers and genres for studying language variation and change. Jurish discusses how the open-source program DiaCollo can be used for diachronic, genre-sensitive collocation profiling. Atwell introduces a range of classical and modern Arabic corpus resources developed by researchers at the University of Leeds. Part II include two chapters that examine language change in specific language usage domains. Taavitsainen traces changes in generic features of English medical writing from 1375 to 1800 using diachronic medical corpora, while Gray and Biber document the patterns of linguistic change in academic writing and discuss the quantitative and functional nature of such changes. The eight chapters in Part III employ multi-genre diachronic corpora to explore how genre affects the analyses and findings of language change and variation at varied linguistic levels and in diverse languages. Overall, this volume provides an excellent state-of-the-art overview of corpus and genre-based studies of language variation and change.

References

Charles, M. (2007). Reconciling top-down and bottom-up approaches to graduate writing: Using a corpus to teach rhetorical functions. *Journal of English for Academic Purposes, 6*, 289–302.

Cortes, V. (2013). The purpose of this study is to: Connecting lexical bundles and moves in research article introductions. *Journal of English for Academic Purposes, 12*, 33–43.

Durrant, P., & Mathews-Aydınlı, J. (2011). A function-first approach to identifying formulaic language in academic writing. *English for Specific Purposes, 30*, 58–72.

Ellis, N. C., & Cadierno, T. (2009). Constructing a second language. *Annual Review of Cognitive Linguistics, 7*, 111–139.

Flowerdew, L. (2005). An integration of corpus-based and genre-based approaches to text analysis in EAP/ESP: Countering criticisms against corpus-based methodologies. *English for Specific Purposes, 24*, 321–332.

Le, T. N. P., & Harrington, M. (2015). Phraseology used to comment on results in the Discussion section of applied linguistics quantitative research articles. *English for Specific Purposes, 39*, 45–61.

Lu, X., Casal, J. E., & Liu, Y. (2020). The rhetorical functions of syntactically complex sentences in social science research article introductions. *Journal of English for Academic Purposes, 44*, 1–16.

Moreno, A. I., & Swales, J. M. (2018). Strengthening move analysis methodology towards bridging the function-form gap. *English for Specific Purposes, 50*, 40–63.

Omidian, T., Shahriari, H., & Siyanova-Chanturia, A. (2018). A cross-disciplinary investigation of multi-word expressions in the moves of research article abstracts. *Journal of English for Academic Purposes, 36*, 1–14.

Swales, J. M. (1990). *Genre analysis: English in academic and research settings.* Cambridge University Press.

Tardy, C. M. (2009). *Building genre knowledge.* Parlor Press.

Xiaofei Lu is Professor of Applied Linguistics and Asian Studies at The Pennsylvania State University. His research interests include corpus linguistics, English for Academic Purposes, second language writing, and computer-assisted language learning. He is the author of *Computational Methods for Corpus Annotation and Analysis* (Springer, 2014) and lead co-editor of *Computational and Corpus Approaches to Chinese Language Learning* (Springer, 2019). His work appears in *American Educational Research Journal, Applied Linguistics, Behavioral Research Methods, Computer Assisted Language Learning, Educational Researcher, English for Specific Purposes, International Journal of Corpus Linguistics, Journal of English for Academic Purposes, Journal of Pragmatics, Journal of Second Language Writing, Language Learning and Technology, Language Resources and Evaluation, Language Teaching Research, Language Testing, ReCALL, TESOL Quarterly,* and *The Modern Language Journal*, among others.

J. Elliott Casal is a Research Scholar in the Case Western Reserve University Department of Cognitive Science. His research interests include corpus linguistics and corpus-based writing pedagogies. His work appears in the *Journal of English for Academic Purposes, Journal of Second Language Writing, Language Learning and Technology, System,* and *CALICO Journal.*

Yingying Liu is a Ph.D. candidate in the Department of Applied Linguistics at The Pennsylvania State University. Her research interests include corpus linguistics, English for Academic Purposes, English phraseology and lexicography, and second language acquisition. Her work appears in *Journal of English for Academic Purposes, Language Teaching,* and *System.*

Embodied Interaction in Second Language Teaching/Learning

Elena Taylor and Dwight Atkinson

Just as in everyday face-to-face social interaction, non-classroom learners, students, and teachers draw on a wide range of embodied tools, including gaze, gesture, facial expression, and body movement. Embodied tools express semantic meaning, nuance, perspective, and emotional valence, thereby guiding the understanding of talk.

In non-classroom interactions involving second language (L2) learners, embodied tools have various learning/teaching functions. Thus, Mori and Hayashi (2006) found that speakers at Japanese conversation tables used "embodied completions"–gestures functioning to complete turns at talk. Studying ESL tutoring situations, Seo and Koshik (2010) found that tutors sometimes used head movements to prompt tutees to self-correct. Atkinson et al. (2007, 2018) showed that embodied sociocognitive alignment facilitated informal learning and teaching opportunities.

Many studies have examined embodiment in classroom teaching and learning. Thus, Smotrova (2017) identified (1) "intentional instructional gestures" and (2) non-pedagogy-specific gestures and body movement used in teaching L2 vocabulary. Other classroom studies of embodied teaching/learning of vocabulary include Belhiah (2013) and Lazaraton (2004).

Embodiment in L2 teaching/learning has primarily been examined from a cognitive viewpoint. This is unfortunate because teaching/learning is socio-affective at its core. Some studies demonstrated affective functions of embodied actions in the classroom. Thus, Nguyen (2007) showed how one ESL teacher used embodied tools such as smiling, gestures, and intonation to maintain a non-threatening and

E. Taylor (✉)
Utah State University, Logan, UT, USA
e-mail: elena.taylor@usu.edu

D. Atkinson
University of Arizona, Tucson, AZ, USA
e-mail: dwightatki@email.arizona.edu

© Springer Nature Switzerland AG 2021
H. Mohebbi and C. Coombe (eds.), *Research Questions in Language Education and Applied Linguistics*, Springer Texts in Education,
https://doi.org/10.1007/978-3-030-79143-8_141

positive classroom environment. Shvidko (2018) examined embodied interaction during L2 writing conferences from an affective angle and found that the teacher/tutor created an affiliative atmosphere by sensitively calibrating her embodied behavior with that of her students.

Embodied interaction in L2 learning/teaching deserves further research attention from multiple points of view, including cognitive, conversation-analytic, socio-affective, and sociocognitive perspectives. Examining multiple functions of various embodied tools will help us better understand the nature of teaching and learning and improve our pedagogical practices in promoting students' language development.

The Research Questions

1. How can embodied interaction facilitate language production in the classroom?
2. How can embodied interaction facilitate language comprehension in the classroom?
3. In what ways does embodied interaction affect classroom management?
4. How can embodied tools help teachers create and maintain teacher-student rapport?
5. Should embodied interaction be integrated into teacher training? If so, how? If not, why not?
6. How can students be taught to better understand teachers' embodied cues?
7. What are the best methodological tools to study embodied classroom interaction?
8. What problems related to embodied interaction can arise in multicultural teaching contexts?
9. What can studies of embodied interaction outside the classroom tell us about studying it in the classroom?
10. How are teaching and learning defined in studies focusing on L2 teaching/learning and embodied interaction?

Suggested Resources

Atkinson, D., Churchill, E., Nishino, T., & Okada, H. (2007). Alignment and interaction in a sociocognitive approach to second language acquisition. *The Modern Language Journal, 91*, 169–188.

The article introduces the concept of alignment and discusses its importance for second language acquisition. The authors argue that alignment is created by various sociocognitive affordances, including participants' embodied actions, and from this perspective they view embodied actions as facilitators of the learning process. To illustrate the concept of alignment in a teaching context, the authors analyzed several episodes presenting interaction between a Japanese high school student and her tutor. In the episodes, embodied actions played a crucial role, allowing the tutor to move the teaching process along and helping the student produce correct responses–thus making their interaction effective from the alignment point of view.

Sert, O., & Jacknick, C. M. (2015). Student smiles and the negotiation of epistemics in L2 classrooms. *Journal of Pragmatics*, *77*, **97–112**.

The purpose of this study was to examine a particular feature of embodied behavior–smiles. Specifically, the researchers looked at how students' smiles in ESL and EFL classrooms helped to resolve interactional trouble caused by the issues related to epistemic status, that is, participants' "relative access to information or knowledge" (p. 100). By analyzing video recordings of interaction in ESL and EFL classrooms, Sert and Jacknick found that students smiled in situations in which they presented themselves as "unknowing participants" (p. 109), in other words, displaying their lack of knowledge, which inevitably led to problems in interaction, most notably disaffiliation and disalignment. Students' smiles in these situations therefore contributed to maintaining affiliation and alignment and preserving the progressivity of interaction.

Shvidko, E. (2018). Writing conference feedback as moment-to-moment affiliative relationship building. *Journal of Pragmatics*, *127*, **20–35**.

The purpose of this study was to explore the affective function of teacher embodied behavior. Specifically, it looked at how teacher embodied tools helped a writing instructor in a university composition course provide feedback on student writing in non-threatening and affiliative ways during individual writing conferences. Shvidko analyzed two instructional instances in conference interaction–providing critical feedback and uttering a directive, and found that the teacher drew on a wide range of embodied interactional tools, including facial expression, gesture, gaze, body position, smile and laughter, that were used in a way that allowed her to minimize her authoritative position, create solidarity with students, and maintain a positive interactional atmosphere at the conferences.

van Compernolle, R., & Smotrova, T. (2013). Corrective feedback, gesture, and mediation in classroom language learning. *Language and Sociocultural Theory*, *1*, **25–47**.

The study explored a mediational function of gesture incorporated in corrective feedback. By providing a detailed analysis of a single case of teacher's error correction in a beginning-level ESL reading class, van Compernolle and Smotrova demonstrated how gestures synchronized with speech can be an effective mediational tool in correcting students' errors. The analyzed instance of the teacher's integration of gesture in corrective feedback showed that although the student benefited from the teacher's correction, which was demonstrated by the accuracy of his subsequent utterance, it was the gesture that mediated the student's learning. Based on the findings of this study, van Compernolle and Smotrova suggested that "researchers interested in corrective feedback as mediation in classroom language teaching and learning would do well to consider at least the potential contribution of speech gesture synchrony when making claims about the function of corrective feedback" (p. 41).

Wang, W., & Loewen, S. (2015). Nonverbal behavior and corrective feedback in nine ESL university-level classrooms. *Language Teaching Research,* https://doi.org/10.1177/1362168815577239.

The study looked at embodied strategies employed by instructors when providing corrective feedback. The researchers identified a wide range of embodied tools, the most common of which were head nod, headshake, and pointing gesture. The results also showed that the types of embodied behavior mainly depended on the nature of the courses and the material used in class. For example, in a reading course, the teacher used a variety of iconic gestures to explain the meanings of verbs found in the text, whereas a grammar teacher frequently employed deictic gestures to explain verb tenses. The findings of the study allowed Wang and Loewen to conclude that understanding of teaching practices without taking into account teachers' embodied behavior is impoverished, and that the teachers' awareness of the types and occurrences of nonverbal tools during corrective feedback can increase the effectiveness of this pedagogical practice.

References

Atkinson, D., Churchill, E., Nishino, T., & Okada, H. (2007). Alignment and interaction in a sociocognitive approach to second language acquisition. *The Modern Language Journal, 91,* 169–188.

Atkinson, D., Churchill, E., Nishino, T., & Okada, H. (2018). Language learning great and small: Environmental support structures and learning opportunities in a sociocognitive approach to second language acquisition/teaching. *The Modern Language Journal, 102,* 471–493.

Belhiah, H. (2013). Using the hand to choreograph instruction: On the functional role of gesture in definition talk. *The Modern Language Journal, 97,* 417–434.

Lazaraton, A. (2004). Gesture and speech in the vocabulary explanations of one ESL teacher: A microanalytic inquiry. *Language Learning, 54*(1), 79–117.

Mori, J., & Hayashi, M. (2006). The achievement of intersubjectivity through embodied completions: A study of interactions between first and second language speakers. *Applied Linguistics, 27,* 195–219.

Nguyen, H. (2007). Rapport building in language instruction: A microanalysis of the multiple resources in teacher talk. *Language and Education, 21*(4), 284–303.

Seo, M., & Koshik, I. (2010). A conversation analytic study of gestures that engender repair in ESL conversational tutoring. *Journal of Pragmatics, 42,* 2219–2239.

Shvidko, E. (2018). Writing conference feedback as moment-to-moment affiliative relationship building. *Journal of Pragmatics, 127,* 20–35.

Smotrova, T. (2017). Making pronunciation visible: Gesture in teaching pronunciation. *TESOL Quarterly, 51,* 59–89.

Elena Taylor is an assistant professor of ESL at Utah State University. Her research interests include interpersonal aspects of language teaching, embodied interaction in the classroom, second language writing, and teacher professional development. Elena's work appears in *TESOL Quarterly, TESOL Journal, Journal of Pragmatics, Journal on Response to Writing, INTESOL*

Journal, and *System*. She has been actively involved in professional organizations, most notably TESOL and AAAL, and has served in various capacities in both organizations. Elena has given presentations at international, national, regional, and local conferences.

Dwight Atkinson is an applied linguist and second language educator who currently works at the University of Arizona, where he is a professor of English. His research and teaching have ranged widely, including work in the following areas: non-mainstream approaches to second language acquisition; second language writing; theories of culture in applied linguistics; qualitative research methods; and the history of scientific writing in English.

Aline Godfroid

What types of knowledge do second-language (L2) learners use to communicate fluently? How do different types of instruction affect L2 learners' linguistic knowledge? Do adult learners use different types of linguistic knowledge than children? Questions like these, about linguistic knowledge representations and language learning, pertain to the implicit (unconscious) and explicit (conscious) dimensions of second language acquisition (SLA). Understanding that distinction is fundamental for researchers and practitioners alike as it carries both theoretical and pedagogical implications.

Implicit knowledge is intuitive and tacit knowledge of the structure of a complex system (e.g., the syntactic structure of a language). Because implicit knowledge is key to communicative competence, many researchers agree that the goal of L2 instruction is to develop learners' implicit knowledge. Some, however, would argue that implicit knowledge is hard for adult, instructed learners to attain (DeKeyser, 2015; Leow, 2015; Spada, 2015). A potential alternative is *explicit knowledge*—conscious and verbalizable knowledge—for instance, being able to say or describe that the verb comes at the end in subordinate clauses in Dutch. Using explicit knowledge in speaking or listening is initially slow and effortful, but it can be sped up with practice. Explicit knowledge that can be retrieved fast and relatively effortlessly is referred to as *automatized explicit knowledge*. Automatized explicit knowledge functions similarly to implicit knowledge in communication; this is why it has been proposed as a more realistic and attainable alternative for adult, instructed learners (DeKeyser, 2015; Leow, 2015; Spada, 2015). In spite of the skepticism about the role of implicit knowledge in adult SLA, some researchers have indeed reported evidence for the acquisition of implicit L2 knowledge (Godfroid, 2016; Leung & Williams, 2011, 2012, 2014; Paciorek & Williams,

A. Godfroid (✉)
Second Language Studies and TESOL program, Department of Linguistics, Languages, and Cultures, Michigan State University, East Lansing, MI, USA
e-mail: godfroid@msu.edu

© Springer Nature Switzerland AG 2021
H. Mohebbi and C. Coombe (eds.), *Research Questions in Language Education and Applied Linguistics*, Springer Texts in Education,
https://doi.org/10.1007/978-3-030-79143-8_142

2015a, 2015b; Rebuschat & Williams, 2012; Williams, 2005; but see Hama & Leow, 2010; Leow & Hama, 2013).

Recent years have seen an increased interest in the learning processes that produce different types of knowledge (i.e., implicit or explicit). Key cognitive learning processes include attention and awareness (Godfroid et al., 2013). With the help of real-time methodologies, which record people's behavior in real time, researchers can tap into L2 learners' cognitive processes as they are happening and use this information to relate it to learning outcomes. *Implicit learning*, then, is a learning process that requires attention to input, but takes place outside of awareness and without intention to learn. *Explicit learning* is a learning process that is conscious and intentional (e.g., learning through forming and testing hypotheses about where the verb is placed in a sentence) and requires both attention and awareness.

A question of current interest is whether learners can simultaneously learn implicitly and explicitly (Bell, 2017). A related question concerns the learning-knowledge or the process–product relationship (Leow, 2015)—that is, to what extent are learning with or without awareness (i.e., explicit or implicit learning) and conscious or unconscious knowledge (i.e., explicit or implicit knowledge) related? In instructed settings, more effort (i.e., more attention, more awareness, a greater depth of processing) often leads to better learning outcomes, but outside the classroom or in purely meaning-focused tasks such as reading a novel, other factors such as input frequency may play a more important role. A question for future research is whether a single set of cognitive learning mechanisms (e.g., statistical learning) can account for the different types of learning observed in different tasks inside and outside the classroom (Andringa & Rebuschat, 2015).

Work on implicit-explicit knowledge and implicit-explicit learning rests on a foundation of valid and reliable measurement. The past two decades have seen an increase in research designed to validate measures of explicit and, especially, implicit knowledge. Currently, there is a broad consensus that oral production affords a relatively pure measure of implicit knowledge. Similarly, the untimed written grammaticality judgment test (GJT) and the metalinguistic knowledge test (e.g., correcting and explaining errors in sentences) are widely regarded as measures of explicit knowledge. The nature of other tasks is contested, specifically the elicited imitation test and the timed written GJT (compare Ellis, 2005; Suzuki and DeKeyser, 2015; and Vafaee et al., 2017). As the field reaches a broader consensus on what different linguistic tests measure (for a synthesis, see Godfroid et al., 2018; Godfroid & Kim, 2021), researchers will be equipped to revisit key questions in SLA and L2 instruction. Is explicit instruction really more effective than implicit instruction (Goo et al., 2015; Norris & Ortega, 2001; Spada & Tomita, 2010)? In what kinds of learners, and under what conditions, can explicit knowledge contribute to implicit knowledge—that is, is there an explicit-implicit knowledge interface? Progress in these areas may shed light on the usefulness, or lack thereof, of explicit grammar instruction for training fluent and competent L2 users.

The Research Questions

1. To what extent can late second-language learners acquire implicit knowledge of a second language?
2. To what extent does attention to linguistic form and "noticing" (Schmidt, 1990) facilitate second language acquisition? Do adult second-language learners need to be aware of linguistic forms in the input to acquire them?
3. What is the relationship between linguistic structure and the nature of second-language learning? Are some structures (e.g., easy or difficult structures) better taught explicitly while others can be acquired more readily from input alone?
4. What teaching methods are most conducive to the development of implicit second-language knowledge? Do explicit and implicit teaching methods result in different types of linguistic knowledge?
5. Is explicit instruction more effective than implicit instruction if the frequency of forms in the input is accounted for?
6. Can explicit knowledge (e.g., from grammar instruction) be beneficial for developing implicit knowledge? In other words, under what conditions, and for what kinds of second-language learners, do explicit and implicit knowledge interface?
7. To what extent can adult second-language learners make up for a possible lack of implicit knowledge through practice and automatization of explicit knowledge?
8. What are valid and reliable measures of implicit, automatized explicit, and explicit knowledge?
9. To what extent do individual differences in implicit and explicit learning aptitudes predict the development of implicit and explicit second-language knowledge?
10. To what extent does the learning context (instructed versus naturalistic) influence the type of knowledge that second-language learners acquire?

Suggested Resources

Hulstijn, J. H., & Ellis, R. (Eds.). (2005). Implicit and explicit second-language learning [Special issue]. *Studies in Second Language Acquisition, 27*(2).

With this seminal collection of research articles, Hulstijn and Ellis put the study of implicit and explicit second-language learning on a firm theoretical basis. The issue featured a balanced mix of theoretical and empirical work. Following an introductory article (Hulstijn, 2005), the special issue included a theoretical review of the explicit-implicit knowledge interface (N. Ellis, 2005) and five empirical studies (R. Ellis, 2005; De Jong, 2005; Robinson, 2005; Tokowicz & MacWhinney, 2005; Williams, 2005), many of which have now become classics.

The article by R. Ellis (2005) ("Measuring Implicit and explicit knowledge of a second language: A psychometric study") marked the beginning of the current wave of test validation research, which has advanced our understanding of how researchers and teachers can measure implicit and explicit knowledge. Williams' (2005) study ("Learning without awareness") has been conceptually replicated and extended several times, with varying results. The research design and proposed findings of this study continue to fuel research on the role of awareness in second-language learning.

Ellis, R., Loewen, S., Elder, C., Erlam, R., Philp, J., & Reinders, H. (Eds.). (2009). *Implicit and explicit knowledge in second language learning, testing, and teaching.* **Bristol, UK: Multilingual Matters.**

This edited volume brings together the output of the Marsden Fund Project, a large-scale research project funded by the New Zealand Royal Society of Arts, which was designed to advance the study of implicit and explicit learning, knowledge, and instruction on multiple fronts. The project had three overarching goals, which are reflected in the structure of the book. Part One presents definitions and R. Ellis' understanding of the issues and relationships between implicit and explicit learning, knowledge, and instruction. Part Two presents the results of the Marsden study proper and includes five proposed measures of implicit and explicit knowledge. In Part Three, the different measures are applied in various ESL/EFL contexts, with the goal of examining the measures' relationship to general language proficiency. Part Four is devoted to form-focused instruction and its effects on implicit and explicit knowledge. The conclusions of the project are presented in Part Five. Given the broad range of topics addressed in this volume, this book will be of interest to a wide range of applied linguistics researchers.

Rebuschat, P. (Ed.). (2015). *Implicit and explicit learning of languages.* **Amsterdam: John Benjamins.**

This volume represents an update to a 1994 edited volume by Nick Ellis carrying the same title (Ellis, N. (Ed.). (1994). *Implicit and explicit learning of languages.* London: Academic Press.) Both volumes bring together psychologists and SLA researchers around the shared topic of implicit and explicit learning. In this new volume, eighteen author teams discuss the topics of implicit-statistical learning, explicit learning, and second language acquisition from within their disciplinary traditions. Contributions are organized into three parts. Part One presents distinct theoretical perspectives. Different schools of thought are represented from SLA and psychology, as well as from the implicit and statistical learning literatures. Part Two focuses on research design and methodology. It includes introductions to two real-time methodologies, eye tracking (Godfroid & Winke, 2015) and event-related potentials (Morgan-Short, Faretta-Stutenberg, & Bartlett-Hsu, 2015), that can bring new insights to the study of implicit and explicit learning and knowledge. In Part Three, theories of implicit and explicit learning are applied to real-world instructional contexts. This section includes a meta-analysis that revisits the relative effectiveness of implicit and explicit instruction (Goo et al., 2015). Readers looking for an in-depth, transdisciplinary overview of big questions in implicit and explicit learning will find this volume particularly informative.

Andringa, S., & Rebuschat, P. (Eds.). (2015). New directions in the study of implicit and explicit learning [Special issue]. *Studies in Second Language Acquisition*, **37(2).**

This thematic issue on new directions in implicit and explicit learning marked the ten-year anniversary of Hulstijn and Ellis' (2005) seminal publication. A notable development over the intervening decade was the rise in real-time, or online, methodologies for studying implicit and explicit learning. Three empirical studies (Andringa & Curcic, 2015; Cintrón-Valentín & Ellis, 2015; Godfroid, Loewen, Jung, Park, Gass, & Ellis, 2015) utilized eye tracking or eye-movement registration to gain a detailed picture of how second-language learners process input, a fourth study (Morgan-Short, Deng, Brill-Schuetz, Faretta-Stutenberg, Wong, & Wong, 2015) relied on brain imaging (fMRI), and a fifth study (Paciorek & Williams, 2015) implemented a reaction-time methodology. The measurement of awareness is central to a paper by Rebuschat, Hamrick, Riestenberg, Sachs, and Ziegler (2015), which nicely synthesizes the research since Williams' (2005) influential study. Caldwell-Harris, Lancaster, Ladd, Dediu, and Christiansen (2015) demonstrate the potential of implicit-statistical learning for lexical tone, an area that has received comparatively less attention in SLA.

Roehr-Brackin, K. (2018). *Metalinguistic awareness and second language acquisition.* **New York: Routledge.**

In this volume, Roehr-Brackin discusses metalinguistic awareness, a concept that includes explicit knowledge, from different theoretical vantage points. The author brings together and synthesizes research from child and adult language learning, which have relied on different conceptualizations of metalinguistic awareness. Drawing on the strengths of both paradigms, the author then outlines new avenues for research and calls for more research with under-studied learner populations. Chapter 1 provides definitions of central concepts in the book. Chapters 2 and 3 are devoted to child language learning and relate metalinguistic awareness (viewed here as a gradient property) to literacy development. Chapters 4, 5, and 6 explore metalinguistic awareness as a part of the explicit-implicit knowledge dichotomy. These chapters address key topics in applied linguistics research, including the explicit-implicit knowledge interface, the effects of explicit instruction, language learning aptitude, and the measurement of explicit knowledge. To conclude, in Chap. 7, the author identifies potential areas of cross-fertilization between child language learning and adult SLA.

References

Andringa, S., & Rebuschat, P. (2015). New directions in the study of implicit and explicit learning: An introduction. *Studies in Second Language Acquisition, 37*, 185–196.

Bell, P. K. (2017). Explicit and implicit learning: Exploring their simultaneity and immediate effectiveness. *Applied Linguistics, 38*, 297–317.

DeKeyser, R. (2015). Skill acquisition theory. In B. VanPatten & J. Williams (Eds.), *Theories in second language acquisition: An introduction* (2nd ed., pp. 94–112). Routledge.

Ellis, R. (2005). Measuring implicit and explicit knowledge of a second language: A psychometric study. *Studies in Second Language Acquisition, 27*, 141–172.

Godfroid, A. (2016). The effects of implicit instruction on implicit and explicit knowledge development. *Studies in Second Language Acquisition, 38*, 177–215.

Godfroid, A., Boers, F., & Housen, A. (2013). An eye for words: Gauging the role of attention in incidental L2 vocabulary acquisition by means of eye-tracking. *Studies in Second Language Acquisition, 35*, 483–517.

Godfroid, A., Kim, K. M., Hui, B., & Isbell, D. (2018). Validating implicit and explicit L2 knowledge measures: A research synthesis. *Paper to the Second Language Research Forum*, Montreal, Canada, October 2018.

Godfroid, A., & Kim, K. M. (2021). The contributions of implicit-statistical learning aptitude to implicit second-language knowledge. *Studies in Second Language Acquisition*. https://doi.org/10.1017/S0272263121000085.

Goo, J., Granena, G., Yilmaz, Y., & Novella, M. (2015). Implicit and explicit instruction in L2 learning: Norris & Ortega (2000) revisited and updated. In P. Rebuschat (Ed.), *Implicit and explicit learning of languages* (pp. 443–482). John Benjamins.

Hama, M., & Leow, R. P. (2010). Learning without awareness revisited: Extending Williams (2005). *Studies in Second Language Acquisition, 32*, 465–491.

Leow, R. P. (2015). *Explicit learning in the L2 classroom: A student-centered approach.* Routledge.

Leow, R. P., & Hama, M. (2013). Implicit learning in SLA and the issue of internal validity. *Studies in Second Language Acquisition, 35*, 545–557.

Leung, J. H. C., & Williams, J. N. (2011). The implicit learning of mappings between forms and contextually derived meanings. *Studies in Second Language Acquisition, 33*, 33–55.

Leung, J. H. C., & Williams, J. N. (2012). Constraints on implicit learning of grammatical form-meaning connections. *Language Learning, 62*, 634–662.

Leung, J. H. C., & Williams, J. N. (2014). Crosslinguistic differences in implicit language learning. *Studies in Second Language Acquisition, 36*, 733–755.

Norris, J., & Ortega, L. (2001). Does type of instruction make a difference? Substantive findings from a meta-analytic review. *Language Learning, 51*, 157–213.

Paciorek, A., & Williams, J. N. (2015). Implicit learning of semantic preferences of verbs. *Studies in Second Language Acquisition, 37*, 359–382.

Paciorek, A., & Williams, J. N. (2015). Semantic generalization in implicit language learning. *Journal of Experimental Psychology: Learning, Memory, and Cognition, 41*, 989–1002.

Rebuschat, P., & Williams, J. N. (2012). Implicit and explicit knowledge in second language acquisition. *Applied Psycholinguistics, 33*, 829–856.

Spada, N. (2015). SLA research and L2 pedagogy: Misapplications and questions of relevance. *Language Teaching, 48*, 69–81.

Spada, N., & Tomita, Y. (2010). Interactions between type of instruction and type of language feature: A meta-analysis. *Language Learning, 60*, 263–308.

Suzuki, Y., & DeKeyser, R. (2015). Comparing elicited imitation and word monitoring as measures of implicit knowledge. *Language Learning, 65*, 860–895.

Vafaee, P., Kachinske, I., & Suzuki, Y. (2017). Validating grammaticality judgment tests: Evidence from two new psycholinguistic measures. *Studies in Second Language Acquisition, 39*, 59–95.

Williams, J. N. (2005). Learning without awareness. *Studies in Second Language Acquisition, 27*, 269–304.

Aline Godfroid is an Associate Professor of Second Language Studies and TESOL at Michigan State University. Her primary research interests are in second language psycholinguistics, with a special emphasis on the study of implicit and explicit knowledge and learning, and in the teaching and learning of vocabulary, quantitative research methods, and eye-tracking methodology. Her research is situated at the intersection of cognitive psychology and second language acquisition and aims to bring second-language psycholinguistics closer to the realities of actual second language learning and teaching. Aline Godfroid is Co-Director of the Second Language Studies Eye-Tracking Lab. She is the author of "Eye tracking in SLA and bilingualism: A research synthesis and methodological guide" (with Routledge) and the recipient of the 2019 TESOL Award for Distinguished Research.

Elvenna Majuddin and Anna Siyanova-Chanturia

The development of the mental lexicon is a mammoth task that language learners face, as it involves the acquisition of thousands of single words as well as units above the word level, known as multi-word expressions (MWEs). A plethora of terminologies and definitions have been proposed. For the purpose of this chapter, we define MWEs as phrases that vary along the continua of frequency, length, fixedness, abstractness and figurativeness/literality, and are recognised as conventional by a proficient language user (Siyanova-Chanturia & van Lancker Sidtis, 2019).

A large proportion of language is made up of MWEs. Hence, effective pedagogical interventions are needed to help second language (L2) learners make large and rapid gains in MWE knowledge. Such pedagogical interventions have, in recent years, been the object of an unprecedented amount of empirical studies. These studies are often categorised under incidental or intentional type of learning.

Despite the prevalence of the incidental-intentional learning dichotomy, there is little consensus as to what learning conditions are considered truly incidental or intentional. One criterion that is often adopted to distinguish between the two types of learning is the expectation of a test (Nation & Webb, 2011). However, as posited by Gass (1999), incidental learning may be more intentional than one may expect. It is still unknown whether learners do in fact pay attention to novel word strings, especially when encountered repeatedly. As such, there is a need to explore whether the absence of test announcement effectively differentiates the two learning conditions.

E. Majuddin (✉) · A. Siyanova-Chanturia
School of Linguistics and Applied Language Studies, Te Herenga Waka,
Victoria University of Wellington, Wellington, New Zealand
e-mail: anna.siyanova@vuw.ac.nz

A. Siyanova-Chanturia
College of Foreign Languages, Ocean University of China, Qingdao, China

© Springer Nature Switzerland AG 2021   831
H. Mohebbi and C. Coombe (eds.), *Research Questions in Language
Education and Applied Linguistics*, Springer Texts in Education,
https://doi.org/10.1007/978-3-030-79143-8_143

In addition, many pedagogical interventions employ input enhancement techniques, such as typographic enhancement, which are meant to draw learners' attention to lexical items while still primarily engaging with content. While some researchers consider these interventions as semi-incidental learning conditions (Pellicer-Sánchez & Boers, 2019), others group them under intentional learning (Szudarski, 2017). What is, perhaps, more important is to determine the quality and amount of attention prompted by each pedagogical intervention, before it is categorised under one type of learning.

Although intentional learning is often said to be more effective than incidental learning, there are few empirical studies that can support this claim. The majority of MWE studies focuses on one type of learning—incidental or intentional—making it difficult for a comparison to be made. Additionally, intervention studies that fall under incidental and semi-incidental learning conditions tend to be short-term interventions or one-off experiments. MWE studies that are longitudinal in nature, on the contrary, mostly concern pedagogic interventions under intentional learning conditions. An example would be studies looking at learners engaging in prolonged MWE-focused activities (e.g., Boers et al., 2006). Thus, little is known about the effects of long-term interventions under the different learning conditions. Comparisons of their longitudinal effects will allow us to determine whether interventions, such as typographic enhancement and glossing, can, in fact, sustain learners' engagement over a period of time, and lead to learning gains that are comparable to those of intentional learning conditions.

Another reason to juxtapose incidental and intentional learning conditions would be to assess how the effects of pedagogic interventions are modulated under the respective learning conditions. Take for example, the use of typographic enhancement. While typographic enhancement has been known to facilitate MWE learning, this has been mostly investigated under the incidental learning condition (i.e., learners were not warned of a MWE test). Therefore, if intentional learning is indeed more effective than incidental learning, the use of typographic enhancement combined with test expectation should result in superior learning gains. Whether this is true, however, has not been established as there is a lack of comparative studies. Further, typographic enhancement may make test announcement redundant, as learners may focus their attention to novel typographically enhanced MWEs even when they do not receive specific test announcement to do so, as shown in Peters (2012). In other words, creating different learning conditions may matter for some, but not all pedagogic interventions. This underscores the need for comparative studies to determine whether the effect of an intervention is indeed modulated by the different learning conditions.

The scarcity of studies which compare MWE learning under the different learning conditions is even more evident in the context of multimodal input. Thus far, there has only been one study which shows that test announcement alters learners' engagement with captioned viewing. In an eye-tracking study, Montero Perez et al. (2015) found that captioned viewing under intentional learning conditions led to longer fixation times. The study also highlighted the role of visual salience in attracting attention. The same question could then be investigated in future comparative studies: Does the absence of a test announcement prior to L2 viewing with typographically enhanced MWEs lead to similar gains as when learners are forewarned of a test?

To determine which learning condition is more effective, learning gains need to be compared. While testing instrument will inevitably depend on the nature of MWEs, there is still no consensus as to what testing instrument might be best for MWE form and meaning. Further, if a learning condition is meant to be truly intentional, will learners benefit from knowing the exact testing instrument at the outset? It will be interesting to find out whether or not the knowledge of *what* will be tested, and *how*, is likely to boost learners' MWE acquisition.

Differentiating the effects of these two learning conditions should not mean that MWE learning has to exclusively take place under one condition. The two learning conditions complement each other, as it is the use of both that is likely to help consolidate learning. The colossal task of learning thousands of MWEs coupled with limited classroom time necessitates prioritising interventions that are worth spending time on. Future empirical studies that address these questions will point to the ways in which classroom time can be used effectively, while still drawing learners' attention as to how incidental learning outside of the classroom can be optimised.

The Research Questions

1. In the realm of MWE learning, can truly incidental and truly intentional learning conditions be established? If so, how can these two conditions be effectively differentiated?
2. Does the absence of test announcement effectively differentiate the two learning conditions?
3. Does the amount and quality of attention given to MWEs under each learning condition differ? If so, in what way?
4. Are short-term interventions aimed at engendering MWE knowledge more effective under intentional learning conditions than incidental learning conditions?
5. Are long-term interventions targeting MWEs more effective under intentional learning conditions than incidental learning conditions?
6. Are the effects of input enhancement techniques on MWE learning similar under the different learning conditions?
7. In what ways do the different learning conditions modulate the effects of input enhancement techniques on MWE learning?
8. How does the absence of test announcement influence MWE uptake from multimodal input such as captioned viewing?

9. What kinds of testing instruments are best suited to measure gains in the knowledge of form and meaning of (different types of) MWEs?
10. If learners are informed of a test on MWE knowledge prior to learning, will pre-empting the format of the test (e.g., multiple-choice, gap-fill, translation task) lead to greater learning gains?

Suggested Resources

Szudarski, P., & Carter, R. (2016). The role of input flood and input enhancement in EFL learners' acquisition of collocations. *International Journal of Applied Linguistics, 26*(2), 245–265.

Expanding the line of enquiry on incidental acquisition of collocations from reading, this study experimentally demonstrates the superiority of a semi-incidental learning condition over a purely incidental learning condition. Two experimental conditions were created with the aim of investigating the effects of input flood and input enhancement on L1-Polish learners' acquisition of collocations. In the input enhancement group, the target collocations, some of which appeared twice, were highlighted. In the purely incidental learning condition, the same target collocations were not highlighted. The results revealed that the input enhancement group outperformed the purely incidental condition on both the form recognition and form recall tests.

Peters, E. (2012). Learning German formulaic sequences: The effects of two attention drawing techniques. *Language Learning Journal, 40*(1), 65–79.

A conceptual replication of Peters (2009), Peters (2012) endeavored to compare the effects of test announcement, as well as typographic salience, on foreign language learners' recall of German MWEs and single words. The experimental group differed from the control group in that participants in the former were explicitly forewarned to pay attention to both MWEs and single words. In both groups, half of the target items were typographically enhanced and accompanied with a gloss. The results revealed that the participants performed better on the enhanced target items, but that explicit instructions to attend to MWEs did not result in superior learning gains. This is reminiscent of the findings of Peters (2009) and provides evidence against the notion that intentional learning is superior to incidental learning.

Sonbul, S., & Schmitt, N. (2013). Explicit and Implicit lexical knowledge: Acquisition of collocations under different input conditions. *Language Learning, 63*(1), 121–159.

To date, this is the only study that investigated how a range of learning conditions affect collocational knowledge. In two experiments that differed in terms of participant profile, three learning conditions were used. In the incidental learning condition, participants read a passage containing the target collocations. The same collocations were taught in a decontextualized, intentional learning condition. Participants in the third experimental group read a passage with the target collocations typographically enhanced. Results of the experiment conducted with non-native speakers indicated that the semi-intentional and intentional learning conditions were more effective compared to the incidental learning condition. This is contradictory to the findings of Peters (2009, 2012), and emphasizes the fact that the relationship between MWE learning conditions and learning gains is not straightforward. Put differently, the inconsistent results brought about by limited reading studies exacerbates the need for more comparative studies on the effects of the different learning conditions on MWE learning.

Montero Perez, M., Peters, E., & Desmet, P. (2015). Enhancing vocabulary learning through captioned video: An eye-tracking study. *The Modern Language Journal*, **99, 308–328**.

This eye-tracking study investigates the effects of both test announcement and types of captioning on the learning of new vocabulary. Looking at both single words and MWEs, this study provides valuable insights into caption-reading behaviour, under both incidental and intentional learning conditions. Participants were divided into full captioning and keyword captioning groups. Under each group, some of the participants were informed of the upcoming tests, while others were unaware of them. The findings suggested that test announcement alters learners' engagement with the input, as participants under the intentional learning conditions spent more time reanalysing the target word area. Further, the intentional learning groups were also found to outperform their counterparts in the meaning recall test. The findings also suggested that visual salience, by way of presenting the target words in isolation, induces longer gaze durations. This study not only underscores the potential of captioned viewing as a way to enhance MWE learning, it further highlights the fact that test announcement could modulate vocabulary learning from multimodal input.

Siyanova-Chanturia, A., & Pellicer-Sánchez, A. (Eds.). (2019) *Understanding formulaic language: A second language acquisition perspective.* **New York: Routledge**.

A comprehensive resource for graduate students and established researchers, this book overviews and provides future directions on topics concerning the acquisition, processing, and use of MWEs in a second language. Three different perspectives are presented: cognitive and psycholinguistic, sociocultural and pragmatic, and pedagogical. Two contributions, in particular, are pertinent to the issues raised in the present chapter. The chapter *Pedagogical approaches to the teaching and learning of formulaic language* by Pellicer-Sánchez and Boers provides a review of empirical studies concerning pedagogical interventions intended to help second language learners acquire different types of MWEs. Adopting test announcement as the criterion that distinguishes between the incidental and intentional learning conditions, the chapter reviews not only pedagogical interventions that fall under both categories, but also those that employ awareness-raising techniques, which the authors categorise as semi-incidental learning condition. The chapter *Testing formulaic language* by Gyllstad and Schmitt argues that there is yet to be an established, widely used testing instrument to measure MWE knowledge. Following a review of main tests that have been used in the literature, the authors identify the key issues that contribute to the difficulties in establishing a standardised MWE test, as well as the principles that need to be considered in the development of future MWE tests.

References

Boers, F., Eyckmans, J., Kappel, J., Stengers, H., & Demecheleer, M. (2006). Formulaic sequences and perceived oral proficiency: Putting a lexical approach to the test. *Language Teaching Research, 10*(3), 245–261.

Gass, S. (1999). Discussion: Incidental vocabulary learning. *Studies in Second Language Acquisition, 21*(2), 319–333.

Montero Perez, M., Peters, E., & Desmet, P. (2015). Enhancing vocabulary learning through captioned video: An eye tracking study. *The Modern Language Journal, 99*, 308–328.

Nation, I. S. P., & Webb, S. (2011). *Researching and analyzing vocabulary*. Heinle, Cengage Learning.

Pellicer-Sánchez, A., & Boers, F. (2019). Pedagogical approaches to the teaching and learning of formulaic language. In A. Siyanova-Chanturia, & A. Pellicer-Sánchez (Eds.), *Understanding formulaic language: A second language acquisition perspective.* (pp. 153–173). Routledge.

Peters, E. (2012). The differential effects of two vocabulary instruction methods on EFL word learning: A study into task effectiveness. *International Review of Applied Linguistics in Language Teaching, 50*(3).

Siyanova-Chanturia, A., & van Lancker Sidtis, D. (2019). What online processing tells us about formulaic language. In A. Siyanova-Chanturia, & A. Pellicer-Sánchez (Eds.), *Understanding formulaic language: A second language acquisition perspective.* (pp. 38–61). Routledge.

Szudarski, P. (2017). Learning and teaching L2 collocations: Insights from research. *TESL Canada Journal, 34*(3), 205–216.

Elvenna Majuddin has a PhD in Applied Linguistics from Victoria University of Wellington (New Zealand). She has taught English in a higher education institution in Malaysia for six years. Her research areas concern the learning of multi-word expressions through watching videos with various caption conditions, under both incidental and intentional learning conditions.

Anna Siyanova-Chanturia is Senior Lecturer in Applied Linguistics at Victoria University of Wellington (New Zealand), and Guest Professor in Linguistics and Applied Linguistics at Ocean University of China (China). Anna's research interests include second language acquisition, psycholinguistics, vocabulary and formulaic language. She has published in applied linguistics and psycholinguistics journals, such as *Applied Linguistics, Language Learning, Studies in Second Language Acquisition, Journal of Experimental Psychology: Learning, Memory and Cognition, Brain and Language,* and others.

Language Processing in the Foreign Language Classroom (From a Cognitive Perspective)

Ronald P. Leow

How foreign/second language (L2) learners process L2 data in the language classroom has been an area of much interest in the (instructed) second language acquisition or (I)SLA strand of research. Indeed, from a cognitive perspective, "SLA research that seeks to probe into learner cognition needs to focus on the identification and explanation of the cognitive processes employed by L2 learners as they learn the L2 …" (Leow, 2015, p. 2). Yet a review of (I)SLA research reveals a relatively small proportion of studies that have employed concurrent data-elicitation procedures (e.g., eye-tracking and think aloud protocols) to elicit online data that provide insights into the cognitive processes employed by L2 learners as they interact with the L2. Those that have employed such concurrent procedures have identified important processes such as (levels of) awareness, activation of prior knowledge, hypothesis testing, rule formulation, metacognition, all related to amount of cognitive effort/engagement or depth of processing (Leow, 2015, 2019).

Language processing in the L2 classroom is typically divided into two dichotomies dependent on the role or lack thereof of awareness during any potential encoding of the linguistic L2 information in the input: implicit (without awareness) or incidental (with or without awareness) learning versus explicit or intentional (with awareness) learning. A comparative analysis of intentional/explicit versus incidental/implicit learning studies (Leow, 2018) reveals a clear superiority of the former over the latter, due to depth of processing and level of awareness.

There have been several cognitive theoretical underpinnings postulated to account for how L2 learners process L2 data (see Leow, 2018 for an overview). However, only two models (Gass, 1997; Leow, 2015) postulate an account of the full learning process from intake to output while Leow (2015) also provides a

R. P. Leow (✉)
Department of Spanish & Portuguese, Georgetown University, Washington, DC, USA
e-mail: leowr@georgetown.edu

© Springer Nature Switzerland AG 2021
H. Mohebbi and C. Coombe (eds.), *Research Questions in Language
Education and Applied Linguistics*, Springer Texts in Education,
https://doi.org/10.1007/978-3-030-79143-8_144

fine-grained explanation of the cognitive processes assumed to be involved at each stage of the L2 learning process.

A recognition of the benefits of explicit language processing and a classroom setting that promotes such processing has led to a recent call to situate ISLA research within the language curriculum (e.g., Leow, 2018; Leow & Cerezo, 2016) in an effort to provide robust pedagogical ramifications. Such ramifications may include the need to have L2 learners cognitively engaged in whatever L2 task or activity they are doing and the designing of computerized problem-solving games that promote deep processing and potential awareness at the level of understanding (e.g., Cerezo et al., 2016). At the same time, there is clearly a need to probe deeper into how L2 learners process different types of linguistic items, be it during interacting with L2 data or feedback, whether proficiency level plays a role, and so on.

The Research Questions

1. Does type of learning (implicit vs. incidental learning vs. explicit) play a role in classroom-based language learning?
2. Does type of cognitive processes L2 learners employ while interacting with L2 data play a role in subsequent learning?
3. Does type of linguistic item play a role in how L2 learners process the L2?
4. Does level of language proficiency play a role in how L2 learners process the L2?
5. What role does prior knowledge play in L2 language processing?
6. Does type of feedback (written or oral, focus or unfocused, direct or indirect etc.) play a role in how L2 learners process the linguistic information in the feedback?
7. What role does type of concurrent data elicitation procedure (think aloud vs. eye-tracking vs. reaction time) play in accessing learner cognitive processes?
8. What role do individual differences play during language processing?
9. What role does modality play in language processing?
10. Does depth of processing play a role in L2 learners' subsequent immediate and delayed retention of L2 data?

Suggested Resources

Bergsleithner, J. M, S. N. Frota & J. Y. Yoshioka (Eds.) (2013). *Noticing and second language acquisition: Studies in honor of Richard Schmidt.* **Honolulu: University of Hawai 'i, National Foreign Language Resource Center.**

This collection of studies honored Richard Schmidt's important contribution to the SLA field, especially in the attentional and awareness strands of research due to his Noticing Hypothesis (1990). Part 1 situates the Noticing Hypothesis in SLA from a theoretical, methodological, empirical, and pedagogical perspective. Part 2 is a series of empirical studies addressing the observation and enhancement of noticing while Part 3 extends the methodological approach to the concurrent procedure of eye-tracking. Part 4 is a mixture of chapters covering the use of subjective measures, the role of individual differences, and approaches to noticing and awareness (cognitive neuroscientific and sociocultural).

Rebuschat, P. (Ed.). (2015). *Implicit and explicit learning of languages***. Amsterdam: John Benjamins.**

This volume brings together eminent researchers from a variety of fields (e.g., cognitive psychology, linguistics, education, cognitive neuroscience, developmental psychology) for a state-of-the-art report on the study of implicit and explicit learning, to critically evaluate key concepts and methodologies, and to determine future directions to take in this interdisciplinary enterprise. The first part provides an array of theoretical perspectives related to the study of implicit and explicit learning. The second part is methodological in nature addressing different research designs associated with the study of type of learning. The third part is pedagogical as it provides practical applications to the instructed setting.

Leow, R. P. (2015). *Explicit learning in the L2 classroom: A student-centered approach***. New York, NY: Routledge.**

This book focuses on the issue of explicit learning in the L2 classroom from a learner-centered perspective. The book reports on the theoretical, methodological, and empirical approaches to (I)SLA research on the constructs of attention and awareness, with a special focus on *how* L2 learners process L2 data. Leow recommends situating the constructs *learning* and *awareness* within an ISLA theoretical framework in an effort to address these constructs at different stages of the learning process. In his own Model of the L2 Learning Process in Instructed SLA, Leow posits that the role of awareness at different stages of the L2 learning process may be dependent upon the role played by depth of processing or *how* the L2 data are processed by the learner. Leow provides pedagogical ramifications for the L2 classroom in relation to promoting L2 learners' cognitive processes while they interact with the L2.

Leow, R. P. (Ed.) (2019). *The Routledge handbook of second language research in classroom learning***. New York, NY: Routledge.**

This Handbook is a comprehensive psycholinguistic approach to the issue of instructed language learning that is uniquely theoretical, methodological, empirical, pedagogical, and curricular. The Handbook first reports the tenets of several models that have postulated the roles of cognitive processes in the L2 learning process, two major methodological data-elicitation procedures to be employed in addressing learner cognitive processes (think aloud protocols and eye-tracking), and conceptual replications and extensions of or new research on several strands of classroom learning or Instructed SLA (ISLA) research, including those that have not methodologically addressed the processing and processes assumed to have played a role, then situates ISLA within a curricular framework, and discusses robust pedagogical ramifications for the instructed setting. The major benefits of this Handbook include a deeper understanding of *how* L2 learners process L2 data while exposed to or interacting with L2 data.

References

Cerezo, L., Caras, A., & Leow, R. P. (2016). Effectiveness of guided induction versus deductive instruction on the development of complex Spanish "gustar" structures: An analysis of learning outcomes and processes. *Studies in Second Language Acquisition, 38*, 265–291.

Gass, S. M. (1997). *Input, interaction, and the second language learner*. Lawrence Erlbaum.

Leow, R. P. (2015). *Explicit learning in the L2 classroom: A student-centered approach*. Routledge.

Leow, R. P. (2018). ISLA: How implicit or how explicit should it be? Theoretical, empirical, and pedagogical/curricular issues. *Language Teaching Research, 23*, 476–493.

Leow, R. P. (Ed.). (2019). *The Routledge handbook of second language research in classroom learning*. Routledge.

Leow, R. P., & Cerezo, L. (2016). Deconstructing the "I" and "SLA" in ISLA: One curricular approach. *Studies in Second Language Learning and Teaching, 6*, 43–63.

Ronald P. Leow is Professor of Applied Linguistics, Director of Spanish Language Instruction, and Director of Graduate Students—Linguistics in the Department of Spanish and Portuguese at Georgetown University. His areas of expertise include language curriculum development, teacher education, Instructed Language Learning, psycholinguistics, cognitive processes in language learning, research methodology, and CALL. Professor Leow has published extensively in prestigious journals and has co-edited several books. His most recent one titled *A psycholinguistic approach to technology and language learning* (de Gruyter Mouton) appeared in 2016 while his single-authored book titled *Explicit learning in the L2 Classroom: A student-centered approach* (Routledge) appeared in 2015. His edited *Routledge handbook of second language research in classroom learning* (Routledge) appeared in 2019.

Mavadat Saidi and Mohadese Khosravi

Intelligence has long been considered as a fixed construct (Smith, 2001) which was measured in terms of the correct answers to the items of IQ tests (Lin, 2006). It was believed that only those individuals with high IQ scores would succeed in the learning process. This view had persisted till the emergence of Multiple Intelligences Theory. Challenging the established monolithic view of intelligence, Gardner (1983) disputed the prevailing conceptualization of intelligence and redefined it as "the ability to find and solve problems, the ability to respond successfully to new situations and the capacity to learn from one's past experiences" (p. 21).

Attempting to widen the scope of human potential beyond the confines of IQ scores (Armstrong, 2000), Gardner postulated that individuals own "a collection of aptitudes" (Gardner, 1993, p. 27) and identified seven types of intelligence including verbal/linguistic, musical, logical/mathematical, spatial/visual, bodily/kinesthetic, interpersonal and intrapersonal, to which natural and existential types were added later. Table 145.1 presents a brief definition of intelligence types.

MI Theory was based on two main claims: (1) that all human beings possess at least eight types of intelligence; and (2) that no two individuals, even identical twins, have the same intelligence profiles (Gardner, 2005). Accordingly, apart from its theoretical innovations, MI Theory gave rise to the hope that more students could achieve their goals in educational settings through identifying their strengths and weaknesses (Gardner, 2004). Indeed, MI Theory tapped into what good teachers always perceive and practice in their classes, "reaching beyond the text and the blackboard to awaken students' minds" (Armstrong, 2000, p. 39).

To implement MI Theory and to create models of practice, many projects have been carried out under the direction of Gardner and his colleagues at Harvard

M. Saidi (✉)
English Department, Shahid Rajaee Teacher Training University, Tehran, Iran
e-mail: m.saidi@sru.ac.ir

M. Khosravi
English Department, Kharazmi University, Tehran, Iran

© Springer Nature Switzerland AG 2021
H. Mohebbi and C. Coombe (eds.), *Research Questions in Language Education and Applied Linguistics*, Springer Texts in Education,
https://doi.org/10.1007/978-3-030-79143-8_145

Table 145.1 Multiple intelligences definitions (Armstrong, 2000, p. 4; Scherer, 1999, p. 4)

Intelligence	Core components
Linguistic-verbal	Sensitivity to the sounds, structure, meanings, and functions of words and language
Logical-mathematical	Sensitivity to, and capacity to discern, logical or numerical patterns; ability to handle long chains of reasoning
Spatial-visual	Capacity to perceive the visual-spatial world accurately and to perform transformations on one's initial perceptions
Bodily-kinesthetic	Ability to control one's body movements and to handle objects skillfully
Musical	Ability to produce and appreciate rhythm, pitch, and timbre; appreciation of the forms of musical expressiveness
Interpersonal	Capacity to discern and respond appropriately to the moods, temperaments, motivations, and desires of other people
Intrapersonal	Access to one's own 'feeling' life and the ability to discriminate among one's emotions; knowledge of one's own strengths and weaknesses
Naturalist	Expertise in distinguishing among members of a species; recognizing the existence of other neighboring species; and charting out the relations, formally or informally, among several species
Existential	Human proclivity to ask fundamental questions about life

University's Project Zero (See Armstrong, 2000). Numerous studies have also addressed multiple intelligences in language learning contexts (See Khosravi & Saidi, 2014). Nevertheless, designing MI-based courses, developing pertinent materials and devising valid and reliable assessment instruments along with the possible relationship between the individuals' multiple intelligences and other influential factors in the process of teaching and learning a language seem to deserve considerable attention and more in-depth research.

The Research Questions

1. What factors should be considered when multiple-intelligences-based activities are developed?
2. How can multiple intelligences be identified? What instruments should be developed to identify the individual learners' intelligences? How can we ensure their validity and reliability?
3. What types of tasks can be developed to target multiple intelligences? How can we control the cognitive complexity of the tasks?
4. What are the contributing factors to mobilizing individual learners' multiple intelligences in both educational and occupational settings?

5. How can individuals benefit from multiple intelligences to choose their appropriate future career? How can we devise placement tests for hiring individuals for the jobs that suit their multiple intelligences?
6. What are the assessment tools in evaluating MI-based classes?
7. How can genetic factors influence the extent of individuals' multiple intelligences?
8. How can socio-cultural factors influence the development of individuals' multiple intelligences?
9. What are the challenges that teachers might face in tackling multiple intelligences in their lesson plans and teaching practices?
10. How can multiple intelligences be incorporated into language learning syllabi and materials?

Suggested Resources

Chen, J., Moran, S., & Gardner, H. (Eds.) (2009). *Multiple Intelligences Around the World***. USA: Jossey-Bass.**

The book covers a wide range of topics related to the basics of multiple intelligences theory. It provides great insights into the influence of the cultural contexts on shaping educational practices all around the world. In five different parts, the contributors present the readers with an overview of the underlying principles of multiple intelligences theory and its applications in Asian and Pacific areas, Europe, South America, and the USA. The last part of the book synthesizes the reasons behind and reflections on applying multiple intelligences theory to the educational policies and practices all around the world. The book is highly recommended to those who need a deeper understanding of multiple intelligences practices and applications in diverse cultural and educational contexts in order to enhance education for all students at all levels.

Gardner, H. (2008). *Multiple Intelligences: New Horizons in Theory and Practice***. USA: Basic Books.**

The book presents an undated version of the first conceptualization of the ideas of multiple intelligences in the 1st edition of 1993. It is highly recommended for readers who want a brief historical account of the early inquiries about IQ and its measurement, different categories of intelligences and the application of multiple intelligences theory in educational settings. Gardner delineates his 25-year-old theory and tries to answer some of the questions poses about multiple intelligences theory's methodological procedures. He also allocated several chapters to answering objections to multiple intelligences theory and expounds on the uses of this theory beyond educational settings. The book covers central arguments about the global applications of multiple intelligences theory, MI in the workplace, an assessment of MI practice in the current conservative educational climate, new evidence about brain functioning, etc.

Kornhaber, M., Fierros, E., & Veenema, S. (2004). *Multiple Intelligences: Best Ideas from Research and Practice.* **USA: Pearson.**

The book provides the teachers and administrators with numerous examples of integrating multiple intelligences theory into their schools and classrooms. It illustrates the implication of multiple intelligences theory in more than 40 schools and presents a detailed account for the relevant experiences, lesson plans and activities, tools and resources, teaching and assessing strategies. It is recommended to the pre-service and in-service teachers who want to realize their students' intelligences and foster their learning and enable them to successfully cope with challenging subjects and contents.

Sternberg, R. J. (2015). Multiple intelligences in the new age of thinking. In *Handbook of intelligence* **(pp. 229–241). Springer, New York, NY.**

The books presents two major theories of intelligence, namely theory of multiple intelligences and theory of successful intelligence. A number of new approaches towards intelligence are presented from an evolutionary perspective. The historical background of the theories are given and they concepts are defined and elaborated. Moreover, new views toward intelligence in the ever changing educational settings are put forth and a host of practical recommendations are provided for researchers and practitioners in relevant area to education. The book provides the interested audience with a bulk of theoretical knowledge and numerous practical suggestions for improving the quality of teaching, learning, and testing practices in the challenging educational environments.

Armstrong, T. (2000). *Multiple Intelligences in the Classroom.* **Alexandria, VA: Association for Supervision and Curriculum Development.**

The book is certainly recommended for readers who are interested in gaining a deep and practical understanding of multiple intelligences theory. It provides a wide range of new multiple intelligences resources, tools and materials. Trying to popularize multiple intelligences theory, Armstrong provides the educational practitioners at all levels with the required strategies and templates to put multiple intelligences into practice in the process of curriculum development, lesson planning, assessment and policy making. Armstrong presents a set of practical tips and examples from real schools and provides the educators with ample ideas for unleashing the students' potential both in educational and professional settings and in their real life.

References

Armstrong, T. (2000). *Multiple intelligences in the classroom.* Association for Supervision and Curriculum Development.

Gardner, H. (1983). *Frames of mind: The theory of multiple intelligences.* Basic Books Inc.

Gardner, H. (1993). *Multiple intelligences: The theory in practice.* Basic Books.

Gardner, H. (2004). *A multiplicity of intelligences: In tribute to Professor Luigi Vigolo.* First published in Scientific American, 1998.

Gardner, H. (2005). Multiple lenses in the mind. In *Paper presented at the ExpoGestian conference,* Bogota Colombia, May 25, 2005.

Khosravi, M., & Saidi, M. (2014). Investigating the possible relationship between multiple intelligences and self-efficacy: The case of Iranian EAP instructors. *Electronic Journal of Foreign Language Teaching, 11*(1), 90–97.

Lin, P. Y. (2006). *Multiple intelligences theory and english language teaching.* Retrieved July 11, 2018 from http://www.52en.com.

Scherer, M. (1999). The constructivist classroom: The understanding pathway: A conversation with Howard Gardner. *Educational leadership, 57*(3). Retrieved July 11, 2018 from http://www.Acsd.org/readingroom/edlead/9911/scherer2.html.

Smith, E. (2001). Implications of multiple intelligences theory for second language learning. *Post-Script, 1*(1), 32–52.

Mavadat Saidi holds a Ph.D. in Teaching English as a Foreign Language from Kharazmi University of Tehran, Iran. She is currently an assistant professor at Shahid Rajaee Teacher Training University, Tehran, Iran. Her areas of interest include English for specific purposes, discourse analysis, systemic functional linguistics, teacher education, and individual differences. She has given several conference presentations and has published papers in both national and international journals.

Mohadese Khosravi got her M.A. in Teaching English as a Foreign Language from Kharazmi University of Tehran, Iran. She currently teaches English to high school students. She is interested in discourse analysis, critical discourse analysis, and learners' individual differences. She has published papers in national and international journals including *International Journal of Language and Applied Linguistics, Electronic Journal of Foreign Language Teaching, Journal of Politeness Research.*

Masatoshi Sato

Peer interaction is a type of interaction that is carried out between second language (L2) learners. Peer interaction is used as a pedagogical tool in communicative classes and online classes, in forms of paired and group activities. From the cognitive-interactionist perspective, researchers have compared peer interaction and other types of interaction, such as learner-native speaker and learner-teacher interactions, and revealed distinct features pertaining to input, corrective feedback, and output (see Philp et al., 2014). From social perspectives, researchers have investigated how learners co-construct L2 knowledge and how social relationships among learners affect the learning processes (see Storch, 2017). Recent research has combined different theoretical frameworks to understand how peer interaction assists L2 learning and how the impact of peer interaction can be enhanced (see Sato & Ballinger, 2016).

The patterns of peer interaction can be mediated by a variety of factors such as task type, pairing patterns based on learners' proficiency, modality of interaction (oral vs. written or face-to-face vs. computer-mediated), and learners' relationships. Overall, research suggests that learners' relationships may be one of the most important factors that determines the ultimate impact of peer interaction on L2 learning. That is, when learners construct collaborative relationships, they tend to engage in more beneficial interaction whereby they produce more language, correct each other's L2 errors in constructive ways, and appreciate each other's contributions to the completion of a given task.

Recent research has examined pedagogical interventions designed to counter some weaknesses of peer interaction. For instance, learners tend to avoid using difficult or infrequent structures during communicative interaction. Priming technique can be a useful tool to ensure that learners' production includes those structures (McDonough et al., 2015). Another upcoming direction pertains to the

M. Sato (✉)
Department of English, Universidad Andres Bello, Santiago, Chile
e-mail: masatoshi.sato@unab.cl

© Springer Nature Switzerland AG 2021
H. Mohebbi and C. Coombe (eds.), *Research Questions in Language Education and Applied Linguistics*, Springer Texts in Education,
https://doi.org/10.1007/978-3-030-79143-8_146

training of learners to give feedback to each other (Sato & Lyster, 2012). Modeling how to interact with each other is another way of enhancing the effectiveness of peer interaction (Kim, 2013). Increasing learners' metacognitive knowledge of peer interaction is yet another approach; learners can be explicitly taught how peer interaction should be carried out and how it benefits their learning (Sato, 2020).

There are a number of theoretical and pedagogical issues related to peer interaction research. First, research has not focused on the teacher's role during peer interaction activities. Given the importance of collaborative relationships among learners, the teacher must play a pivotal role in creating a classroom environment conducive to such learner relationships. Unlike teacher's corrective feedback, feedback providers are L2 learners during peer interaction. To that end, research focusing on the process and impact of provision of feedback has much theoretical potential in understanding peer interaction. Another promising area concerns learner psychology; learners construct different social relationships but why? Discovering what psychological constructs are related to learner relationships may help develop pedagogical interventions designed to enhance learner relationships conducive to learning. Overall, future research should investigate the ways in which peer interaction can be manipulated—cognitively or socially—so as to increase its effectiveness on L2 learning in the classroom.

The Research Questions

1. How does peer interaction differ from other types of interaction such as learner-teacher interaction?
2. How does peer interaction lead to L2 learning?
3. What are learner internal factors (e.g., proficiency, learning background, psychology) that mediate the effectiveness of peer interaction?
4. What are learner external factors (e.g., task, modality, interlocutor, classroom environment) that mediate the effectiveness of peer interaction?
5. How do social relationships among learners relate to the outcome of peer interaction?
6. How can learner relationships be altered to promote collaborative relationships?
7. How can the patterns of peer interaction (input, feedback, and output) be manipulated to increase its effects on L2 learning?
8. How does provision of peer corrective feedback affect the provider's L2 learning?
9. What psychological constructs determine the ways in which L2 learners engage with each other and/or the task?
10. How does the teacher's role affect the effectiveness of peer interaction?

Suggested Resources

Philp, J., Adams, R., & Iwashita, N. (2014). *Peer interaction and second language learning.* **New York: Routledge**.

This is the first monograph focusing on peer interaction. The authors provide a comprehensive review of issues related to peer interaction, such as learners' proficiency levels, L1 use during peer interaction, ages of learners, formats of interaction, and the teacher's role. Primarily written from the interactionist perspective, the book explains how peer interaction functions and how its effectiveness can be enhanced, with a number of excerpts from different data sources. The authors argue that peers and the teacher play different yet important roles in the classroom and the teacher's management is necessary for peer interaction to have a positive impact on L2 learning.

Sato, M. (2020). Metacognitive instruction for collaborative interaction: The process and product of self-regulated learning in the Chilean EFL context. In C. Lambert & R. Oliver (Eds.), *Using tasks in second language teaching: Practice in diverse contexts.* **(pp. 215–236). Clevedon, UK: Multilingual Matters**.

This study incorporated an instructional approach that has rarely been examined in the field of second language teaching/learning—metacognitive instruction. With a quasi-experimental design, the experimental group received metacognitive instruction for collaborative interaction (MICI). MICI was designed to increase the learners' metacognitive knowledge of peer interaction, along with strategy training focusing on collaborative interaction. The results showed that the learners increased the use of collaborative strategies and that they improved their comprehensibility, implying that they became more aware that: (a) their classmates can be a useful learning resource (person knowledge); (b) peer interaction activities can be helpful for their L2 learning (task knowledge); and (c) collaborative strategies increase the benefit of peer interaction (strategy knowledge). The researcher argues that self-regulated learning should be taught in order for learners to take advantage of peer interaction activities.

Sato, M. (2017a). Interaction mindsets, interactional behaviors, and L2 development: An affective-social-cognitive model. *Language Learning*, **67(2), 249–283**.

This article reports on a classroom experiment in which three data sources were used to answer a simple yet important question: Does second language learners' psychology matter for the ways in which they communicate with each other? First, the researcher conducted extensive interviews to determine the participants' psychology towards conversational partners as well as communicative tasks. Then, the learners engaged in communicative tasks, the data of which served as a measure of the level of engagement with each other and with the tasks. Their language development was measured via pre- and post-tests. Based on the results, the researcher proposed the affective-social-cognitive (ASC) model to explain the links among learners' interaction mindsets, interactional behaviors, and language development. The study underscores the importance of incorporating different theoretical frameworks to understand the nature of peer interaction.

Sato, M. (2017b). Oral peer corrective feedback: Multiple theoretical perspectives. In H. Nassaji & E. Kartchava (Eds.), *Corrective feedback in second language teaching and learning: Research, theory, applications, implications* (pp. 19–34). New York, NY: Routledge.

This review article zeros in on corrective feedback that occurs during peer interaction. It focuses on three issues: (a) learners as feedback providers; (b) the impact of social relationships; and (c) the impact of learner psychology. First, the researcher discusses the reciprocal nature of peer interaction. Drawing on Levelt's (1983) perceptual theory of monitoring, the researcher proposes the dual model of peer corrective feedback that accounts for cognitive processes of providers and receivers of feedback. Second, the researcher raises an issue that learners may reject feedback from their peers even when it is accurate. To explain this phenomenon, the researcher invokes sociocultural theory and explains that social relationships formed during communicative interaction may affect the impact of feedback. Also, he posits that learner psychology, interaction mindset in particular, determines the ultimate effectiveness of peer corrective feedback. In the article, several weaknesses of peer feedback are discussed, and solutions are proposed.

Sato, M., & Ballinger, S. (Eds.). (2016). *Peer interaction and second language learning: Pedagogical potential and research agenda*. Amsterdam, The Netherlands: John Benjamins.

This book is the first collection of empirical studies related to peer interaction. Twelve studies are divided into sections focusing on three overall questions: (a) How do interactional patterns and learner characteristics affect L2 learning in peer interaction?; (b) How do tasks and interaction modality affect peer interaction and L2 learning?; and (c) How do learning settings affect peer interaction and L2 learning? The studies, together making up over 500 learners, were conducted in different learning settings (8 different countries) with L2 learners whose first languages vary widely (more than 8), and who are at different educational levels (elementary to adult). In addition to the state-of-the-art introduction chapter outlining issues related to peer interaction, the book includes the concluding chapter that proposes new pathways for researching peer interaction in the classroom.

References

Kim, Y. (2013). Effects of pretask modeling on attention to form and question development. *TESOL Quarterly, 47*(1), 8–35.

McDonough, K., Trofimovich, P., & Neumann, H. (2015). Eliciting production of L2 target structures through priming activities. *The Canadian Modern Language Review, 71*(1), 75–95.

Philp, J., Adams, R., & Iwashita, N. (2014). *Peer interaction and second language learning.* Routledge.

Sato, M. (2020). Metacognitive instruction for collaborative interaction: The process and product of self-regulated learning in the Chilean EFL context. In C. Lambert & R. Oliver (Eds.), *Using tasks in second language teaching: Practice in diverse contexts.* (pp. 215–236). Clevedon, UK: Multilingual Matters. https://doi.org/10.21832/9781788929455-014.

Sato, M. (2017a). Interaction mindsets, interactional behaviors, and L2 development: An affective-social-cognitive model. *Language Learning, 67*(2), 249–283.

Sato, M. (2017b). Oral peer corrective feedback: Multiple theoretical perspectives. In H. Nassaji & E. Kartchava (Eds.), *Corrective feedback in second language teaching and learning: Research, theory, applications, implications* (pp. 19–34). Routledge.

Sato, M., & Ballinger, S. (Eds.). (2016). *Peer interaction and second language learning: Pedagogical potential and research agenda.* John Benjamins.

Sato, M., & Lyster, R. (2012). Peer interaction and corrective feedback for accuracy and fluency development: Monitoring, practice, and proceduralization. *Studies in Second Language Acquisition, 34*(4), 591–262.

Storch, N. (2017). Sociocultural theory in L2 classroom. In S. Loewen & M. Sato (Eds.), *The Routledge handbook of instructed second language acquisition* (pp. 69–84). Routledge.

Masatoshi Sato (Ph.D.: McGill University) is a Professor in the Department of English at Universidad Andrés Bello, Chile. He teaches pre-service and in-service EFL teachers. His research interests include peer interaction, corrective feedback, learner psychology, professional development, and research-pedagogy link. In addition to his publications in international journals, he recently co-edited books from John Benjamins (2016, with Susan Ballinger *Peer Interaction and Second Language Learning*), Routledge (2017, with Shawn Loewen *The Routledge Handbook of Instructed Second Language Acquisition*), and Routledge (2019, with Shawn Loewen *Evidence-Based Second Language Pedagogy*). His co-authored textbook with Shawn Loewen (*A Practical Guide to Second Language Acquisition*) from Cambridge University Press will appear in 2022. He is the recipient of the 2014 ACTFL/MLJ Paul Pimsleur Award. He is currently the Editor of *Language Awareness*.

Plurilingualism in TESOL

Shelley K. Taylor

The Council of Europe/CoE's (2001) construct of "plurilingualism" distinguishes between multilingualism in the sense of languages coexisting at social and individual levels, and the dynamic, evolving linguistic repertoires of "plurilingual" individuals. It frames plurilinguals as social agents with varying degrees of proficiency in several language-varieties, and whose competences are complex or composite, not distinct (CoE, 2001, p. 68). One of Coste, Moore and Zarate's (2009) goals in developing the construct for the CoE (2001) was to inform learners that partial competences counted as part of their full linguistic repertoires. They observed that learners who felt they would never measure up to unattainable yardsticks (becoming 'balanced bilinguals') and (native-speaker/non-native speaker) binaries often felt defeated and stopped studying languages at school; however, like Norton (2013), they also noted that plurilinguals' investment in the language-varieties in their repertoires was subject to change over time and space, and that they developed "competences in a number of languages from desire or necessity... to meet the need to communicate with others" along life's social paths (Coste et al., 2009, p. 17). The various paths they take explain ebbs and flows in their competences over time.

It is important for TESOL educators to understand plurilingualism (Taylor & Snoddon, 2013). With better understanding of the shared conceptual, semantic base of languages, they can see the legitimacy in students drawing on their full linguistic repertoires (e.g., to understand one language, and express themselves in another); they can see beyond the limits of initial teacher education edicts that stress the

S. K. Taylor (✉)
Faculty of Education, The University of Western Ontario, London, ON, Canada
e-mail: taylor@uwo.ca

© Springer Nature Switzerland AG 2021
H. Mohebbi and C. Coombe (eds.), *Research Questions in Language Education and Applied Linguistics*, Springer Texts in Education,
https://doi.org/10.1007/978-3-030-79143-8_147

'language separation ideology' (i.e., not allowing learners to draw on their repertoires as resource for fear of negative transfer); and they can see how setting unattainable goals and binary discourses can lead students (and teachers) to feel insecure in their linguistic competences, and influence their long-term language development. Though educators should view plurilingualism as a resource, not a deficit, they should not adopt Pollyanna views of it promoting 'linguistic equality for all.' Not all language-varieties are equally valued; forces such as linguistic homogenization and sociocultural restrictions on agency may delegitimize competences, and constraints abound (Choi & Ollerhead, 2018; Phillipson, 2019; Selvi, 2010). Still, plurilingualism in TESOL holds much promise.

The Research Questions

1. While plurilingualism in TESOL holds much promise, how can research inform us about the educational and political structures (supports) needed at various levels (curriculum development, language status planning, etc.) to make valorizing and including linguistic diversity more than just an 'add-on' and meet the promise of plurilingualism in TESOL?
2. Are plurilingual approaches better suited to L2/FL learning-as-subject or to language education across the curriculum?
3. Research is needed to hear teachers' and teacher educators' opinions on the conceptual clarity, usefulness, affordances and appeal of plurilingualism in TESOL across age groups, national contexts, and programs (e.g., ESL in bilingual education, language across the curriculum, EAP, etc.). Which research approaches are best suited to gathering this information?
4. It has been suggested that the panoply of terms used following the multilingual (and social) turn in applied linguistics are not helpful, yet each has its own premises. Should an overarching term be agreed upon for pluri-, trans-, metro-, polylingualism, etc., and why? Would adopting an overarching term lose the distinct 'conceptual repertoires' encapsulated in the different terms? Would it promote a mono- ideology that runs counter to the ethos of pluri- approaches? Could national trends, and the rationales underlying those trends, be accounted for if a preferred term is selected (e.g., the predilection of European and a growing number of Canadian researchers to use the term plurilingual, but its underuse in many other national contexts)?
5. There is some slippage between terminology (bilingual, multilingual, plurilingual, translingual) within single edited volumes. To what extent does this reflect conceptualization in the process of 'becoming' or conceptual confusion, and what (if any) role can research play in addressing these issues?

6. Research suggests that presenting plurilinguals as social actors without contextualizing their learning conditions—conditions that may constrain their attempts to develop aspects of their linguistic repertoires—runs the risk of reifying social inequality. How can this issue be addressed?

7. What are the risks of overextending the notion of multi-competence in plurilingualism?

8. How can researchers make the case for plurilingualism in TESOL in higher education and in teacher education, and assist in its implementation?

9. What is the future for plurilingual descriptors across various levels of assessment and in assessment tools other than CEFR scales (Council of Europe, 2018)?

10. What are the findings of international research regarding how to simultaneously support and rein in the role of English to maintain plurilingual ecologies (e.g., in MLE programs)?

Suggested Resources

Council of Europe. (2018). *Common European Framework of Reference for Languages: Learning, teaching, assessment. Companion volume with new descriptors.* **Strasbourg, France: Council of Europe Publishing**.

Since the CoE (2001) introduced plurilingualism, the CEFR has been translated into 40+ languages, and emphasis has shifted from L2/FL learning to language education across the curriculum—a shift that led to increased focus on languages of schooling (internationally and involving migrant populations), and developing curricula, guidelines and resources to promote plurilingualism across languages. The updated CoE (2018) companion volume reflects heightened focus on plurilingualism, bypassing binary (Lx→Ly) assessment to capture dynamic language use (Lx → Ly, Lz and L …). Descriptors were calibrated to reflect individuals' practical functional ability across plurilingual competences from beginner (e.g., A1 –'can use a very limited repertoire in different languages') to highly advanced levels (C2—'can participate effectively in a conversation involving two+ languages' while accommodating language changes and interlocutor needs'; p. 162).

Lau, S., & Stille, S. (Eds.). (2020). *Plurilingual pedagogies: Critical and creative endeavors for equitable language (in) education.* **New York, NY: Springer International Publishing**.

In this edited volume, emerging issues relating to the development and application of *pluri*lingual pedagogies are addressed in theoretical, conceptual and empirical contributions: in conceptual papers featuring Moore, Lin, Kubota, and Piccardo and

North followed by empirical cases divided into three sections on plurilingual engagements for critical learning; for language classrooms, and for higher education, with comments by invited scholars (Li Wei, Cummins and Toohey). The editors' goal is to valorize bi/multilingual learners' languages and the use of *pluri*lingual resources to promote their sense of inclusion, well-being, and self-confidence. Taken together, the contributions provide evidence of educators and researchers engaging in plurilingual practices to dismantle hegemonic discourses related to monolingualism, and to legitimize hybrid forms of expression to promote creative, critical communication and knowledge construction.

Mohanty, A. K. (2019). *The multilingual reality: Living with languages.* **Bristol, UK: Multilingual Matters.**

Mohanty's (2019) book on the "multilingual reality" of plurilingual speakers of indigenous languages living in linguistically complex societies argues for multilingual language education (MLE) from the viewpoints of language, power, and the historic underachievement of minority language children experiencing linguistic domination and subordination in Eastern and Western societies. Mohanty positions these processes historically through snapshots of plurilingual indigenous groups in India that are relevant to plurilingualism in TESOL. This book links fundamental aspects of the construct of plurilingualism (e.g., ties between the dynamics of the multilingual mind and cognition) to plurilingual learners' educational needs beyond monolingual practices and bilingual education to the role English should play in a plurilingual ecology (e.g., MLE programs). It provides much needed insights into plurilingual development in indigenous languages outside of bilingual (Lx/English) development and teaching in western contexts.

Singleton, D. (2018). Multilingualism, multi-competence and (limits to) the interaction between language systems. *Teanga: The Journal of the Irish Association for Applied Linguistics, 25.* https://journal.iraal.ie/index.php/teanga/article/view/46/29.

Singleton (2018) cautions against excessive research zeal for the notion of multi-competence. In his view, the notion has overextended standard views of recognized permeable lines between semantic and conceptual dimensions of language-varieties, and a common underlying conceptual base. He does not support views of 'fusion' at the conceptual level, or of unitary, unbounded and undifferentiated language knowledge in the mind. Singleton (2018) draws on examples of language development, loss and recovery (e.g., selective recovery in cases of aphasia), and the affective dimension of language differentiation to argue that plurilinguals do differentiate between language boundaries in the languages they use in everyday communication. This view merits consideration in broad discussions of (the limits of) plurilingual competence (e.g., CoE, 2018, p. 28).

Snoddon, K., & Weber, J. (Eds.). (2021). *Critical perspectives on plurilingualism in deaf education*. **Bristol, UK: Multilingual Matters.**

In this edited volume, the first author brings the wealth of her experience as past Chair of TESOL's BEIS/TEDS interest section and co-editor of *TESOL Quarterly*'s special issue on "Plurilingualism in TESOL" to the next level; first, exploring partial competences in terms of deaf learners' resourcefulness engaging with multiple semiotic resources when accessing speech and sound and, next, explaining why it is crucial for teachers of deaf students to be highly proficient in standard sign languages (i.e., to develop the range of linguistic repertoires students need to thrive in and beyond educational contexts, given their uneven—if not precarious—access to complex linguistic input). The editors argue, and the contributors provide illustrations, of why a plurilingual approach is needed to develop deaf learners' competences and resourcefulness in multiple languages, modalities, and channels.

References

Choi, J., & Ollerhead, S. (Eds.). (2018). *Plurilingualism in teaching and learning: Complexities across contexts*. Routledge.

Coste, D., Moore, D., & Zarate, G. (2009). *Plurilingual & pluricultural competence*. Council of Europe.

Council of Europe. (2001). *Common European framework of reference for languages: Learning, teaching, assessment*. Cambridge University Press.

Norton, B. (2013). *Identity and language learning: Extending the conversation* (2nd ed.). Multilingual Matters.

Phillipson, R. (2019). *La domination de l'anglais, un défi pour l'Europe [English domination: A challenge for Europe]*. Libre & Solidaire.

Selvi, A. F. (2010). All teachers are equal, but some teachers are more equal than others: Trend analysis of job advertisements in English language teaching. *WATESOL NNEST Caucus Annual Review, 1*, 156–181.

Taylor, S. K., & Snoddon, K. (2013). Plurilingualism in TESOL: Promising controversies. *TESOL Quarterly, 47*(3), 439–445.

Shelley K. Taylor, Professor (Western University, Canada), teaches TESOL and Applied Linguistics at the graduate and preservice levels. Her recent research focusses on language and literacy learning among youth refugees in Canadian tertiary education. Previous research focused on educators orchestrating instructional spaces for students' plurilingual development in multilingual schools, English-medium instruction in the Nordic countries, and plurilingual youths' language development over time and space. She has conducted workshops on trilingual language policy development in Greenland (involving Greenlandic, Danish and English), and mother-tongue based materials development in Nepal for 122 tribal/Indigenous languages. She has published in the *Canadian Journal of Applied Linguistics; Canadian Modern Language Review; Copenhagen Studies in Bilingualism; Intercultural Education; International Journal of Bilingual Education & Bilingualism; Race, Ethnicity & Education,* and *TESOL Quarterly*.

Pragmatics in Language Teaching and Learning

Minh Thi Thuy Nguyen

Instructed pragmatics is a subfield of second language acquisition that investigates how the learning of pragmatic language use occurs as a result of classroom language teaching. Pragmatics is defined as the way individuals achieve communicative intent and attend to interpersonal relationships while using language (e.g. how to disagree with your friends without offending them). Learning pragmatics, therefore, involves learning how to use language appropriately for social interaction. This involves an understanding of how social rules (cultural norms, politeness and taboos) govern choices of language forms in particular contexts of communication, and putting that knowledge into use in real life interaction (Kasper, 2001).

While pragmatics is an important part of the learner's communicative competence, it is also considered one of the most challenging aspects of second language learning. Without an awareness that norms of appropriate language use can vary across languages, cultures and contexts, learners may easily find themselves using language that is socially appropriate for one language, culture or context but not for another. This may bear interactional consequences and reflect negatively on the learner as a person.

Despite its important role in language learning, pragmatics is rarely taught in the second language classroom. An explanation for this neglect is that teachers are not well prepared to teach pragmatics during their teacher education programs (Basturkmen & Nguyen, 2017). There has also been a concern that textbooks do not adequately explain social meanings behind linguistic expressions and the contexts in which these expressions can be used. Textbooks also contain inauthentic language samples, thus making the learning of pragmatics difficult (Nguyen, 2011).

Incidental learning of pragmatics through interaction, however, is not always effective. This is because not all pragmatic norms are noticeable enough for learners to acquire without some sort of guidance. Although a high degree of language

M. T. T. Nguyen (✉)
Department of English & Linguistics, University of Otago, Dunedin, New Zealand
e-mail: minh.nguyen@otago.ac.nz

© Springer Nature Switzerland AG 2021
H. Mohebbi and C. Coombe (eds.), *Research Questions in Language Education and Applied Linguistics*, Springer Texts in Education,
https://doi.org/10.1007/978-3-030-79143-8_148

contact through daily communication may help learners become more fluent language users, it does not always make them more sensitive to subtle pragmatic norms (Taguchi, 2008).

On the other hand, there is accumulating evidence to suggest that instruction that is dedicated to developing explicit understanding of pragmatic norms or making learners attend to and deeply process pragmatic input can be effective in developing pragmatic knowledge (Taguchi, 2015). Instruction that enables pragmatic knowledge to become automatic such as production or comprehension practice is also useful, especially when learners have the opportunity to perform the same task repeatedly (Takimoto, 2012).

As the instructed learning of pragmatics has become increasingly important in the field of language teaching, we can expect greater interest in this area in the future. For example, we can expect future investigations to continue to address how different types of instruction facilitate different areas of pragmatic acquisition (e.g. pragmatic knowledge versus pragmatic processing), or how instruction works for different types of pragmatic targets and learner profiles. Teachers need this information in order to tailor their teaching to suit their particular lesson objectives and classrooms. Teachers also need to know how to help learners transfer their learned knowledge from one domain to another. To this end, future research may explore how strategic learning of pragmatics can complement classroom teaching to promote the transfer (Taguchi, 2018). In recent years, researchers have begun to examine the potential of technologies in supporting self-directed learning of pragmatics (Ishihara, 2007), and undoubtedly this can continue to be a fruitful area for future inquiry.

The Research Questions

1. What types of instruction are most effective for enhancing second language pragmatic knowledge?
2. What types of practice and how much practice are needed for pragmatic knowledge to become automatic?
3. How do different pragmatic features respond to instruction?
4. How does instruction interact with learner characteristics (e.g. agency, motivation, and proficiency) to impact the learning outcome?
5. What are the effective ways of supporting strategic learning of pragmatics?
6. How can technologies be employed to promote the learning and teaching of pragmatics both within and outside of the curriculum?
7. What may effective pragmatics-focused instructional materials look like?
8. What may an effective pragmatics-focused curriculum look like?
9. What do teachers know about teaching pragmatics and what knowledge, skills and competencies do they require to teach pragmatics in the L2 classroom?

10. Does improving teachers' pedagogical content knowledge for teaching pragmatics encourage them to integrate pragmatics-focused instruction in their
teaching to a greater extent?

Suggested Resources

Culpeper, J., McKay, A. & Taguchi, N. (2018). *Second Language Pragmatics:*
from Theory to Practice. **New York: Routledge.**

This book is strongly recommended for readers who want to do research in the field
of second language pragmatics. Its combination of theoretical foundations and
practical advice on how to do research in different areas of pragmatics (production,
comprehension and awareness and interaction) is particularly helpful for novice
researchers and graduate students. The book begins with a brief historical overview
of second language pragmatics as an interdisciplinary field of inquiry that intersects
second language acquisition and pragmatics, including an outline of research
questions typically examined in this field. The book then introduces conceptual
backgrounds on pragmatic production, comprehension, awareness and interaction,
and discusses data collection methods commonly used in researching topics in these
areas. Each method of data collection is illustrated with various examples. Finally,
each chapter also includes a set of discussion questions to encourage readers'
reflection on the different techniques for data collection.

Ishihara, N. & Cohen, A. (2010). *Teaching and Learning Pragmatics: Where*
Language and Culture Meet. **London: Longman-Pearson.**

This book is intended as a practical guide for teachers who would like to explore
ways of teaching and assessing pragmatic language use in the classroom. It is
arguably the most comprehensive teacher's book to date on instructed pragmatics
learning. The book covers a wide range of important topics, from teachers' pragmatics (what do they need to know about teaching pragmatics) and learners'
pragmatics (how to express pragmatic meaning and why), to options in teaching
and assessing pragmatic knowledge and curriculum and materials development.
The book includes a wealth of empirical data, hands-on classroom tasks and discussion questions to encourage teachers to reflect on pedagogical issues under
discussion.

Taguchi, N. & Roever, C. (2017). *Second Language Pragmatics.* **Oxford/New**
York: Oxford University Press.

This book is a much-needed update on theory and research related to second
language pragmatics following Kasper and Rose (2002)'s pioneer volume. The
book brings together current research and developments in second language
pragmatics research as well as identifies gaps and future directions to take the field
further. The book's 10 comprehensive chapters cover a wide range of important

topics, from theories of teaching and learning pragmatics, methodologies for researching pragmatics and insights from current studies to emerging issues in researching second language pragmatics in the era of globalization and multiculturalism. A valuable addition to second language pragmatics scholarship, the book should be of interest to researchers, graduate students and teacher educators who study second language pragmatics.

Taguchi, N. & Sykes, J.M. (eds.) (2013). *Technology in Interlanguage Pragmatics Research and Reaching.* **Philadelphia: John Benjamins.**

This volume brings together nine empirical studies and practical reports on second language pragmatics teaching and research in digitally mediated contexts. It is the only volume to date that addresses the relationship between second language pragmatics and technology. The first five studies address the potential of employing digital technologies for generating and analyzing data on pragmatic language use and expanding the scope of investigation of the field. For example, Taguchi (Chap. 2) and Li (Chap. 3) have demonstrated the ways in which computerized pragmatic tests enable researchers to measure and analyze learners' pragmatic processing ability, which are not normally captured by traditional paper-based tests. The next four studies highlight ways in which digital technologies can create more authentic contexts for teaching and assessing pragmatics. Collectively the studies offer a critical discussion of how technologies may offer a solution to the existing challenges in traditional pragmatics research and pedagogy.

Taguchi, N. (ed.). (2019). *The Routledge Handbook of Second Language Acquisition and Pragmatics.* **New York: Routledge.**

What sets this book apart from other books in the field is its coverage of not only traditionally studied topics such as pragmatic competence, teaching and assessment, but also more emerging areas of pragmatics including interactional pragmatics, intercultural pragmatics, usage-based approaches, corpus linguistics and psycholinguistics. The books' 32 chapters are written in a highly accessible manner, yet without losing their breadth and depth. Each chapter begins with an introduction to a specific topic, followed by a discussion of its theoretical foundations, a critical review of existing literature and evaluation of current practice and concludes with recommendation for future research and key readings. A comprehensive critical survey of the field and its key theories, methods and pedagogies, this book is an essential resource for scholars interested in second language acquisition and pragmatics.

References

Basturkmen, H., & Nguyen, M. (2017). Teaching pragmatics. In A. Barron, P. Grundy, & Y. Guo (Eds.), *The Routledge handbook of pragmatics* (pp. 563–574). Routledge.
Ishihara, N. (2007). Web-based curriculum for pragmatics instruction in Japanese as a foreign language: An explicit awareness-raising approach. *Language Awareness, 16*(1), 21–40.

Kasper, G. (2001). Classroom research on interlanguage pragmatics. In K. Rose & G. Kasper (Eds.), *Pragmatics in language teaching* (pp. 33–60). Cambridge University Press.

Nguyen, M. (2011). Learning to communicate in a globalized world: To what extent do school textbooks facilitate the development of intercultural pragmatic competence? *RELC Journal, 42* (1), 17–30.

Taguchi, N. (2008). Cognition, language contact, and the development of pragmatic comprehension in a study-abroad context. *Language Learning, 58*, 33–71.

Taguchi, N. (2015). Instructed pragmatics at a glance: Where instructional studies were, are, and should be going. *Language Teaching, 48*(1), 1–50.

Taguchi, N. (2018). Pragmatic competence in foreign language education: Cultivating learner autonomy and strategic learning of pragmatics. In I. Walker, D. Chan, M. Nagami, & Bourguignon, C. (Eds), *New perspectives on the development of communicative and related competence in foreign language education* (pp. 53–69). deGruyter.

Takimoto, M. (2012). Assessing the effects of identical task repetition and task-type repetition on learners' recognition and production of second language request downgraders. *Intercultural Pragmatics, 9*, 71–96.

Minh Thi Thuy Nguyen currently teaches TESOL and second language teaching at the University of Otago. Her research interests include pragmatics in second language teaching, interactional competence development, child language learning and language pedagogy. She has published in journals such as *Journal of Pragmatics, Pragmatics, Applied Pragmatics, Intercultural Pragmatics, Multilingua, The Language Learning Journal, Language Awareness, International Review of Applied Linguistics in Language Teaching, Innovation in Language Learning and Teaching* and so on. Her recent co-edited book (with C. V. Le, M. T. H. Nguyen, & R. Bernard) is "*Building teacher capacity in English Language Teaching in Vietnam: Research, Policy and Practice*" (Routledge, 2019). Dr. Nguyen is currently serving on the editorial boards of the *Asian Journal of English Language Teaching* published by The Chinese University of Hong Kong Press, and *Applied Pragmatics* published by John Benjamins.

Kata Csizér

Second language (L2) motivation measuring students' choice, effort and persistence in L2 learning has been an important topic in applied linguistics because of the fact that L2 motivation is one of the outstanding antecedent concepts for success (Dörnyei & Ushioda, 2011). The brief history of this field can be summarized by three major themes. First, social psychological aspects were researched to see to what extent attitudes related to the learning process were shaping students' invested effort in L2 learning and, thus, their ultimate achievement (Gardner, 2010). Second, cognitive-situated notions were included in the research agenda to investigate classroom-related variables in situated manners by including issues related to self-determination theory, attribution theory and self-issues (Csizér & Magid, 2014; Dörnyei & Ushioda, 2011). A third important emerging theme has been how L2 motivation changes over time. Through longitudinal investigations of motivational changes, it can be mapped which constructs/variables have lasting effects on students' L2 motivation, such as, future self-guides, emotions and willingness to engage in the learning. To accommodate these constructs/variables into a single framework, complex dynamic system theory was suggested as useful to investigate motivational processes from minute-to-minute changes (MacIntyre & Serroul, 2015) to semester long fluctuation in dispositions (Piniel & Csizér, 2014) to even longer timescales.

In terms of the various topics investigated in L2 motivation, recent years have brought about a definite shift in the variety of research projects stepping away from the classic, cross-sectional studies looking at one language, usually English, in a single educational setting to more complex and diverse investigations. One such a newly emerging topic is teacher motivation as despite the fact that many studies investigated classroom contexts, teachers often remained in the background of L2

K. Csizér (✉)
Department of English Applied Linguistics, School of English and American Studies,
Eötvös University, Budapest, Hungary
e-mail: wein.kata@btk.elte.hu

© Springer Nature Switzerland AG 2021   865
H. Mohebbi and C. Coombe (eds.), *Research Questions in Language
Education and Applied Linguistics*, Springer Texts in Education,
https://doi.org/10.1007/978-3-030-79143-8_149

motivation studies. Kubanyiova (2009) investigated teachers' selves and how these selves affected professional development. Based on Kubanyiova's work (2009, 2015) a number of scholars extended the investigation of teachers' selves in various directions from motivational profiles to feasible selves (Sahakyan et al., 2017; Thompson & Vásquez, 2015). Another point of view is offered by Hiver (2017; Hiver & Dörnyei, 2017), who conceptualized and researched a notion called teacher immunity. Teacher immunity helps teachers to counteract negative experiences and thus to maintain their own motivation in the long run.

Another important issue is the investigation of a variety of languages and learners learning more than one language. Both Henry (2011, 2014) as well as Csizér and Lukács (2010) found that learning multiple languages had both positive and negative impact on students indicating that not only language choice was an important contributor to L2/L3 motivation but also that the negative influences needed to be counterbalanced. The investigation of languages other than English became an important focal point in a recent *Modern Language Journal* special issue (Ushioda & Dörnyei, 2017) showing that the emergence of English as a lingua franca contributed to L2 motivation research in different ways in different contexts. This results in the fact that L2 motivation in our globalized world should be researched from a social perspective as well. L2 motivation in different contexts does not only mean various classroom-related contexts but also L2 motivation outside the classroom. In other words, L2 motivation needs to be related to explicit and implicit learning in order to remain a relevant L2 research field in the twenty-first century.

The Research Questions

1. What are the main characteristics of students' L2 motivation in various contexts?
2. What characterizes students' L2 motivation and its changes over various timeframes?
3. In what ways does students' willingness to regulate their own learning processes affect their L2 motivation?
4. What relationship can be identified between students' L2 task motivation and their overall achievement?
5. What relationship can be identified between students' L2 motivation and their L2 skills' development and achievement?
6. What impact do contextual variables have on the internal structure of students' L2 motivation?
7. To what extent does language policy affect L2 motivational processes in various contexts?
8. What characterizes the relationship between students' and teachers' L2 motivational processes?

9. What impact does L2 teachers' motivation to teach have on their teaching efficiency?
10. What salient issues can be identified related to the L2 motivation of students with learning differences in various contexts?

Suggested Resources

Lamb, M., Csizér, K., Henry, A., & Ryan, S. (Eds.) (2020). *Palgrave Macmillan handbook of motivation for language learning.* **Basingstoke: Palgrave**.

This volume provides an up-to-date and state-of-the-art summary of the field of L2 motivation. Studies in this handbook are organized into three parts including both theoretical and empirical considerations. The first part provides an overview of the most important theoretical and contextual approaches to L2 motivation research from Gardner's Socio-educational Model to Dörnyei's Directed Motivational Currents. The second part of the handbook includes classroom-related practical overviews of L2 motivation, such as teacher motivation, task motivation and demotivation. The last section of the handbook tries to look over the horizon of current L2 motivation studies and to highlight potentially important future research directions, for example, the investigation of L2 motivation and emotions as well as technology-related issues.

Csizér, K., & Kálmán, Cs. (Eds.) (2019). Language learning experience as a neglected element in L2 motivation research. Special Issue. *Studies in Second Language Learning and Teaching, 6(1)*.

This collection of articles commissioned for a special issue in *Studies in Second Language Learning and Teaching* deals with how language learning experiences shape L2 motivational processes. The special issue starts out with Dörnyei's introductory piece explaining how student engagement establishes a link between students' experiences and their selves. The subsequent empirical studies in the issue include the investigation of language learners around the world studying L2s taking into account various aspects of L2 learning experiences. Some of the focal points in these studies cover teacher-learner interaction as part of learning experience, emotional experience, experiences in study abroad contexts, how seemingly fleeting experiences have powerful effects on L2 motivation as well as how learners' narratives are constructed based on experiences.

Ushioda, E., & Dörnyei, Z. (Eds.) (2017). Beyond global English: Motivation to learn languages in a multicultural world: Introduction to the special issue. *The Modern Language Journal, 101(3), 451–454*.

With English language moving into the position of the lingua franca of our globalized world, it is increasingly important to investigate L2 motivation related to global English as well as to other languages. Hence, this edited issue takes account of the implications to learn languages other than English. The studies include information on the ideal multilingual self and identities, language choice as well as attitudes to languages other than English. Contextual studies describe L2 motivation in Japan, UK, USA and various European contexts. The importance of these studies not only lies in the fact that languages other than English are investigated but also that learners learning multiple languages, which is the norm in many contexts, are researched.

Dörnyei, Z., MacIntyre, P., & Henry, A. (Eds.) (2015). *Motivational dynamics in language learning*. Bristol: Multilingual Matters.

In order to provide a theoretical and empirical overview of motivational dynamics, this edited volume offers an almost equal contribution of conceptual and empirical papers within the complex dynamic system theory's framework. The conceptual papers detail various theoretical issues related to the applicability of the complex dynamic system theory in the field of L2 motivation. The empirical studies apply the dynamic concepts to data collection and analysis and thus show to what extent L2 motivation is indeed a dynamic concept. Through the application of different timescales (from seconds to semesters) one can see not only the changes in L2 motivation but also what stays constant.

Dörnyei, Z., & Ushioda, E. (2011). *Teaching and researching motivation* (2nd ed.). Harlow, UK: Longman.

In this updated version of the first edition of the same title, Zoltán Dörnyei teamed up with Ema Ushioda, another renown L2 motivation researcher, to offer a comprehensive and updated overview of the entire field of L2 motivation. The introduction and discussion of the history of L2 motivation complemented by details of the various interdisciplinary fields of studies related to L2 motivation. Next, practical issues are presented by offering separate sections on motivational strategies, demotivation and teacher motivation. Finally, methodological and research-related information are offered that are highly useful for young and experienced L2 researchers alike. The book uses an accessible and entertaining style that makes it an excellent bedside table book as well.

References

Csizér, K., & Lukács, G. (2010). The comparative analysis of motivation, attitudes and selves: The case of English and German in Hungary. *System, 38*, 1–13.

Csizér, K., & Magid, M. (2014). *The impact of self-concept on language learning*. Multilingual Matters.

Dörnyei, Z., & Ushioda, E. (2011). *Teaching and researching motivation* (2nd ed.). Longman.

Gardner, R. C. (2010). *Motivation and second language acquisition: The socio-educational model*. Peter Lang.

Henry, A. (2011). Examining the impact of L2 English on L3 selves: A case study. *International Journal of Multilingualism, 8*, 235–255.

Henry, A. (2014). The motivational effects of cross linguistic awareness: Developing third language pedagogies to address the negative impact of the L2 on the L3 self-concept. *Innovation in Language Learning and Teaching, 8*, 1–19.

Hiver, P. (2017). Tracing the signature dynamics of language teacher immunity: A retrodictive qualitative modeling study. *The Modern Language Journal, 101*(4), 669–699.

Hiver, P., & Dörnyei, Z. (2017). Language teacher immunity: A double-edged sword. *Applied Linguistics, 38*, 405–423.

Kubanyiova, M. (2009). Possible selves in language teacher development. In Z. Dörnyei & E. Ushioda (Eds.), *Motivation, Language Identity and the L2 Self* (pp. 314–332). Multilingual Matters.

Kubanyiova, M. (2015). The role of teachers' future self guides in creating L2 development opportunities in teacher-led classroom discourse: Reclaiming the relevance of language teacher cognition. *The Modern Language Journal, 99*, 565–584.

MacIntyre, P., & Serroul, A. (2015). Motivation on a per-second timescale: Examining approach-avoidance motivation during L2 task performance. In Z. Dörnyei, P. MacIntyre, & A. Henry (Eds.), *Motivational dynamics in language learning* (pp. 109–138). Multilingual Matters.

Piniel, K., & Csizér, K. (2014). Changes in motivation, anxiety, and self-efficacy during the course of an academic writing seminar. In Z. Dörnyei, P. D. MacIntyre, & A. Henry (Eds.), *Motivational dynamics in language learning* (pp. 164–194). Multilingual Matters.

Sahakyan, T., Lamb, M., & Chambers, G. (2017). Language teacher motivation: From the ideal to the feasible self. In S. Mercer & A. Kostoulas (Eds.), *Language teacher psychology* (pp. 53–70). Multilingual Matters.

Thompson, A. S., & Vásquez, C. (2015). Exploring motivational profiles through language learning narratives. *The Modern Language Journal, 99*, 158–174.

Ushioda, E., & Dörnyei, Z. (Eds.) (2017). Beyond Global English: Motivation to learn languages in a multicultural world. Special issue. *The Modern Language Journal, 101*(3).

Kata Csizér holds a Ph.D. in Language Pedagogy and works as an associate professor in the Department of English and Applied Linguistics at Eötvös University, Budapest. Her main field of research interest is the social psychological aspects of L2 learning and teaching, as well as second and foreign language motivation. She is an expert of L2 motivation research. She has published over 50 academic papers and has co-authored several books on various topics related to social psychological issues in foreign language learning and teaching, including Dörnyei, Z., Csizér, K., & Nemeth, N. (2006). *Motivation, Language Attitudes and Globalization: A Hungarian Perspective*. Clevedon: Multilingual Matters and Csizer, K., & Magid, M. (Eds.). (2014). *The impact of self-concept on language learning*. Bristol: Multilingual Matters and the recent Palgrave Macmillan handbook of motivation for language learning with Martin Lamb, Alastair Henry and Stephen Ryan.

Sociocultural Theory and Second Language Development

150

Matthew E. Poehner and James P. Lantolf

Sociocultural Theory (SCT) originated in the writings of Russian psychologist L. S. Vygotsky (1896–1934). Working at a time when psychology was being established as a scientific discipline, Vygotsky (1997) turned to Marx, and in particular to dialectic materialism, for a method to understand human consciousness and its development. Vygotsky (1987) reasoned that to apprehend consciousness in its entirety, it was necessary to account for biologically endowed capacities, which he termed lower forms of consciousness, as well as their transformation into cultural, higher forms of consciousness. Drawing from Marx, Vygotsky adopted the dialectical view that consciousness arises through participation in socially organized activities, but that this is not fully deterministic as people in turn contribute to such activities, acting with intentions and recognizing themselves as agentive. Particularly important with regard to psychological development, Vygotsky understood our engagement in activity to be mediated by other individuals and by available cultural artifacts, including participation structures, social institutions, conceptual knowledge, and most especially language. Cultural forms of consciousness emerge as these mediating artifacts, which are first encountered externally and through interaction with others, become appropriated, their meanings

M. E. Poehner (✉)
Department of Curriculum and Instruction, The Pennsylvania State University, University Park, PA, USA
e-mail: mep158@psu.edu

J. P. Lantolf
Department of Applied Linguistics, The Pennsylvania State University, University Park, PA, USA
e-mail: jpl7@psu.edu

School of Foreign Studies, Xi'an JiaoTong University, Xi'an China

© Springer Nature Switzerland AG 2021
H. Mohebbi and C. Coombe (eds.), *Research Questions in Language Education and Applied Linguistics*, Springer Texts in Education,
https://doi.org/10.1007/978-3-030-79143-8_150

internalized and serving as resources, or tools, with which we can regulate our psychological activity in order to eventually carry out actions in material reality (Vygotsky, 1987). Recognizing the dialectic relationship between physical tools and signs, the theory proposes that engaging in goal-directed practical activity as an adult requires first acting mentally as a plan is constructed and then implementing the plan in reality (Arievitch, 2017). At the same time, however, by acting on the material reality through tool use, we reshape our understanding of reality as we notice the effects of our actions.

Owing to several decades during which Vygotsky's writings were suppressed by the Soviet government as well as his untimely death, it was not until the late 1970s that an international community of scholars began to gain familiarity with SCT (Kozulin, 1998). Perceived similarities between certain of Vygotsky's proposals and those of his contemporary, Jean Piaget, led some to believe that SCT was primarily concerned with development during childhood, a view reinforced by the fact that some of Vygotsky's most well-known empirical studies involved children. The subsequent publication of more of Vygotsky's writings, however, made clear that his enterprise was to establish psychology as a scientific discipline founded on Marxian principles and that the scope of this general psychology includes all higher forms of consciousness developed throughout the lifespan (Ratner & Silva, 2017). Following Marx, Vygotsky proposed that the appropriate way to understand consciousness scientifically was to track its formation over the course of time (i.e., history). One of the domains where time matters is in the ontogenesis of individuals from infancy through adulthood. This includes the development of conceptual understandings through the study of academic disciplines that enable specialized forms of perceiving, reasoning, and problem-solving.

Over at least the past thirty years, SCT has grown in popularity as a theoretical framework for understanding the developmental impact of teaching and learning activities in all areas of education, including second languages (L2). Beginning with the work of Frawley and Lantolf (1985), L2 researchers have invoked Vygotskian proposals such as mediation, internalization, and psychological tools, among others to understand processes through which L2 abilities develop and the potential for an L2 to regulate psychological activity in new ways. In more recent years, L2 SCT work has embraced Vygotsky's commitment to praxis as the dialectical unity of theory and research with practice (Lantolf & Poehner, 2014). Through research programs such as Dynamic Assessment, which integrates teaching as part of assessment to more fully understand the range of learner L2 abilities, and Concept-based Language Instruction, which reorganizes L2 curricula as concepts learners can internalize and employ as psychological tools, praxis-oriented SCT work aims to develop theoretically informed practices in support of learner L2 development while simultaneously extending and enriching SCT itself.

The Research Questions

1. The concept of mediation is central to Vygotsky's account of human consciousness and its development. Researchers have come to associate, and even conflate, mediation with concepts including scaffolding, assisted performance, corrective feedback, and i + 1. At a conceptual level, how can we distinguish these ideas and also understand them in relation to one another? At a pedagogical level, what instructional practices do these ideas lead us to consider and how do they compel us to think about L2 development?

2. In the area of L2 education, in what ways can SCT as a psychological theory inform theories of language that foreground meaning over form, such as cognitive linguistics as well as systemic functional linguistics as these have been applied to language instruction? How can these theories of language contribute to and enrich the principles of SCT as extended to language pedagogy?

3. Dynamic Assessment (DA) diagnoses learner abilities according to their Zone of Proximal development while non-DA procedures typically interpret abilities according to learner independent performance, that is, development that has already been completed. How do predictions concerning subsequent learner L2 achievement (and difficulties) that are based on DA compare with those based on non-DA? As learners are tracked over time (for instance, when they enter a program of language study), what insights are afforded by these orientations to assessment? Which diagnosis is most relevant to L2 instruction?

4. To date, studies of Concept-based Language Instruction have emphasized interventions targeting a specific language concept. What is the potential to expand beyond this focus to organize an entire coherent meaning-based language curriculum (i.e. one that reveals the essence of communicatively based concepts)? To what degree can conceptual explanations of language features be developed that extend across levels of language instruction and that go beyond aspects of grammar to also include pronunciation, pragmatics, lexical knowledge, figurative language, genre, and so on? Do conceptual explanations developed for a particular language extend to concepts in other languages?

5. How does Concept-based Language Instruction compare with other theoretically motivated approaches to L2 teaching with regard to their effectiveness in promoting learner understanding of and ability to use language?

6. A fundamental principle of Concept-based Language Instruction is that conceptual knowledge must be presented to learners through materialization in the form of a diagram, graphic, digitally, or even with objects such as Cuisenaire rods. What possibilities can be explored regarding the materialization of language concepts? In what ways might some materializations be more effective than others, especially with respect to different concepts (e.g., grammar vs. vocabulary, reading/writing vs. figurative language, etc.)? To what extent does the population of learners (age, level of proficiency) impact the effectiveness of particular approaches to Concept-based Language Instruction?

7. SCT researchers have long emphasized the need to understand interactions among teachers and learners with reference to the ways in which they might mediate learner engagement with language and development of L2 abilities. What models of interaction might prove particularly effective at providing such mediation during specific types of instructional activities? What models might be developed according to SCT principles (e.g., Mediated Development) that could be helpful, for instance, in guiding learners to understand language concepts, their materialization, and their value as tools for regulating language use?

8. Although the Zone of Proximal Development (ZPD) has most frequently been discussed in relation to the development of individuals, some work has explored the relevance of this concept to the development of groups. In what ways can the ZPD be employed in broader contexts, such as at the level of a classroom? What assessment procedures (e.g., Dynamic Assessment) and instructional approaches (Mediated Development, Division of Labor Pedagogy) might allow for the diagnosing and promoting the L2 abilities of the group/class while remaining sensitive to individuals? To what extent might learners be guided to serve as effective peer mediators, co-constructing expertise with one another through differential participation?

9. As the range of contexts in which L2 SCT researchers conduct their work continues to expand and grow more diverse, how can this be more responsive to macro-cultural forms of mediation (i.e. activities, institutions, and practices understood in their cultural, political, and economic environments) in attempting to understand what Vygotsky termed the social situation of development? In what ways does mediation need to change in different political and economic environments in order to appropriately meet learner needs? What are the responsibilities and commitments of researchers as they engage with practitioners in order to devise mediational means of development relevant to particular social situations of development?

10. Recently, SCT research, including SCT-L2 research, has begun to explore the implications of Vygotsky's proposal that consciousness entails the dialectical unity of thinking and emotion. The Russian term Vygotsky employed in conceiving of this unity and its importance is perezhivanie. What are the implications of perezhivanie for understanding the experiences of L2 teachers and learners? In what ways can learners come to regulate their cognitive-emotional functioning through an L2? How might taking account of the cognitive and emotional change inform how researchers conceptualize L2 development? How might it inform educational practices to diagnose and promote learner L2 development as well as teacher education?

Suggested Resources

Johnson, K. E., & Golombek, P. R. (2016). *Mindful L2 teacher education. A Sociocultural perspective on cultivating teachers' professional development.* **New York: Routledge**.

Drawing upon central concepts and principles in SCT and a wealth of experience leading teacher professional development programs, Johnson and Golombek outline a series of activities intended to promote teachers' theoretical knowledge by engaging them in a process of planning for instruction, implementing lessons, and reflecting on their teaching. Particular attention is given to the importance of dialogic interaction with teachers throughout this process in order to mediate their thinking as they encounter points of conflict between, for instance, planned and actual outcomes, theory and practice, and their emerging identity as an L2 educator.

Lantolf, J. P., & Poehner, M. E. (2014). *Sociocultural theory and the pedagogical imperative in L2 education. Vygotskian praxis and the theory practice divide.* **New York: Routledge**.

Through careful analysis of Vygotsky's key writings, including especially his *Historical meaning of the crisis in psychology*, Lantolf and Poehner look beyond previous discussions of Vygotsky's theoretical proposals to explicate his broader enterprise to establish psychology as a scientific discipline. For Vygotsky, this was to be accomplished by following principles of historical materialism, as elaborated by Marx, and employing them as a basis for understanding human consciousness. Lantolf and Poehner emphasize that Vygotsky's commitment to dialectics compelled him to study consciousness through the processes of its development but also to engage with practice, in particular education, as an activity uniquely positioned to guide the development of consciousness through the study of academic disciplines, including language. Lantolf and Poehner include examples of Concept-based Language Instruction and Dynamic Assessment to showcase praxis in the L2 field.

Lantolf, J. P., & Poehner, M. E. (Eds.). With M. Swain. (2018). *The Routledge handbook of sociocultural theory and second language development.* **New York: Routledge**.

Comprising thirty-five chapters authored by leading SCT scholars, the handbook offers a state-of-the-art overview of L2 research informed by Vygotskian theory. It includes individual chapters devoted to central features of the theory, including consciousness, mediation and internalization, and the Zone of Proximal Development. These are then expanded by SCT-L2 researchers to illuminate processes of L2 development as well as to design curricula, create activities, and organize interactions with learners in order to actively intervene in and guide development of L2 abilities. Among the many topics represented are Concept-based Language

Instruction, Dynamic Assessment, technology integrated language learning, and language teacher education. Each chapter reviews the relevant existing research literature, identifies conceptual trends and problems, discusses data or examples, and proposes important areas to be explored in future research.

Mok, N. (2015). Toward an understanding of perezhivanie for sociocultural SLA research. *Language and Sociocultural Theory, 2(2),* **139–160.**

The article explains the meaning of *perezhivanie* and its theoretical significance in the work of Vygotsky as the fundamental unit of consciousness that engages both emotion and thinking as they emerge in concrete social situations. SCT researchers have been debating the precise implications of the conception for the general theory of psychology that Vygotsky attempted to build. The article then surveys a few of the existing publications in SLA research that have taken *perezhivanie* into account and proposes possible future directions for this research.

Poehner, M.E. (2008). *Dynamic Assessment: A Vygotskian approach to understanding and promoting second language development.* **Berlin: Springer.**

The most in-depth introduction of Dynamic Assessment (DA) to the L2 field to date, this book presents the major DA approaches and formats that have emerged in the fields of psychology and general education over the past fifty years. Unlike overviews of DA outside the L2 field, this book situates DA firmly in the theoretical tradition of SCT, identifying specific interpretations of Vygotsky's discussions of the Zone of Proximal Development and how these were subsequently adopted by Western researchers concerned with assessing learner abilities. Poehner proposes a view of DA as the dialectical integration of teaching and assessing, and he illustrates the framework's potential to both diagnose learner emerging abilities and promote their development through examples from a study involving learners of L2 French.

van Compernolle, R. A. (2014). *Sociocultural theory and L2 instructional pragmatics.* **Bristol: Multilingual Matters.**

In the only book-length study to date examining Vygotskian Concept-based Language Instruction, van Compernolle details an instructional enrichment program aimed at university learners of L2 French. The program focused upon the socio-pragmatics of language use in context, in particular the ways in which social distance can be constructed, maintained, and negotiated through strategic selection of linguistic forms. Van Compernolle documents a range of communicative tasks employed in the program, visualizations of relevant concepts, and dialogic interaction with learners as they endeavored to employ the concepts to regulate their interpretation and use of the target language.

References

Arievitch, I. (2017). *Beyond the brain. An agentive activity perspective on mind, development, and learning*. Sense Publishers.

Frawley, W. J., & Lantolf, J. P. (1985). Second language discourse: A Vygotskyan perspective. *Applied Linguistics, 6*, 19–44.

Kozulin, A. (1998). *Psychological tools: A sociocultural approach to education*. Harvard University Press.

Lantolf, J. P., & Poehner, M. E. (2014). *Sociocultural theory and the pedagogical imperative. Vygotskian praxis and the research/practice divide*. Routledge.

Ratner, C., & Silva, D. N. H. (Eds.). (2017). *Vygotsky and Marx: Toward a Marxist psychology*. Routledge.

Vygotsky, L. S. (1987). *The collected works of L. S. Vygotsky. Volume 1: Problems of general psychology, including the volume thinking and speech*. In R. W. Rieber & A. S. Carton (Eds.). Plenum.

Vygotsky, L. S. (1997). *The collected works of L. S. Vygotsky. Volume 3: Problems of the theory and history of psychology*. In R. W. Rieber & J. Wollock (Eds.). Plenum.

Matthew E. Poehner is Professor of World Languages Education and Applied Linguistics at The Pennsylvania State University. His research examines Vygotskian sociocultural theory and its use as a basis for L2 education through frameworks such as dynamic assessment, mediated development, and concept-based language instruction. He has authored numerous journal articles and book chapters and co-authored and co-edited several books on sociocultural theory, language education, and assessment. He is currently associate editor of the journal *Language and Sociocultural Theory* and President of the International Association for Cognitive Education and Psychology.

James P. Lantolf is the Greer Professor in Language Acquisition and Applied Linguistics at The Pennsylvania State University. His is also Director of the Center for Language Acquisition and the Center for Advanced Language Proficiency Education and Research. He also holds a Yangtze River Professorship in Applied Linguistics in the School of Foreign Studies at Xi'an JiaoTong University. He is founding editor of *Language and Sociocultural Theory* and is past President of the American Association for Applied Linguistics.

Kimberly L. Geeslin

Sociolinguistic competence is the ability to employ the variable features of language according to social norms, taking into account the identity of the speaker and other interlocutors. Put simply, competent language users are not just grammatically accurate, they are situationally-appropriate too. Sociolinguistic competence includes, for example, the interpretation of socially-meaningful linguistic cues, and a response to these cues. Native speakers reflect their identity, that of their interlocutors and social facts about the place, purpose and formality of every interaction. In second language education, researchers explored these abilities in the context of what it means to learn to communicate fully in a new language. Canale and Swain (1980) identified three central components of this construct (grammatical, sociolinguistic and strategic competence) and subsequent research has added detail and expanded the areas of focus (e.g., Sun, 2014).

Research on second language sociolinguistic competence now encompasses a range of languages (e.g., Arabic, Chinese, English, French, German, and Spanish), and many areas of grammar. Technological advances have made it possible to study the influence of social and linguistic contexts on the variable realizations of second language sounds (e.g., Dalola & Bullock, 2017) and multiple analyses of interview corpora have made it possible to assess the development of multiple morphosyntactic and phonetic features of a second language (e.g., Regan et al., 2009). Such studies demonstrate differences between native speakers and language learners, but nearly always show development across the time course of the study (or the levels of abilities included in the study) (see Geeslin & Long, 2014 for review).

Learners generally have access to a more limited range of contexts of interaction (Dang & Seals, 2018; Gurzynski-Weiss et al., 2017). Consequently, experiences like study abroad are often important for acquiring socially-indexed patterns of use. Learners who spend time abroad, sometimes for as little as two months of intensive

K. L. Geeslin (✉)
Department of Spanish & Portuguese, Indiana University, Bloomington, IN, USA
e-mail: kgeeslin@indiana.edu

© Springer Nature Switzerland AG 2021
H. Mohebbi and C. Coombe (eds.), *Research Questions in Language Education and Applied Linguistics*, Springer Texts in Education,
https://doi.org/10.1007/978-3-030-79143-8_151

study, develop in the rates of use of markers of regional varieties and informal language, as well as in the linguistic contexts in which those linguistic variants occur (e.g., Adamson & Regan, 1991; Davydova et al., 2017; Kanwit et al., 2015; Terry, 2017). There is further evidence that individual characteristics, such as social networks, beliefs about the value of a stay abroad, and motivation, to name only a few, also play an important role in the acquisition of these socially-meaningful features of language (e.g., Shiri, 2015).

There are additional ways that language teachers can foster the development of sociolinguistic competence. For example, development of sociolinguistic awareness and competence has been linked to inclusion of local or informal varieties of a language in the classroom (Gutiérrez & Fairclough, 2006; Valdman, 1988), the use of authentic discourse in combination with sociolinguistic instruction (Shin & Hudgens Henderson, 2017) and explicit instruction about regional variation (Schoonmaker-Gates, 2017). Likewise, language teachers have been urged to expand the range of "voices" to which learners in the classroom are exposed by including multiple speakers with varied social characteristics using language for a variety of communicative purposes (Geeslin & Long, 2014).

The Research Questions

1. What is sociolinguistic competence?
2. What is the relationship between sociolinguistic and grammatical competence?
3. Is the acquisition and use of geographic markers similar to the acquisition and use of social ones?
4. What role do social networks play in the acquisition and use of sociolinguistic features of a language?
5. What role do individual differences play in the acquisition and use of sociolinguistic features of a language?
6. How do learners come to express their own identities through the variable features in second languages?
7. How is the acquisition of the sociolinguistic factors of language related to access to input?
8. How does study abroad help in the acquisition of sociolinguistic competence?
9. How can sociolinguistic competence be taught?
10. What role should sociolinguistic competence play in teacher training and the assessment of teacher readiness?

Suggested Resources

Adamson, H. D., & Regan, V. M. (1991). The acquisition of community speech norms by Asian immigrants learning English as a second language: A preliminary study. *Studies in Second Language Acquisition*, *13*(1), 1–22.

This classic work remains an excellent model for research on the second language acquisition of variable norms. This study of 31 English-speakers and 14 Cambodian and Vietnamese learners of English, nearly all of whom lived in Philadelphia, examines the variable realization of (ing) in English (e.g., "swimmin'" vs. "swimming"). This variant is conditioned by phonetic context (e.g., preceding segment), grammatical category (e.g., future progressive vs. nominal) and stylistic and social factors, such as formality of the interaction and gender of the speaker. The analysis of sociolinguistic interview data from both groups demonstrated that non-native speakers can acquire the constraints on variable use and, interestingly, at times may overshoot social norms, as exhibited by the increased difference between male and female speakers in monitored, rather than unmonitored speech.

Canale, M., & Swain, M. (1980). Theoretical bases of communicative approaches to second language teaching and testing. *Applied Linguistics*, *1*(1), 1–47.

This foundational work connects theories of language acquisition to second language classroom practices, assessing the degree to which pedagogies meet the needs of learners whose goal is to communicate fully in the target language. The authors take as a point of departure key constructs of the day, such as the distinction between competence and performance, and then move toward a critical analysis of communicative approaches to teaching, including social and integrative theories, for example. The authors identify guiding principles for achieving communicative competence in the classroom and then lay the foundation of our current theoretical understanding of communicative competence. They identify grammatical, sociolinguistic and strategic competence as three basic areas that are essential to communicate fully in the target language. This paper remains the cornerstone of conversations about communicative competence today.

Geeslin, K. L., & Long, A. Y. (2014). Sociolinguistics and second language acquisition: Learning to use language in context. New York, NY: Routledge.

This introductory text provides a comprehensive overview of the connections between second language acquisition and sociolinguistics. Early chapters provide a detailed look at the social aspects of language and how these contribute to a speaker's ability to communicate fully in a second language. The volume later explores several social approaches to second language acquisition and are followed by a critical account of existing research on the second language acquisition of sociolinguistic variation across multiple languages and grammatical structures. The book contains separate chapters dedicated to study abroad, pedagogical norms and targets, and applications for classroom instruction. This text builds from classic works, such as Canale and Swain (1980) and Adamson and Regan (1991) and connects these foundational studies to our present day understanding of how sociolinguistic competence is acquired and how it might be fostered in the second language classroom.

Schoonmaker-Gates, E. (2017). Regional variation in the language classroom and beyond: Mapping learners' developing dialectal competence. *Foreign Language Annals, 50*(1), 177–194.

This empirical study is a model for investigating classroom intervention in the second language acquisition of dialectal competence. The study compares two groups of English-speaking learners of Spanish, only one of which received explicit instruction about the dialects of Spanish through awareness-raising tasks, conversations about dialectal differences, exposure to speech samples, follow-up questions that elicited personal reflection and measures of comprehension, and a dialect-focused project. The group that received explicit instruction improved on the measure of comprehension, whereas the other group did not. However, neither group improved significantly in dialect identification. Looking at individual learners, three learners in the explicit instruction group showed improvement, as did one in the group without instruction. In a follow-up study reported in the same paper, comparing groups with and without previous exposure to a particular dialect of Spanish, the author showed that the group with previous exposure did score higher on measures of recognition.

Terry, K. M. K. (2017). Contact, context, and collocation: The emergence of sociostylistic variation in L2 French learners during study abroad. *Studies in Second Language Acquisition, 39*(3), 553–578.

This multi-factorial analysis of the development of second language sociolinguistic competence by English-speaking learners of French during study abroad, exemplifies the type of work that should be conducted to move our knowledge of sociolinguistic competence and its acquisition forward. Participants spent between a semester and a year in one of three locations in France. Each completed multiple elicitation tasks at least twice during the course of the study. The tasks ranged from production tasks, both open-ended and more focused, to those designed to elicit information about social networks. The Rbrul analysis included both linguistic and extralinguistic factors and measured their influence on a single variable: the realization of /l/ in third person pronouns. Findings show that there is a link between the socially-meaningful variants of /l/ and social networks, as well as other previously investigated linguistic factors.

References

Adamson, H. D., & Regan, V. M. (1991). The acquisition of community speech norms by Asian immigrants learning English as a second language: A preliminary study. *Studies in Second Language Acquisition, 13*(1), 1–22.

Canale, M., & Swain, M. (1980). Theoretical bases of communicative approaches to second language teaching and testing. *Applied Linguistics, 1*(1), 1–47.

Dalola, A., & Bullock, B. E. (2017). On sociophonetic competence: Phrase-final vowel devoicing in native and advanced L2 speakers of French. *Studies in Second Language Acquisition, 39*(4), 769–799.

Dang, T. C. T., & Seals, C. (2018). An evaluation of primary English textbooks in Vietnam: A sociolinguistic perspective. *TESOL Journal, 9*(1), 93–113.

Davydova, J., Tytus, A. E., & Schleef, E. (2017). Acquisition of sociolinguistic awareness by German learners of English: A study in perceptions of quotative *be like*. *Linguistics, 55*(4), 783–812.

Geeslin, K. L., & Long, A. Y. (2014). *Sociolinguistics and second language acquisition: Learning to use language in context*. Routledge.

Gurzynski-Weiss, L., Geeslin, K. L., Long, A. Y., & Daidone, D. (2017). Linguistic variation in instructor provision of oral input. In L. Gurzynski-Weiss (Ed.), *Expanding individual difference research in the interaction approach: Investigating learners, instructors, and researchers* (pp. 226–253). John Benjamins.

Gutiérrez, M., & Fairclough, M. (2006). Incorporating linguistic variation into the classroom. In R. Salaberry & B. A. Lafford (Eds.), *The art of teaching Spanish: Second language acquisition from research to praxis* (pp. 173–191). Georgetown University Press.

Kanwit, M., Geeslin, K. L., & Fafulas, S. (2015). The role of geography in the SLA of variable structures: A look at the present perfect, the copula contrast, and the present progressive in Mexico and Spain. *Probus, 27*(2), 307–348.

Regan, V., Howard, M., & Lemée, I. (2009). *The acquisition of sociolinguistic competence in a study abroad context*. Multilingual Matters.

Schoonmaker-Gates, E. (2017). Regional variation in the language classroom and beyond: Mapping learners' developing dialectal competence. *Foreign Language Annals, 50*(1), 177–194.

Shin, N. L., & Hudgens Henderson, M. (2017). A sociolinguistic approach to teaching Spanish grammatical structures. *Foreign Language Annals, 50*(1), 195–213.

Shiri, S. (2015). The homestay in intensive language study abroad: Social networks, language socialization, and developing intercultural competence. *Foreign Language Annals, 48*(1), 5–25.

Sun, D. (2014). From communicative competence to interactional competence: A new outlook to the teaching of spoken English. *Journal of Language Teaching and Research, 5*(5), 1062–1071.

Terry, K. M. K. (2017). Contact, context, and collocation: The emergence of sociostylistic variation in L2 French learners during study abroad. *Studies in Second Language Acquisition, 39*(3), 553–578.

Valdman, A. (1988). Classroom foreign language learning and language variation: The notion of pedagogical norms. *World Englishes, 7*(2), 221–236.

Kimberly L. Geeslin is Professor at Indiana University in the Department of Spanish and Portuguese. Her research focuses on second language Spanish and the intersection of SLA and sociolinguistics. She co-authored *Sociolinguistics and Second Language Acquisition* (Routledge, 2014) and edited *The Cambridge Handbook of Spanish Linguistics* (Cambridge, 2018) and *The Handbook of Spanish Second Language Acquisition* (Wiley-Blackwell, 2013). She has published research articles in *Studies in Second Language AcquisitionLanguage LearningHispaniaSpanish in ContextBilingualism: Language and CognitionLinguistics* and *Studies in Hispanic and Lusophone Linguistics*.

Rhonda Oliver

When communicating we all employ whatever linguistic features are at our disposal (Jørgensen, 2008). For multilingual speakers, these communicative resources include elements from their various languages, and these can be used concurrently (Baker, 2011) and holistically—a process that has been labelled translanguaging. Baker (2011, p. 288) defines translanguaging as "making meaning, shaping experiences, gaining understanding and knowledge through the use of two (or more) languages".

As a theoretical construct, translanguaging exists in contrast to codeswitching, the latter treating language as discrete with speakers shifting or shuttling between their languages, whereas in the former multilingual meaning making and experiences occur in concert and in fluid ways (Garcia & Wei, 2014). Hence, it is described as a resource and a tool, a communicative strategy that can be used to convey linguistic and social information reflecting the 'integratedness of languages in the daily lives of speakers' (Jonsson, 2017, p. 22). Whilst it is an individual interactive skill, language communities may also regularly engage in translanguaging. The benefit of translanguaging lies with the agency it grants to the multilingual speakers and, unlike codeswitching, it "resists the asymmetries of power" (Garcia & Leiva, 2014, p. 204) and so has the potential to be socially transformative.

Many Australian Aboriginal people, a group who represent 3% of that nation's population, are multilingual, having access to various languages and dialects. They may speak, with varying degrees of proficiency, Standard Australian English (SAE) and Aboriginal English (AE), both dialects of English. In northern parts of Australia, they may also speak Kriol, the name given to a local creole. In addition,

R. Oliver (✉)
School of Education, Curtin University, Perth, West Australia, Australia
e-mail: rhonda.oliver@curtin.edu.au

© Springer Nature Switzerland AG 2021
H. Mohebbi and C. Coombe (eds.), *Research Questions in Language Education and Applied Linguistics*, Springer Texts in Education,
https://doi.org/10.1007/978-3-030-79143-8_152

and particularly for those living in remote communities, they may also speak traditional languages (Eades, 2013). Previous research has described the language practices of Australian Aboriginal people, often through the lens of codeswitching (e.g., Malcolm et al., 1999). Only more recently have investigations been undertaken from a translanguaging perspective. Of particular interest is whether or not, for this minority group, translanguaging can be used educationally to harness support for the development of SAE—the language of power in Australia.

The Research Questions

1. Given its inherent connection to culture, how does translanguaging vary across different cultural groups?
2. Do Australian Aboriginal people use translanguaging strategies?
3. If so, how does it manifest in their language production?
4. What form does it take in different language modalities (written, spoken, gestural)?
5. How does translanguaging represent Australian Aboriginal peoples' 'cultural hybridity'?
6. What different functions does translanguaging serve Australian Aboriginal people?
7. What contribution does it make to the wellbeing of Australian Aboriginal people?
8. Does it really grant 'agency' to them within Australian society?
9. How might it be incorporated into and contribute to educational practices?
10. How might it be used to inform educational assessment practices?

Suggested Resources

Jonsson, C. (2017). Translanguaging and Ideology: Moving Away from a Monolingual Norm. In Paulsard, B., Rosen, J., Straszer, B., & Wedin, A. (Eds.), *New Perspectives on Translanguaging and Education* (pp. 20–37), Bristol, UK: Multilingual Matters.

The purpose of this chapter is to describe translanguaging from an ideological point of view, challenging society norms and in particular the privileging of monolingualism. It describes how the heteroglossic foundation of translanguaging allows multilingual repertoires to be recognized. It does so by highlighting "the fluidity of real-life language practices" (p. 23), the contextual nature of communication and "moves away from a static view of bilingualism and monolinguism" (p. 24). It provides support for the transformational potential of translanguaging. The chapter does this by examining, in depth, such theoretical constructs as languaging, language ideologies, and language norms. Of particular relevance to current debates, the chapter also provides a clear account of the differences between code-switching where "language separation is emphasized" and translanguaging where the "integratedness of languages is the cornerstone" (p. 33).

Rosen, J. (2017). Spaces for Translanguaging in Swedish Education Policy. In Paulsard, B., Rosen, J., Straszer, B., & Wedin, A. (Eds.), *New Perspectives on Translanguaging and Education* **(pp. 38–55), Bristol, UK: Multilingual Matters**.

In this chapter Rosén examines Translanguaging in practice and in this case, exploring how Swedish Education policy has been constructed to reflect this process. To begin she outlines the positive attributes of translanguaging and how it is concerned with language users "participation, socialisation and identity" (p. 43). She describes how it is a process that grants 'agency' to the speakers and how it is a "value" and not just a "tool" (p. 46). She uses the Swedish education policy example as a case study to demonstrate how in contrast to other educational policies, where monolingual norms dominate, this one recognizes "the diverse linguistic language backgrounds of the students and a promotion of these as a foundation for all further learning" (p. 45). This philosophical underpinning helps address the "deficit perspective" (p. 41) of other monolingualised pedagogies.

Garcia, O., & Leiva, C. (2014). Theorizing and Enacting Translanguaging for Social Justice. In Blackledge, A. & Creese, A. (Eds.), *Heteroglossia as Practice and Pedagogy* **(pp. 199–216). Dordrecht: Springer.**

This chapter begins with an introduction to translanguaging, how it emerged from *transculturación* (p. 3) and how it is connected to and supports bilingual education. It also makes a case for the contribution of translanguaging to social justice describing its potential to liberate "the voices of the language minoritized students" (p. 200). Underpinning this process is *languaging* whereby our experiences are shaped and stored in memory for communicative purpose. This is done in a way that resists the "asymmetries" of power in language use. The fluidity of translanguaging is contrasted to static conceptualization of codeswitching. The second part of the chapter provides a case study showing how translanguaging is used with a class of emergent bilinguals—ninth and tenth year high school Spanish speakers in New York. It shows how translanguaging promotes student participation, allowing students to elaborate their ideas and thinking.

Garcia, O., & Kano, N. (2014). Translanguaging as Process and Pedagogy: Developing the English Writing of Japanese Students in the US. In Conteh, J., & Meier, G (Eds.), *The Multilingual Turn in Languages Education: Opportunities and Challenges for Individuals and Societies* **(pp. 258–277). Bristol: Multilingual Matters.**

This chapter has a very pedagogical focus exploring how Japanese high school students (aged 12–16 years) studying in the US can use translanguaging practices as a resource to develop their academic written English proficiency. It address the common unwillingness of teachers to "use the language diversity of their students as a resource" (p. 258) for learning. The participants are a particular cohort, namely those who are 'bi-schooled', that is they attend a mainstream English school during the week, but also attend out-of-school hours Japanese classes. The beginning of the chapter introduces the range of terms that have been used as synonyms for translanguaging. It then describes in detail the study—translanguaging in action—and how it was used by a Japanese teacher to scaffold the participants as they learn to develop their written English, and how this in turn works to support their Japanese literacy skills.

Oliver, R & Nguyen, B. (2017). Aboriginal Youth's Linguistic Success: Translanguaging on Facebook. *The Canadian Modern Language Review/La Revue canadienne des langues vivantes, 73,* **4, 463–487.** https://doi.org/10.3138/cmlr.3890.

This article explores how young bidialectal Australian Aboriginal people use translanguaging practices via social media, and Facebook in particular. Facebook posts written by seven participants (aged 18–25 years) were collected, with permission, over an 18 month period. Data were interrogated by means of discourse and then thematic analysis showing creative and strategic use of both Aboriginal English (AE) and Standard Australian English (SAE). It was also evident that the participants were active agents creating multilingual and bicultural identities, expressing humor, and group and family membership. Their use of translanguaging strategies appeared to "enhance rather than detract from their development of SAE" (p. 463) and enabled them to develop and demonstrate their understanding and knowledge in their different linguistic codes. Such findings highlight the pedagogic potential of the use of translanguaging for teaching language minority students, including Australian Aboriginal students.

References

Baker, C. (2011). *Foundations of bilingual education and bilingualism* (5th ed.). Multilingual Matters.

Eades, D. (2013). *Aboriginal ways of using English*. Aboriginal Studies Press.

Garcia, O., & Leiva, C. (2014). Theorizing and enacting translanguaging for social justice. In A. Blackledge & A. Creese (Eds.), *Heteroglossia as practice and pedagogy* (pp. 199–216). Springer.

Garcia, O., & Wei, Li. (2014). *Translanguaging: Language, bilingualism and education*. Palgrave Macmillan.

Jonsson, C. (2017). Translanguaging and ideology: Moving away from a monolingual norm. In B. Paulsard, J. Rosen, B. Straszer, & A. Wedin (Eds.), *New perspectives on translanguaging and education* (pp. 20–37). Multilingual Matters.

Jørgensen, J. N. (2008). Polylingual languaging around and among children and adolescents. *International Journal of Multilingualism, 5*(3), 161–176.

Malcolm, I. G., Haig, Y., Königsberg, P., Rochecouste, J., Collard, G., Hill, A., & Cahill, R. (1999). *Two-way English: Towards more user-friendly education for speakers of Aboriginal English*. Education Department of Western Australia and Edith Cowan University.

Rhonda Oliver is a professor and Head of the School of Education at Curtin University, Perth, Western Australia. She is widely published in the area of second language acquisition. Internationally she is best known for her work in relation to child language learners. As well as work within the interactionist paradigm, including research about the contribution of negative feedback and negotiation of meaning, she has also conducted numerous pedagogical studies on ESL and mainstream learners in schools and universities. In recent times she has undertaken work in the area of Aboriginal education, particularly for those students who have Standard Australia English as their second language or dialect and has done so in the form of enthnographic case studies and Needs Analysis investigations.

Printed by Printforce, United Kingdom